SPECIMENS

OF THE

PRE-SHAKSPEREAN

DRAMA

Tragedy, comedy, history, pastoral,
pastoral-comical, historical-pastoral,
tragical-historical, tragical-comical-
historical-pastoral, scene individable,
or poem unlimited.

SPECIMENS

OF THE

PRE-SHAKSPEREAN

DRAMA

Selected, Edited and with a Preface by

JOHN MATTHEWS MANLY

IN TWO VOLUMES

Volume II

DOVER PUBLICATIONS, INC., NEW YORK

Published in Canada by General Publishing Company, Ltd., 30 Lesmill Road, Don Mills, Toronto, Ontario.

Published in the United Kingdom by Constable and Company, Ltd., 10 Orange Street, London WC 2.

This Dover edition, first published in 1967, is an unabridged and unaltered republication of the work originally published in 1897 by the Athenaeum Press, a division of Ginn and Company.

Standard Book Number: 486-21859-7
Library of Congress Catalog Card Number: 67-18096

Manufactured in the United States of America
Dover Publications, Inc.
180 Varick Street
New York, N. Y. 10014

PREFATORY NOTE.

THE principles followed in printing these texts have already been stated in the Preface to vol. I, but it seems desirable to repeat some of them here.

Aside from the use of modern conventions in typography, punctuation, and capitals, and the general disregard of long *s* (which is reproduced only occasionally, and then in a footnote), no alteration of the original texts has been admitted without a definite indication. The most general of these indications are the use of italics for expanded contractions (which are not very common in this volume) and the use of square brackets to enclose letters or words added to the original text. In instances in which these general indications are inappropriate the alteration is recorded in a footnote.

The titlepages of the plays, it will be seen, preserve the old spelling, line division, and variation of typography, but none of them is a facsimile in the proper sense of the word. One of them, in fact, — *Cambises*, — may possibly bear little resemblance to the original in typographical appearance, though in other respects it is believed to be correct. The others I believe to be essentially correct in even this respect; but the only ones for which I can vouch with the confidence derived from comparing them myself with the originals are *Campaspe* and *David and Bethsabe*, and they are not exactly facsimiles, but, as it were, translations of ancient typography into modern. Elsewhere in the book no attempt is made to follow the original in the choice of type, except in certain passages of which special mention is made in the footnotes.

The square brackets mentioned above are most frequently used to enclose headings, stage-directions, and lists of *dramatis personae*. The page-headings of the volume, however, though not enclosed in brackets, are not the original headings, as may be learned more definitely from the statements accompanying *Campaspe* and *David and Bethsabe*. In view of the importance of the original stage-directions for the study of the practice of the ancient stage, special pains has been taken to secure accuracy in printing these original directions and in placing the brackets, which indicate additions from whatever source. Between my indications and those of some of those preceding editors who use the same convention a good many discrepancies exist. In only a few instances has it seemed desirable to affirm in a footnote that I have observed the discrepancy; but the benevolent reader may be assured that I have not neglected, as an aid to accuracy in this respect, to read the proof-sheets with the editions of previous editors as well as with the copies made for me from the originals. As the brackets indicate, the old copies usually do not contain a list of *dramatis personae*. But, as the making of such a list is a purely mechanical matter, performed usually by the first modern editor who happened to print the play, I have not credited these lists to their makers, even when adopted by me without modification. In like manner, I have usually omitted to record the authors of bracketed stage-directions.

In recording emendations I have not added to the name of the originator the names of his followers, except for special reasons, as, for instance, when it is proper that the reader should be informed as to the balance of authority. In recording the statements of previous editors in regard to the readings of the original, I have, except in cases of disagreement, omitted as of no authority the name of an editor who clearly follows one of his predecessors without collating or with a merely perfunctory collation. The extent to which variants of spelling are recorded is determined by such various reasons that the reader must be referred to the notes themselves for information. Occasionally, in notes in which variation of spelling is not the matter of record, I have coupled a modern edition with an old one, giving the spelling of the old edition only, and leaving the reader to modernize.

In some instances I shall certainly seem to many to have been over-conservative in refusing to admit to the text various emenda-

tions in metre, spelling, syntax, and vocabulary.   I may plead, in
general, that these emendations are easily accessible in the footnotes, and that I feared to overstep the bound separating the
functions of an editor of texts from those of literary adviser to the
authors.   More specifically, I should reply that by far the larger
part of the emendations here in question belong either to the class
of the unnecessary or to that of the dangerous.   The practice of
normalizing Elizabethan spelling, syntax, and blank verse has
been almost as great a hindrance to students of language and
versification as the introduction of unindicated alterations in stage-
directions has been to students of stage history ; and occasionally
it has given rise to misconceptions in literary questions as well.
As to vocabulary, experience has amply demonstrated that there
exist in the limbo of the footnote enough examples of more than
one word and form discarded as corruptions to establish their
legitimacy and propriety.   And, finally, a reason, perhaps of itself
sufficient, for keeping the original text in these doubtful cases is
that few readers will consult footnotes so long as the text presents
no difficulty or irregularity, whereas almost every one will heed the
warning of the index figure when the text halts ; and thus, in the
long run, the student will by this method become acquainted with
the arguments on both sides and competent to judge whether such
irregularities ought to be retained or removed.

   To Professor Kittredge I am again indebted for aid in reading
the proofs, in establishing and punctuating the text, and in inter-
preting obscure passages.   The footnotes record only a small
part of my obligations to him.

J. M. M.

Providence, Nov. 15, 1897.

CONTENTS OF VOL. II.

———

PART VII.

PART VIII.

PART VII.

ROISTER DOISTER.

BY

NICHOLAS UDALL.

The text is based on Arber's reprint of the unique copy of the old edition. In the footnotes, A. indicates this reprint; C. indicates the edition by W. D. Cooper (Shakespeare Society, 1847). As in vol. I, I have disregarded the punctuation and capitals of the original.

This play seems to have been first printed in 1566, ten years after the death of the author. Whether the extant copy belongs to the first edition cannot be determined, as it lacks both titlepage and colophon.

[*Dramatis Personae.*

RALPH ROISTER DOISTER, *a vain-glorious gull.*
MATHEW MERYGREEKE, *a parasite.*
GAWYN GOODLUCK, *affianced to Dame Custance.*
TRISTRAM TRUSTIE, *his friend.*
DOBINET DOUGHTIE } *servants to Roister Doister.*
HARPAX
TOM TRUPENIE, *servant to Dame Custance.*
SYM SURESBY, *servant to Goodluck.*
A Scrivener.
Musicians.

DAME CHRISTIAN CUSTANCE, *a widow.*
MARGERIE MUMBLECRUST, *her nurse.*
TIBET TALKAPACE } *her maids.*
ANNOT ALYFACE

SCENE: *England. A street or field near Dame Custance's house.*]

4

[ROISTER DOISTER.]

The Prologue.

What creature is in health, eyther yong or olde,
  But som mirth with modestie wil be glad to vse?
As we in thys enterlude shall now vnfolde,
  Wherin all scurilitie we vtterly refuse,
  Auoiding such mirth wherin is abuse,
Knowing nothing more comendable for a mans recreation
Than mirth which is vsed in an honest fashion :   7

For mirth prolongeth lyfe and causeth health ;
  Mirth recreates our spirites and voydeth pensiuenesse ;
Mirth increaseth amitie, not hindring our wealth ;
  Mirth is to be vsed both of more and lesse,
  Being mixed with vertue in decent comlynesse, —
As we trust no good nature can gainsay the same :
Which mirth we intende to vse, auoidyng all blame. 14

The wyse poets long time heretofore
  Vnder merrie comedies secretes did declare,
Wherein was contained very vertuous lore,
  With mysteries and forewarnings very rare.
  Suche to write neither Plautus nor Terence dyd spare,
Whiche among the learned at this day beares the bell :
These with such other therein dyd excell.   21

Our comedie, or enterlude, which we intende to play
  Is named Royster Doyster in-deede,
Which against the vayne-glorious doth inuey,
  Whose humour the roysting sort continually doth feede.
  Thus by your pacience we intende to proceede
In this our enterlude by Gods leaue and grace ;
And here I take my leaue for a certaine space. 28

Actus j. Scæna j.

MATHEWE MERYGREEKE.   *He entreth singing.*

[M. MERY.]   As long lyueth the mery man, they say,
As doth the sory man, and longer by a day.
Yet the grassehopper, for all his sommer pipyng,
Sterueth in winter wyth hungrie gripyng.
Therefore an-other sayd sawe doth men aduise   5
That they be together both mery and wise.
Thys lesson must I practise, or else ere long
Wyth mee, Mathew Merygreeke, it will be wrong.
In-deede men so call me, for, by Him that vs bought,
What-euer chaunce betide, I can take no thought.   10
Yet wisedome woulde that I did my-selfe bethinke
Where to be prouided this day of meate and drinke ;
For know ye, that, for all this merie note of mine,
He might appose me now that should aske where I dine.
My lyuing lieth heere and there, of Gods grace, —   15
Sometime wyth this good man, sometyme in that place,
Sometime Lewis Loytrer biddeth me come neere,
Somewhyles Watkin Waster maketh vs good cheere,
Sometime Dauy Diceplayer, when he hath well cast,
Keepeth reuell-route as long as it will last,   20
Sometime Tom Titiuile maketh vs a feast,
Sometime with Sir Hugh Pye I am a bidden gueast,
Sometime at Nichol Neuerthriues I get a soppe,
Sometime I am feasted with Bryan Blinkinsoppe,
Sometime I hang on Hankyn Hoddydodies sleeue ;   25
But thys day on Ralph Royster Doysters, by hys leeue,
For truely of all men he is my chiefe banker,
Both for meate and money, and my chiefe shootanker.
For, sooth Roister Doister in that he doth say,
And, require what ye will, ye shall haue no nay.   30
But now of Roister Doister somewhat to expresse,
That ye may esteeme him after hys worthinesse!

In these twentie townes, and seke them throughout,
Is not the like stocke, whereon to graffe a loute.
All the day long is he facing and craking   35
Of his great actes in fighting and fraymaking ;
But, when Roister Doister is put to his proofe,
To keepe the Queenes peace is more for his behoofe.
If any woman smyle or cast on hym an eye,
Vp is he to the harde eares in loue by-and-by,   40
And in all the hotte haste must she be hys wife,
Else farewell hys good days, and farewell his life!
Maister Raufe Royster Doister is but dead and gon
Excepte she on hym take some compassion.
Then chiefe of counsell must be Mathew Merygreeke :   45
"What if I for mariage to suche an one seeke?"
Then must I sooth it, what-euer it is ;
For what he sayth or doth can not be amisse.
Holde vp his yea and nay, be his nowne white sonne,
Prayse and rouse him well, and ye haue his heart wonne;   50
For so well liketh he his owne fonde fashions
That he taketh pride of false commendations.
But such sporte haue I with him as I would not leese
Though I should be bounde to lyue with bread and cheese.
For exalt hym, and haue hym as ye lust, in-deede, —   55
Yea, to hold his finger in a hole for a neede.
I can with a worde make him fayne or loth,
I can with as much make him pleased or wroth,
I can, when I will, make him mery and glad,
I can, when me lust, make him sory and sad,   60
I can set him in hope and eke in dispaire,
I can make him speake rough, and make him speake faire.
But I maruell I see hym not all thys same day,
I wyll seke him out. — But, loe! he commeth thys way!
I haue yond espied hym sadly comming,   65
And in loue, for twentie pounde, by hys glommyng!

Actus j. Scæna ij.

[Enter] RAFE ROISTER DOISTER. MATHEW MERYGREEKE [*pretends not to see him*].

R. ROYSTER.   Come, death, when thou wilt, I am weary
     of my life!

M. MERY.   I tolde you, I, we should wowe another wife!

R. ROYSTER.   Why did God make me suche a goodly
     person?

M. MERY.   He is in by the weke, we shall haue sport
     anon.

R. ROYSTER.   And where is my trustie friende, Mathew
     Merygreeke?   5

M. MERY.   I wyll make as I sawe him not; he doth me
     seeke.

R. ROISTER.   I haue hym espyed, me thinketh; yond is
     hee.

Hough, Mathew Merygreeke, my friend, a worde with thee!

M. MERY.   I wyll not heare him, but make as I had
     haste.—

Farewell, all my good friendes, the tyme away doth waste,   10
And the tide, they say, tarieth for no man!

R. ROISTER.   Thou must with thy good counsell helpe me
     if thou can.

M. MERY.   God keepe thee, worshypfull Maister Roister
     Doister!

And fare-well the [1] lustie Maister Roister Doister!

                                [*Pretending to go.*]

R. ROYSTER.   I muste needes speake with thee a worde or
     twaine.   15

M. MERY.   Within a month or two I will be here againe;
Negligence in greate affaires, ye knowe, may marre all.

R. ROISTER.   Attende vpon me now, and well rewarde
     thee I shall.

               [1] *Qy.* the[e].

M. Mery. I haue take my leaue, and the tide is well
    spent.

R. Roister. I die except thou helpe; I pray thee, be
    content!   20

Doe thy parte wel nowe, and aske what thou wilt,

For without thy aide my matter is all spilt.

M. Mery. Then to serue your turne I will some paines
    take

And let all myne owne affaires alone for your sake.

R. Royster. My whole hope and trust resteth onely in
    thee.   25

M. Mery. Then can ye not doe amisse, what-euer it bee.

R. Royster. Gramercies, Merygreeke! most bounde to
    thee I am.

M. Mery. But vp with that heart, and speake out like a
    ramme!

Ye speake like a capon that had the cough now.

Bee of good cheere, anon ye shall doe well ynow!   30

R. Royster. Vpon thy comforte, I will all things well
    handle.

M. Mery. So, loe, that is a breast to blowe out a candle!

But what is this great matter? I woulde faine knowe.

We shall fynde remedie therefore, I trowe.

Doe ye lacke money? Ye knowe myne olde offers,   35

Ye haue always a key to my purse and coffers.

R. Royster. I thanke thee! Had euer man suche a
    frende?

M. Mery. Ye gyue vnto me; I must needes to you lende.

R. Royster. Nay, I haue money plentie all things to dis-
    charge.

M. Mery. [aside] That knewe I ryght well when I made
    offer so large.   40

R. Royster.[1] But it is no suche matter.

M. Mery.   What is it, than?

Are ye in daunger of debte to any man?

If ye be, take no thought nor be not afraide;

---

[1] *Omitted in A., apparently by oversight; it is found in C.*

Let them hardly take thought how they shall be paide.

   R. ROYSTER.   Tut! I owe nought.

   M. MERY.   What then? fear ye imprisonment? 45

   R. ROYSTER.   No.

   M. MERY.   No, i-wist, ye offende not, so to be shent.

But if ye [1] had, the Toure coulde not you so holde

But to breake out at all times ye would be bolde.

What is it? hath any man threatned you to beate?

   R. ROYSTER.   What is he that durst haue put me in that
        heate? 50

He that beateth me — by His armes! — shall well fynde,

That I will not be farre from him nor runne behinde.

   M. MERY.   That thing knowe all men euer since ye ouer-
        threwe

The fellow of the lion which Hercules slewe.

But what is it, than?

   R. ROYSTER.   Of loue I make my mone. 55

   M. MERY. Ah, this foolishe (a!) loue! wilt neare let vs
        alone?

But, bicause ye were refused the last day,

Ye sayd ye woulde nere more be intangled that way.

I would medle no more, since I fynde all so vnkinde.

   R. ROYSTER.   Yea, but I can not so put loue out of my
        minde. 60

   MATH. MER. But is your loue — tell me first, in any
        wise! —

In the way of mariage, or of merchandise?

If it may otherwise than lawfull be founde,

Ye get none of my helpe for a hundred pounde.

   R. ROYSTER.   No, by my trouth, I would haue hir to my
        wife. 65

   M. MERY. Then are ye a good man, and God saue your
        life!

And what or who is she with whome ye are in loue?

   R. ROYSTER.   A woman whome I knowe not by what
        meanes to moue.

<hr>

[1] A. he; C. ye.

M. MERY.   Who is it?

R. ROYSTER.   A woman yond!

M. MERY.   What is hir name?

R. ROYSTER.   Hir yonder.

M. MERY.   Whom?

R. ROYSTER.   Mistresse — ah —

M. MERY.   Fy, fy, for shame!   70
Loue ye, and know not whome, but "hir yonde," "a woman"?
We shall then get you a wyfe — I can not tell whan!

   R. ROYSTER.   The faire woman, that supped wyth vs
      yesternyght,
And I hearde hir name twice or thrice, and had it ryght.

   M. MERY.   Yea, ye may see ye nere take me to good
      cheere with you;   75
If ye had, I coulde haue tolde you hir name now.

   R. ROYSTER.   I was to blame in-deede, but the nexte tyme
      perchaunce —
And she dwelleth in this house.

   M. MERY.   What, Christian Custance?

   R. ROYSTER.   Except I haue hir to my wife, I shall runne
      madde.

   M. MERY.   Nay; vnwise perhaps, but I warrant you for
      madde!   80

   R. ROYSTER.   I am vtterly dead vnlesse I haue my de-
      sire.

   M. MERY.   Where be the bellowes that blewe this sodeine
      fire?

   R. ROYSTER.   I heare she is worthe a thousande pounde
      and more.

   M. MERY.   Yea, but learne this one lesson of me afore:
An hundred pounde of marriage-money, doubtlesse,   85
Is euer thirtie pounde sterlyng, or somewhat lesse.
So that hir thousande pounde, yf she be thriftie,
Is muche neere about two hundred and fiftie.
Howebeit, wowers and widowes are neuer poore!

   R. ROYSTER.   Is she a widowe?   I loue hir better there-
      fore.   90

M. MERY.   But I heare she hath made promise to another.

R. ROYSTER.   He shall goe without hir, and he were my
      brother !

M. MERY.   I haue hearde say, I am right well aduised,
That she hath to Gawyn Goodlucke promised.

R. ROYSTER.   What is that Gawyn Goodlucke?

M. MERY.   A merchant man.   95

R. ROYSTER.   Shall he speede afore me? Nay, sir, by
      sweete Sainct Anne !

Ah, sir, " Backare," quod Mortimer to his sowe;

I wyll haue hir myne owne selfe, I make God a-vow ;

For, I tell thee, she is worthe a thousande pounde.

M. MERY.   Yet a fitter wife for your maship might be
      founde :   100

Suche a goodly man as you might get one wyth lande,

Besides poundes of golde a thousande and a thousande,

And a thousande, and a thousande, and a thousande,

And so to the summe of twentie hundred thousande ;

Your most goodly personage is worthie of no lesse.   105

R. ROYSTER.   I am sorie God made me so comely, doubt-
      lesse,

For that maketh me eche-where so highly fauoured,

And all women on me so enamoured.

M. MERY.   " Enamoured," quod you? haue ye spied out
      that?

Ah, sir, mary, nowe I see you know what is what.   110

" Enamoured," ka? mary, sir, say that againe !

But I thought not ye had marked it so plaine.

R. ROYSTER.   Yes, eche-where they gaze all vpon me and
      stare.

M. MERY.   Yea, Malkyn, I warrant you, as muche as they
      dare.

And ye will not beleue what they say in the streete,   115

When your mashyp passeth by, all such as I meete,

That sometimes I can scarce finde what aunswere to make :

" Who is this ? " sayth one, " Sir Launcelot du Lake ? "

" Who is this ? great Guy of Warwike ? " sayth an-other ;

" No," say I, " it is the thirtenth Hercules brother ; "   120
" Who is this ? noble Hector of Troy ? " sayth the thirde ;
" No, but of the same nest," say I, " it is a birde ; "
" Who is this? greate Goliah, Sampson, or Colbrande? "
" No," say I, " but it is a brute of the Alie Lande ; "
" Who is this? greate Alexander? or Charle le Maigne? "   125
" No, it is the tenth Worthie," say I to them agayne.
I knowe not if I sayd well?
    R. ROYSTER.   Yes, for so I am.
    M. MERY.   Yea, for there were but nine Worthies before
         ye came.
To some others, the thirde Cato I doe you call ;
And so, as well as I can, I aunswere them all.   130
" Sir, I pray you, what lorde or great gentleman is this? "
" Maister Ralph Roister Doister, dame," say I, ywis.
" O Lorde! " sayth she than, " what a goodly man it is !
Woulde Christ I had such a husbande as he is ! "
" O Lorde," say some, " that the sight of his face we lacke! " 135
" It is inough for you," say I, " to see his backe ;
His face is for ladies of high and noble parages.
With whome he hardly scapeth great mariages," —
With muche more than this, and much otherwise.
    R. ROYSTER.   I can thee thanke that thou canst suche
         answeres deuise.   140
But I perceyue thou doste me throughly knowe.
    M. MERY.   I marke your maners for myne owne learnyng,
         I trowe.
But suche is your beautie, and suche are your actes,
Suche is your personage, and suche are your factes,
That all women, faire and fowle, more and lesse,   145
That eye you, they lubbe you, they talke of you doubtlesse ;
Your p[l]easant looke maketh them all merie ;
Ye passe not by but they laugh till they be werie ;
Yea, and money coulde I haue, the truthe to tell,
Of many, to bryng you that way where they dwell.   150
    R. ROYSTER.   Merygreeke, for this thy reporting well of
         mee —

M. MERY.   What shoulde I else, sir? it is my duetie,
    pardee!
R. ROYSTER.   I promise thou shalt not lacke, while I
    haue a grote.
M. MERY.   Faith, sir, and I nere had more nede of a newe
    cote.
R. ROYSTER.   Thou shalte haue one to-morowe, and golde
    for to spende.   155
M. MERY.   Then I trust to bring the day to a good
    ende;
For, as for mine owne parte, hauing money inowe,
I could lyue onely with the remembrance of you.
But nowe to your widowe whome you loue so hotte!
R. ROYSTER.   By Cocke, thou sayest truthe! I had almost
    forgotte.   160
M. MERY.   What if Christian Custance will not haue you,
    what?
R. ROISTER.   Haue me? yes, I warrant you, neuer doubt
    of that;
I knowe she loueth me, but she dare not speake.
M. MERY.   In-deede meete it were some-body should it
    breake.
R. ROISTER.   She looked on me twentie tymes yester-
    night,   165
And laughed so —
M. MERY.   That she coulde not sitte vpright?
R. ROISTER.   No, faith, coulde she not.
M. MERY.   No, euen such a
    thing I cast.
R. ROYSTER.   But, for wowyng, thou knowest, women are
    shamefast.
But, and she knewe my minde, I knowe she would be glad,
And thinke it the best chaunce that euer she had.   170
M. MERY.   Too hir then like a man, and be bolde forth
    to starte!
Wowers neuer speede well that haue a false harte.
R. ROISTER.   What may I best doe?

M. MERY.   Sir, remaine ye a while [here]; [1]
Ere long one or other of hir house will appere.
Ye knowe my minde.

    R. ROYSTER.   Yea, now, hardly, lette me alone!   175

    M. MERY.   In the meane-time, sir, if you please, I wyll
        home,
And call your musitians, for in this your case
It would sette you forth, and all your wowyng grace;
Ye may not lacke your instrumentes to play and sing.

    R. ROYSTER.   Thou knowest I can doe that.

    M. MERY.   As well as
        any-thing.   180
Shall I go call your folkes, that ye may shewe a cast?

    R. ROYSTER.   Yea, runne, I beseeche thee, in all possible
        haste.

    M. MERY.   I goe.   *Exeat.*

    R. ROYSTER.   Yea, for I loue singyng out of measure,
It comforteth my spirites and doth me great pleasure.
But who commeth forth yond from my swete hearte Custance?   185
My matter frameth well, thys is a luckie chaunce.

Actus j. Scæna iij.

MAGE MUMBLE-CRUST, *spinning on the distaffe.* TIBET TALK-APACE,
sowyng. [*The two enter together.*] [*To them later* [2] *comes*] ANNOT
ALYFACE, *knittyng.* R. ROISTER [*remains*].

M. MUMBL.   If thys distaffe were spoonne, Margerie Mum-
    blecrust!

TIB. TALK.   Where good stale ale is, will drinke no water,
    I trust.

M. MUMBL.   Dame Custance hath promised vs good ale
    and white bread.

TIB. TALK.   If she kepe not promise, I will beshrewe hir
    head!
But it will be starke nyght before I shall haue done.   5

---

[1] *Supplied by* C.   [2] *See* l. 27.

R. ROYSTER.   I will stande here a-while, and talke with
  them anon.
I heare them speake of Custance, which doth my heart
  good;
To heare hir name spoken doth euen comfort my blood.
  M. MUMBL.   Sit downe to your worke, Tibet, like a good
   girle.
  TIB. TALK.   Nourse, medle you with your spyndle and
   your whirle!   10
No haste but good, Madge Mumblecrust; for, whip and
  whurre,
The olde prouerbe doth say, neuer made good furre.
  M. MUMBL.   Well, ye wyll sitte downe to your worke
   anon, I trust.
  TIB. TALK.   Soft fire maketh sweete malte, good Madge
   Mumblecrust.
  M. MUMBL.   And swete malte maketh ioly good ale for
   the nones.   15
  TIB. TALK.   Whiche will slide downe the lane without
   any bones.   *Cantet:*

Old browne bread crustes must haue much good mumblyng,
But good ale downe your throte hath good easie tumbling.

R. ROYSTER.   The iolyest wenche that ere I hearde, little
  mouse!
May I not reioyce that she shall dwell in my house? 20
  TIB. TALK.   So, sirrha, nowe this geare beginneth for to
   frame.
  M. MUMBL.   Thanks to God, though your work stand
   stil, your tong is not lame!
  TIB. TALK.   And, though your teeth be gone, both so
   sharpe and so fine,
Yet your tongue can renne on patins as well as mine.
  M. MUMBL.   Ye were not for nought named Tyb Talke-
   apace.   25
  TIB. TALK.   Doth my talke grieue you?   Alack, God
   saue your grace!

M. MUMBL.   I holde a grote ye will drinke anon for this
            geare.

[*Enter* ANNOT ALYFACE, *knitting.*]

TIB. TALK.   And I wyll pray you the stripes for me to
            beare.

M. MUMBL.   I holde a penny, ye will drink without a
            cup.

TIB. TALK.   Wherein-so-ere ye drinke, I wote ye drinke
            all vp.   30

AN. ALYFACE.   By Cock! and well sowed, my good Tibet
            Talke-apace!

TIB. TALK.   And een as well knitte, my nowne Annot
            Alyface!

R. ROYSTER.   See what a sort she kepeth that must be
            my wife!

Shall not I, when I haue hir, leade a merrie life?

TIB. TALK.   Welcome, my good wenche, and sitte here
            by me iust!   35

AN. ALYFACE.   And howe doth our old beldame here,
            Mage Mumblecrust?

TIB. TALK.   Chyde, and finde faultes, and threaten to
            complaine.

AN. ALYFACE.   To make vs poore girles shent, to hir is
            small gaine.

M. MUMBL.   I dyd neyther chyde, nor complaine, nor
            threaten.

R. ROYSTER.   It woulde grieue my heart to see one of
            them beaten.   40

M. MUMBL.   I dyd nothyng but byd hir worke and holde
            hir peace.

TIB. TALK.   So would I, if you coulde your clattering
            ceasse ;

But the deuill can not make olde trotte holde hir tong.

AN. ALYFACE.   Let all these matters passe, and we three
            sing a song!

So shall we pleasantly bothe the tyme beguile now   45
And eke dispatche all our workes ere we can tell how.

Tib. Talk.   I shrew them that say nay, and that shall not
        be I !

M. Mumbl.   And I am well content.

Tib. Talk.   Sing on, then, by-and-by.

R. Royster.   And I will not away, but listen to their
        song.

Yet Merygreeke and my folkes tary very long.   50

Tib, An, and Margerie, doe singe here.

Pipe, mery Annot, etc.[1]

Trilla, trilla, trillarie!
Worke, Tibet; worke, Annot; worke, Margerie!
Sewe, Tibet ; knitte, Annot; spinne, Margerie!
Let vs see who shall winne the victorie.   55

Tib. Talk.   This sleue is not willyng to be sewed, I trowe ;
A small thing might make me all in the grounde to throwe!   57

Then they sing agayne.

Pipe, merrie Annot, etc.

Trilla, trilla, trillarie !
What, Tibet? what, Annot? what, Margerie?
Ye sleepe, but we doe not, that shall we trie.
Your fingers be nombde, our worke will not lie.   62

Tib. Talk.   If ye doe so againe, well, I would aduise you
        nay.

In good sooth, one stoppe more, and I make holy-day.   64

They singe the thirde tyme.

Pipe, mery Annot, etc.

Trilla, trilla, trillarie!
Nowe, Tibbet; now, Annot; nowe, Margerie!
Nowe whippet apace for the maystrie!
But it will not be, our mouth is so drie.   69

Tib. Talk.   Ah, eche finger is a thombe to-day, me thinke !
I care not to let all alone, choose it swimme or sinke !   71

---

[1] *I suppose* etc. *is to be expanded as* Pipe, Tibet ; pipe, Margerie!

They sing the fourth tyme.

            Pipe, mery Annot, etc.
      Trilla, trilla, trillarie!
      When, Tibet? when, Annot? when, Margerie?
      I will not! I can not! No more can I!
      Then giue we all ouer, and there let it lye!   76

            Lette hir caste downe hir vvorke.

   TIB. TALK.   There it lieth; the worste is but a curried
         cote!
Tut, I am vsed therto, I care not a grote!
   AN. ALYFACE.   Haue we done singyng since? then will I
         in againe ;
Here I founde you, and here I leaue both twaine.   *Exeat.* 80
   M. MUMBL.   And I will not be long after. Tib Talke-
         apace!
   TIB. TALK.   What is the[1] matter?
   M. MUMB.   Yond stode a man al this space,
And hath hearde all that euer we spake togyther.
   TIB. TALK.   Mary, the more loute he for his comming
         hither!
And the lesse good he can, to listen maidens talke!   85
I care not and I go byd him hence for to walke ;
It were well done to knowe what he maketh here-away.
   R. ROYSTER.   Nowe myght I speake to them, if I wist
         what to say.
   M. MUMBL.   Nay, we will go both off, and see what he is.

            [*They approach him.*]

   R. ROYSTER.   One that hath hearde all your talke and
         singyng, ywis.   90
   TIB. TALK.   The more to blame you! A good thriftie
         husbande
Woulde elsewhere haue had some better matters in hande.
   R. ROYSTER.   I dyd it for no harme ; but for good loue I
         beare
                  [2] A. ye.

To your dame, Mistresse Custance, I did your talke heare.

And, mistresse nource, I will kisse you for acquaintance.   95

 M. MUMBL. I come anon, sir.

 TIB. TALK.   Faith, I would our dame Custance

Sawe this geare.

 M. MUMBL. I must first wipe al cleane, yea, I must!

 TIB. TALK. Ill chieue it, dotyng foole, but it must be

  cust!

[ROISTER DOISTER kisses MADGE.]

 M. MUMBL. God yelde you, sir! chad not so much ichotte

  not whan,

Nere since chwas bore, chwine, of such a gay gentleman!   100

 R. ROYSTER. I will kisse you, too, mayden, for the good

  will I beare you.

 TIB. TALK. No, forsoth, by your leaue, ye shall not

  kisse me.

 R. ROYSTER. Yes, be not afearde, I doe not disdayne

  you a whit!

 TIB. TALK. Why shoulde I feare you? I haue not so little

  wit;

Ye are but a man, I knowe very well.

 R. ROYSTER.   Why, then?   105

 TIB. TALK. Forsooth, for I wyll not, I vse not to kisse

  men.

 R. ROYSTER. I would faine kisse you too, good maiden,

  if I myght.

 TIB. TALK. What shold that neede?

 R. ROYSTER.   But to honor you, by this light!

I vse to kisse all them that I loue, to God I vowe.

 TIB. TALK. Yea, sir? I pray you, when dyd ye last kisse

  your cowe?   110

 R. ROYSTER. Ye might be proude to kisse me, if ye were

  wise.

 TIB. TALK. What promotion were therein?

 R. ROYSTER.   Nourse is not so nice.

 TIB. TALK. Well, I haue not bene taught to kissing and

  licking.

R. ROYSTER.   Yet I thanke you, mistresse nourse, ye
 made no sticking.

M. MUMBL.   I will not sticke for a kosse with such a man
 as you.   115

TIB. TALK.   They that lust! I will againe to my sewyng
 now.

[Enter ANNOT ALYFACE.]

AN. ALYFAC[E].[1]   Tidings, hough! tidings! Dame Custance greeteth you well!

R. ROYSTER.   Whome? me?

AN. ALYFACE.   You, sir? no, sir; I do no
 suche tale tell.

R. ROYSTER.   But and she knewe me here —

AN. ALYFACE.   Tybet Talke-apace,
Your mistresse Custance and mine must speake with your
 grace.   120

TIB. TALK.   With me?

AN. ALYFACE.   Ye muste come in to hir, out of all
 doutes.

TIB. TALK.   And my work not half done!   A mischief on
 all loutes!

          Ex[eant] am[bo].

R. ROYSTER.   Ah, good sweet nourse!

M. MUMB.   A, good sweete gentleman!

R. ROYSTER.   What?

M. MUMBL.   Nay, I can not tel, sir, but what
 thing would you?

R. ROYSTER.   Howe dothe sweete Custance, my heart of
 gold, tell me how?   125

M. MUMBL.   She dothe very well, sir, and commaunde me
 to you.

R. ROYSTER.   To me?

M. MUMBL.   Yea, to you, sir.

R. ROYSTER.   To me? nurse, tel
 me plain, —
To me?

[1] *So* A.

M. MUMB. Ye!

R. ROYSTER.   That word maketh me aliue again.

M. MUMBL. She commaunde me to one last day, who-ere
it was.

R. ROYSTER. That was een to me and none other, by
the masse!   130

M. MUMBL. I can not tell you surely, but one it was.

R. ROYSTER. It was I and none other; this commeth to
good passe.

I promise thee, nourse, I fauour hir.

M. MUMB.   Een so, sir.

R. ROYSTER. Bid hir sue to me for mariage.

M. MUMBL.   Een so, sir.

R. ROYSTER. And surely for thy sake she shall speede.

M. MUMB.   Een so, sir. 135

R. ROYSTER. I shall be contented to take hir.

M. MUMB.   Een so, sir.

R. ROYSTER. But at thy request and for thy sake.

M. MUMB.   Een so, sir.

R. ROYSTER. And come hearke in thine eare what to say.

M. MUMB.   Een so, sir.

Here lette him tell hir a great long tale in hir eare.

Actus j. Scæna iiij.

[*Enter*] MATHEW MERYGREEKE, DOBINET DOUGHTIE, HARPAX [*and* MUSI-
CIANS *to*] RALPH ROYSTER [*and*] MARGERIE MUMBLECRUST.

M. MERY. Come on, sirs, apace, and quite your-selues
like men,

Your pains shalbe rewarded.

D. DOU.   But I wot not when.

M. MERY. Do your maister worship as ye haue done in
time past.

D. DOUGH. Speake to them; of mine office he shall haue
a cast.

M. MERY. Harpax, looke that thou doe well, too, and thy
fellow!   5

HARPAX.[1]　I warrant, if he will myne example folowe.

M. MERY.　Curtsie, whooresons, douke you and crouche at euery worde !

D. DOUGH.　Yes, whether our maister speake earnest or borde.

M. MERY.　For this lieth vpon his preferment indeede.

D. DOUGH.　Oft is hee a wower, but neuer doth he speede.　10

M. MERY.　But with whome is he nowe so sadly roundyng yond?

D. DOUGH.　With *Nobs nicebecetur miserere* fonde.

[M.][2] MERY.　God be at your wedding, be ye spedde alredie?
I did not suppose that your loue was so greedie.
I perceiue nowe ye haue chose of deuotion;　15
And ioy haue ye, ladie, of your promotion !

R. ROYSTER.　Tushe, foole, thou art deceiued, this is not she.

M. MERY.　Well mocke muche of hir, and keepe hir well, I vise ye.
I will take no charge of such a faire piece keeping.

M. MUMBL.　What ayleth thys fellowe? he driueth me to weeping.　20

M. MERY.　What, weepe on the weddyng day? be merrie, woman !
Though I say it, ye haue chose a good gentleman.

R. ROYSTER.　Kocks nownes, what meanest thou man? tut a whistle !

[M. MERY.][2]　Ah, sir, be good to hir, she is but a gristle !
Ah, sweete lambe and coney !

R. ROYSTER.　　　　　　　Tut, thou art deceiued !　25

M. MERY.　Weepe no more, lady, ye shall be well receiued.
Vp wyth some mery noyse, sirs, to bring home the bride !

R. ROYSTER.　Gogs armes, knaue! art thou madde? I tel thee thou art wide.

---

[1] *In A. this name is not printed in black-letter like the others, but in italics.*

[2] *Supplied by* A.

M. MERY.   Then ye entende by nyght to haue hir home
  brought?

R. ROYSTER.   I tel thee no.

M. MERY.   How then?

R. ROYSTER.   Tis neither ment ne thought.   30

M. MERY.   What shall we then doe with hir?

R. ROYSTER.   Ah, foolish harebraine,
This is not she!

M. MERY.   No is? why then, vnsayde againe!
And what yong girle is this with your mashyp so bolde?

R. ROYSTER.   A girle?

M. MERY.   Yea; I dare say, scarce yet three-
  score yere old.

R. ROYSTER.   This same is the faire widowes nourse of
  whome ye wotte.   35

M. MERY.   Is she but a nourse of a house? hence home,
  olde trotte!
Hence at once!

R. ROYSTER.   No, no!

M. MERY.   What, an please your maship,
A nourse talke so homely with one of your worship?

R. ROYSTER.   I will haue it so: it is my pleasure and will.

M. MERY.   Then I am content.   Nourse, come againe,
  tarry still.   40

R. ROYSTER.   What! she will helpe forward this my sute
  for hir part.

M. MERY.   Then ist mine owne pygs-nie, and blessing on
  my hart!

R. ROYSTER.   This is our best friend, man!

M. MERY.   Then teach hir what to say.

M. MUMBL.   I am taught alreadie.

M. MERY.   Then go, make no delay!

R. ROYSTER.   Yet hark one word in thine eare.

M. MERY.   Back, sirs from his taile!   45
  [Pushing them upon him.]

R. ROYSTER.   Backe, vilaynes! will ye be priuie of my
  counsaile?

M. MERY.　　Backe, sirs! so! I tolde you afore ye woulde
　　be shent!

　　　　　　　　　[*Another push.*]

R. ROYSTER.　　She shall haue the first day a whole pecke
　　of argent.

M. MUMBL.　　A pecke! *Nomine Patris*, haue ye so much
　　spare?

R. ROYSTER.　　Yea, and a carte-lode thereto, or else were
　　it bare,　　　　　　　　　　　　　　　　　　　　　　　50
Besides other mouables, housholde stuffe and lande.

M. MUMBL.　　Haue ye lands too?

R. ROYSTER.　　　　　　　　An hundred marks.

M. MERY.　　　　　　　　　　　　　Yea, a thousand.

M. MUMBL.　　And haue ye cattell too? and sheepe too?

R. ROYSTER.　　　　　　　　　　　Yea, a fewe.

M. MERY.　　He is ashamed the numbre of them to shewe.
Een rounde about him as many thousande sheepe goes　　55
As he and thou and I too haue fingers and toes.

M. MUMBL.　　And how many yeares olde be you?

R. ROYSTER.　　　　　　　　　　Fortie at lest.

M. MERY.　　Yea, and thrice fortie to them!

R. ROYSTER.　　　　　　　　　Nay, now thou dost iest:
I am not so olde, thou misreckonest my yeares.

M. MERY.　　I know that; but my minde was on bullockes
　　and steeres.　　　　　　　　　　　　　　　　　　　60

M. MUMBL.　　And what shall I shewe hir your masterships
　　name is?

R. ROYSTER.　　Nay, she shall make sute ere she know
　　that, ywis!

M. MUMBL.　　Yet let me somewhat knowe.

M. MERY.　　　　　　　　　　This is hee, vnderstand,
That killed the Blewe Spider in Blanchepouder Lande.

M. MUMBL.　　Yea, Iesus, William! zee law! dyd he zo, law?　65

M. MERY.　　Yea, and the last elephant that euer he sawe,
As the beast passed by, he start out of a buske,
And een with pure strength of armes pluckt out his great
　　tuske.

M. MUMBL.   Iesus! *nomine Patris!* what a thing was
        that!

R. ROISTER.   Yea, but, Merygreke, one thing thou hast
        forgot.   70

M. MERY.   What?

R. ROYSTER.   Of thother elephant.

M. MERY.   Oh, hym that fledde away?

R. ROYSTER.   Yea!

M. MERY.   Yea, he knew that his match was in
        place that day.

Tut, he bet the King of Crickets on Christmasse-day,
That he crept in a hole, and not a worde to say!

M. MUMBL.   A sore man by zembletee!

M. MERY.   Why, he wrong a club   75
Once, in a fray, out of the hande of Belzebub.

R. ROYSTER.   And how when Mumfision?

M. MERY.   Oh, your coustrelyng
Bore the lanterne a-fielde so before the gozelyng —
Nay, that is to long a matter now to be tolde!
Neuer aske his name, nurse! I warrant thee, be bolde,   80
He conquered in one day from Rome to Naples,
And woonne townes, nourse, as fast as thou canst make
        apples.

M. MUMBL.   O Lorde, my heart quaketh for feare⸗ he is
        to sore!

R. ROYSTER.   Thou makest hir to much afearde; Mery-
        greeke, no more!

This tale woulde feare my sweete heart Custance right euill.   85

M. MERY.   Nay, let hir take him, nurse, and feare not
        the deuill!

But thus is our song dasht.   Sirs, ye may home againe.

R. ROYSTER.   No, shall they not!   I charge you all here
        to remaine.

The villaine slaues! a whole day ere they can be founde!

M. MERY.   Couche!   On your marybones, whooresons!
        Down to the ground!   90

[*The* MUSICIANS *kneel.*]

Was it meete he should tarie so long in one place
Without harmonie of musike, or some solace?
Who-so hath suche bees as your maister in hys head
Had neede to haue his spirites with musike to be fed.
By your maisterships licence!

[Striking him.]

R. ROYSTER.   What is that? a moate?   95

M. MERY.   No; it was a fooles feather had light on your
coate.

R. ROISTER.   I was nigh no feathers since I came from
my bed.

M. MERY.   No, sir, it was a haire that was fall from your
hed.

R. ROISTER.   My men com when it plese them.

M. MERY.   By your leue!

[Striking him.]

R. ROYSTER.   What is that?

M. MERY.   Your gown was foule spotted with the foot of
a gnat.   100

R. ROISTER.   Their maister to offende they are nothing
afearde.

[MERYGREEKE strikes him.]

What now?

M. MERY.   A lousy haire from your masterships beard.

SERVANTS.[1]   And, sir, for nurses sake pardon this one
offence!

We shall not after this shew the like negligence.

R. ROYSTER.   I pardon you this once; and come sing nere
the wurse!   105

M. MERY.   How like you the goodnesse of this gentleman, nurse?

M. MUMBL.   God saue his maistership that so can his
men forgeue!

And I wyll heare them sing ere I go, by his leaue.

R. ROYSTER.   Mary, and thou shalt, wenche! Come, we
two will daunce!

[1] A. C. Omnes famulæ.

M. MUMBL.   Nay, I will by myne owne selfe foote the
    song perchaunce.
R. ROYSTER.   Go to it, sirs, lustily!
M. MUMBL.   Pipe vp a mery note:
Let me heare it playde, I will foote it, for a grote!   112

Cantent:

[1] Who-so to marry a minion wife
    Hath hadde good chaunce and happe,
Must loue hir and cherishe hir all his life,
    And dandle hir on his lappe.   116

If she will fare well, yf she wyll go gay,
    A good husbande euer styll,
What-euer she lust to doe or to say,
    Must lette hir haue hir owne will.   120

About what affaires so-euer he goe,
    He must shewe hir all his mynde;
None of hys counsell she may be kept froe,[2]
    Else is he a man vnkynde.   124

R. ROYSTER.   Now, nurse, take thys same letter here to
    thy mistresse,
And, as my trust is in thee, plie my businesse.
M. MUMBL.   It shalbe done.
M. MERY.   Who made it?
R. ROYSTER.   I wrote it ech whit.
M. MERY.   Then nedes it no mending.
R. ROYSTER.   No, no!
M. MERY.   No; I know your wit;
I warrant it wel.
M. MUMBL.   It shal be deliuered.
But, if ye speede, shall I be considered?   130
M. MERY.   Whough! dost thou doubt of that?

---

[1] *This song is printed at the end of the volume, under the general heading:* "Certaine Songs to be song by / those which shall vse this Comedie or
Enterlude"; *and is called:* "The Seconde Song."
[2] C. froe; A. free.

MADGE.   What shal I haue?

M. MERY.   An hundred times more than thou canst deuise
to craue.

M. MUMBL.   Shall I haue some newe geare? for my olde
is all spent.

M. MERY.   The worst kitchen wench shall goe in ladies
rayment.

M. MUMBL.   Yea?

M. MERY.   And the worst drudge in the house
shal go better   35
Than your mistresse doth now.

[M. MUMBL.] [1]   Then I trudge with your letter.
                                              [*Exeat.*]

R. ROYSTER.   Now may I repose me: Custance is mine
owne.
Let vs sing and play homeward, that it may be knowne.

M. MERY.   But are you sure that your letter is well
enough? [2]

R. ROYSTER.   I wrote it my-selfe.

M. MERY.   Then sing we to dinner! 140
        Here they sing, and go out singing.

Actus j. Scæna v.

CHRISTIAN CUSTANCE.   MARGERIE MUMBLECRUST.

C. CUSTANCE.   Who tooke thee thys letter, Margerie
Mumblecrust?

M. MUMBL.   A lustie, gay bacheler tooke it me of trust;
And, if ye seeke to him, he will lowe your doing.

C. CUSTANCE.   Yea, but where learned he that manner of
wowing?

M. MUMBL.   If to sue to hym you will any paines take,   5
He will haue you to his wife, he sayth, for my sake.

---

[1] A. MAR.; C. M. Mumbl.

[2] *One would expect the line to read:* But are you sure that your letter
will win her?

C. CUSTANCE.   Some wise gentleman, belike!   I am be-
    spoken;
And I thought verily thys had bene some token
From my dere spouse, Gawin Goodluck, whom, when him
    please,
God luckily sende home to both our heartes ease!   10

    M. MUMBL.   A ioyly man it is, I wote well by report,
And would haue you to him for marriage resort;
Best open the writing, and see what it doth speake.

    C. CUSTANCE.   At thys time, nourse, I will neither reade
    ne breake.

    M. MUMBL.   He promised to giue you a whole pecke of
    golde.   15

    C. CUSTANCE.   Perchaunce lacke of a pynte, when it shall
    be all tolde!

    M. MUMBL.   I would take a gay, riche husbande, and I
    were you!

    C. CUSTANCE.   In good sooth, Madge, een so would I, if
    I were thou.
But no more of this fond talke now; let vs go in;
And see thou no more moue me folly to begin,   20
Nor bring mee no mo letters for no mans pleasure
But thou know from whom.

    M. MUMBL.   I warrant ye, shall be sure!

                           [*Exeant.*]

Actus ij. Scæna j.

[*Enter*] DOBINET DOUGHTIE.

    D. DOUGH.   Where is the house I goe to? before or be-
    hinde?
I know not where nor when nor how I shal it finde.
If I had ten mens bodies and legs and strength,
This trotting that I haue must needes lame me at length.
And nowe that my maister is new set on wowyng,   5
I trust there shall none of vs finde lacke of doyng;
Two paire of shoes a day will nowe be too litle

To serue me, I must trotte to and fro so mickle.
" Go beare me thys token, carrie me this letter," —
Nowe this is the best way, nowe that way is better !   10
"Vp before day, sirs, I charge you, an houre or twaine !
Trudge, do me thys message, and bring worde quicke
          againe ! "
If one misse but a minute, then " His armes and woundes,
I woulde not haue slacked for ten thousand poundes !
Nay, see, I beseeche you, if my most trustie page,   15
Goe not nowe aboute to hinder my mariage ! "
So feruent hotte wowyng, and so farre from wiuing,
I trowe neuer was any creature liuyng.
With euery woman is he in some loues pang ;
Then vp to our lute at midnight, twangledome twang ;   20
Then twang with our sonets, and twang with our dumps,
And heyhough from our heart, as heauie as lead lumpes ;
Then to our recorder with toodleloodle poope,
As the howlet out of an yuie bushe should hoope ;
Anon to our gitterne, thrumpledum, thrumpledum thrum,   25
Thrumpledum, thrumpledum, thrumpledum, thrumpledum
          thrum !
Of songs and balades also he is a maker,
And that can he as finely doe as Iacke Raker ;
Yea, and *extempore* will he dities compose, —
Foolishe Marsias nere made the like, I suppose !   30
Yet must we sing them ; as good stuffe, I vndertake,
As for such a pen-man is well-fyttyng to make.
"Ah, for these long nights, heyhow ! when will it be day?
I feare, ere I come, she will be wowed away."
Then, when aunswere is made that it may not bee,   35
"O death, why commest thou not by-and-by ? " sayth he.
But then, from his heart to put away sorowe,
He is as farre in with some newe loue next morowe.
But in the meane season we trudge and we trot ;
From dayspring to midnyght I sit not nor rest not.   40
And now am I sent to Dame Christian Custance,
But I feare it will ende with a mocke for pastance.

I bring hir a ring, with a token in a cloute;
And, by all gesse, this same is hir house, out of doute.
I knowe it nowe perfect, I am in my right way.   45
And loe yond the olde nourse that was wyth vs last day!

Actus ij. Scæna ij.

MAGE MUMBLECRUST. DOBINET DOUGHTIE.

M. MUMBL.   I was nere so shoke vp afore since I was
   borne!
That our mistresse coulde not haue chid, I wold haue sworne.
And I pray God I die if I ment any harme;
But for my life-time this shall be to me a charme!
   D. DOUGH.   God you saue and see, nurse! and howe is it
   with you?   5
   M. MUMBL.   Mary, a great deale the worse it is, for suche
   as thou!
   D. DOUGH.   For me?   Why so?
   M. MUMB.   Why, wer not thou one of them, say,
That song and playde here with the gentleman last day?
   D. DOUGH.   Yes; and he would know if you haue for him
   spoken;
And prayes you to deliuer this ring and token.   10
   M. MUMBL.   Nowe, by the token that God tokened,
   brother,
I will deliuer no token, one nor other!
I haue once ben so shent for your maisters pleasure
As I will not be agayne for all hys treasure.
   D. DOUGH.   He will thank you, woman.
   M. MUMBL.   I will none of his thanke. 15
                                 Ex[eat.]

   D. DOUGH.   I weene I am a prophete, this geare will
   proue blanke!
But what, should I home againe without answere go?
It were better go to Rome on my head than so.

I will tary here this moneth but some of the house
Shall take it of me, and then I care not a louse.   20
But yonder commeth forth a wenche — or, a ladde ;
If he haue not one Lumbardes touche, my lucke is bad.

Actus ij. Scæna iij.

[Enter] TRUEPENIE. D. DOUGH[TIE *remains*]. TIBET T[ALK-APACE *and*]
ANOT AL[YFACE *enter later*].

TRUPENY.   I am cleane lost for lacke of mery companie,
We gree not halfe well within, our wenches and I ;
They will commaunde like mistresses, they will forbyd ;
If they be not serued, Trupeny must be chyd.
Let them be as mery nowe as ye can desire,   5
With turnyng of a hande our mirth lieth in the mire!
I can not skill of such chaungeable mettle,
There is nothing with them but ʻ in docke, out nettle!ʼ
    D. DOUGH.   Whether is it better that I speake to him
      furst,
Or he first to me?   It is good to cast the wurst.   10
If I beginne first, he will smell all my purpose ;
Otherwise, I shall not neede any-thing to disclose.
    TRUPENY.   What boy haue we yonder?   I will see what
      he is.
    D. DOUGH.   He commeth to me.   It is hereabout, ywis.
    TRUPENY.   Wouldest thou ought, friende, that thou look-
      est so about?   15
    D. DOUGH.   Yea ; but whether ye can helpe me or no, I
      dout.
I seeke to one Mistresse Custance house, here dwellyng.
    TRUPENIE.   It is my mistresse ye seeke too, by your tell-
      ing.
    D. DOUGH.   Is there any of that name heere but shee?
    TRUPENIE.   Not one in all the whole towne that I knowe,
      pardee.   20
    D. DOUGH.   A widowe she is, I trowe?

TRUPENIE.   And what and she be?
D. DOUGH.   But ensured to an husbande?
TRUPENIE.   Yea, so thinke we.
D. DOUGH.   And I dwell with hir husbande, that trusteth
      to be.
TRUPENIE.   In faith, then must thou needes be welcome to
      me ;
Let vs for acquaintance shake handes togither,   25
And, what-ere thou be, heartily welcome hither !

[*Enter* TIBET *and* ANOT.]

TIB. TALK.   Well, Trupenie, neuer but flinging?
AN. ALYFACE.   And frisking?
TRUPENIE.   Well, Tibet and Annot, still swingyng and
      whiskyng?
TIB. TALK.   But ye roile abroade.
AN. ALYFACE.   In the streete euere-where.
TRUPENIE.   Where are ye twaine, in chambers, when ye
      mete me there?   30
But come hither, fooles ; I haue one nowe by the hande,
Seruant to hym that must be our mistresse husbande.
Byd him welcome.
AN. ALYFACE.   To me, truly, is he welcome !
TIB. TALK.   Forsooth, and, as I may say, heartily wel-
      come!
D. DOUGH.   I thank you, mistresse maides.
AN. ALYFACE.   I hope we shal better know.   35
TIB. TALK.   And when wil our new master come?
D. DOUGH.   Shortly, I trow.
TIB. TALK.   I would it were to-morow ; for, till he resorte,
Our mistresse, being a widow, hath small comforte.
And I hearde our nourse speake of an husbande to-day,
Ready for our mistresse, a riche man and a gay ;   40
And we shall go in our Frenche hoodes euery day,
In our silke cassocks, I warrant you, freshe and gay,
In our tricke ferdegews [1] and billiments of golde,

---

[1] A. ferdegews.

Braue in our sutes of chaunge seuen double folde ;
Then shall ye see Tibet, sirs, treade the mosse so trimme, —
Nay, why sayd I treade? ye shall see hir glide and swimme,   46
Not lumperdee clumperdee like our spaniell Rig.

[*She illustrates the modes.*]

TRUPENY.   Mary, then, prickmedaintie, come toste me a
  fig!
Who shall then know our Tib Talke-apace, trow ye?
 AN. ALYFACE.   And why not Annot Alyface as fyne as
  she?   50
 TRUPENY.   And what, had Tom Trupeny a father or none?
 AN. ALYFACE.   Then our prety newe-come man will looke
  to be one.
 TRUPENY.   We foure, I trust, shall be a ioily, mery knot!
Shall we sing a fitte to welcome our friende, Annot?
 AN. ALYFACE.   Perchaunce he can not sing.
 D. DOUGH.   I am at all assayes.
 TIB. TALK.   By Cocke, and the better welcome to vs
  alwayes!   56

Here they sing :

A thing very fitte
For them that haue witte,
And are felowes knitte,
 Seruants in one house to bee,
Is fast[1] for to sitte,
And not oft to flitte,
Nor varie a whitte,
 But louingly to agree.   64

No man complainyng,
Nor other disdayning,
For losse or for gainyng,
 But felowes or friends to bee ;
No grudge remainyng,
No worke refrainyng,

[1] A. Is fast fast; C. As fast..

Nor helpe restrainyng,
    But louingly to agree.   72

No man for despite
By worde or by write
His felowe to twite,
    But further in honestie;
No good turnes entwite,
Nor olde sores recite,
But let all goe quite,
    And louingly to agree.   80

After drudgerie,
When they be werie,
Then to be merie,
    To laugh and sing they be free;
With chip and cherie
Heigh derie derie,
Trill on the berie,
    And louingly to agree.   88

Finis.

TIB. TALK.   Wyll you now in with vs vnto our mistresse
       go?
D. DOUGH.   I haue first for my maister an errand or two.
But I haue here from him a token and a ring;
They shall haue moste thanke of hir that first doth it bring.
    TIB. TALK.   Mary, that will I!
    TRUPENY.   See and Tibet snatch not now!
    TIB. TALK.   And why may not I, sir, get thanks as well
       as you?   *Exeat.*
    AN. ALYFACE.   Yet get ye not all, we will go with you
       both,   95
And haue part of your thanks, be ye neuer so loth!

Exeant omnes.

    D. DOUGH.   So my handes are ridde of it, I care for no
       more.
I may now return home; so durst I not afore.   *Exeat.*

Actus ij.   Scæna iiij.

C. Custance. Tibet. Annot Alyface. Trupeny.

C. Custance.   Nay, come forth all three! and come
  hither, pretie mayde!
Will not so many forewarnings make you afrayde?
 Tib. Talk.   Yes, forsoth.
 C. Custance.   But stil be a runner vp and downe?
Still be a bringer of tidings and tokens to towne?
 Tib. Talk.   No, forsoth, mistresse!
 C. Custance.   Is all your delite and ioy 5
In whiskyng and ramping abroade like a tom-boy?
 Tib. Talk.   Forsoth, these were there too, — Annot and
  Trupenie.
 Trupenie.   Yea, but ye alone tooke it, ye can not denie.
 Annot Aly.   Yea, that ye did!
 Tibet.   But if I had not, ye twaine would.
 C. Custance.   You great calfe, ye should haue more
  witte, so ye should! 10
But why shoulde any of you take such things in hande?
 Tibet.   Because it came from him that must be your
  husbande.
 C. Custance.   How do ye know that?
 Tibet.   Forsoth, the boy
  did say so.
 C. Custance.   What was his name?
 An. Alyface.   We asked not.
 C. Custance.   No did?
 An. Aliface.   He is not farre gone, of likelyhod.
 Trupeny.   I will see. 15
 C. Custance.   If thou canst finde him in the streete,
  bring him to me.
 Trupenie.   Yes.   *Exeat.*
 C. Custance. Well, ye naughty girles, if euer I per-
  ceiue
That henceforth you do letters or tokens receiue

To bring vnto me from any person or place,
Except ye first shewe me the partie face to face,   20
Eyther thou or thou, full truly abye thou shalt.

    TIBET.   Pardon this, and the next tyme pouder me in salt!
    C. CUSTANCE.   I shall make all girles by you twaine to
        beware.
    TIBET.   If euer I offende againe, do not me spare.

But if euer I see that false boy any more,   25
By your mistreshyps licence, I tell you afore,
I will rather haue my cote twentie times swinged
Than on the naughtie wag not to be auenged.

    C. CUSTANCE.   Good wenches would not so rampe abrode
        ydelly,

But keepe within doores, and plie their work earnestly.   30
If one would speake with me that is a man likely,
Ye shall haue right good thanke to bring me worde quickly;
But otherwyse with messages to come in post,
From henceforth, I promise you, shall be to your cost.
Get you in to your work!

    TIB. AN.   Yes, forsoth.
    C. CUSTANCE.   Hence, both twaine;   35
And let me see you play me such a part againe!

[Exeant MAIDS; enter TRUPENY.]

    TRUPENY.   Maistresse, I haue runne past the farre ende
        of the streete,

Yet can I not yonder craftie boy see nor meete.

    C. CUSTANCE.   No?
    TRUPENY.   Yet I looked as farre beyonde the
        people

As one may see out of the toppe of Paules steeple.   40

    C. CUSTANCE.   Hence in at doores, and let me no more be
        vext!
    TRUPENY.   Forgeue me this one fault, and lay on for the
        next!   [Exeat.]
    C. CUSTANCE.   Now will I in too, for I thinke, so God
        me mende,

This will proue some foolishe matter in the ende!   Exeat.

Actus [i]ij.[1] Scæna j.

MATHEWE MERYGREEKE.

M. MERY.   Nowe say thys againe : he hath somewhat to
      dooing
Which followeth the trace of one that is wowing,
Specially that hath no more wit in his hedde
Than my cousin Roister Doister withall is ledde.
I am sent in all haste to espie and to marke   5
How our letters and tokens are likely to warke.
Maister Roister Doister must haue aunswere in haste,
For he loueth not to spende much labour in waste.
Nowe, as for Christian Custance, by this light,
Though she had not hir trouth to Gawin Goodluck plight,   10
Yet rather than with such a loutishe dolte to marie,
I dare say, woulde lyue a poore lyfe solitarie.
But fayne would I speake with Custance, if I wist how,
To laugh at the matter.   Yond commeth one forth now !

Actus iij. Scæna ij.

[*Enter*] TIBET [*to*] M. MERYGREEKE.   CHRISTIAN CUSTANCE [*enters later*].

TIB. TALK.   Ah, that I might but once in my life haue a
      sight
Of him that made vs all so yll-shent, by this light !
He should neuer escape if I had him by the eare,
But euen from his head, I would it bite or teare.
Yea, and if one of them were not inowe,   5
I would bite them both off, I make God auow !
   M. MERY.   What is he whome this little mouse doth so
      threaten ?
   TIB. TALK.   I woulde teache him, I trow, to make girles
      shent or beaten !
   M. MERY.   I will call her.   Maide, with whome are ye so
      hastie ?
            1 *Brackets in* A.

TIB. TALK.   Not with you, sir, but with a little wagpastie,   10
A deceiuer of folkes, by subtill craft and guile.

   M. MERY.   I knowe where she is ; Dobinet hath wrought
       some wile.

   TIB. TALK.   He brought a ring and token which he sayd
       was sent

From our dames husbande, but I wot well I was shent ;

For it liked hir as well, to tell you no lies,   15

As water in hir shyppe, or salt cast in hir eies ;

And yet whence it came neyther we nor she can tell.

   M. MERY.   We shall haue sport anone ; I like this very
      well! —

And dwell ye here with Mistresse Custance, faire maide?

   TIB. TALK.   Yea, mary, doe I, sir ; what would ye haue
      sayd?   20

   M. MERY.   A little message vnto hir by worde of mouth.

   TIB. TALK.   No messages, by your leaue, nor tokens, for-
      soth!

   M. MERY.   Then help me to speke with hir.

   TIBET.   With a good
      wil that.

Here she commeth forth.   Now speake : ye know best what.

[Enter CUSTANCE.]

   C. CUSTANCE.   None other life with you, maide, but
      abrode to skip?   25

   TIB. TALK.   Forsoth, here is one would speake with your
      mistresship.

   C. CUSTANCE.   Ah, haue ye ben learning of mo messages
      now?

   TIB. TALK.   I would not heare his minde, but bad him
      shewe it to you.

   C. CUSTANCE.   In at dores!

   TIB. TALK.   I am gon.   Ex[eat].

   M. MERY.   Dame Custance, God ye saue!

   C. CUSTANCE.   Welcome, friend Merygreeke! and what
      thing wold ye haue?   30

M. MERY. I am come to you a little matter to breake.

C. CUSTANCE. But see it be honest, else better not to speake.

M. MERY. Howe feele ye your-selfe affected here of late?

C. CUSTANCE. I feele no maner chaunge ; but after the
    olde rate.

But wherby do ye meane?

M. MERY.   Concerning mariage.   35

Doth not loue lade you?

    C. CUSTANCE.   I feele no such cariage.

M. MERY. Doe ye feele no pangues of dotage? aunswere
    me right.

C. CUSTANCE. I dote so, that I make but one sleepe all
    the night.

But what neede all these wordes?

M. MERY.   Oh Iesus ! will ye see

What dissemblyng creatures these same women be?   40

The gentleman ye wote of, whome ye doe so loue

That ye woulde fayne marrie him, yf ye durst it moue,

Emong other riche widowes, which are of him glad,

Lest ye for lesing of him perchaunce might runne mad,

Is nowe contented that, vpon your sute making,   45

Ye be as one in election of taking.

    C. CUSTANCE. What a tale is this! that I wote of?
    whome I loue?

M. MERY. Yea, and he is as louing a worme, againe, as a
    doue.

Een of very pitie he is willyng you to take,

Bicause ye shall not destroy your-selfe for his sake.   50

    C. CUSTANCE. Mary, God yelde his mashyp ! What-euer
    he be,

It is gentmanly spoken !

M. MERY.   Is it not, trowe ye?

If ye haue the grace now to offer your-self, ye speede.

    C. CUSTANCE. As muche as though I did! This time it
    shall not neede.

But what gentman is it, I pray you tell me plaine,   55

That woweth so finely?

M. MERY.   Lo where ye be againe,
As though ye knewe him not!

    C. CUSTANCE.   Tush, ye speake in iest!

    M. MERY.   Nay, sure, the partie is in good knacking
        earnest;
And haue you he will, he sayth, and haue you he must.

    C. CUSTANCE.   I am promised duryng my life; that is iust.   60

    M. MERY.   Mary, so thinketh he, vnto him alone.

    C. CUSTANCE.   No creature hath my faith and trouth but
        one,
That is Gawin Goodlucke; and, if it be not hee,
He hath no title this way, what-euer he be,
Nor I know none to whome I haue such worde spoken.   65

    M. MERY.   Ye, knowe him not you by his letter and
        token?

    C. CUSTANCE.   In-dede, true it is that a letter I haue,
But I neuer reade it yet, as God me saue!

    M. MERY.   Ye a woman? and your letter so long vnredde?

    C. CUSTANCE.   Ye may therby know what hast I haue to
        wedde.   70
But now who it is for my hande, I knowe by gesse.

    M. MERY.   Ah well, I, say!

    C. CUSTANCE.   It is Roister Doister, doubtlesse.

    M. MERY.   Will ye neuer leaue this dissimulation?
Ye know hym not?

    C. CUSTANCE.   But by imagination;
For no man there is but a very dolt and loute   75
That to wowe a widowe woulde so go about.
He shall neuer haue me hys wife while he doe liue.

    M. MERY.   Then will he haue you if he may, so mote I
        thriue!
And he biddeth you sende him worde by me,
That ye humbly beseech him ye may his wife be,   80
And that there shall be no let in you, nor mistrust,
But to be wedded on Sunday next, if he lust;
And biddeth you to looke for him.

    C. CUSTANCE.   Doth he byd so?

M. MERY.   When he commeth, aske hym whether he dyd
    or no.

C. CUSTANCE.   Goe say that I bid him keepe him warme
    at home ;   85

For, if he come abroade, he shall cough me a mome.

My mynde was vexed, I shrew his head, sottish dolt !

M. MERY.   He hath in his head —

C. CUSTANCE.   As much braine as a burbolt !

M. MERY.   Well, Dame Custance, if he heare you thus
    play choploge.

C. CUSTANCE.   What will he?

M. MERY.   Play the deuill in the horologe.   90

C. CUSTANCE.   I defye him, loute!

M. MERY.   Shall I tell hym what ye say?

C. CUSTANCE.   Yea, and adde what-so-euer thou canst, I
    thee pray,

And I will auouche it, what-so-euer it bee.

M. MERY.   Then let me alone ; we will laugh well, ye shall
    see ;

It will not be long ere he will hither resorte.   95

C. CUSTANCE.   Let hym come when hym lust, I wishe no
    better sport.

Fare ye well, I will in, and read my great letter ;

I shall to my wower make answere the better.   *Exeat.*

Actus iij. Scæna iij.

MATHEW MERYGREEKE.   [*Enter*] ROISTER DOISTER.

M. MERY.   Nowe that the whole answere in my deuise
    doth rest,

I shall paint out our wower in colours of the best ;

And all that I say shall be on Custances mouth,

She is author of all that I shall speake, forsoth.

But yond commeth Roister Doister nowe, in a traunce.   **5**

R. ROYSTER.   Iuno sende me this day good lucke and good
    chaunce!

I can not but come see how Merygreeke doth speede.

    M. MERY.   I will not see him, but giue him a iutte, in-deede.

[Runs over him.]

I crie your mastershyp mercie!

    R. ROYSTER.   And whither now?

    M. MERY.   As fast as I could runne, sir, in poste against
        you.   10

But why speake ye so faintly, or why are ye so sad?

    R. ROYSTER.   Thou knowest the prouerbe, — bycause I
        can not be had.

Hast thou spoken with this woman?

    M. MERY.   Yea, that I haue!

    R. ROYSTER.   And what, will this geare be?

    M. MERY.   No, so God me saue!

    R. ROYSTER.   Hast thou a flat answer?

    M. MERY.   Nay, a sharp answer.

    R. ROYSTER.   What?   15

    M. MERY.   Ye shall not, she sayth, ·by hir will marry hir
        cat,

Ye are such a calfe, such an asse, such a blocke,

Such a lilburne, such a hoball, such a lobcocke;

And, bicause ye shoulde come to hir at no season,

She despised your maship out of all reason.   20

" Bawawe what ye say," ko I, " of such a ientman !"

" Nay, I feare him not," ko she, " doe the best he can.

He vaunteth him-selfe for a man of prowesse greate,

Where-as a good gander, I dare say, may him beate.

And, where he is louted and laughed to skorne   25

For the veriest dolte that euer was borne,

And veriest lubber, slouen and beast,

Liuing in this worlde from the west to the east,

Yet of himselfe hath he suche opinion

That in all the worlde is not the like minion.   30

He thinketh eche woman to be brought in dotage

With the onely sight of his goodly personage ;

Yet none that will haue hym; we do hym loute and flocke,

And make him, among vs, our common sporting-stocke ;
And so would I now," ko she, " saue onely bicause   35
Better nay, ko I, I lust not medle with dawes."
" Ye are happy," ko I, " that ye are a woman ;
This would cost you your life in case ye were a man."

 R. ROYSTER. Yea, an hundred thousand pound should not
  saue hir life!

 M. MERY. No, but that ye wowe hir to haue hir to your wife. 40
But I coulde not stoppe hir mouth.

 R. ROYSTER.   Heigh how, alas !

 M. MERY. Be of good cheere, man, and let the worlde
  passe!

 R. ROYSTER. What shall I doe or say, nowe that it will
  not bee?

 M. MERY. Ye shall haue choise of a thousande as good
  as shee ;
And ye must pardon hir, it is for lacke of witte.   45

 R. ROYSTER. Yea, for were not I an husbande for hir fitte?
Well, what should I now doe?

 M. MERY.   In faith, I can not tell.

 R. ROYSTER. I will go home and die.

 M. MERY.   Then shall I bidde toll the bell?

 R. ROYSTER. No.

 M. MERY.   God haue mercie on your soule! ah,
  good gentleman,
That er ye shuld th[u]s [1] dye for an vnkinde woman!   50
Will ye drinke once ere ye goe?

 R. ROYSTER.   No, no, I will none.

 M. MERY. How feele your soule to God?

 R. ROISTER.   I am nigh gone.

 M. MERY. And shall we hence streight?

 R. ROYSTER.   Yea.

 M. MERY.   *Placebo dilexi.*
       vt infra.[2]

[1] *Brackets in* A.

[2] *The other version of this burial service is printed in the old copy at
the end of the play, among other songs belonging to the play. For con-
venience I print it at the foot of the next two pages.*

Maister Roister [1] Doister will streight go home and die.

R. ROYSTER.   Heigh how, alas, the pangs of death my
       hearte do breake!   55

M. MERY.   Holde your peace! for shame, sir! a dead man
       may not speake!

Nequando: What mourners and what torches shall we haue?

R. ROYSTER.   None.

M. MERY.   *Dirige:* He will go darklyng to his graue, —
Neque lux, neque crux, neque mourners, *neque* clinke;
He will steale to heauen, vnknowing to God, I thinke.   60
A porta inferi: Who shall your goodes possesse?

R. ROYSTER.   Thou shalt be my sectour, and haue all,
       more and lesse.

M. MERY.   *Requiem æternam:* Now God reward your
       mastershyp!
And I will crie halfepenie-doale for your worshyp.
Come forth, sirs, heare the dolefull newes I shall you tell!   65

      Euocat SERUOS MILITIS.   [*Enter four* SERVANTS.]

Our good maister here will no longer with vs dwell!
But, in spite of Custance, which hath hym weried,
Let vs see his mashyp solemnely buried;
And, while some piece of his soule is yet hym within,

             THE PSALMODIE.

Placebo dilexi,
Maister Roister Doister wil streight go home and die,
Our Lorde Iesus Christ his soule haue mercie vpon:
Thus you see to day a man, to morrow Iohn.
   Yet sauing for a womans extreeme crueltie,
He might haue lyued yet a moneth or two or three,
But in spite of Custance which hath him weried,
His mashyp shall be worshipfully buried.
And while some piece of his soule is yet hym within,
Some parte of his funeralls let vs here beginne.
   Dirige.   He will go darklyng to his graue.
Neque lux, neque crux, nisi solum clinke,
Neuer gentman so went toward heauen I thinke.
   Yet sirs as ye wyll the blisse of heauen win,
When he commeth to the graue lay hym softly in,

   [1] A. Doister; C. Roister.

Some part of his funeralls let vs here begin.   70
Audiui vocem: All men, take heede by this one gentleman
Howe you sette your loue vpon an vnkinde woman ;
For these women be all suche madde, pieuishe elues,
They will not be wonne except it please them-selues.
But, in fayth, Custance, if euer ye come in hell,   75
Maister Roister Doister shall serue you as well.
And will ye needes go from vs thus, in very deede?
   R. ROYSTER.   Yea, in good sadnesse.
   M. MERY.   Now Iesus Christ be your speede!
Good night, Roger, olde knaue! farewell, Roger, olde knaue!
Good night, Roger, old knaue! knaue, knap!   *vt infra.*   80
Pray for the late Maister Roister Doisters soule!
And come forth, parish clarke, let the passing bell toll.

                [*Enter* PARISH CLERK.]

Pray for your mayster, sirs, and for hym ring a peale ; [1]

              Ad SERUOS MILITIS.

He was your right good maister while he was in heale.

> And all men take heede by this one Gentleman,
> How you sette your loue vpon an vnkinde woman :
> For these women be all suche madde pieuish elues,
> They wyll not be woonne except it please them selues.
> But in faith Custance if euer ye come in hell,
> Maister Roister Doister shall serue you as well.
> Good night Roger olde knaue, Farewel Roger olde knaue.
> Good night Roger olde knaue, knaue, knap.
> *Nequando.   Audiui vocem.   Requiem æternam.*

[1] *At the end of the play is printed:*

THE PEALE OF BELLES RONG BY THE PARISH CLERK AND ROISTER
           DOISTERS FOURE MEN.

      The first Bell a Triple.
    When dyed he ?   When dyed he ?

        The seconde.
    We haue hym !   We haue hym !

        The thirde.
  Royster Doyster!   Royster Doyster !

      The fourth Bell.
  He commeth !   He commeth !

      The greate Bell.
    Our owne !   Our owne !

Qui Lazarum.[1]

R. ROYSTER.   Heigh how!

M. MERY.   Dead men go not so fast.   85

In Paradisum.

R. ROYSTER.   Heihow!

M. MERY.   Soft, heare what I haue cast!

R. ROYSTER.   I will heare nothing, I am past.

M. MERY.   Whough, wellaway!

Ye may tarie one houre, and heare what I shall say.

Ye were best, sir, for a-while to reuiue againe

And quite them er ye go.

R. ROYSTER.   Trowest thou so?

M. MERY.   Ye, plain.   90

R. ROYSTER.   How may I reuiue, being nowe so farre
          past?

M. MERY.   I will rubbe your temples, and fette you againe
          at last.

R. ROYSTER.   It will not be possible.

M. MERY.   Yes, for twentie pounde.

[Rubs his head violently.]

R. ROYSTER.   Armes! what dost thou?

M. MERY.   Fet you again out of your sound.

By this crosse, ye were nigh gone in-deede; I might feele   95

Your soule departing within an inche of your heele.

Now folow my counsell.

R. ROYSTER.   What is it?

M. MERY.   If I wer you,

Custance should eft seeke to me ere I woulde bowe.

R. ROYSTER.   Well, as thou wilt haue me, euen so will
          I doe.

M. MERY.   Then shall ye reuiue againe for an houre or
          two.   100

R. ROYSTER.   As thou wilt; I am content, for a little space.

M. MERY.   Good happe is not hastie; yet in space
          comth[2] grace.

---

[1] C. *assigns this to* ROISTER DOISTER.   [2] A. com[e]th.

To speake with Custance your-selfe, shoulde be very well;
What good therof may come, nor I nor you can tell.
But, now the matter standeth vpon your mariage,   105
Ye must now take vnto you a lustie courage.
Ye may not speake with a faint heart to Custance,
But with a lusty breast and countenance,
That she may knowe she hath to answere to a man.
   R. ROYSTER.   Yes, I can do that as well as any can.   110
   M. MERY.   Then, bicause ye must Custance face to face
      wowe,
Let vs see how to behaue your-selfe ye can doe.
Ye must haue a portely bragge, after your estate.
   R. ROISTER.   Tushe, I can handle that after the best rate.

[He swaggers.]

   M. MERY.   Well done! so loe! vp, man, with your head
      and chin!   115
Vp with that snoute, man! so loe! nowe ye begin!
So, that is somewhat like! but, prankie cote, nay, whan!
That is a lustie brute! handes vnder your side, man!
So loe! now is it euen as it should bee!
That is somewhat like for a man of your degree!   120
Then must ye stately goe, ietting vp and downe.
Tut! can ye no better shake the taile of your gowne?
There, loe! suche a lustie bragge it is ye must make!
   R. ROYSTER.   To come behind, and make curtsie, thou
      must som pains take.
   M. MERY.   Else were I much to blame, I thanke your
      mastershyp,   125
The Lorde one day all-to begrime you with worshyp!
Backe, sir sauce! let gentlefolkes haue elbowe roome!
Voyde, sirs! see ye not Maister Roister Doister come?
Make place, my maisters!

[Shoving him about.]

   R. ROYSTER.   Thou iustlest nowe to nigh.
   M. MERY.   Back, al rude loutes!
   R. ROYSTER.   Tush!

M. MERY.   I crie your maship mercy! 130
Hoighdagh! if faire, fine Mistresse Custance sawe you now,
Ralph Royster Doister were hir owne, I warrant you.
    R. ROYSTER.   Neare an M, by your girdle?
    M. MERY.   Your Good Mastershyps
Maistershyp were hir owne Mistreshyps Mistreshyps!
Ye were take vp for haukes, ye were gone, ye were gone!   135
But now one other thing more yet I thinke vpon.
    R. ROYSTER.   Shewe what it is.
    M. MERY.   A wower, be he neuer so poore,
Must play and sing before his bestbeloues doore ;
How much more, than, you!
    R. ROYSTER.   Thou speakest wel, out of dout.
    M. MERY.   And perchaunce that woulde make hir the
            sooner come out.   140
    R. ROYSTER. Goe call my musitians, bydde them high apace.
    M. MERY.   I wyll be here with them ere ye can say trey
            ace.   *Exeat.*
    R. ROYSTER.   This was well sayde of Merygreeke ; I lowe
            hys wit.
Before my sweete hearts dore we will haue a fit,
That if my loue come forth, that I may with hir talke,   145
I doubt not but this geare shall on my side walke.
But lo, how well Merygreeke is returned sence!
            [*Enter* MERYGREEKE *with* MUSICIANS.]
    M. MERY.   There hath grown no grasse on my heele
            since I went hence,
Lo, here haue I brought that shall make you pastance.
    R. ROYSTER.   Come, sirs, let vs sing, to winne my deare
            loue Custance!   150

                    Cantent : [1]

            I mun be maried a Sunday ;
            I mun be maried a Sunday ;
            Who-soeuer shall come that way,
                I mun be maried a Sunday.   154

    [1] *This song is printed at the end of the play in the old copy, and is*
headed : " The fourth Song."

Royster Doyster is my name;
Royster Doyster is my name;
A lustie brute, I am the same,
  I mun be maried a Sunday.   158

Christian Custance haue I founde;
Christian Custance haue I founde,
A wydowe worthe a thousande pounde;
  I mun be maried a Sunday.   162

Custance is as sweete as honey;
Custance is as sweete as honey;
I hir lambe and she my coney,
  I mun be maried a Sunday.   166

When we shall make our weddyng-feast;
When we shall make our weddyng-feast,
There shall bee cheere for man and beast;
  I mun be maried a Sunday.
   I mun be maried a Sunday, etc.   171

M. MERY.   Lo, where she commeth!   Some countenaunce
  to hir make,
And ye shall heare me be plaine with hir for your sake.

Actus iij. Scæna iiij.

CUSTANCE. MERYGREEKE. ROISTER DOISTER.

C. CUSTANCE.   What gaudyng and foolyng is this afore
  my doore?
M. MERY.   May not folks be honest, pray you, though
  they be pore?
C. CUSTANCE.   As that thing may be true, so rich folks
  may be fooles!
R. ROYSTER.   Hir talke is as fine as she had learned in
  schooles.
M. MERY.   Looke partly towarde hir, and drawe a little
  nere.   5

C. CUSTANCE.   Get ye home, idle folkes.

M. MERY.   Why may not we be here?
Nay, and ye will haze, haze ; otherwise, I tell you plaine,
And ye will not haze, then giue vs our geare againe.

   C. CUSTANCE.   In-deede I haue of yours much gay things,
      God saue all !

R. ROYSTER.   Speake gently vnto hir, and let hir take all.   10

M. MERY.   Ye are to tender-hearted; shall she make vs
      dawes ?
Nay, dame, I will be plaine with you in my friends cause.

R. ROYSTER.   Let all this passe, sweete heart, and accept
      my seruice !

C. CUSTANCE.   I will not be serued with a foole, in no
      wise ;
When I choose an husbande, I hope to take a man.   15

M. MERY.   And where will ye finde one which can doe
      that he can?
Now, thys man towarde you being so kinde,
You not to make [1] him an answere somewhat to his minde !

C. CUSTANCE.   I sent him a full answere by you, dyd I
      not? [2]

M. MERY.   And I reported it.

C. CUSTANCE.   Nay, I must speake it againe.   20

R. ROYSTER.   No, no, he tolde it all.

M. MERY.   Was I not metely plaine?

R. ROYSTER.   Yes.

M. MERY.   But I would not tell all; for, faith, if I had,
With you, Dame Custance, ere this houre it had been bad;
And not without cause, for this goodly personage
Ment no lesse than to ioyne with you in mariage.   25

C. CUSTANCE.   Let him wast no more labour nor sute
      about me.

M. MERY.   Ye know not where your preferment lieth, I
      see,
He sending you such a token, ring and letter.

[1] C. Why not make.
[2] *Possibly a line rhyming with this has fallen out.*

C. CUSTANCE.   Mary, here it is, ye neuer sawe a better.

M. MERY.   Let vs see your letter.

C. CUSTANCE.   Holde, reade it, if ye can,   30
And see what letter it is to winne a woman.

M. MERY. [*reads*]   "To mine owne deare coney [1] birde,
          swete heart, and pigsny
Good Mistresse Custance present these by and by."
Of this superscription do ye blame the stile?

C. CUSTANCE.   With the rest as good stuffe as ye redde a
          great while !   35

M. MERY. [*reads.*]   " Sweete mistresse where as I loue you
          nothing at all,
Regarding your substance and richesse chiefe of all,
For your personage, beautie, demeanour and wit,
I commende me vnto you neuer a whit.
Sorie to heare report of your good welfare.   40
For (as I heare say) suche your conditions are,
That ye be worthie fauour of no liuing man,
To be abhorred of euery honest man.
To be taken for a woman enclined to vice.
Nothing at all to Vertue gyuing hir due price.   45
Wherfore concerning mariage, ye are thought
Suche a fine Paragon, as nere honest man bought.
And nowe by these presentes I do you aduertise
That I am minded to marrie you in no wise.
For your goodes and substance, I coulde bee content   50
To take you as ye are.   If ye mynde to bee my wyfe,
Ye shall be assured for the tyme of my lyfe,
I will keepe ye ryght well, from good rayment and fare,
Ye shall not be kepte but in sorowe and care.
Ye shall in no wyse lyue at your owne libertie,   55
Doe and say what ye lust, ye shall neuer please me,
But when ye are mery, I will be all sadde,
When ye are sory, I will be very gladde.

---

[1] *Apparently a comma is needed after* coney; *but, considering the peculiar character of the letter, it seems best to print it without any emendation,
even in punctuation.*

When ye seeke your heartes ease, I will be vnkinde,
At no tyme, in me shall ye muche gentlenesse finde.   60
But all things contrary to your will and minde,
Shall be done: otherwise I wyll not be behinde
To speake. And as for all them that woulde do you wrong
I will so helpe and mainteyne, ye shall not lyue long.
Nor any foolishe dolte, shall cumbre you but I.   65
I, who ere say nay, wyll[1] sticke by you tyll I die,
Thus good mistresse Custance, the lorde you saue and kepe,
From me Roister Doister, whether I wake or slepe.
Who fauoureth you no lesse, (ye may be bolde)
Than this letter purporteth, which ye haue vnfolde."   70

    C. CUSTANCE. Howe by this letter of loue? is it not fine?
    R. ROYSTER. By the armes of Caleys, it is none of
        myne!
    M. MERY. Fie! you are fowle to blame! this is your
        owne hand!
    C. CUSTANCE. Might not a woman be proude of such an
        husbande?
    M. MERY. Ah, that ye would in a letter shew such de-
        spite!   75
    R. ROYSTER. Oh, I would I had hym here, the which did
        it endite!
    M. MERY. Why, ye made it your-selfe, ye tolde me, by
        this light!
    R. ROYSTER. Yea, I ment I wrote it myne owne selfe,
        yesternight.
    C. CUSTANCE. Ywis, sir, I would not haue sent you such
        a mocke.
    R. ROYSTER. Ye may so take it, but I ment it not so, by
        Cocke!   80
    M. MERY. Who can blame this woman to fume and frette
        and rage?
Tut, tut, your-selfe nowe haue marde your owne marriage!
Well, yet, Mistresse Custance, if ye can this remitte,
This gentleman other-wise may your loue requitte.

                 [1] A. uyll.

C. CUSTANCE.   No, God be with you both! and seeke no
   more to me.   *Exeat.*   85
R. ROYSTER.   Wough! she is gone for-euer! I shall hir
   no more see!
M. MERY.   What, weepe? fye, for shame! and blubber?
   For manhods sake,
Neuer lette your foe so muche pleasure of you take!
Rather play the mans parte, and doe loue refraine.
If she despise you, een despise ye hir againe!   90
R. ROYSTER.   By Gosse, and for thy sake I defye hir, in-
   deede!
M. MERY.   Yea, and perchaunce that way ye shall much
   sooner speede;
For one madde propretie these women haue, in fey:
When ye will, they will not; will not ye, then will they.
Ah, foolishe woman! ah, moste vnluckie Custance!   95
Ah, vnfortunate woman! ah, pieuishe Custance!
Art thou to thine harmes so obstinately bent
That thou canst not see where lieth thine high preferment?
Canst thou not lub dis man, which coulde lub dee so well?
Art thou so much thine own foe?
R. ROYSTER.   Thou dost the truth tell.   100
M. MERY.   Wel, I lament.
R. ROYSTER.   So do I.
M. MERY.   Wherfor?
R. ROYSTER.   For this thing:
Bicause she is gone.
M. MERY.   I mourne for an-other thing.
R. ROYSTER.   What is it, Merygreeke, wherfore thou dost
   griefe take?
M. MERY.   That I am not a woman myselfe, for your sake.
I would haue you my-selfe, and a strawe for yond Gill!   105
And mocke much of you though it were against my will.
I would not, I warrant you, fall in such a rage
As so to refuse suche a goodly personage.
R. ROYSTER.   In faith, I heartily thanke thee, Merygreeke.
M. MERY.   And I were a woman—

R. ROYSTER.   Thou wouldest to me seeke. 110
M. MERY.   For, though I say it, a goodly person ye bee.
R. ROYSTER.   No, no.
M. MERY.   Yes, a goodly man as ere I dyd see.
R. ROYSTER.   No, I am a poore homely man, as God
    made mee.
M. MERY.   By the faith that I owe to God, sir, but ye bee!
Woulde I might, for your sake, spende a thousande pound
    land.   115
R. ROYSTER.   I dare say thou wouldest haue me to thy
    husbande.
M. MERY.   Yea ; and I were the fairest lady in the shiere,
And knewe you as I know you and see you nowe here, —
Well, I say no more !
R. ROYSTER.   Gramercies, with all my hart !
M. MERY.   But, since that can not be, will ye play a wise
    parte ?   120
R. ROYSTER.   How should I ?
M. MERY.   Refraine from Custance a-while now,
And I warrant hir soone right glad to seeke to you ;
Ye shall see hir anon come on hir knees creeping,
And pray you to be good to hir, salte teares weeping.
R. ROYSTER.   But what and she come not ?
M. MERY.   In faith, then, farewel she ! 125
Or else, if ye be wroth, ye may auenged be.
R. ROYSTER.   By Cocks precious potsticke, and een so I
    shall !
I wyll vtterly destroy hir and house and all !
But I woulde be auenged, in the meane space,
On that vile scribler, that did my wowyng disgrace.   130
M. MERY.   "Scribler," ko you? in-deede, he is worthy no
    lesse !
I will call hym to you and ye bidde me, doubtlesse.
R. ROYSTER.   Yes, for although he had as many liues
As a thousande widowes, and a thousande wiues,
As a thousande lyons, and a thousand rattes,   135
A thousande wolues, and a thousande cattes,

A thousande bulles, and a thousande calues,
And a thousande legions diuided in halues,
He shall neuer scape death on my swordes point, —
Though I shoulde be torne therfore ioynt by ioynt!   140
    M. MERY.   Nay, if ye will kyll him, I will not fette him ;
I will not in so muche extremitie sette him.
He may yet amende, sir, and be an honest man ;
Therfore pardon him, good soule, as muche as ye can!
    R. ROYSTER.   Well, for thy sake, this once with his lyfe
        he shall passe ;   145
But I wyll hewe hym all to pieces, by the masse !
    M. MERY.   Nay, fayth, ye shall promise that he shall no
        harme haue,
Else I will not fet him.
    R. ROYSTER.   I shall, so God me saue!
But I may chide him a good?
    M. MERY.   Yea, that do, hardely.
    R. ROYSTER.   Go, then.
    M. MERY.   I returne, and bring him to you
        by-and-by.   150

                              Ex[eat].

Actus iij. Scæna v.

ROISTER DOISTER. MATHEWE MERYGREEKE [*enters with*] SCRIUENER
[*during first speech*].

    R. ROYSTER.   What is a gentleman but his worde and his
        promise?
I must nowe saue this vilaines lyfe in any wise,
And yet at hym already my handes doe tickle, —
I shall vneth holde them, they wyll be so fickle.
But lo and Merygreeke haue not brought him sens!   5

      [*Enter* MERYGREEKE *and* SCRIVENER, *talking angrily.*]

    M. MERY.   Nay, I woulde I had of my purse payde fortie
        pens !
    SCRIUENER.   So woulde I, too ; but it needed not that
        stounde.

M. MERY. But the ientman had rather spent fiue thou-
    sande pounde ;
For it disgraced him at least fiue tymes so muche.

SCRIUENER. He disgraced hym-selfe, his loutishnesse is
    suche.   10

R. ROYSTER. Howe long they stande prating! Why
    comst thou not away?

M. MERY. Come nowe to hymselfe, and hearke what he
    will say.

SCRIUENER. I am not afrayde in his presence to appeere.

R. ROYSTER. Arte thou come, felow?

SCRIUENER.   How thinke you? am I not here?

R. ROYSTER. What hindrance hast thou done me, and
    what villanie?   15

SCRIUENER. It hath come of thy-selfe if thou hast had any.

R. ROYSTER. All the stocke thou comest of, later or
    rather,
From thy fyrst fathers grandfathers fathers father,
Nor all that shall come of thee, to the worldes ende,
Though to three-score generations they descende,   20
Can be able to make me a iust recompense
For this trespasse of thine and this one offense!

SCRIUENER. Wherin?

R. ROYSTER.   Did not you make me a letter, brother?

SCRIUENER. Pay the like hire, I will make you suche an-
    other.

R. ROYSTER. Nay, see and these whooreson Phariseys
    and Scribes   25
Doe not get their liuyng by polling and bribes!
If it were not for shame —

SCRIUENER.   Nay, holde thy hands still!

M. MERY. Why, did ye not promise that ye would not
    him spill?

SCRIUENER. Let him not spare me.

R. ROYSTER.   Why, wilt thou strike me again?

SCRIUENER. Ye shall haue as good as ye bring, of me,
    that is plaine!   30

M. MERY. I can not blame him, sir, though your blowes
   wold him greue,
For he knoweth present death to ensue of all ye geue.
R. ROYSTER. Well, this man for once hath purchased thy
   pardon.
SCRIUENER. And what say ye to me? or else I will be
   gon.
R. ROYSTER. I say the letter thou madest me was not
   good.   35
SCRIUENER. Then did ye wrong copy it, of likelyhood.
R. ROYSTER. Yes, out of thy copy worde for worde I
   wrote.
SCRIUENER. Then was it as ye prayed to haue it, I wote,
But in reading and pointyng there was made some faulte.
R. ROYSTER. I wote not; but it made all my matter to
   haulte.   40
SCRIUENER. Howe say you, is this mine originall or no?
R. ROYSTER.· The selfe-same that I wrote out of, so mote
   I go!
SCRIUENER. Loke you on your owne fist, and I will looke
   on this,
And let this man be iudge whether I reade amisse :
" To myne owne dere coney birde, sweete heart, and pigsny,[1] 45
Good mistresse Custance, present these by and by."
How now? doth not this superscription agree?
R. ROYSTER. Reade that is within, and there ye shall the
   fault see.
SCRIUENER. [reads] Sweete mistresse, where as I loue you,
   nothing at all
Regarding your richesse and substance : chiefe of all 50
For your personage, beautie, demeanour and witte
I commende me vnto you : Neuer a whitte
Sory to heare reporte of your good welfare.
For (as I heare say) suche your conditions are,
That ye be worthie fauour : Of no liuing man   55
To be abhorred : of euery honest man

    [1] *This word omitted by mistake in* **A.**

To be taken for a woman enclined to vice
Nothing at all : to vertue giuing hir due price.
Wherfore concerning mariage, ye are thought
Suche a fine Paragon, as nere honest man bought.   60
And nowe by these presents I doe you aduertise,
That I am minded to marrie you : In no wyse
For your goodes and substance : I can be content
To take you as you are : yf ye will be my wife,
Ye shall be assured for the time of my life,   65
I wyll keepe you right well : from good raiment and fare,
Ye shall not be kept : but in sorowe and care
Ye shall in no wyse lyue : at your owne libertie,
Doe and say what ye lust : ye shall neuer please me
But when ye are merrie : I will bee all sadde   70
When ye are sorie : I wyll be very gladde
When ye seeke your heartes ease : I will be vnkinde
At no time : in me shall ye muche gentlenesse finde.
But all things contrary to your will and minde
Shall be done otherwise : I wyl not be behynde   75
To speake : And as for all they that woulde do you wrong,
(I wyll so helpe and maintayne ye) shall not lyue long.
Nor any foolishe dolte shall cumber you, but I,
I, who ere say nay, wyll sticke by you tyll I die.
Thus good mistresse Custance, the lorde you saue and
        kepe.   80
From me Roister Doister, whether I wake or slepe,
Who fauoureth you no lesse, (ye may be bolde)
Than this letter purporteth, which ye haue vnfolde."
Now, sir, what default can ye finde in this letter?
        R. ROYSTER.   Of truth, in my mynde, there can not be a
                better.   85
        SCRIUENER.   Then was the fault in readyng, and not in
                writyng, —
No, nor, I dare say, in the fourme of endityng.
But who read this letter, that it sounded so nought?
        M. MERY.   I redde it, in-deede.
        SCRIUENER,   Ye red it not as ye ought.

R. ROYSTER.   Why, thou wretched villaine ! was all this
    same fault in thee?   90

M. MERY.   I knocke your costarde if ye offer to strike me !

                               [*Strikes him.*]

R. ROYSTER.   Strikest thou in-deede? and I offer but in
    iest.

M. MERY.   Yea, and rappe you againe, except ye can sit
    in rest.

And I will no longer tarie here, me beleue.

R. ROYSTER.   What, wilt thou be angry, and I do thee
    forgeue?   95

Fare thou well, scribler, I crie thee mercie, in-deede !

SCRIUENER.   Fare ye well, bibbler, and worthily may ye
    speede !   [*Exeat.*]

R. ROYSTER.   If it were an-other but thou, it were a
    knaue.

M. MERY.   Ye are an-other your-selfe, sir, the Lorde vs
    both saue!

Albeit, in this matter I must your pardon craue.   100

Alas ! woulde ye wyshe in me the witte that ye haue?

But, as for my fault, I can quickely amende ;

I will shewe Custance it was I that did offende.

R. ROYSTER.   By so doing, hir anger may be reformed.

M. MERY.   But, if by no entreatie she will be turned,   105

Then sette lyght by hir and bee as testie as shee,

And doe your force vpon hir with extremitie.

R. ROISTER.   Come on, therefore, lette vs go home, in
    sadnesse.

M. MERY.   That if force shall neede, all may be in a
    readinesse.

And, as for thys letter, hardely let all go,   110

We wyll know where she refuse you for that or no.

                          Exeant am[*bo*].

Actus iiij. Scæna j.

SYM SURESBY.

SIM SURE.   Is there any man but I, Sym Suresby, alone,
That would haue taken such an enterprise him vpon,
In suche an outragious tempest as this was,
Suche a daungerous gulfe of the sea to passe?
I thinke verily Neptunes mightie godshyp   5
Was angry with some that was in our shyp,
And, but for the honestie which in me he founde,
I thinke for the others sake we had bene drownde.
But fye on that seruant which for his maisters wealth
Will sticke for to hazarde both his lyfe and his health!   10
My maister, Gawyn Goodlucke, after me a day,
Bicause of the weather, thought best hys shyppe to stay;
And, now that I haue the rough sourges so well past,
God graunt I may finde all things safe here at last!
Then will I thinke all my trauaile well spent.   15
Nowe, the first poynt wherfore my maister hath me sent
Is to salute Dame Christian Custance, his wife
Espoused, whome he tendreth no lesse than his life.
I must see how it is with hir, well or wrong,
And whether for him she doth not now thinke long.   20
Then to other friendes I haue a message or tway.
And then so to returne and mete him on the way.
Now wyll I goe knocke, that I may dispatche with speede;
But loe, forth commeth hir-selfe, happily, in-deede!

Actus iiij. Scæna ij.

CHRISTIAN CUSTANCE.   SIM SURESBY.

C. CUSTANCE.   I come to see if any more stirryng be here;
But what straunger is this, which doth to me appere?
SYM SURS.   I will speake to hir: Dame, the Lorde you
    saue and see!

C. CUSTANCE.   What? friende Sym Suresby?   Forsoth,
    right welcome ye be !

Howe doth mine owne Gawyn Goodlucke, I pray the tell?   5

    S. SURESBY.   When he knoweth of your health, he will
        be perfect well.

    C. CUSTANCE.   If he haue perfect helth, I am as I would
        be.

    SIM SURE.   Suche newes will please him well ; this is as
        it should be.

    C. CUSTANCE.   I thinke now long for him.

    SYM SURE.   And he as long for you.

    C. CUSTANCE.   When wil he be at home?

    SYM SURE.   His heart is here een now ;   10
His body commeth after.

    C. CUSTANCE.   I woulde see that faine.

    SIM SURE.   As fast as wynde and sayle can cary it a-maine.
But what two men are yonde comming hitherwarde?

    C. CUSTANCE.   Now I shrew their best Christmasse
        chekes, both togetherward!

Actus iiij. Scæna iij.

[*To*] CHRISTIAN CUSTANCE [*and*] SYM SURESBY [*enter*] RALPH ROISTER
[*and*] MATHEW MERYGREKE.   TRUPENY [*enters later*].

    C. CUSTANCE.   What meane these lewde felowes thus to
        trouble me stil?

Sym Suresby here, perchance, shal therof deme som yll,
And shall suspect in me some point of naughtinesse
And they come hitherward.

    SYM SURE.   What is their businesse?

    C. CUSTANCE.   I haue nought to them, nor they to me, in
        sadnesse.   5

    SIM SURE.   Let vs hearken them ; somewhat there is, I
        feare it.

    R. ROYSTER.   I will speake out aloude, best that she may
        heare it.

M. MERY.   Nay, alas, ye may so feare hir out of hir wit!

R. ROYSTER.   By the crosse of my sworde, I will hurt hir
      no whit!

M. MERY.   Will ye doe no harme, in-deede? shall I trust
      your worde?   10

R. ROYSTER.   By Roister Doisters fayth, I will speake but
      in borde!

SIM SURE.   Let vs hearken them; somwhat there is, I
      feare it.

R. ROYSTER.   I will speake out aloude, I care not who
      heare it:

Sirs, see that my harnesse, my tergat and my shield

Be made as bright now as when I was last in fielde,   15

As white as I shoulde to warre againe to-morrowe;

For sicke shall I be but I worke some folke sorow.

Therfore see that all shine as bright as Sainct George,

Or as doth a key newly come from the smiths forge.

I woulde haue my sworde and harnesse to shine so bright   20

That I might therwith dimme mine enimies sight;

I would haue it cast beames as fast, I tell you playne,

As doth the glittryng grasse after a showre of raine.

And see that, in case I shoulde neede to come to arming,

All things may be ready at a minutes warning;   25

For such chaunce may chaunce in an houre, do ye heare?

M. MERY.   As perchance shall not chaunce againe in
      seuen yeare.

R. ROYSTER.   Now draw we neare to hir, and here what
      shall be sayde!

M. MERY.   But I woulde not haue you make hir too muche
      afrayde.

R. ROYSTER.   Well founde, sweete wife, I trust, for al
      this your soure looke!   30

C. CUSTANCE.   Wife? why cal ye me wife?

SIM SURE.   Wife? this gear goth acrook!

M. MERY.   Nay, Mistresse Custance, I warrant you, our
      letter

Is not as we redde een nowe, but much better;

And, where ye halfe stomaked this gentleman afore
For this same letter, ye wyll loue hym now therefore.   35
Nor it is not this letter, though ye were a queene,
That shoulde breake marriage betweene you twaine, I weene.
    C. CUSTANCE.   I did not refuse hym for the letters sake.
    R. ROYSTER.   Then ye are content me for your husbande
        to take?
    C. CUSTANCE.   You for my husbande to take? nothing
        lesse, truely !   40
    R. ROYSTER.   Yea, say so, sweete spouse, afore straun-
        gers hardly!
    M. MERY.   And, though I haue here his letter of loue
        with me,
Yet his ryng and tokens he sent keepe safe with ye.
    C. CUSTANCE.   A mischiefe take his tokens, and him and
        thee too !
But what prate I with fooles? haue I nought else to doo?   45
Come in with me, Sym Suresby, to take some repast.
    SIM SURE.   I must, ere I drinke, by your leaue, goe in all
        hast
To a place or two with earnest letters of his.
    C. CUSTANCE.   Then come drink here with me.
    SIM SURE.   I thank you.
    C. CUSTANCE.   Do not misse ;
You shall haue a token to your maister with you.   50
    SYM SURE.   No tokens this time, gramercies, God be
        with you!   *Exeat.*
    C. CUSTANCE.   Surely this fellowe misdeemeth some yll
        in me ;
Which thing, but God helpe, will go neere to spill me.
    R. ROYSTER.   Yea, farewell, fellow, and tell thy Maister
        Goodlucke
That he commeth to late of thys blossome to plucke!   55
Let him keepe him there still, or at least wise make no hast ;
As for his labour hither, he shall spende in wast :
His betters be in place nowe !
    M. MERY.   [*aside*]   As long as it will hold.

C. CUSTANCE.   I will be euen with thee, thou beast, thou
  mayst be bolde !
R. ROYSTER.   Will ye haue vs, then?
C. CUSTANCE.   I will neuer haue thee! 60
R. ROYSTER.   Then will I haue you.
C. CUSTANCE.   No, the deuill shal haue thee !
I haue gotten this houre more shame and harme by thee
Then all thy life-days thou canst do me honestie.
M. MERY.   Why, nowe may ye see what it comth too in
  the ende
To make a deadly foe of your most louing frende ! 65
And, ywis, this letter, if ye woulde heare it now —
C. CUSTANCE.   I will heare none of it.
M. MERY.   In faith, would rauishe you.
C. CUSTANCE.   He hath stained my name for-euer, this is
  cleare.
R. ROYSTER.   I can make all as well in an houre.
M. MERY.   As ten yeare.
How say ye? wil ye haue him?
C. CUSTANCE. No.
M. MERY.   Wil ye take him? 70
C. CUSTANCE.   I defie him.
M. MERY.   At my word?
C. CUSTANCE.   A shame take him!
Waste no more wynde, for it will neuer bee.
M. MERY.   This one faulte with twaine shall be mended,
  ye shall see :
Gentle Mistresse Custance now, good Mistresse Custance,
Honey Mistresse Custance now, sweete Mistresse Custance, 75
Golden Mistresse Custance now, white Mistresse Custance,
Silken Mistresse Custance now, faire Mistresse Custance.
C. CUSTANCE.   Faith, rather than to mary with suche a
  doltishe loute,
I woulde matche my-selfe with a begger, out of doute !
M. MERY.   Then I can say no more ; to speede we are
  not like, 80
Except ye rappe out a ragge of your rhetorike.

C. CUSTANCE.　Speake not of winnyng me; for it shall
　　　neuer be so.

R. ROYSTER.　Yes, dame, I will haue you, whether ye will
　　　or no.

I commaunde you to loue me; wherfore shoulde ye not?

Is not my loue to you chafing and burning hot?　　　85

M. MERY.　Too hir! that is well sayd!

R. ROYSTER.　　　　　　　Shall I so breake my braine

To dote vpon you, and ye not loue vs againe?

M. MERY.　Wel sayd yet!

C. CUSTANCE.　　　　Go to, you goose!

R. ROYSTER.　　　　　　　I say, Kit Custance,

In case ye will not haze, — well, better yes, perchaunce!

C. CUSTANCE.　Auaunt, lozell! picke thee hence!

M. MERY.　　　　　　　Wel, sir, ye perceiue,　90

For all your kinde offer, she will not you receiue.

R. ROYSTER.　Then a strawe for hir! and a strawe for
　　　hir againe!

She shall not be my wife, woulde she neuer so faine!

No, and though she would be at ten thousand pounde cost!

M. MERY.　Lo, dame, ye may see what an husbande ye
　　　haue lost!　　　　95

C. CUSTANCE.　Yea, no force; a iewell muche better lost
　　　than founde!

M. MERY.　Ah, ye will not beleue how this doth my heart
　　　wounde!

How shoulde a mariage betwene you be towarde,

If both parties drawe backe and become so frowarde?

R. ROYSTER.　Nay, dame, I will fire thee out of thy house,[1]　100

And destroy thee and all thine, and that by-and-by.

M. MERY.　Nay, for the passion of God, sir, do not so!

R. ROYSTER.　Yes, except she will say yea to that she
　　　sayde no.

C. CUSTANCE.　And what! be there no officers, trow we,
　　　in towne

To checke idle loytrers, braggyng vp and downe?　　　105

---

[1] C. *adds, for the sake of the rhyme,* though I die.

Where be they by whome vacabunds shoulde be represt,
That poore sillie widowes might liue in peace and rest?
Shall I neuer ridde thee out of my companie?
I will call for helpe: what, hough! come forth, Trupenie!

  TRUPENIE. Anon. [*Enters.*] What is your will, mis-
    tresse? dyd ye call me?   110
  C. CUSTANCE. Yea; go runne apace, and, as fast as may
    be,
Pray Tristram Trusty, my moste assured frende,
To be here by-and-by, that he may me defende.

  TRUPENIE. That message so quickly shall be done, by
    Gods grace,
That at my returne ye shall say I went apace. *Exeat.* 115

  C. CUSTANCE. Then shall we see, I trowe, whether ye
    shall do me harme!
  R. ROYSTER. Yes, in faith, Kitte, I shall thee and thine
    so charme
That all women incarnate by thee may beware.

  C. CUSTANCE. Nay, as for charming me, come hither if
    thou dare ;
I shall cloute thee tyll thou stinke, both thee and thy traine, 120
And coyle thee mine owne handes, and sende thee home
    againe.

  R. ROYSTER. Yea, sayst thou me that, dame? dost thou
    me threaten?
Goe we, I will [1] see whether I shall be beaten.

  M. MERY. Nay, for the paishe of God! let me now treate
    peace,
For bloudshed will there be, in case this strife increace. 125
Ah, good Dame Custance, take better way with you!

  C. CUSTANCE. Let him do his worst!

    [ROISTER DOISTER *attacks* CUSTANCE, *and is beaten.*]

M. MERY.   Yeld in time !
R. ROYSTER.   Come hence, thou !

        Exeant ROISTER *et* MERY.

   [1] C. will; A. still; *cf.* Mundus et Infans, l. 9.

Actus iiij. Scæna iiij.

CHRISTIAN CUSTANCE [*alone*]. ANOT ALYFACE, TIBET T., M. MUMBLE-
CRUST [*enter later*].

C. CUSTANCE. So, sirra, if I should not with hym take this
   way,
I should not be ridde of him, I thinke, till doomes-day.
I will call forth my folkes, that, without any mockes,
If he come agayne, we may giue him rappes and knockes.
Mage Mumblecrust, come forth! and Tibet Talke-apace! 5
Yea, and come forth, too, Mistresse Annot Alyface!

    [*Enter the three* SERVANTS.]

ANNOT ALY.   I come.
TIBET.   And I am here.
M. MUMB.   And I am here too at length.
C. CUSTANCE.   Like warriers, if nede bee, ye must shew
   your strength!
The man that this day hath thus begiled you
Is Ralph Roister Doister, whome ye know well inowe,[1] 10
The moste loute and dastarde that euer on grounde trode.
 TIB. TALK.   I see all folke mocke hym when he goth
   abrode.
 C. CUSTANCE.   What, pretie maide? will ye talke when I
   speake?
 TIB. TALK.   No, forsooth, good mistresse.
 C. CUSTANCE.   Will ye my tale breake?
He threatneth to come hither with all his force to fight; 15
I charge you, if he come, on him with all your might!
 M. MUMBL.   I with my distaffe will reache hym one rappe!
 TIB. TALK.   And I with my newe broome will sweepe
   hym one swappe,
And then with our greate clubbe I will reache hym one rappe!
 AN. ALIFACE.   And I with our skimmer will fling him
   one flappe! 20

    [1] C. inowe; A. mowe.

TIB. TALK.   Then Trupenies fireforke will him shrewdly
      fray,
And you with the spitte may driue him quite away.
  C. CUSTANCE.   Go make all ready, that it may be een so.
  TIB. TALK.   For my parte, I shrewe them that last about
      it go !   *Exeant* [SERVANTS].

Actus iiij. Scæna v.

CHRISTIAN CUSTANCE [*alone*].   TRUPENIE [*and*] TRISTRAM TRUSTY [*enter
later*].

  C. CUSTANCE.   Trupenie dyd promise me to runne a great
      pace,
My friend Tristram Trusty to fet into this place.
In-deede he dwelleth hence a good stert, I confesse ;
But yet a quicke messanger might twice since, as I gesse,
Haue gone and come againe.   Ah, yond I spie him now !   5

      [*Enter* TRUPENY *and* TRUSTY.]

  TRUPENY.   Ye are a slow goer, sir, I make God auow ;
My Mistresse Custance will in me put all the blame.
Your leggs be longer than myne ; come apace, for shame !
  C. CUSTANCE.   I can thee thanke, Trupenie ; thou hast
      done right wele.
  TRUPENY.   Maistresse, since I went, no grasse hath
      growne on my hele,   10
But Maister Tristram Trustie here maketh no speede.
  C. CUSTANCE.   That he came at all, I thanke him in very
      deede,
For now haue I neede of the helpe of some wise man.
  T. TRUSTY.   Then may I be gone againe, for none such
      I [a]m.[1]
  TRUPENIE.   Ye may bee by your going ; for no alderman   15
Can goe, I dare say, a sadder pace than ye can.
  C. CUSTANCE.   Trupenie, get thee in, thou shalt among
      them knowe

      [1] *Brackets in* A.

How to vse thy-selfe like a propre man, I trowe.

　　TRUPENY.　I go.　　　　　　　　　　*Ex[eat]*.

　　C. CUSTANCE.　　Now, Tristram Trusty, I thank you right
　　　　much ;

For, at my first sending, to come ye neuer grutch.　　　20

　　T. TRUSTY.　Dame Custance, God ye saue ! and, while my
　　　　life shall last,

For my friende Goodlucks sake ye shall not sende in wast.

　　C. CUSTANCE.　He shal giue you thanks.

　　T. TRUSTY.　　　　　　I will do much for his sake.

　　C. CUSTANCE.　But, alack, I feare, great displeasure shall
　　　　he [1] take !

　　T. TRUSTY.　Wherfore?

　　C. CUSTANCE.　　　　For a foolish matter.

　　T. TRUSTY.　　　　　　　What is your cause?　25

　　C. CUSTANCE.　I am yll accombred with a couple of dawes.

　　T. TRUSTY.　Nay, weepe not, woman, but tell me what
　　　　your cause is.

As concerning my friende is any thing amisse?

　　C. CUSTANCE.　No, not on my part; but here was Sym
　　　　Suresby —

　　T. TRUSTIE.　He was with me and told me so.

　　C. CUSTANCE.　　　　　　And he stoode by　30

While Ralph Roister Doister, with helpe of Merygreeke,

For promise of mariage dyd vnto me seeke.

　　T. TRUSTY.　And had ye made any promise before them
　　　　twaine?

　　C. CUSTANCE.　No ; I had rather be torne in pieces and
　　　　slaine !

No man hath my faith and trouth but Gawyn Goodlucke,　35

And that before Suresby dyd I say, and there stucke ;

But of certaine letters there were suche words spoken —

　　T. TRUSTIE.　He tolde me that too.

　　C. CUSTANCE.　　　　　And of a ring and token,

That Suresby, I spied, dyd more than halfe suspect

That I my faith to Gawyn Goodlucke dyd reiect.　　40

　　　　　　　　[1] C. he ; A. be.

T. TRUSTY.   But there was no such matter, Dame Cus-
    tance, in-deede?

C. CUSTANCE.   If euer my head thought it, God sende
    me yll speede!

Wherfore I beseech you with me to be a witnesse

That in all my lyfe I neuer intended thing lesse.

And what a brainsicke foole Ralph Roister Doister is   45

Your-selfe know well enough.

T. TRUSTY.   Ye say full true, ywis!

C. CUSTANCE.   Bicause to bee his wife I ne graunt nor
    apply,

Hither will he com, he sweareth, by-and-by,

To kill both me and myne, and beate downe my house flat;

Therfore I pray your aide.

T. TRUSTIE.   I warrant you that.   50

C. CUSTANCE.   Haue I so many yeres liued a sobre life

And shewed my-selfe honest, mayde, widowe, and wyfe,

And nowe to be abused in such a vile sorte?

Ye see howe poore widowes lyue, all voyde of comfort!

T. TRUSTY.   I warrant hym do you no harme nor wrong
    at all.   55

C. CUSTANCE.   No; but Mathew Merygreeke doth me
    most appall,

That he woulde ioyne hym-selfe with suche a wretched loute.

T. TRUSTY.   He doth it for a iest, I knowe hym out of
    doubte.

And here cometh Merygreke.

C. CUSTANCE.   Then shal we here his mind.

Actus iiij. Scæna vj.

[Enter] MERYGREKE *[to]* CHRISTIAN CUSTANCE *[and]* TRIST. TRUSTY.

M. MERY.   Custance and Trustie both, I doe you here
    well finde.

C. CUSTANCE.   Ah, Mathew Merygreeke, ye haue vsed
    me well!

M. MERY.   Nowe for altogether ye must your answere
    tell:
Will ye haue this man, woman? or else will ye not?
Else will he come, neuer bore so brymme nor tost so hot.   5
  TRIS. AND CU.   But why ioyn ye with him?
  T. TRUSTY.   For mirth?
  C. CUSTANCE.   Or else in sadnesse?
  M. MERY.   The more fond of you both hardly that[1] mater
    gesse.
  TRISTRAM.   Lo, how say ye, dame?
  M. MERY.   Why do ye thinke, Dame Custance,
That in this wowyng I haue ment ought but pastance?
  C. CUSTANCE.   Much things ye spake, I wote, to main-
    taine his dotage.   10
  M. MERY.   But well might ye iudge I spake it all in
    mockage.
For-why, is Roister Doister a fitte husband for you?
  T. TRUSTY.   I dare say ye neuer thought it.
  M. MERY.   No; to God I vow.
And dyd not I knowe afore of the insurance
Betweene Gawyn Goodlucke and Christian Custance?   15
And dyd not I, for the nonce, by my conueyance,
Reade his letter in a wrong sense for daliance,
That, if you coulde haue take it vp at the first bounde,
We should therat such a sporte and pastime haue founde
That all the whole towne should haue ben the merier?   20
  C. CUSTANCE.   Ill ake your heades both! I was neuer
    werier
Nor neuer more vexte since the first day I was borne!
  T. TRUSTY.   But very well I wist he here did all in scorne.
  C. CUSTANCE.   But I feared therof to take dishonestie.
  M. MERY.   This should both haue made sport and shewed
    your honestie;   25
And Goodlucke, I dare sweare, your witte therin would low.
  T. TRUSTY.   Yea, being no worse than we know it to be
    now.

[1] A. yat; C. the.

M. Mery.   And nothing yet to late ; for, when I come to
      him,
Hither will he repaire with a sheepes looke full grim,
By plaine force and violence to driue you to yelde.   30
    C. Custance.   If ye two bidde me, we will with him
      pitche a fielde,
I and my maides together.
    M. Mery.   Let vs see, be bolde !
    C. Custance.   Ye shall see womens warre.
    T. Trusty.   That fight wil I behold.
    M. Mery.   If occasion serue, takyng his parte full brim,
I will strike at you, but the rappe shall light on him.   35
When we first appeare —
    C. Custance.   Then will I runne away
As though I were afeard.
    T. Trusty.   Do you that part wel play,
And I will sue for peace.
    M. Mery.   And I wil set him on.
Then will he looke as fierce as a Cotssold lyon.
    T. Trusty.   But when gost thou for him?
    M. Mery.   That do I very nowe.   40
    C. Custance.   Ye shal find vs here.
    M. Mery.   Wel, God haue mercy on you!
                               Ex[eat].

T. Trusty.   There is no cause of feare, the least boy in
      the streete —
    C. Custance.   Nay, the least girle I haue will make him
      take his feete.
But hearke ! me thinke they make preparation.
    T. Trusty.   No force, it will be a good recreation.   45
    C. Custance.   I will stand within, and steppe forth
      speedily,
And so make as though I ranne away dreadfully.
                    [Custance *and* Trusty *withdraw.*]

Actus iiij. Scæna vij.

R. ROYSTER. M. MERYGREEKE. C. CUSTANCE. D. DOUGHTIE. HARPAX.
TRISTRAM TRUSTY.[1]

R. ROYSTER. Nowe, sirs, keepe your ray, and see your
    heartes be stoute!
But where be these caitifes? me think they dare not route!
How sayst thou, Merygreeke? What doth Kit Custance
    say?
M. MERY. I am loth to tell you.
R. ROYSTER.   Tushe, speake, man! yea or nay?
M. MERY. Forsooth, sir, I haue spoken for you all that I
    can.   5
But, if ye winne hir, ye must een play the man;
Een to fight it out ye must a mans heart take.
R. ROYSTER. Yes, they shall know, and thou knowest
    I haue a stomacke.
[2][M. MERY.] " A stomacke," quod you? yea, as good as
    ere man had.
R. ROYSTER. I trowe they shall finde and feele that I am
    a lad.   10
M. MERY. By this crosse, I haue seene you eate your
    meate as well
As any that ere I haue seene of or heard tell!
" A stomacke," quod you? he that will that denie,
I know was neuer at dynner in your companie!
R. ROYSTER. Nay, the stomacke of a man it is that I
    meane.   15
M. MERY. Nay, the stomacke of a horse or a dogge, I
    weene.
R. ROYSTER. Nay, a mans stomacke with a weapon
    meane I.

---

[1] *I have not inserted stage directions here, as usual, because I did not
wish to disturb the order of the names. It will be observed that* CUSTANCE
does not enter until l. 41, *and* TRUSTY *not until* l. 76.

[2] *Brackets in* A.

M. MERY.   Ten men can scarce match you with a spoone
in a pie.

R. ROYSTER.   Nay, the stomake of a man to trie in strife.

M. MERY.   I neuer sawe your stomacke cloyed yet in my
lyfe.   20

R. ROYSTER.   Tushe! I meane in strife or fighting to trie.

M. MERY.   We shall see how ye will strike nowe, being
angry.

R. ROYSTER.   Haue at thy pate, then! and saue thy head
if thou may!

M. MERY.   Nay, then, haue at your pate agayne, by this
day!

[They strike at each other.]

R. ROYSTER.   Nay, thou mayst not strike at me againe, in
no wise.   25

M. MERY.   I can not in fight make to you such warrantise.
But, as for your foes here, let them the bargaine bie.

R. ROYSTER.   Nay, as for they, shall euery mothers childe
die!
And in this my fume a little thing might make me
To beate downe house and all, and else the deuill take me!   30

M. MERY.   If I were as ye be, by Gogs deare mother,
I woulde not leaue one stone vpon an-other,
Though she woulde redeeme it with twentie thousand poundes!

R. ROYSTER.   It shall be euen so, by His lily woundes!

M. MERY.   Bee not at one with hir vpon any amendes.   35

R. ROYSTER.   No, though she make to me neuer so many
frendes,
Nor if all the worlde for hir woulde vndertake ;
No, not God hymselfe, neither, shal not hir peace make !
On, therfore! marche forwarde!   Soft; stay a-whyle yet!

M. MERY.   On!

R. ROYSTER.   Tary !

M. MERY.   Forth!

R. ROYSTER.   Back!

M. MERY.   On !

R. ROYSTER.   Soft!   Now forward set!   40

[CUSTANCE *enters, and flees as if in terror.*]

C. CUSTANCE.   What businesse haue we here? out! alas!
      alas!

R. ROYSTER.   Ha, ha, ha, ha, ha!

Dydst thou see that, Merygreeke? how afrayde she was?

Dydst thou see how she fledde apace out of my sight?

Ah, good sweete Custance! I pitie hir, by this light!   45

M. MERY.   That tender heart of yours wyll marre al to-
      gether; [1]

Thus will ye be turned with waggyng of a fether!

R. ROYSTER.   On, sirs, keepe your ray!

M. MERY.   On! forth, while this geare is hot!

R. ROYSTER.   Soft; the armes of Caleys! I haue one
      thing forgot.

M. MERY.   What lacke we now?

R. ROYSTER.   Retire, or else we be all slain!   50

M. MERY.   Backe, for the pashe of God! backe, sirs!
      backe againe!

What is the great mater?

R. ROYSTER.   This hastie forth-goyng

Had almost brought vs all to vtter vndoing;

It made me forget a thing most necessarie.

M. MERY.   Well remembred of a captaine, by Sainct
      Marie!   55

R. ROYSTER.   It is a thing must be had.

M. MERY.   Let vs haue it, then.

R. ROYSTER.   But I wote not where nor how.

M. MERY.   Then wote not I when.

But what is it?

R. ROYSTER.   Of a chiefe thing I am to seeke.

M. MERY.   Tut! so will ye be, when ye haue studied a
      weke.

But tell me what it is.

R. ROYSTER.   I lacke yet an hedpiece.   60

M. MERY.   The kitchen collocauit, the best hennes to
      Grece,

[1] A. altogether.

Runne fet it, Dobinet, and come at once withall!
And bryng with thee my potgunne, hangyng by the wall!

[*Exit* DOBINET.]

I haue seene your head with it, full many a tyme,
Couered as safe as it had bene with a skrine ;   65
And I warrant it saue your head from any stroke,
Except perchaunce to be amased with the smoke ;
I warrant your head therwith, except for the mist,
As safe as if it were fast locked vp in a chist.
And loe, here our Dobinet commeth with it nowe!   70

[*Enter* DOBINET.]

D. DOUGH.   It will couer me to the shoulders well inow.

M. MERY.   Let me see it on.

R. ROYSTER.   In fayth, it doth metely well.

M. MERY.   There can be no fitter thing.   Now ye must
        vs tell
What to do.

R. ROYSTER.   Now forth in ray, sirs, and stoppe no more!

M. MERY.   Now Sainct George to borow !   Drum dubbe-
        a-dubbe afore!   75

[*Enter* TRUSTY.]

T. TRUSTY.   What meane you to do, sir? committe man-
        slaughter?

R. ROYSTER.   To kyll fortie such, is a matter of laughter.

T. TRUSTY.   And who is it, sir, whome ye intende thus to
        spill ?

R. ROYSTER.   Foolishe Custance here forceth me against
        my will.

T. TRUSTY.   And is there no meane your extreme wrath
        to slake?   80
She shall some amendes vnto your good mashyp make.

R. ROYSTER.   I will none amendes.

T. TRUSTY.   Is hir offence so sore?

M. MERY.   And he were a loute, she coulde haue done no
        more :

She hath calde him foole, and dressed him like a foole,
Mocked hym lyke a foole, vsed him like a foole.　　　85
　　T. Trusty.　Well, yet the sheriffe, the iustice or constable,
Hir misdemeanour to punishe might be able.
　　R. Royster.　No, sir; I mine owne selfe will in this
　　　　present cause
Be sheriffe and iustice and whole iudge of the lawes;
This matter to amende, all officers be I shall,　　　90
Constable, bailiffe, sergeant.
　　M. Mery.　　　　　　　And hangman and all.
　　T. Trusty.　Yet a noble courage, and the hearte of a
　　　　man,
Should more honour winne by bearyng with a woman:
Therfore, take the lawe, and lette hir aunswere therto.
　　R. Royster.　Merygreeke, the best way were euen so to do;　95
What honour should it be with a woman to fight?
　　M. Mery.　And what then? will ye thus forgo and lese
　　　　your right?
　　R. Royster.　Nay, I will take the lawe on hir withouten
　　　　grace.
　　T. Trusty.　Or, yf your mashyp coulde pardon this one tres-
　　　　pace,
I pray you forgiue hir.
　　R. Royster.　　　　Hoh?
　　M. Mery.　　　　　　　Tushe! tushe, sir, do not!　100
　　[T. Trusty.]¹　Be good maister to hir.
　　R. Royster.　　　　　Hoh?
　　M. Mery.　　　　　　　　Tush, I say, do not!
And what! shall your people here returne streight home?
　　T. Trustie.　Yea, leuie the campe, sirs, and hence againe,
　　　　eche one!
　　[R. Royster.]²　But be still in readinesse if I happe to
　　　　call;
I can not tell what sodaine chaunce may befall.　　　105
　　M. Mery.　Do not off your harnesse, sirs, I you aduise,
At the least for this fortnight, in no maner wise;

¹ A. omits.　　² Omitted in original, says C.

Perchaunce in an houre when all ye thinke least,
Our maisters appetite to fight will be best.
But soft! ere ye go, haue once at Custance house!   110
   R. ROYSTER.   Soft! what wilt thou do?
   M. MERY.   Once discharge my harquebouse;
And, for my heartes ease, haue once more with my potgoon.
   R. ROYSTER.   Holde thy handes, else is all our purpose
     cleane fordoone.
   M. MERY.   And it cost me my life!
   R. ROYSTER.   I say thou shalt not!
   M. MERY.   By the matte, but I will! Haue once more
     with haile-shot!   [*Shoots.*] 115
I will haue some penyworth; I will not leese all!

Actus iiij. Scæna viij.

M. MERYGREEKE. C. CUSTANCE. R. ROISTER. TIB. T. AN. ALYFACE.
M. MUMBLECRUST. TRUPENIE. DOBINET DOUGHTIE. HARPAX. *Two
drummes with their ensignes.*[1]

   C. CUSTANCE.   What caitifes are those that so shake my
     house-wall?
   M. MERY.   Ah, sirrha! now, Custance, if ye had so muche
     wit,
I woulde see you aske pardon and your-selues submit.
   C. CUSTANCE.   Haue I still this adoe with a couple of
     fooles?
   M. MERY.   Here ye what she saith?
   C. CUSTANCE.   Maidens, come forth with your tooles!   5

        [*The* MAIDS *enter, armed.*]

   R. ROYSTER.   In a-ray —
   M. MERY.   Dubba-dub, sirrha!
   R. ROYSTER.   In a-ray
They come sodainly on vs.
   M. MERY.   Dubbadub!

   [1] CUSTANCE *comes out at the beginning of the scene; the* MAIDS *enter
later.*

R. ROYSTER.   In a-ray !
That euer I was borne!   We are taken tardie !
   M. MERY.   Now, sirs, quite our-selues like tall men and
      hardie.
   C. CUSTANCE.   On afore, Truepenie ! holde thyne owne,
      Annot!   10
On towarde them, Tibet! for scape vs they can not.
Come forth, Madge Mumblecrust ! so ! stand fast togither !
   M. MERY.   God sende vs a faire day.
   R. ROYSTER.   See, they marche on hither !
   TIB. TALK.   But, mistresse !
   C. CUSTANCE.   What sayst thou? [1]
   TIB. [TALK.]   Shall I go fet our goose ?
   C. CUSTANCE.   What to do?
   TIB. [TALK.]   To yonder captain I will
      turne hir loose :   15
And she gape and hisse at him as she doth at me,
I durst ieoparde my hande she wyll make him flee.

                 [*They fight.*]

   C. CUSTANCE.   On! forward!
   R. ROYSTER.   They com!
   M. MERY.   Stand!
   R. ROYSTER.   Hold!
   M. MERY.   Kepe!
   R. ROYSTER.   There !
   M. MERY.   Strike !
   R. ROYSTER.   Take heede !
   C. CUSTANCE.   Wel sayd, Truepeny !
   TRUPENY.   Ah, whooresons!
   C. CUSTANCE.   Wel don, in-deede!
   M. MERY.   Hold thine owne, Harpax ! downe with them,
      Dobinet!   20
   C. CUSTANCE.   Now, Madge! there, Annot! now sticke
      them, Tibet!
   TIB. TALK.   All my chiefe quarell is to this same little
      knaue
               [1] A. you.

That begyled me last day; nothyng shall him saue!

 D. DOUGH. Downe with this litle queane that hath at
  me such spite!

Saue you from hir, maister, it is a very sprite! 25

 C. CUSTANCE. I my-selfe will Mounsire graunde captaine
  vndertake!

 R. ROYSTER. They win grounde!

 M. MERY.   Saue your-selfe, sir, for Gods sake!

 R. ROYSTER. Out! alas, I am slaine! helpe!

 M. MERY.   Saue your-self!

 R. ROYSTER.   Alas!

 M. MERY. Nay, then, haue at you, mistresse!

 R. ROYSTER.   Thou hittest me, alas!

 M. MERY. I wil strike at Custance here.

 R. ROYSTER.   Thou hittest me!

 M. MERY.   So I wil! 30

Nay, Mistresse Custance!

 R. ROYSTER.   Alas, thou hittest me still!

Hold!

 M. MERY. Saue your-self, sir.

 R. ROYSTER.   Help! out! alas, I am slain!

 M. MERY. Truce! hold your hands! truce for a pissing-
  while or twaine!

Nay, how say you, Custance? for sauing of your life,

Will ye yelde, and graunt to be this gentmans wife? 35

 C. CUSTANCE. Ye tolde me he loued me; call ye this
  loue?

 M. MERY. He loued a-while euen like a turtle-doue.

 C. CUSTANCE. Gay loue, God saue it, so soone hotte, so
  soone colde!

 M. MERY. I am sory for you : he could loue you yet, so
  he coulde.

 R. ROYSTER. Nay, by Cocks precious, she shall be none
  of mine! 40

 M. MERY. Why so?

 R. ROYSTER.   Come away; by the matte, she is
  mankine!

I durst aduenture the losse of my right hande
If shee dyd not slee hir other husbande.
And see, if she prepare not againe to fight!

    M. MERY.   What then?   Sainct George to borow, our
        Ladies knight!   45
    R. ROYSTER.   Slee else whom she will, by Gog, she shall
        not slee mee!
    M. MERY.   How then?
    R. ROYSTER.   Rather than to be slaine, I will flee.
    C. CUSTANCE.   Too it againe, my knightesses! downe
        with them all!
    R. ROYSTER.   Away! away! away! she will else kyll vs
        all!
    M. MERY.   Nay, sticke to it, like an hardie man and a tall.   50
    R. ROYSTER.   Oh, bones! thou hittest me! Away! or else
        die we shall!
    M. MERY.   Away, for the pashe of our sweete Lord Iesus
        Christ!
    C. CUSTANCE.   Away, loute and lubber! or I shall be thy
        priest!

          [ROISTER DOISTER *and his* MEN *flee.*][1]

So this fielde is ours, we haue driuen them all away!

    TIB. TALK.   Thankes to God, mistresse, ye haue had a
        faire day!   55
    C. CUSTANCE.   Well, nowe goe ye in, and make your-selfe
        some good cheere.
    ALL.[2]   We goe.

          [*Exeant* MAIDS.]

    T. TRUST.   Ah, sir, what a field we haue had heere!
    C. CUSTANCE.   Friend Tristram, I pray you, be a witnesse
        with me.
    T. TRUSTY.   Dame Custance, I shall depose for your
        honestie.

And nowe fare ye well, except some-thing else ye wolde.   60

---

      [1] A. Exeant om.   [2] A. *Omnes pariter.*

C. CUSTANCE.   Not now ; but, when I nede to sende, I
          will be bolde.   *Exeat.*
I thanke you for these paines.   And now I wyll get me in ;
Now Roister Doister will no more wowyng begin.
                                                    Ex[eat].

Actus v. Scæna j.

GAWYN GOODLUCKE.   SYM SURESBY.

[G. GOODL.]   Sym Suresby, my trustie man, nowe aduise
          thee well,
And see that no false surmises thou me tell :
Was there such adoe about Custance, of a truth?
     SIM SURE.   To reporte that I hearde and sawe, to me is
          ruth,
But both my duetie and name and propretie   5
Warneth me to you to shewe fidelitie.
It may be well enough, and I wyshe it so to be ;
She may hir-selfe discharge and trie hir honestie ;
Yet their clayme to hir, me thought, was very large,
For with letters, rings and tokens they dyd hir charge :   10
Which when I hearde and sawe, I would none to you bring.
     G. GOODL.   No, by Sainct Marie, I allowe thee in that
          thing!
Ah, sirra, nowe I see truthe in the prouerbe olde :
All things that shineth is not by-and-by pure golde.
If any doe lyue a woman of honestie,   15
I would haue sworne Christian Custance had bene shee.
     SIM SURE.   Sir, though I to you be a seruant true and iust,
Yet doe not ye therfore your faithfull spouse mystrust ;
But examine the matter, and if ye shall it finde
To be all well, be not ye for my wordes vnkinde.   20
     G. GOODL.   I shall do that is right, and as I see cause why.
But here commeth Custance forth ; we shal know by-and-by.

Actus v. Scæna ij.

C. Custance. Gawyn Goodlucke. Sym Suresby.

C. Custance.   I come forth to see and hearken for newes
     good,
For about this houre is the tyme, of likelyhood,
That Gawyn Goodlucke, by the sayings of Suresby,
Would be at home; and lo, yond I see hym, I!
What, Gawyn Goodlucke, the onely hope of my life,   5
Welcome home, and kysse me, your true espoused wife!
     Ga. Good.   Nay, soft, Dame Custance! I must first, by
          your licence,
See whether all things be cleere in your conscience.
I heare of your doings to me very straunge.
     C. Custance.   What, feare ye that my faith towardes
          you should chaunge?   10
     Ga. Good.   I must needes mistrust ye be elsewhere en-
          tangled,
For I heare that certaine men with you haue wrangled
About the promise of mariage by you to them made.
     C. Custance.   Coulde any mans reporte your minde
          therein persuade?
     Ga. Good.   Well, ye must therin declare your-selfe to
          stande cleere,   15
Else I and you, Dame Custance, may not ioyne this yere.
     C. Custance.   Then woulde I were dead and faire layd
          in my graue!
Ah, Suresby, is this the honestie that ye haue?
To hurt me with your report, not knowyng the thing?
     Sim Sure.   If ye be honest, my wordes can hurt you
          nothing;   20
But what I hearde and sawe, I might not but report.
     C. Custance.   Ah, Lorde, helpe poore widowes, destitute
          of comfort!
Truly, most deare spouse, nought was done but for pastance.

G. Good.   But such kynde of sporting is homely daliance.

C. Custance.   If ye knewe the truthe, ye would take all
    in good parte.   25

Ga. Good.   By your leaue, I am not halfe-well skilled in
    that arte.

C. Custance.   It was none but Roister Doister, that
    foolishe mome.

Ga. Good.   Yea, Custance !   " Better," they say, " a badde
    scuse than none."

C. Custance.   Why, Tristram Trustie, sir, your true and
    faithfull frende,

Was priuie bothe to the beginning and the ende ;   30
Let him be the iudge and for me testifie.

Ga. Good.   I will the more credite that he shall verifie.
And, bicause I will the truthe know een as it is,
I will to him my-selfe, and know all without misse.
Come on, Sym Suresby, that before my friend thou may   35
Auouch the same wordes which thou dydst to me say.

                  Exeant [*all but* Custance].

Actus v. Scæna iij.

Christian Custance.

C. Custance.   O Lorde, howe necessarie it is nowe-of-dayes,
That eche bodie liue vprightly all maner wayes ;
For, lette neuer so little a gappe be open,
And be sure of this, the worst shall be spoken !
Howe innocent stande I in this for deede or thought !   5
And yet see what mistrust towardes me it hath wrought !
But thou, Lorde, knowest all folkes thoughts and eke intents ;
And thou arte the deliuerer of all innocentes.
Thou didst helpe the aduoutresse that she might be amended,
Much more then helpe, Lorde, that neuer yll intended !   10
Thou didst helpe Susanna, wrongfully accused,
And no lesse dost thou see, Lorde, how I am now abused.
Thou didst helpe Hester, when she should haue died,
Helpe also, good Lorde, that my truth may be tried !

Yet, if Gawin Goodlucke with Tristram Trusty speake,　　15
I trust of yll report the force shall be but weake.
And loe! yond they come, sadly talking togither;
I wyll abyde, and not shrinke, for their comming hither.

Actus v. Scæna iiij.

GAWYN GOODLUCKE. TRISTRAM TRUSTIE. C. CUSTANCE. SYM SURESBY.[1]

GA. GOOD.　And was it none other than ye to me reporte?

TRISTRAM.　No; and here were ye wished to haue seene
the sporte.

GA. GOOD.　Woulde I had, rather than halfe of that in
my purse.

SIM SURE.　And I doe muche reioyce the matter was no
wurse;

And, like as to open it I was to you faithfull,　　5
So of Dame Custance honest truth I am ioyfull;
For God forfende that I shoulde hurt hir by false reporte.

GA. GOOD.　Well, I will no longer holde hir in discom-
forte.

C. CUSTANCE.　Nowe come they hitherwarde, I trust all
shall be well.

GA. GOOD.　Sweete Custance, neither heart can thinke
nor tongue tell　　10
Howe much I ioy in your constant fidelitie.
Come nowe, kisse me, the pearle of perfect honestie!

C. CUSTANCE.　God lette me no longer to continue in lyfe
Than I shall towardes you continue a true wyfe!

GA. GOODL.　Well now, to make you for this some parte
of amendes,　　15
I shall desire first you, and then suche of our frendes
As shall to you seeme best, to suppe at home with me,
Where at your fought fielde we shall laugh and mery be.

SIM SURE.　And, mistresse, I beseech you, take with me
no greefe,

---

[1] *The three men advance together towards* CUSTANCE.

I did a true mans part, not wishyng you repreefe.   20

    C. CUSTANCE.   Though hastie reportes through surmises growyng

May of poore innocentes be vtter ouerthrowyng,

Yet, bicause to thy maister thou hast a true hart,

And I know mine owne truth, I forgiue thee for my part.

    GA. GOODL.   Go we all to my house; and of this geare no more!   25

Goe prepare all things, Sym Suresby; hence, runne afore!

    SIM SURE.   I goe.   *Ex[eat]*.

    G. GOOD.   But who commeth yond? M. Merygreeke?

    C. CUSTANCE.   Roister Doisters champion, I shrewe his best cheeke.

    T. TRUSTY.   Roister Doister selfe, your wower, is with him, too;

Surely some-thing there is with vs they haue to doe.   30

Actus v. Scæna v.

[*Enter*] M. MERYGREEKE [*and*] RALPH ROISTER [*to*] GAWYN GOODLUCKE, TRISTRAM TRUSTIE [*and*] C. CUSTANCE.

    M. MERY.   Yond I see Gawyn Goodlucke, to whom lyeth my message;

I will first salute him after his long voyage,

And then make all thing well concerning your behalfe.

    R. ROYSTER.   Yea, for the pashe of God!

    M. MERY.   Hence out of sight, ye calfe,

Till I haue spoke with them, and then I will you fet,   5

    R. ROYSTER.   In Gods name!

    M. MERY.   What, Master Gawin Goodluck, wel met!

And from your long voyage I bid you right welcome home.

    GA. GOOD.   I thanke you.

    M. MERY.   I come to you from an honest mome.

    GA. GOOD.   Who is that?

    M. MERY.   Roister Doister, that doughtie kite.

C. CUSTANCE.　Fye! I can scarce abide ye shoulde his
　　name recite.　　　　　　　　　　　　　　　　　　10

M. MERY.　Ye must take him to fauour, and pardon all
　　past;

He heareth of your returne, and is full yll agast.

GA. GOOD.　I am ryght well content he haue with vs some
　　chere.

C. CUSTANCE.　Fye vpon him, beast! then wyll not I be
　　there!

GA. GOOD.　Why, Custance do·ye hate hym more than
　　ye loue me?　　　　　　　　　　　　　　　　　　15

C. CUSTANCE.　But for your mynde, sir, where he were
　　would I not be!

T. TRUSTY.　He woulde make vs al laugh.

M. MERY.　　　　　　　　　　Ye nere had better sport.

GA. GOOD.　I pray you, sweete Custance, let him to vs
　　resort.

C. CUSTANCE.　To your will I assent.

M. MERY.　　　　　　　　　Why, suche a foole it is

As no man for good pastime would forgoe or misse.　　20

G. GOODL.　Fet him to go wyth vs.

M. MERY.　　　　　　　　　He will be a glad man.

　　　　　　　　　　　　　　　　　　　　Ex[eat].

T. TRUSTY.　We must, to make vs mirth, maintaine hym
　　all we can.

And loe, yond he commeth, and Merygreeke with him!

C. CUSTANCE.　At his first entrance ye shall see I wyll
　　him trim;

But first let vs hearken the gentlemans wise talke.　　25

T. TRUSTY.　I pray you marke if euer ye sawe crane so
　　stalke.

Actus v. Scæna vj.

R. Roister.   M. Merygreeke.   C. Custance.   G. Goodlucke.   T.
Trustie.   D. Doughtie.   Harpax.[1]

R. Royster.   May I then be bolde?

M. Mery.   I warrant you, on my worde;
They say they shall be sicke but ye be at theyr borde.

R. Royster.   Thei wer not angry, then?

M. Mery.   Yes, at first, and made strange;
But, when I sayd your anger to fauour shoulde change,
And therewith had commended you accordingly,   5
They were all in loue with your mashyp by-and-by,
And cried you mercy that they had done you wrong.

R. Royster.   For-why no man, woman, nor childe can
          hate me long.

M. Mery.   "We feare," quod they, "he will be auenged
          one day,
Then for a peny giue all our liues we may."   10

R. Royster.   Sayd they so in-deede?

M. Mery.   Did they? yea, euen with one voice.
" He will forgiue all," quod I; oh, how they did reioyce!

R. Royster.   Ha, ha, ha!

M. Mery.   "Goe fette hym," say they, "while he is in
          good moode,
For, haue his anger who lust, we will not, by the roode!"   15

R. Royster.   I pray God that it be all true that thou
          hast me tolde,
And that she fight no more.

M. Mery.   I warrant you; be bolde,
Too them, and salute them!

R. Royster.   Sirs, I greete you all well!

Omnes.   Your maistership is welcom!

C. Custance.   Sauyng my quarell;
For, sure, I will put you vp into the Eschequer.   20

M. Mery.   Why so? better nay; wherfore?

---

[1] Doughtie *and* Harpax *do not enter until* l. 43.

C. Custance.   For an vsurer.

R. Royster.   I am no vsurer, good mistresse, by His
armes!

M. Mery.   When tooke he gaine of money to any mans
harmes?

C. Custance.   Yes, a fowle vsurer he is, ye shall see els.

R. Royster.   Didst not thou promise she would picke no
mo quarels?   25

C. Custance.   He will lende no blowes but he haue in
recompence
Fiftene for one; whiche is to muche, of conscience!

R. Royster.   Ah, dame, by the auncient lawe of armes,
a man
Hath no honour to foile [1] his handes on a woman.

C. Custance.   And, where other vsurers take their gaines
yerely,   30
This man is angry but he haue his by-and-by.

Ga. Goodl.   Sir, doe not for hir sake beare me your
displeasure.

M. Mery.   Well, he shall with you talke therof more at
leasure.
Vpon your good vsage, he will now shake your hande.

R. Royster.   And much heartily welcome from a straunge
lande!   35

M. Mery.   Be not afearde, Gawyn, to let him shake your
fyst!

Ga. Goodl.   Oh the moste honeste gentleman that ere I
wist!
I beseeche your mashyp to take payne to suppe with vs!

M. Mery.   He shall not say you nay and I too, by Iesus!
Bicause ye shall be friends, and let all quarels passe.   40

R. Royster.   I wyll be as good friends with them as ere
I was.

M. Mery.   Then let me fet your quier that we may haue
a song.

R. Royster.   Goe.   [*Exeat.*]

---

[1] *Both* A. *and* C. *have* foile, *not* foile; *cf.* Cymbeline, ii, 3, 126.

G. GOODLUCK.   I haue hearde no melodie all this yeare
long.

[Enter MERYGREEKE *with* MUSICIANS.]

M. MERY.   Come on, sirs, quickly!

R. ROYSTER.   Sing on, sirs, for my frends sake!

D. DOUGH.   Cal ye these your frends?

R. ROYSTER.   Sing on, and no mo words make!   45

Here they sing.

GA. GOOD.   The Lord preserue our most noble Queene of
renowne,
And hir virtues rewarde with the heauenly crowne.

C. CUSTANCE.   The Lorde strengthen hir most excellent
Maiestie,
Long to reigne ouer vs in all prosperitie.

T. TRUSTY.   That hir godly proceedings the faith to
defende   50
He may stablishe and maintaine through to the ende.

M. MERY.   God graunt hir, as she doth, the Gospell to
protect,
Learning and vertue to aduaunce, and vice to correct.

R. ROYSTER.   God graunt hir louyng subiects both the
minde and grace
Hir most godly procedyngs worthily to imbrace.   55

HARPAX.   Hir Highnesse most worthy counsellers God
prosper
With honour and loue of all men to minister.

OMNES.   God graunt the Nobilitie hir to serue and loue,
With all the whole Commontie, as doth them behoue.

Amen.

FINIS.

A Ryght

Pithy, Pleaſaunt and me
rie Comedie: In-

tytuled *Gammer gur-*
tons Nedle: Played on
Stage, not longe
ago in Chri-
ſtes

Colledge in Cambridge.

Made by M^r. S. M^r. of Art.

Imprented at London in
Fleeteſtreat beneth the Con-
duit at the ſigne of S. John
Euangeliſt by Tho-
mas Colwell.

Printed from the earliest extant edition (Thomas Colwell, London, 1575), which, however, was probably not the first edition, for "a playe intituled Dyccon of Bedlam, &c.," was licensed to Colwell in 1562. In the footnotes, Co. indicates the 1575 edition; Dods. indicates the edition in Dodsley's "Old Plays" (1825); Haz. indicates Hazlitt's edition of Dodsley. In this, as in the other plays printed in this volume, only significant variants are recorded.

The titlepage is a reprint, but not a facsimile, of the old titlepage.

For a discussion of date and authorship, see vol. III.[1a]

The Names of the Speakers in this Comedie.

> Diccon, *the Bedlem.*
> Hodge, *Gammer Gurtons seruante.*
> Tyb, *Gammer Gurtons mayde.*
> Gammer Gurton.
> Cocke,[1] *Gammer Gurtons boye.*
> Dame Chatte.
> Doctor Rat, *the Curate.*
> Mayster Baylye.
> Doll, *Dame Chattes mayde.*
> Scapethryft,[2] *Mayst Beylies seruante.*

> *Mutes.*

> [Scene: *A village in England.*]

> God Saue the Queene![3]

1 Co. Docke.   3 *Omitted by* Dods. Haz.
2 Co. Scapethryk.

1aSee Publisher's Note.

[GAMMER GURTONS NEDLE.]

The Prologue.

As Gammer Gurton, with manye a wyde styche,
Sat pesynge *and* patching of Hodg her [1] mans briche,
By chance or misfortune, as shee her geare tost,
In Hodge lether bryches her needle shee lost.
When Diccon the bedlem [2] had hard by report   5
That good Gammer Gurton was robde in thys sorte,
He quyetly perswaded with her in that stound
Dame Chat, her deare gossyp, this needle had found.
Yet knew shee no more of this matter, alas!
Then knoeth Tom, our clarke, what the priest saith at masse.   10
Here-of there ensued so fearfull a fraye
Mas Doctor was sent for, these gossyps to staye,
Because he was Curate, and estemed full wyse:
Who found that he sought not, by Diccons deuice.
When all thinges were tombled and cleane out of fassion,   15
Whether it were by fortune, or some other constellacion,
Sodenlye the neele Hodge found by the prickynge,
And drew it [3] out of his bottocke, where he felt [4] it stickynge.
Theyr hartes then at rest with perfect securytie,
With a pot of good nale they stroake vp theyr plauditie.   20

[1] Co. Hodgher.   [3] Dods. *omits* it.
[2] Dods. bedlam.   [4] Dods. found.

The fyrst Acte. The fyrst Sceane.

[A street or field near Gammer Gurton's *house.]*

[Enter] Diccon.

Diccon. Many a myle haue I walked, diuers and sundry waies,
And many a good mans house haue I bin at in my daies;
Many a gossips cup in my tyme haue I tasted,
And many a broche and spyt haue I both turned and basted;
Many a peece of bacon haue I had out of thir balkes   5
In ronnyng ouer the countrey with long and were walkes;
Yet came my foote neuer within those doore-cheekes,
To seeke flesh or fysh, garlyke, onyons or leekes,
That euer I saw a sorte in such a plyght
As here within this house appereth to my syght.   10
There is howlynge and scowlyng,[1] all cast in a dumpe,[2]
With whewling and pewling, as though they had lost a trump;
Syghing and sobbing, they weepe and they wayle :
I meruell in my mynd what the deuill they ayle.
The olde trot syts groning, with alas! and alas!   15
And Tib wringes her hands, *and* takes on in worse case,
With poore Cocke, theyr boye. They be dryuen in such fyts
I feare mee the folkes be not well in theyr wyts.
Aske them what they ayle, or who brought them in this staye,
They aunswer not at all but alacke! and welaway!   20
Whan I saw it booted not, out at doores I hyed mee,
And caught a slyp of bacon, when I saw that[3] none spyed mee,
Which I intend not far hence, vnles my purpose fayle,
Shall serue for a shoinghorne to draw on two pots of ale.

[1] Dods. schowlyng.
[2] Co. abumpe.
[3] Dods. *omits* that.

The fyrst Acte.   The second Sceane.

[*The same place.*]

[*Enter*] HODGE [*to*] DICCON.

HODGE.   See! so cham arayed with dablynge in the durt!
She that set me to ditchinge, ich wold she had the squrt![1]
Was neuer poore soule that such a life had!
Gogs bones, thys vylthy glaye hase drest mee to[2] bad!
Gods soule, see how this stuffe teares!   5

[*Examining the rents in his breeches.*]

Iche were better to bee a bearward and set to keepe beares!
By the masse, here is a gasshe! a shamefull hole in-deade!
And one stytch teare furder, a man may thruste in his heade.
        DICCON.   By my fathers soule, Hodge, if I shulde now be
                sworne,
I can not chuse but say thy breech is foule be-torne!   10
But the next remedye in such a case and hap
Is to plaunche on a piece as brode as thy cap.
        HODGE.   Gogs soule, man, tis not yet two dayes fully
                ended
Synce my dame Gurton, chem[3] sure, these breches amended!
But cham made such[4] a drudge, to trudge at euery neede,   15
Chwold rend it though it were stitched wath[5] sturdy pac-
                threede.
        DICCON.   Hoge, let thy breeches go, and speake and tell
                mee soone
What deuill ayleth Gammer Gurton and Tib, her mayd, to
                frowne.
        HODGE.   Tush, man, thart deceyued! tys theyr dayly
                looke;
They coure so ouer *th*e coles theyr eyes be bleard with smooke.   20

---

[1] Dods. squirt.   [3] Dods. cham.
[2] Dods. too.
[4] Co. suce; *corr. by* Dods., *who gives* Co. *as* succ.
[5] Co. what; Dods. *prints* wath, *without note.*

DICCON.   Nay, by the masse, I perfectly perceiued, as I
          came hether,
That eyther Tib *and* her dame hath ben by the eares together,
Or els as great a matter, as thou shalt shortly see.
    HODGE.   Now iche beseeche our Lord they neuer better
          agree!
    DICCON.   By Gogs soule, there they syt as still as stones
          in the streite,   25
As though they had ben take*n* with fairies or els w*ith* some
          il sprite.[1]
    HODGE.   Gogs hart, I durst haue layd my cap to a crowne
Chwould lerne of some prancome as sone as ich come to
          town!
    DICCON.   Why, Hodge, art thou inspyred? or dedst thou
          therof here?
    HODGE.   Nay; but ich saw such a wonder as ich saw nat
          this vii yere: 30
Tome Tannkards cow — be Gogs bones! — she set me vp
          her saile,
And flynging about his halfe-aker,[2] fysking with her taile,
As though there had ben in her ars a swarme of bees.
And chad not cryed, "Tphrowh, hoore!" shead lept out of
          his lees.
    DICCON.   Why, Hodg, lies the connyng in Tom Tan-
          kards cowes taile?   35
    HODGE.   Well, ich chaue hard some say such tokens do
          not fayle.
But ca[n]st *tho*u not tell,[3] in faith, Diccon, why she frownes,
          or wher-at?
Hath no man stolne her ducks or henes, or gelded Gyb, her
          cat?
    DICCON.   What deuyll can I tell, man? I cold not haue
          one word;
They gaue no more hede to my talk then thou woldst to a
          lorde.   40

_____

[1] Dods. spreet.   [3] Co. till.
[2] Dods. *reads* halse aker, *and suggests* halse anker.

HODGE.   Iche cannot styll but muse what meruaylous
thinge it is!

Chyll in and know my-selfe what matters are amys.

DICCON.   Then farewell, Hodge, a-while, synce thou doest
inward hast,

For I will into the good-wyfe Chats, to feele how the ale
dooth [1] taste.

[*Exit* DICCON.]

The fyrst Acte.   The thyrd Sceane.

[*The same place.*]

HODGE [*is met by*] TYB.

HODGE.   Cham agast, by the masse! ich wot not what to
do.

Chad nede blesse me well before ich go them to!

Perchaunce some felon sprit may haunt our house indeed,

And then chwere but a [2] noddy to venter where cha no neede!

TIB.   Cham worse then mad, by the masse, to be at this
staye!   5

Cham chyd, cham blamd, and beaton [3] all thoures on the
daye,

Lamed and hunger-storued, prycked vp all in iagges,

Hauyng no patch to hyde my backe, saue a few rotten ragges!

HODGE.   I say, Tyb, — if thou be Tyb, as I trow sure
thou bee, —

What deuyll make-a-doe is this betweene our dame and thee?   10

TYB.   Gogs breade, Hodg, thou had a good turne thou
warte not here this while! [4]

It had ben better for some of vs to haue ben hence a myle!

My gammer is so out of course and frantyke all at ones

That Cocke, our boy, *and* I, poore wench, haue felt it on our
bones.

[1] Dods. does.   [2] Co. at.   [3] Co. beat on.

[4] *In* Co. *this is the last line of A. iii. recto, and* here *is the end of the
line.* Dods. *prints* this while, *without note.*

HODGE.   What is the matter — say on, Tib! — wherat
   she taketh so on?   15

TYB.   She is vndone, she sayth ; alas! her ioye and life is
   gone!

If shee here not of some comfort, she is, sayth,[1] but dead, —

Shall neuer come within her lyps one inch of meate ne
   bread!

HODGE.   Byr Ladie, cham not very glad to see her in this
   dumpe.

Cholde a noble her stole hath fallen *and* shee hath broke her
   rumpe!   20

TYB.   Nay, and that were the worst! — we wold not greatly
   care

For bursting of her huckle-bone or breakyng of her chaire ;

But greatter, greater, is her grief, as, Hodge, we shall all
   feele!

HODGE.   Gogs woundes, Tyb! my gammer has neuer
   lost her neele?

TYB.   Her neele.

HODGE.   Her neele?

TIB.   Her neele.[2]   25

By him that made me, it is true, Hodge, I tell thee!

HODGE.   Gogs sacrament, I would she had lost tharte
   out of her bellie!

The deuill, or els his dame, they ought her, sure, a shame!

How a murryon came this chaunce — say, Tib! — vnto our
   dame?

TYB.   My gammer sat her downe on her pes, *and* had
   me reach thy breeches,   30

And by-*and*-by, — a vengeance in it! — or she had take two
   stitches

To clap [3] a clout vpon thine ars, by chaunce a-syde she leares,

And Gyb, our cat, in the milke-pan she spied ouer head and
   eares.

---

[1] Dods. *emends to* shee sayth she is.
[2] *In* Co. Dods. *these two words are part of the following line.*
[3] Dods. clout.

"Ah, hore! out, thefe!"[1] she cryed aloud, *and* swapt the
    breches downe.
Up went her staffe, and out leapt Gyb at doors into the
    towne.   35
And synce that time was neuer wyght cold set their eies vpo*n*
    it.
Gogs malison chave Cocke and I byd twenty times light on it.
   HODGE.   And is not, the*n*, my breches sewid vp, to-morow
     *tha*t I shuld were?
     TYB.   No, in faith, Hodge, thy breeches lie, for al this,
     neuer the nere.
   HODGE.   Now a ve*n*geance light on al *th*e sort, *tha*t better
     shold haue kept it, —   40
The cat, the house, and Tib, our maid, *tha*t better shold haue
    swept it!
Se where she co*m*meth crawling! Come on, in twenty deuils
    way!
Ye haue made a fayre daies worke, haue you not? pray you
    say!

The fyrst Acte.   The iiij Sceane.

[The same place.]

[Enter] GAMMER *[to]* HODGE *[and]* TYB. COCKE *[comes later]*.

   GAMMER.[2]   Alas, Hoge,[3] alas!   I may well cursse and
    ban
This daie, that euer I saw it, with Gyb and the mylke-pan!
For these and ill lucke to-gather, as knoweth Cocke, my
    boye,
Haue stacke away my deare neele, and robd me of my ioye, —
My fayre, longe, strayght neele, that was myne onely treas-
    ure!   5
The fyrst day of my sorow is, and last end of my pleasure!

---

[1] Dods. these.
[2] *Here and below* Co. *regularly has* Gāmer.
[3] *Omitted by* Dods.

HODGE.   Might ha kept it when ye had it! but fooles will
  be fooles styll!

Lose that is vast in your handes? — ye neede not; but ye
  will!

GAMMER.   Go hie thee, Tib, and run, thou hoore, to thend
  here of the towne!

Didst cary out dust in thy lap; seeke wher thou porest it
  downe,[1]   10

And, as thou sawest me roking[2] in the asshes where I
  morned,

So see in all the heaps of dust thou leave no straw vnturned.

TYB.   That chal, Gammer, swythe and tyte, and sone be
  here agayne!

[*Goes to the dust-pile.*]

GAMMER.   Tib, stoope, *and* loke downe to *th*e ground!
  To it, *and* take some paine!

HODGE.   Here is a prety matter, to see this gere how it
  goes.   15

By Gogs soule, I thenk you wold loes your ars and it were
  loose!

Your neele lost? it is a[3] pitie you shold lack care and endlesse sorow!

Gogs deth, how shall my breches be sewid?   Shall I go thus
  to-morow?

GAMMER.   Ah, Hodg, Hodg! if that ich cold find my
  neele, by the reed,

Chould sow thy breches, ich promise *tha*t,[4] w*ith* full good
  double threed,   20

And set a patch on either knee shuld last this monethes
  twaine.

Now God *and* good Saint Sithe I praye to send it home
  againe!

HODGE.   Wherto serued your hands *and* eies, but this
  your neele to kepe?

---

[1] Co. dowde; *corr. by* Dods.   [3] *Omitted by* Dods.
[2] *Qy.* raking.   [4] Dods. the, *which is, perhaps, better.*

What deuill had you els to do? ye kept,[1] ich wot, no sheepe!
Cham faine a-brode to dyg and delue, in water, myre and
    claye,   25
Sossing and possing in the durte styll from day to daye;
A hundred thinges that be abrode, cham set to see them weele,
And foure of you syt idle at home, and can not keepe a neele!
    GAMMER.   My neele, alas! ich lost it, Hodge, what time
        ich me vp-hasted
To saue the milke set vp for the, which Gib, our cat, hath
    wasted.   30
    HODGE.   The deuill he burst both Gib and Tib, with all
        the rest!
Cham alwayes sure of the worst end, who-euer haue the best!
Where ha you ben fidging abrode since you your neele lost?
    GAMMER.   Within the house, and at the dore, sitting by
        this same post,
Wher I was loking a long howre, before these folks came
    here;   35
But, welaway! all was in vayne, my neele is neuer the nere!
    HODGE.   Set[2] me a candle; let me seeke, and grope
        where-euer it bee.
Gogs hart, ye be so folish, ich thinke, you knowe it not when
    you it see!
    GAMMER.   Come hether, Cocke! what, Cocke, I say!

               [*Enter* COCKE.]

COCKE.   Howe, Gammer!
    GAMMER.   Goe hye the soone
And grope behynd the old brasse pan, whych thing when
    thou hast done,[3]   40
Ther shalt thou fynd an old shooe, wher-in, if thou looke well,
Thou shalt fynd lyeng an inche of a[4] whyte tallow-candell;
Lyght it and brynge it tite awaye.
    COCKE.   That shalbe done anone.

---

[1] Dods. keep.   [2] *Qy.* Fet *or* Get.
[3] *These two lines as four in* Co. Dods. Haz., *ending* say, Gammer, pan,
done.   [4] *Omitted by* Dods.

[Goes into the house.]

GAMMER.   Nay, tary, Hodg, til thou hast light, and then
   weele seke ech one.

HODGE.   Cum away, ye horsen boy, are ye a slepe? ye
   must haue a crier!   45

COCKE.   Ich cannot get the candel light: here is almost
   no fier.

HODGE.   Chil hold the a peny chil make *th*e come if *tha*t
   ich may catch thine eares!

Art deffe, thou horson boy?   Cocke, I say, why canst not
   heares? [1]

GAMMER.   Beate hym not, Hodge, but help the boy, and
   come you two together.

[HODGE *goes into the house.*]

The i Acte. The v Sceane.

[The same place.]

GAMMER [*alone*].   [*Enter*] TYB, [*then*] COCKE, [*then*] HODGE.

GAMMER.   How now, Tyb? quycke, lets here what newes
   thou hast brought hether!

[TYB *returns from the dust-pile.*]

TYB.   Chaue tost and tumbled yender heap ou[e]r *and*
   ouer againe,

And winowed it through my fingers, as me*n* wold winow
   grain, —

Not so much as a hens turd but in pieces I tare it,

Or what-so-euer clod or clay I found, I did not spare it, —   5

Lokyng within, and eke without, to fynd your neele, alas!

But all in vaine and without help, — your neele is where it was.

GAMMER.   Alas, my neele! we shall neuer meete! adue!
   adue, for aye!

TYB.   Not so, Gammer, we myght it fynd if we knew
   where it laye.

[1] Dods. hear's.

[Enter Cocke from the house.]

COCKE.   Gogs crosse, Gammer, if ye will laugh, looke in
  but at the doore,   10
And see how Hodg lieth tomblynge and tossing amids the
  floure,
Rakyng there some fyre to find amonge the asshes dead,
Where there is not one sparke so byg as a pyns head.
At last in a darke corner two sparkes he thought he sees,
Whiche were,[1] indede, nought els but Gyb our cats two eyes.   15
" Puffe! " quod Hodg, thinking therby to haue fyre without
  doubt;
With that Gyb shut her two eyes, *and* so the fyre was out.
And by-and-by them opened, euen as they were before;
With that the sparkes appered, euen as they had done of
  yore.
And, euen as Hodge blew the fire, as he did thincke,   20
Gyb, as she felt the blast, strayght-way began to wyncke,
Tyll Hodge fell of swering, as came best to his turne,
The fier was sure bewicht, and therfore wold not burne.
At last Gyb vp the stayers, among the old postes and pinnes,
And Hodge he hied him after till broke were both his
  shinnes, —   25
Cursynge and swering othes, were neuer of his makyng,
That Gyb wold fyre the house if that shee were not taken.
 GAMMER.   See, here is all the thought that the foolysh
  urchyn taketh!
And Tyb, me thinke, at his elbowe almost as mery maketh!
This is all the wyt ye haue, when others make their mone.   30
Come downe, Hodge! where art thou? *and* let the cat alone!
 HODGE.   Gogs harte, helpe and come vp! Gyb in her tayle
  hath fyre,
And is like to burne all if shee get a lytle hier!
Cum downe, quoth you? nay, then you might count me a
  patch!
The house cometh downe on your heads if it take ons *th*e
  thatch.   35
      1 Co. where.

GAMMER.   It is the cats eyes, foole, that shineth in the
      darke!

HODGE.   Hath the cat, do you thinke, in euery eye a
      sparke?

GAMMER.   No, but they shyne as lyke fyre as euer man see.

HODGE.   By the masse, and she burne all, yoush beare
      the blame for mee!

GAMMER.   Cum downe, *and* help to seeke here our neele,
      that it were found.   40

Downe, Tyb, on thy[1] knees, I say!   Downe, Cocke, to the
      ground!

To God I make a-vowe, and so to good Saint Anne,

A candell shall they haue a-peece, get it where I can,

If I may my neele find in one place or in other.

HODGE.   Now a vengeaunce on Gib lyght, on Gyb and
      Gybs mother,   45

And all the generacyon of cats both far and nere!

[2] Looke on the ground, horson? thinks then [3] the neele is here?

COCKE.   By my trouth, Gammer, me thought your neele
      here I saw,

But, when my fyngers toucht it, I felt it was a straw.

TYB.   See, Hodge! whats tys? may it not be within it?   50

HODGE.   Breake it, foole, with thy hand, and see and thou
      canst fynde it.

TYB.   Nay, breake it you, Hodge, accordyng to your word.

HODGE.   Gogs sydes! fye, it styncks! it is a cats tourd!

It were well done to make thee eate it, by the masse!

GAMMER.   This matter amendeth not; my neele is still
      where it wasse.   55

Our candle is at an ende; [4] let vs all in quight,

And come another tyme, when we haue more lyght!

                              [*Exeunt omnes.*]

      [1] Co. tho; Dods. thy.
      [2] *Line* 48 *does not make necessary the transfer of this to Gammer.*
      [3] Dods. thou.
      [4] Co. anende.

The ii Acte.

Fyrste a songe:

Backe and syde, go bare, go bare;
   Booth foote and hande, go colde:
But, bellye, God sende thee good ale ynoughe,
   Whether it be newe or olde!   4

I can not eate but lytle meate,
   My stomacke is not good;
But, sure, I thinke that I can dry[n]cke
   With him that weares a hood.
Thoughe I go bare, take ye no care,
   I am nothinge a-colde,
I stuffe my skyn so full within
   Of ioly good ale and olde.   12

Backe and syde, go bare, go barc;
   Booth foote and hand, go colde:
But, belly, God send the good ale inoughe,
   Whether it be new or olde!   16

I loue no [1] rost, but a nut-browne toste
   And a crab layde in the fyre;
A lytle bread shall do me stead,
   Much breade I not desyre.
No froste nor snow, no winde, I trowe,
   Can hurte mee if I wolde,
I am so wrapt and throwly lapt
   Of ioly good ale and olde.   24

Backe and syde, go bare, &c.

And Tyb, my wyfe, that as her lyfe
   Loueth well good ale to seeke,
Full ofte drynkes shee tyll ye may see
   The teares run downe her cheeke; [2]

---

[1] Co. to; Dods. no.   [2] Co. Dods. cheekes; Haz. cheek,

Then dooth she trowle to mee the bowle,
 Euen as a mault-worme shuld,
And sayth, " Sweete hart, I tooke my part
 Of this ioly good ale and olde."   32

Backe and syde, go bare, &c.

Now let them drynke tyll they nod and winke,
 Euen as good felowes shoulde doe ;
They shall not mysse to haue the blisse
 Good ale doth bringe men to.
And all poore soules that haue scowred boules
 Or haue them lustely trolde,
God saue the lyues of them and theyr wyues,
 Whether they be yonge or olde !   40

Backe and syde, go bare, &c.

The fyrst Sceane.

[*The same street, near* DAME CHAT'S *house.*]

[*Enter*] DICCON [*from* DAME CHAT'S]. HODGE [*enters later*].

DICCON.   Well done, be [1] Gogs malt! well songe, and well
  sayde !
Come on, mother Chat, as thou art [2] true mayde !
One fresh pot of ale lets see, to make an ende,
Agaynst this colde wether my naked armes to defende !

[*Drinks.*]

This gere it warms the soule! Now, wind, blow on thy [3]
  worst !   5
And let vs drink and swill till that our bellies burste !
Now were he a wyse man, by cunnynge colde defyne [4]
Which way my iourney lyeth or where Dyccon will dyne !
But one good turne I haue : be it by nyght or daye,
South, east, north or west, I am neuer out of my waye !   10

[1] Dods. by.   [3] Co. the ; Dods. thy.
[2] Dods. *inserts* a.   [4] Co. defyne ; Dods. defyne.

[Enter Hodge.]

HODGE.   Chym goodly rewarded, cham I not, do you
    thyncke?
Chad a goodly dynner for all my sweate and swyncke!
Neyther butter, cheese, mylke, onyons, fleshe nor fyshe,
Saue thys poor [1] pece of barly bread, — tis a pleasant costly
    dishe!
DICCON.   Haile, fellow Hodge, *and* will [2] to fare w*it*h thy
    meat, if *tho*u [3] haue any!   15
But, by thy words, as I the*m* smelled, thy daintrels be not
    manye.
HODGE.   Daintrels, Dicco*n*? Gogs soule, ma*n*, saue this
    pece of dry horsbred,
Cha [4] byt no byt this lyue-longe daie, no crome come in my
    hed.
My gutts they yawle, crawle, and all my belly rumbleth,
The puddynges can not lye styll, ech one ouer other tum-
    bleth.   20
By Gogs harte, cham so vexte [5] and in my belly pende
Chould one peece were at the spittlehouse, another at *th*e
    castels ende!
DICCON.   Why, Hodge, was there none at home thy din-
    ner for to set?
HODGE.   Godgs bread, Diccon, ich came to late, was
    nothing ther to get!
Gib — a fowle feind might on her light! — lickt *th*e milke-
    pan so clene, —   25
See, Diccon, twas not so well washt this vii yere, as ich
    wene!
A pestilence lyght on all ill lucke! chad thought yet, for all
    thys,
Of a morsell of bacon behynde the dore at worst shuld not
    misse;

---

[1] *Omitted by* Dods.
[2] Dods. *emends to* well.
[3] Dods. you.
[4] *Misprinted* Chat *in* Dods.
[5] *The* x *is broken.*

But when ich sought a slyp to cut, as ich was wont to do,
Gogs soule, Diccon, Gyb, our cat, had eate the bacon to!   30

Which bacon Diccon stole, as is declared before.

DICCON.   Ill[1] luck, quod he? mary, swere it, Hodg! This
          day *th*e trueth to[2] tel,
Thou rose not on thy right syde, or els blest thee not wel.
Thy mylk slopt vp, thy baco*n* filtched, — that was to bad
          luck, Hodg!
HODGE.   Nay, nay, ther was a fowler fault: my ga*m*mer
          ga me *th*e dodge![3]
Seest not how cha*m* rent *and* torn, my heels, my knees *and*
          my breech?   35
Chad thought, as ich sat by the fire, help here *and* there a
          stitch;
But there ich was powpte indeede.
     DICCON.   Why, Hodge?
     HODGE.   Bootes not, man, to tell.
Cham so drest amonst a sorte of fooles chad better be in
          hell!
My gammer, cham ashamed to say, by God, serued me not
          weele!
     DICCON.   How so, Hodge?
     HODGE.   Hase she not gone, trowest
          now,[4] and lost her neele?   40
     DICCON.   Her eele, Hodge? Who fysht of late? That
          was a dainty dysh!
     HODGE.   Tush, tush, her neele! her neele! her neele,
          man! tys neyther flesh nor fysh.
A lytle thing with an hole in the end, as bright as any syller,
Small, longe, sharpe at the poynt, *and* straight as any pyller.
     DICCON.   I know not what a deuil *th*ou me*n*est, *th*ou
          bringst me more in doubt!   45
     HODGE.   Knowest not w*ith* what Tom Tailers ma*n* sits
          broching throughe a clout?

[1] Co. All; Dods. Ill.   [3] Co. dogde.
[2] *Omitted by* Dods. Haz.   [4] Dods. now thou, *without note.*

A neele, neele,[1] a neele! my gammers neele is gone!

DICCON. Her neele, Hodge? now I smel thee! *that* was
    a chaunce alone!

By *th*e masse, *tho*u hadst a shamefull losse *and* it wer but for
    thy breches!

HODGE. Gogs soule, man, chould giue a crown chad it
    but iii stitches!   50

DICCON. How sayest *tho*u, Hodg? what shuld he haue,
    again thy neele [2] got?

HODGE. Bem vathers soule, and chad it, chould giue him
    a new grot!

DICCON. Canst thou keepe counsaile in this case?

HODGE.   Els chwold my tonge [3] were out.

DICCON. Do thou [4] but then by my aduise, *and* I will
    fetch it w*ith*out doubt.

HODGE. Chyll runne, chyll ryde, chyll dygge, chyl delue,
    chill toyle, chill trudge, shalt see;   55

Chill hold, chil drawe, chil pull, chill pynche, chill kneele on
    my bare knee;

Chill scrape, chill scratche, chill syfte, chyll seeke, chill
    bowe, chill bende, chill sweate,

Chil stoop, chil stur, chil cap, chil knele, chil crepe on ha*n*ds
    and feete;

Chil be thy bondman, Diccon, ich sweare by sunne and
    moone.

And channot sum-what to stop this gap, cham vtterly vndone!   60

Pointing behind to his torne breeches.[5]

DICCON. Why, is ther any special cause thou takest
    hereat such sorow?

HODGE. Kristian [6] Clack, Tom Simsons maid, bi the
    masse, coms hether to-morow!

Chamnot able to say, betweene vs what may hap, —

She smyled on me the last Sonday when ich put of my cap.

---

[1] Dods. a neele.

[2] Dods. nedle.

[3] Co. thonge; Dods. tonge.

[4] Co. than; *emend. by* Dods.

[5] Co. kreeches; *corr. silently by* Dods.

[6] Dods. Kirstian.

DICCON. Well, Hodge, this is a matter of weight, *and*
     must be kept close;   65
It might els turne to both our costes, as the world now
     gose.
Shalt sware to be no blab, Hodge!
    HODGE.   Chyll, Diccon!
    DICCON.   Then, go to!
Lay thine hand here; say after me as thou shalt here me do.
Haste no booke?
    HODGE.   Cha no booke, I!
    DICCON.   Then needes must force vs both
Upon my breech to lay thine hand, and there to take thine
     othe.   70

    [He recites the oath line by line, and HODGE *repeats it after him.]*

HODGE. I, Hodge, breechelesse,
Sweare to Diccon, rechelesse,
    By the crosse that I shall kysse,
To kepe his counsaile close,
And alwayes me to dispose
    To worke that his pleasure is.   76

    Here he kesseth [1] *Diccons breeche.*

DICCON. Now, Hodge, see thou take heede
And do as I thee byd,
    For so I iudge it meete;
This nedle againe to win,
There is no shift therin
    But coniure vp a spreete.   82

HODGE. What, the great deuill? Diccon, I saye!
DICCON. Yea, in good faith, that is the waye, —
    Fet with some prety charme.
HODGE. Softe, Diccon, be not to hasty yet,
By the masse, for ich begyn to sweat!
    Cham afrayde of some [2] harme!   88

---

[1] Co. kessech.
[2] Co. syme; *corr. by* Dods.

[DICCON *draws a magic circle.*]

DICCON.   Come hether then, and sturre the nat
One inche out of this cyrcle plat,
    But stande as I thee teache.
HODGE.   And shall ich be here safe from theyr clawes?

[*He seeks a safe place.*]

DICCON.   The mayster deuill with his longe pawes
    Here to thee can not reache.   94

Now will I settle me to this geare.
HODGE.   I saye, Diccon! heare me, heare!
    Go softely to thys matter!
DICCON.   What deuyll, man? art afraide of nought?
HODGE.   Canst not tarrye a lytle thought
    Tyll ich make a curtesse of water?   100

DICCON.   Stand still to it!   Why shuldest thou feare hym?
HODGE.   Gogs sydes, Diccon, me thinke ich heare him!
    And tarrye, chal mare all!
DICCON.   The matter is no worse then I tolde it.
HODGE.   By the masse, cham able no longer to holde it!
    To[1] bad! iche must beraye the hall!   106

DICCON.   Stand to it, Hodge! sture not, you horson!
What deuyll? be thine ars-strynges brusten?
    Thy-selfe a-while but staye;
The deuill — I smell hym — wyll be here anone.
HODGE.   Hold him fast, Diccon, cham gone! cham gone!
    Chyll not be at that fraye!   112

[*Exit* HODGE *running.*]

The ii Acte.   The ii Sceane.

[*The same place.*]

DICCON [*alone*].   [DAME] CHAT [*enters later*].

DICCON.   Fy, shytten knaue! and out vpon thee!
Aboue all other loutes fye on thee!
    Is not here a clenly prancke?

---

[1] Dods. *changes to* So.

But thy matter was no better,
Nor thy presence here no sweter,
    To flye I can the thanke.   6

Here is a matter worthy glosynge
Of Gammer Gurtons nedle losynge,
    And a foule peece of warke !
A man, I thyncke, myght make a playe,
And nede no worde to this they saye,
    Being but halfe a clarke.   12

Softe, let me alone ! I will take the charge
This matter further to enlarge
    Within a tyme shorte.
If ye will marke my toyes, and note,
I will geue ye leaue to cut my throte
    If I make not good sporte.   18

[Approaches DAME CHAT'S *door.]*

Dame Chat, I say ! where be ye? within?
   CHAT.   Who haue we there maketh such a din?
   DICCON.   Here is a good fellow, maketh no great daunger.
   CHAT.   What? Diccon? Come nere, ye be no straunger !
We be fast set at trumpe, man, hard by the fyre :
Thou shalt set[1] on the king, if thou come a litle nyer.
   DICCON.   Nay, nay, there is no tarying, I must be gone
      againe.   25
But, first, for you in councel I haue a word or twaine.
   CHAT.   Come hether, Dol ! Dol, sit downe and play this
      game,
And, as thou sawest me do, see thou do euen the same.
There is five[2] trumps beside[3] the queene, — *th*e hindmost
    *th*ou shalt finde her.
Take hede of Sim Glouers wife, she hath an eie behind her !   30
Now, Diccon, say your will.
   DICCON.   Nay, softe a litle yet !
I wold not tel it my[4] sister, the matter is so great.

---

¹ *Qy.* fet.   ² Co. 5.   ⁸ Dods. besides.   ⁴ Dods. tell me.

There I wil haue you sweare by our dere Lady of Bullaine,
S. Dunstone and S. Donnyke, with the three Kinges of
      Kullaine,
That ye shal keepe it secret.

    CHAT.   Gogs bread, that will I doo!   35
As secret as mine owne thought, by God, and the deuil
      two![1]

    DICCON.   Here is Gammer Gurton, your neighbour, a sad
      and heuy wight, —
Her goodly faire red cock at home was stole this last night.

    CHAT. Gogs soule, her cock with the yelow legs, *tha*t
      nightly crowed[2] so iust?

    DICCON.   That cocke is stollen.

    CHAT.   What! was he fet out of the hens ruste? 40

    DICCON.   I can not tel where *th*e deuil he was kept, vnder
      key or locke;
But Tib hath tykled in Gammers eare that you shoulde steale
      the cocke.

    CHAT. Haue I, stronge hoore? By bread and salte —

    DICCON.   What, softe, I say! be styl!
Say not one word for all this geare.

    CHAT.   By the masse, that I wyl!
I wil haue the yong hore by the head, *and* the old trot by *th*e
      throte!   45

    DICCON.   Not one word, Dame Chat, I say, not one word,
      for my cote!

    CHAT.   Shall such a begars brawle as *tha*t, thinkest *tho*u,
      make me a theefe?
The pocks light on her hores sydes, a pestlence *and* a[3] mis-
      cheefe!
Come out, thou hungry, nedy bytche! O that my nails be
      short!

    DICCON.   Gogs bred, woma*n*, hold your peace, this gere
      wil els passe sport!   50
I wold not for an hundred pound this matter shuld be knowen,

---

[1] Dods. *corrects spelling to* too.
[2] Dods. crowded.   [3] Dods. *omits* a.

That I am auctour of this tale or haue abrode it blowen!
Did ye not sweare ye wold be ruled, before the tale I tolde?
I said ye must all secret keepe, and ye said sure ye wolde.

    CHAT.   Wolde you suffer, your-selfe, Diccon, such a sort
      to reuile you,   55
With slaunderous words to blot your name, *and* so to defile
    you?

    DICCON.   No, goodwife Chat, I wold be loth such drabs
      shulde blot my name;
But yet ye must so order all *tha*t Diccon beare no blame.

    CHAT.   Go to, then! what is your rede? say on your
      minde, ye shall mee rule herein.

    DICCON.   Godamercye to[1] Dame Chat! in faith, thou
      must the gere begin.   60
It is twenty pound to a goose-turd, my Gammer will not tary
But hetherward she comes as fast as her legs can her cary
To brawle with you about her cocke; for well I hard Tib say
The cocke was rosted in your house to breafast yesterday,
And, when ye had the carcas eaten, the fethers ye out flunge, 65
And Doll, your maid, the legs she hid a foote depe in the
    dunge.

    CHAT.   Oh gracyous God! my harte it[2] burstes!

    DICCON.   Well, rule your-selfe a space!
And Gammer Gurton, when she commeth anon into thys
    place,
Then to the queane, lets see, tell her your mynd *and* spare
    not,
So shall Diccon blamelesse bee; and then, go to, I care not! 70

    CHAT.   Then hoore, beware her throte! I can abide no
      longer![3]
In faith, old witch, it shalbe seene, which of vs two be
    stronger!
And, Diccon, but at your request, I wold not stay one howre.

    DICCON.   Well, keepe it in till she be here, and then out let
      it powre!
In the meane-while get you in, and make no wordes of this. 75

---

    [1] Dods. *omits* to.   [2] Co. is; Dods. it.   [3] Co. lenger.

More of this matter w*ith*-in this howre to here you shall not
    misse.

Because I knew[1] you are my freind, hide it I cold not,
    doubtles.

Ye know your harm, see ye be wise about your owne busines!
So fare ye well!

    CHAT.   Nay, soft, Diccon, and drynke! What,
    Doll, I say!

Bringe here a cup of the best ale; lets see, come quicly
    a-waye!   80
                [*They go into the house.*]

The ii Actt.   The iii Sceane.

[*The same place.*]

[*Enter*] HODGE [*immediately after*] DICCON.

DICCON. Ye see, masters, *tha*t one end tapt of this my
    short deuise!

Now must we broche tother,[2] to, before the smoke arise.

And, by the time they haue a-while run, I trust ye need not
    craue it,

But, loke, what lieth in both their harts, ye ar like, sure, to
    haue it.
                [*Enter* HODGE.]

    HODGE. Yea, Gogs soule, art aliue yet? What, Diccon,
    dare ich come?   5

    DICCON. A man is wel hied[3] to trust to the, I wil say
    nothing but mum.

But, and ye come any nearer, I pray you see all be sweete!

    HODGE. Tush, man, is Gammers neele found? That
    chould gladly weete!

    DICCON. She may tha*n*ke thee it is not fou*n*d, for if *tho*u
    had kept thy sta*n*ding,

The deuil he wold haue fet it out, euen, Hodg, at thy co*m*-
    maunding.   10

---

[1] Dods. know.   [3] *Qy.* paied.
[2] Co. thoter; Dods. t'other.

HODGE.   Gogs hart! *and* cold he tel nothing wher the
neele might be found?

DICCON.   Ye folysh dolt, ye were to seek, ear we had got
our ground ;

Therfore his tale so doubtfull was that I cold not perceiue it.

HODGE.   Then ich se wel somthing was said, chope one
day yet to haue it.

But, Diccon, Diccon, did not the deuill cry " ho ! ho ! ho "?   15

DICCON.   If *tho*u hadst taryed where thou stoodst, thou
woldest haue said so.

HODGE.   Durst swere of a boke, chard him rore, streight
after ich was gon.

But tel me, Diccon, what said *th*e knaue? let me here it
anon !

DICCON.   The horson talked to mee I know not well of
what :

One whyle his tonge it ran and paltered of a cat ;   20

Another whyle he stamered styll vppon a rat ;

Last of all, there was nothing but euery word chat! chat!

But this I well perceyued, before I wolde him rid,

Betweene chat and the rat and the cat, the nedle is hyd.

Now, wether Gyb, our cat, haue eate it in her mawe,   25

Or Doctor Rat, our curat, haue found it in the straw,

Or this Dame Chat, your neighbour, haue stollen it, God hee
knoweth !

But by *th*e morow at this time we shal learn how the matter
goeth.

HODGE.   Canst not learn to-night, man?   Seest not what
is here?

Pointyng behind to his torne breeches.

DICCON.   Tys not possyble to make it sooner appere.   30

HODGE.   Alas, Diccon, then chaue no shyft but — least
ich tary to longe —

Hye me to Sym Glouers shop, theare to seeke for a
thonge,

Ther-with this breech to tatche and tye as ich may.

DICCON.   To-morow, Hodg, if we chaunce to meete, shalt [1]
 see what I will say.

     [Exit HODGE.]

The ii Acte.   The iiii Sceane.

    [*The same place.*]

   [*To*] DICCON [*enter*] GAMMER [GURTON].

DICCON.   Now this gere must forward goe, for here my
 gammer commeth.
Be still a-while *and* say nothing, make here a litle romth !

    [*Enter* GAMMER GURTON.]

GAMMER.   Good Lord, shall neuer be my lucke my neele
 agayne to spye ?
Alas the whyle, tys past my helpe! where tis, still it must
 lye !

DICCON.   Now, Iesus, Gammer Gurto*n*, what driueth you
 to this sadnes?   5
I feare me, by my conscience, you will sure fall to madnes.

GAMMER.   Who is that?   What, Diccon?   Cham lost,
 man, fye! fye !

DICCON.   Mary, fy on them *tha*t be worthy ! but what
 shuld be your troble?

GAMMER.   Alas, the more ich thinke on it, my sorow it
 waxeth [2] doble !
My goodly tossing sporyars neele chaue lost ; ich wot not
 where.   10

DICCON.   Your neele? whan?

GAMMER.   My neele, alas, ich myght full ill [3] it spare !
As God him-selfe he knoweth, nere one besyde chaue.

DICCON.   If this be all, good Gammer, I warrant you all
 is saue.

GAMMER.   Why, know you any tydings which way my
 neele is gone ?

---

[1] Dods. shall. [2] *The* x *is broken in* Co. [3] Dods. *omits* ill.

DICCON. Yea, that I do, doubtlesse, as ye shall here
    anone.   15
A see a thing this matter toucheth, within these xx howres,
Euen at this gate, before my face, by a neyghbour of yours :
She stooped me downe, *and* vp she toke a nedle or a pyn.
I durst be sworne it was euen yours, by all my mothers kyn.
   GAMMER. It was my neele, Diccon, ich wot ; for here,
    euen by this poste,   20
Ich sat, what time as ich vp-starte, and so my neele is [1] loste.
Who was it, leiue son? speke, ich pray the, *and* quickly
    tell me that!
   DICCON. A suttle queane as any in thys towne, your
    neyghbour here, Dame Chat.
   GAMMER. Dame Chat, Diccon? Let me be gone, chil
    thyther in post-haste.
   DICCON. Take my councell yet or ye go, for feare ye
    walke in wast !   25
It is a murrion crafty drab, and froward to be pleased ;
And ye take not the better way, our [2] nedle yet ye lese [3] it.
For when she tooke it vp, euen here before your doores,
" What, soft, Dame Chat," quoth I, " that same is none of
    yours ! "
" Auant," quoth she, " syr knaue ! what pratest thou of that
    I fynd?   30
I wold *tho*u hadst kist me I wot whear," — she ment, I know,
    behind.
And home she went as brag as it had ben a bodelouce,
And I after as bold as it had ben the goodman of the house.
But there and ye had hard her how she began to scolde —
The tonge it went on patins, by hym that Iudas solde !   35
Ech other worde I was a knaue, and you a hore of hores,
Because I spake in your behalfe and sayde the neele was
    yours.
   GAMMER. Gogs bread, and thinks *th*e callet thus to kepe
    my neele me fro?

---

[1] Dods. it.   [2] Dods. *changes to* your.
[3] Co. Dods. lose ; Haz. *omits* it.

DICCON.   Let her alone, and she minds non other but
  eue*n* to dresse you so!

GAMMER.   By the masse, chil rather spend the cote that is
  on my backe!   40

Thinks the false quean by such a slyght [1] that chill my neele
  lacke?

DICCON.   Slepe not you[r] [2] gere, I counsell you, but of
  this take good hede:

Let not be knowen I told you of it, how well soeuer ye spede!

GAMMER.   Chil in, Diccon, a cleene aperne to take and
  set before me;

And ich may my neele once see, chil, sure, remember the!   45

[*Exit* GAMMER GURTON.]

The ii Acte.   The v Sceane.

[*The same place.*]

DICCON.

DICCON.   Here will the sporte begin: if these two once
  may meete,

Their chere, durst lay money, will proue scarsly sweete!

My gammer, sure, entends to be vppon her bones

With staues or with clubs or els with coble-stones.

Dame Chat, on the other syde, if she be far behynde,   5

I am right far deceiued, she is geuen to it of kynde.

He that may tarry by it a-whyle, and that but shorte,

I warrant hym, trust to it, he shall see all the sporte.

Into the towne will I, my frendes to vysit there,

And hether straight againe, to see thend of this gere.   10

In the meane-time, felowes, pype vpp your fiddles! I saie,
  take them,

And let your freyndes here such mirth as ye can make them!

[1] Co. flygh; Dods. *gives* Co. *as* slygh, *and reads* slight.
[2] Dods. *gives reading of* Co. *and corrects to* slip not your.

The iii Acte.   The i Sceane.

[The same place.]

[Enter] HODGE *[returning from Sym Glover's].*

HODGE.   Sym Glouer, yet gramercy! cham meetlye well-
 sped now,
Thart euen as good a felow as euer kyste a cowe!
Here is a thonge[1] in-dede ; by *the* masse, though ich speake
 it,
Tom Tankards great bald curtal, I thinke, could not breake
 it!
And when he spyed my neede to be so straight and hard,   5
Hays lent me here his naull to set the gyb forward.
As for my gammers neele, the flyenge feynd go weete!
Chill not now go to the doore, againe with it to meete.
Could make shyfte good inough and chad a candels ende ;
The cheefe hole in my breeche with these two chil amende.   10

The iii Acte.   The ii Sceane.

[The same place.]

[Enter] GAMMER *[to]* HODGE.

GAMMER.   How, Hodge! mayst nowe be glade, cha
 newes to tell thee.
Ich knowe who hais my neele ; iche trust soone shalt it see.
 HODGE.   The deuyll thou does! Hast hard, Gammer, in-
 deede, or doest but iest?
 GAMMER.   Tys as true as steele, Hodge.
 HODGE.   Why, knowest well where dydst leese it?
 GAMMER.   Ich know who found it and tooke it vp, shalt
 see or it be longe.   5
 HODGE.   Gods Mother dere, if that be true, far-wel both
 naule an[2] thong!

<hr>

[1] Co. thynge; *corr. by* Dods.   [2] Dods. and.

But who hais it, Gammer? say on![1] Chould faine here it
　　disclosed.

GAMMER. That false fixen,[2] that same Dame Chat, that
　　counts her-selfe so honest!

HODGE. Who tolde you so?

GAMMER.　　　　　　　That same did Diccon the bed-
　　lam, which saw it done.

HODGE. Diccon? it is a vengeable knaue, Gammer; tis a
　　bonable horso*n*!　　　　　　　　　　　　　　　　　10

Can do mo things then that, els cham deceyued euill:

By the masse, ich saw him of late cal vp a great blacke
　　deuill!

O, the knaue cryed "ho! ho!" He roared, and he thundred.

And yead bene here, cham sure yould murrenly ha wondred!

GAMMER. Was not thou afraide, Hodge, to see him in this
　　place?　　　　　　　　　　　　　　　　　　　15

HODGE. No; and chad come to me, chould haue laid
　　him on the face, —

Chould haue, promised him!

GAMMER.　　　But, Hodge, had he no hornes, to pushe?

HODGE. As long as your two armes! Saw ye neuer Fryer
　　Rushe

Painted on a cloth, with a side long cowes tayle,

And crooked clouen feete, and many a hoked nayle?　　20

For al the world, if I shuld iudg, chould recken him his
　　brother.

Loke, euen what face Frier Rush had, the deuil had such
　　another!

GAMMER. Now [3] Iesus mercy, Hodg! did Diccon in him
　　bring?

HODGE. Nay, Gammer, heare me speke, chil tel you a
　　greater thing:

The deuil, when Diccon had [4] him, — ich hard him wondrous
　　weel, —　　　　　　　　　　　　　　　　　25

---

[1] Dods. say? one.

[2] Dods. fixen; *in* Co., *through mutilation of* f *and* x, *it now looks like*
firen.　　　　　　[3] Co. New; Dods. Now.　　　　[4] Dods. bad.

Sayd plainly here before vs that Dame Chat had your neele.
> GAMMER.   Then let vs go and aske her wherfore she
>   minds to kepe it;

Seing we know so much, tware a madnes now to slepe it.
> HODGE.   Go to her, Ga*m*mer; see ye not where she
>   stands in her doores?

Byd her geue you the neele, — tys none of hers but yours!   30

The iii Acte.   The iii Sceane.

[*The same place.*]

GAMMER [*goes to* DAME] CHAT.   HODGE [*follows*].

> GAMMER.   Dame Chat, cholde praye the fair, let me haue
>   *tha*t is mine!

Chil not this twenty yeres take one fart that is thyne.
Therfore giue me mine owne, *and* let me liue besyde the!
> CHAT.   Why art thou crept fro*m* home hether to mine
>   own doores to chide me?

Hence, doting drab, auaunt, or I shall set the further!   5
Intends thou and that[1] knaue mee in my house to murther?
> GAMMER.   Tush, gape not so on[2] me, woman! shalt not
>   yet eate mee!

Nor all the frends thou hast in this shall not intreate mee!
Mine owne goods I will haue, and aske the on[3] beleue.[4]
What, woman! pore folks must haue right, though the thing
>   you agreue.   10

> CHAT.   Giue thee thy right, and hang thee vp, w*ith* al thy
>   baggers broode!

What, wilt thou make me a theefe, and say I stole thy good?
> GAMMER.   Chil say nothing, ich warra*n*t thee, but that ich
>   ca*n* proue it well.

Thou fet[5] my good euen from my doore, cham able this to
>   tel!

---

[1] Dods. this.   [4] Haz. by'r leave.
[2] Co. no; Dods. *keeps* no *and omits* me; *the text is due to* Haz.
[3] Dods. *changes to* no.   [5] Co. fet; Dods. fet.

CHAT.   Dyd I, olde witche, steale oft was thine? how
should that thing be knowen?   15

GAMMER.   Ich can not tel; but vp thou tokest it, as
though it had ben thine owne.

CHAT.   Mary, fy on thee, thou old gyb, with al my very
hart!

GAMMER.   Nay, fy on thee, *tho*u rampe, thou ryg, with al
that take thy parte!

CHAT.   A vengeaunce on those lips *tha*t laieth such things
to my charge!

GAMMER.   A vengeance on those callats hips whose con-
scie*n*ce is so large!   20

CHAT.   Come out, hogge!

GAMMER.   Come out, hogge, and let me
haue [1] right!

CHAT.   Thou arrant witche!

GAMMER.   Thou bawdie bitche, chil
make thee cursse this night!

CHAT.   A bag and a wallet!

GAMMER.   A carte for a callet!

CHAT.   Why, wenest thou thus to preuaile?
I hold thee a grote I shall patche thy coate!

GAMMER.   Thou warte as
good kysse my tayle! [2]

Thou slut, *tho*u kut, *tho*u rakes, *tho*u iakes! will not shame
make *th*e [3] bide? [4]   25

CHAT.   Thou skald, thou bald, thou rotten, *tho*u glotton!
I will no lenger chyd! [5]

But I will teache the to kepe home.

GAMMER.   Wylt thou, drunken beaste?

HODGE.   Sticke to her, Gammer, take her by the head,
chil warrant you thys feast!

Smyte, I saye, Gammer!   Byte, I say, Gammer!   I trow ye
wyll be keene! [2]

---

[1] Co. Dods. let haue me.   [3] Co. y^u; Dods. thee.
[2] *This line as three in* Co.   [4] Dods. *reads* hide [thee].
[5] Co. chyd the; Dods. chyd thee; *see preceding note.*

Where be your nayls? claw her by the iawes! pull me out
    bothe her eyen!   30
Gogs bones, Gammer, holde vp your head!
CHAT.   I trow, drab, I shall dresse thee.
Tary, *tho*u knaue, I hold the a grote I shall make these
    hands blesse thee!
Take *tho*u this, old hore, for a-mends, *and* lerne thy tonge
    well to tame,
And say thou met at this bickering, not thy [1] fellow, but thy
    dame!

            [GAMMER *falls down.*]

HODGE.   Where is the strong stued hore? chil geare a
    hores marke!   35
Stand out ones way, that ich kyll none in the darke!
Up, Gammer, and ye be alyue! chil feygh[t] [2] now for vs
    bothe.
Come no nere me, thou scalde callet! to kyll the ich wer loth.
    CHAT.   Art here agayne, thou hoddy-peke! What, Doll,
    bryng me out my spitte!
    HODGE.   Chill broche thee wyth this, bim father soule,
    chyll coniure that foule sprete!   40
Let dore stand, Cock! why coms in-deede? kepe dore, *tho*u
    horson boy!
    CHAT.   Stand to it, *tho*u dastard, for thine eares! Ise
    teche *th*e, a [3] sluttish toye!
    HODGE.   Gogs woundes, hore, chil make the auaunte!
    Take heede, Cocke, pull in the latche!
    CHAT.   I faith, sir loose-breche, had ye taried, ye shold
    haue found your match!

          [HODGE *flees;* GAMMER *attacks.*]

GAMMER.   Now ware thy throte, losell, thouse pay [4] for al!

           [DAME CHAT *falls.*]

HODGE.   Well said, Gammer, by my soule.   45

---

[1] Co. *repeats* thy.   [3] Dods. *omits* a.
[2] *Corr. by* Dods.   [4] Co. pray; Dods. pay.

Hoyse her, souse her, bounce her, trounce her, pull out her
    throte-boule! [1]

CHAT. Comst behynd me, thou withered witch? *And* I
    get once on foote,

Thouse pay for all, *tho*u old tarlether! Ile teach the what
    longs to it!

Take *th*e this to make vp thy mouth til time thou come by
    more!

[GAMMER *falls; exit* DAME CHAT.]

HODGE. Up, Gammer, stand on your feete; where is the
    old hore?   50

Faith, woulde chad her by the face, choulde cracke her callet
    crowne!

GAMMER. A, Hodg, Hodg, where was thy help, when
    fixen had me downe?

HODGE. By the masse, Gammer, but for my staffe, Chat
    had gone nye to spyl you!

Ich think the harlot had not cared, and chad not com, to kill
    you.

But shall we loose our neele thus?

GAMMER.   No, Hodge, chwarde lothe doo soo. 55

Thinkest thou chill take that at her hand? No, Hodg, ich
    tell the, no!

HODGE. Chold yet this fray wer wel take vp, *and* our own
    neele at home.

Twill be my chaunce els some to kil, wher-euer it be, or
    whome!

GAMMER. We haue a parson, Hodge, thou knoes, a man
    estemed wise,

Mast Doctor Rat; chil for hym send, and let me here his
    aduise.   60

He will her shriue for all this gere, *and* geue her penaunce
    strait;

Wese haue our neele, els Dame Chat comes nere w*ith*-in
    heaue*n* gate!

---

[1] Dods. houle, *which* Haz. *modernizes as* hole.

HODGE.   Ye, mary, Gammer, *tha*t ich think best.   Wyll
        you now for him send?

The sooner Doctor Rat be here, the soner wese ha an ende.

And here, Gammer! Dyccons deuill, as iche remember well,   65

Of cat, and Chat and Doctor Rat a felloneus tale dyd tell.

Chold you forty pound, that is the way your neele to get
        againe!

GAMMER.   Chil ha him strait!   Call out *th*e boy, wese
        make him take the payn.

HODGE.   What, Coke, I saye!   Come out!   What deuill!
        canst not here?

COCKE.[1]   How now, Hodg?   How does, Gammer?   Is yet
        the wether cleare?   70

What wold chaue me to doo?

GAMMER.   Come hether, Cocke, anon!

Hence swythe to Doctor Rat, hye the that thou were gone!

And pray hym come speke with me, cham not well at ease.

Shalt haue him at his chamber, or[2] els at Mother Bees;

Els seeke him at Hob Fylchers[3] shop, for, as charde it reported, 75

There is the best ale in al the towne, and now is most resorted.

COCKE.   And shall ich brynge hym with me, Gammer?

GAMMER.   Yea, by-and-by, good Cocke.

COCKE.[4]   Shalt see that shalbe here anone, els let me haue
        on[5] the docke!

                    [*Exit* COCKE.]

HODGE.   Now, Gammer, shal we two go in, and tary for
        hys commynge?

What deuill, woman, plucke vp your hart, *and* leue of al this
        glo*m*ming!   80

Though she were stronger at *th*e first, as ich thinke ye did
        find her,

Yet there ye drest the dronke*n* sow, what time ye cam behind
        her,

---

[1] Co. Ga*m*mer; *corr. by* Dods.   [2] Co. of; Dods. or.

[3] Co. Hobfylchers *as one word, here and below.*

[4] Dods. *says* Co. *assigns this to* HODGE; *not so my copyist.*

[5] Ço. one; *corr. by* Haz.

GAMMER.   Nay, nay, cham sure she lost not all, for, set
  thend [1] to *th*e beginni*n*g,
And ich doubt not but she [2] will make small bost of her
  winning.
     [They go towards GAMMER'S *house.*]

The iii Acte. The iiii Sceane.

    [*The same place, near* GAMMER GURTON'S *door.*]

   TYB [*meets*] HODGE [*and*] GAMMER. COCKE [*returns later*]

TYB. See, Ga*m*mer, Ga*m*mer, Gib, our cat, cha*m* afraid
  what she ayleth!
She standes me gasping behind the door, as though her winde
  her faileth.
Now let [3] ich doubt what Gib shuld mean, *tha*t now she doth
  so dote.
  HODGE. Hold hether! Ichould twenty pound your neele
   is in her throte!
Grope her, ich say! Me thinkes ich feele it. Does not
  pricke your hand?   5
  GAMMER. Ich can feele nothing.
  HODGE.   No? Ich know thars [4]
   not within this land
A muryner cat then Gyb is, betwixt the Tems and Tyne;
Shase as much wyt in her head almost as chaue in mine!
  TYB. Faith, shase eaten some-thing that wil not easely
  downe.
Whether she gat it at home or abrode in the towne   10
Iche can not tell.
  GAMMER.   Alas, ich feare it be some croked pyn!
And then farewell Gyb, she is vndone, and lost al saue the
  skyn.
  HODGE. Tys [5] your neele, woman, I lay! [6] Gogs soule,
   geue me a knyfe,

---

[1] Dods. them.   [4] Dods. that 's.
[2] Dods. he.   [5] Co. Tyb; *corr. by* Dods.
[3] Haz. *changes to* mot. [6] Dods. say.

And chil haue it out of her mawe, or els chal lose my lyfe!

GAMMER.   What! Nay, Hodg, fy! kil not our cat, tis al
the cats we ha now!   15

HODGE.   By the masse, Dame Chat hays me so moued
iche care not what I kyll, ma God a-vowe!

Go to then, Tyb! to this gere! holde vp har[1] tayle, and
take her!

Chil see what deuil is in her guts, chil take the[2] paines to
rake her!

GAMMER.   Rake a cat, Hodge? what woldst thou do?

HODGE.   What! thinckst that cham not able?

Did not Tom Tankard rake his curtal toure day, standing in
the stable?   20

[*Enter* COCKE.]

GAMMER.   Soft, be content, lets here what newes Cocke
bringeth from Maister Rat!

COCKE.   Gammer, chaue ben ther-as you bad, you wot
wel about what.

Twill not be long before he come, ich durst sweare of a
booke.

He byds you see ye be at home, and there for him to looke.

GAMMER.   Where didst thou find him, boy? was he not
wher I told thee?   25

COCKE.   Yes, yes, euen at Hob Filchers house, by him
that[3] bought and solde me;

A cup of ale had in his hand, and a crab lay in the fyer.

Chad much a-do to go and come, al was so ful of myer.

And, Gammer, one thing I can tel, Hob Filchers naule was
loste,

And Doctor Rat found it againe, hard beside the doore-
poste.   30

I chould a penny can say something your neele againe to fet.[4]

GAMMER.   Cham glad to heare so much, Cocke, then
trust he wil not let

----

[1] Dods. her.   [3] Co. *the*; Dods. that.
[2] Co. *th*u; Dods. the.   [4] Co. fet; Dods. fet.

To helpe vs herein best he can; therfore, tyl time he come,
Let vs go in.   If there be aught to get, thou shalt haue some.

The iiij Acte.   The i Sceane.[1]

[The same place.]

[Enter] Doctor Rat. Gammer Gurton *[is at work]*.

D. Rat.   A man were better twenty times be a bandog
    and barke
Then here among such a sort be parish-priest or clarke!
Where he shal neuer be at rest one pissing-while a day
But he must trudge about the towne this way and that way:
Here to a drab, there to a theefe, his shoes to teare and rent,   5
And, that which is worst of al, at euery knaues commaunde-
    ment!
I had not sit the space to drinke two pots of ale
But Gammer Gurtons sory boy was straite-way at my taile,
And she was sicke, and I must come, to do I wot not what!
If once her fingers-end but ake, trudge! call for Doctor Rat! 10
And when I come not at their call, I only therby loose;
For I am sure to lacke therfore a tythe-pyg or a goose.
I warrant you, when truth is knowen, *and* told they haue
    their tale,
The matter where-about I come is not worth a half-peny-
    worth of ale.
Yet must I talke so sage and smothe as though I were a
    glosier, 15
Els, or the yere come at an end, I shalbe sure the loser.

[He sees Gammer Gurton.*]*

What! worke ye, Gammer Gurton? Hoow, here is your frend
    M[ast][2] Rat!
Gammer.   A, good M[ast] Doctor, cha trobled, cha
    trobled you, chwot wel that!

---

[1] Co. The ij Acte. The iiii Sceane; Dods. The Fourth Acte. The First
Sceane.   [2] Dods. doctor.

D. RAT.   How do ye, woman? be ye lustie, or be ye not
    wel at ease?

GAMMER.   By Gys, master, cham not sick,[1] but yet chaue
    a disease.   20

Chad a foule [2] turne now of late, chill tell it you, by Gigs!

D. RAT.   Hath your browne cow cast her calfe or your
    sandy sow her pigs?

GAMMER.   No; but chad ben as good they had as this
    ich wot weel.

D. RAT.   What is the matter?

GAMMER.   Alas, alas, cha lost my good neele!

My neele, I say!   And, wot ye what? a drab came by and
    spied it,   25

And, when I asked hir for the same, the filth flatly denied it.

D. RAT.   What was she that—?

GAMMER.   A dame, ich warrant you!   She
    began to scold and brawle —

Alas, alas!   Come hether, Hodge!   This wr[e]tche can tell
    you all.

The iiii Acte.   The ii Sceane.

[The same place.]

[Enter] HODGE *[to]* DOCTOR RAT *[and]* GAMMER.   DICCON *[enters later]*.[3]

HODGE.   God morow, Gaffer Vicar!

[D. RAT.][4]   Come on, fellow, let vs heare.

Thy dame hath sayd to me thou knowest of all this geare;

Lets see what thou canst saie.

HODGE.   Bym fay, sir, that ye shall!

What matter so-euer here was done, ich can tell your maship
    [all].

---

[1] Co. sich; Dods. sick.

[2] Co. foule; Dods. foule.

[3] Co. *has also* CHAT; *but she does not enter until the point at which I begin Scene iii; see below,* p. 135.

[4] *Not in* Co.; *supplied by* Dods., *without note.*

My Gammer Gurton heare, see now,   5
    Sat her downe at this doore, see now,
And, as she began to stirre her, see now,
    Her neele fell in the floore, see now;
And, while her staffe shee tooke, see now,
    At Gyb, her cat, to flynge, see now,   10
Her neele was lost in the floore, see now.
    Is not this a wondrous thing, see now?
Then came the queane, Dame Chat, see now,
    To aske for hir blacke cup, see now;
And euen here at this gate, see now,   15
    She tooke that neele vp, see now.
My gammer then she yeede, see now,
    Hir neele againe to bring, see now,
And was caught by the head, see now.
    Is not this a wondrous thing, see now?   20
She tare my gammers cote, see now,
    And scratched hir by the face, see now;
Chad thought shad stopt hir throte, see now.
    Is not this a wondrous case, see now?
When ich saw this, ich was wrothe,[1] see now,   25
    And start betwene them twaine, see now;
Els, ich durst take a booke-othe, see now,
    My gammer had bene slaine, see now.
    GAMMER.   This is euen the whole matter, as Hodge has
        plainly tolde,
And chould faine be quiet for my part, that chould.   30
But helpe vs, good master, — beseech ye that ye do, —
Els shall [2] we both be beaten and lose our neele too.
    D. RAT.   What wold ye haue me to doo?   Tel me, that
        I were gone;
I will do the best that I can, to set you both at one.
But be ye sure Dame Chat hath this your neele founde?   35
    GAMMER.   Here comes the man that see hir take it vp of
        the ground;

---

[1] Co. worthe; Dods. wrothe.
[2] Co. shalt; Dods. shall.

Aske him your-selfe, Master Rat, if ye beleue not me.
And helpe me to my neele, for Gods sake and saint charite!

[Enter DICCON.]

D. RAT.   Come nere, Diccon, and let vs heare what thou
can expresse.
Wilt *tho*u be sworne *tho*u seest Dame Chat this womans
neele haue?   40
DICCON.   Nay, by S. Benit, wil I not; then might ye
thinke me raue!
GAMMER.   Why, didst not *tho*u tel me so euen here? Canst
*tho*u for shame deny it?
DICCON.   I, mary, Gammer; but I said I wold not abide
by it.
D. RAT.   Will you say a thing, and not sticke to it to trie
it?
DICCON.   "Stick to it," quoth you, Master Rat? mary,
sir, I defy it!   45
Nay, there is many an honest man, when he suche blastes
hath blowne
In his freindes eares, he woulde be loth the same by him
were knowne.
If such a toy be vsed oft among the honestie,
It may be-seme a simple man of [1] your and my degree.
D. RAT.   Then we be neuer the nearer, for all that you
can tell!   50
DICCON.   Yes, mary, sir, if ye will do by mine aduise and
counsaile.
If Mother Chat se al vs here, she knoweth how the matter
goes ;
Therfore I red y[o]u three go hence, and within keepe close,
And I will into Dame Chats house, and so the matter vse,
That, or you cold go twise to church, I warant you here
news.   55
She shall looke wel about hir, but, I durst lay a pledge,
Ye shal of Gammers neele haue shortly better knowledge.

¹ Co. if: Dods. of.

GAMMER.   Now, gentle Diccon, do so; and, good sir, let
   vs trudge.

D. RAT.   By the masse, I may not tarry so long to be your
   iudge.

DICCON.   Tys but a litle while, man; what! take so much
   paine!   60

If I here no newes of it, I will come sooner [1] againe.

HODGE.   Tary so much, good Master Doctor, of your
   gentlenes!

D. RAT.   Then let vs hie vs inward; and, Diccon, speede
   thy busines!

                    [*Exeunt.*]

[The iiij Act.   The iij Scene.] [2]

[*The same place, near* DAME CHAT'S *door.*]

[DICCON *approaches* DAME CHAT'S.]

DICCON.   Now, sirs, do you no more, but kepe my counsaile iuste,

And Docter Rat shall thus catch some good, I trust.

But Mother Chat, my gossop, talke first with-all I must;

For she must be chiefe captaine to lay the Rat in the dust.

[*Enter* DAME CHAT.]

God deuen, Dame Chat, in faith, and wel met in this place!   5

CHAT.   God deuen, my friend Diccon; whether walke ye
   this pace?

DICCON.   By my truthe, euen to you, to learne how the
   world goeth.

Hard ye no more of the other matter, say me now, by your
   troth!

CHAT.   O yes, Diccon, here the olde hoore *and* Hodge,
   that great knaue —

---

[1] Haz. *emends to* soon here.

[2] *On the principle adopted in this play, a new scene should begin here;
but it is not so indicated in the old copy;* Haz. *says the scene should begin
with* l. 5.

But, in faith, I would thou hadst sene, — O Lord, I drest
    them braue !   10
She bare me two or three souses behind in the nape of the
    necke,
Till I made hir olde wesen to answere againe, " kecke " ! [1]
And Hodge, that dirty dastard that at hir elbow standes, —
If one paire of legs had not bene worthe two paire of hands,
He had had his bearde shauen, if my nayles wold haue
    serued !   15
And not without a cause, for the knaue it well deserued.
    DICCON.   By the masse, I can the thank, wench, *tho*u
        didst so wel acquite the!
    CHAT.   And thadst seene him, Diccon, it wold haue made
        *th*e beshite the
For laughter.   The horsen dolt at last caught vp a club,
As though he would haue slaine the master-deuil, Belsabub,   20
But I set him soone inward.
    DICCON.   O Lorde, there is the thing
That Hodge is so offended!   That makes him starte and
    flyng !
    CHAT.   Why, makes the knaue any moyling, as ye haue
        sene or hard ?
    DICCON.   Euen now I sawe him last, — like a mad-man he
        farde,
And sware by heauen and hell he would a-wreake his sorowe,   25
And leue you neuer a hen on-liue by viii of the clock to-
    morow.
Therfore marke what I say, and my wordes see that ye trust :
Your hens be as good as dead if ye leaue them on the ruste !
    CHAT.   The knaue dare as wel [2] go hang himself as go
        vpon my grou*n*d !
    DICCON.   Wel, yet take hede, I say! I must tel you my
        tale round.   30
Haue you not about your house, behind your furnace or leade,
A hole where a crafty knaue may crepe in for neade? [3]

---

[1] Co. kicke; Dods. kecke.   [3] Co. neades; Dods. neade.
[2] Co. wol; Dods. wel.

CHAT.   Yes, by the masse, a hole broke down euen wit*h*in
these ii dayes.

DICCON.   Hodge he intendes this same night to slip in
there-a-wayes.

CHAT.   O Christ, that I were sure of it! in faith, he shuld
haue his mede !   35

DICCON.   Watch wel, for the knaue wil be there as sure
as is your crede.

I wold spend my-selfe a shilling to haue him swinged well.

CHAT.   I am as glad as a woman can be of this thing to
here tell.

By Gogs bones, when he co*m*meth, now that I know the
matter,

He shal sure at the first skip to leape in scalding water, —   40

With a worse turne besides !   When he will, let him come!

DICCON.   I tell you as my sister, you know what meaneth
" mum " !

                                                      [*Exit* DAME CHAT.]

[The iiij Act.   The iiij Scene.]¹

[*The same place.*]

[DICCON *awaits* DOCTOR RAT.]

[DICCON.]   Now lacke I but my doctor to play his part
againe.

And lo,² where he commeth towards, — per aduenture, to his
paine !

D. RAT.   What good newes, Diccon, fellow? is Mother
Chat at home?

DICCON.   She is, syr, and she is not, but it please her to
whome.

Yet dyd I take her tardy, as subtle³ as she was !   5

D. RAT.   The thing that thou wentst for, hast thou
brought it to passe?

---

¹ *This scene, as the brackets indicate, is not marked in* Co.
² Co. to; Dods. lo.   ³ Co. Haz. subtle; Dods. suble.

DICCON. I haue done that I haue done, be it worse, be it
 better!
And Dame Chat at her wyts ende I haue almost set her.
 D. RAT. Why, hast thou spied the neele? Quickly, I
 pray thee, tell!
 DICCON. I haue spyed it, in faith, sir, I handled my-selfe
 so well.   10
And yet the crafty queane had almost take my trumpe.
But, or all came to an ende, I set her in a dumpe!
 D. RAT. How so, I pray thee, Diccon?
 DICCON.   Mary, syr, will ye heare?
She was clapt downe on the backside, by Cocks Mother dere,
And there she sat sewing a halter or a bande,   15
With no other thing saue Gammers nedle in her hande.
As soone as any knocke, if the filth be in doubte,
She needes but once puffe, and her candle is out.
Now I, sir, knowing of euery doore the pin,
Came nycely, and said no worde till time I was within;   20
And there I sawe the neele, euen with these two eyes.
Who-euer say the contrary, I will sweare he lyes!
 D. RAT. O Diccon, that I was not there then in thy steade!
 DICCON. Well, if ye will be ordred and do by my reade,
I will bring you to a place, as the house standes,   25
Where ye shall take the drab with the neele in hir handes.
 D. RAT. For Gods sake, do so, Diccon, and I will gage
 my gowne
To geue thee a full pot of the best ale in the towne!
 DICCON. Follow me but a litle, and marke what I will say;
Lay downe your gown beside you; go to, come on your way! 30
Se ye not what is here? — a hole wherin ye may creepe
Into the house, and sodenly vnwares among them leape.
There shal ye finde the bitchfox and the neele together.
Do as I bid you, man, come on your wayes hether!
 D. RAT. Art thou sure, Diccon, the swil-tub standes not
 here-aboute?   35
 DICCON. I was within my-selfe, man, euen now, there is
 no doubt.

Go softly, make no noyse, giue me your foote, sir John!
Here will I waite vpon you tyl you come out anone.

[DOCTOR RAT *climbs into the house.*]

D. RAT.   Helpe, Diccon! out, alas! I shal be slaine
among them!

DICCON.   If they giue you not the nedle, tel them that ye
will ha*n*g them.   40

Ware that! Hoow, my wenches! haue ye caught the foxe
That vsed to make reuel among your hennes and cocks?
Saue his life yet for his order, though he susteine some paine.
Gogs bread, I am afraide, they wil beate out his braine!

[*Exit* DICCON.   DOCTOR RAT *comes out in disarray.*]

D. RAT.   Wo worth the houre that I came heare!   45
And wo worth him that wrought this geare!
A sort of drabs and queanes haue me blest!
Was euer creature halfe so euill drest?
Who-euer it wrought and first did inuent it,
He shall, I warrant him, erre long repent it!   50
I will spend all I haue, without my skinne,
But he shall be brought to the plight I am in!
Master Bayly, I trow, and he be worth his eares,
Will snaffle these murderers and all that them beares.
I will surely neither byte nor suppe   55
Till I fetch him hether, this matter to take vp.

[*Exit.*]

The v Acte.   The i Sceane.

[*A room in the house of the* BAILIE.]

MASTER BAYLY.   DOCTOR RAT.   [SCAPETHRYFT *and* MUTES.]

BAILIE.   I can perceiue none other, I speke it from my hart,
But either ye ar in al the fault or els in *th*e greatest part.

D. RAT.   If it be counted his fault, besides all his greeues,
When a poore man is spoyled and beaten among theeues,
Then I confesse my fault herein, at this season;   5

But I hope you wil not iudge so much against reason.

    BAILY.   And me thinkes, by your owne tale, of all that ye
        name,

If any plaid the theefe, you were the very same.

The women they did nothing, as your words make probation,

But stoutly withstood your forcible inuasion.   10

If that a theefe at your window to enter should begin,

Wold you hold forth your hand and helpe to pull him in?

Or wold you[1] kepe him out? I pray you, answere me.

    D. RAT.   Mary, kepe him out, and a good cause why!

But I am no theefe, sir, but an honest learned clarke.   15

    BAILY.   Yea, but who knoweth that, when he meets you
        in the darke.

I am sure your learning shines not out at your nose.

Was it any maruaile though the poore woman arose

And start vp, being afraide of that was in her purse?

Me thinke you may be glad that you[r][2] lucke was no
        worse.   20

    D. RAT.   Is not this euill ynough, I pray you, as you
        thinke?

            Showing his broken head.

    BAILY.   Yea, but a man in the darke, if[3] chaunces do
        wincke,

As soone he smites his father as any other man,

Because for lacke of light discerne him he ne can.

Might it not haue ben your lucke *with* a spit to haue ben
        slaine?   25

    D. RAT.   I thinke I am litle better, my scalpe is clouen to
        the braine.

If there be all the remedy, I know who beares the k[n]ockes.[4]

    BAILY.   By my troth, and well worthy besides to kisse
        the stockes,

To come in on the backe-side, when ye might go about!

---

[1] Co. you wold; *corr. by* Dods.
[2] *Corr. by* Dods.
[3] Co. of; Dods. if; Haz. *changes to* oft.
[4] *Corr. by* Dods.

I know non such, vnles they long to haue their braines knockt
    out.   30
  D. RAT.   Well, wil you be so good, sir, as talke with
    Dame Chat,
And know what she intended?   I aske no more but that.
  BAYLY.   Let her be called, fellow, because of Master
    Doctor.
I warrant in this case she wil be hir owne proctor ;

[Exit SCAPETHRYFT.]

She will tel hir owne tale in metter or in prose,   35
And byd you seeke your remedy and so go wype your nose !

The v Acte.   The ii Sceane.

[The same place.]

M. BAYLY, CHAT, D. RAT, GAMMER, HODGE, DICCON, [SCAPETHRYFT
and MUTES are present during the scene, GAMMER, HODGE and DICCON
coming in later].

BAYLY.   Dame Chat, Master Doctor vpon you here com-
    plained [1]
  That you *and* your maides shuld him much misorder,
And taketh many an oth that no word he [2] fained,[3]
    Laying to your charge how you thought him to murder ;
    And, on his part againe, that same man saith furder
He neuer offended you in word nor intent :
To heare you answer hereto, we haue now for you sent.   7

  CHAT.   That I wold haue murdered him? fye on him,
    wretch !
And euil mought he [4] thee for it, our Lord I besech.[5]
I will swere on al the bookes that opens and shuttes,
He faineth this tale out of his owne guttes ;
For this seuen weekes with me, I am sure, he sat not downe.

---

[1] Co. complained ; Dods. complaineth.
[2] Haz. be.   [4] Co. be ; Dods. he.
[3] Co. Dods. fained.   [5] Co. besēch.

Nay, ye haue other minions, in the other end of the towne,
Where ye were liker to catch such a blow
Then any-where els, as farre as I know!   15

    BAILY.   Be-like then, Master Doctor, you[r] [1] stripe there
        ye got not !

    D. RAT.   Thinke you I am so mad that where I was bet
        I wot not?

Will ye beleue this queane before she hath tryd it?
It is not the first dede she hath done and afterward denide
    it.

    CHAT.   What, man, will you say I broke your head?   20
    D. RAT.   How canst thou proue the contrary?
    CHAT.   Nay, how prouest thou that I did the deade?
    D. RAT.   To plainly, by S. Mary!

This profe, I trow, may serue though I no word spoke!

Showing his broken head.

    CHAT.   Bicause thy head is broken, was it I that it broke?   25
I saw thee, Rat, I tel thee, not once within this fortnight.

    D. RAT.   No, mary, thou sawest me not, for-why thou
        hadst no light ;

But I felt thee, for al the darke, beshrew thy smothe cheekes !
And thou groped me, this wil declare any day this six weekes.

Showing his heade.

    BAILY.   Answere me to this, M[ast] Rat: when caught
        you this harme of yours?   30

    D. RAT.   A-while a-go, sir, God he knoweth, *with*-in les
        the*n* these ii houres.

    BAILY.   Dame Chat, was there none with you — confesse,
        i faith ! — about that season?

What, woman ! let it be what it wil, tis neither felony nor
    treason.

    CHAT.   Yes, by my faith, Master Bayly, there was a
        knaue not farre

Who caught one good philup on the brow with a dore-barre, —   35

[1] *Corr. by* Dods.

And well was he worthy, as it semed to mee ;
But what is that to this man, since this was not hee ?

    BAILY.   Who was it then ?   Lets here !

    D. RAT.   Alas ! sir, aske you that ?
Is it not made plain inough by the owne mouth of Dame
    Chat ?
The time agreeth, my head is broken, her tong can not lye ;   40
Onely vpon a bare nay she saith it was not I.

    CHAT.   No, mary, was it not indeede ; ye shal here by
    this one thing :
This after-noone a frend of mine for good wil gaue me warn-
    ing,
And bad me wel loke to my ruste and al my capons pennes,
For, if I toke not better heede, a knaue wold haue my hennes ;   45
Then I, to saue my goods, toke so much pains as him to
    watch,
And, as good fortune serued me, it was my chaunce him for
    to catch.
What strokes he bare away, or other what was his gaines,
I wot not, but sure I am he had something for his paines !

    BAILY.   Yet telles thou not who it was.

    CHAT.   Who it was ? a false theefe,   50
That came like a false foxe my pullaine to kil and mischeefe !

    BAILY.   But knowest thou not his name ?

    CHAT.   I know it.   But what than ?
It was that crafty cullyon, Hodge, my Gammer Gurtons man.

    BAILIE.   Call me the knaue hether, he shal sure kysse the
    stockes ;
I shall teach him a lesson for filching hens or cocks !   55

             [*Exit* SCAPETHRYFT.]

    D. RAT.[1]   I meruaile, Master Bayly, so bleared be your
    eyes ;
An egge is not so ful of meate as she is ful of lyes.
When she hath playd this pranke to excuse al this geare,
She layeth the fault in such a one as I know was not there.

        [1] *In* Co. *this precedes* l. 55.

CHAT.   Was he not thear?   Loke on his pate, that shalbe
        his witnes!   60
D. RAT.   I wold my head were half so hole, I wold seeke
        no redresse!

[Enter GAMMER GURTON.]

BAILY.   God blesse you, Gammer Gurton!
GAMMER.   God dylde you, master mine!
BAILY.   Thou hast a knaue w*ith*-in thy ho[u]se, — Hodge,
        a seruant of thine.
They tel me that busy knaue is such a filching one
That hen, pig, goose or capon thy neighbour can haue none.   65
GAMMER.   By God, cham much ameued to heare any such
        reporte!
Hodge was not wont, ich trow, to haue him in that sort.
CHAT.   A theeuisher knaue is not on-liue, more filching nor
        more false ;
Many a truer man then he hase hanged vp by the halse! [1]
And thou, his dame, — of al his theft thou art the sole re-
        ceauer.   70
For Hodge to catch and thou to kepe I neuer knew none
        better.
GAMMER.   Sir reuerence of your masterdome, and you
        were out a-doore,
Chold be so bolde, for al hir brags, to cal hir arrant whoore!
And ich knew Hodge so bad as tow, ich wish me endlesse
        sorow
And chould not take the pains to hang him vp before to-
        morow !   75
CHAT.   What haue I stolne fro*m* the or thine, thou il-
        fauored olde trot?
GAMMER.   A great deale more, by Gods blest, then cheuer
        by the got !
That thou knowest wel, I neade not say it.
BAILY.   Stoppe there, I say !
And tel me here, I pray you, this matter by the way :

[1] Co. halfe; Dods. halse.

How chaunce Hodge is not here?   Him wol[d]e I faine haue
  had.   80
 GAMMER.   Alas, sir, heel be here anon ; ha be handled to
  bad!
 CHAT.   Master Bayly, sir, ye be not such a foole, wel I
  know,
But ye perceiue by this lingring there is a pad in the straw.

> *Thinking that* HODG *his head was broke, and that* GAMMER *wold not let
> him come before them.*

 GAMMER.   Chil shew you his face, ich warrant the, — lo
  now where he is !

> [*Enter* HODGE, *wearing his torn best breeches, and covering the rent
> with his hands.*]

 BAILIE.   Come on, fellow!   It is tolde me thou art a
  shrew, i-wysse.   85
Thy neighbours hens *tho*u takest, and playes the two-legged
  foxe ;
Their chikens *and* their capons to, *and* now and then their
  cocks.
 HODGE.   Ich defy them al that dare it say ; cham as true
  as the best!
 BAILY.   Wart not *tho*u take within this houre in Dame
  Chats hens nest?
 HODGE.   Take there?   No, master, chold not do 't for a
  house-ful of gold !   90
 CHAT.   Thou, or the deuil in thy cote, sweare this I dare
  be bold.
 D. RAT.   Sweare me no swearing, quean, the deuill he geue
  the sorow!
Al is not worth a gnat thou canst sweare till to-morow.
Where is the harme he hath?   Shew it, by Gods bread !
Ye beat him, with a witnes, but the stripes light on my head!   95
 HODGE.   Bet me?   Gogs blessed body, chold first, ich
  trow, haue burst the.
Ich thinke, and chad my hands loose, callet, chould haue
  crust the!

CHAT.   Thou shitte*n* knaue, I trow *tho*u knowest *th*e ful
weight of my fist ;

I am fowly deceiued onles thy head *and* my doore-bar kyste !

HODGE.   Hold thy chat, whore, *tho*u criest so loude can
no man els be hard.   100

CHAT.   Well, knaue, *and* I had the alone, I wold surely
rap thy costard !

BAYLY.   Sir, answer me to this : is thy head whole or
broken?

CHAT.   Yea, Master Bayly, blest be euery good token !

HODGE.   Is my head whole?   Ich warra*n*t you tis neither
scuruy nor scald !

What, you foule beast, does think tis either pild or bald?   105

Nay, ich thanke God, chil not, for al that thou maist spend,

That chad one scab on my narse as brode as thy fingers end.

BAYLY.   Come nearer heare !

HODGE.   Yes, that iche dare.

BAYLY.   By Our Lady, here is no harme

Hodges head is hole ynough, for al Dame Chats charme.

CHAT.   By Gogs blest, how-euer the thing he clockes or
smolders,   110

I know the blowes he bare away either w*ith* head or
shoulders.

Camest *tho*u not, knaue, within this houre creping into my
pens,

And there was caught within my hous gropi*n*g among my
hens?

HODGE.   A plage both on thy hens *and* the! A carte,
whore, a carte !

Chould I were ha*n*ged as hie as a tree *and* chware as false
as *tho*u art!   115

Geue my Ga*m*mer again her washical *tho*u stole away in thy
lap!

GAMMER.   Yea, Maister Baily, there is a thing you know
not on, may hap :

This drab she kepes away my good, *th*e deuil he might her
snare !

Ich pray you that ich might haue a right action on her.

CHAT.   Haue I thy good, old filth, or any such old sowes? 120
I am as true, I wold thou knew, as skin betwene thy browes !

GAMMER.   Many a truer hath be*n* hanged, though you
escape the daunger !

CHAT.   Thou shalt answer, by Gods pity, for this thy
foule slaunder !

BAILY.   Why, what ca*n* ye charge hir withal?   To say so
ye do not well.

GAMMER.   Mary, a ve*n*geance to hir hart, *th*e whore hase
stoln my neele !   125

CHAT.   Thy nedle, old witch? how so?   It were almes thy
skul to knock !

So didst thou say the other day that I had stolne thy cock
And rosted him to my breakfast, — which shal not be for-
gotten,
The deuil pul out thy lying tong and teeth that be so rotten !

GAMMER.   Geue me my neele !   As for my cocke, chould
be very loth   130
That chuld here tel he shuld hang on thy false faith and
troth.

BAILY.   Your talke is such I can scarse learne who shuld
be most in fault.

GAMMER.   Yet shal ye find no other wight saue she, by
bred *and* salt !

BAILY.   Kepe ye content a-while, se that your tonges ye
holde ;
Me thinkes you shuld remembre this is no place to scolde. 135
How knowest thou, Ga*m*mer Gurton, Dame Chat thy nedle
had?

GAMMER.   To name you, sir, the party, chould not be
very glad.

BAILY.   Yea, but we must nedes heare it, *and* therfore say
it boldly.

GAMMER.   Such one as told the tale full soberly and
coldly,
Euen he that loked on — wil sweare on a booke —   140

What time this drunken gossip my faire long neele vp tooke:
Diccon, Master, the bedlam, cham very sure ye know him.

    BAILIE.   A false knaue, by Gods pitie! ye were but a
        foole to trow him.

I durst auenture wel the price of my best cap
That, when the end is knowen, all wil turne to a iape.   145
Tolde he not you that, besides, she stole your cocke that
        tyde?

    GAMMER.   No, master, no indede; for then he shuld
        haue lyed!

My cocke is, I thanke Christ, safe and wel a-fine.

    CHAT.   Yea, but that ragged[1] colt, that whore, that Tyb
        of thine,

Said plainly thy cocke was stolne, *and* in my house was
        eaten.   150
That lying cut is lost, that she is not swinged and beaten, —
And yet for al my good name it were a small amendes!
I picke not this geare, hearst thou, out of my fingers endes;
But he that hard it, told me, who thou of late didst name, —
Diccon, whom al men knowes, — it was the very same.   155

    BAILY.   This is the case: you lost your nedle about the
        dores,

And she answeres againe she hase no cocke of yours;
Thus, in you[r] talke and action, from that you do intend
She is whole fiue mile wide from that she doth defend.
Will you saie she hath your cocke?

    GAMMER.   No, mary,[2] sir, that chil not! 160

    BAYLY.   Will you confesse hir neele?

    CHAT.   Will I? no, sir, will I not!

    BAYLY.   Then there lieth all the matter.

    GAMMER.   Soft, master, by the way!

Ye know she could do little and she cold not say nay.

    BAYLY.   Yea, but he that made one lie about your cock-
        stealing,

Wil not sticke to make another, what time lies be in dealing. 165

        [1] Dods. rogged; Haz. rugged.
        [2] Co. mery; Dods. mary.

I weene the ende wil proue this brawle did first arise
Upon no other ground but only Diccons lyes.

CHAT.   Though some be [1] lyes, as you belike haue espyed
          them,
Yet other some be true; by proof I haue wel tryed them.

BAYLY.   What other thing beside this, Dame Chat.

CHAT.   Mary, syr, euen this: 170
The tale I tolde before, the selfe-same tale it was his;
He gaue me, like a frende, warning against my losse,
Els had my hens be stolne eche one, by Gods crosse!
He tolde me Hodge wold come, and in he came indeede;
But, as the matter chaunsed, with greater hast then speede.   175
This truth was said, and true was found, as truly I report.

BAYLY.   If Doctor Rat be not deceiued, it was of another
          sort.

D. RAT.   By Gods Mother, thou and he be a cople of
          suttle foxes!
Betweene you and Hodge I beare away the boxes.
Did not Diccon apoynt the place wher thou shuldst stand to
          mete him?   180

CHAT.   Yes, by the masse, and, if he came, bad me not
          sticke to speet hym.

D. RAT.   Gods sacrament, the villain knaue hath drest vs
          round about,
He is the cause of all this brawle, that dyrty, shitten loute!
When Gammer Gurton here complained, and made a ruful
          mone,
I heard him sweare that you had gotten hir nedle that was
          gone;   185
And this to try, he furder said, he was ful loth, how-be-it
He was content with small adoe to bring me where to see it.
And where ye [2] sat, he said ful certain, if I wold folow his
          read,
Into your house a priuy way he wold me guide and leade,
And where ye had it in your hands, sewing about a clowte;   190
And set me in the backe-hole, therby to finde you oute.

----

[1] Co. he; Dods. be.   [2] Dods. he.

And, whiles I sought a quietnes, creping vpon my knees,
I found the weight of your dore-bar for my reward and fees.
Such is the lucke that some men gets while they begin to mel
In setting at one such as were out, minding to make al wel.   195

HODGE.   Was not wel blest, Ga*m*mer, to scape *tha*t
scoure?   *And* chad ben there,
The*n* chad ben drest, be-like, as ill, by the masse, as Gaffar
Vicar.

BAYLY.   Mary, sir, here is a sport alone.   I loked for
such an end.

If Di*c*con had not playd the knaue, this had ben sone
amend.
My Gammer here he made a foole, and drest hir as she was ;   200
And goodwife Chat he set to scole,[1] till both parties[2] cried
alas ;
And D[octor] Rat was not behind, whiles Chat his crown did
pare ;
I wold the knaue had be*n* starke blind, if Hodg had not his
share !

HODGE.   Cham meetly wel-sped alredy amongs, cham
drest like a coult!

And chad not had the better wit, chad bene made a doult.   205

BAYLY.   Sir knaue, make hast Diccon were here ; fetch
him where-euer he bee!

[*Exit* SCAPETHRYFT.]

CHAT.   Fie on the villaine! fie! fie! *tha*t makes vs thus
agree !

GAMMER.   Fie on him knaue, with al my hart! now fie!
and fie againe !

D. RAT.   Now "fie on him !" may I best say, whom he
hath almost slaine.

[*Enter* DICCON.]

BAYLY.   Lo where he commeth at hand ; belike he was
not fare !   210

Diccon, heare be two or three thy company can not spare.

---

[1] Dods. *changes to* scold.   [2] Dods. parts.

DICCON.　God blesse you, and you may be blest, so many
　　al at once!

CHAT.　Come, knaue, it were a good deed[1] geld the, by
　　Cockes bones!

Seest not thy handiwarke?　Sir Rat, can ye forbeare him?

DICCON.　A vengeance on those hands lite![2] for my hands
　　cam not nere hym.　　　　　　　　　　　　　　　215

The horsen priest hath lift the pot in some of these alewyues
　　chayres,

That his head wolde not serue him, belyke, to come downe
　　the stayres.

BAILY.　Nay, soft! thou maist not play *th*e knaue *and*
　　haue this language to!

If thou thy tong bridle a-while, the better maist thou do.

Confesse the truth, as I shall aske, and cease a-while to fable;　220

And for thy fault, I promise the, thy handling shalbe reason-
　　able.

Hast thou not made a lie or two, to set these two by the
　　eares?

DICCON.　What if I haue? fiue hundred such haue I seene
　　within these seuen yeares.

I am sory for nothing else but that I see not the sport

Which was betwene them when they met, as they them-selues
　　report.　　　　　　　　　　　　　　　　　　225

BAYLY.　The greatest thing — Master Rat, ye se how he
　　is drest!

DICCON.　What deuil nede he be groping so depe in
　　goodwife Chats hens nest?

BAYLY.　Yea, but it was thy drift[3] to bring him into *th*e
　　briars.

DICCON.　Gods bread, hath not such an old foole wit to
　　saue his eares?

He showeth himselfe herein, ye see, so very a coxe　　　230

The cat was not so madly alured by the foxe

To run into the snares was set for him, doubtlesse;

For he leapt in for myce, and this sir John for madnes.

---

[1] Dods. *inserts* to.　　　　[2] Dods. life.　　　　[3] Dods. drif.

D. RAT.   Well, and ye shift no better, ye losel, lyther
and lasye,
I will go neare, for this, to make ye leape at a dasye.   235
In the kings name, Master Bayly, I charge you set him fast!
DICCON.   What, fast at cardes, or fast on-slepe?   It is
the thing [1] I did last.
D. RAT.   Nay, fast in fetters, false varlet, according to
thy deedes!
BAYLY.   Master doctor, ther is no remedy I must intreat
you needes
Some other kinde of punishment.
D. RAT.   Nay, by all halowes!   240
His punishment, if I may iudg, shalbe naught els but the
gallous.
BAYLY.   That ware to sore, a spiritual man to be so
extreame !
D. RAT.   Is he worthy any better, sir? how do ye iudge
and deame?
BAYLY.   I graunt him wort[h]ie punishment, but in no
wise so great.
GAMMER.   It is a shame, ich tel you plaine, for such false
knaues intreat !   245
He has almost vndone vs al, — that is as true as steele.
And ye[t], for al this great ado, cham neuer the nere my
neele !
BAYLY.   Canst *tho*u not say any-thing to that, Diccon,
with least or most?
DICCON.   Yea, mary, sir, thus much I can say : wel, the
nedle is lost !
BAYLY.   Nay, canst not thou tel which way that nedle
may be found?   250
DICCON.   No, by my [2] fay, sir, though I might haue an
hundred pound.
HODGE.   Thou lier lickdish, didst not say the neele wold
be gitten?

1 Dods. king; Co. Haz. thing.
2 Dods. *omits* my.

DICCON.   No, Hodge, by the same token, you were [1] that
     time beshittene
For feare of Hobgobiling, — you wot wel what I meane;
As long as it is sence, I feare me yet ye be scarce cleane.   255
   BAYLY.   Wel, Master Rat, you must both learne, *and*
     teach vs, to forgeue.
Since Diccon hath confession made *and* is so cleane shreue,
If ye to me conscent, to amend this heauie chaunce,
I wil inioyne him here some open kind of penaunce, —
Of this condition: where ye know my fee is twenty pence 260
For the bloodshed, I am agreed with you here to dispence, —
Ye shal go quite, so that ye graunt the matter now to run
To end with mirth among vs al, euen as it was begun.
   CHAT.   Say yea, Master Vicar, *and* he shal sure confes to
     be your detter,
And al we that be heare present wil loue you much the better. 265
   D. RAT.   My part is the worst; but, since you al here-on
     agree,
Go euen to, Master Bayly, — let it be so for mee!
   BAYLY.   How saiest thou, Diccon, art content this shal on
     me depend?
   DICCON.   Go to, M[ast] Bayly, say on your mind, I know
     ye are my frend.
   BAYLY.   Then marke ye wel: to recompence this thy
     former action, — 270
Because thou hast offended al, — to make them [2] satisfaction,
Before their faces here kneele downe, *and*, as I shal the
     teach, —
For thou shalt take on [3] othe of Hodges leather breache:
First, for Master Doctor, vpon paine of his cursse,
Where he wil pay for al, thou neuer draw thy pursse, 275
And, when ye meete at one pot, he shall haue the first pull,
And thou shalt neuer offer him the cup but it be full;
To goodwife Chat thou shalt be sworne, euen on the same
     wyse,

---

[1] Co. where; Dods. were.   [3] Dods. an.
[2] Dods. the; Co. Haz. them.

If she refuse thy money once, neuer to offer it twise, —
Thou shalt be bound by the same here, as thou dost take it,   280
When thou maist drinke of free cost, thou neuer forsake it ;
For Gammer Gurtons sake, againe, sworne shalt thou bee
To helpe hir to hir nedle againe, if it do lie in thee,
And likewise be bound by the vertue of that
To be of good abering to Gib, hir great cat ;   285
Last of al, for Hodge the othe to scanne,
Thou shalt neuer take him for fine gentleman.

HODGE.   Come on, fellow Diccon, chalbe euen with thee
   now !
BAYLY.   Thou wilt not sticke to do this, Diccon, I trow?
DICCON.   No, by my fathers skin, my hand downe I lay it!   290
Loke, as I haue promised, I wil not denay it.
But, Hodge, take good heede now thou do not beshite me !

And gaue[1] *him a good blow on the buttocke.*

HODGE.   Gogs hart, thou false villaine, dost thou bite mee?
BAYLY.   What, Hodge, doth he hurt the or euer he begin?
HODGE.   He thrust me into the buttocke with a bodkin or
   a pin !   295

[*He finds the needle.*]

I saie, Gammer ! Gammer !
GAMMER.   How now, Hodge, how now?
HODGE.   Gods malt, Gammer Gurton !
GAMMER.   Thou art mad, ich trow !
HODGE.   Will you see ! the deuil, Gammer !
GAMMER.   The deuil, sonne?   God
   blesse vs !
HODGE.   Chould[2] iche were hanged, Gammer !
GAMMER.   Mary, se[3] ye might dresse vs.
HODGE.   Chaue it, by the masse, Gammer !
GAMMER.   What? not
   my neele, Hodge?   300
HODGE.   Your neele, Gammer ! your neele !
GAMMER.   No, fie, dost but dodge !

  [1] Haz. give.   [2] Haz. *inserts* [if].   [3] *Qy.* so.

HODGE.   Cha found your neele, Gammer, here in my
hand be it!

GAMMER.   For al the loues on earth, Hodge, let me see it!

HODGE.   Soft, Gammer!

GAMMER.   Good Hodge!

HODGE.   Soft, ich say; tarie a while!

GAMMER.   Nay, sweete Hodge, say truth, and do not me
begile!   305

HODGE.   Cham sure on it, ich warrant you; it goes no
more a-stray.

GAMMER.   Hodge, when I speake so faire, wilt stil say
me nay?

HODGE.   Go neare the light, Gammer; this ¹ wel! in faith,
good lucke!

Chwas almost vndone, twas so far in my buttocke!

GAMMER.   Tis min owne deare neele, Hodge, sykerly I
wot!   310

HODGE.   Cham I not a good sonne, Gammer? cham I not?

GAMMER.   Christs blessing light on thee, hast made me
for-euer!

HODGE.   Ich knew that ich must finde it els choud a had
it neuer!

CHAT.   By my troth, Gossyp Gurton, I am euen as glad

As though I mine owne selfe as good a turne had!   315

BAYLY.   And I, by my concience, to see it so come forth,

Reioyce so much at it as three nedles be worth!

D. RAT.   I am no whit sory to see you so reioyce!

DICCON.   Nor I much the gladder for al this noyce!

Yet say, " Gramercy, Diccon," for springing of the game.²   320

GAMMER.   Gramercy, Diccon, twenty times!   O how glad
cham!

If that chould do so much, your masterdome to come hether,

Master Rat, goodwife Chat and Diccon, together, —

Cha but one halfpeny, as far as iche know it,

And chil not rest this night till ich bestow it;   325

---

¹ Haz. 'tis.

² *Should this line be spoken by the* BAILY ?

If euer ye loue me, let vs go in and drinke!

    BAYLY.   I am content, if the rest thinke as I thinke.

Master Rat, it shalbe best for you if we so doo;

Then shall you warme you and dresse your-self too.

    DICCON.   Soft, syrs, take vs with you, the company shalbe
        the more!   330

As proude coms behinde, they say, as any goes before!

[Turning to the audience.]

But now, my good masters, since we must be gone

And leaue you behinde vs here all alone, —

Since at our last ending thus mery we bee,

For Gammer Gurtons nedle sake let vs haue a plaudytie!   335

    FINIS.   GURTON.   PERUSED AND ALOWED, &C.

Imprinted at London

in Fleeteſtreate beneath the Conduite

at the ſigne of S. John Euangeliſt, by

Thomas Colwell.

1575.

PART VIII.

A Lamentable Tragedie,

mixed full of plefant mirth
containing the Life

of Cambifes King of Percia,

from the beginning of his kingdome
unto his Death,

his one good deede of execution,
after that, many wicked deedes
and tyrannous murders

committed by and through him,
and laft of all,

his odious death by Gods Iuftice appointed,

Done in fuch order as foloweth.

By Thomas Prefton.

This play was licensed to John Allde in 1569. From his edition both Hawkins
("Origin of the English Drama," I, 243 ff.) and Hazlitt (Dodsley's "Old Plays,"
IV, 157 ff.) printed. I print from the second edition, by Edward Allde, the existence of which Hawkins doubted. Insignificant variants in Hawkins and Hazlitt
are not recorded; *u* and *v* are reduced to modern usage. The titlepage is, of
course, not a facsimile.

THE DIVISION OF THE PARTS.

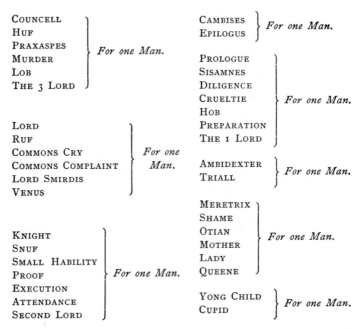

COUNCELL
HUF
PRAXASPES
MURDER
LOB
THE 3 LORD
} *For one Man.*

LORD
RUF
COMMONS CRY
COMMONS COMPLAINT
LORD SMIRDIS
VENUS
} *For one Man.*

KNIGHT
SNUF
SMALL HABILITY
PROOF
EXECUTION
ATTENDANCE
SECOND LORD
} *For one Man.*

CAMBISES
EPILOGUS
} *For one Man.*

PROLOGUE
SISAMNES
DILIGENCE
CRUELTIE
HOB
PREPARATION
THE 1 LORD
} *For one Man.*

AMBIDEXTER
TRIALL
} *For one Man.*

MERETRIX
SHAME
OTIAN
MOTHER
LADY
QUEENE
} *For one Man.*

YONG CHILD
CUPID
} *For one Man.*

[A LAMENTABLE TRAGEDIE.]

[Prologue.]

The PROLOGUE *entreth.*

Agathon, he whose counsail wise to princes weale extended,
By good advice unto a prince three things[1] he hath com-
    mended:
First is that he hath government and ruleth over men;
Secondly, to rule with lawes, eke iustice, saith he then;
Thirdly, that he must wel conceive he may not alwaies
    raigne.   5
Lo, thus the rule unto a prince Agathon squared plaine!
Tullie the wise, whose sapience in volumes great doth tell,
Who in wisedom in that time did many men excel,
"A prince," saith he, "is, of himselfe, a plaine and speaking
    law;
The law, a schoolmaister devine," — this by his rule I drawe.   10
The sage and wittie Seneca his words therto did frame:
"The honest exercise of kings, men wil insue the same;
But, contrariwise, if that a king abuse his kingly seat,
His ignomie and bitter shame in fine shal be more great."
In Percia there raignd a king, who Cirus hight by name,   15
Who did deserve, as I do read, the lasting blast of fame;
But he when Sisters Three had wrought to shere his vital
    threed,
As heire due to take the crowne Cambises did proceed.
He in his youth was trained up by trace of vertues lore;
Yet, being king, did cleane forget his perfect race before.   20

[1] E. Allde, 3 things.

Then, cleaving more unto his wil, such vice did immitate
As one of Icarus his kinde : forewarning then did hate,
Thinking that none could him dismay, ne none his fact could
     see.
Yet at the last a fall he tooke, like Icarus to be.
Els, as the fish, which oft had take the pleasant bait from
     hooke,   25
In safe did spring, and pearce the streames, when fisher fast
     did looke
To hoist up from the watry waves unto the dried land,
Then skapte, at last by suttle bait come to the fishers hand ;
Even so this King Cambises heere, when he had wrought his
     wil,
Taking delight the innocent his guiltlesse blood to spil,   30
Then mighty Jove would not permit to prosecute offence,
But, what mesure the king did meat, the same did Jove com-
     mence,
To bring to end with shame his race, — two yeares[1] he did
     not raign.
His cruelty we wil delate, and make the matter plaine.
Craving that this may suffise now your patience to win,   35
I take my way.   Beholde, I see the players comming in.

FINIS.

A COMMEDY OF KING CAMBISES.

First enter CAMBISES, the king, KNIGHT, and COUNCELLOR.

CAMB. My Counsaill grave and sapient, with lords of
     legall traine,
Attentive ears towards me[2] bend, and mark what shalbe
     sain ;
So you likewise, my valiant knight, whose manly acts doth
     flie
By brute of Fame, that[3] sounding tromp doth perce the azur
     sky ;

---

[1] E. Allde, 2 yeares.   [2] Haw. Haz. *omit* me.   [3] Haw. Haz. the.

My sapient words, I say, perpend, and so your skil delate!   5
You know that Mors vanquished hath Cirus, that king of
    state,
And I, by due inheritance, possesse that princely crowne,
Ruling by sword of mighty force in place of great renowne.
You knowe, and often have heard tell, my fathers worthy
    facts, —
A manly Marsis heart he bare, appearing by his acts.   10
And what? shall I to ground let fall my fathers golden praise?
No, no! I meane for to attempt this same more large to raise.
In that, that I, his sonne, succeed his kingly seat, as due,
Extend your councell unto me in that I aske of you:
I am the king of Persia, a large and fertile soile;   15
The Egyptians against us repugne as varlets slave and vile;
Therefore I mean with Marsis hart with wars them to fre-
    quent,
Them to subdue as captives mine, — this is my hearts intent;
So shall I win honors delight, and praise of me shall go.
My Councell, speake, — and, lordings, eke : — is it not best
    do so?   20
    Counc.   O puisant king, your blisful words deserves
        abundant praise,
That you in this doo go about your fathers fame to raise.
O blisful day, that king so yoong such profit should conceive,
His fathers praise and his to win from those that wold
    deceive !
Sure, my true and soveraigne king, I fall before you prest,   25
Answere to give, as dutie mine, in that your Grace request.
If that your heart adicted be the Egyptians to convince,
Through Marsis aid the conquest wun, then deed of hapy
    prince
Shall pearce the skies unto the throne of the supernal seat,
And merite there a just reward of Jupiter the Great.   30
But then your Grace must not turne backe from this pre-
    tenced will;
For to proceed in vertuous life imploy indevour stil;
Extinguish vice, and in that cup to drinke have no delight;

To martiall feats and kingly sport [1] fix all your whole delight.

    KING.   My Councel grave, a thousand thanks with hart I
        do you render,   35
That you my case so prosperous intirely doo tender!
I wil not swerve from those your steps whereto you wold me
    train.
But now, my lord and valiant knight, with words give
    answer plain :
Are you content with me to go the Marsis games to try?

    LORD.   Yea, peerelesse prince, to aid your Grace my-selfe
        wil live and die.   40

    KNIGHT.   And I, for my hability, for feare will not turne
        backe,
But, as the ship against the rocks, sustaine and bide the
    wracke.

    KING.   O willing harts, a thousand thanks I render unto
        you!
Strik up your drums with corage great, we wil march foorth
    even now!

    COUNC.   Permit, O king, few wordes to heer, — my duty
        serves no lesse ;   45
Therefore give leave to Councel thine his mind for to expresse!

    KING.   Speake on, my Councel ; what it be, you shal have
        favor mine.

    COUNC.   Then wil I speake unto your Grace, as duty doth
        me bind.
Your Grace doth meane for to attempt of war the manly art;
Your Grace therein may hap receive, with others, for your
    part,   50
The dent of death, — in those affaires all persons are alike, —
The heart couragious oftentimes his detriment doth seeke :
Its best therefore for to permit a ruler of your land
To sit and judge with equity when things of right are skand.

    KING.   My Grace doth yeeld to this your talke ; to be thus
        now it shall.   55
My knight, therefore prepare your-selfe Sisamnes for to call :

---

[1] Haw. Haz. sports.

A iudge he is of prudent skil, even he shal beare the sway
In absence mine, when from the land I do depart my way.
   KNIGHT. Your knight before your Grace even heer him-
       self hath, redy prest
With willing heart for to fulfil as your Grace made request.   60
   COUNC. Pleaseth your Grace, I judge of him to be a man
       right fit;
For he is learned in the law, having the gift of wit;
In your Graces precinct I do not view for it a meeter man;
His learning is of good effect, bring proofe thereof I can.
I doo not know what is his life, — his conscience hid from me; 65
I dout not but the feare of God before his eies to be.
   LORD. Report declares he is a man that to himselfe is nie,
One that favoureth much the world and sets to much [1] thereby.
But this I say of certainty: if hee your Grace succeed
In your absence but for a-while, he wil be warnd indeed   70
No injustice for to frequent, no partiall iudge to proove,
But rule all things with equitie, to win your Graces love.
   KING. Of that he shall a warning have my heasts for to
       obay;
Great punishment for his offence against him will I lay.

             [*Enter* SISAMNES.]

   COUNC. Behold, I see him now agresse and enter into
       place!   75
   SISAM. O puissant prince and mighty king, the gods pre-
       serve your Grace!
Your Graces message came to me, your wil purporting forth;
With grateful mind I it receiv'd according to mine oath,
Erecting then my-selfe with speed before your Graces eies,
The tenor of your princely wil from you for to agnise.   80
   KING. Sisamnes, this the whole effect the which for you
       I sent:
Our mind it is to elevate you to great preferment.
My Grace, and gracious Councel eke, hath chose you for this
       cause,

---

[1] Haw. Haz. to much sets. *Here and below I give the spelling of* Haw.

In iudgement you do office beare, which have the skil in
      lawes ;
We thinke that you accordingly by justice rule wil deale,   85
That for offence none shal have cause, of wrong you to
      appeale.
    SISAM.   Abundant thankes unto your Grace for this benig-
      nity !
To you, his Councel, in like case, with lords of clemency !
What-so your Grace to me permits, if I therein offend,
Such execution then commence, and use it to this end,   90
That all other, by that my deed, example so may take,
To admonish them to flee the same by feare it may them
      make !
    KING.   Then, according to your words,[1] if you therein
      offend,
I assure you, even from my brest correction shall extend.
From Persia I meane to go into the Egypt land,   95
Them to convince by force of armes, and win the upper hand.
While I therefore absent shall be, I doe you full permit,
As governour in this my right, in that estate to sit,
For to detect, and eke correct, those that abuse my grace.
This is the totall of my wil ; give answere in this case !   100
    SISAM.   Unworthy much, O prince, am I, and for this
      gift unfit ;
But, sith that it hath pleasd your Grace that I in it must sit,
I do avouch, unto my death, according to my skil,
With equity for to observe your Graces mind and wil,
And nought from it to swarve, indeed, but sincerely to stay ;   105
Els let me tast the penalty, as I before did say.
    KING.   Wel then, of this authoritie I give you ful posses-
      sion.
    SISAM.   And I will it fulfil, also, as I have made profes-
      sion.
    KING.   My Councel, then let us depart a small stay [for]
      to make ;
To Egypt land now forth with speed my voyage will I take.   110

[1] Haw. Haz. word.

Strike up your drums, us to rejoyce to hear the warlike
    sound.
Stay you heere, Sisammes, judge, and looke wel to your
    bound!

       Exeunt KING, LORD *and* COUNCELL.

  SISAM. Even now the king hath me extold and set me up
    aloft;
Now may I weare the bordred [1] guard and lie [2] in downe-bed
    soft;
Now may I purchase house and land, and have all at my wil; 115
Now may I build a princely place, my mind for to fulfil;
Now may I abrogate the law as I shall thinke it good;
If any-one me now offend, I may demaund his blood.
According to the proverbe old, my mouth I wil up-make,
Now it doth lie all in my hand to leave or els to take,   120
To deale with justice to my [3] bound, and so to live in hope.
But oftentimes the birds be gone, while one for nest doth
    grope.
Doo well or il, I dare avouch, some evil on me wil speake.
No, truly, yet I do not meane the kings precepts to breake;
To place I meane for to returne my duty to fulfil.   125

                   Exit.[4]

    Enter the VICE, [AMBIDEXTER,] *with an old capcase on his head, an olde*
    paile about his hips for harnes, a scummer and a potlid by his side, and
    a rake on his shoulder.

AMB. Stand away, stand away, for the passion of God!
    Harnessed I am, prepared to the field;
I would have bene content at home to have bod,
    But I am sent forth with my speare and shield.
I am appointed to fight against a snaile,   130

  [1] Haw. Haz. brodered.
  [2] Haw. Haz. lay.
  [3] *So* Haw. Haz.; E. Allde, me.
  [4] *As this play is not divided into acts and scenes, and as the events occur
apparently in a place which is now a council-chamber, now a street, and
now a garden, it seems improper to subdivide the play or to indicate
changes of scene. When necessary for intelligibility, the location is an-
nounced in the text.*

And Wilken Wren the ancient shall beare;
I dout not but against him to prevaile, —
   To be a man my deeds shall declare!
If I overcome him, then a butter-flie takes his part.
   His weapon must be a blew-specked [1] hen;   135
But you shall see me overthrow him with a fart.
   So, without conquest, he shall go home againe!
If I overcome him, I must fight with a flie,
   And a blacke-pudding the flies weapon must be.
At the first blow on the ground he shall lie,   140
   I wil be sure to thrust him through the mouth to the
     knee!
To conquest these fellowes the man I wil play.
   Ha, ha, ha! now ye wil make me to smile.
. . . .[2]

   To see if I can all men beguile.   145
Ha! my name? My name would ye so faine know?
   Yea, iwis, shal ye, and that with al speed! —
I have forgot it, therefore I cannot show.
   A! a! now I have it, I have it, in-deed!
My name is Ambidexter: I signifie one   150
   That with both hands finely can play;
Now with King Cambises, and by-and-by gone, —
   Thus doo I run this way and that way.
For, while I meane with a souldier to be,
   Then give I a leape to Sisamnes the iudge, —   155
I dare avouch you shall his destruction see!
   To all kinde of estates I meane for to trudge.
Ambidexter? Nay, he is a fellow, if ye knew all!
Cease for awhile; heereafter heare more ye shall!

    Enter three ruffins, HUF, RUF *and* SNUF, *singing.*[3]

   HUF. Gogs flesh and his wounds, these warres reioyce
     my hart!   160
By His wounds, I hope to doo well, for my part:

---

[1] Haw. Haz. speckled.   [2] *A line missing, as* Haw. *pointed out.*
[3] *The song is not given.*

By Gogs hart, the world shall goe hard[1] if I doo not shift;
At some olde carles budget I meane for to lift!

   RUF.   By His flesh, nose, eyes and eares,
I will venter void of all cares!   165
He is not a souldier that doth feare any doubt
If that he would bring his purpose about.

   SNUF.   Feare that feare list, it shall not be I.
By Gogs wounds, I will make some necke stand awry!
If I loose my share, I sweare by Gogs hart,   170
Then let another take up my parte!

   HUF.   Yet I hope to come the richest souldier away.

   RUF.   If a man aske ye, ye may hap to say nay.

   SNUF.   Let all men get what they can, not to leese I hope;
Wheresoever I goe, in eche corner I will grope.   175

   AMB.   What and ye run in[2] the corner of some prittie
           maide?

   SNUF.   To grope there, good fellow, I will not be afraid.

   HUF.   Gogs wounds, what art thou that with us doost mel?
Thou seemest to be a souldier, the truth to tel;
Thou seemest to be harnessed I cannot tel how,   180
I thinke he came lately from riding some cow.
Such a deformed slave did I never see!
Ruf, doost thou know him? I pray thee, tel me!

   RUF.   No, by my troth, fellow Huf, I never see him
           before!

   SNUF.   As for me, I care not if I never see him more.   185
Come, let us run his arse against the poste!

   AMB.   A, ye slaves! I will be with you at oste![3]
Ah, ye knaves! I wil teach ye how ye shal me deride!

Heere let him swinge them about.

Out of my sight! I can ye not abide!
Now, goodman poutchmouth, I am a slave with you?   190
Now have at ye a-fresh, againe, even now!
Mine arse against the poste you will run?

        [1] Haw. Haz. evil.   [2] Haw. Haz. into.
        [3] Haw. at the oste; Haz. at the host.

But I wil make you from that saying to turn!

HUF.   I beseech ye hartely to be content!

RUF.   I insure you, by mine honesty, no hurt we ment!   195
Besides that, againe, we do not know what ye are.
Ye know that souldiers their stoutnes will declare ;
Therefore, if we have anything offended,
Pardon our rudenes, and it shalbe amended.

AMB.   Yea, Gods pittie, begin ye to intreat me?   200
Have at ye once againe ! by the masse, I will beat ye.

Fight againe.

HUF.   Gogs hart, let us kill him!   Suffer no longer!

Draw their swords.

SNUF.   Thou slave, we will see if thou be the stronger !

RUF.   Strike of his head at one blow !
That we be souldiers, Gogs hart, let him know!   205

AMB.   O the passion of God, I have doon, by mine honestie!
I will take your part heerafter, verily.

ALL.   Then come,[1] let us agree !

AMB.   Shake hands with me, I shake hands with thee.
Ye are full of courtesie, that is the best.   210
And you take great paine, ye are a mannerly guest.
Why, maisters, doo you not know me? the truth to me tel !

ALL.   No, trust us ; not very well.

AMB.   Why, I am Ambidexter, whom many souldiers doo
love.

HUF.   Gogs hart, to have thy company needs we must
prove !   215
We must play with both hands, with our hostes and host,
Play with both hands, and score on the poste ;
Now and then, with our captain, for many a delay,
We wil not sticke with both hands to play.

AMB.   The honester man, ye [2] may me trust !   220

Enter MERETRIX, with a staffe on her shoulder.

MER.   What, is there no lads heere that hath a lust
To have a passing trul to help at their need?

[1] Haw. Haz. content.   [2] Haw. Haz. ye, ye; E. Allde *has only one* ye.

Huf. Gogs hart, she is come, indeed!
What, Mistres Meretrix, by His wounds, welcome to me!
    Mer. What wil ye give me? I pray you, let me see.   225
    Ruf. By His hart, she lookes for gifts by-and-by!
    Mer. What? Maister Ruf? I cry you mercy!
The last time I was with you, I got a broken head,
And lay in the street all night for want of a bed!
    Snuf. Gogs wounds, kisse me, my trull so white!   230
In thee, I sweare, is all my delight!
If thou shouldst have had a broken head for my sake,
I would have made his head to ake!
    Mer. What? Maister Ambidexter? Who looked for you?
    Amb. Mistres Meretrix, I thought not to see you heere
        now.   235
There is no remedy, — at meeting I must have a kisse!
    Mer. What, man, I wil not sticke for that, by Gisse!

Kisse.

    Amb. So now, gramercy! I pray thee be gone!
    Mer. Nay, soft, my freend, I meane to have one!
Nay, soft! I sweare, and if ye were my brother,   240
Before I let go, I wil have another!

Kisse, kisse, kisse.

    Ruf. Gogs hart, the whore would not kisse me yet!
    Mer. If I be a whore, thou art a knave; then it is quit!
    Huf. But hearst thou, Meretrix? With who this night
        wilt thou lye?
    Mer. With him that giveth the most money.   245
    Huf. Gogs hart, I have no money in purse, ne yet in
        clout!
    Mer. Then get thee hence and packe, like a lout!
    Huf. Adieu, like a whore!   *Exit* Huf.
    Mer.   Farwell, like a knave![1]
    Ruf. Gogs nailes, Mistres Meretrix, now he is gone,
A match ye shall make straight with me: 250
I wil give thee sixpence to lye one night with thee.

---

[1] *The rhyme seems to demand some such word as* whoreson.

MER.   Gogs hart, slave, doost thinke [1] I am a sixpeny iug?
No, wis ye, Jack, I looke a little more smug!
   SNUF.   I will give her xviii pence to serve me first.
   MER.   Gramercy, Snuf, thou art not the wurst!   255
   RUF.   By Gogs hart, she were better be hanged, to for-
     sake me and take thee!
   SNUF.   Were she so? that shall we see!
   RUF.   By Gogs hart, my dagger into her I will thrust!
   SNUF.   A, ye boy, ye would doo it and ye durst!
   AMB.   Peace, my maisters; ye shall not fight.   260
He that drawes first, I will him smite.
   RUF.   Gogs wounds, Maister Snuf, are ye so lusty?
   SNUF.   Gogs sides, Maister Ruf, are ye so crusty?
   RUF.   You may happen to see!
   SNUF.   Doo what thou darest to me!   265

> *Heer draw and fight. Heere she must lay on and coyle them both; the*
> VICE *must run his way for feare;* SNUF *fling down his sword and*
> *buckler and run his way.*

MER.   Gogs sides, knaves! seeing to fight ye be so rough,
Defend yourselves, for I will give ye both inough!
I will teach ye how ye shall fall out for me!
Yea, thou slave, Snuf! no more blowes wilt thou bide?
To take thy heeles a time hast thou spied?   270
Thou villaine, seeing Snuf has gone away,
A little better I meane thee to pay!

> *He falleth downe; she falleth upon him, and beats him, and taketh away*
> *his weapon.*[2]

   RUF.   Alas, good Mistres Meretrix, no more!
My legs, sides and armes with beating be so sore!
   MER.   Thou a souldier, and loose thy weapon?   275
Goe hence, sir boy; say a woman hath thee beaten!
   RUF.   Good Mistres Meretrix, let me my weapon have;
Take pittie on me, mine honestie to save!
If it be knowne this repulse I sustaine,
It will redound to my ignomy and shame.   280

---

[1] Haw. Haz. dost thou think.   [2] E. Allde weapons.

MER.   If thou wilt be my man, and waite upon me,
This sword and buckler I wil give thee.
    RUF.   I will doo all at your commaundement;
As servant to you I wilbe obedient.
    MER.   Then let me see how before me you can goe.   285
When I speake to you, you shall doo so :
Of with your cap at place and at boord, —
"Forsooth, Mistres Meretrix," at every word.
Tut! tut ! in the campe such souldiers there be ;
One good woman would beat away two or three!   290
Wel, I am sure customers tarry at home.
Manerly before, and let us be gone !   *Exeunt.*

        Enter AMBIDEXTER.

AMB.   O the passion of God, be they heer still or no ?
I durst not abide to see her beat them so !
I may say to you I was [1] in such a fright,[2]   295
Body of me, I see the heare of my head stand upright !
When I saw her so hard upon them lay on,[3]
O the passion of God, thought I, she wil be with me anon !
I made no more [4] adoo, but avoided the thrust,
And to my legs began for to trust ;   300
And fell a-laughing to my-selfe, when I was once gone :
It is wisdome, quoth I, by the masse, to save one !
Then into this place I intended to trudge,
Thinking to meete Sisamnes the judge.
Beholde where he commeth !   I will him meet,   305
And like a gentleman I meane him to greet.

        [*Enter* SISAMNES.]

SISAM.   Since that the Kings Graces Maiestie in office did
      me set,
What abundance of wealth to me might I get !
Now and then some vantage I atchive ; much more yet may
      I take,
But that I fear unto the king that some complaint will make. 310

---

[1] *So* Haw. Haz.; E. Allde, wis.
[2] *So* Haw. Haz.; E. Allde, flight.
[3] Haw. Haz. *omit* on.
[4] *So* Haw. Haz.; E. Allde, mare.

AMB.   Jesu, Maister Sisamnes, you are unwise!

SISAM.   Why so?   I pray thee,[1] let me agnise.

What, Maister Ambidexter, is it you?

Now welcome to me, I make God a-vow!

   AMB.   Jesu, Maister Sisamnes, with me you are wel ac-
      quainted!   315

By me rulers may be trimly painted.

Ye are unwise if ye take not time while ye may :

If ye wil not now, when ye would ye shall have nay.

What is he that of you dare make exclamation,

Of your wrong-dealing[2] to make explication?   320

Can you not play with both hands, and turn with the winde?

   SISAM.   Beleeve me, your words draw deepe in my mind :

In collour wise unto this day, to bribes I have inclined ;

More the same for to frequent, of truth I am now minded.

Behold, even now unto me suters doo proceed.   325

[Enter SMALL HABILITIE.]

   SM. HAB.   I beseech you heer, good Maister Judge, a
      poor man's cause to tender ;

Condemne me not in wrongfull wise that never was offender!

You know right wel my right it is.   I have not for to give.

You take away from me my due, that should my corps
      releeve.

The commons of you doo complaine ; from them you devo-
      cate,[3]   330

With anguish great and grevos words their harts do pene-
      trate.

The[4] right you sell[5] unto the wrong, your private gain to
      win ;

You violate the simple man, and count it for no sinne.

   SISAM.   Hold thy tung, thou pratling knave, and give to
      me reward,

[1] Haw. Haz. ye.
[2] Haw. Haz. dealings.
[3] New Eng. Dict. <i>suggests</i> derogate.
[4] Haz. <i>changes to</i> From.
[5] Haw. fel ; E. Allde, Haz. fell

Els, in this wise, I tell thee truth, thy tale wil not be heard.   335
Ambidexter, let us goe hence, and let the knave alone.

AMB.   Farwell, Small Habilitie, for helpe now get you
        none ;
Bribes hath corrupt him good lawes to polute.   [*Exeunt.*]

SM. HAB.   A naughty man that will not obay the kings
            constitute !
With hevy hart I wil return, til God redresse my pain.   340

Exit. Enter SHAME, *with a trump blacke.*

SHAME.   From among the grisly ghosts I come from ti-
          rants testy train ;
Unseemely Shame, of sooth, I am, procured to make plaine
The odious facts and shameles deeds[1] Cambises king doth
    use.
All pietie and vertuous life he doth it cleane refuse ;
Lechery and drunkennes he doth it much frequent ;   345
The tigers kinde to imitate he hath given full consent.
He nought esteems his Counsel grave ne vertuous bringing-
    up,
But dayly stil receives the drink of damned Vices cup.
He can bide no instruction, he takes so great delight
In working of iniquitie for to frequent his spight.   350
As Fame doth sound the royal trump of worthy men and
    trim,
So Shame doth blow with strained blast the trump of shame
    on him.

Exit [with a blast of the trumpet].

Enter the KING, LORD, PRAXASPES *and* SISAMNES.

KING.   My Iudge, since my departure hence, have you
         used iudgement right?
If faithful steward I ye finde, the same I wil requite.

SISAM.   No doubt your Grace shal not once hear that I
          have done amis.   355

PRAX.   I much reioyce to heare so good newes as this.

----

[1] *I omit* that.

Enter COMMONS CRY *running in; speake this verse; and[1] goe out*
againe hastily.

COM. CRY.   Alas, alas, how are the commons oppressed
    By that vile iudge, Sisamnes by name !
I doo not know how it should be redressed ;
    To amend his life no whit he dooth frame.   360
We are undoone and thrown out of doore,
    His damnable dealing dooth us so torment ;
At his hand we can finde no releefe nor succour.
    God graunt him grace for to repent!

Run away crying.

KING.   What doleful cries be these, my *lord*, that sound
    do in mine[2] eare?   365
Intelligence if you can give, unto your king declare.
To me it seemeth my commons al they doo lament and cry
Out of[3] Sisamnes, iudge, most cheefe, even now standing us
    by.
PRAX.   Even so, O king, it seemd to me, as you rehear-
    sall made ;
I doubt the iudge culpable be in some respect or trade.   370
SISAM.   Redouted king, have no mistrust, no whit your
    minde dismay ;
There is not one that can me charge or ought against me
    lay.

Enter COMMONS COMPLAINT, *with* PROOFE *and* TRIALL.

COM. COMP.   Commons Complaint I represent, with thrall
    of dolfull state.
My urgent cause erected foorth my greefe for to dilate,
Unto the king I wil prepare my miserie to tell,   375
To have releefe of this my greefe and fettered feet so fel.
Redoubted prince and mighty king, myself I prostrat heere !
Vouchsafe, O king, with me to beare for this that I appeere !
With humble sute I pardon crave of your Most Royall Grace,
To give me leave my minde to break before you in this place. 380

---

[1] Haw. Haz. *omit* and.   [3] Haz. *changes to* at.
[2] *So* E. Allde, Haw.; Haz. my, *without note.*

KING.   Commons Co*m*plaint, keep nothing back, fear not
      thy tale to tel.
What-ere he be within this land that hath not used thee wel,
As princes mouth shal sentence give, he shal receive the
      same.
Unfolde [1] the secrets of thy brest, for I extinguish blame.
    COM. COMP.   God preserve your Royall Grace, and send
      you blisful daies,   385
That all your deeds might stil accord to give the [2] god[s] the
      praise!
My complaint is, O mighty king, against that iudge you by,
Whose careles deeds, gain to receive, hath made the co*m*-
      mons cry :
He, by taking bribes and gifts, the poore he doth oppresse,
Taking releefe from infants yong, widows and fatherles.   390
    KING.   Untrustfull [3] traitor and corrupt iudge, how likest
      thou this complaint?
Forewarning I to thee did give, of this to make restraint.
And hast thou doon this divelish deed mine ire for to augment?
I sentence give, thou Judas judge, thou shalt thy deed repent.
    SISAM.   O pusant prince, it is not so! his complaint I
      deny.   395
    COM. COMP.   If it be not so, most mighty king, in place
      then let me dye !
Behold that I have brought with me both Proof and Triall
      true,
To stand even heere, and sentence give what by him did
      insue.
    PROOF.   I, Proof, do him in this appeal: he did the com-
      mons wrong ;
Unjustly he with them hath delt, his greedy was so strong ;   400
His hart did covet in to get, he cared not which way ;
The poor did leese their due and right, because they want [4]
      to pay

---

[1] E. Allde *misprints* Unforde.
[2] Haz. *changes to* to.   [4] Haz. *changes to* wont.
[3] *So* E. Allde, Haw.; Haz. Untruthful, *without note.*

Unto him for bribes, indeed, — this was his wonted use.
Whereas your Grace good lawes did make, he did the same
　　abuse.

　　TRIALL.　I, Triall, heer to verifie what Proof dooth now
　　　　unfolde,　　　　　　　　　　　　　　　　　　　　405
To stand against him in his wrong as now I dare be bolde.

　　KING.　How likest thou this, thou caitive vile? Canst
　　　　thou the same deny?

　　SISAM.　O noble king, forgive my fact! I yeeld to thy
　　　　mercy.

　　KING.　Complaint[1] and Proof, redresse will I all this your
　　　　misery.
Depart with speed, from whence you came, and straight com-
　　maund by me　　　　　　　　　　　　　　　　　　410
The execution-man to come before my Grace with haste.

　　ALL.　For to fulfil this your request no time we meane to
　　　　waste.
　　　　　　　　　　Exeunt they three.

　　KING.　My lord, before my Grace goe call Otian, this
　　　　iudges sonne,
And he shal heare and also see what his father hath doon.
The father he shal suffer death, the sonne his roome succeed; 415
And, if that he no better prove, so likewise shall he speed.

　　PRAX.　As your Grace hath commaundment given, I mean
　　　　for to fulfil.
　　　　　　　　　　Step aside and fetch him.

　　KING.　Accursed iudge, couldst thou consent to do this
　　　　cursed ill?
According unto thy demaund, thou shalt, for this thy gilt,
Receive thy death before mine eyes, — thy blood it shalbe
　　spilt.　　　　　　　　　　　　　　　　　　　　　420
　　　　　　　　[Enter PRAXASPES with OTIAN.]

　　PRAX.　Beholde, O king, Sisamnes sonne before you doth
　　　　appere.

　　KING.　Otian, this is my minde, therefore to me come
　　　　neere :

　　　　　[1] *So* Haw. Haz. ; E. Allde, Complaints.

Thy father heer for judgment wrong procured hath his death,
And thou, his son, shalt him succeed when he hath lost his
   breth ;
And, if that thou dost once offend, as thou seest thy father
   have,   425
In like wise thou shalt suffer death, — no mercy shal thee save.
 Otian. O mighty king, vouchsafe your grace my father
   to remit ;
Forgive his fault, his pardon I doo aske of you as yet.
Alas! although my father hath your princely hart offended,
Amends for misse he wil now make, and faults shalbe
   amended.   430
In-stead of his requested life, pleaseth your Grace take mine!
This offer I as tender childe, so duty doth me binde.
 King. Doo not intreat my grace no more, for he shal dye
   the death.
Where is the execution-man him to bereave of breath?

Enter EXECUTION.

 Exec. At hand, and if it like your Grace, my duty to
   dispatch,   435
In hope that I, when deede is doone, a good reward shall
   catch.
 King. Dispatch with sword this iudges life; extinguish
   fear and cares :
So doon, draw thou his cursed skin strait over both his eares.
I wil see the office done, and that before mine eyes.
 Exec. To doo the thing my king commaunds I give the
   enterprise.   440
 Sisam. Otian, my sonne, the king to death by law hath
   me condemned,
And you in roome and office mine his Graces wil hath placed ;
Use iustice, therefore, in this case, and yeeld unto no wrong,
Lest thou do purchase the like death ere ever it be long.
 Otian. O father deer, these words to hear, — that you [1]
   must dye by force,   445

[1] Haw. Haz. thou.

Bedews my cheeks with stilled teares, — the king hath no remorce.

The greevous greefes [1] and strained sighes my hart doth breake in twaine,

And I deplore, most woful childe, that I should see you slaine.

O false and fickle frowning dame, that turneth as the winde,

Is this the joy in fathers age thou me assignest to finde?   45(

O dolefull day, unhappy houre, that loving childe should see

His father deer before his face thus put to death should be!

Yet, father, give me blessing thine, and let me once imbrace

Thy comely corps in foulded arms, and kisse thy ancient face!

    Sisam.   O childe, thou makes my [2] eyes to run, as rivers doo, by streame;   455

My leave I take of thee, my sonne; beware of this my beame!

    King.   Dispatch even now, thou man of death; no longer seem to stay!

    Exec.   Come, *Master* Sisamnes, come on your way!

My office I must pay; forgive therefore my deed.

    Sisam.   I doo forgive it thee, my freend; dispatch therefore with speed!   460

Smite him in the neck with a sword to signifie his death.

    Prax.   Beholde, O king, how he dooth bleed, being of life bereft!

    King.   In this wise he shall not yet be left.

Pull his skin over his eares [3] to make his death more vile.

A wretch he was, a cruell theefe, my commons to beguile!

Flea [4] him with a false skin.

    Otian.   What childe [5] is he of natures mould could bide the same to see, —   465

His father flead in this wise?   Oh, how it greeveth me!

---

[1] Haw. Haz. greef; E. Allde, greefes.
[2] Haw. Haz. mine.
[3] Haw. eares; Haz. ears; E. Allde, eyes.
[4] *So* E. Allde, Haw.; Haz. Flays, *without note.*
[5] *Misprinted* thilde *by* E. Allde.

KING. Otian thou seest thy father dead, and thou art in
    his roome :

If thou beest proud, as he hath beene, even thereto shalt thou
    come.

    OTIAN. O king, to me this is a glasse : with greefe in it I
        view

Example that unto your Grace I doo not prove untrue.   470

    PRAX. Otian, convay your father hence to tomb where he
        shall lye.

    OTIAN. And if it please your lordship, it shall be done
        by-and-by.

Good execution-man, for need, helpe me with him away.

    EXEC. I wil fulfill, as you to me did say.

They take him away.

    KING. My l*ord*, now that my Grace hath seen that finisht
        is this deed,   475

To question mine give tentive eare, and answere make with
    speed :

Have not I doon a gratious deed, to redresse my co*m*mons
    woe?

    PRAX. Yea, truely, if it please your Grace, you have
        indeed doon so.

But now, O king, in freendly wise I councel you in this, —

Certain vices for to leave that in you placed is :   480

The vice of drunkennes, Oh king, which doth you sore infect,

With other great abuses, which I wish you to detect.

    KING. Peace, my lord ! what needeth this? Of this I
        will not heare !

To pallace now I will returne, and thereto make good cheere.

God Baccus he bestows his gifts, we have good store of wine ; 485

And also that the ladies be both passing brave and fine.

But stay ! I see a lord now come, and eke a valiant knight.

What news, my lord? To see you heer my hart it doth delight.

Enter LORD *and* KNIGHT *to meet the* KING.

    LORD. No news, O king ; but of duty come to wait upon
        your Grace.

KING.   I thank you, my lord and loving knight; I pray
       you with me trace.   490
My lords and knight, I pray ye tel, — I wil not be offended, —
Am I worthy of any crime once to be reprehended?

PRAX.   The Persians much doo [1] praise your Grace, but
       one thing discommend,
In that to wine subject you be, wherein you doo offend,
Sith that the might of wine effect doth oft subdue your brain.[2]   495
My counsel is, to please their harts from it you would refrain.

LORD.   No, no, my lord, it is not so; for of this prince
       they tel,
For vertuous proofe and princely facts Cirus he doth excel.
By that his Grace by conquest great the Egiptians did
       convince,
Of him report abroad doth passe to be a worthy prince.   500

KNIGHT.   In person of Cresus I answer make, we may not
       his Grace compare
In whole respect for to be like Cirus, the kings father,
In-so-much your Grace hath yet no childe as Cirus left
       behinde,
Even you I meane, Cambises king, in whom I favour finde.

KING.   Cresus said well in saying so; but, Praxaspes, tel
       me why   505
That to my mouth in such a sort thou should avouch a lye,
Of drunkenes me thus to charge!   But thou with speed shalt
       see
Whether that I a sober king or els a drunkard be.
I know thou hast a blisful babe, wherein thou doost delight, —
Me to revenge of these thy words I wil go wreke this spight: 510
When I the most have tasted wine, my bow it shalbe bent, —
At hart of him even then to shoote is now my whole intent;
And, if that I his hart can hit, the king no drunkard is;
If hart of his I doo not kill, I yeeld to thee in this.
Therefore, Praxaspes, fetch to me thy youngest son with speed.   515
There is no way, I tell thee plaine, but I wil doo this deed.

     1 Haw. Haz. *omit* doo.
     2 *Were this in any play but* Preston's, *I would emend it.*

PRAX.   Redoubted prince, spare my sweet childe, he is
    mine only joy!
I trust your Grace to infants [1] hart no such thing will imploy.
If that his mother hear of this, she is so nigh her flight
In clay her corps wil soone be shrinde to passe from worlds
    delight.   520
KING.   No more adoe!   Go fetch me him; it shalbe as I
    say.
And if that I doo speak the word, how dare ye once say nay?
PRAX.   I wil go fetch him to your Grace; but so, I trust,
    it shall not be!
KING.   For feare of my displeasure great, goe fetch him
    unto me.
           [Exit PRAXASPES.]

Is he gone?   Now, by the gods, I will doo as I say!   525
My lord, therefore fill me some wine, I hartely you pray,
For I must drinke to make my braine somewhat intoxicate, —
When that the wine is in my head, O, trimly I can prate.
LORD.   Heere is the cup, with filled wine, thereof to take
    repast.
KING.   Give it me, to drinke it off, and see no wine be
    wast.   530
           Drink.

Once againe inlarge this cup, for I must tast it stil.[2]

           Drink.

By the gods, I think of plesant wine I cannot take my fill!
Now drink is in, give me my bow and arrows from sir knight;
At hart of childe I meane to shoot, hoping to cleve it right.
KNIGHT.   Behold, O king, where he doth come, his infant
    yong in hand.   535
           [*Enter* PRAXASPES, *with the* CHILD.]
PRAX.   O mighty king, your Grace behest with sorrow I
    have scand,

      [1] *So* E. Allde, Haw.; Haz. infant, *without note.*
      [2] Haz. *changes to* it still taste.

And brought my childe fro mothers knee, before you to
    appeer,
And she thereof no whit doth know that he in place is heer.
    KING.   Set him up, my marke to be; I will shoot at his
    hart.
    PRAX.   I beseech your Grace not so to doo! set this
    pretence a-part!   540
Farewel, my deer and loving babe! come, kisse thy father
    deer!
A greevous sight to me it is to see thee slaine even heere.
Is this the gaine now from the king for giving councell
    good, —
Before my face with such despight to spil my sons hart-blood?
O heavy day to me this is, and mother in like case!   545
YONG CHILDE.   O father, father, wipe your face,
    I see the teares run from your eye:
My mother is at home sowing of a band;
    Alas! deere father, why doo you cry?
    KING.   Before me as a mark now let him stand,   550
I wil shoot at him my minde to fulfill.
    YONG CHILDE.   Alas, alas! father wil you me kill?
Good Master king, doo not shoot at me, my mother loves
    me best of all.
    KING.   I have despatched him, down he doth fall!

Shoot.

As right as a line his hart I have hit.   555
Nay, thou shalt [1] see, Praxaspes, stranger newes yet.
My knight, with speed his hart cut out and give it unto me.
    KNIGHT.   It shalbe doon, O mighty king, with all seleritie.
    LORD.   My lord Praxaspes, this had not been but your
    tung must be walking;
To the king of correction you must needs be talking!   560
    PRAX.   No correction, my lord; but councel for the best.
    KNIGHT.   Heere is the hart, according to your Graces
    behest.

    1 E. Allde, Haw. shalt; Haz. shall, *without note.*

KING. Beholde, Praxaspes, thy sonnes owne hart! O,
how well the same was hit!

After this wine to doo this deed I thought it very fit.

Esteem thou maist right well therby no drunkard is the king 565

That in the midst of all his cups could doo this valiant thing.

My lord and knight, on me attend; to pallace we will goe,

And leave him heer to take his son when we are gone him
fro.

ALL. With al our harts we give consent to wait upon your
Grace.   [*Exeunt.*]

PRAX. A wofull man, O Lord, am I, to see him in this
case!   570

My daies, I deem, desires their end; this deed wil help me
hence, —

To have the blossoms of my feeld destroyed by violence!

Enter MOTHER.

MOTHER. Alas, alas! I doo heare tell the king hath kild
my sonne!

If it be so, wo worth the deed that ever it was doone!

It is even so; my lord I see, how by him he dooth weepe. 575

What ment I, that from hands of him this childe I did not
keepe?

Alas! husband and lord, what did you meane, to fetch this
childe away?

PRAX. O lady wife, I little thought for to have seene this
day.

MOTHER. O blisful babe, O joy of womb, harts comfort
and delight!

For councel given unto the king is this thy just require?   580

O hevy day and dolefull time, these mourning tunes to make!

With blubred eies, into mine[1] armes from earth I wil thee
take,

And wrap thee in mine apron white! — But, oh my heavy
hart,

The spiteful pangs that it sustains wold make it in two to part,

[1] E. Allde, Haw. mine; Haz. my.

The death of this my sonne to see!   O hevy mother now,   585
That from thy sweet and sugred joy to sorrow so shouldst
     bow !
What greef in womb did I retain before I did thee see!
Yet at the last, when smart was gone, what joy wert thou to
     me!
How tender was I of thy food, for to preserve thy state!
How stilled I thy tender hart at times early and late !   590
With velvet paps I gave thee suck with issue from my brest,
And danced thee upon my knee to bring thee unto rest.
Is this the joy of thee I reap?   O king, of tigers brood!
O tigers whelp, hadst thou the hart to see this childs hart-
     blood?
Nature inforseth me, alas! in this wise to deplore,   595
To wring my hands, — O wel-away, that I should see this
     houre!
Thy mother yet wil kisse thy lips, silk-soft and pleasant
     white,
With wringing hands lamenting for to see thee in this plight!
My lording deer, let us goe home our mourning to augment.
    PRAX.   My lady deer, with heavy hart to it I doo consent, 600
Between us both the childe to bere unto our lordly place.

                                   Exeunt.
          Enter AMBIDEXTER.

    AMB.   Indeed, as ye say, I have been absent a long space.
But is not my cosin Cutpurse with you in the meane-time?
To it! to it, cosin, and doo your office fine!
How like you Sisamnes for using of me?   605
He plaid with both hands, but he sped ilfavourdly!
The king himselfe was godly uptrained ;
He professed vertue, but I think it was fained.
He plaies with both hands, good deeds and ill ;
But it was no good deed Praxaspes sonne for to kill.   610
As he for the good deed on the iudge was commended,
For all his deeds els he is reprehended.
The most evill-disposed person that ever was
All the state of his life he would not let passe ;

Some good deeds he will doo, though they be but few : 615
The like things this tirant Cambises doth shew.
No goodnes from him to none is exhibited,
But still malediction [1] abroad is distributed ;
And yet ye shall see in the rest of his race
What infamy he will work against his owne grace. 620
Whist! no more words! heere comes the kings brother.

Enter LORD SMIRDIS, *with* ATTENDANCE *and* DILIGENCE.

SMIR. The kings brother by birth am I, issued from Cirus
loynes :
A greefe to me it is to heare of this the king repines.
I like not well of those his deeds that he dooth still frequent ;
I wish to God that other waies his minde he could content. 625
Yong I am, and next to him ; no moe of us there be :
I would be glad a quiet realme in this his reign to see.
ATT. My lord, your good a[nd] willing hart the gods wil
recompence,
In that your minde so pensive is for those his great offence.
My lord, his Grace shall have a time to paire and to amend. 630
Happy is he that can escape and not his Grace offend.
DIL. If that wicked vice he could refraine, from wasting
wine forbere,
A moderate life he would frequent, amending this [2] his square.
AMB. My lord, and if your Honor it shall please,
I can informe you what is best for your ease : 635
Let him alone, of his deeds doo not talke,
Then by his side ye may quietly walke ;
After his death you shalbe king,
Then may you reforme eche kinde of thing ;
In the meane-time live quietly, doo not with him deale ; 640
So shall it redound much to your weale.
SMIR. Thou saist true, my freend ; that is the best ;
I do not know whether he love me or doo me detest.
ATT. Lea[r]ne from his company all that you may.
I, faithfull Attendance, wil your Honor obay ; 645

---

[1] E. Allde, Haw. malediction ; Haz. maledictions.
[2] Kittredge *conjectures* thus.

If against your Honor he take any ire,
His Grace is as like to kindle his fire
To your Honors destruction as otherwise.

    DIL.   Therefore, my lord, take good advise,
And I, Diligence, your case wil so tender   650
That to his Grace your Honor shalbe none offender.

    SMIR.   I thank you both, intire freends ; with my Honor
        stil remaine.

    AMB.   Beholde where the king doth come with his train!

Enter KING, *and a*[1] LORD.

    KING.   O lording deer and brother mine, I joy your state
        to see,
Surmising much what is the cause you absent thus from me.   655

    SMIR.   Pleaseth your Grace, no absence I, but redy to
        fulfill,
At all assaies, my prince and king, in that your Grace me
        will.
What I can doo in true defence to you, my prince, aright,
In readines I alwaies am to offer, foorth my might.

    KING.   And I the like to you againe doo heer avouch
        the same.   660

    ALL.   For this your good agreement heer, now praised be
        Gods name!

    AMB. [*to* SMIRDIS]   But heare ye, noble prince ; harke in
        your eare :
It is best to doo as I did declare.

    KING.   My lord and brother Smirdis, now this is my minde
        and will :
That you to court of mine returne, and there to tary still   665
Till my returne within short space your Honor for to greet.

    SMIR.   At your behest so wil I doo till time againe we
        meet.
My leave I take from you, O king; even now I doo departe.

Exeunt SMIRDIS, ATTENDANCE *and* DILIGENCE.

    KING.   Farwel, lord and brother mine! farwel with all my
        hart !

[1] Haw. Haz. one ; E. Allde, a,

My lord, my brother Smerdis is of youth and manly plight,   670
And in his sweet and pleasant face my hart doth take
    delight.
   LORD. Yea, noble prince, if that your Grace before his
    Honor dye,
He wil succeede, a vertuous king, and rule with equitie.
   KING. As you have said, my lord, he is cheefe heire next
    my Grace;
And, if I dye to-morrow, next he shall succeed my place.   675
    AMB. And if it please your Grace, O king, I heard him
     say:
For your death unto the god[s] day and night he did pray;
He would live so vertuously and get him such a praise
That Fame by trump his due deserts in[1] honor should up-
    raise.
He said your Grace deserved had the cursing of all men,   680
That ye should never after him get any praise againe.
   KING. Did he speake thus of my Grace, in such despight-
    ful wise?
Or els doost thou presume to fill my princely eares with lyes?
   LORD. I cannot think it in my hart that he would report
    so.
   KING. How saist thou? speake the truth: was it so or
    no?   685
    AMB. I thinke so, if it please your Grace, but I cannot
    tell.
   KING. Thou plaist with both hands, now I perceive well!
But, for to put al doubts aside and to make him leese his
    hope,
He shall dye by dint[2] of swoord or els by choking rope.
Shall he succeed when I am gone, to have more praise then I? 690
Were he father, as brother, mine, I swere that he shal dye.
To pallaice mine I will therefore, his death for to pursue.
                                  Exit.
    AMB. Are ye gone? Straightway I will follow you.
How like ye now, my maisters? Dooth not this geere cotten?

---

[1] Haw, Haz. his,   [2] Haw. Haz. dent.

The proverbe olde is verified: soone ripe, and soone rotten! 695
He wil not be quiet til his brother be[1] kild,
His delight is wholly to have his blood spild.
Mary, sir, I tolde him a notable lye;
If it were to doo againe,[2] I durst not doo it, I!
Mary, when I had doon, to it I durst not stand; 700
Thereby ye may perceive I use to play with eche hand.
But how now, cosin Cutpursse, with whom play you?
Take heed, for his hand is groping even now!
Cosin, take heed, if you doo secretly grope;
If ye be taken, cosin, ye must looke through a rope. 705

Exit.

Enter LORD SMIRDIS *alone.*

SMIR.   I am wandring alone, here and there to walke;
    The Court is so unquiet, in it I take no joy.
Solitary to my-selfe now I may talke.
    If I could rule, I wist what to say.

Enter CRUELTY *and* MURDER *with bloody hands.*

CRUEL.   My coequall partner, Murder, come away; 710
From me long thou maist not stay.
    MURD.   Yes, from thee I may stay, but not thou from me:
Therefore I have a prerogative above thee.
    CRUEL.   But in this case we must togither abide.
Come, come! Lord Smirdis I have spide: 715
Lay hands on him with all festination,
That on him we may worke our indignation!

[They seize him.]

SMIR.   How now, my freends? what have you to doo
    with me?
    MURD.   King Cambises hath sent us unto thee,
Commaunding us straightly, without mercy or favour, 720
Upon thee to bestow our behaviour,
With cruelty to murder you and make you away.

Strike him in divers places.

---

[1] Haz. he, *probably a misprint.*
[2] *Before* I Haw. Haz. *have* man, *which is not in* E. Allde.

SMIR.   Yet pardon me, I hartely you pray !
Consider, the king is a tirant tirannious,
And all his dooings be damnable and parnitious :   725
Favour me therfore ; I did him never offend.

A little bladder of vineger prickt.[1]

CRUEL.   No favour at all ; your life is at an end.
Even now I strike, his body to wound, —
Beholde, now his blood springs out on the ground!
MURD.   Now he is dead, let us present him to the king.   730
CRUEL.   Lay to your hand, away him to bring.
                                        Exeunt.
Enter AMBIDEXTER.

AMB.   O the passion of God, yonder is a hevy Court :
Some weepes, some wailes, and some make great sport.
Lord Smirdis by Cruelty and Murder is slaine ;
But, Jesus ! for want of him how some doo complaine !   735
If I should have had a thousand pound, I could not forbeare
        weeping.
Now Jesus have his blessed soule in keeping!
Ah good Lord ! to think on him, how it dooth me greeve !
I cannot forbeare weeping, ye may me beleeve.   *Weep.*
O my hart ! how my pulses doo beate,   740
With sorrowfull lamentations I am in such a heate !
Ah, my hart, how for him it doth sorrow !
Nay, I have done, in faith, now, and God give ye [2] good
        morrow !
Ha, ha !   Weep?   Nay, laugh, with both [3] hands to play !
The king through his cruelty hath made him away, —   745
But hath not he wrought a most wicked deed,
Because king after him he should not proceed,
His owne naturall brother, and having no more,
To procure his death by violence sore ?
In spight, because his brother should never be king,   750
His hart, being wicked, consented to this thing.

[1] Haz. *puts this stage-direction after* l. 729.
[2] Haw. Haz. you ; *so often.*
[3] *Misprinted* buth *in* E. Allde.

Now hath he no more brothers nor kinred alive.
If the king use this geere still, he cannot long thrive.

Enter HOB *and* LOB.

HOB.   Gods hat, neighbour,[1] come away! its time to
market to goe!

LOB.   Gods vast, naybor, zay ye zo?   755
The clock hath stricken vive, ich think by Laken!
Bum vay, vrom sleep cham not very well waken!
But, naybor Hob, naybor Hob, what have ye to zel?

HOB.   Bum troth, naybor Lob, to you I chil tel:
Chave two goslings and a chine of good [2] porke, —   760
There is no vatter between this and Yorke, —
Chave a pot of strawberies and a calves head, —
A zennight zince, to-morrow, it hath been dead.

LOB.   Chave a score of egges and of butter a pound;
Yesterday a nest of goodly yong rabits I vound.   765
Chave vorty things mo, of more and of lesse, —
My brain is not very good them to expresse.
But, Gods hat, naybor, wotst what?

HOB.   No, not wel, naybor; whats that?

LOB.   Bum vay, naybor, maister king is a zhrode lad!   770
Zo God help me, and holidam, I think the vool be mad!
Zome zay he deale cruelly: his brother he did kill,
And also a goodly yung lads hart-blood he did spill.

HOB.   Vorbod of God, naybor! has he plaid zuch a volish
deed?

AMB.   Goodman Hob and goodman Lob, God be your
speed!   775
As you two towards market doo[3] walke,
Of the kings cruelty I did heare you talke;
I insure you he is a king most vile and parnitious, —
His dooings and life are odious and vicious.

LOB.   It were a good deed zome-body would break his
head.   780

---

1 Haz. neighbours.   8 Haz. *changes to* did.
2 E. Allde *omits* good.

Hob. Bum vay, naybor Lob, I chuld he were dead!

Amb. So would I, Lob and Hob, with all my hart!

[*Aside*] [1] Now with both hands will you see me play my parte. —

A, ye whorson traitorly knaves,

Hob and Lob, out upon you, slaves!   785

Lob. And thou calst me knave, thou art another!

My name is Lob, and Hob my next naybor.

Amb. Hob and Lob! a, ye cuntry patches!

A, ye fooles, ye have made wrong matches!

Ye have spoken treason against the kings Grace, —   790

For it I will accuse ye before his face;

Then for the same ye shalbe martered, —

At the least ye shalbe hangd, drawne and quartered.

Hob. O gentleman, ye shal have two peare-pyes, and tel not of me!

Lob. By God, a vat gooce chil give thee: 795

I think no hurt, by my vathers soule I sweare!

Hob. Chave lived wel all my life-time, my naybors among;

And now chuld be loth to come to zuch wrong, —

To be hanged and quartered the greefe would be great!

Lob. A foule evil on thee, Hob! Who bid thee on it treat?   800

Vor it was thou that first did him name.

Hob. Thou lyest like a varlet and thou zaist the zame!

It was zuch a foolish Lob as thou.

Lob. Speak many words, and, by Cods nailes I vow,

Upon thy pate my staffe I will lay!   805

Amb. [*aside*] [1] By the masse, I will cause them to make a fray. —

Yea, Lob, thou saist true: all came through him.

Lob. Bum vay, thou Hob,[2] a little would make me thee [3] trim!

Give thee a zwap [4] on thy nose till thy hart ake!

---

[1] *Supplied by* Haz., *without note.*   [3] All edd. ye.
[2] *Misprinted* Hod *in* E. Allde.   [4] Haw. zawp.

Hob.   If thou darest, doo it !   Els, man, cry " creke ! "   810
I trust, before thou hurt me,
With my staffe chil make a Lob of thee !

> *Heer let them fight with their staves, not come neer an-other by three or
> foure yardes ; the* Vice *set them on ꞉s hard as he can ; one of their wives
> come out, and all to-beat the* V꞉c꞉; *he run away.*

> *Enter* Marian may-be-good, Hobs *wife, running in with a broome, and
> parte them.*

Marian.   O the body of me, husband Hob, what meane
          ye to fight?
For the passion of God, no more blowes smite !
Neighbours and freends so long, and now to fall out?   815
What ! in your age to seeme so stout?
If I had not parted ye, one had kild another.
     Lob.   I had not cared, I swere by Gods Mother !
     Marián.   Shake hands againe at the request of me ;
As ye have been freends, so freends still be.   820
     Hob.   Bum troth, cham content and zaist word, neighbour
          Lob.
     Lob.   I am content ; agreed, neighbor Hob !

> *Shake hands and laugh hartely one at another.*

Marian.   So, get you to market ; no longer stay.
And with yonder knave let me make a fray.
     Hob.   Content, wife Marian, chill doo as thou doost say ;   825
But busse me, ich pray thee, at going away !

> *Exeunt* Hob, Lob.

Marian. Thou whorson knave, and prickeard boy, why
          didst thou let them fight?
If one had kild another heer, couldst thou their deaths re-
          quite ?
It beares a signe by this thy deed a cowardly knave thou art,
Els wouldst thou draw that weapon thine, like a man [1] them
          to parte.   830
     Amb.   What, Marian-may-be good, are you come prattling?

---

[1] E. Allde, knaue.

Ye may hap get a box on the eare with your talking.
If they had kild one another, I had not cared a pease.

Heer let her swinge him in[1] *her broome; she gets him down, and he her*
down, — thus one on the top of another make pastime.

MARIAN.   A, villain, my-selfe on thee I must ease!
Give me a box on the eare? that will I try.   835
Who shalbe maister, thou shalt see by-and-by!
   AMB.   O, no more, no more, I beseech you hartily!
Even now I yeeld, and give you the maistry.

Run his way out while she is down.

MARIAN.   A, thou [2] knave, doost thou throw me down and
            run thy [3] way?
If he were heere againe, oh, how I would him pay!   840
I will after him; and, if I can him meet,
With these my nailes his face I wil greet.   [*Exit.*]

Enter VENUS *leading out her sonne,* CUPID, *blinde : he must have a bow*
and two shafts, one headed with golde and th' other headed with lead.

VENUS.   Come foorth, my sonne, unto my words attentive
            eares resigne;
What I pretend, see you frequent, to force this game of mine.
The king a kinswoman hath, adornd with beauty store;   845
And I wish that Dianas gifts they twain shal keep no more,
But use my silver sugred game their ioyes for to augment.
When I doo speak, to wound his hart, Cupid my son, con-
            sent!
And shoot at him the shaft of love, that beares the head of
            golde,
To wound his hart in lovers wise, his greefe for to unfolde.   850
Though kin she be unto his Grace, that nature me expell,
Against the course thereof he may in my game please me
            wel.
Wherfore, my sonne, doo not forget; forthwith pursue the
            deed!
   CUPID.   Mother, I meane for to obay as you have whole
            decreed;

1 Haz. *changes to* with.   2 Haz. *omits* thou.   3 E. Allde, the.

But you must tel me, mother deere, when I shal arrow draw, 855
Els your request to be attaind wil not be worth a straw;
I am blinde and cannot see, but stil doo shoot by gesse, —
The poets wel, in places store, of my might doo expresse.

    VENUS.   Cupid my son, when time shall serve that thou
        shalt do this deed,
Then warning I to thee wil give; but see thou shoot with
        speed.   860

        Enter a LORD, *a* LADY, *and a* WAITING-MAID.[1]

    LORD.   Lady deer, to king a-kin, forthwith let us proceed
To trace abroad the beauty feelds, as erst we had decreed.
The blowing buds, whose savery sents our sence wil much
        delight;
The sweet smel of musk white-rose to please the appetite;
The chirping birds, whose pleasant tunes therein shal hear [2]
        record,   865
That our great joy we shall it finde in feeld to walk abroad;
On lute and cittern there to play, a heavenly harmony:
Our eares shall heare, hart to content, our sports to beautify.[3]

    LADY.   Unto your words, most comely lord, my-selfe sub-
        mit doo I;
To trace with you in feeld so green I meane not to deny.   870

        Heere trace up and downe playing.

    MAID.   And I, your waiting-maid, at hand with diligence
        will be,
For to fulfil with hart and hand, when you shal commaund
        me.

        Enter KING, LORD, *and* KNIGHT.

    KING.   Come on, my lord and knight; abroad our mirth
        let us imploy;
Since he is dead, this hart of mine in corps I feel it joy.
Should brother mine have raigned king when I had yeelded
        breth?   875

---

[1] *So* E. Allde.   [2] *Qy.* bear.
[3] *So* E. Allde; Haz. *prints* beautify, *but says,* "Old copy, beautie":
beautie *is the reading of* Haw.; *whether it be that of* J. Allde *I cannot say.*

A thousand brothers I rather had to put them all to death.
But, oh beholde, where I doo[1] see a lord and lady faire!
For beauty she most worthy is to sit in princes chaire.
 Venus. Shoot forth, my son; now is the time that thou
   must wound his hart.
 Cupid. Content you, mother; I will doo my parte. 880

   Shoote there, and goe out Venus *and* Cupid.

 King. Of truth, my lord, in eye of mine all ladies she doth
   excell.
Can none reporte what dame she is, and to my Grace it tell?
 Lord. Redouted prince, pleaseth your Grace, to you she
   is a-kin,
Cosin-iarmin nigh of birth, by mothers side come in.
 Knight. And that her waiting-maiden is, attending her
   upon. 885
He is a lord of princes court, and wil be there anon.
They sport themselves in pleasant feeld, to former used use.
 King. My lord and knight, of truth I speak: my hart it
   cannot chuse
But with my lady I must speake and so expresse my minde.
My lord and ladyes, walking there, if you wil favour finde, 890
Present your-selves unto my Grace, and by my side come
   stand.
 First Lord. We wil fulfil, most mighty king, as your
   Grace doth commaund.
 King. Lady deere, intelligence my Grace hath got of late,
You issued out of mothers stocke and kin unto my state.
According to rule of birth you are cosin-jarmin mine; 895
Yet do I wish that farther of this kinred I could finde,
For Cupid he, that eylesse boy, my hart hath so enflamed
With beauty you me to content the like cannot be named;
For, since I entred in this place and on you fixt mine eyes,
Most burning fits about my hart in ample wise did rise. 900
The heat of them such force doth yeeld, my corps they
   scorch, alas !

   [1] *So* E. Allde, Haw.; Haz. do I.

And burns the same with wasting heat, as Titan doth the
    gras.
And, sith this heat is kindled so and fresh in hart of me,
There is no way but of the same the quencher you must be.
My meaning is that beauty yours my hart with love doth
    wound ;   905
To give me love minde to content, my hart hath you out-
    found ;
And you are she must be my wife, els shall I end my daies.
Consent to this, and be my queen, to weare the crown with
    praise !
    LADY.   If it please your Grace, O mighty king, you shall
        not this request ;
It is a thing that Natures course doth utterly detest,   910
And high it would the god[s] displease, — of all that is the
    woorst.
To graunt your Grace to marry so, it is not that I durst.
Yet humble thanks I render now unto you, mighty king,
That you vouchsafe to great estate so gladly would me bring.
Were it not it were offence, I would it not deny,   915
But such great honor to atchive my hart I would apply.
Therefore, O king, with humble hart in this I pardon crave :
My answer is : in this request your minde ye may not have.
    KING.   May I not? nay, then, I will, by all the gods I
        vow !
And I will mary thee as wife, — this is mine answere now.   920
Who dare say nay what I pretend, who dare the same with-
    stand,
Shal lose his head and have reporte as traitor through my
    land.
There is no nay ; I wil you have, and you my queene shalbe.
    LADY.   Then, mighty king, I crave your Grace to heare
        the words of me :
Your councel take of lordings wit, the lawes aright peruse ;   925
If I with safe may graunt this deed, I will it not refuse.
    KING.   No, no ! what I have said to you, I meane to have
        it so ;

For councel theirs I mean not, I, in this respect to goe.
But to my pallaice let us goe, the mariage to prepare;
For, to avoid my wil in this, I can it not forbeare. 930
    LADY.   O God, forgive me, if I doo amisse!
The king by compultion inforceth me this.
    MAID.   Unto the the gods for your estate I will not cease
        to pray,
That you may be a happy queen and see most joyfull day.
    KING.   Come on, my lords, with gladsome harts let us re-
        ioyce with glee! 935
Your musick shew to joy this deed at the request of me!
    BOTH.   For to obey your Graces words our Honors doo
        agree.   *Exeunt.*
               Enter AMBIDEXTER.

    AMB.   O the passion of me! mary, as ye say, yonder is a
        royal court;
There is triumphing and sporte upon sporte, —
Such loyall lords, with such lordly exercise, 940
Frequenting such pastime as they can devise,
Running at tilt, iusting, with running at the ring,
Masking and mumming, with eche kinde of thing, —
Such daunsing, such singing, with musicall[1] harmony,
Beleeve me, I was loth to absent their company. 945
But wil you beleeve? Jesu, what hast they made till they
        were maried!
Not for a milion of pounds one day longer they would have
        tared!
Oh! there was a banquet royall and superexcellent, —
Thousands and thousands at that banquet was spent.
I muse of nothing but how they can be maried so soone; 950
I care not if I be maried before to-morrow at noone,
If mariage be a thing that so may be had.
How say you, maid? to marry me wil ye be glad?
Out of doubt, I beleeve it is some excellent treasure, —
Els to the same belongs abundant pleasure. 955
Yet with mine eares I have heard some say:

      [1] *Misprinted* muūcall *in* E. Allde.

"That ever I was maried, now cursed be the day!"
Those be they [that]¹ with curst wives be matched.
That husband for haukes met of them is up-snatched,
Head broke with a bedstaffe, face all to-be-scratched ; — ²   960
"Knave!" "slave!" and "villain!" a coylde cote now and
     than, —
When the wife hath given it,³ she wil say, "Alas, goodman!'
Such were better unmarried, my maisters, I trow,
Then all their life after be matched with a shrow.

Enter Preparation.

PREP.   With speed I am sent all things to prepare,   965
My message to doe as the king did declare.
His Grace doth meane a banquet to make,
Meaning in this place repast for to take.
Wel, the cloth shalbe laid, and all things in redines,
To court to return, when doon is my busines.   970
    AMB.   A proper man and also a ⁴ fit
For the kings estate to prepare a banquet!
    PREP.   What, Ambidexter?   Thou art not unknowen!
A mischeefe on all good faces, so that I curse not mine owne!
Now, in the knaves name, shake hands with me.   975
    AMB.   Wel said, goodman pouchmouth ; your reverence I
     see.
I will teach ye, if your manners no better be!
A, ye slave, the king doth me a gentleman allow ;
Therefore I looke that to me ye should ⁵ bow.

Fight.

    PREP.   Good Maister Ambidexter, pardon my behaviour ;   980
For this your deed ⁶ you are a knave for your labour!
    AMB.   Why, ye stale counterly villain, nothing but knave?

Fight.

    PREP.   I am sorry your maistership offended I have ;
Shake hands, that betweene us agreement may be.

---

¹ E. Allde *omits* that.   ⁵ Haw. Haz. shall.
² *So* E. Allde, Haw.; Haz. be all-to scratched.
³ *So* E. Allde, Haw.; Haz. in.
⁴ E. Allde *omits* a.   ⁶ E. Allde, deeds.

I was over-shot with my-selfe, I doo see. 985
Let me have your helpe this furniture to provide
The king from this place wil not long abide.

Set the fruit on the boord.

AMB.　Content : it is the thing that I would wish ;
I my-selfe wil goe fetch one [1] dish.

Let the VICE fetch [2] a dish of nuts and let them fall in the bringing of
them in.

PREP.　Clenly, Maister Ambidexter ; for faire on the
　　　ground they lye. 990
AMB.　I will have them up againe by-and-by.
PREP.　To see all in redines I will put you in trust ;
There is no nay, to the court needs I must.

Exit PREPARATION.

AMB.　Have ye no doubt, sir, but all shalbe wel.
Mary, sir, as you say, this geer dooth excell ! 995
All things is in a readines, when they come hither, —
The kings Grace and the queene both togither.
I beseech ye, my maisters, tell me, is it not best
That I be so bolde as to bid a guest?
He is as honest a man as ever spurd cow, — 1000
My cosin Cutpursse, I meane ; I beseech ye, judge you.
Beleeve me, cosin, if to be the kings guest ye could be taken,
I trust that offer will never [3] be forsaken.
But, cosin, because to that office ye are not like to come,
Frequent your exercises, a horne on your thum, 1005
A quick eye, a sharpe knife, at hand a receiver ;
But then take heed, cosin, ye be a clenly convayour.
Content your-selfe, cosin ; for this banquet you are unfit,
When such as I at the same am unworthy [4] to sit.

Enter KING, QUEENE, *and his traine.*[5]

KING.　My queen and lords, to take repast, let us attempt
　　　the same ;
　　　　　　　　　　　　　　　　　　　　　　1010

[1] Haw. Haz. on.　　　　　[4] Haw. Haz. am not worthy.
[2] E. Allde, fetch ; Haw. fet ; Haz. set.
[3] Haw. Haz. would not.　　[5] Haw. Haz. Queen, Lords, &c.

Heer is the place ; delay no time, but to our purpose frame.

QUEENE.   With willing harts your whole behest we minde
for to obay.

ALL.   And we, the rest of princes traine, will doo as you
doo say.

Sit at the banquet.

KING.   Me think mine eares doth wish the sound of
musicks harmony ;

Heer, for to play before my Grace, in place I would them
spy.   1015

Play at the banquet.

AMB.   They be at hand, sir, with sticke and fiddle ;

They can play a new daunce, called Hey-diddle-diddle.

KING.   My queene, perpend ; what I pronounce, I wil
not violate,

But one thing which my hart makes glad I minde to
explicate :

You know in court uptrained is a lyon very yong ;   1020

Of one litter two whelps beside, as yet not very strong ;

I did request one whelpe to see and this young lyon fight ;

But lion did the whelpe convince by strength of force and
might.

His brother whelpe, perceiving that the lion was too good,

And he by force was like to see the other whelp his blood,   1025

With force to lyon he did run, his brother for to helpe, —

A wonder great it was to see that freendship in a whelpe ! —

So then the whelps between them both the lyon did convince,

Which thing to see before mine eyes did glad the hart of
prince.

At this tale tolde, let the QUEENE *weep.*

QUEENE.   These words to heare makes stilling teares
issue from christall eyes.   1030

KING.   What, doost thou meane, my spouse, to weep for
losse of any prise?

QUEENE.   No, no, O king, but as you see freendship in
brothers whelp,

When one was like to have repulse, the other yeelded helpe.
And was this favour shewd in dogs, to shame of royall king?
Alack, I wish these eares of mine had not once heard this
    thing! 1035
Even so should you, O mighty king, to brother beene a stay,
And not, without offence to you, in such wise him to slay.
In all assaies it was your part his cause to have defended,
And, who-so-ever had him misused, to have them repre-
    hended.
But faithfull love was more in dog then it was in your
    Grace. 1040
    KING. O cursed caitive vicious and vile, I hate thee in
      this place!
This banquet [now] is at an end; take all these things
    away.
Before my face thou shalt repent the words that thou dost
    say.
O wretch most vile, didst thou the cause of brother mine so
    tender
The losse of him should greeve thy hart, — he being none
    offender? 1045
It did me good his death to have, so will it to have thine;
What freendship he had at my hands, the same even thou
    shalt finde.
I give consent, and make a-vow, that thou shalt dye the
    death;
By Cruels sword and Murder fel even thou shalt lose thy [1]
    breth.
Ambidexter, see with speed to Cruelty ye goe; 1050
Cause him hither to approche, Murder with him also.
    AMB. I am redy for to fulfil,
If that it be your Graces will.[2]
    KING. Then nought oblight my message given; absent
      thy-selfe away.
    AMB. Then in this place I will no longer stay. 1055

[1] Haw. Haz. the.
[2] *These two lines as one in all the editions.*

[*Aside*] [1] If that I durst, I would mourne your case ;
But, alas! I dare not, for feare of his Grace.

Exit AMBIDEXTER.

KING.   Thou cursed Iill, by all the gods I take an othe
and swere,
That flesh of thine these hands of mine in peeces small could
tere ;
But thou shalt dye by dent of sword : there is no freend ne
fee   1060
Shall finde remorce at princes hand to save the life of thee.
QUEENE.   O mighty king *and* husband mine, vouchsafe
to heare me speak,
And licence give to spouse of thine her patient minde to
breake !
For tender love unto your Grace my words I did so frame ;
For pure love doth hart of king me violate and blame.   1065
And to your Grace is this offence that I should purchase
death ?
Then cursed time that I was queene, to shorten this my
breth !
Your Grace doth know, by mariage true I am your wife and
spouse,
And one to save anothers helth at trothplight made our
vowes ;
Therefore, O king, let loving queen at thy hand finde
remorse,   1070
Let pitie be a meane to quench that cruell raging force,
And pardon, plight from princes mouth, yeeld grace unto
your queen,
That amity with faithfull zeal may ever be us between !
KING.   A, caitive vile, to pitie thee my hart it is not bent,
Ne yet to pardon your offence it is not mine intent.   1075
FIRST LORD.   Our mighty prince, with humble sute of
your Grace this [2] I crave,

---

[1] Haz. *supplies* aside *at the beginning of the preceding line, but that
line may have been a reply to the king.*

[2] *So* E. Allde, Haw.; Haz. of you this grace.

That this request it may take place, your favour for to have.
Let mercy yet aboundantly the life of queen preserve,
Sith she in[1] most obedient wise[2] your Graces will doth
    serve.
As yet your Grace but while with her hath had cohabitation, 1080
And sure this is no desert why to yeeld her indignation.
Therefore, O king, her life prolong, to joy her daies in blisse!
    SECOND LORD.   Your Grace shal win immortall fame in
        graunting unto this.
She is a queene whose goodly hue excelles the royall rose,
For beauty bright Dame Nature she a large gift did
    dispose.   1085
For comelines who may compare?   Of all she beares the bell.
This should give cause to move your Grace to love her very
    wel.
Her silver brest[3] in those your armes to sing the songs of
    love, —
Fine qualities most excellent to be in her you prove ;
A precious pearle of prise to prince, a iewell passing all.   1090
Therefore, O king, to beg remorce on both my knees I fall ;
To graunt her grace to have her life, with hart I doo desire.
    KING.   You villains twain, with raging force ye set my
        hart on fire!
If I consent that she shall dye, how dare ye crave her life?
You two to aske this at my hand dooth much inlarge my
    strife.   1095
Were it not for shame, you two should dye, that for her life
    do sue!
But favour mine from you is gone ; my lords, I tell you true.
I sent for Cruelty of late ; if he would come away,
I would commit her to his hands his cruell part to play.
Even now I see where he dooth come ; it dooth my hart
    delight.   1100

---

[1] *So* E. Allde, Haw.; Haz. is.
[2] *So* Haw.; Haz. wife; *my collator makes no remark as to the reading
of* E. Allde.
[3] Haz. breasts; E. Allde, Haw. brest.

Enter CRUELTY *and* MURDER.

CRUEL.   Come, Murder, come; let us goe foorth with
         might;
Once againe the kings commaundement we must fulfill.
   MURD.   I am contented [1] to doo it with a good will.
   KING.   Murder and Cruelty, for both of you I sent,
With all festination your offices to frequent.   1105
Lay holde on the queene; take her to your power,
And make her away within this houre!
Spare for no feare, I doo you full permit.
So I from this place doo meane for to flit.
   BOTH.   With couragious harts, O king, we will obay.   1110
   KING.   Then come, my lords, let us departe away.
   BOTH THE LORDS.   With hevy harts we will doo all your
         Grace dooth say.   *Exeunt* KING *and* LORDS.
   CRUEL.   Come, lady and queene, now are you in our
         handling;
In faith, with you we will use no dandling.
   MURD.   With all expedition I, Murder, will take place;   1115
Though thou be a queene, ye be under my grace.
   QUEENE.   With patience I will you both obay.[2]
   CRUEL.   No more woords, but goe with us away![2]
   QUEENE.   Yet, before I dye, some psalme to God let me
         sing.
   BOTH.   We be content to permit you that thing.   1120
QUEENE. [*sings*]   Farwell, you ladies of the court,
      With all your masking hue!
I.doo forsake these brodered gardes
      And all the fashions new,
The court and all the courtly train   1125
      Wherin I had delight;
I banished am from happy sporte,
      And all by spitefull spite;
Yet with a ioyfull hart to God
      A psalme I meane to sing,   1130

---

[1] *Misprinted* contended *in* E. Allde.
[2] *In* E. Allde *these two words are interchanged.*

Forgiving all [men] and the king
　　Of eche kinde of thing.

Sing and exeunt.

Enter AMBIDEXTER *weeping.*

AMB. A, a, a, a! I cannot chuse but weepe for the queene!
Nothing but mourning now at the court there is seene.
Oh, oh, my hart, my hart! O, my bum will break! 　1135
Very greefe so torments me that scarce I can speake.
Who could but weep for the losse of such a lady?
That cannot I doo, I sweare by mine honestie.
But, Lord! so the ladies mourne, crying "Alack!"
Nothing is worne now but onely black: 　1140
I beleeve all [the][1] cloth in Watling Street to make gowns
　　would not serve, —
If I make a lye, the devill let ye[2] starve!
All ladyes mourne, both yong and olde;
There is not one that weareth a points woorth of golde.
There is a sorte for feare for[3] the king doo pray 　1145
That would have him dead, by the masse, I dare say.
What a king was he that hath used such tiranny!
He was akin to Bishop Bonner, I think verily!
For both their delights was to shed blood,
But never intended to doo any good. 　1150
Cambises put a iudge to death, — that was a good deed, —
But to kill the yong childe was worse to proceed,
To murder his brother and then his owne wife, —
So help me God and holidom, it is pitie of his life!
Heare ye? I will lay twenty thousand pound 　1155
That the king himselfe dooth dye by some wound.
He hath shed so much blood that his will be shed;
If it come so[4] to passe, in faith, then is he sped.

Enter the KING, *without a gowne, a swoord thrust up into his side,*
bleeding.

KING. Out! alas! what shal I doo? my life is finished!
Wounded I am by sodain chaunce, my blood is minished. 　1160

---

[1] *Supplied by* Haz.　　　　[3] *So* E. Allde, Haw.; Haz. of.
[2] *So* E. Allde, Haw.; Haz. me.　[4] E. Allde *omits* so.

Gogs hart, what meanes might I make, my life to preserve?
Is there nought to be my helpe? nor is there nought to
    serve?
Out upon the court and lords that there remaine!
To help my greefe in this my case wil none of them take
    paine?
Who but I in such a wise his deaths wound could have
    got?   1165
As I on horse back up did leap, my sword from scabard
    shot,
And ran [1] me thus into the side, as you right well may see, —
A marvels chaunce unfortunate that in this wise should be!
I feele my-selfe a-dying now, of life bereft am I,
And Death hath caught me with his dart, for want of blood
    I spy.   1170
Thus gasping heer on ground I lye; for nothing I doo
    care;
A just reward for my misdeeds my death doth plaine declare.

Heere let him quake and stir.

   AMB.   How now, noble king? pluck up your hart!
What, will you dye, and from us depart?
Speake to me and ye be alive!   1175
He cannot speak. But beholde, now with Death he doth
    strive.
Alas, good king! alas, he is gone!
The devill take me if for him I make any mone.
I did prognosticate of his end, by the masse;
Like as I did say, so is it come to passe!   1180
I wil be gone; if I should be found heere,
That I should kill him it would appeer.
For feare with his death they doo me charge,
Farwell, my maisters, I will goe take barge;
I meane to be packing; now is the tide;   1185
Farwell, my maisters, I will no longer abide!
                         Exit AMBIDEXTER.

[1] *So* E. Allde, Haw.; Haz. run.

Enter three LORDS.

FIRST LORD.   Beholde, my lords, it is even so as he to
    us did tell :

His Grace is dead, upon the ground, by dint [1] of sword most
    fel.

SECOND LORD.   As he in saddle would have lept, his
    sword from sheath did goe, [2]

Goring him up into the side, — his life was ended so.   1190

THIRD LORD.   His blood so fast did issue out that nought
    could him prolong ;

Yet, before he yeelded up the ghost, his hart was very
    strong.

FIRST LORD.   A just reward for his misdeeds the God
    above hath wrought,

For certainly the life he led was to be counted nought.

SECOND LORD.   Yet a princely buriall he shall have,
    according his estate ;   1195

And more of him heere at this [3] time we have not to dilate.

THIRD LORD.   My lords, let us take him up, to carry him
    away !

BOTH.   Content we are with one accord to doo as you
    doo say.

Exeunt all.

EPILOGUE. [4]

Right gentle audience, heere have you perused
    The tragicall history of this wicked king.
According to our duty, we have not refused,
    But to our best intent exprest everything.
    We trust none is offended for this our dooing ;
Our author craves likewise, if he have squared amisse,
By gentle admonition to know where the fault is.   1205

His good will shall not be neglected to amend the same.
    Praying all to beare, therefore, with this [3] simple deed

---

1 Haw. Haz. dent.   3 Haw. Haz. his.
2 *Misprinted* gee *in* E. Allde.   4 Haw. Haz. Epilogus.

Untill the time serve a better he may frame, —
    Thus yeelding you thanks, to end we decreed
    That you so gently have suffered us to proceed,
In such patient wise as to heare and see, —
We can but thank ye therfore, we can doo no more, we ! —   1212

As duty bindes us, for our noble Queene let us pray,
    And for her Honorable Councel, the truth that they may
        use,
To practice iustice and defend her Grace eche day ;
    To maintain Gods woord they may not refuse,
    To correct all those that would her Grace *and* Graces
        lawes abuse ;
Beseeching God over us she may raigne long,
To be guided by truth and defended from wrong.   1219

"Amen," quod Thomas Prefton.

Imprinted at London
by Edward Allde.

The Tragidie of Ferrex

and Porrex,

ſet forth without addition or alteration but altogether as the ſame was ſhewed
on ſtage before the Queenes Maieſtie,
about nine yeares past, *vz.*, the
xviij day of Ianuarie 1561.
by the Gentlemen of the
Inner Temple.

Seen and allowed &c.

Imprinted at London by
Iohn Daye, dwelling ouer
Alderſgate.

This play, under the title *Gorboduc*, was licensed to William Griffith in 1565 and printed by him in the same year. In 1570 it appeared under the title *Ferrex and Porrex*, with an address from the publisher, John Day, declaring the first edition to have been surreptitious and defective. In 1590 it was reprinted from the first edition with a few modernizations of spelling and diction. These three editions are indicated in the footnotes by A., B., and C.

The first edition was carefully reprinted for the Shakespeare Society in 1847 by W. D. Cooper. The second edition was reprinted in modernized spelling by R. W. Sackville-West in 1859 (*The Works of Thomas Sackville, Lord Buckhurst*). In 1883 Miss Lucy Toulmin Smith published a critical edition (*Englische Sprach- und Literaturdenkmale*, vol. I.), with the variants of the three old editions.

In spelling I have followed the second edition; in punctuation, capitalization, use of stage-directions, etc., I have followed modern usage. In the footnotes will be found the significant variants of the first edition, and a few of the more interesting readings of the third. The three modern editions are indicated in the footnotes by Co., S.-W., and Sm., respectively.

The Names of the Speakers.

GORBODUC, *king of Great Brittaine.*
VIDENA, *queene, and wife to king Gorboduc.*
FERREX, *elder sonne to king Gorboduc.*
PORREX, *yonger sonne to king Gorboduc.*
CLOTYN, *duke of Cornewall.*
FERGUS, *duke of Albanye.*
MANDUD, *duke of Loegris.*[1]
GWENARD, *duke of Cumberland.*
EUBULUS, *secretarie to the king.*[2]
AROSTUS, *a counsellor to the king.*[3]
DORDAN, *a counsellor assigned by the king to his eldest sonne, Ferrex.*
PHILANDER, *a counsellor assigned by the king to his yongest[4] sonne, Porrex.*
      Both being of the olde kinges counsell before.
HERMON, *a parasite remaining with Ferrex.*
TYNDAR, *a parasite remaining with Porrex.*
NUNTIUS, *a messenger of the elder brothers death.*
NUNTIUS, *a messenger of Duke Fergus rising in armes.*
MARCELLA, *a lady of the queenes priuie-chamber.*
CHORUS, *foure auncient and sage men of Brittaine.*

[SCENE: *Britain.*]

[1] A. Leagre.   [3] A. of King Gorboduc.
[2] A. *adds* Gorboduc.   [4] A. yonger.

The P[rinter][1] to the Reader.[2]

Where this Tragedie was for furniture of part of the grand Christmasse in the Inner Temple first written about nine yeares agoe by the Right Honourable Thomas, now Lorde Buckherst, and by T. Norton, and after shewed before her Maiestie, and neuer intended by the authors therof to be published; yet one W. G. getting a copie therof at some yongmans hand that lacked a litle money and much discretion, in the last great plage, *an*[*no*] 1565, about v yeares past, while the said lord was out of England, and T. Norton farre out of London, and neither of them both made priuie, put it forth excedingly corrupted, — euen as if by meanes of a broker, for hire, he should haue entised into his house a faire maide and done her villanie, and after all-to-bescratched her face, torne her apparell, berayed and disfigured her, and then thrust her out of dores dishonested. In such plight, after long wandring, she came at length home to the sight of her frendes, who scant knew her but by a few tokens and markes remayning. They — the authors, I meane — though they were very much displeased that she so ranne abroad without leaue, whereby she caught her shame, as many wantons do, yet seing the case, as it is, remedilesse, haue, for common honestie and shamefastnesse, new apparelled, trimmed and attired her in such forme as she was before. In which better forme since she hath come to me, I haue harbored her for her frendes sake and her owne; and I do not dout her parentes the authors will not now be discontent that she goe abroad among you good readers, so it be in honest companie. For she is by my encouragement and others somewhat lesse ashamed of the dishonestie done to her,

---

[1] *Letters in brackets supplied by* Miss Smith.
[2] *This Address is omitted by* S.-W.; *in* B. Sm. *it follows* The Argument.

because it was by fraude and force. If she be welcome among you and gently enterteined in fauor of the house from whense she is descended and of her owne nature courteously disposed to offend no man, her frendes will thanke you for it. If not, but that she shall be still reproched with her former missehap, or quarelled at by enuious persons, she, poore gentlewoma[n],[1] wil surely play Lucreces part, and of her-self die for shame ; and I shall wishe that she had taried still at home with me, where she was welcome, for she did neuer put me to more charge but this one poore blacke gowne lined with white that I haue now geuen her to goe abroad among you withall.

THE ARGUMENT OF THE TRAGEDY.[2]

Gorboduc, king of Brittaine, diuided his realme in his life-time to his sonnes, Ferrex and Porrex ; the sonnes fell to discention ;[3] the yonger killed the elder ; the mother, that more dearely loued the elder, for reuenge killed the yonger ; the people, moued with the crueltie of the fact, rose in rebellion and slew both father and mother ; the nobilitie assembled and most terribly destroyed the rebels ; and afterwardes, for want of issue of the prince, whereby the succession of the crowne became vncertaine, they fell to ciuill warre, in which both they and many of their issues were slaine, and the land for a long time almost desolate and miserably wasted.

[1] *Letter in brackets supplied by* Miss Smith.
[2] *In* B. Sm. *this is on the back of the titlepage.*
[3] A. to dyuision and discention.

[GORBODUC; OR, FERREX AND PORREX.]

The Order of the Domme Shew before the First Act, and the Signification Thereof.

First the musicke of violenze began to play, during which came in vpon the stage sixe wilde men, clothed in leaues; of whom the first bare in his necke a fagot of small stickes, which they all, both seuerally and together, assayed with all their strengthes to breake, but it could not be broken by them. At the length, one of them plucked[1] out one of the stickes and brake it, and the rest plucking out all the other stickes one after an-other did easely breake them,[2] the same being seuered, which, being conioyned, they had before attempted in vaine. After they had this done, they departed the stage; and the musicke ceased. Hereby was signified that a state knit in vnitie doth continue strong against all force, but being diuided is easely destroyed: As befell vpon Duke Gorboduc diuiding his land to his two sonnes, which he before held in monarchie, and vpon the discention of the brethren to whom it was diuided.

Actus Primus. Scena Prima.

[A room in GORBODUC's *palace.]*

VIDENA. FERREX.

VID. The silent night, that bringes the quiet pawse,
From painefull trauailes of the wearie day,
Prolonges my carefull thoughtes, and makes me blame
The slowe Aurore, that so for loue or shame
Doth long delay to shewe her blushing face;   5
And now the day renewes my griefull plaint.

FERR. My gracious lady and my mother deare,
Pardon my griefe for your so grieued minde,

---

[1] C. S.-W. pulled.   [2] A. *omits* them.

215

To aske what cause tormenteth so your hart.

    VID.   So great a wrong, and so vniust despite,   10
Without all cause, against all course of kinde!

    FERR.   Such causelesse wrong and so vniust despite
May haue redresse, or, at the least, reuenge.

    VID.   Neither, my sonne ; such is the froward will,
The person such, such my missehappe and thine.   15

    FERR.   Mine know I none but grief for your distresse.

    VID.   Yes, mine for thine, my sonne.   A father?   No ;
In kinde a father, not[1] in kindliness.

    FERR.   My father?   Why, I know nothing at all
Wherein I have misdone vnto his Grace.   20

    VID.   Therefore the more vnkinde to thee and mee !
For, knowing well, my sonne, the tender loue
That I haue euer borne and beare to thee,
He, greued thereat, is not content alone
To spoile thee of my sight,[2] my chiefest ioye ;   25
But thee of thy birthright and heritage,
Causelesse, vnkindly and in wrongfull wise,
Against all lawe and right, he will bereaue :
Halfe of his kingdome he will geue away.

    FERR.   To whom?

    VID.   Euen to Porrex, his yonger sonne,   30
Whose growing pride I do so sore suspect
That, being raised to equall rule with thee,
Mee thinkes I see his envious hart to swell,
Filled with disdaine and with ambicious hope.[3]
The end the goddes do know, whose altars I   35
Full oft haue made in vaine of cattell slaine
To send the sacred smoke to Heauens throne
For thee, my sonne, if thinges do[4] so succede
As now my ielous mind misdemeth sore.

    FERR.   Madam, leaue care and carefull plaint for me.   40
Just hath my father bene to euery wight ;
His first vniustice he will not extend

---

    [1] A. but not.   [3] A. pride.
    [2] *Qy.* To spoile me of thy sight.   [4] A. *omits* do.

To me, I trust, that geue no cause therof.
My brothers pride shall hurt him-selfe, not me.
    VID.   So graunt the goddes! But yet thy father so   45
Hath firmely fixed his vnmoued minde
That plaintes and prayers can no whit auaile, —
For those haue I assaied, — but euen this day
He will endeuour to procure assent
Of all his counsell to his fonde deuise.   50
    FERR.   Their ancestors from race to race haue borne
True fayth to my forefathers and their seede ;
I trust they eke will beare the like to me.
    VID.   There resteth all. But, if they faile there-of,
And if the end bring forth an ill[1] successe,   55
On them and theirs the mischiefe shall befall ;
And so I pray the goddes requite it them,
And so they will, for so is wont to be.
When lordes, and trusted rulers vnder kinges,
To please the present fancie of the prince,   60
With wrong transpose the course of gouernance,
Murders, mischiefe or ciuill sword at length,
Or mutuall treason, or a iust reuenge
When right-succeding line returnes againe,
By Ioues iust iudgement and deserued wrath   65
Bringes them to cruell[2] and reprochfull death
And rootes their names and kindredes from the earth.
    FERR.   Mother, content you ; you shall see the end.
    VID.   The end? Thy end, I feare! Ioue end me first!

Actus Primus.   Scena Secunda.

[*The council-chamber of* GORBODUC.]

GORBODUC. AROSTUS. PHILANDER. EUBULUS.

    GORB.   My lords, — whose graue aduise and faithful aide
Haue long vpheld my honour and my realme,
And brought me to[3] this age from tender yeres,

---

[1] A. euill.   [2] A. ciuill.   [3] A. C. from.

Guidyng so great estate with great renowme, —
Nowe more importeth mee than [1] erst to vse   5
Your fayth and wisedome, — whereby yet I reigne, —
That, when by death my life and rule shall cease,
The kingdome yet may with vnbroken course
Haue certayne prince, by whose vndoubted right
Your wealth and peace may stand in quiet stay ;   10
And eke that they whome nature hath preparde,
In time to take my place in princely seate,
While in their fathers tyme their pliant youth
Yeldes to the frame of skilfull gouernance,
Maye so be taught and trayned in noble artes,   15
As, what their fathers which haue reigned before
Haue with great fame deriued downe to them,
With honour they may leaue vnto their seede ;
And not be thought,[2] for their vnworthy life
And for their lawless swaruynge out of kinde,   20
Worthy to lose what lawe and kind them gaue ;
But that they may preserue the common peace —
The cause that first began and still mainteines
The lyneall course of kinges inheritance —
For me, for myne, for you, and for the state,   25
Whereof both I and you haue charge and care.
Thus do I meane to vse your wonted fayth
To me and myne, and to your natiue lande.
My lordes, be playne, without all wrie respect
Or poysonous craft to speake in pleasyng wise,   30
Lest, as the blame of yll-succedyng thinges
Shall light on you, so light the harmes also.
  AROS.   Your good acceptance so, most noble king,
Of suche our [3] faithfulnesse as heretofore
We haue employed in dueties to your Grace   35
And to this realm, whose worthy head you are,
Well proues that neyther you mistrust at all
Nor we shall neede in [4] boasting wise to shewe

---

[1] A. C. the.   [3] A. C. your.
[2] A. C. taught.   [4] A. C. no.

Our trueth to you, nor yet our wakefull care
For you, for yours, and for our natiue lande.   40
Wherefore, O kyng, — I speake as one for [1] all,
Sithe all as one do beare you egall faith, —
Doubt not to vse our [2] counsells and our [2] aides,
Whose honours, goods and lyues are whole auowed,
To serue, to ayde and to defende your Grace.   45
   GORB. My lordes, I thanke you all.   This is the case :
Ye know, the gods, who haue the soueraigne care
For kings, for kingdomes and for common-weales,
Gaue me two sonnes in my more lusty age,
Who nowe in my decayeing [3] yeres are growen   50
Well towardes ryper state of minde and strength
To take in hande some greater princely charge.
As yet they lyue and spende their [4] hopefull daies
With me and with their mother here in courte.
Their age nowe asketh other place and trade,   55
And myne also doth aske an-other chaunge :
Theirs to more trauaile, myne to greater ease.
Whan fatall death shall ende my mortall life,
My purpose is to leaue vnto them twaine
The realme diuided in two [5] sondry partes :   60
The one Ferrex, myne elder sonne, shall haue,
The other shall the yonger,[6] Porrex, rule.
That both my purpose may more firmely [7] stande
And eke that they may better rule their charge,
I meane forthwith to place them in the same,   65
That in my life they may both learne to rule
And I may ioy to see their ruling well.
This is, in summe, what I woulde haue ye wey :
First, whether ye allowe my whole deuise
And thinke it good for me, for them, for you,   70
And for our countrey, mother of vs all ;

---

1 A. C. for one as.   5 A. B. C. into two.
2 A. C. their.   6 A. C. other.
3 A. deceyuyng.   7 A. framelie.
4 B. C. *omit* their.

And, if ye like it and allowe it well,
Then, for their guydinge and their gouernaunce,
Shew forth such meanes of circumstance [1]
As ye thinke meete to be both knowne and kept.   75
Loe, this is all; now tell me your aduise.

 AROS. And this is much, and asketh great aduise;
But, for my part, my soueraigne lord and kyng,
This do I thinke: your Maiestie doth know
How, vnder you, in iustice and in peace,   80
Great wealth and honour long we haue enioy'd,
So as we can not seeme with gredie mindes
To wisshe for change of prince or gouernaunce;
But, if we [2] lyke your purpose and deuise,
Our lyking must be deemed to proceede   85
Of rightfull reason and of heedefull care,
Not for ourselues, but for the [3] common state,
Sithe our owne state doth neede no better change.
I thinke in all as erst your Grace hath saide.
Firste, when you shall vnlode your aged mynde   90
Of heuye care and troubles manifolde,
And laye the same vpon my lordes your sonnes,
Whose growing yeres may beare the burden long, —
And long I pray the goddes to graunt it so! —
And in your life while you shall so beholde   95
Their rule, their vertues and their noble deedes,
Suche as their kinde behighteth to vs all,
Great be the profites that shall growe therof :
Your age in quiet shall the longer last ;
Your lasting age shalbe their longer stay ;   100
For cares of kynges that rule, as you have ruled,
For publique wealth and not for priuate ioye,
Do wast mannes lyfe, and hasten crooked age
With furrowed face and with enfeebled lymmes
To draw on creepyng death a swifter pace.   105

---

 [1] *This line has only four feet; the insertion of* to me *or* I pray *after*
forth *would restore the metre.*
 [2] A. C. ye.   [3] A. our.

They two yet yong, shall beare the parted [1] reigne
With greater ease than one, nowe olde, alone
Can welde the whole, for whom muche harder is
With lessened strength the double weight to beare.
Your eye, your counsell, and the graue regarde   110
Of father,[2] yea, of such a fathers name,
Nowe at beginning of their sondred reigne,
When is the [3] hazarde of their whole successe,
Shall bridle so their force of youthfull heates,
And so restreine the rage of insolence,   115
Whiche most assailes the yonge and noble minds,
And so shall guide and traine in tempred stay
Their yet greene, bending wittes with reuerent awe,
As [4] — now inured with vertues at the first, —
Custome, O king, shall bring delightfulnesse;   120
By vse of vertue, vice shall growe in hate.
But, if you so dispose it that the daye
Which endes your life shall first begin their reigne,
Great is the perill what will [5] be the ende,
When such beginning of such liberties,   125
Voide of suche stayes [6] as in your life do lye,
Shall leaue them free to randon [7] of their will,
An open praie to traiterous flatterie, —
The greatest pestilence of noble youthe;
Whiche perill shalbe past, if in your life   130
Their tempred youthe with aged fathers awe
Be brought in vre of skilfull stayednesse;
And in your life their liues disposed so,
Shall length your noble life in ioyfulnesse.
Thus thinke I that your Grace hath wisely thought,   135
And that your tender care of common weale
Hath bred this thought, so to diuide your lande
And plant your sonnes to beare the present rule

---

[1] A. C. partie.   [5] C. shall.
[2] A. C. fathers.   [6] A. C. states.
[3] A. When it is.   [7] A. C. to free randon.
[4] A. C. And.

While you yet liue to see their rulinge well,
That you may longer lyue by ioye therein.   140
What furder [1] meanes behouefull are and meete,
At greater [2] leisure may your Grace deuise,
When all haue said, and when we be agreed
If this be best to part the realme in twaine
And place your sonnes in present gouernement;   145
Whereof, as I haue plainely said my mynde,
So woulde I here the rest of all my lordes.

    PHIL.   In part I thinke as hath bene said before;
In parte, agayne, my minde is otherwise.
As for diuiding of this realme in twaine,   150
And lotting out the same in egall partes
To either of my lordes your Graces sonnes,
That thinke I best for this your realmes behofe,
For profite and aduauncement of your sonnes,
And for your comforte and your honour eke.   155
But so to place them while your life do [3] last,
To yelde to them your royall gouernaunce,
To be aboue them onely in the name
Of father, not in kingly state also,
I thinke not good for you, for them, nor vs.   160
This kingdome, since the bloudie ciuill fielde
Where Morgan slaine did yeld his conquered parte
Unto his cosins sworde in Camberland,
Conteineth all that whilome did suffice
Three noble sonnes of your forefather Brute.   165
So your two sonnes it maye suffice also. [4]
The moe, the stronger, if they gree in one.
The smaller compasse that the realme doth holde,
The easier is the swey thereof to welde,
The nearer justice to the wronged poore,   170
The smaller charge, — and yet ynoughe for one.
And, whan the region is diuided so
That brethren be the lordes of either parte,

---

[1] C. further.   [3] C. doth.
[2] A. great.   [4] A. C. also suffice,

Such strength doth Nature knit betwene them both
In sondrie bodies by conioyned loue   175
That, not as two, but one of doubled force,
Eche is to other as a sure defence ;
The noblenesse and glory of the one
Doth sharpe the courage of the others mynde
With vertuous enuie to contende for praise.   180
And suche an egalnesse hath Nature made
Betwene the brethren of one fathers seede
As an vnkindly wrong it seemes to bee
To throwe the brother [1] subiect vnder feete
Of him whose peere he is by course of kinde.   185
And Nature, that did make this egalnesse,
Ofte so repineth [2] at so great a wrong
That ofte she rayseth vp a grudginge griefe
In yonger brethren at the elders state,
Wherby both townes and kingdomes haue ben rased,   190
And famous stockes of royall bloud destroied :
The brother, that shoulde be the brothers aide
And haue a wakefull care for his defence,
Gapes for his death, and blames the lyngering yeres
That draw [3] not forth his ende with faster course ; 195
And oft, impacient of so longe delayes,
With hatefull slaughter he preuentes [4] the Fates,
And heapes [5] a iust rewarde for brothers bloode,
With endlesse vengeaunce, on his stocke for aye.
Suche mischiefes here are wisely mette withall,   200
If egall state maye nourishe egall loue,
Where none hath cause to grudge at others good.
But nowe the head to stoupe beneth them bothe,
Ne kind ne reason ne good ordre beares.
And oft it hath ben seene, where Natures course [6]   205

---

[1] A. C. other.

[2] Dods. *says* C. *has* sore pineth ; Sm. *records no such variant.*

[3] Sm. *gives reading of* A. C. *as* brings ; Co. *prints* A. bring ; Dods. *gives*
C. *as* brings.   [5] A. C. keepes.

   [4] A. presentes.   [6] A. C. that where nature.

Hath ben peruerted in disordered wise,
When fathers cease to know that they should rule,
The [1] children cease to know they should obey ;
And often ouerkindly tendernesse
Is mother of vnkindly stubbornnesse.   210
I speake not this in enuie or reproche,
As if I grudged the glorie of your sonnes, —
Whose honour I besech the goddes encrease ! —
Nor yet as if I thought there did remaine
So filthie cankers in their noble brestes   215
Whom I esteeme — which is their greatest praise —
Undoubted children of so good a kyng ;
Onelie I meane to shewe, by [2] certeine rules
Whiche Kinde hath graft within the mind of man,
That Nature hath her ordre and her course,   220
Which being broken doth corrupt the state
Of myndes and thinges, euen in the best of all.
My lordes your sonnes may learne to rule of you ;
Your owne example in your noble courte
Is fittest guyder of their youthfull yeares.   225
If you desire to see [3] some present ioye
By sight of their well rulynge in your lyfe,
See them obey, so shall you see them rule :
Who-so obeyeth not with humblenesse
Will rule with outrage and with insolence.   230
Longe maye they rule, I do beseche the goddes ;
But [4] longe may they learne, ere they begyn to rule !
If Kinde and Fates [5] woulde suffre, I would wisshe
Them aged princes and immortall kinges.
Wherfore, most noble kynge, I well [6] assent,   235
Betwene your sonnes that you diuide your realme,
And, as in kinde, so match them in degree.
But, while the goddes prolong your royall life,
Prolong your reigne ; for therto lyue you here,

---

[1] A. C. And.   [2] A. C. my.   [3] A. C. seeke.
[4] S.-W. *omits* but, *for the metre; the omission of* they *would obtain the same effect.*   [5] C. saies.   [6] C. will.

And therfore haue the goddes so long forborne　　　240
To ioyne you to them-selues, that still you might
Be prince and father of our common-weale.
They, when they see your children ripe to rule,
Will make them roume, and will remoue you hence,
That yours, in right ensuynge of your life,　　　245
Maye rightly honour your immortall [1] name.
　　　EUB.　Your wonted true regarde of faithfull hartes
Makes me, O kinge, the bolder to presume
To speake what I conceiue within my brest,
Although the same do not agree at all　　　250
With that which other here my lordes haue said,
Nor which yourselfe haue seemed best to lyke.
Pardon I craue, and that my wordes be demde
To flowe from hartie zeale vnto your Grace,
And to the safetie of your common-weale.　　　255
To parte your realme vnto my lordes your sonnes
I thinke not good for you, ne yet for them,
But worste of all for this our natiue lande.
Within [2] one land one single rule is best :
Diuided reignes [3] do make diuided hartes,　　　260
But peace preserues the countrey and the prince.
Suche is in man the gredy minde to reigne,
So great is his desire to climbe alofte,
In worldly stage the stateliest partes to beare,
That faith and iustice and all kindly loue　　　265
Do yelde vnto desire of soueraignitie
Where egall state doth raise an egall hope
To winne the thing that either wold attaine.
Your Grace remembreth how in passed yeres
The mightie Brute, first prince of all this lande,　　　270
Possessed the same and ruled it well in one ;
He, thinking that the compasse did suffice
For his three sonnes three kingdoms eke to make,
Cut it in three, as you would now in twaine ;

---

[1] A. C. mortall.　　　　[3] C. regions.
[2] A. C. For with.

But how much Brittish [1] bloud hath since bene spilt,   275
To ioyne againe the sondred vnitie ;
What princes slaine before their timely houre ; [2]
What wast of townes and people in the lande ;
What treasons heaped on murders and on spoiles,
Whose iust reuenge even yet is scarcely ceased,   280
Ruthefull remembraunce is yet rawe [3] in minde!
The gods forbyd the like to chaunce againe !
And you, O king, geue not the cause therof !
My lord Ferrex, your elder sonne, perhappes,
Whome kinde and custome geues a rightfull hope   285
To be your heire and to succeede your reigne,
Shall thinke that he doth suffre greater wrong
Than he perchaunce will beare, if power serue.
Porrex, the younger, so vpraised [4] in state,
Perhappes in courage will be raysed also.   290
If flatterie, then, whiche fayles not to assaile
The tendre mindes of yet vnskilfull youth,
In one shall kindle and encrease disdaine,
And [5] enuie in the others harte enflame,
This fire shall waste their loue, their liues, their land,   295
And ruthefull ruine shall destroy them both.
I wishe not this, O kyng, so to befall,
But feare the thing that I do most abhorre.
Geue no beginning to so dreadfull ende ;
Kepe them in order and obedience,   300
And let them both, by now obeying you,
Learne such behauiour as beseemes their state, —
The elder, myldenesse in his gouernaunce,
The yonger, a yelding contentednesse.
And kepe them neare vnto your presence still,   305
That they, restreyned by the awe of you,
May liue in compasse of well tempred staye
And passe the perilles of their youthfull yeares.
Your aged life drawes on to febler tyme,

---

[1] A. C. Brutish.   [3] A. C. had.   [5] C. In.
[2] A, C, honour.   [4] A. C. vnpaised.

Wherin you shall lesse able be to beare   310
The trauailes that in youth you haue susteyned
Both in your persones and your realmes defence.
If, planting now your sonnes in furder partes,
You sende them furder from your present reach,
Lesse shall you know how they them-selues demeane ;[1]   315
Traiterous corrupters of their plyant youth
Shall have, vnspied, a muche more free accesse ;
And, if [2] ambition and inflamed disdaine
Shall arme the one, the other, or them both,
To ciuill warre or to vsurping pride,   320
Late shall you rue that you ne recked before.
Good is, I graunt, of all to hope the best,
But not to liue still dreadlesse of the worst.
So truste the one that the other be foresene.
Arme not vnskilfulnesse with princely power ;   325
But you, that long haue wisely ruled the reignes
Of royaltie within your noble realme,
So holde them, while the gods for our auayles
Shall stretch the thred of your prolonged daies.
To soone he clambe into the flaming carre   330
Whose want of skill did set the earth on fire.
Time, and example of your noble Grace,
Shall teach your sonnes both to obey and rule.
When time hath taught them, time shal make them place, —[3]
The place that now is full : and so, I pray,   335
Long it remaine, to comfort of vs all!
    GORB.   I take your faithful harts in thankful part.
But, sithe I see no cause to draw my minde
To feare the nature of my louing sonnes,
Or to misdeme that enuie or disdaine   340
Can there worke hate where nature planteth loue,
In one selfe purpose do I still abide.
My loue extendeth egally to both ;
My lande suffiseth for them both also.
Humber shall parte the marches of theyr realmes :   345

---

[1] A. C. demaund.   [2] A. C. of.   [3] A. C. pace.

The sotherne part the elder shall possesse ;
The no[r]therne shall Porrex, the yonger, rule.
In quiet I will passe mine aged dayes,
Free from the trauaile and the painefull cares
That hasten age vpon the worthiest kinges.   350
But, lest the fraude that ye do seeme to feare
Of flattering tongues corrupt their tender youth,
And wrythe them to the wayes of youthfull lust,
To climyng pride or to reuenging hate,
Or to neglecting of their carefull charge,   355
Lewdely to lyue in wanton recklessnesse,
Or to oppressing of the rightfull cause,
Or not to wreke the wronges done to the poore,
To treade downe truth or fauour false deceite,
I meane to ioyne to eyther of my sonnes   360
Some one of those whose long approued faith
And wisdome tryed may well assure my harte
That mynyng fraude shall finde no way to crepe
Into their fensed eares with graue aduise.
This is the ende, and so I pray you all   365
To beare my sonnes the loue and loyaltie
That I haue founde within your faithfull brestes.
   AROS.   You nor your sonnes, our soueraign lord, shal want
Our faith and seruice while our liues do last!

                                            Exeunt.

CHORUS.

When settled stay doth holde the royall throne
    In stedfast place by knowen and doubtles right,
And chiefely when discent on one alone
    Makes single and vnparted reigne to light,
Eche chaunge of course vnioynts the whole estate,
And yeldes it thrall to ruyne by debate.   6

The strength that, knit by faste [1] accorde in one,
    Against all forrein power of mightie foes

                1 A. C. laste.

Could of it-selfe defende it-selfe alone,
    Disioined once, the former force doth lose.
The stickes that, sondred, brake so soone in twaine,
In faggot bounde attempted were in vain.   12

Oft tender minde, that leades the parciall eye
    Of erring parentes in their childrens loue,
Destroyes the wrongly loued childe thereby.
    This doth the proude sonne of Apollo proue,
Who, rashely set in chariot of his sire,
Inflamed the parched earth with heauens fire.   18

And this great king, that doth deuide his land
    And chaunge the course of his discending crowne
And yeldes the reigne into his childrens hande,
    From blisfull state of ioye and great renowne
A myrrour shall become to princes all
To learne to shunne the cause of suche a fall.   24

End of the First Act.

The Order and Signification of the Domme Shew before the Second Acte.

First, the musicke of cornettes began to playe, during which came in vpon the
stage a king accompanied with a nombre of his nobilitie and gentlemen ; and, after
he had placed him-self in a chaire of estate prepared for him, there came and kneled
before him a graue and aged gentelman, and offred vp a cuppe vnto him of wyne
in a glasse, which the king refused ; after him commes a braue and lustie yong
gentleman and presentes the king with a cup of golde filled with poyson, which the
king accepted, and, drinking the same, immediatly fell downe dead vpon the stage,
and so was carried thence away by his lordes and gentelmen ; and then the musicke
ceased. Hereby was signified, that, as glasse by nature holdeth no poyson, but is
clere and may easely be seen through, ne boweth by any arte : so a faythfull counsellour holdeth no treason, but is playne and open, ne yeldeth to any vndiscrete
affection, but geueth[1] holsome counsell, which the yll-aduised prince refuseth.
The delightfull golde filled with poyson betokeneth flattery, which vnder faire
seeming of pleasaunt wordes beareth deadly poyson, which destroieth[2] the prince
that receyueth it ; as befell in the two brethren, Ferrex and Porrex, who, refusing
the holsome aduise of grave counsellours, credited these yong paracites, and brought
to[3] them-selues death and destruction therby.

[1] C. giueth.   [2] *So* A. C. ; B. destroyed.   [3] C. vnto.

Actus Secundus. Scena Prima.

[The court of FERREX.]

FERREX. HERMON. DORDAN.

FERR.   I meruaile much what reason ledde the king,
My father, thus without all my desert,
To reue me halfe the kingdome, which by course
Of law and nature should remayne to me.
  HER.   If you with stubborne and vntamed pryde   5
Had stood against him in rebelling wise,
Or if with grudging minde you had enuied
So slow a slidyng of his aged yeres,
Or sought before your time to haste the course
Of fatall death vpon his royall head,   10
Or stained your stocke with murder of your kyn,
Some face of reason might perhaps haue seemed
To yelde some likely cause to spoyl ye thus.
  FERR.   The wrekeful gods powre on my cursed head
Eternall plagues and neuer-dying woes,   15
The hellish prince adiudge my dampned ghost
To Tantales thirste, or proude Ixions wheele,
Or cruell gripe to gnaw my growing harte,
To during tormentes and vnquenched flames,
If euer I conceyued so foule a thought   20
To wisshe his ende of life, or yet of reigne!
  DOR.   Ne yet your father, O most noble prince
Did euer thinke so fowle a thing of you;
For he, with more than fathers tendre loue,
While yet the fates do lende him life to rule, —   25
Who long might lyue to see your ruling well, —
To you, my lorde, and to his other sonne,
Lo, he resignes his realme and royaltie:
Which neuer would so wise a prince haue done,
If he had once misdemed that in your harte   30
There euer lodged so vnkinde a thought.

But tendre loue, my lorde, and setled truste
Of your good nature and your noble minde
Made him to place you thus in royall throne,
And now to geue you half his realme to guide, —   35
Yea, and that halfe which in [1] abounding store
Of things that serue to make a welthy realme,
In stately cities, and in frutefull soyle,
In temperate breathing of the milder heauen,
In thinges of nedefull vse, which frendly sea   40
Transportes by traffike from the forreine partes,
In flowing wealth, in honour and in force,
Doth passe the double value of the parte
That Porrex hath allotted to his reigne.
Such is your case; such is your fathers loue.   45
    FERR.   Ah loue, my frendes, — loue wrongs not whom he
        loues!
    DOR.   Ne yet he wrongeth you, that geueth you
So large a reigne ere that the course of time
Bring you to kingdome by discended right,
Which time perhaps might end your time before.   50
    FERR.   Is this no wrong, say you, to reaue from me
My [2] natiue right of halfe so great a realme,
And thus to matche his yonger sonne with me
In egall power and in as great degree?
Yea, and what sonne?   The sonne whose swelling pride   55
Woulde neuer yelde one poinct of reuerence
Whan I the elder and apparaunt heire
Stoode in the likelihode to possesse the whole;
Yea, and that sonne which from his childish age
Enuieth myne honour and doth hate my life.   60
What will he now do, when his pride, his rage,
The mindfull malice of his grudging harte,
Is armed with force, with wealth and kingly state?
    HER.   Was this not wrong, — yea, yll-aduised wrong,
To giue so mad a man so sharpe a sworde?   65
To so great perill of so great missehappe

---

[1] A. C. within.   [2] Co. By; *perhaps a misprint.*

Wide open thus to set so large a waye?
    DOR.   Alas, my lord, what griefull thing is this,
That of your brother you can thinke so ill?
I neuer saw him vtter likelie signe   70
Whereby a man might see or once misdeme
Such hate of you ne such unyelding pride.
Ill is their counsell, shamefull be their ende,
That, raysing such mistrustfull feare in you,
Sowing the seede of such vnkindly hate,   75
Trauaile by treason[1] to destroy you both.
Wise is your brother, and of noble hope,
Worthie to welde a large and mightie realme :
So much a stronger frende haue you therby,
Whose strength is your strength, if you gree in one.   80
    HER.   If Nature and the goddes had pinched so
Their flowing bountie and their noble giftes
Of princelie qualities from you, my lorde,
And powrde them all at ones in wastfull wise
Upon your fathers yonger sonne alone,   85
Perhappes there be that in your preiudice
Would say that birth should yeld to worthinesse.
But, sithe in eche good gift and princelie arte[2]
Ye are his matche, and in the chiefe of all,
In mildenesse and in sobre gouernaunce,   90
Ye farre surmount ; and sith there is in you
Sufficing skill and hopefull towardnesse
To weld the whole and match your elders prayse,
I see no cause why ye should loose the halfe ;
Ne would I wisshe you yelde to such a losse,   95
Lest your milde sufferaunce of so great a wronge
Be deemed cowardishe and simple dreade,
Which shall geue courage to the fierie head
Of your yonge brother to inuade the whole.
While yet, therfore, stickes in the peoples minde   100
The lothed wrong of your disheritaunce ;
And ere your brother haue, by settled power,

      [1] A. C. reason.   [2] A. C. acte.

By guilefull cloke of an alluring showe,
Got him some force and fauour in the[1] realme;
And while the noble queene, your mother, lyues,   105
To worke and practise all for your auaile, —
Attempt redresse by armes, and wreake your-self
Upon his life that gayneth by your losse,
Who nowe, to shame of you, and griefe of vs,
In your owne kingdome triumphes ouer you.   110
Shew now your courage meete for kingly state,[2]
That they which haue auowed to spend theyr goods,
Their landes, their liues and honours in your cause,
May be the bolder to mainteyne your parte,
When they do see that cowarde feare in you   115
Shall not betray ne faile their faithfull hartes.
If once the death of Porrex ende the strife,
And pay the price of his vsurped reigne,
Your mother shall perswade the angry kyng.
The lords, your frends, eke shall appease his rage;   120
For they be wise, and well they can forsee
That ere longe time your aged fathers death
Will bryng a time when you shall well requite
Their frendlie fauour, or their hatefull spite,
Yea, or their slackenesse to auaunce your cause.   125
" Wise men do not so hang on passing state
" Of present princes, chiefely in their age,
" But they will further cast their reaching eye
" To viewe and weye the times and reignes to come."[3]
Ne is it likely, though the kyng be wrothe,   130
That he yet will or that the realme will beare
Extreme reuenge vpon his onely sonne;
Or, if he woulde, what one is he that dare
Be minister to such an enterprise?
And here you be now placed in your owne,   135

---

[1] A. C. this.   [2] A. C. estate.
[3] *Here and elsewhere in the play quotation-marks are used, after the
fashion of the time, to call particular attention to certain sententious
remarks.*

Amyd your frendes, your vassalles and your strength.
We shall defende and kepe your person safe,
Till either counsell turne his tender minde
Or age or sorrow end his werie dayes.
But, if the feare of goddes and secrete grudge   140
Of Natures law, repining at the fact,
Withholde your courage from so great attempt,
Know ye that lust of kingdomes hath no law :
The goddes do beare and well allow in kinges
The thinges [that] [1] they abhorre in rascall routes.   145
" When kinges on slender quarrells runne to warres,
" And then, in cruell and vnkindely wise,
" Commaund theftes, rapes, murders of innocentes,
" The [2] spoile of townes, ruines [3] of mighty realmes, —
" Thinke you such princes do suppose [4] them-selues   150
" Subiect to lawes of Kinde and feare of gods? "
Murders and violent theftes in priuate men [5]
Are hanious crimes and full of foule reproch,
Yet none offence, but deckt with glorious name
Of noble conquestes, in the handes of kinges.   155
But, if you like not yet so hote deuise,
Ne list to take such vauntage of the time,
But, though with perill of your owne estate,[6]
You will not be the first that shall inuade ;
Assemble yet your force for your defence,   160
And, for your safetie, stand vpon your garde.
    DOR.   O Heauen! was there euer heard or knowen
So wicked counsel to a noble prince?
Let me, my lorde, disclose vnto your Grace
This hainous tale, what mischiefe it containes, —   165
Your fathers death, your brothers and your owne,

---

[1] *According to* Co. Dods. Haw., *the reading of* B. *is* thinges that they ;
but according to S.-W. Sm., *it is* thinges they.
    [2] A. C. To.
    [3] A. C. and reignes.
    [4] A. C. suppresse.
    [5] *In* A. C. *the order of lines is* 154, 155, 152, 153.
    [6] A. C. with great perill of your state.

Your present murder and eternall shame.
Heare me, O king, and suffer not to sinke
So high a treason in your princely brest!
   FERR.　The mightie goddes forbid that euer I　　170
Should once conceaue such mischiefe in my hart.
Although my brother hath bereft my realme,
And beare perhappes to me an [1] hatefull minde,
Shall I reuenge it with his death, therefore?
Or shall I so destroy my fathers life　　　175
That gaue me life?　The gods forbid, I say.
Cease you to speake so any more to me;
Ne you, my frend, with answere once repeate
So foule a tale, — in silence let it die!
What lord or subiect shall haue hope at all　　180
That vnder me they safely shall enioye
Their goods, their honours, landes and liberties,
With whom neither one onely brother deare
Ne father dearer could enioye their liues?
But, sith I feare my yonger brothers rage,　　185
And sith perhappes some other man may geue
Some like aduise to moue his grudging head
At mine estate, — which counsell may perchaunce
Take greater force with him than this with me, —
I will in secrete so prepare myselfe　　　190
As, if his malice or his lust to reigne
Breake forth in [2] armes or sodeine violence,
I may withstand his rage and keepe mine owne.

                 [*Exeunt* FERREX *and* HERMON.]

   DOR.　I feare the fatall time now draweth on,
When ciuil hate shall end the noble line　　195
Of famous Brute and of his royall seede.
Great Ioue, defend the mischiefes now at hand!
O that the secretaries wise aduise
Had erst bene heard, when he besought the king
Not to diuide his land nor send his sonnes　　200

   [1] *According to* Sm., A. *has* and.　　　[2] A. C. with.

To further partes from presence of his court,
Ne yet to yelde to them his gouernaunce.
Lo, such are they now in the royall throne
As was rashe [1] Phaeton in Phœbus carre ;
Ne then the fiery stedes did draw the flame   205
With wilder randon through the kindled skies
Than traitorous counsell now will whirle about
The youthfull heades of these vnskilfull kinges.
But I hereof their father will enforme.
The reuerence of him perhappes shall stay   210
The growing mischiefes while they yet are greene.
If this helpe not, then woe vnto them-selues,
The prince, the people, the diuided land !

                                                        [*Exit.*]

Actus Secundus.   Scena Secunda.

[*The court of* PORREX.]

PORREX.   TYNDAR.   PHILANDER.

PORR.   And is it thus? and doth he so prepare
Against his brother as his mortall foe?
And now while yet his aged father liues?
Neither regardes he him nor feares he me?
Warre would he haue? and he shall haue it so!   5
    TYND.   I saw myselfe the great prepared store
Of horse, of armour [2] and of weapon [3] there ;
Ne bring I to my lorde reported tales
Without the ground of seen and searched trouth.
Loe, secrete quarrels runne about his court,   10
To bring the name of you, my lorde, in hate.
Ech man almost can now debate the cause
And aske a reason of so great a wrong :
Why [4] he, so noble and so wise a prince,
Is, as vnworthy, reft his heritage,   15

---

[1] C. that.   [3] A. C. weapons.
[2] A. C. armours,   [4] A. C. While.

And why the king, misseledde by craftie meanes,
Diuided thus his land from course of right.
The wiser sort holde downe their griefull heades.
Eche man withdrawes from talke and company
Of those that haue bene knowne to fauour you.   20
To hide the mischiefe of their meaning there,
Rumours are spread of your preparing here.
The rascall numbers of [the] [1] vnskilfull sort
Are filled with monstrous tales of you and yours.
In secrete I was counselled by my frendes   25
To hast me thence, and brought you, as you know,
Letters from those that both can truely tell
And would not write vnlesse they knew it well.

   PHIL.   My lord, yet ere you moue [2] vnkindly warre,
Send to your brother to demaund the cause.   30
Perhappes some traitorous tales haue filled his eares
With false reportes against your noble Grace :
Which once disclosed shall end the growing strife,
That els, not stayed with wise foresight in time,
Shall hazarde both your kingdomes and your liues.   35
Send to your father eke ; he shall appease
Your kindled mindes, and rid you of this feare.

   PORR.   Ridde me of feare ?   I feare him not at all,
Ne will to him ne to my father send.
If danger were for one to tary there,   40
Thinke ye it safetie to returne againe?
In mischiefes such as Ferrex now intendes,
The wonted courteous lawes to messengers
Are not obserued, which in iuste warre they vse.
Shall I so hazard any one of mine?   45
Shall I betray my trusty frendes [3] to him,
That haue [4] disclosed his treason vnto me?
Let him entreate that feares ! I feare him not.
Or shall I to the king, my father, send?
Yea, and send now, while such a mother liues,   50

<hr />

[1] *Inserted from* C.; *according to* Co., *it is also found in* A.
[2] A. C. nowe.   [3] A. C. friende.   [4] A. C. hath.

That loues my brother and that hateth me?
Shall I geue leasure, by my fonde delayes,
To Ferrex to oppresse me all[1] vnware?
I will not.   But I will inuade his realme
And seeke the traitour prince within his court.   55
Mischiefe for mischiefe is a due reward :
His wretched head shall pay the worthy price
Of this his treason and his hate to me.
Shall I abide, and treate,[2] and send, and pray,
And holde my yelden throate to traitours knife,   60
While I, with valiant minde and conquering force,
Might rid myselfe of foes and winne a realme?
Yet rather, when I haue the wretches head,
Then to the king, my father, will I send.
The bootelesse case may yet appease his wrath ;   65
If not, I will defend me as I may.

                                   [*Exeunt* PORREX *and* TYNDAR.]

   PHIL.   Lo, here the end of these two youthful kings,
The fathers death, the ruine of their realmes ![3]
" O most vnhappy state of counsellers
" That light on so vnhappy lordes and times   70
" That neither can their good aduise be heard,
" Yet must they beare the blames of ill successe."
But I will to the king, their father, haste,
Ere this mischiefe come to the[4] likely end,
That, — if the mindfull wrath of wrekefull gods,   75
Since mightie Ilions fall not yet appeased
With these poore remnantes of the Troian name,
Haue not determined by[5] vnmoued fate
Out of this realme to rase the Brittishe line, —
By good aduise, by awe of fathers name,   80
By force of wiser lordes, this kindled hate
May yet be quentched ere it consume us all.

                                                  [*Exit.*]

---

1 A. C. at.   4 A. C. that.
2 A. C. abide, entreate.   5 A. C. determinedlie.
3 A. C. the reigne of their two realmes.

Chorus.

When youth, not bridled with a guiding stay,
  Is left to randon of their owne delight
And welds whole realmes by force of soueraign sway,[1]
  Great is the daunger of vnmaistred might,
Lest skillesse rage throwe downe with headlong fall
Their lands, their states, their liues, them-selues and al.   6

When growing pride doth fill the swelling brest,
  And gredy lust doth rayse the climbing minde,
Oh hardlie maye the perill be represt:
  Ne feare of angrie goddes, ne lawes kinde,
Ne countries care can fiered hartes restrayne,
Whan force hath armed enuie and disdaine.   12

When kinges of foresette will neglect the rede
  Of best aduise and yelde to pleasing tales
That do their fansies noysome humour feede,
  Ne reason nor regarde of right auailes:
Succeding heapes of plagues shall teach, to late,
To learne the mischiefes of misguided state.   18

Fowle fall the traitour false that vndermines
  The loue of brethren to destroye them both;
Wo to the prince that pliant eare enclynes
  And yeldes his mind to poysonous tale that floweth
From flattering mouth, and woe to wretched land
That wastes it-selfe with ciuil sworde in hand!   24

Loe thus it is, poyson in golde to take
And holsome drinke in homely cuppe forsake.

End of the Second Act.

[1] A. C. fraie.

The Order and Signification of the Domme Shewe before the Thirde Act.

Firste the musicke of flutes began to playe, during which came in vpon the stage a company of mourners all clad in blacke, betokening death and sorowe to ensue vpon the ill-aduised misgouernement and discention of bretherne : as befell vpon the murder of Ferrex by his yonger brother.   After the mourners had passed thryse about the stage, they departed ; and than the musicke ceased.[1]

Actus Tertius.   Scena Prima.

[*The court of* GORBODUC.]

GORBODUC, EUBULUS, AROSTUS [*are present at the opening of the scene*].

PHILANDER [*and*] NUNTIUS [*enter later*].[2]

GORB.   O cruel Fates, O mindful wrath of goddes !
Whose vengeance neither Simois stayned [3] streames
Flouing with bloud of Troian princes slaine,
Nor Phrygian fieldes made ranck with corpses dead
Of Asian kynges and lordes, can yet appease ;   5
Ne slaughter of vnhappie Pryams race,
Nor Ilions fall made leuell with the soile,
Can yet suffice ; but still-continued rage
Pursues our lyues, and from the farthest seas
Doth chase the issues of destroyed Troye.   10
" Oh, no man happie till his ende be seene."
If any flowing wealth and seemyng ioye
In present yeres might make a happy wight,
Happie was Hecuba, the wofullest wretch
That euer lyued to make a myrrour of ;   15
And happie Pryam with his noble sonnes ;
And happie I, till nowe, alas, I see

---

[1] Sm. *gives reading of* A. *as* caused ; Co. *prints* ceased, *without note*.
[2] Sm. *drops the names of* PHILANDER *and the* MESSENGER *from the heading of the scene on the ground that they are not present at the beginning, but it is customary in plays of this date to give the names of all who appear during the scene.*   [3] A. C. streined.

And feele my most vnhappye wretchednesse!
Beholde, my lordes, read ye this letter here!
Loe, it conteins the ruine of our [1] realme,   20
If timelie speede prouide not hastie helpe.
Yet, O ye goddes, if euer wofull kyng
Might moue ye [2] kings of kinges, wreke it on me
And on my sonnes, not on this giltlesse realme!
Send down your wasting flames from wrathful skies   25
Te reue me and my sonnes the hatefull breath!
Read, read, my lordes!   This is the matter why
I called ye nowe to haue your good aduyse.

The letter from DORDAN, *the Counsellour of the elder prince.*

EUBULUS *readeth the letter:*

" My Soueraigne Lord, what I am loth to write,
But lothest am to see, that I am forced   30
By letters nowe to make you vnderstande :
My lord Ferrex, your eldest sonne, misledde
By traitorous fraude [3] of yong vntempred wittes,
Assembleth force agaynst your yonger sonne,
Ne can my counsell yet withdrawe the heate   35
And furyous panges of hys enflamed head.
Disdaine, sayth he, of his disheritance [4]
Armes him to wreke the great pretended wrong
With ciuyll sword vpon his brothers life.
If present helpe do not restraine this rage,   40
This flame will wast your sonnes, your land and you.
  Your Maiesties faithfull and most humble subiect,
                              DORDAN."

  AROS.   O king, appease your griefe and stay your plaint!
Great is the matter, and a wofull case ;
But timely knowledge may bring timely [5] helpe.
Sende for them both vnto your presence here :   45

───────────

[1] C. this.   [4] A. C. inheritaunce.
[2] A. C. you.   [5] C. manly.
[3] A. C. traitours framde.

The reuerence of your honour, age and state,
Your graue aduice, the awe of fathers name,
Shall quicklie knit agayne this broken peace.
And, if in either of my lordes your sonnes
Be suche vntamed and vnyelding pride   50
As will not bende vnto your noble hests, —
If Ferrex, the elder sonne, can beare no peere,
Or Porrex, not content, aspires to more
Than you him gaue aboue his natiue right, —
Ioyne with the iuster side ; so shall you force   55
Them to agree, and holde the lande in stay.
    EUB.   What meaneth this?   Loe, yonder comes in hast
Philander from my lord your yonger sonne.

[Enter PHILANDER.]

    GORB.   The goddes sende ioyfull newes!
    PHIL.   The mightie Ioue
Preserue your Maiestie, O noble king!   60
    GORB.   Philander, welcome !   But how doth my son?
    PHIL.   Your sonne, sir, lyues, and healthie I him left.
But yet, O king, the [1] want of lustfull health
Could not be halfe so griefefull to your Grace
As these most wretched tidynges that I bryng.   65
    GORB.   O heauens, yet more? not [2] ende of woes to me?
    PHIL.   Tyndar, O king, came lately from the court
Of Ferrex to my lord your yonger sonne,
And made reporte of great prepared store
For [3] warre, and sayth that it is wholly ment   70
Agaynst Porrex, for high disdayne that he
Lyues now a king and egall in degree
With him that claimeth to succede the whole
As by due title of discending right.
Porrex is nowe so set on flaming fire,   75
Partely with kindled rage of cruell wrath,
Partely with hope to gaine a realme thereby,
That he in hast prepareth to inuade

<hr>

[1] A. C. this.   [2] A. C. no.   [3] A. C. Of.

His brothers land, and with vnkindely warre
Threatens the murder of your elder sonne ;   80
Ne could I him perswade that first he should
Send to his brother to demaunde the cause,
Nor yet to you to staie this [1] hatefull strife.
Wherfore, sithe there no more I can be hearde,
I come my-selfe now to enforme your Grace,   85
And to beseche you, as you loue the life
And safetie of your children and your realme,
Now to employ your wisdome and your force
To stay this mischiefe ere it be to late.

   GORB.   Are they in armes? would he not sende to [2] me?   90
Is this the honour of a fathers name?
In vaine we trauaile to asswage their mindes,
As if their hartes, whome neither brothers loue
Nor fathers awe nor kingdomes cares can moue,
Our counsels could withdraw from raging heat.   95
Ioue slay them both and end the cursed line !
For, though perhappes feare of such mightie force
As I, my lordes, ioyned with your noble aides,
Maye yet raise shall represse [3] their present heate,
The secret grudge and malice will remayne.   100
The fire not quenched, but kept in close restraint,
Fedde still within, breakes forth with double flame.
Their death and myne must peaze the angrie gods.

   PHIL.   Yelde not, O king, so much to weake dispeire ;
Your sonnes yet lyue, and long, I trust, they shall.   105
If Fates had taken you from earthly life
Before beginning of this ciuyll strife,
Perhaps your sonnes in their vnmaistered youth,
Loose from regarde of any lyuing wight,
Would runne on headlong, with vnbridled race,   110
To their owne death, and ruine of this realme ;
But, sith the gods, that haue the care for kinges,
Of thinges and times dispose the order so
That in your life this kindled flame breakes forth,

        [1] A. C. his.   [2] A. C. for.   [3] A. expresse.

While yet your lyfe, your wisdome and your power   115
May stay the growing mischiefe and represse
The fierie blaze of their inkindled[1] heate,
It seemes — and so ye ought to deeme thereof —
That louyng Ioue hath tempred so the time
Of this debate to happen in your dayes   120
That you yet lyuing may the same appeaze
And adde it to the glory of your latter[2] age,
And they, your[3] sonnes, may learne to liue in peace.
Beware, O king, the greatest harme of all,
Lest by your waylefull plaints your hastened death   125
Yelde larger[4] roume unto their[5] growing rage.
Preserue your life, the onely hope of stay.
And, if your Highnes herein list to vse
Wisdome or force, counsell or knightly aide,
Loe, we, our persons, powers and lyues, are yours :   130
Use us tyll death, O king ! we are your owne.
    EUB.   Loe, here the perill that was erst forsene,
When you, O king, did first deuide your lande
And yelde your present reigne vnto your sonnes.
But now, O noble prince, now is no time   135
To waile and plaine, and wast your wofull life.
Now is the time for present good aduise.
Sorow doth darke the iudgement of the wytte.
" The hart vnbroken, and the courage free
" From feble faintnesse of bootelesse despeire,   140
" Doth either ryse to safetie or renowme
" By noble valure of vnuanquisht minde
" Or yet doth perishe in more happy sort."
Your Grace may send to either of your sonnes
Some one both wise and noble personage,   145
Which with good counsell and with weightie name
Of father shall present before their eyes

---

[1] C. vnkindled.   [4] Co. *gives* B. *as* large; *but* Sm. *has* larger.
[2] *The omission of* latter *would reduce this Alexandrine to a decasyllabic
line, but the word appears in all the editions, as* Co. *points out.*
[3] C. your; A. B. our.   [5] Co. *gives* C. *as* this.

Your hest, your life, your safetie and their owne,
The present mischiefe of their deadly strife ;
And, in the while, assemble you the force   150
Which your commaundement and the spedy hast
Of all my lordes here present can prepare.
The terrour of your mightie power shall stay
The rage of both, or yet of one at lest.

[*Enter* Nuntius.]

NUNT. O king, the greatest griefe that euer prince dyd
              heare,[1]   155
That euer wofull messenger did tell,
That euer wretched lande hath sene before,
I bryng to you.   Porrex, your yonger sonne,
With soden force inuaded hath the lande
That you to Ferrex did allotte to rule,   160
And with his owne most bloudy hand he hath
His brother slaine, and doth possesse his realme.
GORB. O Heauens, send down the flames of your reuenge !
Destroy, I say, with flash of wrekefull fier
The traitour sonne, and then the wretched sire !   165
But let vs go, that yet perhappes I may
Die with reuenge, and peaze the hatefull gods.

[*Exeunt.*]

CHORUS.

The lust of kingdome [2] knowes no sacred faith,
        No rule of reason, no regarde of right,
No kindely loue, no feare of heauens wrath ;
        But with contempt of goddes, and mans despite,   4
Through blodie slaughter doth prepare the waies
        To fatall scepter and accursed reigne.
The sonne so lothes the fathers lingering daies,
        Ne dreades his hand in brothers blode to staine.   8

─────────

[1] *This Alexandrine also is easy to reduce.*
[2] A. C. kingdomes.

O wretched prince, ne doest thou yet recorde
    The yet fresh murthers done within the lande[1]
Of thy forefathers, when the cruell sworde
    Bereft Morgan his life with cosyns hand ?   12
Thus fatall plagues pursue the giltie race,
    Whose murderous hand, imbrued with giltlesse blood,
Askes vengeaunce still[2] before the heauens face,
    With endlesse mischiefes on the cursed broode.   16
The wicked childe thus[3] bringes to wofull sire
    The mournefull plaintes, to wast his very[4] life.
Thus do the cruell flames of ciuyll fier
    Destroy the parted reigne with hatefull strife.
And hence doth spring the well from which doth flow
The dead black streames of mourning, plaints and woe.   22

End of the Third Act.

The Order and Signification of the Domme Shew before the Fourth Act.

    First the musick of howboies began to plaie, during which there came from vnder the stage, as though out of hell, three Furies, Alecto, Megera and Ctesiphone,[5] clad in black garmentes sprinkled with bloud and flames, their bodies girt with snakes, their heds spred with serpentes in-stead of heare ; the one bearing in her hand a snake, the other a whip, and the third a burning firebrand ; ech driuing before them a king and a queene, which, moued by furies, vnnaturally had slaine their owne children : the names of the kings and queenes were these, Tantalus, Medea, Athamas, Ino, Cambises, Althea. After that the Furies and these had passed about the stage thrise, they departed; and than the musicke ceased. Hereby was signified the vnnaturall murders to follow, that is to say, Porrex slaine by his owne mother, and of King Gorboduc and Queene Viden, killed by their owne subiectes.

[1] A. lands.	[4] A. wery; C. weary.
[2] A. C. *omit* still.	[5] *So* A. B. C.
[3] A. C. this.	

Actus Quartus.   Scena Prima.

[*A room in* Gorboduc's *palace.*]

Viden *sola.*

[Vid.]   Why should I lyue, and linger forth my time
In longer life to double my distresse?
O me most wofull wight, whom no mishappe
Long ere this day could haue bereued hence!
Mought not these handes by fortune or by fate   5
Haue perst this brest, and life with iron reft?
Or in this palace here, where I so long
Haue spent my daies, could not that happie houre
Once, once haue hapt in which these hugie frames
With death by fall might haue oppressed me?   10
Or should not this most hard and cruell soile,
So oft where I haue prest my wretched steps,
Sometime had ruthe of myne accursed life,
To rende in twayne, and[1] swallow me therin?
So had my bones possessed now in peace   15
Their happie graue within the closed grounde,
And greadie wormes had gnawen this pyned hart
Without my feeling payne ; so should not now
This lyuing brest remayne the ruthefull tombe
Wherin my hart yelden to death is graued,   20
Nor driery thoughts, with panges of pining griefe,
My dolefúll minde had not afflicted thus.
O my beloued sonne, O my swete childe,
My deare Ferrex, my ioye, my lyues delyght!
Is my beloued[2] sonne, is my sweete childe,   25
My deare Ferrex, my ioye, my lyues delight,
Murdered with cruell death?   O hatefull wretch,
O heynous traitour both to heauen and earth!
Thou, Porrex, thou this damned dede hast wrought!

---

[1] B. *omits* and.   [2] A. C. welbeloued.

Thou, Porrex, thou shalt dearely bye [1] the same!   30
Traitour to kinne and kinde, to sire and me,
To thine owne fleshe, and traitour to thy-selfe,
The gods`on thee in hell shall wreke their [2] wrath,
And here in earth this hand shall take reuenge
On thee, Porrex, thou false and caitife wight!   35
If after bloud so eigre were thy thirst,
And murderous minde had so possessed thee,
If such hard hart of rocke and stonie flint
Liue [3] in thy brest that nothing els could like
Thy cruell tyrantes thought but death and bloud,   40
Wilde sauage beasts, mought not their [4] slaughter serue
To fede thy gredie will, and in the middest
Of their entrailes to staine thy deadly handes
With bloud deserued, and drinke thereof thy fill?
Or, if nought els but death and bloud of man   45
Mought please thy lust, could none in Brittaine land,
Whose hart betorne [5] out of his panting [6] brest
With thine owne hand, or worke what death thou wouldest,
Suffice to make a sacrifice to peaze [7]
That deadly minde and murderous thought in thee,   50
But he who in the selfesame wombe was wrapped
Where thou in dismall hower receiuedst life?
Or, if nedes, nedes, thy [8] hand must [9] slaughter make,
Moughtest thou not haue reached a mortall wound,
And with thy sword haue pearsed this cursed wombe   55
That the accursed Porrex brought to light,
And geuen me a iust reward therefore?
So Ferrex yet [10] sweete life mought haue enioyed,
And to his aged father comfort brought
With some yong sonne, in whom they both might liue.   60

---

[1] A. C. abye.   [6] A. louyng; C. louing.
[2] Co. *gives* B. *as* the; *but* Sm. *has* their.
[3] A. lyued; C. liued.   [7] A. appeaze; C. appease.
[4] A. C. the.   [8] C. this.
[5] Co. *prints* be torne.   [9] C. might.
[10] Sm. *gives* A. C. *as* if; Co. *prints* A. *as* of.

But whereunto waste I this ruthfull speche
To thee that hast thy brothers bloud thus shed?
Shall I still thinke that from this wombe thou sprong?
That I thee bare? or take thee for my sonne?
No, traitour, no!   I thee refuse for mine.   65
Murderer, I thee renounce; thou art not mine.
Neuer, O wretch, this wombe conceiued thee,
Nor neuer bode I painfull throwes for thee.
Changeling to me thou art and not my childe,
Nor to no wight that sparke of pitie knew.   70
Ruthelesse, vnkinde, monster of natures worke,
Thou neuer suckt the milke of womans brest,
But from thy birth the cruell tigers [1] teates
Haue nursed thee; [2] nor yet of fleshe and bloud
Formde is thy hart, but of hard iron wrought;   75
And wilde and desert woods bredde thee to life.
But canst thou hope to scape my iust reuenge?
Or that these handes will not be wrooke [3] on thee?
Doest thou not know that Ferrex mother liues,
That loued him more dearly than her-selfe?   80
And doth she liue, and is not venged on thee?   [*Exit.*]

Actus Quartus.   Scena Secunda.

[*The court of* GORBODUC.]

GORBODUC [*and*] AROSTUS.   EUBULUS, PORREX [*and*] MARCELLA [*enter later*].

GORB.   We marvell much wherto this lingring stay
Falles out so long.   Porrex vnto our court
By order of our letters is returned,
And Eubulus receaued from vs by hest
At his arrivall here to geue him charge   5
Before our presence straight to make repaire, —
And yet we haue [4] no worde whereof he stayes.
AROS.   Lo, where he commes and Eubulus with him.

---

[1] A. C. tigres.   [3] A. wrekte.
[2] A. C. *omit* thee.   [4] C. heare.

[Enter EUBULUS *and* PORREX.]

EUB.   According to your Highnesse hest to me,
Here haue I Porrex brought euen in such sort   10
As from his weried horse he did alight,
For that your Grace did will such hast therein.
  GORB.   We like and praise this spedy will in you
To worke the thing that to your charge we gaue.
Porrex, if we so farre should swarue from kinde   15
And from those¹ boundes which lawe of nature sets
As thou hast done by vile and wretched deede
In cruell murder of thy brothers life,
Our present hand could stay no longer² time,
But straight should bathe this blade in bloud of thee,   20
As iust reuenge of thy detested crime.
No, we should not offend the lawe of kinde
If now this sworde of ours did slay thee here ;
For thou hast murdered him whose heinous death
Euen natures force doth moue vs to reuenge   25
By bloud againe, and³ iustice forceth vs
To measure death for death, thy due desert.
Yet, sithens thou art our childe, and sith as yet
In this hard case what worde thou canst alledge
For thy defence by vs hath not bene heard,   30
We are content to staye our will for that
Which iustice biddes vs presently to worke,
And geue thee leaue to vse thy speche at full,
If ought thou haue to lay for thine excuse.
  PORR.   Neither, O king, I can or will denie   35
But that this hand from Ferrex life hath reft, —
Which fact how much my dolefull hart doth waile,
Oh would it mought as full appeare to sight
As inward griefe doth poure it forth to me !
So yet, perhappes, if euer ruthefull hart,   40
Melting in tears within a manly brest,
Through depe repentance of his bloudy fact,

¹ C. these.   ² A. lenger.   ⁸ A. but.

If euer griefe, if euer wofull man
Might moue regreite with sorrowe of his fault,
I thinke the torment of my mournefull case,   45
Knowen to your Grace as I do feele the same,
Would force euen wrath her-selfe to pitie me.
But, as the water troubled with the mudde
Shewes not the face which els the eye should see,
Euen so your irefull minde with stirred thought   50
Cannot so perfectly discerne my cause.
But this vnhappe, amongest so many happes,
I must content me with, most wretched man,
That to my-selfe I must reserue[1] my woe
In pining thoughtes of mine accursed fact,   55
Since I may not shewe here[2] my smallest griefe
Such as it is, and as my brest endures.
Which I esteeme the greatest miserie
Of all missehappes that fortune now can send :
Not that I rest in hope with plaint and teares   60
To[3] purchase life ; for to the goddes I clepe
For true recorde of this my faithfull speche, —
Neuer this hart shall haue the thoughtfull dread
To die the death that by your Graces dome,
By iust desert, shall be pronounced to me,   65
Nor neuer shall this tongue once spend the[4] speche
Pardon to craue, or seeke by sute to liue.
I meane not this as though I were not touchde
With care of dreadfull death, or that I helde
Life in contempt ; but that I know the minde   70
Stoupes to no dread, although the fleshe be fraile.
And, for my gilt, I yelde the same so great
As in my-selfe I finde a feare to sue
For graunt of life.
　　GORB.　　　　　　In vaine, O wretch, thou shewest
A wofull hart !　Ferrex now lies in graue,   75
Slaine by thy hand.

---

[1] A. C. referre.　　　[3] A. C. Should.　　　[4] A. C. this.
[2] Co. *says* B, *omits* here : *but* Sm. *prints it, without remark.*

PORR.   Yet this, O father, heare;
And then I end.   Your Majestie well knowes
That, when my brother Ferrex and my-selfe
By your owne hest were ioyned in gouernance
Of this your Graces realme of Brittaine land,   80
I neuer sought nor trauailled for the same,
Nor[1] by my-selfe, nor by no frend I wrought,
But from your Highnesse will alone it sprong,
Of your most gracious goodnesse bent to me.
But how my brothers hart euen then repined   85
With swollen disdaine against mine egall rule,
Seing that realm which by discent should grow
Wholly to him allotted halfe to me,
Euen in your Highnesse court he now remaines,
And with my brother then in nearest place,   90
Who can recorde what proofe thereof was shewde
And how my brothers enuious hart appearde.
Yet I, that iudged it my part to seeke
His fauour and good will, and loth to make
Your Highnesse know the thing which should haue brought 95
Grief to your Grace, and your offence to him,
Hoping my[2] earnest sute should soone haue wonne
A louing hart within a brothers brest,
Wrought in that sort that for a pledge of loue
And faithful hart, he gaue to me his hand.   100
This made me thinke that he had banisht quite
All rancour from his thought, and bare to me
Such hartie loue as I did owe to him.
But, after once we left your Graces court,
And from your Highness presence liued apart,   105
This egall rule still, still, did grudge him so,
That now those enuious sparkes which erst lay raked
In liuing cinders of dissembling brest
Kindled so farre within his hart[3] disdaine
That longer could he not refraine from proofe   110
Of secrete practise to depriue me[4] life

---

[1] A. C. Or.   [2] A. C. by.   [3] A. hartes.   [4] A. my.

By poysons force ; and had bereft me so,
If mine owne seruant, hired to this fact
And moued by trouth with hate[1] to worke the same,
In[2] time had not bewrayed it vnto me.   115
Whan thus I sawe the knot of loue vnknitte,
All honest league and faithfull promise broke,
The law of kinde and trouth thus rent in twaine,
His hart on mischiefe set, and in his brest
Blacke treason hid, then, then did I despeire   120
That euer time could winne him frend to me.
Then saw I how he smiled with slaying knife
Wrapped vnder cloke, then saw I depe deceite
Lurke in his face and death prepared for me.
Euen nature moued me than to holde my life   125
More deare to me than his, and bad this hand, —
Since by his life my death must nedes ensue,
And by his death my life to[3] be preserued, —
To shed his bloud, and seeke my safetie so ;
And wisedome willed me without protract   130
In spedie wise to put the same in vre.
Thus haue I tolde the cause that moued me
To worke my brothers death ; and so I yeld
My life, my death, to iudgement of your Grace.

    GORB.   Oh cruel wight, should any cause preuaile   135
To make thee staine thy hands with brothers bloud?
But what of thee we will resolue to doe
Shall yet remaine vnknowen.   Thou in the meane
Shalt from our royall presence banisht be
Untill our princely pleasure furder shall   140
To thee be shewed.   Depart therefore our sight,
Accursed childe !   [*Exit* PORREX.]   What cruell destenie,
What froward fate hath sorted vs this chaunce,
That euen in those where we should comfort find,
Where our delight now in our aged dayes   145
S[h]ould rest and be, euen there our onely griefe

---

[1] Dods. Co. *say* B. *omits* hate.
[2] A. If.   [3] Dods. Co. *say* B. *has* mote.

And depest sorrowes to abridge our life,
Most pyning cares and deadly thoughts do grow? [1]
   AROS.   Your Grace should now in these graue yeres of
      yours
Haue found ere this the price of mortall ioyes :   150
How short they be, how fading here in earth,
How full of chaunge, how brittle our estate,
Of nothing sure saue onely of the death,
To whom both man and all the world doth owe
Their end at last.   Neither should [2] natures power   155
In other sort against your hart preuaile
Than as the naked hand whose stroke assayes
The armed brest, where force doth light in vaine.
   GORB.   Many can yelde right sage and graue [3] aduise
Of pacient sprite to others wrapped in woe,   160
And can in speche both rule and conquere kinde,
Who, if by proofe they might feele natures force,
Would shew them-selues men, as they are in-dede,
Which now wil nedes be gods.   But what doth meane
The sory chere of her that here doth come?   165

               [*Enter* MARCELLA.]

   MARC.   Oh where is ruth or where is pitie now?
Whither is gentle hart and mercy fled?
Are they exiled out of our stony brestes,
Neuer to make returne?   Is all the world
Drowned in bloud and soncke in crueltie?   170
If not in women mercy may be found,
If not, alas! within the mothers brest
To her owne childe, to her owne fleshe and bloud,
If ruthe be banished thence, if pitie there
May haue no place, if there no gentle hart   175
Do liue and dwell, where should we seeke it then?
   GORB.   Madame, alas! what meanes your woful tale?
   MARC.   O sillie woman I, why to this houre
Haue Kinde and Fortune thus deferred my breath,

---

   [1] A. C. graue.   [2] A. C. shall.   [3] A. C. graue and sage.

That I should liue to see this dolefull day?   180
Will euer wight beleue that such hard hart
Could rest within the cruell mothers brest
With her owne hand to slay her onely sonne?
But out! alas! these eyes behelde the same,
They saw the driery sight, and are become   185
Most ruthfull recordes of the bloudy fact.
Porrex, alas! is by his mother slaine,
And with her hand — a wofull thing to tell!—
While slumbring on his carefull bed he restes,
His hart, stabde[1] in with knife, is reft of life.   190
   GORB.   O Eubulus, oh draw this sword of ours,
And pearce this hart with speed!   O hatefull light,
O lothsome life, O sweete and welcome death!
Deare Eubulus, worke this we thee besech.
   EUB.   Pacient your Grace, perhappes he liueth yet,   195
With wound receaued, but not of certaine death.
   GORB.   O let us then repayre vnto the place,
And see if Porrex liue, or[2] thus be slaine.

        [Exeunt GORBODUC *and* EUBULUS.]

   MARC.   Alas, he liueth not!   It is to true
That, with these eyes, of him a perelesse prince,   200
Sonne to a king, and in the flower of youth,
Euen with a twinke[3] a senselesse stocke I saw.
   AROS.   O damned deede!
   MARC.   But heare hys[4] ruthefull end!
The noble prince, pearst with the sodeine wound,
Out of his wretched slumber hastely start,   205
Whose strength now fayling, straight he ouerthrew, —
When in the fall his eyes euen new[5] vnclosed
Behelde the queene, and cryed to her for helpe.
We then, alas! the ladies which that time
Did there attend, seing that heynous deede,   210

<hr>

[1] A. C. stalde.   [3] Dods. Co. *say* B. *has* twinkle.
[2] A. C. if that Porrex or.   [4] A. C. this.
[5] Dods. Co. *say* B. *has* now; Sm. *says* B. new, C. now.

And hearing him oft call the wretched name
Of mother, and to crye to her for aide
Whose direfull hand gaue him the mortall wound,
Pitying — alas ! for nought els could we do, —
His ruthefull end, ranne to the wofull bedde,   215
Dispoyled straight his brest, and, all we might,
Wiped in vaine with napkins next at hand
The sodeine streames of bloud that flushed fast
Out of the gaping wound.   O what a looke,
O what a ruthefull stedfast eye, me thought,   220
He fixt vpon my face, which to my death
Will neuer part fro me, when with a braide
A deepe-fet sigh he gaue, and therewithall
Clasping his handes, to heauen he cast his sight !
And straight — pale death pressing within his face —   225
The flying ghost his mortall corpes forsooke.
   Aros.   Neuer did age bring forth so vile a fact !
   Marc.   O hard and cruell happe, that thus assigned
Unto so worthy a wight so wretched end !
But most hard, cruell hart, that could consent   230
To lend the hatefull destenies that hand
By which, alas, so heynous crime was wrought !
O queene of adamant, O marble brest,
If not the fauour of his comely face,
If not his princely chere and countenance,   235
His valiant actiue armes, his manly brest,
If not his faire and seemely personage,
His noble limmes in such proportion[1] cast
As would have wrapt a sillie womans thought, —
If this mought not haue moued thy bloudy hart   240
And that most cruell hand the wretched weapon
Euen to let fall, and kiste him in the face,
With teares for ruthe to reaue such one by death, —
Should nature yet consent to slay her sonne ?
O mother, thou to murder thus thy childe !   245
Euen Ioue with iustice must with lightning flames

---

[1] A. preparacion.

From heauen send downe some strange reuenge on thee.
Ah noble prince, how oft haue I behelde
Thee mounted on thy fierce and traumpling stede,
Shining in armour bright before the tilt,   250
And with thy mistresse sleue tied on thy helme,
And charge thy staffe to please thy ladies eye,
That bowed the head-peece of thy frendly foe!
How oft in armes on horse to bend the mace!
How oft in armes on foote to breake the sworde!   255
Which neuer now these eyes may see againe.
    AROS.   Madame, alas, in vaine these plaints are shed!
Rather with me depart, and helpe to swage [1]
The thoughtfull griefes that in the aged king
Must needes by nature growe, by death of this   260
His onely sonne, whom he did holde so deare.
    MARC.   What wight is that which saw that I did see,
And could refraine to waile with plaint and teares?
Not I, alas! that hart is not in me.
But let vs goe, for I am greued anew   265
To call to minde the wretched fathers woe.   *[Exeunt.]*

CHORUS.

Whan greedy lust in royall seate to reigne
    Hath reft all care of goddes and eke of men,
And cruell hart, wrath, treason and disdaine
    Within [2] ambicious brest are lodged, then
Beholde how mischiefe wide her-selfe displayes,
And with the brothers hand the brother slayes.   6

When bloud thus shed doth staine the [3] heauens face,
    Crying to Ioue for vengeance of the deede,
The mightie God euen moueth from his place,
    With wrath to wreke : then sendes he forth with spede
The dreadfull Furies, daughters of the night,
    With serpentes girt, carying the whip of ire,
With heare of stinging snakes, and shining bright

---

[1] A. C. asswage.   [2] A. C. Within the.   [3] A. C. this.

With flames and bloud, and with a brand of fire.
These, for reuenge of wretched murder done,
Do make [1] the mother kill her onely sonne.   16

Blood asketh blood, and death must death requite :
    Ioue by his iust and euerlasting dome
Iustly hath euer so requited it.
    The [2] times before recorde, and times to come
Shall finde it true, and so doth present proofe
Present before our eyes for our behoofe.   22

O happy wight that suffres not the snare
    Of murderous minde to tangle him in blood ;
And happy he that can in time beware
    By others harmes, and turne it to his good ;
But wo to him that, fearing not to offend,
Doth serue his lust and will not see the end.   28

End of the Fourth Act.

The Order and Signification of the Domme Shew before the Fifth Act.

First the drommes and fluites began to sound, during which there came forth
vpon the stage a company of hargabusiers and of armed men all in order of
battaile.   These, after their peeces discharged, and that the armed men had three
times marched about the stage, departed ; and then the drommes and fluits did
cease.   Hereby was signified tumults, rebellions, armes and ciuill warres to follow : as fell in the realme of Great Brittayne, which by the space of fiftie yeares
and more continued in ciuill warre betwene the Nobilitie after the death of King
Gorboduc and of his issues, for want of certayne limitacion in the [3] succession
of the crowne, till the time of Dunwallo Mollmutius, who reduced the land to
monarchie.

Actus Quintus.   Scena Prima.

[*The court of* GORBODUC.]

CLOTYN.   MANDUD.   GWENARD.   FERGUS.   EUBULUS.

CLO.   Did euer age bring forth such tirants harts ?
The brother hath bereft the brothers life,

---

[1] C. Dooth cause.   [2] A. C. These.   [3] B. *omits* the.

The mother she hath died her cruell handes
In bloud of her owne sonne, and now at last
The people, loe! forgetting trouth and loue,   5
Contemning quite both law and loyall hart,
Euen they haue slaine their soueraigne lord and queene.

    MAND.   Shall this their traitorous crime vnpunished rest?
Euen yet they cease not, caryed on[1] with rage,
In their rebellious routes to threaten still   10
A new bloud-shed vnto the princes kinne,
To slay them all, and to vproote the race
Both of the king and queene: so are they moued
With Porrex death, wherin they falsely charge
The giltlesse king, without desert at[2] all,   15
And traitorously haue murdered him therfore,
And eke the queene.

    GWEN.   Shall subjectes dare with force
To worke reuenge vpon their princes fact?
Admit the worst that may, — as sure in this
The deede was fowle, the queene to slay her sonne, —   20
Shall yet the subiect seeke to take the sworde,
Arise agaynst his lord, and slay his king?
O wretched state, where those rebellious hartes
Are not rent out euen from their liuing breastes,
And with the body throwen vnto the foules   25
As carrion foode, for terrour of the rest!

    FERG.   There can no punishment be thought to great
For this so greuous cryme; let spede therfore
Be vsed therin, for it behoueth so.

    EUB.   Ye all, my lordes, I see, consent in one,   30
And I as one consent with ye in all.
I holde it more than neede with sharpest law
To punish this[3] tumultuous bloudy rage;
For nothing more may shake the common state
Than sufferance of vproares without redresse,   35
Wherby how some kingdomes of mightie power,

---

[1] A. C. out.   [3] A. C. the.
[2] Dods. Co. *say* B. *omits* at.

After great conquestes made, and florishing
In fame and wealth, haue ben to ruine brought,
I pray to Ioue that we may rather wayle
Such happe in them than witnesse in our-selues.   40
Eke fully with the duke my minde agrees,
[1] That no cause serues wherby the subiect maye
Call to accompt the doynges of his prince,
Muche lesse in bloode by sworde to worke reuenge,
No more then maye the hande cut of the heade.   45
In acte nor speache, no, not in secrete thoughte,
The subiect maye rebell against his lorde,
Or iudge of him that sittes in Cæsars seate,
With grudging mind to [2] damne those he mislikes.
Though kinges forget to gouerne as they ought,   50
Yet subiectes must obey as they are bounde.
But now, my lordes, before ye farder wade,
Or spend your speach what sharpe reuenge shall fall
By iustice plague on these rebellious wightes,
Me thinkes ye rather should first search the way   55
By which in time the rage of this vproare
Mought be repressed and these great tumults ceased.
Euen yet the life of Brittayne land doth hang
In traitours balaunce of vnegall weight.
Thinke not, my lordes, the death of Gorboduc,   60
Nor yet Videnaes bloud will cease their rage.
Euen our owne lyues, our wiues and children deare, [3]
Our countrey, dearest of all, in daunger standes
Now to be spoiled, now, now, made desolate,
And by our-selues a conquest to ensue.   65
For, geue once swey vnto the peoples lustes
To rush forth on, and stay them not in time,
And, as the streame that rowleth downe the hyll,
So will they headlong ronne with raging thoughtes
From bloud to bloud, from mischiefe vnto moe,   70
To ruine of the realm, them-selues, and all, —

[1] *Lines 42–49 omitted in* B.; *see Notes.*
[2] A. C. doo.   [3] A. C. *omit* deare.

So giddy are the common peoples mindes,
So glad of chaunge, more wauering than the sea.
Ye see, my lordes, what strength these rebelles haue,
What hugie nombre is assembled still;   75
For, though the traiterous fact for which they rose
Be wrought and done, yet lodge they still in field;
So that how farre their furies yet will stretch
Great cause we haue to dreade.   That we may seeke
By present battaile to represse their power,   80
Speede must we vse to leuie force therfore;
For either they forthwith will mischiefe worke
Or their rebellious roares forthwith will [1] cease:
These violent thinges may haue no lasting long. [2]
Let vs therfore vse this for present helpe,   85
Perswade by gentle speach, and offre grace
With gift of pardon, saue vnto the chiefe,
And that vpon condicion that forthwith
They yelde the captaines of their enterprise,
To beare such guerdon of their traiterous fact   90
As may be both due vengeance to them-selues
And holsome terrour to posteritie.
This shall, I thinke, scatter [3] the greatest part
That now are holden with desire of home,
Weried in field with cold of winters nightes,   95
And some, no doubt, striken with dread of law.
When this is once proclamed, it shall make
The captaines to mistrust the multitude,
Whose safetie biddes them to betray their heads, —
And so much more bycause the rascall routes   100
In thinges of great and perillous attemptes
Are neuer trustie to the noble race.
And, while we treate and stand on termes of grace,
We shall both stay their furies rage the while
And eke gaine time, whose onely helpe sufficeth   105
Withouten warre to vanquish rebelles power.

<hr>

[1] Dods. Co. *say* C. *has* must.
[2] A. C. londe.   [3] A. C. flatter.

In the meane while make you in redynes
Such band of horsemen as ye may prepare.
Horsemen, you know, are not the commons strength
But are the force and store of noble men ;   110
Wherby the vnchosen and vnarmed sort
Of skillesse [1] rebelles, whome none other power
But nombre makes to be of dreadfull force,
With sodeyne brunt may quickely be opprest.
And, if this gentle meane of proffered grace   115
With stubborne hartes cannot so farre auayle
As to asswage their desperate courages,
Then do I wish such slaughter to be made
As present age and eke posteritie
May be adrad with horrour of reuenge   120
That iustly then shall on these rebelles fall.
This is, my lords,[2] the sum of mine aduise.

   CLO.   Neither this case admittes debate at large,
And, though it did, this speach that hath ben sayd
Hath well abridged the tale I would haue tolde.   125
Fully with Eubulus do I consent
In all that he hath sayd ; and, if the same
To you, my lordes, may seeme for best aduise,
I wish that it should streight be put in vre.

   MAND.   My lordes, than let vs presently depart   130
And follow this that liketh vs so well.

[Exeunt all but FERGUS.]

   FERG.   If euer time to gaine a kingdome here
Were offred man, now it is offred mee.
The realme is reft both of their king and queene,
The ofspring of the prince is slaine and dead,   135
No issue now remaines, the heire vnknowen ;
The people are in armes and mutynies ;
The nobles they are busied how to cease
These great rebellious tumultes and vproares ;
And Brittayne land, now desert left alone   140

----

[1] A. C. skillishe.   [2] *So* A. C.; B. lord.

Amyd these broyles, vncertayne where to rest,
Offers her-selfe vnto that noble hart
That will or dare pursue to beare her crowne.
Shall I that am the Duke of Albanye,
Discended from that line of noble bloud   145
Which hath so long florished in worthy fame
Of valiaunt hartes, such as in noble brestes
Of right should rest aboue the baser sort,
Refuse to venture [1] life to winne a crowne?
Whom shall I finde enmies that will withstand   150
My fact herein, if I attempt by armes
To seeke the same [2] now in these times of broyle?
These dukes power can hardly well appease
The people that already are in armes.
But, if perhappes my force be once in field,   155
Is not my strength in power aboue the best
Of all these lordes now left in Brittayne land?
And, though they should match me with power of men,
Yet doubtfull is the chaunce of battailles ioyned.
If victors of the field we may depart,   160
Ours is the scepter then of Great Brittayne;
If slayne amid the playne this body lye, [3]
Mine enmies yet shall not deny me this,
But that I dyed geuing the noble charge
To hazarde life for conquest of a crowne.   165
Forthwith therefore will I in post depart
To Albanye and raise in armour there
All power I can; and here my secret friendes
By secret practise shall sollicite still
To seeke to wynne to me the peoples hartes.   170
                                                    Exit.

[1] A. C. aduenture.
[2] A. C. Fame.
[3] A. C. be.

Actus Quintus. Scena Secunda.

[The court.]

EUBULUS *[alone]*. CLOTYN, MANDUD, GWENARD, AROSTUS, *[and]* NUN-
TIUS *[enter later]*.

[EUB.]   O Ioue, how are these peoples harts abusde!
What blind fury thus headlong caries them,
That, though so many bookes, so many rolles,
Of auncient time recorde what greuous plagues
Light on these rebelles aye, and though so oft   5
Their eares haue heard their aged fathers tell
What iuste reward these traitours still receyue, —
Yea, though them-selues haue sene depe death and bloud
By strangling cord and slaughter of the sword
To such assigned, yet can they not beware,   10
Yet can [1] not stay their lewde [2] rebellious handes,
But, suffring too [3] fowle treason to distaine
Their wretched myndes, forget their loyall hart,
Reiect all truth, and rise against their prince?
A ruthefull case, that those, whom duties bond,[4]   15
Whom grafted law by nature, truth and faith
Bound to preserue their countrey and their king,
Borne to defend their common-wealth and prince, —
Euen they should geue consent thus to subuert
Thee,[5] Brittaine land, and from thy [5] wombe should spring,[6]   20
O native soile, those that will needs destroy
And ruyne thee, and eke them-selues in fine !
For lo, when once the dukes had offred grace
Of pardon sweete, the multitude missledde
By traitorous fraude of their vngracious heades,   25
One sort that saw the dangerous successe
Of stubborne standing in rebellious warre
And knew the difference of princes power

---

[1] A. C. can they.   [4] A. C. bounde.
[2] A. C. *omit* lewde.   [5] A. C. the.
[3] A. to; C. too; B. loe.   [6] A. C. bring.

From headlesse nombre of tumultuous routes,
Whom common countreies care and priuate feare   30
Taught to repent the errour [1] of their rage,
Layde handes vpon the captaines of their band
And brought them bound vnto the mightie dukes ;
An-other [2] sort, not trusting yet so well
The truth of pardon, or mistrusting more   35
Their owne offence than that they could conceiue
Such hope of pardon for so foule misdede,
Or for that they their captaines could not yeld,
Who, fearing to be yelded, fled before,
Stale home by silence of the secret night ;   40
The thirde, vnhappy and enraged [3] sort
Of desperate hartes, who, stained in princes bloud,
From trayterous furour could not be withdrawen
By loue, by law, by grace, ne yet by feare,
By proffered life, ne yet by threatned death,   45
With mindes hopelesse of life, dreadlesse of death,
Carelesse of countrey and awelesse of God,
Stoode bent to fight as Furies did them moue,
With violent death to close their traiterous life.
These all by power of horsemen were opprest,   50
And with reuenging sworde slayne in the field
Or with the strangling cord hangd on the tree,
Where yet their [4] carryen carcases do preach [5]
The fruites that rebelles reape of their vproares
And of the murder of their sacred prince.   55
But loe, where do approche the noble dukes
By whom these tumults haue ben thus appeasde.

[*Enter* CLOTYN, MANDUD, GWENARD *and* AROSTUS.]

    CLO.   I thinke the world will now at length beware,
And feare to put on armes agaynst their prince.
    MAND.   If not, those trayterous hartes that dare [6] rebell,   60

---

[1] A. C. terrour.   [4] A. C. the.
[2] B. And other.   [5] A. C. proche.
[3] A. C. vnraged.   [6] A. doo.

Let them beholde the wide and hugie fieldes
With bloud and bodies spread of[1] rebelles slayne,
The lofty[2] trees clothed with the[3] corpses dead
That strangled with the corde do hang theron.

    AROS. A iust rewarde, such as all times before   65
Haue euer lotted to those wretched folkes.

    GWEN. But what meanes he that commeth here so fast?

[Enter NUNTIUS.]

    NUNT. My lordes, as dutie and my trouth doth moue
And of my countrey worke a[4] care in mee,
That, if the spending of my breath auailed   70
To do the seruice that my hart desires,
I would not shunne to imbrace a present death,
So haue I now, in that wherein I thought
My trauayle mought performe some good effect,
Ventred my life to bring these tydinges here :   75
Fergus, the mightie Duke of Albanye,
Is now in armes, and lodgeth in the fielde
With twentie thousand men ; hether he bendes
His spedy marche, and mindes to inuade the crowne ;
Dayly he gathereth strength, and spreads abrode   80
That to this realme no certeine heire remaines,
That Brittayne land is left without a guide,
That he the scepter seekes for nothing els
But to preserue the people and the land,
Which now remaine as ship without a sterne.   85
Loe, this is that which I haue here to say.[5]

    CLO. Is this his fayth? and shall he falsely thus
Abuse the vauntage of vnhappie times?
O wretched land, if his outragious pride,
His cruell and vntempred wilfulnesse,   90
His deepe dissembling shewes of false pretence,
Should once attaine the crowne of Brittaine land!

---

1 A. C. with.   4 A. C. and.
2 A. C. lustie.   5 A. C. hereto saide.
3 A. C. *omit* the.

Let vs, my lordes, with timely force resist
The new attempt of this our common foe,
As we would quench the flames of common fire.   95
    MAND.   Though we remaine without a certain prince
To weld the realme or guide the wandring rule,
Yet now the common mother of vs all,
Our natiue land, our countrey, that conteines
Our wiues, children,[1] kindred, our-selues, and all   100
That euer is or may be deare to man,
Cries vnto vs to helpe our-selues and her.
Let us aduaunce our powers to represse
This growing foe of all our liberties.
    GWEN.   Yea, let vs so, my lordes, with hasty speede.   105
And ye, O goddes, send vs the welcome death,
To shed our bloud in field, and leaue us not
In lothesome life to lenger out our dayes [2]
To see the hugie heapes of these vnhappes
That now roll downe vpon the wretched land,   110
Where emptie place of princely gouernaunce,
No certaine stay now left of doubtlesse heire,
Thus leaue this guidelesse realme an open pray
To endlesse stormes and waste of ciuill warre!
    AROS.   That ye, my lordes, do so agree in one   115
To saue your countrey from the violent reigne
And wrongfully vsurped tyrannie
Of him that threatens conquest of you all,
To saue your realme, and in this realme your-selues,
From forreine thraldome of so proud a prince,   120
Much do I prayse, and I besech the goddes
With happy honour to requite it you.
But, O my lordes, sith now the heauens wrath
Hath reft this land the issue of their prince,
Sith of the body of our late soueraigne lorde   125
Remaines no moe since the yong kinges be slaine,
And of the title of discended crowne

---

[1] *The rhythm of the line would be improved, as* Kittredge *suggests, by reading:* Our children, wiues.   [2] A. lyues; C. liues.

Uncertainly the diuerse mindes do thinke
Euen of the learned sort, and more vncertainly
Will parciall fancie and affection deeme, —   130
But most vncertainly will climbing pride
And hope of reigne withdraw to[1] sundry partes
The doubtfull right and hopefull lust to reigne, —
When once this noble seruice is atchieued
For Brittaine land, the mother of ye all,   135
When once ye haue with armed force represt
The proude attemptes of this Albanian prince
That threatens thraldome to your natiue land,
When ye shall vanquishers returne from field
And finde the princely state an open pray   140
To gredie lust and to vsurping power,
Then, then, my lordes, if euer kindly care
Of auncient honour of your auncesters,
Of present wealth and noblesse of your stockes,
Yea, of the liues and safetie yet to come   145
Of your deare wiues, your children and your-selues,
Might moue your noble hartes with gentle ruth,
Then, then, haue pitie on the torne estate,
Then helpe to salue the welneare hopelesse sore!
Which ye shall do, if ye your-selues withholde   150
The slaying knife from your owne mothers throate.
Her shall you saue, and you and yours in her,
If ye shall all with one assent forbeare
Once to lay hand or take vnto your-selues
The crowne, by colour of pretended right   155
Or by what other meanes so-euer it be,
Till first by common councell of you all
In Parliament the regall diademe
Be set in certaine place of gouernaunce.
In which your Parliament, and in your choise,   160
Preferre the right, my lordes, without[2] respect
Of strength or[3] frendes or what-soeuer cause
That may set forward any others part;

---

[1] A. C. from.   [2] B. with.   [3] A. C. of.

For right will last, and wrong cannot endure.
Right meane I his or hers vpon whose name　　165
The people rest by meane of natiue line
Or by the vertue of some former lawe,
Already made their title to aduaunce.
Such one, my lordes, let be your chosen king,
Such one, so borne within your natiue land,　　170
Such one preferre, and in no wise admitte
The heauie yoke of forreine gouernaunce.
Let forreine titles yelde to publike wealth ;
And with that hart wherewith ye now prepare
Thus to withstand the proude inuading foe,　　175
With that same hart, my lordes, keepe out also
Vnnaturall thraldome of strangers reigne,
Ne suffer you against the rules of kinde
Your mother land to serue a forreine prince.
　　EUB.　Loe here the end of Brutus royall line,　　180
And loe the entry to the wofull wracke
And vtter ruine of this noble realme !
The royall king and eke his sonnes are slaine,
No ruler restes within the regall seate,
The heire, to whom the scepter longes, unknowen ;　　185
That to eche [1] force of forreine princes power
Whom vauntage of our [2] wretched state may moue [3]
By sodeine armes to gaine so riche a realme,
And to the proud and gredie minde at home
Whom blinded lust to reigne leades to aspire,　　190
Loe, Brittaine realme is left an open pray,
A present spoyle by conquest to ensue !
Who seeth not now how many rising mindes
Do feede their thoughts with hope to reach a realme?
And who will not by force attempt to winne　　195
So great a gaine, that hope perswades to haue?
A simple colour shall for title serue :
Who winnes the royall crowne will want no right,

[1] C. the.　　　　[3] A. C. *omit* may moue.
[2] A. C. your.

Nor such as shall display by long discent
A lineall race to proue him lawfull[1] king.   200
In the meane-while these ciuil armes shall rage,
And thus a thousand mischiefes shall vnfolde,
And farre and neare spread the, O Brittaine Land!
All right and lawe shall cease; and he that had
Nothing to-day to-morrowe shall enioye   205
Great heapes of golde,[2] and he that flowed in wealth,
Loe, he shall be bereft[3] of life and all;
And happiest he that then possesseth least.
The wiues shall suffer rape, the maides defloured,
And children fatherlesse shall weepe and waile.   210
With fire and sworde thy natiue folke shall perishe.
One kinsman shall bereaue an-others life;
The father shall vnwitting slay the sonne;
The sonne shall slay the sire and know it not.
Women and maides the cruell souldiers sword   215
Shall perse to death, and sillie children, loe,
That playing[4] in the streetes and fieldes are found,
By violent hand shall close their latter day.
Whom shall the fierce and bloudy souldier
Reserue to life? whom shall he spare from death?   220
Euen thou, O wretched mother, halfe aliue,
Thou shalt beholde thy deare and onely childe
Slaine with the sworde while he yet suckes thy brest:
Loe, giltlesse bloud shall thus eche-where be shed.
Thus shall the wasted soile yelde forth no fruite,   225
But dearth and famine shall possesse the land.
The townes shall be consumed and burnt with fire,
The peopled cities shall waxe desolate;
And thou, O Brittaine,[5] whilome in renowme,
Whilome in wealth and fame, shalt thus be torne,   230
Dismembred thus, and thus be rent in twaine,
Thus wasted and defaced, spoyled and destroyed.

---

[1] A. C. him-selfe a.   [4] B. C. play.
[2] A. C. good.   [5] A. C. O Brittaine Land.
[3] A. C. reft.

These be the fruites your ciuil warres will bring.
Hereto it commes when kinges will not consent
To graue aduise, but followe wilfull will.   235
This is the end when in fonde [1] princes hartes
Flattery preuailes, and sage rede hath no place.
These are the plages when murder is the meane
To make new heires vnto the royall crowne.
Thus wreke the gods when that the mothers wrath   240
Nought but the bloud of her owne childe may swage.
These mischiefes spring [2] when rebells will arise
To worke reuenge and iudge their princes fact.
This, this ensues when noble-men do faile
In loyall trouth, and subiectes will be kinges.   245
And this doth growe when, loe, vnto the prince
Whom death or sodeine happe of life bereaues
No certaine heire [3] remaines, such certaine heire
As not all-onely is the rightfull heire
But to the realme is so made knowen [4] to be,   250
And trouth therby vested in subiectes hartes
To owe fayth there where right is knowen to rest.
Alas, in Parliament what hope can be,
When is of Parliament no hope at all,
Which, though it be assembled by consent,   255
Yet is not likely with consent to end?
While eche one for him-selfe or for his frend,
Against his foe, shall trauaile what he may,
While now the state left open to the man
That shall with greatest force inuade the same,   260
Shall fill ambicious mindes with gaping hope,
When will they once with yelding hartes agree?
Or, in the while, how shall the realme be vsed?
No, no; then Parliament should haue bene holden,
And certeine heirs appointed to the crowne,   265
To stay the [5] title of [6] established right

---

[1] A. C. yonge.
[2] A. C. springes.
[3] A. C. certeintie.
[4] A. vnknowen; C. vnknowne.
[5] A. C. their.
[6] Dods. Co. *say* B. *has* on.

And in the people plant [1] obedience,[2]
While yet the prince did liue, whose name and power
By lawfull sommons and authoritie
Might make a Parliament to be of force,   270
And might haue set the state [3] in quiet stay.
But now, O happie man whom [4] spedie death
Depriues of life, ne is enforced to see
These hugie mischiefes and these miseries,
These ciuil warres, these murders and these wronges   275
Of iustice.   Yet must God [5] in fine restore
This noble crowne vnto the lawfull heire ;
For right will always liue and rise at length,
But wrong can neuer take deepe roote, to last.

THE END OF THE TRAGEDY.

[1] A. C. plant the people in.   [4] C. what.
[2] *Misprinted* obedienhos *in* Sm.   [5] A. C. Ioue.
[3] C. Realme.

CAMPASPE

Played before the Queenes
Maieſtie on *Twelfe*
day at Night:

By her MAIESTIES
Children, and the Chil-
dren of *Paules.*

Vignette, with
motto: " *Mollia*
cum duris "

LONDON,
Printed by *William Stansby,*
for *Edward Blount,*
1632.

Printed from "Sixe Covrt Comedies," Edward Blount, London, 1632. The readings of the quartos are given on the authority of Fairholt, "The Dramatic Works of John Lilly," London, 1858. The titlepage is not a facsimile.

[DRAMATIS PERSONAE.

ALEXANDER, *King of Macedon.*

HEPHESTION, *his General.*

CLYTUS
PARMENIO } *Soldiers.*
MILECTUS
PHRYGIUS

MELIPPUS, *Chamberlain to Alexander.*

ARISTOTLE
PLATO
DIOGENES
CRISIPPUS
CRATES } *Philosophers.*
CLEANTHES
ANAXARCHUS
CRYSUS

APELLES, *a Painter.*

SOLINUS
SYLVIUS } *Citizens of Athens.*

PERIM
MILO } *Sons to Sylvius.*
TRICO

GRANICHUS, *Servant to Plato.*

MANES, *Servant to Diogenes.*

PSYLLUS, *Servant to Apelles.*

Page to Alexander.

Citizens.

Soldiers.

CAMPASPE
TIMOCLEA } *Theban Captives.*

LAIS, *a Courtezan.*

SCENE: *Athens.*]

274

[CAMPASPE.] [1]

The Prologue at the Blacke-Friers.

They that feare the stinging of waspes make fannes of pea-cocks tailes, whose spots are like eyes; and Lepidus, which could not sleepe for the chattering of birds, set vp a beast whose head was like a dragon: and wee, which stand in awe of report, are compelled to set before our owle Pallas shield, thinking by her vertue to couer the others deformity. It was a signe of famine to Ægypt when Nylus flowed lesse than twelue cubites or more than eighteene: and it may threaten despaire vnto vs if wee bee lesse courteous than you looke for or more cumbersome. But, as Theseus, being promised to be brought to an eagles nest, and, trauailing all the day, found but a wren in a hedge, yet said, "This is a bird": so, we hope, if the shower of our swelling mountaine seeme to bring forth some elephant, performe but a mouse, you will gently say, "This is a beast." Basill softly touched yieldeth a sweete sent, but chafed in the hand, a ranke sauour: we feare, euen so, that our labours slily [2] glanced on will breed some con-

---

[1] *In the first quarto* (1584) *the title of this play is* "A moste excellent Comedie of Alexander, Campaspe, and Diogenes, played before the Queene's Maiestie on twelfe day at night, by her Maiesties Children, and the Children of Paules. Imprinted at London, for Thomas Cadman, 1584." *In the second edition, issued the same year by the same publisher, the title is changed to* "Campaspe," *and the play is said to have been given* "on new yeares day at night." *The title* "Campaspe" *was retained in the third quarto*, 1591, *and in* Blount's *edition. In* Blount, *however, the run-ning title is,* "A tragicall Comedie of / Alexander and Campaspe."

[2] *So* Bl., *and* F. *records no variant; but qy.* slightly.

tent, but examined to the proofe, small commendation. The haste in performing shall be our excuse. There went two nights to the begetting of Hercules; feathers appeare not on the phœnix vnder seuen moneths; and the mulberie is twelue in budding: but our trauailes are like the hares, who at one time bringeth forth, nourisheth, and engendreth againe, or like the brood of trochilus, whose egges in the same moment that they are laid become birds. But, howsoeuer we finish our worke, we craue pardon if we offend in matter, and patience if wee transgresse in manners. Wee haue mixed mirth with councell, and discipline with delight, thinking it not amisse in the same garden to sow pot-hearbes that wee set flowers. But wee hope, as harts that cast their hornes, snakes their skins, eagles their bils, become more fresh for any other labour: so, our charge being shaken off, we shall be fit for greater matters. But, least, like the Myndians, wee make our gates greater than our towne, and that our play runs out at the preface, we here conclude, — wishing that, although there be in your precise iudgements an vniuersall mislike, yet we may enioy by your wonted courtesies a generall silence.

The Prologue at the Court.

We are ashamed that our bird, which fluttereth by twilight seeming a swan, should bee proued a bat, set against the sun. But, as Iupiter placed Silenus asse among the starres, and Alcibiades couered his pictures, being owles and apes, with a curtaine imbroidered with lions and eagles: so are we enforced vpon a rough discourse to draw on a smooth excuse, resembling lapidaries who thinke to hide the cracke in a stone by setting it deepe in gold. The gods supped once with poore Baucis; the Persian kings sometimes shaued stickes: our hope is your Highnesse wil at this time lend an eare to an idle pastime. Appion, raising Homer from hell, demanded only who was his father; and we, calling Alexander from his graue, seeke only who was his loue. Whatsoeuer wee present, we wish it may be thought the dancing of Agrippa his shadowes, who, in the moment they were seene, were of any shape one would conceiue ; or lynces, who, hauing a quicke sight to discerne, haue a short memory to forget. With vs it is like to fare as with these torches, which giuing light to others consume themselues : and we shewing delight to others shame our-selues.

Actus primus. Scæna prima.

[The audience-chamber of the palace.]

CLITUS [*and*] PARMENIO [*near the door*]. TIMOCLEA [*and*] CAMPASPE [*are brought in later as prisoners*]. ALEXANDER [*on the throne, attended by*] HEPHESTION.

CLYT. Parmenio, I cannot tell whether I should more commend in Alexanders victories courage or courtesie, in the one being a resolution without feare, in the other a liberalitie aboue custome. Thebes is razed, the people not racked ; towers throwne downe, bodies not thrust aside : a conquest without 5 conflict, and a cruell warre in a milde peace.

PARME. Clytus, it becommeth the sonne of Philip to bee none other than Alexander is ; therefore, seeing in the father a full perfection, who could haue doubted in the sonne an excellency? For, as the moone can borrow nothing else of 10 the sunne but light : so, of a sire in whom nothing but vertue was, what could the childe receiue but singular? It is for turkies to staine each other, not for diamonds : in the one to bee made a difference in goodnesse, in the other no comparison. 15

CLYTUS. You mistake mee, Parmenio, if, whilest I commend Alexander, you imagine I call Philip into question ; vnlesse, happily, you coniecture — which none of iudgement will conceiue — that, because I like the fruit, therefore I heaue at the tree, or, coueting to kisse the childe, I therefore goe 20 about to poyson the teat.

PARME. I, but, Clytus, I pe[r]ceiue you are borne in the east, and neuer laugh but at the sunne rising : which argueth,

though a dutie where you ought, yet no great deuotion where
you might. 25

CLYTUS. We will make no controuersie of that which there
ought to be no question ; onely this shall be the opinion of vs
both, that none was worthy to be the father of Alexander but
Philip, nor any meete to be the sonne of Philip but Alexander.

[*Enter* SOLDIERS *with spoils and* TIMOCLEA, CAMPASPE *and other prisoners.*]

PARME. Soft, Clytus ! behold the spoiles and prisoners. A 30
pleasant sight to vs, because profit is ioyned with honour ; not
much painfull to them, because their captiuitie is eased by
mercie.

TIMO. [*aside*] Fortune, thou didst neuer yet deceiue vertue,
because vertue neuer yet did trust fortune! Sword *and* fire 35
will neuer get spoyle where wisdome and fortitude beares
sway. O Thebes, thy wals were raised by the sweetnesse of
the harpe, but rased by the shrilnes of the trumpet. Alexander had neuer come so neer the wals, had Epaminondas walkt
about the wals; and yet might the Thebanes haue beene 40
merry in their streets, if hee had beene to watch their towers.
But destinie is seldome foreseene, neuer preuented. We are
here now captiues, whose neckes are yoaked by force, but
whose hearts cannot yeeld by death. — Come, Campaspe and
the rest, let vs not be ashamed to cast our eyes on him on 45
whom we feared not to cast our darts.

PARME. Madame, you need not doubt; it is Alexander
that is the conquerour.

TIMO. Alexander hath ouercome, not conquered.

PARME. To bring all vnder his subiection is to conquer. 50

TIMO. He cannot subdue that which is diuine.

PARME. Thebes was not.

TIMO. Vertue is.

CLYTUS. Alexander, as hee tendreth vertue, so hee will
you. He drinketh not bloud, but thirsteth after honour ; hee 55
is greedie of victorie, but neuer satisfied with mercie ; in fight
terrible, as becommeth a captaine ; in conquest milde, as
beseemeth a king : in all things — than which nothing can be
greater — hee is Alexander.

CAMPAS. Then, if it be such a thing to be Alexander, I 60
hope it shall be no miserable thing to be a virgin. For, if hee
saue our honours, it is more than to restore our goods ; and
rather doe I wish he preserue our fame than our liues : which
if he doe, we will confesse there can be no greater thing than
to be Alexander. 65

ALEX. Clytus, are these prisoners? Of whence these spoiles?

CLYT. Like your Maiestie, they are prisoners, and of
Thebes.

ALEX. Of what calling or reputation?

CLYT. I know not, but they seeme to be ladies of honour. 70

ALEX. I will know. Madam, of whence you are I know,
but who I cannot tell.

TIMO. Alexander, I am the sister of Theagines, who fought
a battell with thy father before the citie of Chieronie,[1] where
he died — I say, which none can gainsay — valiantly. 75

ALEX. Lady, there seeme in your words sparkes of your
brothers deedes, but worser fortune in your life than his death ;
but feare not, for you shall liue without violence, enemies or
necessitie. But what are you, faire ladie? another sister to
Theagines? 80

CAMPAS. No sister to Theagines, but an humble handmaid to Alexander, born of a meane parentage but to extreme
fortune.

ALEX. Well, ladies, — for so your vertues shew you, whatsoeuer your births be, — you shall be honorably entreated. 85
Athens shall be your Thebes ; and you shall not be as abiects
of warre, but as subiects to Alexander. Parmenio, conduct
these honourable ladies into the citie ; charge the souldiers not
so much as in words to offer them any offence, and let all
wants bee supplied so farre forth as shall be necessarie for 90
such persons and my prisoners.

Exeunt PARME[NIO] &° CAPTIUI.

[ALEX.] Hephestion,[2] it resteth now that wee haue as
great care to gouerne in peace as conquer in warre, that, while

---

[1] *So* first and second edd.; Bl. Chyeronte.
[2] *In* Blount *this is printed as if it were the name of the speaker.*

armes cease, arts may flourish, and, ioyning letters with
launces, wee endeuour to bee as good philosophers as soul- 95
diers, knowing it no lesse prayse to bee wise than commend-
able to be valiant.

HEPHEST. Your Maiestie therein sheweth that you haue
as great desire to rule as to subdue. And needs must that
commonwealth be fortunate whose captaine is a philosopher 100
and whose philosopher a captaine. *Exeunt.*

Actus primus.   Scæna secunda.

[The market-place.]

MANES. GRANICHUS. PSYLLUS.

MANES. I serue in-stead of a master a mouse, whose
house is a tub, whose dinner is a crust, and whose bed is a
boord.

PSYLLUS. Then art thou in a state of life which philosophers commend : a crum for thy supper, an hand for thy   5
cup, and thy clothes for thy sheets; for *Natura paucis
contenta.*

GRANI. Manes, it is pitie so proper a man should be cast
away vpon a philosopher; but that Diogenes, that dogge,
should haue Manes, that dog-bolt, it grieueth nature and   10
spiteth art: the one hauing found thee so dissolute — absolute, I would say — in bodie, the other so single — singular — in minde.

MANES. Are you merry? It is a signe by the trip of
your tongue and the toyes of your head that you haue done 15
that to-day which I haue not done these three dayes.

PSYLLUS. Whats that?

MANES. Dined.

GRANI. I thinke Diogenes keepes but cold cheare!

MANES. I would it were so ; but he keepeth neither hot 20
nor cold.

GRANI. What then? luke-warme? That made Manes
runne from his master the last day.

PSYLLUS.	Manes had reason, for his name foretold as much.	25

MANES.	My name? how so, sir boy?

PSYLLUS.	You know that it is called *mons, a mouendo,* because it stands still.

MANES.	Good.

PSYLLUS.	And thou art named Manes, *a manendo,* because thou runnest away.	30

MANES.	Passing reasons! I did not run away, but retire.

PSYLLUS.	To a prison, because thou wouldst haue leisure to contemplate.

MANES.	I will proue that my bodie was immortal, because it was in prison.	35

GRANI.	As how?

MANES.	Did your masters neuer teach you that the soule is immortall?

GRANI.	Yes.	40

MANES.	And the bodie is the prison of the soule?

GRANI.	True.

MANES.	Why then, this: [1] — to make my body immortall, I put it in prison.

GRANI.	Oh, bad!	45

PSYLLUS.	Excellent ill!

MANES.	You may see how dull a fasting wit is. Therefore, Psyllus, let vs goe to supper with Granichus. Plato is the best fellow of all philosophers. Give me him that reades in the morning in the schoole and at noone in the kitchin.	50

PSYLLUS.	And me!

GRANI.	Ah, sirs, my master is a king in his parlour for the body, and a god in his studie for the soule. Among all his men he commendeth one that is an excellent musition; then stand I by and clap another on the shoulder and say,	55 "This is a passing good cooke."

MANES.	It is well done, Granichus; for giue mee pleasure that goes in at the mouth, not the eare, — I had rather fill my guts than my braines.

[1] F. thus.

PSYLLUS.   I serue Apelles, who feedeth mee as Diogenes   60
doth Manes ; for at dinner the one preacheth abstinence, the
other commendeth counterfaiting.   When I would eat meate,
he paints a[1] spit, and when I thirst, " O," saith he, " is not
this a faire pot ? " and points to a table which containes the
Banquet of the Gods, where are many dishes to feed the eye,   65
but not to fill the gut.

GRANI.   What doest thou then?

PSYLLUS.   This doth hee then, — bring in many examples
that some haue liued by sauours, and proueth that much
easier it is to fat by colours, and telles of birdes that haue   70
beene fatted by painted grapes in winter, and how many haue
so fed their eyes with their mistresse picture that they neuer
desired to take food, being glutted with the delight in their
fauours.   Then doth he shew me counterfeites, such as haue
surfeited with their filthy and lothsome vomites, and with   75
the riotous Bacchanalls of the god Bacchus and his disorderly
crew, which are painted all to the life in his shop.   To conclude, I fare hardly, though I goe richly ; which maketh me,
when I should begin to shadow a ladies face, to draw a
lambs head, and sometime to set to the body of a maid a   80
shoulder of mutton, for *Semper animus meus est in patinis.*

MANES.   Thou art a god to mee ; for, could I see but a
cookes shop painted, I would make mine eyes fatte as butter ;
for I haue nought but sentences to fill my maw : as, *Plures
occidit crapula quam gladius ; Musa ieiunantibus amica ;*   85
Repletion killeth delicatly ; and an old saw of abstinence by[2]
Socrates, — The belly is the heads graue.   Thus with sayings, not with meate, he maketh a gallimafray.

GRANI.   But how doest thou then liue?

MANES.   With fine iests, sweet ayre and the dogs almes.   90

GRA.   Well, for this time I wil stanch thy gut, and among
pots and platters thou shalt see what it is to serue Plato.

---

[1] Bl. *omits* a.

[2] *All the old editions omit* by ; *it appears in* Dodsley, *and a sixteenth
century hand inserted it in ink in a copy of the* third ed. *now in the Garrick Collection.*

PSYLLUS.   For ioy of it, Granichus, lets sing.

MANES.   My voice is as cleare in the euening as in the morning.   95

GRANI.   An-other commoditie of emptines!

Song.[1]

GRAN.   O for a bowle of fatt canary,
    Rich Palermo, sparkling sherry,
Some nectar else from Iuno's daiery:
    O, these draughts would make vs merry!   100

PSIL.   O for a wench! — I deale in faces
    And in other dayntier things.
Tickled am I in her embraces, —
    Fine dancing in such fairy-ringes.   104

MA.   O for a plump fat leg of mutton,
    Veale, lambe, capon, pigge *and* conney!
None is happy but a glutton;
    None an asse but who wants money.   108

CH[ORUS].   Wines, indeed, *and* girles are good,
    But braue victuals feast the bloud.
For wenches, wine and lusty cheere
    Ioue would leape downe to surfet heere.   112

[*Exeunt.*]

Actus primus.   Scæna tertia.

[ALEXANDER'S *palace.*]

MELIPPUS, PLATO, ARISTOTLE, CRYSIPPUS, CRATES, CLEANTHES, ANAX-
ARCHUS, ALEXANDER, HEPHESTION, PARMENIO, CLYTUS [*and*] DIOGE-
NES [*appear during the scene*].   [MELIPPUS *alone.*]

MELIP.   I had neuer such adoe to warne schollers to come before a king!   First, I came to Crisippus, a tall, leane old madman, willing him presently to appeare before Alexander. Hee stood staring on my face, neither mouing his eyes nor

1 *The songs were first given in* Bl.

his body.   I urging him to giue some answer, hee tooke vp a   5
booke, sate downe, and saide nothing.   Melissa, his maide,
told mee it was his manner, and that oftentimes shee was fain
to thrust meat into his mouth, for that he would rather sterue
than cease studie.   Well, thought I, seeing bookish men are
so blockish and great clearkes such simple courtiers, I will   10
neither be partaker of their commons nor their commendations.   From thence I came to Plato and to Aristotle and to
diuers others, none refusing to come sauing an olde obscure
fellow, who, sitting in a tub turned towardes the sunne, read
Greeke to a young boy.   Him when I willed to appeare be-   15
fore Alexander, he answered, " If Alexander would faine see
mee, let him come to mee ; if learne of me, let him come to
mee ; whatsoeuer it be, let him come to mee."   " Why," said
I, " he is a king."   He answered, " Why, I am a philosopher."   " Why, but he is Alexander ! "   " I ; but I am Di-   20
ogenes."   I was halfe angry to see one so crooked in his
shape to bee so crabbed in his sayings ; so, going my way, I
said, " Thou shalt repent it, if thou comest not to Alexander."
" Nay," smiling answered hee, " Alexander may repent it, if
hee come not to Diogenes : vertue must be sought, not   25
offered."   And, so, turning himselfe to his cell, hee grunted
I know not what, like a pig vnder a tub.   But I must bee
gone, the philosophers are comming.   *Exit.*

    [*Enter* PLATO, ARISTOTLE, CRYSIPPUS, CRATES, CLEANTHES, *and* ANAX-
      ARCHUS.]

    PLATO.   It is a difficult controuersie, Aristotle, and rather
to be wondred at than beleeued, how natural causes should   30
worke supernaturall effects.

    ARIST.   I do not so much stand vpon the apparition is
seene in the moone, neither the Demonium of Socrates, as
that I cannot by naturall reason giue any reason of the ebbing
and flowing of the sea ; which makes me in the depth of my   35
studies to crie out, *O ens entium, miserere mei!*

    PLATO.   Cleanthes and you attribute so much to nature
by searching for things which are not to be found, that,
whilest you studie a cause of your owne, you omit the occa-

sion it-selfe.   There is no man so sauage in whom resteth   40
not this diuine particle : that their[1] is an omnipotent, eternall
and diuine mouer, which may be called God.

CLEANT.   I am of this minde, that that first mouer, which
you terme God, is the instrument of all the mouings which
we attribute to nature.   The earth, which is masse, swimmeth[2]   45
on the sea, seasons diuided in themselues, fruits growing in
themselues, the maiestie of the skie, the whole firmament of
the world, *and* whatsoeuer else appeareth miraculous, — what
man almost of meane capacitie but can proue it natural?

ANAXAR.   These causes shall be debated at our philosophers   50
feast, in which controuersie I will take part with Aristotle
that there is *Natura naturans*, and yet not God.

CRATES.[3]   And I with Plato that there is *Deus optimus
maximus*, and not Nature.

[*Enter* ALEXANDER *and* HEPHESTION.]

ARIST.   Here commeth Alexander.   55

ALEX.   I see, Hephestion, that these philosophers are
here attending for vs.

HEPHEST.   They are not philosophers if they know[4] not
their duties.

ALEX.   But I much meruaile Diogenes should bee so   60
dogged.

HEP.   I doe not thinke but his excuse will be better than
Melippus message.

ALEX.   I will goe see him, Hephestion, because I long to
see him that would Alexander to come, to whom all the world   65
is like to come. — Aristotle and the rest, sithence my comming
from Thebes to Athens, from a place of conquest to a pallace
of [5] quiet, I haue resolued with my-selfe in my court to haue
as many philosophers as I had in my camp souldiers.   My
court shalbe a schoole, wherein I will haue vsed as great   70
doctrine in peace as I did in warre discipline.

---

[1] *A mere error ;*   Bl.'s *spelling is, in general, very good.*
[2] *Qy.* swimming.　　[4] Third ed. knewe.
[3] Bl. Craterus.　　[5] Bl. *omits* of.

AR.   We are all here ready to be commanded, *and* glad
we are that we are commanded, for that nothing better be-
c[o]mmeth kings than literature, which maketh them come as
neare to the gods in wisdome as they doe in dignitie.   75

ALEX.   It is so, Aristotle, but yet there is among you, yea,
and of your bringing vp, that sought to destroy Alexander, —
Calistenes, Aristotle, whose treasons against his prince shall
not be borne out with the reasons of his philosophie.

AR.   If euer mischief entred into the heart of Calistenes,   80
let Calistenes suffer for it; but that Aristotle euer imagined
any such thing of Calistenes, Aristotle doth denie.

ALEX.   Well, Aristotle, kindred may blinde thee, *and*
affection me ; but in kings causes I will not stand to schollers
arguments.   This meeting shalbe for a commandement that   85
you all frequent my court.   Instruct the young with rules,[1]
confirme the olde with reasons; let your liues bee answerable
to your learnings, least my proceedings be contrary to my
promises.

HEPHEST.   You said you would aske euery one of them a   90
question which yesternight none of vs could answere.

ALEX.   I will.   Plato, of all beasts which is the subtilest?

PLATO.   That which man hitherto neuer knew.

ALEX.   Aristotle, how should a man be thought a god?

ARIST.   In doing a thing vnpossible for a man.   95

ALEX.   Crisippus, which was first, the day or the night?

CRISIP.   The day, by a day.

ALEX.   Indeede strange questions must haue strange
answers.   Cleanthes, what say you, is life or death the
stronger?   100

CLEA.   Life, that suffereth so many troubles.

ALEX.   Crates, how long should a man liue?

CRATES.   Till hee thinke it better to die than to liue.

ALE.   Anaxarchus, whether doth the sea or the earth bring
forth most creatures?   105

---

[1] *So the quartos;* Bl. rulers, — *probably not in allusion to the educa-
tional apparatus with which, not many years ago, the love of learning
was inculcated.*

ANAX.　The earth, for the sea is but a part of the earth.

ALEX.[1]　Hephestion, me thinkes they haue answered all well; and in such questions I meane often to trie them.

HEPHEST.　It is better to haue in your court a wise man than in your ground a golden mine.　Therefore would I leaue war, to study wisdom, were I Alexander. 110

ALEX.　So would I, were I Hephestion.　But come, let vs goe and giue release, as I promised, to our Theban thralls.[2]

　　　　　　　　　　　　　　　　　　　　Exeunt.

PLATO.　Thou art fortunate, Aristotle, that Alexander is thy scholler. 115

ARIST.　And all you happy that he is your soueraigne.

CRISIP.　I could like the man well, if he could be contented to bee but a man.

ARISTO.　He seeketh to draw neere to the gods in knowledge, not to be a god. 120

　　　　　　　　[*Enter* DIOGENES.][3]

PLATO.　Let vs question a little with Diogenes why he went not with vs to Alexander.　Diogenes, thou didst forget thy duety, that thou wentst not with vs to the king.

DIOGE.　And you your profession, that went to the king.

PL.　Thou takest as great pride to be peeuish as others do glory to be vertuous. 125

DIOG.　And thou as great honour, being a philosopher, to be thought court-like as others shame, that be courtiers, to be accounted philosophers.

ARIST.　These austere manners set aside, it is well knowne that thou didst counterfeite money. 130

DIOG.　And thou thy manners, in that thou didst not counterfeite money.

ARIST.　Thou hast reason to contemne the court, being both in bodie and minde too crooked for a courtier. 135

DIOG.　As good be crooked and indeuour to make my-selfe

---

[1] Bl. Ala.

[2] *So the quartos;* Bl. thrall.

[3] *In the Garrick copy of the third edition this stage-direction is inserted in ink by the hand of* W. Neile, *a contemporary of* Lyly.

straight, from the court, as bee straight and learne to be crooked at the court.

CR.   Thou thinkest it a grace to be opposite against Alex-
ander.   140

DIOG.   And thou to be iump with Alexander.

ANAX.   Let vs goe, for in contemning him we shal better please him than in wondering at him.

ARIST.   Plato, what doest thou thinke of Diogenes.

PLATO.   To be Socrates furious.   Let vs goe.   145

Exeunt PHILOSOPHI.

Actus secundus.   Scæna prima.

[The market-place.]

DIOGENES, PSYLLUS, MANES, GRANICHUS [*and* CITIZENS].

PS.   Behold, Manes, where thy master is, seeking either for bones for his dinner or pinnes for his sleeues.   I will goe salute him.

MANES.   Doe so; but mum! not a word that you saw Manes.   5

GRANI.   Then stay thou behinde, and I will goe with Psyllus.

[They go to DIOGENES.*]*

PSYL.   All hayle, Diogenes, to your proper person!

DI.   All hate to thy peeuish conditions.

GRANI.   O dogge!   10

PSYL.   What doest thou seeke for here?

DIOG.   For a man and a beast.

GRANI.   That is easie without thy light to bee found: be not all these men?

DIOG.   Called men.   15

GR.   What beast is it thou lookest for?

DIOG.   The beast my man Manes.

PSYL.   Hee is a beast indeed that will serue thee.

DIOG.   So is he that begat thee.

GRA.   What wouldest thou do, if thou shouldst find   20
Manes?

DIOG. Giue him leaue to doe as hee hath done before.

GR. Whats that?

DIOG. To run away.

P[SYL]. Why, hast thou no neede of Manes?   25

DIO. It were a shame for Diogenes to haue neede of Manes and for Manes to haue no neede of Diogenes.

GRANI. But put the case he were gone, wouldst thou entertaine any of vs two?

DIOG. Vpon condition.   30

PSYLLUS. What?

DIOG. That you should tell me wherefore any of you both were good.

GRANI. Why, I am a scholler and well seene in philosophy.   35

PSYLLUS. And I a prentice and well seene in painting.

DIOG. Well then, Granichus, be thou a painter to amend thine ill face; *and* thou, Psyllus, a philosopher to correct thine euill manners. But who is that? Manes?

MANES. I care not who I were, so I were not Manes.   40

GRANI. You are taken tardie.

PSYL. Let vs slip aside, Granichus, to see the salutation betweene Manes and his master.

[They stand aside.]

DIOG. Manes, thou knowest the last day I threw away my dish, to drinke in my hand, because it was superfluous;   45 now I am determined to put away my man and serue my-selfe, *quia non egeo tui vel te.*

MANES. Master, you know a-while agoe I ran away; so doe I meane to doe againe, *quia scio tibi non esse argentum.*

DIOG. I know I haue no money, neither will haue euer[1] a   50 man, for I was resolued long sithence to put away both my slaues, — money and Manes.

MANES. So was I determined to shake of both my dogges, — hunger *and* Diogenes.

[1] *So* Bl.; Quartos, will I haue euer.

PSYLLUS. O sweet consent betweene a crowde and a   55
Iewes-harpe !

GRANI.   Come, let vs reconcile them.

PSYL.   It shall not neede, for this is their vse : now doe
they dine one vpon another.   *Exit* DIOGENES.

GRANI.   How now, Manes, art thou gone from thy   60
master?

MANES.   No; I did but now binde my-selfe to him.

PS.   Why, you were at mortall iarres.

MANES.   In faith, no ; we brake a bitter iest one vpon
another.   65

GRANI.   Why, thou art as dogged as he.

PSYLLUS.   My father knew them both little whelps.

MANES.   Well, I will hie me after my master.

GRANI.   Why, is it supper-time with Diogenes?

MANES.   I, — with him at all time when he hath meate.   70

PSYL.   Why then, euery man to his home ; and let vs
steale out againe anone !

GRANI.   Where shall we meete?

PSY.   Why, at *Alae* [1] *vendibili suspensa haedera non est
opus.*   75

MANES.   O Psyllus, *habeo te loco parentis;* thou blessest
me.   *Exeunt.*

Actus secundus.   Scæna secunda.

[*The market-place.*]

ALEXANDER, HEPHESTION [*and*] PAGE [*walking*].   DIOGENES [*in the
background*].   APELLES [*enters at the end of the scene*].

ALEX.   Stand aside, sir boy, till you be called.   Hephestion, how doe you like the sweet face of Campaspe?

HEPHEST.   I cannot but commende the stout courage of
Timoclea.

ALEX.   Without doubt Campaspe had some great man to   5
her father.

1 Bl. Ala.

HEPHEST.   You know Timoclea had Theagines to her
brother.

ALEX.   Timoclea still in thy mouth? art thou not in loue?

HEPHEST.   Not I.   10

ALEX.   Not with Timoclea, you meane.   Wherein you
resemble the lapwing, who crieth most where her nest is not :
and so you lead me from espying your loue with Campaspe, —
you crie Timoclea.

HEPHEST.   Could I as well subdue kingdomes as I can   15
my thoughts, or were I as far from ambition as I am from
loue, all the world would account mee as valiant in armes as
I knovv my-selfe moderate in affection.

ALEX.   Is loue a vice?

HEPHEST.   It is no vertue.   20

ALEX.   Well, novv shalt thou see what small difference I
make betweene Alexander and Hephestion.   And, sith thou
hast beene alvvaies partaker of my triumphes, thou shalt bee
partaker of my torments.   I loue, Hephestion, I loue !   I
loue Campaspe, — a thing farre vnfit for a Macedonian, for a   25
king, for Alexander.   Why hangest thou downe thy head,
Hephestion, blushing to heare that which I am not ashamed
to tell?

HEPHEST.   Might my words craue pardon and my counsell credit, I would both discharge the duetie of a subiect,   30
for so I am, *and* the office of a friend, for so I will.

ALEX.   Speake, Hephestion ; for, whatsoeuer is spoken,
Hephestion speaketh to Alexander.

HEPHEST.   I cannot tell, Alexander, whether the report
be more shamefull to be heard or the cause sorrowful to be   35
beleeued.   What, is the son of Philip, king of Macedon, become the subiect of Campaspe, the captiue of Thebes?   Is
that minde whose greatnes the world could not containe drawn
within the compasse of an idle alluring eie?   Wil you handle
the spindle with Hercules, when you should shake the speare   40
with Achilles?   Is the warlike sound of drum *and* trump
turned to the soft noise of lyre *and* lute? the neighing of
barbed steeds, whose lowdnes filled the aire with terrour and

whose breathes dimmed the sun with smoake, conuerted to
delicate tunes and amorous glances? O Alexander, that soft   45
and yeelding minde should not bee in him whose hard and
vnconquerd heart hath made so many yeeld. But you loue!
Ah griefe! But whom? Campaspe. Ah shame! a maide
forsooth vnknowne, vnnoble, and who can tell whether im-
modest? whose eyes are framed by art to enamour and whose   50
heart was made by nature to enchant. I; but she is beautifull. Yea; but not therefore chaste. I; but she is comely
in all parts of the bodie. But shee may bee crooked in some
part of the minde. I, but shee is wise. Yea; but she is a
woman. Beautie is like the black-berry, which seemeth red   55
when it is not ripe, — resembling precious stones that are
polished with honie, which, the smoother they looke, the
sooner they breake. It is thought wonderfull among the sea-
men that mugill, of all fishes the swiftest, is found in the
belly of the bret, of all the slowest: and shall it not seeme   60
monstrous to wise men that the heart of the greatest conquerour of the world should be found in the hands of the
weakest creature of nature? of a woman? of a captiue? Her-
myns haue faire skins, but foule liuers; sepulchres fresh
colours, but rotten bones: women faire faces, but false   65
hearts. Remember, Alexander, thou hast a campe to gouerne,
not a chamber. Fall not from the armour of Mars to the
armes of Venus, from the fierie assaults of warre to the
maidenly skirmishes of loue, from displaying the eagle in
thine ensigne to set downe the sparrow. I sigh, Alexander,   70
that, where fortune could not conquer, folly should ouercome.
But behold all the perfection that may bee in Campaspe: a
haire curling by nature, not art, sweete alluring eyes, a faire
face made in despite of Venus, and a stately port in disdaine
of Iuno, a wit apt to conceiue and quicke to answere, a skinne 75
as soft as silke and as smooth as iet, a long white hand, a
fine little foot, — to conclude, all parts answerable to the best
part. What of this? Though she haue heauenly gifts, vertue and beautie, is shee not of earthly metall, flesh and bloud?
You, Alexander, that would be a god, shew your-selfe in this   80

worse than a man, so soone to be both ouerseene and ouer-
taken in a woman, whose false teares know their true times,
whose smooth words wound deeper than sharpe swords.
There is no surfet so dangerous as that of honie, nor any
poyson so deadly as that of loue: in the one physicke cannot 85
preuaile, nor in the other counsell.

ALEX. My case were light, Hephestion, and not worthy
to be called loue, if reason were a remedie, or sentences could
salue that sense cannot conceiue. Little do you know and
therefore sleightly doe you regard the dead embers in a priuate 90
person or liue coales in a great prince, whose passions and
thoughts doe as farre exceed others in extremetie as their
callings doe in maiestie. An eclipse in the sunne is more
than the falling of a starre: none can conceiue the torments
of a king vnlesse he be a king, whose desires are not inferiour 95
to their dignities. And then iudge, Hephestion, if the agonies
of loue be dangerous in a subiect, whether they be not more
than deadly vnto Alexander, whose deepe and not-to-bee-con-
ceiued sighes cleaue the heart in shiuers, whose wounded
thoughts can neither be expressed nor endured. Cease then, 100
Hephestion, with arguments to seeke to refell that which with
their deitie the gods cannot resist; and let this suffice to
answere thee, that it is a king that loueth, and Alexander,
whose affections are not to bee measured by reason, being
immortall, nor, I feare me, to be borne, being intolerable. 105

HEPHEST. I must needs yeeld, when neither reason nor
counsell can bee heard.

ALEX. Yeeld, Hephestion, for Alexander doth loue, and
therefore must obtaine.

HEPHEST. Suppose shee loues not you? Affection com- 110
meth not by appointment or birth, and then as good hated
as enforced.

ALEX. I am a king, and will command.

HEPHEST. You may, to yeeld to lust by force, but to consent to loue by feare you cannot. 115

ALEX. Why? What is that which Alexander may not
conquer as he list?

HEPHEST.   Why, that which you say the gods cannot resist, — loue.

ALEX.   I am a conqueror, shee a captiue; I as fortunate 120
as shee faire; my greatnesse may answere her wants and the
gifts of my mind the modestie of hers: is it not likely then
that she should loue?   Is it not reasonable?

HEPHEST.   You say that in loue there is no reason; and
therefore there can be no likelyhood.   125

ALEX.   No more, Hephestion!   In this case I will vse
mine owne counsell, and in all other thine aduice: thou mayst
be a good souldier, but neuer good louer.   Call my page.
[*Enter* PAGE.]   Sirrha, goe presently to Apelles and will him to
come to me without either delay or excuse.   130

PAGE.   I goe.   [*Exit.*]

ALEX.   In the meane season, to recreate my spirits, being
so neere, wee will goe see Diogenes.   And see where his tub
is!   Diogenes!

DIOG.   Who calleth?   135

ALEX.   Alexander.   How happened it that you would not
come out of your tub to my palace?

DIOG.   Because it was as farre from my tub to your
palace as from your palace to my tub.

ALEX.   Why then, doest thou owe no reuerence to kings? 140

DIOG.   No.

ALEX.   Why so?

DIOG.   Because they be no gods.

ALEX.   They be gods of the earth.

DIOG.   Yea, gods of earth.   145

ALEX.   Plato is not of thy minde.

DIOG.   I am glad of it.

ALEX.   Why?

DIOG.   Because I would haue none of Diogenes minde
but Diogenes.   150

ALEX.   If Alexander haue any-thing that may pleasure
Diogenes, let me know, and take it.

DIOG.   Then take not from mee that you cannot giue
mee, — the light of the world.

ALEX.   What doest thou want?   155
DIOG.   Nothing that you haue.
ALEX.   I haue the world at command.
DIOG.   And I in contempt.
ALEX.   Thou shalt liue no longer than I will.
DIOG.   But I shall die, whether you will or no.   160
ALEX.   How should one learne to bee content?
DIOG.   Vnlearne to couet.

ALEXAND.   Hephestion, were I not Alexander, I would
wish to bee Diogenes!

HEPHEST.   He is dogged, but discreet; I cannot tell how 165
sharpe, with a kind of sweetnes; full of wit, yet too-too
wayward.

ALEX.   Diogenes, when I come this way againe, I will
both see thee and confer with thee.

DIOG.   Doe.   170

[*Enter* APELLES.]

ALEX.   But here commeth Apelles. How now, Apelles,
is Venus face yet finished?

APEL.   Not yet; beautie is not so soone shadowed whose
perfection commeth not within the compasse either of cunning or of colour.   175

ALEX.   Well, let it rest vnperfect, and come you with
mee where I will shew you that finished by nature that you
haue beene trifling about by art.

[*Exeunt.*]

Actus tertius.   Scæna prima.

[*The shop of* APELLES.]

APELLES [*and*] CAMPASPE. [PSYLLUS *in the background.*]

APEL.   Ladie, I doubt whether there bee any colour so
fresh that may shadow a countenance so faire.

CAMP.   Sir, I had thought you had bin commanded to
paint with your hand, not to glose with your tongue. But,
as I haue heard, it is the hardest thing in painting to set   5

downe a hard fauour; which maketh you to despaire of my
face : and then shall you haue as great thankes to spare your
labour as to discredit your art.

APEL.   Mistris, you neither differ from your-selfe nor
your sexe ; for, knowing your owne perfection, you seeme to   10
dispraise that which men most commend, drawing them by
that meane into an admiration, where feeding them-selues,
they fall into an extasie ; your modestie being the cause of
the one, and of the other your affections.

CAMP.   I am too young to vnderstand your speech, though   15
old enough to withstand your deuise.   You haue bin so long
vsed to colours [1] you can doe nothing but colour.

APEL.   Indeed, the colours I see, I feare, will alter the
colour I haue.   But come, madam, will you draw neere? for
Alexander will be here anon.   Psyllus, stay you here at the   20
window.   If any enquire for me, answere, *Non lubet esse
domi.*

                    Exeunt [APELLES *and* CAMPASPE].

Actus tertius.   Scæna secunda.

                    [*The street before* APELLES' *shop.*]

                    PSYLLUS [*alone*].   MANES [*enters later*].

PSYLLUS.   It is alwayes my masters fashion when any
faire gentlewoman is to be drawne within to make me to stay
without.   But if hee should paint Iupiter like a bull, like a
swanne, like an eagle, then must Psyllus with one hand grind
colours and with the other hold the candle.   But let him   5
alone!   The better hee shadowes her face, the more will he
burne his owne heart.   And now if any man could meet with
Manes, who, I dare say, lookes as leane as if Diogenes
dropped out of his nose —

                    [*Enter* MANES.]

MANES.   And here comes Manes, who hath as much   10
meate in his maw as thou hast honestie in thy head.

                    [1] *Misprinted* toc olours *in* Bl.

PSYLLUS.   Then I hope thou art very hungry.

MANES.   They that know thee know that.

PSYLLUS.   But doest thou not remember that wee haue
certaine liquor to conferre withall?   15

MANES.   I ; but I haue businesse, I must goe cry a thing.

PSYLLUS.   Why, what hast thou lost?

MANES.   That which I neuer had, — my dinner.

PSYLLUS.   Foule lubber, wilt thou crie for thy dinner?

MANES.   I meane I must crie, not as one would say,   20
" crie," but " crie," — that is make a noyse.

PSYLLUS.   Why, foole, that is all one ; for, if thou crie,
thou must needs make a noyse.

MANES.   Boy, thou art deceiued : " crie " hath diuers
significations, and may be alluded to many things ; " knaue "   25
but one, and can be applyed but to thee.

PSYLLUS.   Profound Manes!

MANES.   Wee Cynickes are mad fellowes.   Didst thou not
finde I did quip thee?

PSYLLUS.   No, verily ; why, what's a quip?   30

MANES.   Wee great girders call it a short saying of a
sharpe wit, with a bitter sense in a sweet word.

PSYLLUS.   How canst thou thus diuine, diuide, define, dispute, and all on the sodaine?

MANES.   Wit will haue his swing!   I am bewitcht, in-   35
spired, inflamed, infected!

PSYLLUS.   Well, then will not I tempt thy gybing spirit.

MANES.   Doe not, Psyllus, for thy dull head will bee but a
grindstone for my quicke wit, which if thou whet with ouer-
thwarts, *perijsti, actum est de te!*   I haue drawne bloud at   40
ones braines with a bitter bob.

PSYLLUS.   Let me crosse my-selfe ; for I die if I crosse
thee.

MANES.   Let me doe my businesse.   I my-selfe am afraid
lest my wit should waxe warme, and then must it needs con-   45
sume some hard head with fine and prettie iests.   I am sometimes in such a vaine that, for want of some dull pate to
worke on, I begin to gird my-selfe.

PSYLLUS.   The gods shield me from such a fine fellow, whose words melt wits like waxe.   50

MANES.   Well then, let vs to the matter.   In faith, my master meaneth to-morrow to flie.

PSYLLUS.   It is a iest.

MANES.   Is it a iest to flie?   Shouldst thou flie so soone, thou shouldst repent it in earnest.   55

PSYLLUS.   Well, I will be the cryer.

MANES AND PSYLLUS.   (*one after another*)   O ys!   O ys! O ys!   All manner of men, women or children that will come to-morrow into the market-place betweene the houres of nine and ten shall see Diogenes the Cynicke flie.[1]   60

PSYLLUS.   I doe not thinke he will flie.

MANES.   Tush! say " flie."

PSYLLUS.   Flie.

MANES.   Now let vs goe; for I will not see him againe till midnight, — I haue a backe way into his tub.   65

PSYLLUS.   Which way callest thou the backe way, when euery way is open?

MANES.   I meane to come in at his backe.

PSYLLUS.   Well, let vs goe away, that we may returne speedily.   70

Exeunt.

Actus tertius.   Scæna tertia.

[*The shop of* APELLES.]

APELLES [*and*] CAMPASPE.

APEL.   I shall neuer draw your eyes well, because they blinde mine.

CAMP.   Why then, paint mee without eyes, for I am blind.

APEL.   Were you euer shadowed before of any?

CAMP.   No; and would you could so now shadow me that   5 I might not be perceiued of any !

APEL.   It were pitie but that so absolute a face should furnish Venus temple amongst these pictures.

---

[1] *As* F. *points out,* PSYLLUS *stops upon reaching this word.*

CAMP.   What are these pictures?

APEL.   This is Laeda, whom Ioue deceiued in likenesse of   10
a swan.

CAMP.   A faire woman, but a foule deceit.

APEL.   This is Alcmena, vnto whom Iupiter came in
shape of Amphitrion her husband, and begate Hercules.

CAMP.   A famous sonne, but an infamous fact.   15

APEL.   Hee might doe it, because he was a god.

CAMP.   Nay, therefore it was euill done because he was a
god.

APEL.   This is Danae, into whose prison Iupiter drizled a
golden showre, and obtained his desire.   20

CAMP.   What gold can make one yeeld to desire?

APEL.   This is Europa, whom Iupiter rauished ; this,
Antiopa.

CAMP.   Were all the gods like this Iupiter?

APEL.   There were many gods in this like Iupiter.   25

CAMP.   I thinke in those dayes loue was well ratified
among men on earth, when lust was so full authorised by the
gods in heauen.

APEL.   Nay, you may imagine there were women passing
aimable, when there were gods exceeding amorous.   30

CAMP.   Were women neuer so faire, men would be false.

APEL.   Were women neuer so false, men would be fond.

CAMP.   What counterfeit is this, Apelles?

APEL.   This is Venus, the goddesse of loue.

CAMP.   What, bee there also louing goddesses?   35

APEL.   This is shee that hath power to command the very
affections of the heart.

CAMP.   How is she hired? by prayer, by sacrifice, or
bribes?

APEL.   By prayer, sacrifice and bribes.   40

CAMP.   What prayer?

APEL.   Vowes irreuocable.

CAMP.   What sacrifice?

APEL.   Hearts euer sighing, neuer dissembling.

CAMP.   What bribes?   45

APEL.   Roses and kisses.   But were you neuer in loue?
CAMP.   No, nor loue in me.
APEL.   Then haue you iniuried many.
CAMP.   How so?
APEL.   Because you haue beene loued of[1] many.   50
CAMP.   Flattered perchance of some.
    APEL.   It is not possible that a face so faire and a wit so
sharpe, both without comparison, should not be apt to loue.
    CAMP.   If you begin to tip your tongue with cunning, I
pray dip your pensill in colours and fall to that you must doe,   55
not that you would doe.

Actus tertius.   Scæna quarta.

[*The market-place or a street, and the shop of* APELLES.]

[*Enter*] CLYTUS [*and*] PARMENIO ; [*to them*] ALEXANDER [*and*] HEPHES-
TION.   CRYSUS [*and*] DIOGENES [*enter unobserved*].   APELLES [*and*]
CAMPASPE *remain from Scene iii*].

CLYTUS.   Parmenio, I cannot tell how it commeth to passe
that in Alexander now-a-dayes there groweth an vnpatient
kind of life : in the morning he is melancholy, at noone solemne, at all times either more sowre or seuere than hee was
accustomed.   5
    PARME.   In kings causes I rather loue to doute than con-
iecture, and thinke it better to bee ignorant than inquisitive :
they haue long eares and stretched armes, — in whose heads
suspition is a proofe, and to be accused is to be condemned.
    CLYTUS.   Yet betweene vs there can be no danger to find   10
out the cause, for that there is no malice to withstand it.   It
may be an vnquenchable thirst of conquering maketh him
vnquiet ; it is not vnlikely his long ease hath altered his
humour ; that he should be in loue it is impossible.[2]

---

[1] *In my copy of* Blount *the* "f" *of this word, which stands at the outer
margin, has disappeared.*

[2] First ed. not impossible; Fairholt *follows* Blount *in his text, but says
in his note that the* first ed. *is right.*

PAR. In loue, Clytus? No, no! it is as farre from his   15
thought as treason in ours. He, whose euer-waking eye,
whose neuer-tired heart, whose body patient of labour, whose
minde vnsatiable of victorie hath alwayes beene noted, cannot so soone be melted into the weake conceites of loue.
Aristotle told him there were many worlds ; and that he hath   20
not conquered one that gapeth for all, galleth Alexander.
But here he commeth.

[*Enter* ALEXANDER *and* HEPHESTION.]

ALEX. Parmenio and Clytus, I would haue you both
readie to goe into Persia about an ambassage no lesse prof-
itable to me than to your-selues honourable.   25

CLYTUS. Wee are readie at all commands, wishing nothing else but continually to be commanded.

ALEX. Well then, withdraw your-selues till I haue further
considered of this matter.   *Exeunt* CLYTUS *and* PARMENIO.

[ALEX.] Now wee will see how Apelles goeth forward. I   30
doubt me that nature hath ouercome art, and her countenance his cunning.

HEPHEST. You loue, and therefore think any-thing.

ALEX. But not so farre in loue with Campaspe as with
Bucephalus, if occasion serue either of conflict or[1] conquest.   35

HEPHEST. Occasion cannot want if will doe not. Behold
all Persia swelling in the pride of their owne power, the
Scythians carelesse what courage or fortune can do, the
Egyptians dreaming in the southsayings of their augures
and gaping ouer the smoake of their beasts intralls. All   40
these, Alexander, are to be subdued, if that world be not
slipped out of your head which you have sworne to conquer
with that hand.

ALEX. I confesse the labours fit for Alexander, and yet
recreation necessarie among so many assaults, bloudie   45
wounds, intolerable troubles. Giue me leaue a little, if not
to sit, yet to breath. And doubt not but Alexander can,

[1] F. or of ; Bl. of.

when he will, throw affections as farre from him as hee can
cowardise.   But behold Diogenes talking with one at his tub.

CRYSUS.   One penny, Diogenes; I am a Cynicke.   50

DIOG.   Hee made thee a begger that first gaue thee any-
thing.

CRYSUS.   Why, if thou wilt giue nothing, no-bodie will
giue thee.

DIOG.   I want nothing, till the springs drie and the earth   55
perish.

CRYSUS.   I gather for the gods.

DIOG.   And I care not for those gods which want money.

CRYSUS.   Thou art not a right Cynick, that wilt giue
nothing.   60

DIOG.   Thou art not, that wilt begge any-thing.

CRYSUS.   Alexander! King Alexander! give a poore Cynick a groat!

ALEX.   It is not for a king to giue a groat.

CRYSUS.   Then giue me a talent.   65

ALEX.   It is not for a begger to aske a talent; away!
[*Approaches* APELLES *and* CAMPASPE.]   Apelles!

APEL.   Here.

ALEX.   Now, gentlewoman, doth not your beautie put the
painter to his trumpe?   70

CAMP.   Yes, my lord; seeing so disordered a countenance,
hee feareth hee shall shadow a deformed counterfeite.

ALEX.   Would he could colour the life with the feature!
And, mee thinketh, Apelles, were you as cunning as report
saith you are, you may paint flowres as well with sweet smels   75
as fresh colours, obseruing in your mixture such things as
should draw neere to their sauours.

APEL.   Your Maiestie must know, it is no lesse hard to
paint sauours than vertues; colours can neither speake nor
thinke.   80

ALEX.   Where doe you first begin, when you draw any
picture?

APEL.   The proportion of the face in iust compasse as I
can.

ALEX. I would begin with the eye, as a light to all the 85
rest.

APEL. If you will paint, as you are a king, your Maiestie
may begin where you please; but, as you would bee a painter,
you must begin with the face.

ALEX. Aurelius would in one houre colour foure faces. 90

APEL. I maruaile in halfe an houre hee did not foure.

ALEX. Why, is it so easie?

APEL. No; but he doth it so homely.

ALEX. When will you finish Campaspe?

APEL. Neuer finish; for alwayes in absolute beauty there 95
is somewhat aboue art.

ALEX. Why should not I by labour be as cunning as
Apelles?

APEL. God shield you should haue cause to be so cunning
as Apelles! 100

ALEX. Me thinketh foure colours are sufficient to shadow
any countenance; and so it was in the time of Phydias.

APEL. Then had men fewer fancies and women not so
many fauours. For now, if the haire of her eye-browes be
blacke, yet must the haire of her head be yellow; the attire 105
of her head must bee different from the habit of her bodie,
else would the picture seeme like the blazon of ancient
armory, not like the sweet delight of new-found amiablenesse.
For, as in garden-knots diuersitie of odours make a more
sweete sauour, or as in musique diuers strings cause a more 110
delicate consent: so in painting, the more colours, the better
counterfeit, — obseruing black for a ground and the rest for
grace.

ALEX. Lend me thy pensill, Apelles: I will paint, and
thou shalt iudge. 115

APEL. Here.

ALEX. The coale breakes.

APEL. You leane too hard.

ALEX. Now it blackes not.

APEL. You leane too soft. 120

ALEX. This is awrie.

APEL.   Your eye goeth not with your hand.

ALEX.   Novv it is worse.

APEL.   Your hand goeth not with your minde.

ALEX.   Nay, if all be too hard or soft, — so many rules 125
and regards that ones hand, ones eye, ones minde must all
draw together, I had rather bee setting of a battell than blot-
ting of a boord.   But how haue I done here?

APEL.   Like a king.

ALEX.   I thinke so; but nothing more vnlike a painter. 130
Well, Apelles, Campaspe is finished as I wish.   Dismisse her,
and bring presently her counterfeit after me.

APEL.   I will.

[ALEXANDER *and* HEPHESTION *leave* APELLES.]

ALEX.   Now, Hephestion, doth not this matter cotton as
I would?   Campaspe looketh pleasantly; libertie will en- 135
crease her beautie, and my loue shall aduance her honour.

HEPHEST.   I will not contrarie your Maiestie; for time
must weare out that loue hath wrought, *and* reason weane
what appetite nursed.

[*Exit* CAMPASPE.]

ALEX.   How stately shee passeth by, yet how soberly, a 140
sweete consent in her countenance, with a chaste disdaine, desire mingled with coynesse, and — I cannot tell how to terme
it — a curst yeelding modesty.

HEPHEST.   Let her passe.

ALEX.   So shee shall for the fairest on the earth!   145

Exeunt.

Actus tertius.   Scæna quinta.

[*The house of* APELLES.]

PSYLLUS [*and*] MANES.   APELLES [*enters later*].

PSYLLUS.   I shall be hanged for tarrying so long.

MANES.   I pray God my master be not flowne before I
come!

PSYLLUS.   Away, Manes! my master doth come!

[Exit MANES; *enter* APELLES.]

APEL.   Where haue you beene all this while?   5
PSYLLUS.   No-where but here.
APEL.   Who was here sithens my comming?
PSYLLUS.   No-bodie.
APEL.   Vngracious wag, I perceiue you haue beene a-loy-
tering! was Alexander no-bodie?   10
PSYLLUS.   He was a king; I meant no meane bodie.
APEL.   I will cudgell your bodie for it, and then I will say
it was no bodie, because. it was no honest bodie.   Away! in!

Exit PSYLLUS.

[APEL.]   Vnfortunate Apelles! and therefore vnfortunate
because Apelles!   Hast thou by drawing her beautie brought   15
to passe that thou canst scarce draw thine owne breath?   And
by so much the more hast thou increased thy care by how
much the more thou hast [1] shewed thy cunning?   Was it not
sufficient to behold the fire, and warme thee, but with
Satyrus thou must kisse the fire and burne thee?   O, Cam-   20
paspe, Campaspe!   Art must yeeld to nature, reason to appetite, wisdome to affection.   Could Pigmalion entreate by
prayer to haue his iuory turned into flesh, *and* cannot Apelles
obtaine by plaints to haue the picture of his loue changed
into life?   Is painting so farre inferiour to caruing? or dost   25
thou, Venus, more delight to bee hewed with chizels then
shadowed with colours?   What Pigmalion, or what Pyrgo-
teles, or what Lysippus is hee that euer made thy face so
faire or spread thy fame so farre as I?   Vnlesse, Venus, in
this thou enuiest mine art, that in colouring my sweet Cam-   30
paspe I have left no place by cunning to make thee so
amiable!   But, alas! shee is the paramour to a prince!
Alexander, the monarch of the earth, hath both her body and
affection.   For what is it that kings cannot obtaine by
prayers, threats and promises?   Will not shee thinke it better   35
to sit vnder a cloth of estate, like a queene, than in a poore
shop, like a huswife; and esteeme it sweeter to be the concu-

[1] Bl. hast thou hast.

bine of the lord of the world than spouse to a painter in
Athens?   Yes, yes, Apelles, thou maist swimme against the
streame with the crab, *and* feede against the winde with the   40
deere, and pecke against the steele with the cockatrice:
starres are to be looked at, not reached at; princes to be
yeelded vnto, not contended with ; Campaspe to be honoured,
not obtained, to be painted, not possessed of thee.   O faire
face!   O vnhappy hand, *and* why didst thou drawe it — so   45
faire a face?   O beautiful countenance! the expres image of
Venus, but somewhat fresher, — the only patterne of that
eternitie which Iupiter dreaming a-sleepe could not conceiue
againe waking!   Blush, Venus, for I am ashamed to ende
thee!   Now must I paint things vnpossible for mine art, but   50
agreeable with my affections, — deepe and hollow sighes, sad
and melancholie thoughtes, woundes and slaughters of conceits, a life posting to death, a death galloping from life, a
wauering constancie, an vnsetled resolution, — and what not,
Apelles?   And what but Apelles?   But, as they that are   55
shaken with a feauer are to be warmed with cloathes, not
groanes, and as he that melteth in a consumption is to be
recured by colices, not conceits: so the feeding canker of
my care, the neuer-dying worme of my heart is to bee killed
by counsell, not cries, by applying of remedies, not by reply-   60
ing of reasons.   And, sith in cases desperate there must be
vsed medicines that are extreame, I will hazard that little life
that is left to restore the greater part that is lost; *and* this
shall be my first practice, — for wit must worke where authoritie is not: As soone as Alexander hath viewed this portrai-   65
ture, I will by deuise giue it a blemish, that by that meanes
she may come againe to my shop; *and* the*n* as good it were
to vtter my loue and die with deniall as conceale it and liue
in despaire.   69

Song by APELLES.

Cvpid and my Campaspe playd
At cardes for kisses ; Cupid payd.
He stakes his quiuer, bow *and* arrows,

His mothers doues *and* teeme of sparows ;
Looses them too.   Then downe he throwes
The corrall of his lippe, the rose   75
Growing on 's cheek, — but none knows how, —
With these the cristall of his brow,
And then the dimple of his chinne ;
All these did my Campaspe winne.
At last hee set her both his eyes ;   80
Shee won, and Cupid blind did rise.
        O Loue, has shee done this to thee?
        What shall, alas ! become of mee?

Actus quartus.   Scæna prima.

[*The market-place.*]

Solinus, Psyllus, Granichus, Manes [*walking about*].   Diogenes [*concealed in his tub*].   Populus [*enters later*].

So.   This is the place, the day, the time, that Diogenes hath appointed to flie.

Psyl.   I will not loose the flight of so faire a foule as Diogenes is though my master cudgell my no body as he threatened.   5

Gran.   What, Psyllus, will the beast wag his wings to-day?

Psyl.   Wee shall heare, for here commeth Manes.   Manes, will it be?

Manes.   Be?   He were best be as cunning as a bee, or   10
else shortly he will not bee at all!

Gran.   How is hee furnished to flie? hath he feathers?

Ma.   Thou art an asse!   Capons, geese and owles haue feathers ; he hath found Dedalus old waxen wings, and hath beene peecing them this moneth, he is so broad in the shoul-   15
ders.   O, you shall see him cut the ayre euen like a tortoys !

Soli.   Me thinkes so wise a man should not bee so mad.
His body must needs be too heauie.

Manes.   Why, hee hath eaten nothing this seuen-night
but corke and feathers.   20

PSYL. Touch him, Manes.

MANES. Hee is so light that hee can scarce keepe him from flying at midnight.

POPULUS intrat.

MANES. See, they begin to flocke, and behold, my master bustels himselfe to flie!   25

DIOG. You wicked and bewitched Athenians, whose bodies make the earth to groane, and whose breathes infect the ayre with stench, come ye to see Diogenes flie? Diogenes commeth to see you sinke. Yea,[1] call me dogge! So I am, for I long to gnaw the bons in your skins. Yee tearme   30 mee an hater of men. No; I am a hater of your manners. Your liues, dissolute, not fearing death, will proue your deaths desperat, not hoping for life. What do you else in Athens but sleepe in the day and surfeit in the night? Backe-gods in the morning with pride, in the euening belly-gods with   35 gluttony! You flatter kings and call them gods: speak truth of your-selues and confesse you are diuels. From the bee you haue taken not the honey but the wax to make your religion, framing it to the time, not to the truth. Your filthy lust you colour vnder a courtly colour of loue, iniuries abroad   40 vnder the title of policies at home; and secret malice creepeth vnder the name of publike iustice. You haue caused Alexander to drie vp springs and plant vines, to sow rocket and weed endiff, to sheare sheepe and shrine foxes. All conscience is sealed at Athens: swearing commeth of a hot   45 mettle, lying of a quick wit, flattery of a flowing tongue, vndecent talke of a merry disposition. All things are lawfull at Athens: either you think there are no gods or I must think ye are no men. You build as though you should liue for-euer and surfeit as though you should die to-morrowe. None   50 teacheth true philosophie but Aristotle, because hee was the kings schoole-master! O times! O men! O corruption in manners! Remember that greene grasse must turne to drie hay. When you sleepe, you are not sure to wake; and when

<hr>

[1] Qy. yee.

you rise, not certaine to lie downe. Looke you neuer so high, 55
your heads must lie leuel with your feet. Thus haue I flowne
ouer your disordered liues ; and, if you will not amend your
manners, I will studie to flie further from you, that I may bee
neerer to honestie.

SOLI. Thou rauest, Diogenes; for thy life is different 60
from thy words. Did not I see thee come out of a brothell
house? Was it not a shame?

DIOG. It was no shame to goe out; but a shame to
goe in.

GRANI. It were a good deede, Manes, to beate thy 65
master.

MANES. You were as good eate my master.

ONE OF THE PEOPLE. Hast thou made vs all fooles, and
wilt thou not flie?

DIOG. I tell thee, vnlesse thou be honest, I will flie. 70

PEOPLE. Dog, dog, take a bone!

DIOG. Thy father need feare no dogs, but dogs thy father.

PEOPLE. We will tell Alexander that thou reprouest him
behinde his back.

DIOG. And I will tell him that you flatter him before his 75
face.

PEOPLE. Wee will cause all the boyes in the streete to
hisse at thee.

DIOG. Indeede, I thinke the Athenians haue their children readie for any vice, because they bee Athenians. 80

MANES. Why, master, meane you not to flie?

DIOG. No, Manes, not without wings.

MANES. Euery-body will account you a lyar.

DIOG. No, I warrant you, for I will alwayes say the
Athenians are mischeuous. 85

PSYL. I care not; it was sport enough for mee to see
these old huddles hit home.

GRANI. Nor I.

PSY. Come, let vs goe; and hereafter when I meane to
rayle vpon any-body openly, it shall be giuen out I will flie. 90

Exeunt.

Actus quartus.   Scæna secunda.

[A room in the palace.]

CAMPASPE *[alone]*.   APELLES *[enters later]*.

CAMPASPE. *(sola)* Campaspe, it is hard to iudge whether
thy choyce be more vnwise or thy chance vnfortunate.   Doest
thou preferre — ? but stay! vtter not that in wordes which
maketh thine eares to glow with thoughts.   Tush! better thy
tongue wagge than thy heart breake.   Hath a painter crept   5
further into thy minde than a prince?   Apelles than Alexander?   Fond wench, the basenes of thy minde bewraies the
meannesse of thy birth.   But, alas! affection is a fire which
kindleth as well in the bramble as in the oake, and catcheth
hold where it first lighteth, not where it may best burne.   10
Larkes, that mount aloft in the ayre, build their neasts below
in the earth : and women that cast their eyes vpon kings may
place their hearts vpon vassalls.   A needle will become thy
fingers better tha*n* a lute, *and* a distaffe is fitter for thy hand
than a scepter.   Antes liue safely till they haue gotten wings,   15
and iuniper is not blowne vp till it hath gotten an high top :
the meane estate is without care as long as it continueth
without pride.   But here co*m*meth Apelles, — in whom I
would there were the like affection!

APELL.   Gentlewoman, the misfortune I had with your   20
picture will put you to some paines to sit againe to be painted.

CAMP.   It is small paines for mee to sit still, but infinite
for you to draw still.

APEL.   No, madame ; to painte Venus was a pleasure,
but to shadow the sweete face of Campaspe it is a heauen.   25

CAMP.   If your tongue were made of the same flesh that
your heart is, your words would bee as your thoughts are ;
but such a common thing it is amongst you to commend that
oftentimes for fashion sake you call them beautiful whom
you know blacke.   30

APEL.   What might men doe to be beleeued?[1]

---

[1] Bl. beceued.

CAMP.   Whet their tongue on their hearts.

APEL.   So they doe, and speake as they thinke.

CAMP.   I would they did!

APEL.   I would they did not!   35

CAMP.   Why, would you haue them dissemble?

APEL.   Not in loue, but their loue.   But will you giue mee leaue to aske you a question without offence?

CAMP.   So that you will answere mee another without excuse.   40

APEL.   Whom doe you loue best in the world?

CA.   He that made me last in the world.

APEL.   That was a god.

CAMP.   I had thought it had beene a man.   But whom doe you honour most, Apelles?   45

APEL.   The thing that is likest you, Campaspe.

CAMP.   My picture?

APEL.   I dare not venture vpon your person.   But come, let vs go in ; for Alexander will thinke it long till we returne.

Exeunt.

Actus quartus.   Scæna tertia.

[*The palace.*]

CLYTUS. PARMENIO.

CLYT.   We heare nothing of our embassage, — a colour, belike, to bleare our eyes or tickle our eares or inflame our hearts.   But what doth Alexander in the meane season but vse for *tantara sol-fa-la,* for his hard couch downe-beds, for his handfull of water his standing-cup of wine?   5

PAR.   Clytus, I mislike this new delicacie *and* pleasing peace.   For what else do we see now than a kind of softnes in euery mans minde, bees to make their hiues in souldiers helmets, our steeds furnished with foot-clothes of gold in-steede of sadles of steele, more time to be required to scowre   10 the rust of our weapons tha*n* there was wont to be in subdu-ing the countries of our enemies?   Sithence Alexander fell from his hard armour to his soft robes, behold the face of

his court: youths that were wont to carry deuices of victory
in their shields engraue now posies of loue in their ringes ;   15
they that were accustomed on trotting horses to charge the
enemie with a launce, now in easie coches ride vp and downe
to court ladies ; in-steade of sword and target to hazard their
liues, vse pen and paper to paint their loues ; yea, such a
feare and faintnesse is growne in court that they wish rather   20
to heare the blowing of a horne to hunt than the sound of a
trumpet to fight.   O Philip, wert thou aliue to see this alteration, — thy men turned to women, thy souldiers to louers,
gloues worne in veluet caps in-stead of plumes in grauen
helmets, — thou wouldest either dye among them for sorrow   25
or confound them for anger !

    CLYT.   Cease, Parmenio, least in speaking what becommeth
thee not, thou feele what liketh thee not : truth is neuer without a scracht face ; whose tongue, although it cannot be cut
out, yet must it be tied vp.   30

    PA.   It grieueth me not a little for Hephestion, who
thirsteth for honour, not ease ; but such is his fortune and
neerenesse in friendship to Alexander that hee must lay a
pillow vnder his head, when hee would put a target in his
hand.   But let vs draw in, to see how well it becomes them   35
to tread the measures in a daunce that were wont to set the
order for a march.   *Exeunt.*

Actus quartus.   Scæna quarta.

[The shop of APELLES.]

APELLES.   CAMPASPE.

    APEL.   I haue now, Campaspe, almost made an ende.
    CAMP.   You told mee, Apelles, you would neuer end.
    APEL.   Neuer end my loue, for it shalbe eternall.
    CAMP.   That is, neither to haue beginning nor ending.
    APEL.   You are disposed to mistake ; I hope you do not   5
mistrust.

CAMP. What will you say, if Alexander perceiue your loue?

APEL. I will say it is no treason to loue.

CAMP. But how if hee will not suffer thee to see my person.   10

APEL. Then will I gaze continually on thy picture.

CAMP. That will not feede thy heart.

APEL. Yet shall it fill mine eye. Besides, the sweet thoughts, the sure hopes, thy protested faith, wil cause me   15 to embrace thy shadow continually in mine armes, of the which, by strong imagination, I will make a substance.

CAMP. Wel, I must be gone. But this assure your-selfe, that I had rather be in thy shop grinding colours than in Alexanders court following higher fortunes.   20

[*She leaves him.*]

CAMPASPE *alone.*

[CAMP.] Foolish wench, what hast thou done? That, alas! which cannot be vndone; and therefore I feare me vndone. But content is such a life I care not for aboundance. O Apelles, thy loue commeth from the heart, but Alexanders from the mouth! The loue of kings is like the   25 blowing of winds, which whistle sometimes gently among the leaues, *and* straight-waies turne the trees vp by the rootes; or fire, which warmeth afarre off, and burneth neerehand; or the sea, which maketh men hoise their sailes in a flattering calme, and to cut their mastes in a rough storme.   30 They place affection by times, by policy, by appoyntment. If they frowne, who dares call them vnconstant; if bewray secrets, who will tearme them vntrue; if fall to other loues, who trembles not if he call them vnfaithfull? In kings there can bee no loue but to queenes, for as neere must they meete   35 in maiestie as they doe in affection. It is requisite to stande aloofe from kings loue, Ioue, and lightening!   *Exit.*

Actus quartus.   Scæna quinta.

[*The shop of* APELLES.]

APELLES.   [ALEXANDER'S] PAGE.

APEL.   Now, Apelles, gather thy wits together.   Campaspe is no lesse wise then faire; thy-selfe must be no lesse cunning then faithfull.   It is no small matter to be riuall with Alexander.

[*Enter* PAGE.]

PAG.   Apelles, you must come away quickly with the   5
picture, the king thinketh that, now you haue painted it, you play with it.

APEL.   If I would play with pictures, I haue enough at home.

PAGE.   None perhaps you like so well.   10

APEL.   It may be I haue painted none so well.

PA.   I haue knowen many fairer faces.

APEL.   And I many better [1] boyes.   *Exeunt.*

Actus quintus.   Scæna prima.

[*The market-place;* DIOGENES' *tub*.]

DIOGENES, SYLUIUS, PERIM, MILO, TRICO, MANES.

SY.   I haue brought my sons, Diogenes, to be taught of thee.

DIOG.   What can thy sonnes doe?

SYLU.   You shall see their qualities.   Dance, sirha!

Then PERIM *danceth.*

How like you this? doth he well?   5

DIOG.   The better, the worser.

SYLUI.   The musicke very good.

DIOG.   The musitions very bad, who onely study to haue their strings in tune, neuer framing their manners to order.

[1] Bl. bettes.

SYLUI.   Now shall you see the other : tumble, sirha !   10

MILO *tumbleth.*

How like you this?   Why do you laugh?

DIOG.   To see a wagge that was borne to breake his neck by destinie to practise it by art.

MILO.   This dogge will bite me ; I will not be with him.

DIOG.   Feare not, boy; dogges eate no thistles.   15

PERIM.   I maruell what dogge thou art, if thou be a dogge.

DIOG.   When I am hungry, a mastife ; and when my belly is full, a spannell.

SYLUI.   Dost thou beleeue that there are any gods, that   20
thou art so dogged?

DIOG.   I must needs beleeue there are gods ; for I thinke thee an enemie to them.

SYLUI.   Why so?

DIOG.   Because thou hast taught one of thy sonnes to rule   25
his legges and not to follow learning, the other to bend his bodie euery way and his minde no way.

PERIM.   Thou doest nothing but snarle and barke, like a dogge.

DIO.   It is the next vvay to driue away a theefe.   30

SYLUI.   Now shall you heare the third, who sings like a nightingale.

DIOG.   I care not; for I haue a nightingale to[1] sing her-selfe.

SYL.   Sing, sirha!   35

TRYCO *singeth:*

Song.

What bird so sings, yet so dos wayle?
O 't is [2] the rauish'd nightingale.
" Iug, iug, iug, iug, tereu," shee cryes ;
And still her woes at midnight rise.

[1] Bl. *omits* to.
[2] Bl. t' is.

Braue prick-song! who is 't now we heare?   40
None but the larke so shrill and cleare.
How at heauens gats she claps her wings,
The morne not waking till shee sings!
Heark, heark, with what a pretty throat
Poore Robin red-breast tunes his note!   45
Heark how the iolly cuckoes sing
" Cuckoe," to welcome in the spring, —
" Cuckoe," to welcome in the spring!

SYL.   Loe, Diogenes, I am sure thou canst not doe so
much.   50

DI.   But there is neuer a thrush but can.

SY.   What hast thou taught Manes, thy man?

DI.   To be as vnlike as may be thy sons.

MANES.   He hath taught me to fast, lie hard and run
away.   55

SYL.   How sayest thou, Perim? wilt thou bee with him?

PERIM.   I, so he will teach me first to runne away.

DIOG.   Thou needest not be taught, thy legges are so
nimble.

SYLUI.   How sayest thou, Milo? wilt thou be with him?   60

DIOG.   Nay, hold your peace; hee shall not.

SILUI.   Why?

DIOG.   There is not roome enough for him and me to
tumble both in one tub.

SYLUI.   Well, Diogenes, I perceiue my sonnes brooke not   65
thy manners.

DIOG.   I thought no lesse, when they knew my vertues.

SYLUI.   Farewell, Diogenes; thou neededst not haue
scraped rootes, if thou wouldst haue followed Alexander.

DIOG.   Nor thou haue followed Alexander, if thou hadst   70
scraped rootes.   *Exeunt.*

Actus quintus.   Scæna secunda.

[*The shop of* APELLES.]

APELLES *alone.*

[APEL.]   I feare mee, Apelles, that thine eyes haue
blabbed that which thy tongue durst not! What little
regard hadst thou! whilest Alexander viewed the counterfeit
of Campaspe, thou stoodest gazing on her countenance.   If
he espie, or but suspect, thou must needs twice perish, — with   5
his hate and thine owne loue.   Thy pale lookes when he
blushed, thy sad countenance when he smiled, thy sighes
when he questioned, may breed in him a ielousie, perchance
a frenzie.   O loue! I neuer before knew what thou wert,
and now hast thou made me that I know not what my-selfe   10
am!   Onely this I know, that I must endure intolerable
passions for vnknowne pleasures.   Dispute not the cause,
wretch, but yeeld to it; for better it is to melt with desire
than wrastle with loue.   Cast thy-selfe on thy carefull bed,
be content to liue vnknown *and* die vnfound.   O Campaspe,   15
I haue painted thee in my heart! Painted? nay, contrary
to mine arte, imprinted! and that in such deepe characters
that nothing can rase it out, vnlesse it rubbe my [1] heart out.

Exit.

Actus quintus.   Scæna tertia.

[*The market-place.*]

MILECTUS, PHRYGIUS, LAIS [*walking*].   DIOGENES [*in his tub*].

MIL.   It shall goe hard but this peace shall bring vs some
pleasure.

PHRI.   Downe with armes, and vp with legges! This is
a world for the nonce !

LAIS.   Sweet youths, if you knew [2] what it were to saue   5
your sweet blood, you would not so foolishly go about to

---

[1] Quartos *and* Bl. thy; *corr. by* Dods.   [2] Bl. know.

spend it.   What delight can there be in gashing, to make foule
scarres in faire faces and crooked maimes in streight legges,
as though men, being borne goodly by nature, would of purpose become deformed by folly?   And all, forsooth, for a   10
new-found tearme called "valiant,"—a word which breed-
eth more quarrels than the sense can commendation.

MIL.   It is true, Lais, a feather-bed hath no fellow.   Good
drinke makes good blood, and shall pelting words spill it?

PHRY.   I meane to enjoy the world, and to draw out my   15
life at the wire-drawers, not to curtall it off at the cutlers.

LA.   You may talke of vvarre, speake bigge, conquer
vvorlds vvith great words; but stay at home, vvhere in-steade
of alarums you shall haue dances, for hot battailes with fierce
men gentle skirmishes with faire women.   These pevvter   20
coates can neuer sit so well as satten doublets.   Beleeue me,
you cannot conceiue the pleasures of peace vnlesse you despise the rudenes of warre.

MIL.   It is so.   But see Diogenes prying ouer his tub!
Diogenes, what sayest thou to such a morsell? [*Pointing to* LAIS.]   25

DIOG.   I say I would spit it out of my mouth, because it
should not poyson my stomacke.

PHRY.   Thou speakest as thou art; it is noe meate for dogges.

DIOG.   I am a dogge, and philosophy rates me from carrion.

LAIS.   Vnciuil wretch, whose manners are answerable to   30
thy calling, the time was thou vvouldest haue had my company, had it not beene, as thou saidst, too deare!

DI.   I remember there was a thing that I repented mee of,
and now thou hast told it.   Indeed it vvas too deare of nothing, and thou deare to no-bodie.   35

LAYS.   Downe, villaine, or I will haue thy head broken!

MILE.   Will you couch?   [*Beating him.*]

PHRY.   Auant, curre!   Come, sweet Lays, let vs goe to
some place and possesse peace.   But first let vs sing; there
is more pleasure in tuning of a voyce than in a volly of shot.   40

[*They sing.*]

MILEC.   Now let .vs make hast, least Alexander finde vs
here!   *Exeunt.*

Actus quintus.　Scæna quarta.

[*The market-place.*]¹

ALEXANDER, HEPHESTION, PAGE [*together*].　DIOGENES [*in the back-ground*].　APELLES [*and*] CAMPASPE [*enter when called*].

ALEX.　Me thinketh, Hephestion, you are more melancholy than you were accustomed, but I perceiue it is all for Alexander.　You can neither brooke this peace nor my pleasure. Bee of good cheare ; though I winke, I sleepe not.

HEPHEST.　Melancholy I am not, nor well content ; for, I 　5 know not how, there is such a rust crept into my bones with this long ease that I feare I shall not scowre it out with infinite labours.

ALEX.　Yes, yes, if all the trauailes of conquering the world will set either thy bodie or mine in tune, we will vnder- 　10 take them.　But what thinke you of Apelles?　Did yee euer see any so perplexed?　Hee neither answered directly to any question nor looked stedfastly vpon any-thing.　I hold my life the painter is in loue.

HEPHEST.　It may be ; for commonly we see it incident in 　15 artificers to be enamoured of their. owne workes, as Archidamus of his wooden doue, Pygmalion of his iuorie image, Arachne of his vvooden swanne, — especially painters, who, playing with their owne conceits, now coueting ² to draw a glancing eie, then a rolling, novv a vvinking, still mending it, 　20 neuer ending it, till they be caught vvith it, and then, poore soules ! they kisse the colours vvith their lips vvith vvhich before they vvere loth to taint their fingers.

ALEX.　I will find it out.　Page, goe speedily for Apelles, will him to come hither ; and, when you see vs earnestly in 　25 talke, sodainly crie out : " Apelles shop is on fire ! "

PAGE.　It shall be done.

---

¹ *I have so assigned this scene because it can be so played, not because this was the intention of the author, who seems rather to have conceived one of those scenes in which all places lie adjacent to one another.*

² *Qy. read* couet.

ALEX.   For-get not your lesson.   [*Exit* PAGE.]

HEPH.   I maruell what your deuise shalbe.

ALEX.   The euent shall proue.   30

HEPH.   I pittie the poore painter, if he be in loue.

ALEX.   Pitie him not, I pray thee.   That seuere grauity set aside, what doe you thinke of loue?

HEPH.   As the Macedonians doe of their hearbe beet, which, looking yellow in the ground and blacke in the hand, 35 thinke it better seene than toucht.

ALEX.   But what doe you imagine it to be?

HEPH.   A word, by superstition thought a god, by vse turned to an humour, by selfe-will made a flattering madnesse.

ALEX.   You are too hard-hearted to thinke so of loue.   40 Let vs goe to Diogenes.   [*They approach the tub.*]   Diogenes, thou mayst thinke it somewhat that Alexander commeth to thee againe so soone.

DIOG.   If you come to learne, you could not come soone enough; if to laugh, you be come too soone.   45

HEPH.   It would better become thee to be more courteous *and* frame thy-self to please.

DIOG.   And you better to bee lesse, if you durst displease.

ALEX.   What doest thou thinke of the time we haue here?

DIOG.   That we haue little *and* lose much.   50

ALEX.   If one be sicke, what wouldst thou haue him doe?

DIOG.   Bee sure that hee make not his physician his heire.

ALEX.   If thou mightest haue thy will, how much ground would content thee?

DIOG.   As much as you in the end must be contented 55 withall.

ALEX.   What, a world?

DIOG.   No; the length of my bodie.

ALEX.   Hephestion, shall I bee a little pleasant with him?

HEPH.   You may, but hee will be very peruerse with you. 60

ALEX.   It skils [1] not; I cannot be angry with him.   Diogenes, I pray thee what doest thou thinke of loue?

DIOG.   A litle worser than I can of hate.

---

[1] First ed. skilleth.

ALEX.   And why?

DIOG.   Because it is better to hate the things which make   65
to loue than to loue the things which giue occassion of hate.

ALEX.   Why, bee not women the best creatures in the
world?

DIOG.   Next men and bees.

ALEX.   What doest thou dislike chiefly in a woman?   70

DIOG.   One thing.

ALEX.   What?

DIOG.   That she is a woman.

ALEX.   In mine opinion thou wert neuer borne of a woman,
that thou thinkest so hardly of women.   But now commeth   75
Apelles, who, I am sure, is as farre from thy thoughts as thou
art from his cunning.   Diogenes, I will haue thy cabin remoued neerer to my court, because I will be a philosopher.

DIOG.   And when you haue done so, I pray you remoue
your court further from my cabin, because I will not be a   80
courtier.

[Enter APELLES.]

ALEX.   But here commeth Apelles.   Apelles, what peece
of worke haue you now in hand?

APEL.   None in hand, if it like your Maiestie ; but I am
deuising a platforme in my head.   85

ALEXAND.   I thinke your hand put it in your head.   Is it
nothing about Venus?

APELLES.   No ; but some-thing aboue [1] Venus.

PAGE.   Apelles ! Apelles ! looke about [1] you, your shop is
on fire!   90

APEL.   Aye mee ! if the picture of Campaspe be burnt, I
am vndone.

ALEX.   Stay, Apelles ; no haste.   It is your heart is on
fire, not your shop ; and, if Campaspe hang there, I would
shee were burnt.   But haue you the picture of Campaspe?   95

---

[1] *In* Bl. *these two words (each standing at the end of a line) are interchanged.* F. *prints as I do ; but, as he has no note, I do not know whether
he follows one of the older editions, or corrects by conjecture.*

Belike you loue her well, that you care not though all be lost,
so she be safe.

APEL.   Not loue her? — but your Maiestie knowes that
painters in their last workes are said to excell themselues ;
and in this I haue so much pleaseᵈ my-selfe that the shadow   100
as much delighteth mee, being an artificer, as the substance
doth others, that are amorous.

ALEX.   You lay your colours grosly.   Though I could not
paint in your shop, I can spie into your excuse.   Be not
ashamed, Apelles ; it is a gentlemans sport to be in loue. —   105
[*To the* PAGE.]   Call hither Campaspe. — Me thinkes I might
haue beene made priuie to your affection ; though my counsell had not bin necessary, yet my countenance might haue
beene thought requisite.   But Apelles, forsooth, loueth vnder
hand, yea, and vnder Alexanders nose, and — but I say no   110
more !

APEL.   Apelles loueth not so ; but he liueth to doe as
Alexander will.

[*Enter* CAMPASPE.]

ALEX.   Campaspe, here is newes !   Apelles is in loue with
you.   115

CAMP.   It pleaseth your Maiestie to say so.

ALEX.   Hephestion, I will trie her too.   Campaspe, for
the good qualities I know in Apelles and the vertue I see in
you, I am determined you shall enioy one another.   How say
you, Campaspe?   Would you say, " I "?   120

CAMP.   Your hand-maid must obey if you command.

ALEXAN.   Thinke you not, Hephestion, that shee would
faine be commanded?

HEPH.   I am no thought-catcher, but I ghesse vnhappily.

ALEX.   I will not enforce marriage where I cannot com-   125
pell loue.

CAMP.   But your Maiestie may moue a question where
you be willing to haue a match.

ALEX.   Beleeue me, Hephestion, these parties are agreed ;
they would haue mee both priest and witnesse.   Apelles,   130
take Campaspe !   Why moue yee not?   Campaspe, take

Apelles! Will it not be? If you be ashamed one of the
other, by my consent you shall neuer come together. But
dissemble not, Campaspe : doe you loue Apelles?

CAMP.   Pardon, my lord; I loue Apelles.   135

ALEX.   Apelles, it were a shame for you, being loued so
openly of so faire a virgin, to say the contrarie. Doe you
loue Campaspe?

APEL.   Onely Campaspe!

ALEX.   Two louing wormes, Hephestion! I perceiue 140
Alexander cannot subdue the affections of men, though[1]
conquer their countries. Loue falleth, like a dew, as well
vpon the low grasse as vpon the high cedar. Sparkes haue
their heat, ants their gall, flies their spleene. Well, enioy
one another. I giue her thee frankly, Apelles. Thou shalt 145
see that Alexander maketh but a toy of loue and leadeth
affection in fetters, vsing fancie as a foole to make him sport
or a minstrell to make him merry. It is not the amorous
glance of an eye can settle an idle thought in the heart. No,
no, it is childrens game, a life for seamsters and schollers : 150
the one, pricking in clouts, haue nothing else to thinke on ;
the other, picking fancies out of books, haue little else to
maruaile at. Go, Apelles, take with you your Campaspe,
Alexander is cloyed with looking on that which thou won-
drest at.   155

APEL.   Thankes to your Maiestie on bended knee : you
haue honoured Apelles !

CAMP.   Thankes, with bowed heart: you haue blessed
Campaspe.
                Exeunt [APELLES *and* CAMPASPE].

ALEX.   Page, goe warne Clytus and Parmenio and the 160
other lords to be in a readinesse ; let the trumpet sound ;
strike[2] vp the drumme ; and I will presently into Persia.
[*Exit* PAGE.] How now, Hephestion? is Alexander able to
resist loue as he list?

HEPH.   The conquering of Thebes was not so honourable 165
as the subduing of these thoughts.

<hr>

[1] F. though he, *without note*.   [2] *Misprinted* trike *in* F.

ALEX.   It were a shame Alexander should desire to command the world, if he could not command himselfe.   But
come, let vs goe.   I will trie whether I can better beare my
hand with my heart than I could with mine eye.   And, good   170
Hephestion, when all the world is wonne and euery country
is thine and mine, either find me out another to subdue, or,
of my word, I will fall in loue !   *Exeunt.*

FINIS.

The Epilogue at the Blacke-Friers.

Where the rain-bow toucheth the tree, no caterpillars will
hang on the leaues ; where the glo-worme creepeth in the
night, no adder will goe in the day : wee hope, in the eares
where our trauailes be lodged, no carping shall harbour in
those tongues.   Our exercises must be as your iudgement is :   5
resembling water, which is alwayes of the same colour into
what it runneth.   In the Troyan horse lay couched souldiers,
with children : and in heapes of many words, we feare, diuers
vnfit, among some allowable.   But, as Demosthenes with
often breathing vp the hill amended his stammering, so wee   10
hope with sundrie labours against the haire to correct our
studies.   If the tree be blasted that blossomes, the fault is
in the winde and not in the root : and if our pastimes bee
misliked that haue beene allowed,[1] you must impute it to the
malice of others and not our endeuour.   And so we rest in   15
good case, if you rest well content !

The Epilogue at the Court.

We cannot tell whether wee are fallen among Diomedes
birdes or his horses, — the one receiued some men with sweet
notes, the other bit all men with sharpe teeth.   But, as

---

[1] *It is obvious from this, even if it were not antecedently probable, that,*
although the Epilogue at the Court *stands last, the performance at the*
Court came first.

Homers gods conueyed them into cloudes whom they would
haue kept from curses, and as Venus, least Adonis should be   5
pricked with the stings of adders, couered his face with the
wings of swannes, so, wee hope, being shielded with your
Highnesse countenance, wee shall, though[1] heare the neighing, yet not feele the kicking of those iades, and receiue,
though no prayse, — which wee cannot deserue, — yet a par-   10
don, which in all humilitie we desire.   As yet we cannot tell
what we should tearme our labours, iron or bullion; only it
belongeth to your Maiestie to make them fit either for the
forge or the mint, currant by the stampe or counterfeit by the
anuill.   For, as nothing is to be called white vnlesse it had   15
beene named white by the first creature, so can there be
nothing thought good in the opinion of others vnlesse it be
christened good by the iudgement of your-selfe.   For our-
selues, againe, we are like these torches of waxe, of which,
being in your Highnesse hands, you may make doues or   20
vultures, roses or nettles, laurels for a garland or ealder for
a disgrace.

1 F. *accepts* Dods. *emendation of inserting* we; *but it seems unnecessary.*

FINIS.

THE

SCOTTISH

HISTORIE OF JAMES THE

fourth, flaine at *Flodden:*

Entermixed with a pleafant Comedie, presented by

Oboram King of *Fayeries:*

As it hath bene fundrie times publikely
plaide.

Written by *Robert Greene*, Maifter of Arts.

Omne tulit punctum.

Vignette.

LONDON
Printed by Thomas Creede. 1598.

May, 1594, a year and a half after the death of the author, this play was licensed for printing, but no copy of that edition is known to exist. I print from the same copy of Creede's edition (Mitford's copy, now in the British Museum) that was used by Dyce. In the footnotes I have pointed out the most important differences between my copyist's reading of Creede's edition (Cr.) and Dyce's edition (D.); but there are in the Scotch passages, which Dyce usually reproduced accurately, many insignificant differences of spelling, which I have noted only exceptionally. Grosart's edition (*Works of Robert Greene*, vol. XIII) is indicated by G.

[DRAMATIS PERSONAE.

OBERON, *King of Fairies.*
BOHAN, *a Scottish misanthrope.*

SLIPPER
NANO } *his sons.*

Fairies and other mutes.

KING OF SCOTS.
KING OF ENGLAND.

DOUGLAS
MORTON } *Scottish nobles.*
ROSS

BISHOP OF ST. ANDREWS.

SIR BARTRAM
SIR CUTHBERT ANDERSON } *Scottish gentlemen.*

EUSTACE, *an English gentleman.*
ATEUKIN, *a parasite.*

ANDREW
SLIPPER } *his servants.*

JAQUES, *a Frenchman.*
NANO, *the queen's dwarf.*
A Lawyer.
A Merchant.
A Divine.
Lord Percy, Samles, Purveyor, Herald, Scout,
    Noblemen, Soldiers, Huntsmen, &c.
DOROTHEA, *queen of Scots.*
COUNTESS OF ARRAN.
IDA, *her daughter.*
LADY ANDERSON.
Ladies and Servants.

SCENE: *Scotland.*]

328

THE SCOTTISH HYSTORIE OF IAMES THE FOURTH, SLAINE AT FLODDEN.

[The Induction.]

Musicke playing within.

[1] *Enter after* [1] OBERON,[2] *King of Fayries, an* [3] *antique, who dance about a tombe plac'st conueniently on the stage, out of the which suddainly starts vp as they daunce* BOHAN, *a Scot, attyred like a ridstall man, from whom the antique flyes.*[4] OBERON *manet.*

BOHAN. Ay say, whats thou?

OBERON. Thy friend, Bohan.

BOHAN. What wot I or reck I that? Whay, guid man, I reck no friend, nor ay reck no foe; als ene to me! Git the ganging, and trouble not may whayet, or ays gar the recon   5
me nene of thay friend, by the Mary masse, sall I!

OBER. Why, angrie Scot, I visit thee for loue : then what mooues thee to wroath?

BOHAN. The deele awhit reck I thy loue. For I knowe too well that true loue tooke her flight twentie winter sence   10
to heauen; whither till ay can, weele I wot, ay sal nere finde loue. An thou lou'st me, leaue me to my-selfe. But what were those puppits that hopt and skipt about me year-whayle?

OBERON. My subiects.

BOH. Thay subiects? whay, art thou a king?   15

OBER. I am.

BOHAN. The deele thou art! whay, thou look'st not so

---

[1] Cr. G. After; D. Aster.

[2] Cr. G. Oberō.   [4] *So* Cr; G. Antique[s] flye; D. Antics fly.

[3] D. G. *having read* after *as a name or title are obliged to change* an *to* and. *They also change* antique *to* antiques.

big as the king of clubs nor so sharpe as the king of spades
nor so faine as the king a daymonds.¹ Be the masse, ay take
thee to bee the king of false harts : therefore, I rid thee,   20
away! or ayse so curry your kingdome that yous be glad to
runne to saue your life.

OBER.   Why, stoycall Scot, do what thou dar'st to me :
heare is my brest, strike!

BOH.   Thou wilt not threap me. This whiniard has gard   25
many better me*n* to lope the*n* thou. But how now? Gos
sayds! what, wilt not out? Whay, thou wich! thou deele!
Gads fute, may whiniard!

OBER.   Why, pull, man! But what an twear out, how then?

BOH.   This then, thou weart best begon first; for ayl so   30
lop thy lyms that thouse go with half a knaues carkasse to
the deele.

OBER.   Draw it out. Now strike, foole. Canst thou not?

BOH.   Bread ay Gad, what deele is in me? Whay, tell mee,
thou skipiack : what art thou?   35

OBER.   Nay, first tell me what thou wast from thy birth,
what thou hast past hitherto, why thou dwellest in a tombe
and leauest the world ; and then I will release thee of these
bonds ; before, not.

BOH.   And not before, then needs must needs sal! I was   40
borne a gentleman of the best bloud in all Scotland, except
the king. When time brought me to age, and death tooke
my parents, I became a courtier ; where, though ay list not
praise my-selfe, ay engraued the memory of Boughon on the
skin-coate of some of them, and reueld with the proudest.   45

OBER.   But why, liuing in such reputation, didst thou leaue
to be a courtier?

BOH.   Because my pride was vanitie, my expence losse, my
reward faire words and large promises, *and* my hopes spilt,
for that after many yeares seruice one outran me, — and what   50
the deele should I then do there? No, no ; flattering knaues
that can cog and prate fastest speede best in the court.

OBER.   To what life didst thou then betake thee?

¹ Cr. G. Adaymonds.

BOH. I then chang'd the court for the countrey, and the wars for a wife; but I found the craft of swaines more vile 55 then the knauery of courtiers, the charge of children more heauie then seruants, and wiues tongues worse then the warres it-selfe; and therefore I gaue ore that, *and* went to the citie to dwell, *and* there I kept a great house with smal cheer, but all was nere the neere. 60

OBER. And why?

BOH. Because in seeking friends I found table-guests to eate me *and* my meat, my wiues gossops to bewray the secrets of my heart, kindred to betray the effect of my life. Which when I noted, — the court ill, the country worse, and 65 the citie worst of all, — in good time my wife died, ay wood she had died twentie winter sooner, by the masse! — leauing my two sonnes to the world, I shut[1] my-selfe into this tombe, where, if I dye, I am sure I am safe from wilde beasts, but, whilest I liue, cannot be free fro*m* ill companie. 70 Besides, now I am sure, gif all my friends faile me, I sall haue a graue of mine owne prouiding. This is all. Now what art thou?

OBER. Oberon, King of Fayries, that loues thee because thou hatest the world; and, to gratulate thee, I brought those 75 antiques to shew thee some sport in daunsing, which thou haste loued well.

BOHAN. Ha, ha, ha! thinkest thou those puppits can please me? whay, I haue two sonnes, that with one Scottish gigge shall breake the necke of thy antiques. 80

OBER. That I would faine see.

BOHA. Why, thou shalt. Howe, boyes!

Enter SLIPPER *and* NANO.

Haud your clacks, lads; trattle not for thy life, but gather vppe your legges and daunce me forthwith a gigge worth the sight. 85

SLIP. Why, I must talk, on[2] I dy fort; wherefore was my tongue made?

---

[1] G. and shutting; D. "*some words wanting.*"
[2] D. *emends to* an.

BOHA.   Prattle, an thou darst, one word more, and ais dab
this whiniard in thy wembe.

OBER.   Be quiet, Bohan! Ile strike him dumbe, and his   90
brother too; their talk shal not hinder our gyg.   Fall to it;
dance, I say, ma*n*!

BOH.   Dance, humer;[1] dance, ay rid thee!

The two dance a gig deuised for the nonst.

Now get you to the wide world with more the*n* my father
gaue me, — thats, learning enough, both kindes, knauerie *and*   95
honestie; and that I gaue you spend at pleasure.

OBER.   Nay, for their sport I will giue them this gift: to
the dwarfe I giue a quicke witte, prettie[2] of body, and a
warrant[3] his preferment to a princes service, where by his
wisdome he shall gaine more loue then co*m*mon; and to log-   100
gerhead your sonne I giue a wandering life, and promise he
shall neuer lacke, and auow that,[4] if in all distresses he call
vpon me, to helpe him.   Now let them go.

Exeunt with curtesies.

BOH.   Now, king, if thou bee a king, I will shew thee
whay I hate the world by demonstration.   In the yeare 1520   105
was in Scotland a king overruled with parasites, misled by
lust, *and* many circumstances too long to trattle on now,
much like our court of Scotland this day.   That story haue
I set down; gang with me to the gallery, *and* Ile shew thee
the same in action by guid fellowes of our country-men; and   110
then, when thou seest that, iudge if any wise man would not
leaue the world if he could.

OBER.   That will I see; lead, and Ile follow thee.

Exeunt.

[1] *In his note on this passage* G. *says:* " Dyce, *in his first edition,
printed* ' Heimore' *from a modern text.*"   *This is misleading, especially
when taken in connection with* G.'s *statement that the Huth copy of this
play is unique.   What* Dyce *says is that in the copy he used for his first
edition the leaf containing this passage is modern.   As I print from the
copy used by* Dyce, *I abandon it and follow* G. *from* l. 50 *above to the end
of this Induction.*

[2] G. prettie[ness].   [3] D. G. awarrant.   [4] D. *strikes out* that.

OF IAMES THE FOURTH.[1]

Laus Deo detur in eternum!

Actus[2] primus.   Scena prima.

[*The Scottish court.*]

Enter[3] *the* KING OF ENGLAND, *the* KING OF SCOTS, DORITHE, *his queen, the* COUNTESSE, LADY IDA, *with other* LORDS; *and* ATEUKIN *with them, aloofe.*

K. OF SCOTS.   Brother of England, since our neighboring
          land
And neare alliance doth [4] inuite our loues,
The more I think vpon our last accord,
The more I greeue your suddaine parting hence.
First, lawes of friendship did confirme our peace ;   5
Now, both the seale of faith and marriage-bed,
The name of father, and the style of friend.
These force in me affection full confirmd,
So that I greeue — and this my heartie griefe
The heauens record, the world may witnesse well —   10
To loose your presence, who are now to me
A father, brother and a vowed friend.
     K. OF ENG.   Link all these louely stiles, good king, in one ;
And, since thy griefe exceeds in my depart,
I leaue my Dorithea to enioy   15
Thy whole compact of [5] loues and plighted vowes.
Brother of Scotland, this is my ioy, my life,
Her fathers honour and her countries hope,
Her mothers comfort and her husbands blisse.
I tell thee, king, in louing of my Doll   20
Thou bindst her fathers heart and all his friends
In bands of loue that death cannot dissolue.

---

[1] *Omitted by* D. G.   [2] Cr. Attus.
[3] In Cr. *the stage-direction precedes* Actus primus.
[4] D. *changes to* do.
[5] D. *inserts* of; G. *reads* compact[ed]. *In* Cr. l. 15 *ends here.*

K. OF SCOTS.   Nor can her father loue her like to me.
My liues light and the comfort of my soule,
Faire Dorithea, that wast Englands pride,   25
Welcome to Scotland!   And, in signe of loue,
Lo, I inuest thee with the Scottish crowne.
Nobles and ladies, stoupe vnto your queene ;
And trumpets sound, that heralds may proclaime
Faire Dorithea peerlesse queene of Scots !   30
    ALL.   Long liue and prosper our faire q[ueene] of Scots !

Enstall and crowne her.

    DOR.   Thanks to the King of Kings for [1] my dignity ;
Thanks to my father, that prouides so carefully ;
Thanks to my lord and husband for this honor ; [2]
And thanks to all that loue their king and me!   35
    ALL.   Long liue faire Dorithea, our true queene !
    K. OF E.   Long shine the sun of Scotland in her pride,
Her fathers comfort and faire Scotlands bride !
But, Dorithea, since I must depart
And leaue thee from thy tender mothers charge,   40
Let me aduise my louely daughter first
What best befits her in a forraine land :
Liue, Doll, for many eyes shall looke on thee ;
Haue [3] care of honor and the present state,
For she that steps to height of maiestie   45
Is euen the marke whereat the enemy aimes.
Thy vertues shall be construed to vice,
Thine affable discourse to abiect minde ;
If coy, detracting tongues will call thee proud :
Be therefore warie in this slippery state ;   50
Honour thy husband, loue him as thy life ;
Make choyce of friends — as eagles of their yoong —
Who sooth no vice, who flatter not for gaine,
But loue such friends as do the truth maintaine.

---

[1] G. *inserts* this.   [2] G. honour.
[3] D. *emends to* With, *on account of the previous line.*

Thinke on these lessons when thou art alone,　　　55
And thou shalt liue in health when I am gone.
　　Dor.　I will engraue these preceps [1] in my heart;
And, as the wind with calmnesse woes you hence,
Euen so I wish the heauens, in all mishaps,
May blesse my father with continuall grace.　　　60
　　K. of E.　Then, son, farwell;
The fauouring windes inuites [2] vs to depart; [3]
Long circumstance in taking princely leaues
Is more officious then conuenient.
Brother of Scotland, loue me in my childe!　　　65
You greet me well, if so you will her good.
　　K. of Sc.　Then, louely Doll, and all that fauor me,
Attend to see our English friends at sea;
Let all their charge depend vpon my purse:
They are our neighbors, by whose kind accord　　　70
We dare attempt the proudest potentate.
Onely, faire countesse, and your daughter, stay;
With you I haue some other thing to say.

　　　Exeunt all saue the King, *the* Countesse, Ida, Ateukin, *in all royaltie.*

　　K. of S. [*aside*]　So let them tryumph that haue cause to
　　　ioy!
But, wretched king, thy nuptiall knot is death,　　　75
Thy bride the breeder of thy countries ill;
For, thy false heart dissenting from thy hand,
Misled by loue, hast [5] made another choyce, —
Another choyce, euen when thou vowdst thy soule
To Dorithea, Englands choysest pride.　　　80
O then thy wandring eyes bewitcht thy heart!
Euen in the chappell did thy fancie change,
When, periur'd man, though faire Doll had thy hand,

---

1 *This perhaps represents the pronunciation.*
2 D. *changes to* invite.
3 Lines 61, 62 *as one in* Cr.
4 *In G. these three words precede* saue.
5 D. *emends to* hath.

The Scottish Idaes bewtie [1] stale thy heart!
Yet feare and loue hath [2] tyde thy readie tongue   85
From blabbing forth the passions of thy minde,
Lest [3] fearefull silence haue in suttle lookes
Bewrayd the treason of my new-vowd loue.
Be faire and louely, Doll, but here 's the prize,
That lodgeth here, and entred through mine eyes.   90
Yet, how-so-ere I loue, I must be wise!—
Now, louely countesse, what reward or grace
May I imploy [4] on you for this your zeale
And humble honors done vs in our court
In entertainment of the English king?   95

COUNTESSE.   It was of dutie, prince, that I haue done ;
And what in fauour may content me most
Is that it please your Grace to giue me leaue
For to returne vnto my countrey home.

K. OF SCOTS.   But, louely Ida, is your mind the same?   100

IDA.   I count of court, my lord, as wise men do :
Tis fit for those that knowes [5] what longs thereto.
Each person to his place : the wise to art,
The cobler to his clout, the swaine to cart.

K. OF SC.   But, Ida, you are faire, and bewtie [6] shines   105
And seemeth best where pomp her pride refines.

IDA.   If bewtie [7]— as I know there 's none in me —
Were sworne my loue, and I his life should be,
The farther from the court I were remoued,
The more, I thinke, of Heauen I were beloued.   110

K. OF SCOTS.   And why? [8]

IDA.   Because the court is counted Venus net,
Where gifts and vowes for stales are often set.
None, be she chaste as Vesta, but shall meete
A curious toong to charme her eares with sweet.   115

---

[1] G. beauty.   [5] D. *changes to* know.
[2] D. *changes to* have.   [6] G. beautie.
[3] D. G. *change to* 'Less.   [7] G. beutie.
[4] D. *changed to* impose ; *but later restored the text.*
[8] *The play contains Alexandrines, but, as short lines are even more common, I leave these two syllables as a line.*

K. OF SCOTS.　Why, Ida, then I see you set at naught,
The force of loue.

　IDA.　　　　　In sooth this is my thogt,
Most gratious[1] king, that they that little proue[2]
Are mickle blest from bitter sweets of loue.
And weele I wot, I heard a shepheard sing　　　　120
That, like a bee, loue hath a little sting.
He lurkes in flowres, he pearcheth on the trees,
He on kings pillowes'bends his prettie knees ;
The boy is blinde but when he will not spie ;
He hath a leaden[3] foote, and wings to flie :　　　125
Beshrow me yet, for all these strange effects,
If I would like the lad, that so infects.

　K. OF SCOTS. [aside]　Rare wit, fair face, what hart could
　　　more desire?
But Doll is faire, and doth concerne thee neere.[4]
Let Doll be faire, she is wonne ; but I must woe　　130
And win faire Ida ; theres some choyce in two. —
But, Ida, thou art coy.

　IDA.　　　　　And why, dread king?

　K. OF SCOTS.　In that you will dispraise so sweet a thing
As loue.　Had I my wish —

　IDA.　　　　　What then?

　K. OF SCOTS.　　　　　Then would I place
His arrow[5] here, his bewtie in that face.[6]　　　135

　IDA.　And were Apollo moued and rulde by me,
His wisedome should be yours, and mine his tree.

　K. OF SCOTS.　But here returnes our traine.　Welcome,
　　　faire Doll![7]
How fares our father? is he shipt and gone?

Enters the traine backe.[8]

---

[1] G. gracious.　　　　　　[4] *Qy.* nigher, *for rhyme.*

[2] *In* Cr. ll. 117, 118 *as three, ending* loue, king, proue.

[3] G. leaded.　　　　　　[5] G. arrows.

[6] *In* Cr. ll. 132–135 *as seven, ending* coy, king, sweet, wish, then, here,
face.　　　　　　　　　[7] *In* Cr. *these three words are in* l. 139.

[8] G. *silently transfers this stage-direction* (*with* Enter *for* Enters) *to the
middle of* l. 138.

DOR.   My royall father is both shipt and gone ;   140
God and faire winds direct him to his home !
   K. OF SC.   Amen, say I ! [*aside*] Wold thou wert with him
     too !
Then might I haue a fitter time to woo. —
But, Countesse, you would be gone : therfore farwell !
Yet, Ida, if thou wilt, stay thou behind,   145
To accompany my queene ;
But, if thou[1] like the pleasures of the court —
[*Aside*] Or if she likte me, tho she left the court, —
What should I say ? I know not what to say. —
You may depart. And you, my curteous queene,   150
Leaue me a space ; I haue a waighte cause
To thinke vpon.[2]   [*Aside*] Ida! It nips me neere ;
It came from thence, I feele it burning heere.

       Exeunt all sauing the KING *and* ATEUKIN.

   K. OF SCOT.   Now am I free from sight of common eie,
Where to my-selfe I may disclose the griefe   155
That hath too great a part in mine affects.
   ATEU.   And now is my time by wiles *and* words to rise
Greater then those that thinks[3] themselues more wise.
   K. OF SCOTS.   And first, fond king, thy honor doth engraue
Vpon thy browes the drift of thy disgrace :   160
Thy new-vowd loue in sight of God and men
Linke[4] thee to Dorithea during life ;
For who more faire and vertuous then thy wife.
Deceitfull murtherer of a quiet minde,
Fond loue, vile lust, that thus misleads vs men   165
To vowe our faithes, and fall to sin againe !
But kings stoupe not to euery common thought.
Ida is faire and wise, fit for a king ;
And for faire Ida will I hazard life,
Venture my kingdome, countrey,[5] and my crowne, —   170

---

   [1] G. *inserts* not.   [5] G. country.
   [2] *In* Cr. *these three words are in* l. 151.
   [3] D. *changes to* think.
   [4] D. *changes to* Links ; G. *takes* Linke *as optative.*

Such fire hath loue to burne a kingdome downe!
Say Doll dislikes that I estrange my loue, —
Am I obedient to a womans looke?
Nay, say her father frowne when he shall heare
That I do hold faire Idaes loue so deare, —   175
Let father frowne and fret, and fret and die,
Nor earth nor heauen shall part my loue and I.
Yea, they shall part vs, but we first must meet,
And wo and win, and yet the world not seet.
Yea, ther 's the wound!   *And*, wounded with that thoght,   180
So let me die; for all my drift is naught!

    ATEU.   Most gratious and imperiall Maiestie. —
[*Aside*] A little flattery more were but too much![1]

    K. OF S.   Villaine, what art thou
That thus darest interrupt a princes secrets.[2]   185

    ATEU.   Dread king, thy vassall is a man of art,
Who knowes by constellation of the stars,
By oppositions and by dire[3] aspects,
The things are past and those that are to come.

    K. OF S.   But where 's thy warrant to approach my pres-
        ence?   190

    ATEU.   My zeale and ruth to see your Graces wrong
Makes me lament I did detract so long.

    K. OF S.   If thou knowst thoughts, tell me what mean
        I now?

    ATEU.   Ile calculate the cause
Of those your Highnesse smiles[4] and tell your thoughts.   195

    K. OF S.   But, least thou spend thy time in idlenesse
And misse the matter that my mind aimes at,
Tell me:[5] what star was opposite when that was thought?

He strikes him on the eare.

    ATEU.   Tis inconuenient, mightie[6] potentate,

---

[1] Cr. *gives this line to the* KING; *I accept* D.'s *transfer of it to*
ATEUKIN.   [3] Cr. drie; D. dry; *corr. by* G.
  [2] *In* Cr. ll. 184, 185 *as one.*   [4] *In* Cr. l. 194 *ends here.*
  [5] D. *gets rid of the Alexandrine by making a separate line of these two*
words.   [6] G. mighty.

Whose lookes resembles [1] Ioue in maiestie,   200
To scorne the sooth of science with contempt.
I see in those imperiall lookes of yours
The whole discourse of loue: Saturn combust
With direfull lookes at your natiuitie
Beheld faire Venus in her siluer orbe.   205
I know by certaine exiomies [2] I haue read
Your Graces griefs, *and*, further, can expresse
Her name [3] that holds you thus in fancies bands.

   K. OF S.   Thou talkest wonders.

   ATEU.   Nought but truth, O king.
Tis Ida is the mistresse of your heart,   210
Whose youth must take impression of affects ;
For tender twigs will bowe, and milder mindes
Will yeeld to fancie, be they followed well.

   K. OF S.   What god art thou, composde in humane shape,
Or bold Trophonius, to decide our doubts?   215
How knowst thou this?

   ATEU.   Euen as I know the meanes
To worke your Graces freedome and your loue.
Had I the mind, as many courtiers haue,
To creepe into your bosome for your coyne
And beg rewards for euery cap and knee,   220
I then would say : if that your Grace would giue
This lease, this manor or this pattent seald,
For this or that I would effect your loue ;
But Ateukin [4] is no parasite, O prince !
I know your Grace knowes schollers are but poore ;   225
And therefore, as I blush to beg a fee,
Your Mightinesse is so magnificent
You cannot chuse but cast some gift apart
To ease my bashfull need that cannot beg.

---

[1] D. G. resemble, *without note.*

[2] D. G. *modernize to* axioms.

[3] *In* Cr. *these two words are in* l. 207.

[4] *Here, and often elsewhere, a dissyllable ; for discussion of* Fleay's *inference, see Notes.*

As for your loue, oh, might I be imployd,   230
How faithfully would Ateukin compasse it!
But princes rather trust a smoothing tongue
Then men of art that can accept the time.
   K. OF SCOTS.   Ateu[kin], — if so thy name, for so thou
      saist, —
Thine art appeares in entrance of my loue;   235
And, since I deeme thy wisedom matcht with truth,
I will exalt thee; and thy-selfe alone
Shalt be the agent to dissolue my griefe.
Sooth is, I loue, and Ida is my loue;
But my new marriage nips me neare, Ateukin,   240
For Dorithea may not brooke th' abuse.
   ATEU.   These lets are but as moaths[1] against the sun,
Yet not so great; like dust before the winde,
Yet not so light.[2]   Tut! pacifie your Grace:
You haue the sword and scepter in your hand,   245
You are the king, the state depends on you,
Your will is law.   Say that the case were mine, —
Were she my sister whom your Highnesse loues,
She shou'd[3] consent, for that our liues, our goods,
Depend on you.   And, if your queene repine,   250
Although my nature cannot brooke of blood,
And schollers grieue to heare of murtherous deeds, —
But if the lambe should let the lyons[4] way,
By my aduise the lambe should lose her life.
Thus am I bold to speake vnto your Grace,   255
Who am too base to kisse your royall feete;
For I am poore, nor haue I land or[5] rent
Nor countenance here in court; but, for my loue,
Your Grace shall find none such within the realme!
   K. OF S.   Wilt thou effect my loue? shal[6] she be mine?   260

---

[1] D. motes; G. *thinks* moathes (moaths) *a misprint.*
[2] G. *proposes* the dust . . . is not.
[3] G. should.
[4] G. lyon's.
[5] D. G. nor, *without note.*   [6] G. shall.

ATEU.   Ile gather moly, rocus [1] and the earbes
That heales [2] the wounds of body and the minde;
Ile set out charmes and spels; nought else [3] shalbe left
To tame the wanton if she shall rebell:
Giue me but tokens of your Highnesse trust.   265
    K. OF S.   Thou shalt haue gold, honor and wealth inough;
Winne [4] my loue, and I will make thee great.
    ATEU.   These words do make me rich, most noble prince;
I am more proude of them then any wealth.
Did not your Grace suppose I flatter you,   270
Beleeue me I would boldly publish this:
Was neuer eye that sawe a sweeter face,
Nor neuer eare that heard a deeper wit;
Oh God, how I am rauisht in your woorth!
    K. OF S.   Ateu[kin], follow me; loue must haue ease.   275
    ATEU.   Ile kisse your Highnesse feet; march when you
        please.   *Exeunt.*

[Act first.   Scene second.]

[*The market-place.*] [5]

Enter SLIPPER, NANO, *and* ANDREW, *with their billes, readie written, in
    their hands.*

ANDREW.   [6] Stand back, sir; mine shall stand highest!
    SLIP.   Come vnder mine arme, sir, or get a footstoole;
Or else, by the light of the moone, I must come to it.
    NANO.   Agree, my maisters; euery man to his height!
Though I stand lowest, I hope to get the best maister.   5

---

1 Cr. Moly-rocus; Mitford, moly, crocus; *but this seems doubtful.*
2 D. *changes to* heal.   3 D. G. *reject* else.
4 Winne me my, etc., *would restore the metre; but lines of nine syllables are common in* Greene *and* Peele.   D. *suggests* thou *or* but *as missing;* G. *accepts* thou.
5 *But the author probably had in mind some such place as St. Paul's,
London.*
6 *From here to the entrance of* ATEUKIN D. G. *print as prose; but as
some of it seems to be a rude sort of verse, and as* Cr. *begins each line with
a capital, I preserve the line-division of* Cr.

ANDR.   Ere I will stoupe to a thistle, I will change turnes ;
As good lucke comes on the right hand as the left ;
Here 's for me !

[SLIP.]   And me !

[NANO.]   And mine ! [1]

> [*They post their bills.*]

ANDR.   But tell me, fellowes, till better occasion come :
Do you seeke maisters?   10

AMBO.   We doo.

ANDR.   But what can you do worthie preferment?

NANO.   Marry I can smell a knaue from a rat.

SLIP.   And I can licke a dish before a cat.

ANDR.   And I can finde two fooles vnsought.   15
How like you that?
But in earnest now, tell me : of what trades are you two?

SLIP.   How meane you that, sir?   Of what trade?
Marry, Ile tell you, I haue many trades :
The honest trade when I needs must,   20
The filching trade when time serues,
The cousening trade as I finde occasion.
And I haue more qualities : I cannot abide a ful cup vnkist,
A fat capon vncaru'd,
A full purse vnpickt,   25
Nor a foole to prooue a iustice, as you do.

ANDR.   Why, sot, why calst thou me foole?

NANO.   For examining wiser then thy-selfe.

ANDR.   So doth many more then I in Scotland.

NANO.   Yea, those are such as haue more autthoritie [2] then
        wit,   30
And more wealth then honestie.

SLIP.   This is my little brother with the great wit, ware
        him !
But what canst thou do, tel me, that art so inquisitiue of vs?

---

[1] Cr. D. *assign* Here 's for me, and me, and mine *to* ANDREW.   G.'s
assignment, adopted above, is supported by the repetition of ANDR. *before*
l. 9.   G. *indicates in no way that he has emended* Cr.

[2] G. *does not notice the misprint.*

Andr.   Any-thing that concernes a gentleman to do, that
        can I do.
Slip.   So you are of the gentle trade?   35
Andr.   True.
Slip.   Then, gentle sir, leaue vs to our-selues;
For heare comes one as if he would lack a seruant ere he
        went.[1]   *Ent[er]* Ateu[kin].
[Ateu.]   Why so, Ateukin, this becomes thee best:
Wealth, honour, ease, and angelles in thy chest.   40
Now may I say, as many often sing:
No fishing to the sea, nor seruice to a king.
Vnto this high promotions[2] doth belong,
Meanes to be talkt[3] of in the thickest throng.
And first, to fit the humors of my lord,   45
Sweete layes and lynes of loue I must record;
And such sweete lynes and louelayes Ile endite
As men may wish for, and my leech[4] delight.
And next, a traine of gallants at my heeles,
That men may say the world doth run on wheeles;   50
For men of art that rise by indirection
To honour and the fauour of their king,
Must vse all meanes to saue what they haue got,
And win their fauours whom he[5] neuer knew.
If any frowne to see my fortunes such,   55
A man must beare a little, — not too much!
But in good time! — these billes partend,[6] I thinke,
That some good fellowes do for seruice seeke.
    Read: " If any gentleman, spirituall or temperall, will en-
tertaine out of his seruice, a yong[7] stripling of the age of 30   60
yeares, thet[6] can sleep with the soundest, eate with the hun-
griest, work with the sickest,[8] lye with the lowdest, face with

---

1 D. G. *print a stage-direction:* Andrew stands aside, *which is not in
the copy made for me.*   5 D. G. *change to* they.
    2 D. G. *change to* promotion.   6 *So* Cr.
    3 *So* G.; Cr. talke; D. talk'd.   7 G. Young.
    4 D. *emends to* liege, *which is, of course, the meaning.*
    8 D. *had a friend who conjectured* sickerest, *which instigated* D. *to con-
jecture* stoutest.

the proudest, &c.,[1] that can wait in a gentlemans chamber
when his maister is a myle of, keepe his stable when tis
emptie and his purse when tis full, and hath many qualities   65
woorse then all these, let him write his name and goe his
way, and attendance shall be giuen."

ATEU.   [2] By my faith, a good seruant! which is he?

SLIP.   Trulie, sir, that am I.

ATEU.   And why doest thou write such a bill?   70
Are all these qualities in thee?

SLIP.   O Lord, I, sir, and a great many more,
Some better, some worse, some richer, some porer.
Why, sir, do you looke so? do they not please you?

ATEU.   Trulie, no; for they are naught, and so art thou;   75
If thou hast no better qualities, stand by!

SLIP.   O, sir, I tell the worst first; but, and you lack a man,
I am for you, ile tell you the best qualities I haue.

ATEU.   Be breefe then.

SLIP.   If you need me in your chamber,   80
I can keepe the doore at a whistle; in your kitchin,
Turne the spit and licke the pan and make the fire burne.
But if in the stable —

ATEU.[3] Yea, there would I vse thee.

SLIP.   Why, there you kill me, there am I![4]   85
And turne me to a horse *and* a wench, and I haue no peere!

ATEU.   Art thou so good in keeping a horse?
I pray thee, tell me how many good qualities hath a horse.

SLIP.   Why, so, sir: a horse hath two properties of a
      man, —
That is, a proude heart, and a hardie stomacke;   90
Foure properties of a lyon, — a broad brest, a stiffe docket
(Hold your nose, master!), a wild countenance, and foure [5]
      good legs;

[1] *As* D. *suggests in regard to another passage* (*see* p. 350, *below*), *the
actor was allowed to interpret this* &c. *liberally.*

[2] *From here to the end of the scene* D. G. *print as prose; I follow* Cr.

[3] Cr. Steu.   [5] Cr. G. 4.

[4] D., *probably not observing that this is a bit of slang, supposes the loss
of some words;* Mitford *suggested* there am I a per se.

Nine properties of a foxe, nine of a hare, nine of an asse,
And ten of a woman.

    Ateu.   A woman? why, what properties of a woman hath
        a horse?   95

    Slip.   O, maister, know you not that?
Draw your tables, and write what wise I speake:
First, a merry countenance ;
Second, a soft pace ;
Third, a broad forehead ;   100
Fourth, broad buttockes ;
Fift, hard of ward ; [1]
Sixt, easie to leape vpon ;
Seuenth, good at long iourney ;
Eight, mouing vnder a man ;   105
Ninth, alway busie with the mouth ;
Tenth, euer chewing on the bridle.

    Ateu.   Thou art a man for me.   Whats thy name?
    Slip.   An auncient name, sir, belonging to the
Chamber and the night-gowne.   Gesse you that.   110
    Ateu.   Whats that? Slipper?
    Slip.   By my faith, well gest ; and so tis indeed.
Youle be my maister?
    Ateu.   I meane so.
    Slip.   Reade this first.   115
    Ateu. [*reads*] " Pleaseth it any gentleman to entertaine
A seruant of more wit then [2] stature,
Let them subscribe, and attendance shall be giuen."
What of this?
    Slip.   He is my brother, sir, and we two were borne to-
        gither,   120
Must serue togither, and will die togither
Though we be both hangd.
    Ateu.   Whats thy name?
    Nano.   Nano.
    Ateu.   The etimologie of which word is " a dwarfe."   125
Art not thou the old Stoykes son that dwels in his tombe?

---

[1] G. warde.   [2] G. than.

AMBO.   We are.

ATEU.   Thou art welcome to me.

Wilt thou giue thy-selfe wholly to be at my disposition?

NANO.   In all humilitie I submit my-selfe.   130

ATEU.   Then will I deck thee princely, instruct thee courtly,

And present thee to the queene as my gift.

Art thou content?

NANO.   Yes, and thanke your Honor too.

SLIP.   Then welcome, brother, and fellow now!   135

ANDR.   May it please your Honor to abase your eye so
          lowe

As to looke either on my bill or my-selfe.

ATEU.   What are you?

AN.   By birth a gentleman, in profession a scholler,

And one that knew your Honor in Edenborough   140

Before your worthinesse cald you to this reputation.

                    By me, Andrew Snoord.

ATEU. Andrew, I remember thee ; follow me,

And we will confer further ; for my waightie affaires

For the king commands [1] me to be briefe at this time.   145

Come on, Nano ; Slipper, follow!   *Exeunt.*

[Act first.   Scene third.]

[*The house of* SIR BARTRAM.]

Enter SIR BARTRAM, *with* EUSTAS *and others, booted.*

S. BAR.   But tell me louely Eustas, as thou lou'st me :

Among the many pleasures we haue past

Which is the rifest in thy memorie

To draw the ouer to thine auncient friend?

EU.   What makes Sir Bartram thus inquisitiue?   5

Tell me, good knight : am I welcome or no?

SIR BAR.   By sweet S. Andrew and may sale I sweare,

As welcom is my honest Dick to me

---

[1] D. *changes to* command.

As mornings sun or as the[1] watry moone
In merkist night when we the borders track.   10
I tell thee, Dick, thy sight hath cleerd my thoughts
Of many banefull troubles that there woond.
Welcome[2] to Sir Bartram as his life !
Tell me, bonny Dicke : hast got a wife?

     EUST.   A wife?   God shield, Sir Bartram ! that were ill   15
To leaue my wife and wander thus astray.
But time and good aduise, ere many yeares,
May chance to make my fancie bend that way.
What newes in Scotland?   Therefore came I hither, —
To see your country, and to chat togither.   20

     SIR BAR.   Why, man, our countries blyth, our king is well,
Our queene so-so, the nobles well and worse ;
And weele are they that were[3] about the king ;
But better are the country gentlemen.
And I may tell thee, Eustace, in our liues   25
We old men neuer saw so wondrous change.
But leaue this trattle, and tell me what newes
In louely England with our honest friends.

     EUST.   The king, the court and all our noble friends
Are well, and God in mercy keepe them so !   30
The northren lords and ladies here-abouts
That knowes[4] I came to see your queen and court
Commends[5] them to my honest friend Sir Bartram, —
And many others that I haue not seene.
Among the rest, the Countesse Elinor,   35
From Carlile,[6] where we merry oft haue bene,
Greets well my lord, and hath directed me,
By message, this faire ladies face to see.

[1] *So* D. G.; Cr. a.

[2] D. *suggests* As welcome *here, and* But tell *in next line;* G. Aye welcome *here and* me my bonny *in next line. I regard them as nine-syllabled lines.*

[3] D. *emends to* are, *perhaps rightly.*

[4] D. *changes to* know.

[5] D. *changes to* commend.

[6] *In* Cr. *these two words are in* l. 35.

[Showing a picture.]

SIR BAR.   I tell thee, Eustace, lest [1] mine old eyes daze,
This is our Scottish moone and euenings pride;   40
This is the blemish of your English bride.
Who sailes by her are sure of winde at will;
Her face is dangerous, her sight is ill.
And yet, in sooth, sweet Dicke, it may be said:
The king hath folly; their 's vertue in the mayd.   45
    EUST.   But knows my friend this portrait? be aduisd.
    SIR BAR.   Is it not Ida the Countesse of Arains [2] daughters?
    EUST.   So was I told by Elinor of Carlile.
But tell me, louely Bartram: is the maid
Euil-inclind, misled, or concubine   50
Vnto the king or any other lord? [3]
    BA.   Shuld I be brief *and* true, the*n* thus, my Dicke:
All Englands grounds yeelds [4] not a blyther lasse,
Nor Europ can not match [5] her for her gifts
Of vertue, honour, beautie, and the rest;   55
But our fo*n*d king, not knowing sin in lust,
Makes loue by endlesse meanes and precious gifts,
And men that see it dare not sayt, my friend,
But wee may wish that it were otherwise.
But I rid thee to view the picture still;   60
For by the persons sights [6] there hangs som ill.
    EUST. [7]   Oh, good Sir Bartram, you suspect I loue —
Then were I mad — her [8] whom I neuer sawe!
But, how-so-ere, I feare not entisings;

---

[1] D. G. *change to* 'less.

[2] G. Arain's.

[3] *In* Cr. ll. 49–51 *as two, ending* inclind, lord.

[4] D. *changes to* yield.

[5] Cr. can art; D. *emends to* can surpass.

[6] D. *emends to* sight (*not to* right, *as* G. *says*), *which is better* (*cf.* l. 43);
G. *keeps* sights, *but thinks it means* eyes.

[7] D. G. *say* Cf. *assigns* ll. 62–67 *to* BARTRAM; *my copyist, who never
undertakes to correct errors of the original, wrote* B, *and then erased it
and wrote* EUST.

[8] Cr. hee; *corr. by* D.

Desire will giue no place vnto a king :   65
Ile see her whom the world admires so much,
That I may say with them, there liues none such.
   BAR.   Be Gad, and sal both see and talke with her;
And, when th' hast done, what-ere her beautie be,
Ile warant [1] thee her vertue [2] may compare   70
With [3] proudest she that waits vpon your queen.

[Enter SERVANT.]

   SERV.[4]   My ladie intreats your Worship in to supper.
   BA.   Guid, bony Dick, my wife will tel thee more,
Was neuer no man [5] in her booke before :
Be Gad, shees blyth, faire, lewely,[6] bony, &c.[7]   75
Exeunt.

[The End of the First Act.]

[CHORUS.]

Enter BOHAN and the FAIRY KING after the First Act, to them a rownd
of fairies, or some prittie dance.

   BOH.   Be Gad, gramersis, little king, for this !
This sport is better in my exile life
Then euer the deceitfuil werld could yeeld.
   OBER.   I tell thee, Bohan, Oberon is king
Of quiet, pleasure, profit and content,   5
Of wealth, of honor and of all the world ;
Tide to no place, — yet all are tide to one.[8]
Liue thou in [9] this life, exilde from world and men,
And I will shew thee wonders [10] ere we part.

---

  [1] G. warrant.   [2] D. G. vertues.
  [3] So Cr.; D. G., silently, With the ; I suppose with to have absorbed the
unstressed the, just as this often absorbs unstressed is.
  [4] Cr. EU.; corr. by D.
  [5] D. in his first edition suggests woman ; but apparently EUSTACE is
meant.   [6] G. changes to lovely.
  [7] D. suggests that the player was here to extemporize ; see above, p. 345.
G. plausibly suggests that it means " he goes out talking."
  [8] D. changes to me ; but he misses the thought.
  [9] D. G. reject in.   [10] Cr. wonters ; corr. silently by D.

Boh.   Then marke my story[1] and the strange doubts[2]   10
That follow flatterers, lust and lawlesse will,
And then say I haue reason to forsake
The world,[3] and all that are within the same.
Gow shrowd vs in our harbor, where weele[4] see
The pride of folly as it ought to be.   15

Exeunt.

After the First Act.[5]

[1.]

Ober.   Here see I good fond actions in thy gyg
And meanes to paint the worldes in-constant waies ;
But turne thine ene, see what[6] I can commaund.

*Enter two battailes strongly fighting: the one, Semiramis ;[7] the other,
Stabrobates ;[8] she flies, and her crowne is taken, and she hurt.*

[*Exeunt.*]

Boh.   What gars this din of mirk and balefull harme,
Where euery weane is all betaint with bloud?   5
Ober.   This shewes thee, Bohan, what is worldly pompe.
Simeramis, the proud Assirrian queene,

---

[1] Cr. stay; *emend. by* D.

[2] *Qy.* defeats; D. *suggests* debates.

[3] *In* Cr. *these two words are in* l. 12.

[4] *So* G.; Cr. we ele.

[5] D. *suggests that the three dumb-shows inserted here may perhaps have
been meant for production after the first, second, and third acts. This
may be true.* G., *misunderstanding* gyg, *thinks it clear that the first dumb-
show should follow the "jig" in the* Induction, *but admits that his hypothesis does not explain the presence of "2" and "3," or even the last line of
this section. It seems highly probable that they were composed as substitutes for three (or more) of the inter-scenes with dances ; perhaps they came
into the printer's hands on a loose sheet of* MS. *Cf.* p. 354, n. 1.

[6] Cr. which for; *emend. by* D.

[7] Cr. Simi Ramis; *corr. by* D.; D. G. *read* Cr. *here as* Simi Ranus,
and l. 7 *as* Simeranus.

[8] Cr. Staurobates; *corr. by* D.

When Ninus died, did tene in[1] her warres
Three millions of footemen to the fight,
Fiue hundreth thousand horse, of armed chars   10
A hundreth thousand more; yet in her pride
Was hurt and conquered by Stabrobates.[2]
Then what is pompe?
    BOHAN.   I see thou art[3] thine ene,
Thou bonny king, if princes fall from high :
My fall is past, vntill[4] I fall to die.   15
Now marke my talke, and prosecute my gyg.

2.

    OBER.   How shuld these crafts withdraw thee from the
        world?
But looke my Bohan, pompe[5] allureth [thee].

Enter CIRUS, KINGS[6] *humbling themselues ; himselfe crowned, by* OLIUE
PAT;[7] *at last dying, layde in a marbell tombe with this inscription :*

Who-so thou bee that passest by, — [8]
For I know one shall passe, — knowe I
Am[9] Cirus [king] of Persia,   5
And I prithee[10] leaue me not thus like a clod of clay[11]
Wherewith my body[12] is couered.   *All exeunt.*

---

[1] *Qy.* into; D. G. *emend to* levy in.
[2] Cr. S. Taurobates; *corr. by* D.
[3] G. *suggests* hast *for* art.
[4] G. vntil.
[5] G. *inserts* again.
[6] Cr. king; *corr. silently by* D.
[7] *So* Cr.; G. *emends to* Oliue and Palm; *but in* Cr. *Roman type is used
as for proper names ; I conjecture* ASPATIA, *cf.* Bacon and Bungay, 1141, —
the confusion in regard to CYRUS *is easily intelligible.*
[8] By *is not in* Cr., *but was supplied by* D.
[9] Cr. D. I am.
[10] G. *changes to* and I pray, *and transfers to* l. 5.
[11] *Whichever version of this inscription the author may have had in
mind, this line ought to read:* Envy me not this clod of clay.
[12] G. *says* Cr. *has* bydy.

Enter the KING *in great pompe, who reads it, &° issueth, crieth :* Vermeum.[1]

BOHA.   What meaneth this?

OBER.   Cirus of Persia,
Mightie in life, within a marbell graue,
Was layde to rot, whom Alexander once   10
Beheld in-tombde,[2] and weeping did confesse
Nothing in life could scape from wrechednesse :[3]
Why then boast men?

BOH.   What recke I then of life,
Who makes [4] the graue my home,[5] the earth my wife :
But marke mee more.[6]   15

3.

BOH.   I can no more, my patience will not warpe
To see these flatterers [7] how they scorne and carpe.

OBER.   Turne but thy head.

Enter four [8] KINGS *carr[y]ing crowns,* LADIES *presenting odors to* POTEN-
TATE[9] *in-thrond, who suddainly is slaine by his* SERUANTS *and thrust
out ; and so they eate.   Exeunt.*

[BOH.] [10]   Sike [11] is the werld, but whilke is he I sawe?

OBER.   Sesostris, who was conquerour of the werld,   5
Slaine at the last, and stampt on by his slaues.

BOH.   How blest are peur men then that know their
        graue[s] ! [12]
Now marke the sequell of my gig.

---

[1] D. G. *accept* Mitford's *emendation* Ver meum ; *but it seems unsuited
to the occasion ; see Notes,* vol. III, *on* Vermeum (*i.e.,* Vermium).

[2] G. in tombe.   [3] G. wretchednesse.

[4] *So* Cr. *according to* D. *and my copyist ; but* G. *says* make.

[5] *So* Collier ; G. *says* Cr. *has* tumbe, D. *says* tombe, *my copyist* tomb.

[6] D. G., *apparently forgetting that this is an invitation to see another
act of* BOHAN'S *play, assign this line to* OBERON.

[7] Cr. flatteries ; *corr. by* D.

[8] Cr. our ; *corr. by* D.

[9] Cr. Potentates ; *corr. by* D.

[10] *In* Cr. BOHAN *is, by mistake, omitted ; corr. by* D.

[11] G. Sicke.   [12] *Corr. by* D.

[4.] [1]

BOH.[2]   An he [3] weele meete ends : the mirk and sable night
Doth leaue the pering morne to prie abroade.
Thou nill me stay ; haile then thou pride of kings,
I ken the world, and wot well worldly things.
Marke thou my gyg, in mirkest termes that telles   5
The loathe of sinnes, and where corruption dwells.
Haile me ne mere with showes of gudlie sights;
My graue is mine, that rids me from despights.[4]

[5.]

[BOH.]   Accept my gig, guid king, and let me rest;
The graue with guid men is a gay-built nest.
     OBER.   The rising sunne doth call me hence away ;
Thankes for thy gyg, I may no longer stay.
But, if my traine did wake thee from thy rest,   5
So shall they sing thy lullabie to nest.

Actus secundus.   Schena prima.

[*The house of the* COUNTESS OF ARRAN.]

Enter the COUNTESSE OF ARRAIN,[5] *with* IDA, *her daughter, in theyr porch,
sitting at worke.*[6]

A song.[7]

COUNT.   Faire Ida, might you chuse the greatest good
Midst all the world, in blessings that abound,

---

[1] Kittredge *points out that* 3. 8 *indicates the end of the passage relating
to the third dumb-show* (*cf.* 1. 16 ; 2. 15) *and is inconsistent with* 5. 1 *and*
4, *and that the presence of* BOH. *before* 4. 1 *is another proof that a new
section begins here. We have, therefore, not three, but four substitutes for
the speeches of the* CHORUS, *which now appear at the ends of the Acts. But*
4. 5 *implies that there is more of the play,* BOHAN'S " gyg," *to come, whereas
the whole passage here set apart as* 5 *seems to belong after the Fifth Act ;
and it will be observed that this extension of* Kittredge's *suggestion not
only provides a* CHORUS *for each Act, but also clears up many obscurities of
the text. The brevity of these speeches can be no argument against this
theory; see the end of Act iii.*

[2] *So* Cr.,*according to my copyist, but* D. G. *do not print or mention the
name.*   [3] G. *omits* he.   [4] G. dispights.   [5] G. Arran.
     [6] G. work.   [7] *The song is not given.*

Wherein, my daughter, shuld [1] your liking be?

IDA.   Not in delights or pompe or maiestie.

COUNT.   And why?

IDA.   Since these are meanes to draw the minde   5
From perfect good and make true iudgement blind.

COUNT.   Might you haue wealth, and fortunes ritchest
store?

IDA.   Yet would I, might I chuse, be honest poore;
For she that sits at fortunes feete alowe
Is sure she shall not taste a further woe;   10
But those that prancke one top of fortunes ball
Still feare a change, and, fearing, catch a fall.

COUNT.   Tut, foolish maide, each one contemneth need.

IDA.   Good reason why, they know not good indeed.

COUNT.   Many marrie, then, on whom distresse doth loure.   15

IDA.   Yes, they that vertue deeme an honest dowre.
Madame, by right this world I may compare
Vnto my worke, wherein with heedfull care
The heauenly workeman plants with curious hand —
As I with needle draw — each thing one land   20
Euen as hee list: some men like to the rose
Are fashioned fresh, some in their stalkes do close,
And borne do suddaine die; some are but weeds,
And yet from them a secret good proceeds.
I with my needle, if I please, may blot   25
The fairest rose within my cambricke plot:
God with a becke can change each worldly thing,
The poore to earth,[2] the begger to the king.
What then hath man wherein hee well may boast,
Since by a becke he liues, a louer [3] is lost?   30

Enter EUSTACE *with letters.*

COUNT.   Peace, Ida, heere are straungers neare at hand.

EUST.   Madame, God speed!

COUNT.   I thanke you, gentle squire.

EUST.   The countrie [4] Countesse of Northumberland

---

[1] G. shold.   [3] Mitford *suggested* flower.
[2] D. G. *change to* rich. [4] *Qy.* courteous.

Doth greete you well, and hath requested mee
To bring these letters to your ladiship.   35

He carries the letter[s].

COUNT.   I thanke her Honour and your-selfe, my friend.

Shee receiues and peruseth them.

I see she meanes you good, braue gentleman,
Daughter, the Ladie Elinor salutes
Your-selfe as well as mee; then for her sake
T'were good you entertaind that courtiour well.   40
    IDA.   As much salute as may become my sex
And hee in vertue can vouchsafe to thinke
I yeeld him for the courteous countesse sake.
Good sir, sit downe; my mother heere and I
Count time mispent an endlesse vanitie.   45
    EUST. [*aside*] Beyond report the wit, the faire, the shape!—
What worke you heere, faire mistresse? may I see it?
    ID.   Good sir, looke on; how like you this compact?
    EUST.   Me thinks in this I see true loue in act:
The woodbines [1] with their leaues do sweetly spred,   50
The roses blushing prancke them in their red,
No flower but boasts the beauties of the spring;
This bird hath life indeed, if it could sing.
What meanes, faire mistres, had you in this worke?
    IDA.   My needle, sir.
    EUST.   In needles then there lurke [2]   55
Some hidden grace, I deeme, beyond my reach.
    ID.   Not grace in the*m*, good sir, but those that teach.
    EUST.   Say that your needle now were Cupids sting,—
[*Aside*] But ah! her eie must bee no lesse,
In which is heauen and heauenlinesse,   60
In which the foode of God is shut,
Whose powers the purest mindes do glut.
    IDA.   What if it were?
    EUST.   Then see a wondrous thing:

[1] G. woodbins.
[2] Cr. lurkes; *emend. by* D.; *but possibly a perfect rhyme was not intended.*

I feare me you would paint in Tereus [1] heart
Affection in his power and chiefest part.[2]   65

IDA.   Good Lord, sir, no ; for hearts but pricked soft
Are wounded sore, for so I heare it oft.

EUST.   What recks the wound,[3] where but your happy eye
May make him liue whom Ioue hath iudgd to die.

IDA.   Should life *and* death within this needle lurke,   70
Ile pricke no hearts, Ile pricke vpon my worke.

Enter ATEUKIN,[4] *with* SLIPPER, *the clowne.*

COUN.   Peace, Ida ! I perceiue the fox at hand.

EUST.   The fox? why, fetch your [5] hounds *and* chace him
          hence.

COUNT.   Oh, sir, these great men barke at small offence.
Come, will it please you to enter, gentle sir?   75
                                        Offer to exeunt.

ATEU.[6]   Stay, courteous ladies ; fauour me so much
As to discourse a word or two apart.

COUNT.   Good sir, my daughter learnes this rule of mee,
To shun resort and straungers companie ;
For some are shifting mates that carrie letters ;   80
Some, such as you, too good, because our betters.

SLIP.   Now I pray you, sir, what a-kin are you to a pick-
rell?

ATEU.   Why, knaue?

SLIP.   By my troth, sir, because I neuer knew a proper   85
scituation fellow of your pitch fitter to swallow a gudgin.

ATEU.   What meanst thou by this?

SLIP.   " Shifting fellow," sir ; these be thy words, " shifting
fellow ": this gentlewoman, I feare me, knew your[7] bringing vp.

ATEU.   How so?   90

SLIP.   Why, sir, your father was a miller that could shift
for a pecke of grist in a bushell, and you[8] a faire-spoken

---

1 Cr. Teueus ; *emend. by* D.
2 Cr. parts ; *emend. by* D.; *but see note on* l. 55.
3 Cr. fecond ; *emend. by* D.   6 *In* Cr. ATEU. *is before* l. 75; *corr. by* D.
4 *Misprinted* Ateuken *in* Cr.   7 G. you[r].
5 Cr. our ; D. G. your.   8 D. you['re].

gentleman that can get more land by a lye then an honest
man by his readie mony.

ATEU.   Catiue, what sayest thou?   95

SLIP.   I say, sir, that if shee call you shifting knaue, you
shall not put her to the proofe.

ATEU.   And why?

SLIP.   Because, sir, liuing by your wit as you doo,[1] shifting
is your letters pattents; it were a hard matter for mee to get   100
my dinner that day wherein my maister had not solde a dozen
of deuices, a case of cogges and a shute of shifts in the
morning.   I speak this in your [2] commendation, sir, *and* I
pray you so take it.

ATEU.   If I liue, knaue, I will bee reuenged!   What   105
gentleman would entertaine a rascall, thus to derogate from
his honour?   [*Beats him.*]

IDA.   My lord, why are you thus impatient?

ATEU.   Not angrie, Ida, but I teach this knaue
How to behaue himselfe among his betters.   110
Behold, faire countesse, to assure your stay,
I heere present the signet of the king,
Who now by mee, faire Ida, doth salute you;
And, since in secret I haue certaine things
In his behalfe, good madame, to impart,   115
I craue your daughter to discourse a-part.

COUNT.   Shee shall in humble dutie bee addrest
To do his Highnesse will in what shee may.

ID.   Now, gentle sir, what would his Grace with me?

ATEU.   Faire, comely nimph, the beautie of your face,   120
Sufficient to bewitch the heauenly powers,
Hath wrought so much in him that now of late
He findes himselfe made captiue vnto loue;
And, though his power and maiestie requires [3]
A straight commaund before an humble sute,   125
Yet hee his mightinesse doth so abase
As to intreat your fauour, honest maid.

IDA.   Is hee not married, sir, vnto our queen?

---

[1] G. do.   [2] G. you[r].   [3] D. *changes to* require.

ATEU.   Hee is.

IDA.   And are not they by God accurst
That seuer them whom hee hath knit in one?   130

ATEU.   They bee; what then?   Wee seeke not to displace
The princesse from her seate; but, since by loue
The king is made your owne, hee [1] is resolude
In priuate to accept your dalliance,
In spight of warre,[2] watch, or worldly eye.   135

IDA.   Oh how hee talkes! as if hee [3] should not die!
As if that God in iustice once could winke
Vpon that fault I am a-sham'd to thinke!

ATEU.   Tut, mistresse, man at first was born to erre;
Women are all not formed to bee saints.   140
Tis impious for to kill our natiue king,
Whom by a little fauour wee may saue.

IDA.   Better then liue vnchaste, to liue [4] in graue.

ATEU.   Hee shall erect your state *and* wed you well.

IDA.   But can his warrant keep my soule from hell?   145

ATEU.   He will inforce, if you resist his sute.

ID.   What tho?   The world may shame to him account [5]
To bee a king of men and worldly pelfe,
Yet [6] hath no [7] power to [7] rule and guide himselfe.

ATEU.[8]   I know you, gentle ladie, and the care   150
Both of your honour and his Graces health
Makes me confused in this daungerous state.

IDA.   So counsell him, but sooth thou not his sinne;
Tis vaine alurement that doth make him loue.
I shame to heare; bee you a-shamde to mooue.   155

COUNT. [*aside*]   I see my daughter growes impatient;
I feare me hee pretends some bad intent.

ATEU.   Will you dispise the king *and* scorne him so?

IDA.   In all allegeance I will serue his Grace,

---

[1] Cr. shee; *corr. by* D.   [3] Cr. shee; D. G. hee.
[2] *Qy.* wary; D. *suggests, and* G. *accepts,* warre or.
[4] D. G. *change to* lie.   [5] *Qy.* impute.
[6] G. *inserts* [h'].
[7] *In* Cr. *these two words are interchanged; corr. by* D.
[8] *In* Cr. ATEU. *precedes* l. 149; *corr. by* D.

But not in lust, — oh, how I blush to name it!   160

   ATEU. [*aside*]   An endlesse worke is this; how should I
     frame it?

They discourse priuately.

   SLIP.   Oh, mistresse, may I turne a word vpon you?

   COUNT.[1]   Friend, what wilt thou?

   SLIP.   Oh what a happie gentlewoman bee you trulie! the
world reports this of you, mistresse, — that a man can no   165
sooner come to your house but the butler comes with a blacke-
iack, and sayes : " Welcome, friend ; heeres [2] a cup of the best
for you." Verilie, mistresse, you are said to haue the best
ale in al Scotland.

   COUNT.   Sirrha, go fetch him drinke. [*A* SERVANT *brings drink.*]   170
How likest thou this?

   SLIP.   Like it, mistresse? why this is quincy quarie, pepper
de watchet, single goby, of all that euer I tasted! Ile prooue
in this ale and tost the compasse of the whole world.   First,
this is the earth; it lies [3] in the middle a faire browne tost, a   175
goodly countrie for hungrie teeth to dwell vpon; next, this is
the sea, a faire [4] poole for a drie tongue to fish in; now come
I, *and*, seing the world is naught, I diuide it thus; *and*, because the sea cannot stand without the earth, as Arist[otle]
saith, I put them both into their first chaos, which is my   180
bellie.   And so, mistresse, you may see your ale is become a
myracle.

   EUSTACE.   A merrie mate, madame, I promise you!

   COUNT.   Why sigh you, sirrah?

   SLIP.   Trulie, madam, to think vppon the world, which   185
since I denounced it, keepes such a rumbling in my stomack
that vnlesse your cooke giue it a counterbuffe with some of
your rosted capons or beefe, I feare me I shal become a loose
body, so daintie, I thinke, I shall neither hold fast before nor
behinde.   190

   COUNT.   Go, take him in, and feast this merrie swaine.
Syrrha, my cooke is your phisitian :

    [1] Cr. ATEU.; *corr. by* D.; G. COUNT., *without note.*
    [2] G. heere 's.   [3] Cr. ties; *corr. by* D.   [4] G. fair.

He hath a purge for to disiest the world.

[Exeunt SLIPPER and SERVANT.]

ATEU.   Will you not, Ida, grant his Highnesse this?

IDA.   As I haue said, in dutie I am his ;   195
For other lawlesse lusts, that ill beseeme him,
I cannot like, and good I will not deeme him.[1]

COUNT.   Ida, come in ; and, sir, if so you please,
Come take a homelie widdowes [2] intertaine.

IDA.   If he haue no great haste, he may come nye ;   200
If haste, tho he be gone, I will not crie.

Exeunt [all but ATEUKIN].

ATEU.   I see this labour lost, my hope in vaine ;
Yet will I trie an-other drift. againe.   [Exit.]

[Act second.   Scene second.]

[The court.]

Enter the BISHOP OF S. ANDREWES, EARLE DOUGLAS, MORTON, with others, one way, with the Queene [DOROTHEA] with DWARFE [3] an-other way.

B. S. ANDR.   Oh wrack of common-weale! Oh wretched
            state!

DOUG.   Oh haplesse flocke,[4] whereas the guide is blinde?

They all are in a muse.[5]

MORT.   Oh heedlesse youth, where counsaile is dispis'd.[6]

DOROT.   Come, prettie knaue, and prank it by my side :
Lets see your best attendaunce out of hande.   5

DWARFE.   Madame, altho my lims are very small,
My heart is good; Ile serue you therewithall.

DORO.   How if I were assaild? what couldst thou do?

DWARF.   Madame, call helpe, and boldly fight it to.
Altho a bee be but a litle [7] thing,   10

<hr>

[1] D. suggests 'em.   [5] G. prints this as if it followed l. 3 in Cr.
[2] G. widowes.   [6] G. despis'd.
[3] Cr. DWARFES, which D. changes to NANO, saying that there is no other dwarf in the play ; the others might be mutes, and consequently not be specifically mentioned elsewhere ; but the emendation seems certain.
[4] G. flock.   [7] G. little.

You know, faire queen, it hath a bitter sting.

DOR.   How couldst thou do me good, were I in greefe?

DWAR.   Counsell, deare princes, is a choyce releefe :

Tho Nestor wanted force, great was his wit;

And, tho I am but weake, my words are fit.   15

S. AND. [aside]   Like to a ship vpon the ocean seas,

Tost in the doubtfull streame without a helme,

Such is a monarke without good aduice.

I am ore-heard! Cast raine vpon thy tongue;

Andrewes, beware, reproofe will breed a scar!   20

MOR.   Good day, my lord.

B. S. AND.   Lord Morton, well ymet!

Whereon[1] deemes[2] Lord Douglas all this while?

DOUG. Of that which yours and my poore heart doth
          break,

Altho feare shuts our mouths, we dare not speake.

DOR. [aside]   What meane these princes sadly to consult? 25

Somewhat, I feare, betideth them amisse,

They are so pale in lookes, so vext in minde. —

In happie houre, the[3] noble Scottish peeres,

Haue I incountred you!   What makes you mourne?

B. S. AND.   If we with patience may attention[4] gaine,   30

Your Grace shall know the cause of all our griefe.

DOR.   Speake on, good father; come and sit by me :

I know thy care is for the common good.

B. S. AND.   As fortune, mightie princes, reareth some

To high estate and place in common-weale,   35

So by diuine bequest to them is lent

A riper iudgement and more searching eye,

Whereby they may discerne the common harme ;

For, where importunes[5] in the world are most,

Where all our profits rise and still increase,   40

---

1 *This is a nine-syllabled line, unless we read* Whereupon.

2 D. *suggests, and* G. *accepts,* dreames.

3 D. G. *change to* ye ; *it is not a mistake, cf.* v. I, 31.

4 Cr. attentiue ; *emend. by* D.

5 D. G. *accept* Collier's *emendation,* our fortunes.

There is our minde, thereon we meditate, —
And what we do partake of good aduice,
That we imploy for to concerue the same.
To this intent these nobles and my-selfe,
That are, or should bee, eyes of common-weale,   45
Seeing his Highnesse reachlesse course of youth,
His lawlesse and vnbridled vaine in loue,
His to intentiue trust too flatterers,
His abiect care of councell and his friendes,
Cannot but greeue ; and, since we cannot drawe   50
His eye or iudgement to discerne his faults,
Since we haue spake [1] and counsaile is not heard,
I, for my part, — let others as they list, —
Will leaue the court, and leaue him to his will,
Least with a ruthfull eye I should behold   55
His ouerthrow, which, sore I feare, is nye.

    Doro.   Ah, father, are you so estranged from loue,
From due alleageance to your prince and land,
To leaue your king, when most he needs your help?
The thriftie husbandmen are neuer woont,   60
That see their lands vnfruitfull, to forsake them ;
But, when the mould is barraine and vnapt,
They toyle, they plow and make the fallow fatte.
The pilot in the dangerous seas is knowne ;
In calmer waues the sillie sailor striues.   65
Are you not members, lords, of common-weale?
And can your head, your deere annointed king,
Default ye, lords, except your-selues do faile?
Oh, stay your steps, returne and counsaile him !

    Doug.   Men seek not mosse vpon a rowling stone,   70
Or water from the siue, or fire from yce,
Or comfort from a rechlesse monarkes [2] hands.
Madame, he sets vs light, that seru'd in court
In place of credit in his fathers dayes :
If we but enter presence of his Grace,   75
Our payment is a frowne, a scoffe, a frumpe,

    [1] D. *changes to* spoke.   [2] G. monarches.

Whilst flattering Gnato prancks it by his side,
Soothing the carelesse king in his misdeeds.
And, if your Grace consider your estate,
His life should vrge you too, if all be true.   80
    DORO.[1]   Why, Douglas, why?
    DOUG.   As if you haue not heard
His lawlesse loue to Ida growne of late,
His carelesse [2] estimate of your estate!
    DORO.   Ah, Douglas, thou misconstrest his intent:
He doth but tempt his wife, he tryes [3] my loue.   85
This iniurie pertaines to me, not to you.
The king is young, and, if he step awrie,
He may amend, and I will loue him still.
Shou'd [4] we disdaine our vines because they sprout
Before their time? or young men if they straine   90
Beyo*n*d their reach?   No; vines that bloome and spread
Do promise fruites, and young men that are wilde
In age growe wise.   My freendes [5] and Scottish peeres,
If that an English princesse may preuaile,
Stay, stay with him!   Lo how my zealous prayer   95
Is plead with teares!   Fie, peeres! will you hence?
    S. AND.   Madam, tis vertue in your Grace to plead;
But we that see his vaine vntoward course,
Cannot but flie the fire before it burne,
And shun the court before we see his fall.   100
    DORO.   Wil you not stay?   Then, lordings, fare you well!
Tho you forsake your king, the Heauens, I hope,
Will fauour him through mine incessant prayer.
    DWAR.   Content you, madam; thus old Ouid sings:
Tis foolish to bewaile recurelesse things.   105
    DOROTHEA.   Peace,[6] dwarffe;   these words my patience
        moue.
    DWAR.   All-tho [7] you charme my speech, charme not my
        loue!

---

[1] *So* D. G.; *my copyist* DOUG., *perhaps by mistake.*
[2] G. careless.   [4] G. Should.   [5] G. frendes.   [7] G. Altho.
[3] G. tryes.   [6] G. *inserts* foolish, *for metre.*

Exeunt NANO, DOROTHEA.[1]

Enter the KING OF SCOTS ;[2] *the* NOBLES, *spying him, returnes.*

K. OF S.   Douglas, how now? why changest thou thy
    cheere?

DOUGL.   My priuate troubles are so great, my liege,
As I must craue your licence for a while   110
For to intend mine owne affaires at home.   *Exit.*[3]

KING.   You may depart.   But why is Morton sad?

MOR.   The like occasion doth import me too :
So I desire your grace to giue me leaue.

K. OF S.   Well, sir, you may betake you to your ease.   115

                              [*Exit* MORTON.]

When such grim syrs are gone, I see no let
To worke my will.

S. ANDR.[4]   What, like the eagle then,
With often flight wilt thou thy feathers loose?
O king, canst thou indure to see thy court
Of finest wits and iudgements dispossest,   120
Whilst cloking craft with soothing climbes so high
As each bewailes ambition is so bad?
Thy father left thee, with estate and crowne,
A learned councell to direct thy court,[5]
These careleslie, O king, thou castest off,   125
To entertaine a traine of sicophants.
Thou well mai'st [6] see, although thou wilt not see,
That euery eye and eare both sees and heares
The certaine signes of thine incontinence.[7]
Thou art alyed vnto the English king   130
By marriage, — a happie friend indeed,

---

[1] D. *gives this :* Exeunt QUEEN *and* NANO, *and says, in his first edition :*
"the 4to Dwarfs"; *my copyist gives it exactly as here printed ;* G. *prints*
Exeunt NANO *and* DOROTHEA, *but brackets it as if* Cr. *had nothing.*

[2] Cr. Enter the KING OF SCOTS, ARIUS.

[3] G. *prints* Exit DOUGLAS *in brackets as if* Cr. *had nothing.*

[4] Cr. S. ATTEN.; *corr. by* D., *who, however, read* Cr. *as* 8 ATTEN., *as
does* G.

[5] D. G. *change to* course.

[6] G. maist.   [7] Cr. inconstinence; *corr. silently by* D.

If vsed well; if not, a mightie foe.
Thinketh your Grace he can indure and brooke
To haue a partner in his daughters loue?
Thinketh your Grace the grudge of priuie wrongs 135
Will not procure him chaunge his smiles to threats?
Oh, be not blinde to good! call home your lordes;
Displace these flattering Gnatoes, driue them hence!
Loue, and with kindnesse take your wedlocke-wife,
Or else, — which God forbid! — I feare a change. 140
Sinne cannot thriue in courts without a plague.

   K. OF S. Go pack thou too, vnles thou me*n*d thy talk!
On paine of death, proud bishop, get you gone,
Vnlesse you headlesse mean to hoppe away!

   S. AND.[1] Thou God of heaue*n* preuent my countries fall! 145

                                             Exit.[2]

   K. OF S. These staies and lets to pleasure plague my
          thoughts,
Forcing my greeuous wounds a-new to bleed.
But care, that hath transported me so farre,
Faire Ida, is disperst in thought of thee,
Whose answere yeeldes me life, or breeds my death! 150
Yond comes the messenger of weale — or woe!   *Enter* GNATO.[3]
Ateukin,[4] what newes?

   ATEU. The adament, o king, will not be filde
But by it-selfe, and beautie that exceeds
By some exceeding [5] fauour must be wrought: 155
Ida is coy as yet, and doth repine,
Obiecting marriage, honour, feare and death;
Shee 's holy, wise and too precise for me.

   K. OF S. Are these thy fruites of wits? [6] thy sight in art?
Thine eloquence? thy pollicie? thy drift? 160
To mocke thy prince? the*n*, catiue, packe [7] thee hence,
And let me die deuoured in my loue!

---

[1] Cr. S. ATTEN.; D. G. *as before.*   [5] G. ex[c]eeding.
[2] Cr. G. Exeunt.   [6] D. *changes to* wit.
[3] *So* ATEUKIN *is often called.*   [7] G. pack.
[4] *In* Cr. *printed in the margin as if the name of the speaker.*

ATEU.   Good Lord, how rage gainsayeth reasons power!
My deare, my gracious and beloued prince,
The essence of my soule,[1] my God on earth,   165
Sit downe and rest your-selfe; appease your wrath,
Least with a frowne yee wound me to the death!
Oh that I were included in my graue,
That eyther now to saue my princes life
Must counseli crueltie or loose my king!   170
    K. OF S.   Why, sirrha, is there meanes to mooue her
        minde?
    ATEU.   Oh, should I not offend my royall liege —
    K. OF S.   Tell all, spare nought,[2] so I may gaine my loue.
    ATEU.   Alasse, my soule, why art thou torne in twaine
For feare thou talke a thing that should displease?   175
    K. OF S.   Tut! speake what-so thou wilt; I pardon thee.
    ATEU.   How kinde a word! how courteous is his Grace!
Who would not die to succour such a king?
My liege, this louely mayde of modest minde
Could well incline to loue, but that shee feares   180
Faire Dorotheas power.   Your Grace doth know
Your wedlocke is a mightie let to loue.
Were Ida sure to bee your wedded wife,
That then the twig would bowe you might command.
Ladies loue presents, pompe and high estate.   185
    K. OF S.   Ah, Ateukin, how shuld we display[3] this let?
    ATEU.   Tut, mightie prince! oh that I might bee whist!
    K. OF S.   Why dalliest thou?
    ATEU.   I will not mooue my prince!
I will preferre his safetie before[4] my life:
Heare mee, O[5] king! tis Dorotheas death   190
Must do you good.
    K. OF S.   What, murther of my queene?

---

[1] Cr. sute; *emend. by* Collier.   [2] G. naught.
[3] D. *emends to* displace; distroy *is also possible; but* display *may be
right:* Greene *was a " student in Phisicke."*
[4] D. 'fore, *without note; adopted by* G.
[5] G. Hear me, ô; Cr. Heare mee, o'.

Yet to enioy my loue, what is my queene?
Oh, but my vowe and promise to my queene!
I, but my hope to gaine a fairer queene!
With how contrarious thoughts am I with-drawne!   195
Why linger I twixt hope and doubtfull feare?
If Dorothe[1] die, will Ida loue?

    ATEU.   Shee will, my lord.

    K. OF S. Then let her die! Deuise, aduise the meanes;[2]
Al likes me wel that lends me hope in loue.

    ATEU.   What, will your Grace consent? then let mee
        worke!   200
Theres heere in court a Frenchman, Iaques calde,
A fit performer of our enterprise,
Whom I by gifts and promise will corrupt,
To slay the queene, — so that your Grace will seale
A warrant for the man to saue his life.   205

    K. OF S. Nought shall he want. Write thou, and I wil
        signe.
And, gentle Gnato, if my Ida yeelde,
Thou shalt haue what thou wilt; Ile giue the straight
A barrony,[3] an earledome, for reward.

    ATEU. Frolicke, young king, the lasse shall bee[4] your owne! 210
Ile make her blyth and wanton by my wit.

                                  Exeunt.

        [*The End of the Second Act.*]

            [CHORUS.]

           Enter BOHAN *with* OBIRON.[5]

    BOH. So, Oberon, now it beginnes[6] to worke in kinde!
The auncient lords, by leauing him alone,[7]
Disliking of his humors and despight,[8]

    [1] G., *following* D., Dorothe[a].
    [2] *Two lines in* Cr.
    [3] G. barony.   [7] Cr. aliue; *emend. by* D.
    [4] G. be.   [8] Cr. refpight; *emend. by* D.
    [5] *Immediately under this* Cr. *has* 3 Act; *omitted by* D., *without note.*
    [6] D. *suggests* 'gins, *to get rid of the Alexandrine.*

Lets [1] him run headlong, till his flatterers,
Sweeting [2] his thoughts of lucklesse [3] lust   5
With vile perswations [4] and alluring words,
Makes [5] him make way by murther to his will.
Iudge, fairie king : hast heard a greater ill?
   OBER.   Nor seen [6] more vertue in a countrie mayd.
I tell the, Bohan, it doth make me merrie [7]   10
To thinke the deeds the king meanes to performe !
   BOHA.   To change that humour, stand and see the rest :
I trow my sonne Slipper will shewes a iest.

> *Enter* SLIPPER *with a companion, boy* [8] *or wench, dauncing a hornpipe,
> and daunce out againe.*

   BOHA.   Now, after this beguiling of our thoughts
And changing them from sad to better glee,   15
Lets to our sell, and sit and see thee [9] rest ;
For I beleeue this iig will prooue no iest.   *Exit* CHORUS.[10]

Actus tertia.[11]   Schena prima.

[*The court.*]

Enter SLIPPER *one way, and* S[IR] BARTRAM *another way.*

   BAR.   Ho, fellow! stay, and let me speake with thee.
   SLI.   Fellow? frend, thou doest disbuse [12] me ; I am a
gentlema*n*.
   BAR.   A gentleman? how so?
   SLIP.   Why, I rub horses, sir.   5

---

[1] D. *changes to* Let.   [3] Collier, D. lawless.
[2] Walker, D. soliciting ; Collier, suiting ; G. sweetning ; *I incline to the
first.*   [4] G. perswasions.
[5] D. *changes to* Make.
[6] Cr. fend ; *emend. by* D. ; found *is also a possibility.*
[7] D. *emends to* sorry, *which is probably right ; but cf. Act iv, Chorus.*
[8] Cr. bog ; *corr. by* D ; G. boy, *without note.*
[9] G. the.
[10] *In* Cr. *this word stands in the next line, immediately before* Actus;
the MS. *may have misled the printer.   I emend* Exeunt *to* Exit.
[11] Cr. 3.   [12] *So* Cr. ; D. *changes to* abuse.

BAR.   And what of that?

SIP.   Oh simple-witted! marke my reason: they that do
good seruice in the common-weale are gentlemen; but such
as rub horses do good seruice in the common-weale: ergo,
tarbox, Maister courtier, a horse-keeper is a gentleman.   10

BAR.   Heere [1] is ouermuch wit in good earnest! [2]
But, sirrha, where is thy maister?

SLIP.   Neither aboue ground nor vnder ground,
Drawing out red into white,
Swallowing that downe without chawing   15
That was neuer made without treading.[2]

BAR.   Why, where is hee then?

SLIP.   Why, in his seller, drinking a cup of neate and
briske claret in a boule of siluer. Oh, sir, the wine runnes
trillill down his throat, which cost the poore vintnerd [3] many a   20
stampe before it was made. But I must hence, sir; I haue
haste.

BAR.   Why, whither now, I prithee?

SLIP.   Faith, sir, to Sir Siluester, a knight hard by, vppon
my maisters arrand, whom I must certifie this: that the   25
lease of Est Spring shall bee confirmed; and therefore must
I bid him prouide trash, for my maister is no friend without
mony.

BAR. [aside]   This is the thing for which I sued so long,
This is the lease which I by Gnatoes meanes [4]   30
Sought to possesse by pattent from the king;
But hee, iniurious man, who liues by crafts
And selles kings fauours for who will giue most,
Hath taken bribes of mee, yet couertly
Will sell away the thing pertaines to mee.   35
But I haue found a present helpe, I hope,
For to preuent his purpose and deceit. —
Stay, gentle friend!

SLIP.   A good word! thou haste won me:

---

[1] G. Here.   [4] G. means.
[2-2] In Cr. *each of these is a separate line, beginning with a capital.*
[3] G. *says this is a misprint.*

This word is like a warme caudle [1] to a colde stomacke!　　　40

BAR.　Sirra, wilt thou for mony and reward
Conuay me certaine letters out of hand
From out thy maisters pocket?

SLIP.　Will I, sir? why, were it to rob my father, hang my
mother, or any such-like trifles, I am at your commaunde-　45
ment, sir.　What will you giue me, sir?

S. BAR.　A hundreth pounds.

SLIP.　I am your man : giue me earnest.　I am dead at a
pocket, sir ; why, I am a lifter, maister, by my occupation.

S. BAR.　A lifter? what is that?　　　50

SLIP.　Why, sir, I can lift a pot as well as any man, and
picke a purse as soone [2] as any theefe in my countrie.

S. BAR.　Why, fellow, hold! heere is earnest :
Ten pound to assure thee.　Go, dispatch,
And bring it me to yonder tauerne thou seest ;　　　55
And assure thy-selfe thou shalt both haue
Thy skin full of wine, and the rest of thy mony.

SLIP.　I will, sir.　Now, roome for a gentleman, my
　　　maisters !
Who giues mee mony for a faire new angell, a trimme new
　　　angell?　　　　　　　　　　　　　　*Exeunt.*

[Act third.　Scene second.]

[ATEUKIN'S *stable.*]

Enter ANDREW *and* PURUEYER.[3]

PUR.　Sirrha, I must needes haue your maisters horses,
The king cannot bee vnserued.

AND.　Sirrha, you must needs go without them,
Because my maister must be serued.

PUR.　Why, I am the kings purueyer,　　　5
And I tell thee I will haue them.

AND.　I am Ateukins seruant, Signior Andrew,
And I say thou shalt not haue them.

---

[1] Cr. candle; *corr. by* D.　　　[2] Cr. affoone.　　　[3] G. Purueyor.

PUR.   Heeres my ticket ; denie it if thou darst.

AND.   There is the stable ; fetch them out if thou darst.   10

PUR.   Sirrha, sirrha, tame your tongue, least I make you !

AND.   Sirrha, sirrha, hold your hand, least I bum you !

PUR.   I tell thee, thy maisters geldings are good,
And therefore fit for the king.

AN.   I tell thee, my maisters horses haue gald backes,   15
And therefore cannot fit the king.
Purueyr,[1] purueyer, puruey thee of more wit ! Darst thou
presume to wrong my lord Ateukin,[2] being the chiefest man
in court?

PUR.   The more vnhappie common-weale,   20
Where flatterers are chiefe in court !

AND.   What sayest thou?

PUR.   I say thou art too presumtuous,[3]
And the officers shall schoole thee.

AND.   A figge for them and thee, purueyer !   25
They seeke a knot in a ring that would wrong
My maister or his seruants in this court.

Enter IAQUES.

PUR.   The world is at a wise passe
When nobilitie is a-fraid of a flatterer !

IAQ.   Sirrha, what be you that parley contra Monsieur my   30
lord Ateukin? *En bonne foy*, prate you gainst[4] syr *Altesse*,
mee maka your test[5] to leap from your shoulders ; per ma
foy, cy fere-ie.[6]

AND.   Oh Signior captaine, you shewe your-selfe a forward and friendly gentleman in my maisters behalfe ! I will   35
cause him to thanke you.

IAQ.   *Poultron*, speake me one parola against my bon

1 G. Purueyer.   3 G. presumptuous.
2 Cr. Ateukins ; *corr. silently by* D.   4 D. G. against.
5 D. tête ; G. teste, *a better form for the date. In the French passages
I record* D.'s *readings both when they are really significant and when*
Cr. *is not readily intelligible to the ordinary reader. The Italics in all
such passages are those of* Cr.
6 D. c'y ferai-je ; *but* Greene *probably intended* si.

gentilhome, I shal estrampe[1] your guttes and thumpe your
backa that you no poynt mannage this tenne ours.[2]

PUR.   Sirrha, come open me the stable,   40
And let mee haue the horses!
And, fellow, for all your French bragges, I will doo my dutie.

AND.   Ile make garters of thy guttes,
Thou villaine, if thou enter this office!

IAQ.   Mort lieu,[3] take me that cappa   45
Pour uostre[4] labeur!   Be gonne, villein, in the mort!

[Exit JAQUES.]
PUR.   What, will you resist mee then?
Well, the Councell, fellow, shall know of your insolency.

Exit.
ANDR.   Tell them what thou wilt, and eate that I can best
spare from my backe-partes, and get you gone with a ven-   50
geance.

Enter GNATO.
ATEU.   Andrew.

ANDR.   Sir?

ATEU.   Where be my writings I put in my pocket last
night?   55

ANDR.   Which, sir? your anno[t]ations[5] vpon Matchauell?

ATEU.   No, sir; the letters pattents for East Spring.

AN.   Why, sir, you talk wonders to me, if you ask that
question.

ATEU.   Yea, sir, and wil worke wonders too with[6] you   60
vnlesse you finde them out.   Villaine, search me them out
and bring them me, or thou art but dead!

ANDR.   A terrible word in the latter end of a sessions!
Master, were you in your right wits yesternight?

ATEU.   Doest thou doubt it?   65

ANDR.   I, and why not, sir? for the greatest clarkes are
not the wisest,[7] and a foole may dance in a hood as well as a

---

[1] G. *gives* Cr. *as* shall astrampe.   [5] *Corr. silently by* D.

[2] D. *prints* ours; *his textual principle would seem to require* hours.

[3] D. Mort dieu.   [6] Cr. which; *corr. by* D.

[4] Cr. nostre; D. votre, *without note.*

[7] *The proverb usually has* the wisest men.

wise man in a bare frock.   Besides, such as giue themselues
to Philautia,[1] as you do, maister, are so cholericke of com-
plection that that which they burne in fire ouer night they   70
seeke for with furie the next morning.   Ah, I take care of
your worship! this common-weale should haue a great losse
of so good a member as you are.

    ATEU.   Thou flatterest me.

    ANDR.   Is it flatterie in me, sir, to speake you faire?   75
What is it then in you to dallie with the king?

    ATEU.   Are you prating, knaue?
I will teach you better nurture!
Is this the care you haue of my wardrop,
Of my accounts and matters of trust?   80

    ANDR.   Why alasse sir, in times past your garments haue
beene so well inhabited as your tenants woulde giue no place
to a moathe to mangle them; but since you are growne
greater and your garments more fine and gaye, if your garments are not fit for hospitallitie, blame your pride, and com-   85
mend my cleanlinesse.   As for your writings, I am not for
them, nor they for mee.

    ATEU.   Villaine, go, flie, finde them out!
If thou loosest them, thou loosest my credit.

    AND.   Alasse, sir, can I loose that you neuer had?   90

    ATEU.   Say you so?   Then hold, feel you that you neuer
        felt!   [*Strikes him.*]

[*Enter* JAQUES.]

    IA.   Oh, monsieur, aies patience,[2] pardon your pouure
        vallet;
Me bee at your commaundement.

    ATEU.   Signior Iaques, wel met; you shall commaund me.
Sirra, go cause my writings be proclamed in the market-
        place;   95
Promise a great reward to them that findes [3] them.
Looke where I supt and euery-where.

<hr>

  [1] Cr. Plulantia; *emend. by* Collier.   [3] D. *changes to* find.
  [2] Cr. patient; *corr. silently by* D.

AND. I will, sir. [*Aside*] Now are two knaues well met,
and three well parted !   If you conceiue mine enigma,
gentlemen, what shal[1] I bee then ?   Faith, a plaine [1] harpe- 100
shilling.   *Exit.*[2]

ATEU.   Sieur Iaques, this our happy meeting rids[3]
Your friends and me of care and greeuous toyle ;
For I, that looke into deserts of men
And see among the souldiers in this court   105
A noble forward minde, and iudge thereof,
Cannot but seeke the meanes to raise them vp
Who merrit credite in the common-weale.
To this intent, friend Iaque[s], I haue found
A meanes to make you great and well-esteemd   110
Both with the king and with the best in court;
For I espie in you a valiant minde,
Which makes mee loue, admire and honour you.
To this intent, — if so your trust and faith,
Your secrecie be equall with your force, —   115
I will impart a seruice to thy-selfe,
Which if thou doest effect, the king, my-selfe,
And what or hee or [4] I with him can worke
Shall be imployd in what thou wilt desire.

IAQ.   Me sweara by my ten bones, my Singniar,[5] to be 120
loyal to your lordships [6] intents, affaires ; ye, my monsignieur,
que non ferai-ie pour your pleasure?[7]   By my sworda, me
be no babillard.[8]

ATEU.   Then hoping one thy truth, I prithe see
How kinde Ateukin is to forward thee.[9]   125
Hold ! take this earnest-pennie of my loue !
And marke my words : the king by me requires
No slender seruice, Iaques, at thy hands, —
Thou must by priuie practise make away

---

[1] G. *has the modern spelling.*
[2] Cr. Exeunt ; *corr. silently by* D.
[3] Cr. hides ; D. *emends to* hinders.
[4] Cr. and.
[5] G. *says* Cr. Signiar.
[6] G. lordship's.
[8] Cr. babie Lords ; *corr. by* D.
[9] Cr. mee ; *corr. by* D.
[7] Cr. my monsignieur, *qui non fera ic pour.* Yea pleasure? *corr. by* D.

The queene, faire Dorethea, as she sleepes, 130
Or how thou wilt, so she be done to death.
Thou shalt not want promotion heare in court.

    IAQ.   Stabba the woman? Per ma foy, monsignieur, me
thrusta my weapon into her belle, so me may be gard[1] per le
roy! 135
Mee do[2] your seruice,
But me no be hanged pur my labor!

    ATEU.   Thou shalt haue warrant, Iaques, from the king :
None shall outface, gainsay and wrong my friend.
Do not I loue thee, Iaques? Feare not then! 140
I tell thee, who-so[3] toucheth thee in ought,
Shall iniure me ; I loue, I tender thee ;
Thou art a subiect fit to serue his Grace.
Iaques, I had a written warrant once,
But that, by great misfortune, late is lost. 145
Come, wend we to S. Andrewes, where his Grace
Is now in progresse, where he shall assure
Thy safetie and confirme thee to the act.

    IAQUES.   We will attend your Noblenesse.   *Exeunt.*

[Act third.   Scene third.]

[The palace.]

Enter SIR BARTRAM, DOROTHEA, *the queene,* NANO, LORD ROSS. LADIES,
ATTENDANTS.

    DORO.   Thy credite, Bartram, in the Scottish court,
Thy reuerend yeares, the stricknesse of thy vowes,
All these are meanes sufficient to perswade ;
But loue, the faithfull lincke of loyall hearts,
That hath possession of my constant minde, 5
Exiles all dread, subdueth vaine suspect.[4]

    [1] G. guard.
    [2] Cr. de ; G. do, *without note.*
    [3] *In the numerous instances in which I hyphenate a word which appears
in* G. *as a single word, the parts are separate in* Cr.
    [4] *So* G. ; Cr. supect.

Me thinks no craft should harbour in that brest
Where maiestie and vertue is [1] instaled.
Me thinke [2] my beautie should not cause my death.

BAR.   How gladly, soueraigne [3] princesse, would I erre,   10
And binde [4] my shame to saue your royall life!
Tis princely in your-selfe to thinke the best,
To hope his Grace is guiltlesse of this crime;
But, if in due preuention you default,
How blinde are you that were forwarnd before!   15

DORO.   Suspition without cause deserueth blame.

BAR.   Who sees [5] and shunne not harmes, deserue the
same.
Beholde the tenor of this traiterous plot.

[*Presents the warrant.*]

DORO.   What should I reade?   Perhappes he wrote it
not.

BAR.   Heere is his warrant, vnder seale and signe,   20
To Iaques, borne in France, to murther you.

DORO.   Ah, carelesse king, would God this were not thine!
What tho I reade?   Ah, should I thinke it true?

ROSSE.   The hand and seale confirmes [6] the deede is his.

DORO.   What know I tho if now he thinketh this?   25

NANO.   Madame, Lucretius saith that to repent
Is childish, [7] wisdome to preuent.

DORO.   What tho?

NANO.   Then cease your teares, that haue dismaid you,
And crosse the foe before hee haue betrayed you.

BAR.   What needes this [8] long suggestion [9] in this cause,   30
When euery circumstance confirmeth trueth?
First, let the hidden mercie from aboue
Confirme your Grace, since by a wondrous meanes
The practise of your daungers came to light;

[1] D. G. are, *without note.*
[2] D. *changes to* Methinks.
[3] G. soueraign.
[4] D. *suggests* find; G. *emends to* bide.
[5] D. *emends to* see.
[6] D. *changes to* confirm.
[7] Cr. G. shildish.
[8] D. *changes to* need these; G. needes these.
[9] Cr. suggestions.

Next, let the tokens of app[r]ooued [1] trueth   35
Gouerne and stay your thoughts, too much seduc't
And marke the sooth, and listen the intent.
Your Highnesse knowes, and these my noble lords
Can witnesse this, that whilest your husbands [2] sirre
In happie peace possest the Scottish crowne,   40
I was his sworne attendant heere in court ;
In daungerous fight I neuer fail'd my lord ;
And since his death, and this your husbands raigne,
No labour, dutie haue I left vndone
To testifie my zeale vnto the crowne.   45
But now my limmes are weake, mine eyes are dim,
Mine age vnweldie and vnmeete for toyle ;
I came to court in hope, for seruice past,
To gaine some lease to keepe me, beeing olde.
There found I all was vpsie-turuy turnd,   50
My friends displac'st, the nobles loth to craue.
Then sought I to the minion of the king,
Ateukin,[3] who, allured by a bribe,
Assur'd me of the lease for which I sought ;
But see the craft! when he had got the graunt,   55
He wrought to sell it to Sir Siluester
In hope of greater earnings from his hands.
In briefe, I learnt his craft, and wrought the meanes,
By one his needie seruants,[4] for reward,
To steale from out his pocket all the briefes ;   60
Which hee perform'd, and with reward resignd.
Them when I read, — now marke the power of God ! —
I found this warrant seald, among the rest,
To kill your Grace, — whom God long keepe aliue!
Thus, in effect, by wonder are you sau'd.   65
Trifle not then, but seeke a speadie [5] flight ;
God will conduct your steppes, and shield the right.

---

[1] G. approued.   [2] G. husband's.
[3] Cr. G. Auteukin.
[4] D. *emends to* servant ; *it is a confusion of two constructions.*
[5] Cr. speakie ; *corr. silently by* D. G.

Dor.   What should I do? ah, poore vnhappy queen,
Borne to indure what fortune can containe ! [1]
Ah lasse,[2] the deed is too apparent [3] now!   70
But, oh mine eyes, were you as bent to hide
As my poore heart is forward to forgiue,
Ah cruell king, my loue would thee acquite![4]
Oh, what auailes to be allied and matcht
With high estates, that marry but in shewe?   75
Were I baser [5] borne, my meane estate
Could warrant me from this impendent harme ; [6]
But to be great and happie, these are twaine.
Ah, Rosse, what shall I do? how shall I worke?

Rosse.   With speedie letters to your father send,   80
Who will reuenge you, and defend your right.

Dor.   As if they kill not me, who with him fight !
As if his breast be toucht, I am not wounded!
As if he waild, my ioyes were not confounded!
We are one heart, tho rent by hate in twaine ;   85
One soule, one essence doth our weale containe :
What then can conquer him that kils not me?

Rosse.   If this aduice displease, then, madame, flee.

Dor.   Where may I wend or trauel without feare?

Rosse.[7]   Where not, in changing this attire you weare?   90

Dor.   What, shall I clad me like a country maide?

Na.   The pollicie is base, I am affraide.

Dor.   Why, Nano?

Na.   Aske you why?   What, may a queene
March foorth in homely weede and be not seene?
The rose, although in thornie shrubs she spread,   95
Is still the rose, her beauties waxe not dead :
And noble mindes, altho the coate be bare,
Are by their semblance knowne, how great they are.

---

[1] G. *changes to* contrive.   [2] G. Ahlasse.
[3] G. apparant.   [4] Cr. acquire; *corr. silently by* D. G.
[5] D. *proposes* If I were baser *or* Were I baser; G. Were I but baser;
I retain the nine-syllabled line.
[6] Cr. *apparently* harnie.   [7] Cr. Na.; *corr. by* G.

BAR.   The dwarfe saith true.

DOR.   What garments likste thou than?

NA.   Such as may make you seeme a proper man.   100

DOR.   He makes me blush and smile, tho I am sad.

NA.   The meanest coat for saftie [1] is not bad.

DOR.   What, shall I iet in breeches, like a squire?
Alasse, poore dwarfe, thy mistresse is vnmeete.[2]

NA.   Tut! go me thus, your cloake before your face,   105
Your sword vpreard with queint *and* comely grace.
If any come and question what you bee,
Say you, " a man," and call for witnesse mee.

DOR.   What should I weare a sword? to what intent?

NA.   Madame, for shewe ; [3] it is an ornament;   110
If any wrong you, drawe : a shining blade
Withdrawes a coward theefe that would inuade.

DOR.   But, if I strike, and hee should strike againe,
What should I do?   I feare I should bee slaine.

NANO.   No ; take it single on your dagger so :   115
Ile teach you, madame, how to ward a blow.

DO.   How litle shapes much substance may include !
Sir Bartram, Rosse, yee ladies and my friends,
Since presence yeelds me death, and absence life,
Hence will I flie, disguised like a squire,   120
As one that seekes to liue in Irish warres.
You, gentle Rosse, shal [3] furnish my depart.

ROSS.   Yea, prince, *and* die with you with all my hart!
Vouchsafe me, then, in all extreamest states,
To waight on you and serue you with my best.   125

DOR.   To me pertaines the woe : liue then [4] in rest!
Friends, fare you well ; keepe secret my depart ;
Nano alone shall my attendant bee.

NAN.   Then, madame, are you mand, I warrant ye !
Giue me a sword, and, if there grow debate,   130
Ile come behinde and breake your enemies pate.

ROSS.   How sore wee greeue [3] to part so soone away !

---

[1] G. safetie.   [2] D. *thinks* 103, 104 *must rhyme ;* G. *denies it.*
[3] G. *has the modern spelling.*   [4] D. *changes to* thou.

Dor.   Greeue not for those that perish if they stay!

Nano.   The time in words mispent is litle woorth;

Madam walke on, and let them bring vs foorth.   135

Exeunt.

[*The End of the Third Act.*]

Chorus.

Enter Boh[an].

[Boh.]   So these sad motions makes [1] the faire [2] sleepe.[3]

And sleep hee shall in quiet and content;

For it would make a marbell melt and weepe

To see these treasons gainst the innocent.

But, since shee scapes by flight to saue her life,

The king may chance repent she was his wife.   6

The rest is ruthfull; yet, to beguilde [4] the time,

Tis [5] interlast with merriment and rime.   *Exeunt.*

Actus quartus.   Schena prima.

[*A forest.*]

After a noyse of hornes and showtings, enter certaine Huntsmen (*if you please, singing*) *one way ; another way* Ateukin *and* Iaques.[6]

Ateu.   Say, gentlemen, where may wee finde the king?

Hunts.   Euen heere at hand on hunting ; [7]

And at this houre hee taken hath a stand

To kill a deere.

Ateu.   A pleasant worke in hand !

Follow your sport, and we will seeke his Grace.   5

Hunts.   When such him seeke, it is a wofull case !

Exeunt Huntsmen *one way ;* Ateu. *and* Iaq. *another.*

---

[1] D. G. make, *without note.*   [2] D. *normalizes to* fairy.

[3] *The sleep of* Oberon *is against* D.'s *suggestion that one of the pageants printed at the end of Act I belongs here, except, of course, as a substitute for this passage.*   [4] *So* Cr.; D. G. *change to* beguile.

[5] G. 'Tis.   [7] G. *inserts* he is bent.

[6] Cr. Ateukin *and* Iaques, Gnato ; *but, as* D. *points out, "* Gnato *is only another name for* Ateukin."

[Act fourth.   Scene second.]

[THE COUNTESS OF ARRAN'S *park*.]

Enter EUSTACE, IDA, *and the* COUNTESSE.

COUNT.   Lord Eustace, as your youth *and* vertuous life
Deserues a faire,[1] more faire and richer wife,
So, since I am a mother, and do wit
What wedlocke is, and that which longs to it,
Before I meane my daughter to bestow,   5
Twere meete that she and I your state did know.
  EUST.   Madame, if I consider Idas woorth,
I know my portions merit[2] none so faire.
And yet I hold in farme and yearly rent
A thousand pound, which may her state content.   10
  COUNT.   But what estate, my lord, shall she possesse?
  EUST.   All that is mine, graue Countesse, *and* no lesse.
But, Ida, will you loue?
  IDA.   I cannot hate.
  EUST.   But will you wedde?
  IDA.   Tis Greeke to mee, my lord;
Ile wish you well, and thereon take my word.   15
  EUST.   Shall I some signe of fauour then receiue?
  IDA.   I, if her ladiship will giue me leaue.
  COUNT.   Do what thou wilt.
  IDA.   Then, noble English peere,
Accept this ring, wherein my[3] heart is set, —
A constant heart, with burning flames befret;   20
But vnder written this, *O morte dura;*
Heereon when so you looke with eyes *pura,*
The maide you fancie most will fauour you.
  EUST.   Ile trie this heart, in hope to finde it true.   24

---

[1] D. *changes to* deserve a far.
[2] D. *changes to* portion merits.
[3] Walker *conjectures* a; *the conjectures of* Walker *and* Collier *are all recorded by* D.

Enter certaine HUNTSMEN *and* LADIES.

HUNTS.   Widdowe countesse, well ymet!
    Euer may thy ioyes bee many!
Gentle Ida, faire beset,[1]
    Faire and wise, not fairer any!   28
Frolike huntsmen of the game
    Willes [2] you well, and giues [3] you greeting.
IDA.   Thanks, good woodman, for the same
    And our sport and merrie meeting!   32
HUNTS.   Vnto thee we do present
    Siluer heart with arrow wounded.
EUST.   This doth shadow my lament,
    Both [with] [4] feare and loue confounded.   36
LADIES.   To the mother of the mayde,
    Faire as th' lillies,[5] red as roses,
Euen so many goods are saide
    As her-selfe in heart supposes.   40
   COUNT.   What are you, friends, that thus doth [6] wish vs
      wel?
   HUNTS.   Your neighbours nigh, that haue on hunting
      beene,
Who, vnderstanding of your walking foorth,
Prepare this traine to entertaine you with:
This Ladie Douglas, this Sir Egmond is.   45
   COUNT.   Welcome, ye ladies, and thousand thanks for this!
Come, enter you a homely widdowes house;
And, if mine entertainment please you, let vs [7] feast.
   HUNTS.   A louely ladie neuer wants a guest.

---

[1] D. *accepts* Walker's *change to the Scotch* sair beset; *but, as* G. *points out, the* HUNTSMAN *does not speak Scotch, nor take so melancholy a view of love and marriage as this phrase would imply.*

[2] D. *changes to* Will.

[3] D. *changes to* give.

[4] *Supplied by* D.; G. [With] both.

[5] G. th' lilies.

[6] D. *changes to* do.

[7] D. *thinks* let vs *an interpolation;* G. *says* " = let's."

Exeunt; mane[n]t EUSTACE, IDA.

EUST.   Stay, gentle Ida : tell me what you deeme !   50
What, doth this hast [1] this tender heart [2] beseeme?

IDA.   Why not, my lord? since nature teacheth art
To sencelesse beastes to cure their greeuous smart :
Dicta[m]num [3] serues to close the wound againe.

EUST.   What helpe for those that loue?

IDA.   Why, loue againe.   55

EUST.   Were I the hart —

IDA.   Then I the hearbe would bee :
You shall not die for help ; come, follow me !

                                        Exeunt.

[Act fourth.   Scene third.]

[*The forest.*]

Enter ANDREW *and* IAQUES.

IAQ.   *Mon deiu*, what *malheure* be this ! me come a the
chamber, Signior Andrew, *mon deiu*, taka my *poinyard en
mon* [4] *maine* to giue the *estocade* to the *damoisella ; per ma
foy*, there was no person, — *elle cest en alle.* [5]

AND.   The woorse lucke, Iaques ! But, because I am thy   5
friend, I will aduise the somewhat towards the attainement of
the gallowes.

IAQ.   Gallowes? what be that?

AN.   Marrie, sir, a place of great promotion, where thou
shalt by one turne aboue ground rid the world of a knaue,   10
and make a goodly ensample for all bloodie villaines of thy
profession.

IAQ. [6]   *Que ditte vous,* [7] *Monsieur Andrew ?*

----

[1] D. G. *change to* hart ; G. *thinks something is omitted.*
[2] D. *prints* hart, *without note.*
[3] *Corr. by* D.   [4] D. ma, *without note.*
[5] D. *corrects the spelling to* elle s'est en allée.
[6] *Supplied by* D., *without note.*
[7] D. G. Que dites vous.

AND. I say, Iaques, thou must keep this path, and high
thee, for the q[ueene], as I am certified, is departed with her   15
dwarfe, apparelled like a squire. Ouertake her, Frenchman,
stab her; Ile promise thee this dubblet shall be happy.

IAQ. *Purquoy?*

AND. It shall serue a iolle gentleman,
Sir Dominus Monsignior Hangman.   20

IAQ. *Cest*[1] *tout vn;* me will *rama pour le*[2] *monoy.* [*Exit.*]

AND. Go, and the rot consume thee! Oh, what a trim
world is this! My maister liu[e]s by cousoning the king; I by
flattering him; Slipper, my fellow, by stealing; and I by lying: is not this a wylie accord, gentlemen? This last night 25
our iolly horsekeeper, beeing well stept in licor, confessed to
me the stealing of my maisters writings, and his great reward.
Now dare I not bewraye him, least he discouer my knauerie;
but this[3] haue I wrought: I vnderstand he will passe this
way to prouide him necessaries; but, if I and my fellowes   30
faile not, wee will teach him such a lesson as shall cost him
a chiefe place on pennilesse-bench for his labour. But yond
he comes!

Enter SLIPPER, *with a* TAILOR, *a* SHOOMAKER, *and a* CUTLER.

SLIP. Taylor!

TAYL. Sir?   35

SLIP. Let my dubblet bee white northren, fiue groates the
yard; I tell the I will bee braue.

TAYL. It shall, sir.

SLIP. Now, sir, cut it me like the battlements of a custerd,
ful[4] of round holes; edge me the sleeues with Couentry-blew, 40
and let the lynings bee[5] of tenpenny locorum.

TAYL. Very good, sir.

SLIP. Make it the amorous cut, a flappe before.

TAYL. And why so? that fashion is stale.

SLIP. Oh, friend, thou art a simple fellow! I tell thee, a 45

[1] G. C'est, *without note.*
[2] G. la, *without note, following* D., *who, of course, normalizes his text.*
[3] D. G. thus, *without note,*   [4] G. full.   [5] G. be,

flap is a great friend to a storrie,[1] it stands him in stead of
cleane napery ; and, if a mans shert bee torne, it is a present
penthouse to defend him from a cleane huswifes scoffe.

TAY.   You say sooth, sir.

SLIP.   Holde, take thy mony : there is seuen shillings for   50
the dubblet, and eight for the breeches.   Seuen and eight ;
birladie, thirtie-sixe is a faire deale[2] of mony !

TAYL.   Farwell, sir.

SLIP.   Nay, but stay, taylor.

TAYL.   Why, sir?   55

SLIPPER.   Forget not this speciall mate :[3]
Let my back-parts bee well linde,
For there come many winter stormes from a windie bellie, I
tell thee.   [*Exit* TAILOR.]   Shoo-maker!

SHOE-MA.   Gentleman, what shoo will it please you to   60
haue?

SLIP.   A fine, neate calues leather, my friend.

SHOO.   Oh, sir, that is too thin ; it will not last you.

SLIP.   I tell thee, it is my neer kinsman, for I am Slipper,
which hath his best grace in summer to bee suted in kalu[e]s[4]   65
skins.   Guidwife Clarke[5] was my grandmother, and Goodman
Neatherleather mine vnckle, but my mother, good woman,
alas! she was a Spaniard, and being wel tande and drest by
a good fellow an English-man, is growne to some wealth : as,
when I haue but my vpper-parts clad in her husbands costlie   70
Spanish leather, I may bee bold to kisse the fayrest ladies
foote in this countrey.

SHOO.   You are of high birth, sir.
But haue you all your mothers markes on you?

SLIP.   Why, knaue?   75

SHOOMAKER.   Because, if thou come of the bloud of the

---

[1] *A word unknown to* D. *and to me ;* G. *suggests "*florrie = flurry,*" but
apparently had no very definite meaning in mind.   It seems barely possible
that* stottie *is the right reading ; see Notes.*

[2] G. deal.   [3] D. *emends to* make, *perhaps rightly.*

[4] Cr. lakus ; *emend. by* Kittredge ; D. G. *accept* Collier's *suggestion of*
jackass.   [5] Collier, D. G. Calfe ; *qy.* Barke ; *see Notes.*

Slippers, you should haue a shoomakers alle thrust through
your eare.   *Exit.*[1]

SLIP.   Take your earnest, friend, and be packing,
And meddle not with my progenators.   Cutler!   80
CUTLER.   Heare, sir.
SLIP.   I must haue a rapier and dagger.[2]
CUTLER.   A rapier and dagger you meane, sir?
SLIPPER.   Thou saiest true, but it must haue a verie
faire edge.   85
CUTLER.   Why so, sir?
SLIP.   Because it may cut by himselfe; for trulie, my
freende, I am a man of peace, and weare weapons but for
facion.
CUTLER.   Well, sir, giue me earnest, I will fit you.   90
SLIP.   Hold, take it; I betrust thee, friend; let me be
welarmed.[3]
CUTLER.   You shall.   *Exit* CUTLER.
SLIP.   Nowe what remaines?   Theres twentie crownes
for house,[4] three crownes for houshol stuffe, six pence to buie   95
a constables-staffe.   Nay, I will be the chiefe of my parish!
There wants nothing but a wench, a cat, a dog, a wife and a
seruant, to make an hole familie.   Shall I marrie with Alice,
good-man Grimshaues daughter?   Shee is faire, but indeede
her tongue is like clocks on Shrouetuesday, alwaies out of 100
temper.   Shall I wed Sisley of the Whighton?   Oh, no!
she is like a frog in a parcely-bed, as scittish as an ele; if I
seek to hamper her, she wil horne me.   But a wench must
be had, Maister Slip[per]!   Yea, and shal be, deer
friend!   105
AND.   I now wil driue him from his contemplations.   Oh
my mates, come forward; the lamb is vnpent, the fox shal
preuaile.

---

[1] G., *following* D., *transfers this, without note, to* l. 80.

[2] *As* D. *points out, there must have been something peculiar in* SLIPPER'S
pronunciation of these words. D. G. *accept* Collier's *emendation* reaper
and digger, *but with hesitation.*

[3] G. wel armed.   [4] *So* Cr.; D. G. a house.

Enter three ANTIQUES, *who dance round and take* SLIPPER *with them.*

SLIP.   I will, my freend,[1] and I thanke you heartilie ; pray
keepe your curtesie, I am yours in the way of an hornepipe. 110
They are strangers, I see, they vnderstand not my language;
wee, wee.[2]

> *Whilest they are dauncing,* ANDREW *takes away his money, and the other*
> ANTIQUES *depart.*

SLIP.   Nay, but, my friends, one hornpipe further ! a reflu-
ence backe, and two doubles forward! What! not one
crosse-point against Sundayes? What, ho, sirrha ! you gone,[3] 115
you with the nose like an eagle, and you be a right Greeke,
one turne more! Theeues! theeues! I am robd! theeues!
Is this the knauerie of fidlers?[4]   Well, I will then binde the
hole credit of their occupatio*n* on a bagpiper, and he for my
money.   But I will after, and teach[5] them to caper in a 120
halter that haue cousoned me of my money.

Exit.[6]

[Act fourth.   Scene fourth.]

[*The forest.*]

Enter NANO, DOROTHEA, *in mans apparell.*

DORO.   Ah, Nano, I am wearie of these weedes;
     Wearie to weeld this weapon that I bare;
Wearie of loue, from whom my woe proceedes ;
     Wearie of toyle, since I haue lost my deare :
O wearie life, where wanteth[7] no distresse,
But euery thought is paide with heauinesse !   6

NA.   Too much of wearie, madame, if you please !

---

[1] D. G. friend[s], *which, though possible, seems unnecessary.*

[2] D., *in his first edition, says :* " *Perhaps this is not an exclamation, but
a misprint for* well, well." *Later he thought it French, as in* iv. 5, 5 ; *this
opinion is, of course, correct.*

[3] *Qy.* yon ; D. G. *emend to* gome.   [4] G. fiddlers.

[5] Cr. reach; *corr. silently by* D. G.

[6] Cr. Exeunt; *corr. silently by* D.

[7] Cr. wanted ; *corr. by* D. ; G. *prefers* wanted.

Sit downe; let wearie dye, and take your ease.

    DOROT.   How looke I, Nano? like a man or no?

    NANO.   If not a man, yet like a manlie shrowe.   10

    DORO.   If any come and meete vs on the way,

What should we do if they inforce vs stay?

    NA.   Set cap a-huffe, and challenge him the field.

Suppose the worst, the weake may fight to yeeld.

    DOROT.   The battaile, Nano, in this troubled minde   15

Is farre more fierce then euer we may finde.

The bodies [1] wounds by medicines may be eased,

But griefes of mindes [2] by salues are not appeased.

    NA.   Say, madame, will you heare your Nano sing?

    DOR.   Of woe, good boy, but of no other thing.   20

    NA.   What if I sing of fancie? will it please?

    DOR.   To such as hope successe such noats breede ease.

    NA.   What if I sing, like Damon, to my sheepe?

    DOR.   Like Phillis, I will sit me downe to weepe.

    NA.   Nay, since my songs afford such pleasure small,   25

Ile sit me downe, and sing you none at all.

    DORO.   Oh be not angrie, Nano.

    NANO.   Nay, you loath

To thinke on that which doth content vs both.

    DORO.   And [3] how?

    NANO.   You scorne desport when you are wearie,

And loath my mirth who liue to make you merry.   30

    DORO.   Danger and fear withdraw me from delight.

    NA.   Tis vertue to contemne fals Fortunes spight.

    DO.   What shuld I do to please thee, friendly squire?

    NA.   A smile a day, is all I will require;

And, if you pay me well the smiles you owe me,   35

Ile kill this cursed care, or else beshrowe me!

    DORO.[4]   We are descried! oh Nano,[4] we are dead!

---

[1] G. bodie's.   [2] D. *changes to* mind.

[3] D. *suggests* As; G. *says,* " = An' "; *I take it as* And.

[4] Cr. DOUG. . . . Mano; *corr. silently by* D.

Enter IAQUES, *his sword drawne.*

NANO.   Tut, yet you walk, you are not dead indeed.
Drawe me your sword, if he your way withstand,
And I will seeke for rescue out of hand.   40

   DO.[1]   Run, Nano, runne! preuent thy princes death!

   NA.   Feare not, Ile run all danger out of breath.

   IAQ.   Ah, you *calletta!* you *strumpet! ta,*[2] *Matresse
Doretie, este vous surprius?*[3]   Come, say your pater noster,
car vous est mort[4] *par ma foy.*   45

   DO.   *Callet?*[5] *me? strumpet?*   *Catiue* as thou art!
But euen a princesse borne, who scorne thy threats.[6]
Shall neuer French-man say an English mayd
Of threats of forraine force will be afraid.

   IAQ.   You no *dire vostre prieges?*[7] *vrbleme mechante*   50
famme,[8] *guarda* your *bresta! there! me make you die on
my morglay.*

   DORO.   God sheeld me, helplesse[9] princes and a wife,

They fight, and shee is sore wounded.[10]

And saue my soule, altho I loose my life!
Ah, I am slaine! some piteous power repay   55
This murtherers cursed deed that doth me slay!

   IAQ.   *Elle est tout mort.*   Me will runne *pur* a wager,
for feare me be *surpryes* and *pendu* for my labour.   Bein,[11]

---

   [1] *In* Cr. *this is prefixed to* l. 40; *corr. by* D.

   [2] *Qy.* ha; G. *emends to* la.   [3] D. êtes vous surprise.

   [4] D. car vous êtes morte.   [5] D. *suggests* Callest.

   [6] *So* Cr.; D. *prints:* [I'm no strumpet] but euen a princesse born,
                              Who scorne[s] thy threats —

   [7] D. votres prières; G. *points out that* Greene's *Italian gets the better of
his French.*

   [8] Cr. vrbleme merchants famme; D. *emends to* morbleu, mechante
femme.

   [9] G. haplesse.

   [10] D. G. *transfer this, and place it after* l. 54.

   [11] Cr. Be in; D. Bien; *I accept* D.'s *emendation (for the retention of
the spelling of* Cr. *see above,* iv. 3, ll. 1, 2), *although* Cr. *has here Roman
type, as if it were English.   That it is English, and is addressed to his
sword or himself, seems unlikely.*

Ie meu alera[1] *au roy auy cits me affaires,*[2] *Ie serra vn*
chiualier, for this daies trauaile.   60

                                                   Exit.

Enter NANO [*and*] S[IR] CUTBERT ANDERSON, *his sword drawne.*

S. CUTH.   Where is this poore distressed gentleman?

NANO.   Here, laid on ground, and wounded to the death.
Ah, gentle heart, how are these beautious lookes
Dimd by the tyrant cruelties of death !
Oh wearie soule, breake thou from forth my brest,   65
And ioyne thee with the soule I honoured most !

S. CUT.   Leaue mourning, friend ; the man is yet aliue.
Some[3] helpe me to conuey him to my house.
There will I see him carefully recured,
And send[4] priuie search to catch the murtherer.   70

NANO.   The God of heauen reward the, curteous knight

Exeunt ; and they beare out DOROTHEA.

[Act fourth.   Scene fifth.]

[*Another part of the same forest.*]

Enter the KING OF SCOTS, IAQUES, ATEUKIN, ANDREW ; IAQUES *running*
with his swoord one way, the KING *with his traine an-other way.*

K. OF S.   Stay, Iaques ; feare not ; sheath thy murthering
            blade!
Loe, here thy king and friends are come abroad
To saue thee from the terrors of pursuite :
What, is she dead ?

IAQ.   Wee, Monsieur, elle is[5] blesse per lake teste, oues   5
les espanles.[6]   I warrant she no trouble you.

---

[1] G. *gives* Cr. *as* vlera.

[2] D. je m'en allerai au roi lui dire mes affaires. *It seems improbable that*
lui dire *was the original of* auy cits, *which rather suggests some form of*
aviser. *It is hard to conjecture what such a French scholar as* Greene *wrote.*

[3] *Unless servants entered with* SIR CUTHBERT, — *which is possible, al-*
though none are mentioned in the stage-directions, — *this is to be emended*
to Come.   [4] G. send [forth].   [5] D. est, *without note.*

[6] D., *in his first edition, prints* par . . . la tête sur les épaules ; *later he*
printed par la tête *over* les épaules, — *so* G., *retaining* teste, *however.*

ATEU.   Oh then, my liege, how happie art thou growne,
How fauoured of the heauens, and blest by loue!
Mee thinkes I see faire Ida in thine armes,
Crauing remission for her late contempt;[1]   10
Mee thinke I see her blushing steale a kisse,
Vniting both your soules by such a sweete;
And you, my king, suck nectar from her lips.
Why then delaies your Grace to gaine the rest
You long desired?   Why loose we forward time?   15
Write, make me spokesman now, vow marriage:
If she deny your fauour, let me die.

ANDR.   Mightie and magnificent potentate, giue credence
to mine honorable good lord, for I heard the midwife sweare
at his natiuitie that the faieries gaue him the propertie of the   20
Thracian stone: for who toucheth it is exempted from griefe,
and he that heareth my maisters counsell is alreadie[2] possessed of happinesse.   Nay, — which is more myraculous —
as the noble-man in his infancie lay in his cradle, a swarme
of bees laid honey on his lippes in token of his eloquence,   25
for *melle dulcior*[3] *fluit oratio.*

ATEU.   Your Grace must beare with imperfections:
This is exceeding loue that makes him speake.

K. OF S.   Ateukin, I am rauisht in conceit!
And yet deprest againe with earnest thoughts: 30
Me thinkes this murther soundeth in mine eare
A threatning noyse of dire and sharp reuenge.
I am incenst with greefe, yet faine would ioy;
What may I do to end me of these doubts?

ATEU.   Why, prince, it is no murther in a king   35
To end an-others life to saue his owne,
For you are not as common people bee,
Who die and perish with a fewe mens[4] teares;
But, if you faile, the state doth whole default:
The realme is rent in twaine in such a losse.[5]   40

---

[1] Cr. attempt; *corr. by* D.   [4] Cr. mans; *corr. by* D.
[2] Cr. alreadle.   [5] *So* G.; Cr. alosse.
[3] Cr. dulcier; *corr. by* D., *without note.*

And Aristotle holdeth this for true :
Of euills [1] needs we must chuse the least.
Then better were it that a woman died
Then all the helpe of Scotland should be blent.
Tis pollicie, my liege, in euerie state   45
To cut off members that disturbe the head.
And [2] by corruption generation growes ;
And contraries maintaine the world and state.
    K. OF S.   Enough, I am confirmed ! Ateukin, come ;
Rid [3] me of loue, and rid me of my greefe :   50
Driue thou the tyrant from this tainted brest,
Then may I triumph in the height of ioy.
Go to mine Ida, tell her that I vowe
To raise her head and make her honours great.
Go to mine Ida, tell her that her haires   55
S[h]albe [4] embellished [5] with orient pearles,
And crownes of saphyrs compassing her browes
Shall warre [6] with those sweete beauties of her eyes.
Go to mine Ida, tell her that my soule
Shall keepe her semblance closed in my brest ;   60
And I, in touching of her milke-white mould,
Will thinke me deified in such a grace.
I like no stay ; go write, and I will signe.
Reward me Iaques, giue him store of crownes.[7]
And, sirrha Andrew, scout thou here in court,   65
And bring me tydings if thou canst perceiue
The least intent of muttering in my traine ;
For either those that wrong thy lord or thee [8]
Shall suffer death.   *Exit the* KING.[9]

---

[1] *Qy. insert* twain ; D. *suggests* needeth *for* needs ; G. *reads* need[ful].

[2] G. *wishes to read* As.

[3] G. *thinks this a misprint for* Rede.

[4] G. Shall be.   [5] Cr. embollished ; *corr. silently by* D.

[6] Cr. weare ; *corr. by* D.

[7] Cr. crowne ; *corr. by* D.

[8] *Qy.* me ; *but* KITTREDGE *suggests that this clause is addressed to* ATEUKIN.

[9] *He does not go until after* ATEUKIN'S *speech ;* D. G. *transfer the stage-direction accordingly.*

ATEU.   How much, ô mightie king,
Is thy Ateukin bound to honour thee!   70
Bowe thee,[1] Andrew; bend thine sturdie knees.
Seest thou not here thine onely god on earth?
    IAQ.   Mes ou est mon argent, signior?
    ATEU.   Come, follow me.   His graue, I see, is made,
That thus on suddain he hath left vs here.[2]   75
Come, Iaques, we wil[3] haue our packet soone dispatcht
And you shall be my mate vpon the way.
    IAQ.   Com vous plera,[4] monsieur.   *Exeunt.*
    ANDR.   Was neuer such a world, I thinke, before,
When sinners seeme to daunce within a net :   80
The flatterer and the murtherer they grow big ;
By hooke or crooke promotion now is sought.
In such a world, where men are so misled,
What should I do but, as the prouerbe saith,
Runne with the hare, and hunt[5] with the hound?   85
To haue two meanes beseemes a wittie man :
Now here in court I may aspire and clime
By subtiltie for[6] my maisters death ;
And, if that faile, well fare an-other drift :
I will in secret certaine letters send   90
Vnto the English king, and let him know
The order of his daughters ouerthrow,[7]
That, if my maister crack his credit here, —
As I am sure long flattery cannot hold, —
I may haue meanes within the English court   95
To scape the scourge that waits on bad aduice.   *Exit.*

[*The End of the Fourth Act.*]

---

[1] G. *inserts* then, *for metre.*
[2] D. G. *mark this as an* "aside." *I do not understand the passage;*
His Grace, I see, is madde *suggests itself as an emendation.*
[3] G. will.   [4] G. *gives* Cr. *as* Come vous plora.
[5] G. *inserts* too.
[6] D. *suggests* before.
[7] G. *says* Cr. *misprints* ouerthtow.

CHORUS.

Enter BOHAN *and* OBIRON.

OBER.   Beleue me, bonny Scot, these strange euents
Are passing pleasing ; may they end as well!
  BOHA.   Else say that Bohan hath a barren skull
If better motions yet then any past
Do not, more glee[1] to make, the fairie greet.   5
But my small son made prittie hansome[2] shift
To saue the queene, his mistresse, by his speed.
  OBIRO.   Yea, and your laddie,[3] for his sport he made,
Shall see, when least he hopes, Ile stand his friend,
Or else hee capers in a halters end.   10
  BOHA.   What, hang my son?   I trowe not, Obiran!
Ile rather die then see him woe begon.

Enter a rownd, or some daunce, at pleasure.

OBER.   Bohan, be pleasd, for, do they what they will,
Heere is my hand Ile saue thy son from ill.
                                   Exeunt.[4]

Actus quintus.   Schena prima.

[SIR CUTHBERT ANDERSON'S *house.*]

Enter the QUEENE *in a night gowne,* LADIE ANDERSON, *and* NANO.

LA. AND.   My gentle friend, beware, in taking aire,
Your walkes growe not offensiue to your woundes.
  DO.   Madame, I thank you of your courteous care ;
My woundes[5] are well-nigh clos'd, tho sore they are.
  L. AND.   Me thinks these closed wounds should breed
          more griefe,   5
Since open wounds haue cure, and finde reliefe.
  DOR.   Madame, if vndiscouered wounds you meane,
They are not curde, because they are not seen.

---

[1] G. *changes to* gree (= agree), *and takes* greet *as meaning* weep.
[2] G. handsome.   [3] Cr. you Ladie ; D. G. [and] yon laddie.
[4] Cr. Exit ; *corr. silently by* D.   [5] G. wounds.

L. AND.   I meane the woundes which do the heart subdue.
NANO.   Oh, that is loue !   Madame, speake I not true?   10

LADIE ANDERSON [1] ouerheares.

LA. AND.   Say it were true, what salue for such a sore?
NANO.   Be wise, and shut such neighbours out of dore.
LA. AND.   How if I cannot driue him from my brest?
NANO.   Then chaine him well, and let him do his best.
S. CUTH. [<i>aside</i>] In ripping vp their wounds I see their wit,   15
But, if these woundes be cured, I sorrow it.
DORO.   Why are you so intentiue to behold
My pale and wofull lookes, by care controld?
LA. AND.   Because in them a readie way is found
To cure my care and heale my hidden wound.   20
NANO.   Good maister, shut your eyes, keepe that conceit,
Surgeons giue quoine to get a good receit.
DORO.   Peace, wanton son, this ladie did amend
My woundes : mine eyes her hidden griefe shall end.
NANO.[2]   Looke not too much ; it is a waightie case   25
Where-as a man puts on a maidens face ;
For many times, if ladies weare [3] them not,
A nine moneths wound with little worke is got.
S. CUTH.   Ile breake off their dispute, least loue proceed
From couert smiles to perfect loue indeed.   30

[Enter SIR CUTHBERT.]

NANO.   The cats abroad, stirre not, the [4] mice bee still!
L. AND.   Tut! wee can flie such cats when so we will.
S. CUTH.   How fares my guest? take cheare, nought shall
       default
That eyther doth concerne your health or ioy.
Vse me : my house, and what is mine[5] is yours.   35

<hr/>

[1] <i>So</i> Cr. D. G.; <i>I regard it as a mistake for</i> SIR CUTHBERT; D. <i>indi-
cates the entry of</i> SIR CUTHBERT <i>before</i> l. 1 ; D. <i>before</i> l. 15.

[2] <i>In</i> Cr. <i>this line is assigned to</i> DOROTHEA; D. G. <i>follow</i> Cr.

[3] D. G. <i>correct the spelling to</i> ware.

[4] <i>It is perhaps only by an oversight that</i> D. G. <i>do not alter this to</i> ye;
see ii. 2, 28 ; v. 3, 1.   [5] D. changes to as.

DORO.   Thanks,[1] gentle knight; and, if all hopes be true,
I hope ere long to do as much for you.

    S. CUTH.   Your vertue doth acquite me of that doubt.
But, courteous sir, since troubles calles[2] me hence,
I must to Edenbourg vnto the king,   40
There to take charge, and waight him in his warres.
Meane-while, good madame, take this squire in charge,
And vse him so as if it were my-selfe.

    L. AND.   Sir Cutbert, doubt not of my dilligence.
Meane-while, till your returne God send you health.   45

    DORO.   God blesse his Grace, and, if his cause be iust,
Prosper his warres ; if not, hee 'l mend, I trust.
Good sir, what mooues the king to fall to armes?

    S. CUTH.   The king of England forrageth his land,
And hath besieged Dambar[3] with mightie force ;   50
[4] What other newes are common in the court,
Reade you these letters, madame ; tell the squire
The whole affaires of state, for I must hence.   *Exit.*

    DORO.   God prosper you, and bring you backe from thence!
Madame, what newes?

    LA. AND.   They say the queene is slaine.   55

    DORO.   Tut! such reports more false then trueth containe.

    L. AND.   But these reports haue made his nobles leaue
      him.

    DORO.   Ah, carelesse men, and would they so deceiue him?

    LA. AND.   The land is spoylde, the commons fear the
      crosse,
All crie against the king, their cause of losse ;   60
The English king subdues and conquers all.

    DORO.   Ah lasse![5] this warre growes great on causes small.

    L. AND.   Our court is desolate, our prince alone,
Still dreading death.

---

1 G. Thankes.   2 D. *changes to* call.

3 Cr. Dambac ; D. *emends to* Dunbar.

4 D. G., *regarding this as a direct question, transfer the line to* DORO-
THEA ; *but there is no occasion to alter the text.*

5 G. Ahlasse.

DORO.   Woes me! for him I mourne.[1]
Helpe! now helpe![2] a suddaine qualme   65
Assayles my heart.
    NANO.   Good madame, stand his[3] friend ;
Giue vs some licor to refresh his[3] heart.
    L. AND.   Daw thou him[3] vp, ande[4] I will fetch thee foorth
Potions of comfort to represse[5] his[3] paine.   *Exit.*
    NANO.   Fie, princesse! faint on euery fond report?   70
How well-nigh had you opened your estate!
Couer these sorrowes with the vaile of ioy,
And hope the best, for-why this warre will cause
A great repentance in your husbands minde.
    DORO.   Ah, Nano, trees liue not without their sap ;   75
And Clitia[6] cannot blush but on the sunne ;
The thirstie earth is broke with many a gap,
And lands are leane, where riuers do not runne :
Where soule is reft from that it loueth best,
How can it thriue or boast of quiet rest?   80
Thou knowest the princes losse must be my death,
His griefe, my griefe, his mischiefe must be mine.
Oh, if thou loue me, Nano, high to court!
Tell Rosse, tell Bartram, that I am aliue ;
Conceale thou yet the place of my aboade.   85
Will[7] them, euen as they loue their queene,
As they are charie of my soule and ioy,
To guard the king, to serue him as my lord.
Haste thee, good Nano,[8] for my husbands care
Consumeth mee and wounds mee to the heart.   90
    NANO.   Madame, I go, yet loth to leaue you heere.
                                               Exit.[9]

[1] Cr. moune ; D. G. moane.
[2] D. *says* "*something is lacking*," *and* G. *reads* Helpe [me] now helpe [me, for].   [4] G. and.
[3] Cr. her ; D. *charges the confusion to the transcriber.*
[5] G. repress.   [6] D. Clytie, *without note* ; G. Clytia.
[7] D. *proposes* But will *or* And will, *for metre.*
[8] Cr. Nana ; D. G. Nano.
[9] Cr. Exeunt ; G. *silently transfers it to* l. 93, *and prints* Exit [NANO], *as if* Cr. *had* Exit.

DOR.   Go thou with speed, euen as thou holdst me deare ;
Returne in haste.

Enter LADIE ANDERSON.

L. AN.   Now, sir, what cheare? come tast this broth I
  bring.

DORO.   My griefe is past ; I feele no further sting.   95

L. AND.   Where is your dwarfe?   Why hath he[1] left you,
  sir ?

DORO.   For some affaires ; hee is not traueld farre.

L. AND.   If so you please, come in and take your rest.

DORO.   Feare keepes awake a discontented brest.

Exeunt.

[Act fifth.   Scene second.]

[*Before the house of the* COUNTESS OF ARRAN.]

After a solemne seruice, enter from the WIDDOWES *house a seruice, musical
songs of marriages, or a maske, or what prettie triumph you list ; to
them,* ATEUKIN *and* IAQUES.[2]

ATE.   What means this triumph, frend? why are these
  feasts?

SERUI.   Faire Ida, sir, was marryed yesterday
Vnto Sir Eustace ; and, for that intent,
Wee feast and sport it thus to honour them.
And, if you please, come in and take your part ;   5
My ladie is no niggard of her cheare.   *Exit.*[3]

IAQ.   *Monsigneur,* why be you so sadda? *fette bon chere ;
foutre[4] de ce monde !*

ATEU.   What! was I borne to bee the scorne of kinne?
To gather feathers like to a[5] hopper-crowe   10

---

[1] G. hee.

[2] Cr. ATEUKIN *and* GNATO ; *corr. by* D ; G. and [his] GNATO [=
IAQUES].   [4] G. *says* Cr. *has* fontre.

[3] *So* Cr. ; D. G. [Exit with other Reuellers.   D., *of course, does not pro-
fess to follow the original in stage-directions ;* G. *does, but here, as often,
his single bracket indicates that the stage-direction is not in* Cr. *while his
spelling indicates that it is.*   [5] G., *following* D.'s *suggestion, omits* a.

And loose them in the height of all my pompe?
Accursed man, now is my credite lost!
Where is [1] my vowes I made vnto the king?
What shall become of mee, if hee shall heare
That I haue causde him kill a vertuous queene,   15
And hope in vaine for that which now is lost?
Where shall I hide my head?   I knowe the Heauens
Are iust, and will reuenge ; I know my sinnes
Exceede compare.   Should I proceed in this,
This Eustace must a-main [2] be made away.   20
Oh, were I dead, how happy should I bee!

   IAQ.   *Est ce donque a tell poynt vostre estat?*   Faith,
then adeiu Scotland! adeiu Signior Ateukin! me will homa
to France, and no be hanged in a strange country.   *Exit.*

   ATEU.   Thou doest me good to leaue me thus alone,   25
That galling griefe and I may yoake in one.
Oh, what are subtile [3] meanes to clime on high,
When euery fall swarmes with exceeding shame?
I promist Idaes loue vnto the prince,
But shee is lost, and I am false forsworne ;   30
I practis'd Dorotheas haplesse death,
And by this practise haue commenst a warre, —
Oh cursed race of men that traficque guile,
And, in the end, themselues and kings beguile!
A-shamde to looke vpon my prince againe,   35
A-shamde of my suggestions and aduise,
A-shamde of life, a-shamde that I haue erde,
Ile hide my-selfe, expecting for my shame !
Thus God doth worke with those that purchase [4] fame
By flattery, and make their prince their game. [5]   40
                                                    Exeunt.

---

[1] D. *emends to* are.   [3] G. subtle.
[2] Cr. a man; *corr. by* D.   [4] *So* G.; Cr. purſchase.
   [5] D. *prints* gain, *and suggests* game; *according to my copyist,* game *is
the reading of* Cr., *but* G. *says* Cr. *has* gaine, *and he prefers that reading.*

[Act fifth.   Scene third.]

Enter the KING OF ENGLAND, LORD PERCEY, SAMLES, *and others.*

ARIUS.[1]   Thus farre, the[2] English peeres, haue we dis-
playde
Our wauing ensignes with a happy warre ;
Thus neerely hath our furious rage reuengde
My daughters death vpon the traiterous Scot ;
And now before Dambar our campe is pitcht,   5
Which if it yeeld not to our compromise,[3]
The plough[4] shall furrow where the pallace stood,
And furie shall enuy[5] so high a power
That mercie shall bee bannisht[6] from our swords.

    DOUG.   What seekes the English king?   10
    ARIUS.   Scot, open those·gates, and let me enter in ;
Submit thy-selfe and thine vnto my grace,
Or I will put each mothers sonne to death,
And lay this cittie leuell with the ground.

    DOUG.   For what offence, for what default of ours   15
Art thou incenst so sore against our state?
Can generous hearts in nature bee so sterne
To pray on those that neuer did offend?
What tho[7] the lyon, king of brutish race,
Through outrage sinne, shall lambes be therefore slaine?   20
Or is it lawfull that the humble die
Because the mightie do gainsay the right?
O English king, thou bearest in thy crest[8]
The king of beasts, that harmes not yeelding ones,

---

[1] *In this scene the speeches marked* ARIUS *belong to the* KING OF ENG-
LAND ; *see Notes,* vol. III, *and cf. above,* p. 365, n. 2.

[2] D. *changes to* then ; G. *to* ye ; *cf. above,* p. 396, n. 4.

[3] *Misprinted* compremise *in* Cr.

[4] Cr. place ; *emend. by* D.   [7] G. though.

[5] D. *suggests, and* G. *accepts,* enjoy, *which is probably right.*

[6] G. banisht.   [8] Cr. brest ; *emend. by* D.

The roseall crosse is spred within thy field, 25
A signe of peace, not of reuenging warre :
Be gracious then vnto this little towne,
And, tho we haue withstood thee for a while
To shew[1] alleageance to our liefest liege,
Yet, since wee know no hope of any helpe, 30
Take vs to mercie, for wee yeeld our-selues.
    ARI. What, shall I enter then, and be your lord?
    DOUG. We will submit vs to the English king.

They descend downe, open the gates, and humble them.

    ARIUS. Now life and death dependeth on my sword :
This hand now reard, my Douglas, if I list,[2] 35
Could part thy head and shoulders both in twaine ;
But, since I see thee wise and olde in yeares,
True to thy king, and faithfull in his warres,
Liue thou and thine. Dambar is too too small,
To giue an entrance to the English king. 40
I, eaglelike, disdaine these little foules,
And looke on none but those that dare resist.
Enter your towne as those that liue by me.
For others, that resist, — kill, forrage, spoyle !
Mine English souldiers, as you loue your king, 45
Reuenge his daughters death, and do me right.

Exeunt.

[Act fifth. Scene fourth.][3]

[Near the Scottish camp.]

Enter the LAWYER, *the* MERCHANT, *and the* DIUINE.

    LAWYER. My friends, what thinke you of this present
        state ?
Were euer seene such changes in a time ?

---

[1] G. show.   [2] Cr. G. D. lift.

[3] *I have assigned this to the place indicated at the end. But it has no connection with the play nor any special appropriateness to it ; it is merely a débat, foisted into the play — perhaps by* Greene *himself.*

The manners and the fashions of this age
Are, like the ermine-skinne, so full of spots
As sooner [1] may the Moore bee washed white   5
Then these corruptions bannisht from this realme.
   MERCH.   What sees Mas Lawyer in this state amisse?
   LAW.   A wresting power that makes a nose of wax
Of grounded lawe, a damde and subtile drift
In all estates to clime by others losse,   10
An eager thrift [2] of wealth, forgetting trueth.
Might I ascend vnto the highest states,
And by discent discouer euery crime,
My friends, I should lament, and you would greeue,
To see the haplesse ruines of this realme.   15
   DIU.   O Lawyer, thou haste curious eyes to prie
Into the secret [3] maimes of their estate ;
But, if thy vaile of error were vnmaskt,
Thy-selfe should see your sect do maime her most.
Are you not those that should maintaine the peace,   20
Yet onely are the patrones of our strife?
If your profession haue his ground and spring
First from the lawes of God, then countriees [4] right,
Not any-waies inuerting natures power,
Why thriue you by contentions?   Why deuise you   25
Clawses and subtile reasons to except?
Our state was first, before you grew so great,
A lanterne to the world for vnite ; [5]
Now they that are befriended and are rich,
Op-presse [6] the poore.   Come Homer without quoine,   30
He is not heard.   What shall we terme this drift, —
To say the poore mans cause is good and iust,
And yet the rich man gaines the best in lawe?
It is your guise — the more the world laments ! —
To quoine prouisoes to beguile your lawes ;   35

---

[1] Cr. As soone ; *emend. by* D.   [4] G. countries.
[2] D. *emends to* thirst, *which is probably right ;* G. *prints* thrift, *as read-*
ing of Cr.   [5] G. vnitie.
[3] Cr. *misprints* secrets.   [6] Cr. Or presse ; *corr. by* D.

To make a gay pretext of due proceeding,
When you delay your common-pleas for yeares.
Mark what these dealings lately here haue wrought :
The craftie men haue purchaste greatmens[1] lands ;
They powle, they pinch, their tennants are vndone.   40
If these complaine, by you they are vndone ;
You fleese them of their quoine, their children beg,
And many want, because you may bee rich.
This scarre is mightie, Maister Lawyer !
Now war[2] hath gotten head within this land,   45
Marke but the guise : the poore man that is wrongd
Is readie to rebell; hee spoyles, he pilles, —
We need no foes to forrage that wee haue ;
The lawe, say they, in peace consumed vs,
And now in warre wee[3] will consume the lawe.   50
Looke to this mischiefe, lawyers !   Conscience knowes
You liue amisse : amend it, least you end !
    LAW.   Good Lord, that these[4] diuines should see so farre
In others faults, without amending theirs !
Sir, sir, the generall defaults in state —   55
If you would read before you did correct —
Are by a hidden working from aboue
By their successiue changes still remoued.[5]
Were not the lawe by contraries maintainde,
How could the trueth from falsehood be discernde?   60
Did wee not tast[6] the bitternesse of warre,
How could wee knowe the sweet effects of peace?
Did wee not feele the nipping winter frostes,
How should we know the sweetnesse of the spring?
Should all things still remaine in one estate,   65
Should not in greatest arts some scarres be found?
Were all vpright, vn-changd,[7] what world were this?
A chaos, made of quiet, yet no world,

---

1 G. great mens.   4 Cr. their ; *emend. by* D.
2 Cr. man ; *emend. by* D.   5 Cr. remainde ; *emend. by* D.
3 G. we.   6 G. taste.
7 Cr. and changd ; D. *emends* and *to* nor.

Because the parts thereof did still accord.
This matter craues a variance not a speech.[1]   70
But, sir Diuine, to you: looke on your maimes,
Diuisions, sects, your simonies [2] and bribes,
Your cloaking with the great for feare to fall, —
You shall perceiue you are the cause of all.
Did each man know there were a storme at hand,   75
Who would not cloath him well to shun the wet?
Did prince and peere, the lawyer and the least,
Know what were sinne, without a partiall glose,
Wee'd [3] need no long discouery [4] then of crimes,
For each would mend, aduis'de by holy men.   80
Thus I [5] but slightly shadow out your sinnes;
But, if they were depainted out of [6] life,
Alasse, wee both had wounds inough to heale!
    MERCH.   None of you both, I see, but are in fault;
Thus simple men, as I, do swallow flies.   85
This graue diuine can tell vs what to do,
But wee may say: "Phisitian [7] mend thy-selfe;"
This lawyer hath a pregnant wit to talke,
But all are words, I see no deeds of woorth.
    LAW.   Good Merchant, lay your fingers on your mouth;   90
Be not a blab, for feare you bite your-selfe.
What should I terme your state but euen the way
To euery ruine in this common-weale?
You bring vs in the meanes of all excesse,
You rate it and retale [8] it as you please,   95
You sweare, forsweare, and all, to compasse wealth;
Your mony is your God, your hoord your heauen.
You are the groundworke of contention :
First, heedlesse youth by you is ouerreacht,
Wee are corrupted by your many crownes;   100
The gentlemen whose titles you haue bought

1 *Qy.* peace.   5 *Supplied by* D.   6 D. G. for.
2 Cr. summonies; *corr. silently by* D.   7 G. Physitian.
8 Cr. Wee; *emend. by* D.   8 Cr. retalde; *corr. by* D.
4 D. *changes to* discoursing; G. *rightly defends the text.*

Loose all their fathers toyle within a day,
Whilst Hob, your sonne, and Sib, your nutbrowne childe,
Are gentle-folkes, and gentles are beguilde.
This makes so many noble maides [1] to stray,   105
And take sinister courses in the state.

Enter a SCOUT.

SCOUT.   My friends, begone and if you loue your liues!
The King of England marcheth heere at hand;
Enter the campe, for feare you bee surprisde.
DIUINE.   Thankes, gentle scout. God mend that is amisse, 110
And place true zeale whereas corruption is!   *Exeunt.*

[Act fifth.   Scene fifth.]

[*The house of* SIR CUTHBERT ANDERSON.]

Enter DOROTHEA, LADIE ANDERSON *and* NANO.

DORO.   What newes in court, Nano? let vs know it.
NANO.   If so please my lord, I straight will shew it:
The English king hath all the borders spoyld,
Hath taken Morton prisoner, and hath slaine
Seuen thousand Scottish lords [2] not farre from Tweade.[3]   5
DORO.   A wofull murther, and a bloodie deed!
NANO.   The king,[4] our liege, hath sought by many meanes
For to appease his enemie by prayers.
Nought will preuaile vnlesse hee can restore
Faire Dorothea, long supposed dead.   10
To this intent he hath proclaimed late
That who-so-euer returne the queene to court
Shall haue a thousand markes for his reward.
L. AND.   He loues her then, I see, altho inforst,
That would bestow such gifts for to regaine her.   15
Why sit you sad, good sir?   Be not dismaide.

1 D. *emends to* minds.
2 D. G. *accept* Collier's *emendation*, lads.
3 Cr. Twearde; D. G. Tweed, *without note.*
4 Cr. Thinking; *corr. by* D.

NA.   Ile lay my life this man would be a maide.

DOR. [*to* NANO]   Faine would I shewe my-selfe, and change
        my tire.

AND.   Whereon diuine you, sir?

NA.   Vppon desire.

Madam marke but my skill : Ile lay my life   20

My maister here will prooue a married wife.

DORO. [*to* NANO]   Wilt thou bewray me, Nano?

NANO.   Madam, no :

You are a man, and like a man you goe ;

But I, that am in speculation seene,

Know you would change your state to be a queene.   25

DOR.   Thou art not, dwarffe,[1] to learne thy mistresse mind :

Faine would I with [2] thy-selfe disclose my kind,

But yet I blush.

NA.   What? blush you, madam, than,

To be your-selfe, who are a fayned man?

Let me alone.[3]   30

LA. AND.   Deceitfull beautie, hast thou scornd me so?

NANO.   Nay, muse not, madam,[4] for she tels you true.

LA. AND.   Beautie bred loue, and loue hath bred my
        shame.

N.   And womens faces work more wrongs then these.

Take comfort, madam, to cure your[5] disease.   35

And yet [s]he loues a man as well as you,

Onely this difference : she [6] cannot fancie too.[7]

LA. AN.   Blush, greeue and die, in thine insaciat lust !

DO.   Nay, liue, and ioy that thou hast won a friend

That loues thee as his life, by good [8] desert.   40

LA. AND.   I ioy, my lord, more then my tongue can tell.

Although not as I desir'd,[9] I loue you well ;

But modestie, that neuer blusht before,

---

[1] G. dwarfe.   [2] D. *suggests* wish.

[3] Lines 45-77 (?) *should follow this ; the confusion was caused by* Let
me alone.   [4] Cr. maiden ; *emend. by* D.   [5] Cr. our ; *emend. by* D.

[6] Cr. she ; D. G. *change to* he.   [7] G. two.   [8] Cr. god ; D. good.

[9] *The verse hobbles ; perhaps read* Though *for* Although (*with* D. G.)
or wish'd *for* desir'd.

Discouer my false heart! I say no more.
Let me alone.

  Doro.   Good Nano, stay a while.[1]   45
Were I not sad, how kindlie could I smile
To see how faine I am to leaue this weede;
And yet I faint to shewe my-selfe indeede.
But danger hates delay; I will be bold:
Faire ladie, I am not, [as you][2] suppose,   50
A man, but euen that queene[3] — more haplesse I!—
Whom Scottish king appointed hath[4] to die;
I am the haplesse princesse for whose right
These kings in bloudie warres reuenge dispight;
I am that Dorothea whom they seeke,   55
Yours bounden for your kindnesse and releefe.
And, since you are the meanes that saue my life,
Your-selfe and I will to the camp repaire,
Whereas your husband shal enioy reward,
And bring me to his Highnesse once againe.   60

  An. Pardon, most gratious princesse, if you please,
My rude discourse and homelie entertaine;
And, if my words may sauour any worth,
Vouchsafe my counsaile in this waightie cause:
Since that our liege hath so vnkindly dealt,   65
Giue him no trust, returne vnto your syre,
There may you safelie liue in spight of him,

  Doro. Ah, ladie, so wold worldly counsell work;
But constancie, obedience and my loue,
In that my husband is my lord and chiefe,   70
These call me to compassion of his state.[5]
Disswade me not, for vertue will not change.

  An. What woonderous constancie is this I heare?
If English dames their husbands loue so deer,
I feare me in the world they haue no peere.   75

  Na. Come, princes, wend, and let vs change your weede,
I long to see you now a queene indeede.   *Exeunt.*

---

1 *This confirms* p. 407, n. 3. 2 *Supplied by* D. 3 Cr. qeene; G. queene.
4 G. *changes to* had. 5 Cr. estate; *emend. by* D.

[Act fifth.   Scene sixth.]

[The Scottish camp.]

Enter the KING OF SCOTS, *the* ENGLISH HERAULD *&* LORDS.

K. OF S.   He would haue parly, lords.   Herauld, say he
shall.
And get thee gone.   Goe, leaue me to my-selfe.

[Exeunt HERALD *and* LORDS.]¹

Twixt loue and feare continuall is ² the warres :
The one assures me of my Idaes loue,
The other moues me for my murthred queene.   5
Thus finde I greefe of that whereon I ioy,
And doubt in greatest hope, and death in weale.
Ah lasse ! ³ what hell may be compared with mine,
Since in extreames my comforts do consist?
Warre then will cease, when dead ones are reuiued!   10
Some then will yeelde, when I am dead for hope!
Who doth disturbe me?   Andrew!   ANDREW *enter, with* SLIPPER.
ANDR.   I, my liege.
K. OF S.   What newes?
ANDR.   I thinke my mouth was made at first
To tell these tragique tales, my liefest lord.
K. OF S.   What, is Ateukin dead? tell me the worst!   15
ANDR.   No ; but your Ida — ⁴ shall I tell him all? —
Is married late — ah, shall I say to whom?
My maister sad — for-why he shames the court —
Is fled away, — ah, most vnhappie flight!
Onelie my-selfe, — ah, who can loue you more? —   20
To shew my dutie, — dutie past beliefe ! —
Am come vnto your Grace, oh gratious liege,
To let you know — oh, would it weare not thus ! —

¹ *No stage-direction in* Cr.; D. *has* Exit Herald — Lords retire, *which*
G. *repeats without brackets, as if it were in* Cr.
² D. *changes to* are.   ³ G. Ahlasse.
⁴ G. *inserts* and; *for what reason, I know not.*

That loue is vain, and maids soone lost and wonne.

    K. of S.   How haue the partial heauens the*n* dealt with
        me,   25
Boading my weale, for to abase my power !
Alas, what thronging thoughts do me oppresse !
Iniurious loue is partiall in my right,
And flattering tongues by whom I was misled
Haue laid a snare to spoyle my state and me.   30
Methinkes I heare my Dorotheas goast
Howling reuenge for my accursed hate ;
The gosts[1] of those my subiects that are slaine
Pursue me, crying out, " Woe, woe, to lust ! "
The foe pursues me at my pallace doore ;   35
He breakes my rest and spoyles me in my camp.
Ah, flattering broode of sicophants, my foes,
First shall my dire reuenge begin on you !
I will reward thee, Andrew.

    Slip.   Nay, sir, if you be in your deeds of charitie, re-   40
member me : I rubd M. Ateukins horse heeles, when he rid
to the medowes.[2]

    K. of S.   And thou shalt haue thy recompence[3] for that. —
Lords, beare them to the prison ; chaine them fast,
Vntil we take some order for their deathes.   45

               [Enter Lords *and seize them.*]

    And.   If so your Grace in such sort giue rewards,
Let me haue nought ; I am content to wait.

    Slip.   Then I pray, sir, giue me all ; I am as ready for a
reward as an oyster for a fresh tide ; spare not me, sir.

    K. of S.   Then hang them both as traitors to the king.   50

    Slip.   The case is altered, sir, Ile none of your gifts.
What, I take a reward at your hands, maister ? Faith, sir,
no ! I am a man of a better conscience.

    K. of S.   Why dallie you ? go draw them hence away.

    Slip.   Why, alas, sir, I wil[4] go away. I thanke you, gentle   55

---

[1] Cr. gifts ; *corr. by* D.   [3] G. recompense.
[2] *Qy.* widowes.   [4] G. will.

friends; I pray you spare your pains, I will not trouble his
Honors maistership, Ile run away.

> *Enter* Oberon,[1] *and* Antiques, *and carrie away the* Clowne; *he makes
> pots*[2] *and sports and scornes.*

Why stay you?   Moue me not ; let search be made
For vile Ateukin ; who-so findes him out
Shall haue fiue hundreth markes for his reward.   60
Away with them, lords !   Troupes, about[3] my tent!
Let all our souldiers stand in battaile ray,
For, lo! the English to their parley come.

> *March ouer brauelie: first, the English hoste, the sword caried before the
> King by* Percy; *the Scottish on the other side,*[4] *with all their pompe
> brauelie.*

K. of S.   What seekes the King of England in this land?
K. of Eng.   False traiterous Scot, I come for to reuenge   65
My daughters death : I come to spoyle thy wealth,
Since thou hast spoyld me of my marriage ioy ;
I come to heape thy land with carkasses,
That this thy thriftie[5] soyle, choakt vp with blood,
May thunder forth reuenge vpon thy head ;   70
I come to quit thy louelesse[6] loue with death.
In briefe, no meanes of peace shall ere be found,
Except I haue my daughter or thy head.
K. of S.   My head, proud king?   Abase thy prancking
            plumes![7]
So striuing[8] fondly, maiest thou catch thy graue.   75
But, if true iudgement do direct thy course,

---

[1] Cr. Adam; *corr. by* D.   *If any actor of this date named Adam were
known, one would be inclined to assign the part of* Oberon *to him, as* G.
does. D. G. *transfer this stage-direction to* l. 61.

[2] D. *conjectures and reads* mops, *having previously conjectured* pouts;
but see Nares, *s. v.*   [4] Cr. otherside.

[3] Cr. Away with the Lords troupes about; D. *emends to* Away with
them! Lords, troop about.   [5] D. thirsty; G. thirftie (= thirsty).

[6] D. *accepts* Collier's *emendation* lawless; G. *rightly defends the text.*

[7] Cr. plaines; *emend. by* D.

[8] *In* G, *the* u *is inverted.*

These lawfull reasons should deuide [1] the warre :
Faith, not by my consent thy daughter dyed.

 K. OF E. Thou liest, false Scot ! thy agents haue confest
   it !

These are but fond delayes, thou canst not thinke   80
A meanes to [2] reconcile me for thy friend ;
I haue thy parasites confession pend.
What then canst thou alleage in thy excuse?

 K. OF S. I will repay the raunsome for her bloud.

 K. OF E. What, thinkst thou, catiue, I wil sel my child? 85
No ; if thou be a prince and man-at-armes,
In singule combat come and trie thy right ;
Else will I prooue thee recreant to thy face!

 K. OF S. I tooke [3] no combat, false iniurious king!
But, since thou needlesse art inclinde to warre,   90
Do what thou darest : we are in open field ;
Arming thy [4] battailes I wil [5] fight with thee.

 K. OF E. Agreed. Now trumpets sound a dreadfull
   charge !

Fight for your princesse, [6] braue English-men !

 [K. OF SCOTS.] [7] Now for your lands, your children and
   your wiues,   95
My Scottish peeres, and lastly for your king!

  Alarum sounded ; both the battailes offer to meet ; &c, as the kings are
  ioyning battaile, enter SIR CUTBER[T] *and* [8] LADY CUTBERT, *with the*
  queene, DOROTHEA, *richly attired,* [*and* NANO].

S. CUT. Stay, princes, wage not warre ! A priuie grudge
Twixt such as you, most high in maiestie,

  [1] D. *first suggested* decide, *later* This lawful reason should divert ; *but*
deuide *may be right.*   [2] Cr. for to ; *corr. by* D.
  [3] *So* Cr. ; D. *emends to* brook ; seeke *seems about as likely.*
  [4] *So* Cr. ; D. *emends to* Arming my ; Among thy *seems possible.*
  [5] G. will.
  [6] D. *inserts* my, *for metrical reasons ; various other monosyllables are*
possible, if any is needed.
  [7] *Not in* Cr. ; *supplied by* D. ; G.'s *statement that* D. *"gives these two*
lines to the KING OF ENGLAND*" is erroneous.*
  [8] Cr. to his ; *corr. by* D. *in his first edition ;* G. and the.

Afflicts both nocent and the innocent.
How many swordes, deere princes, see I drawne !   100
The friend against his friend, a deadly friend ;[1]
A desperate diuision in those lands
Which if they ioyne in one commaund the world.
Oh, stay!   With reason mittigate your rage,
And let an old man, humbled on his knees,   105
Intreat a boone, good princes, of you both.

    K. OF EN.   I condiscend, for-why thy reuerend years
Import some newes of truth and consequence ;
[2] I am content, for Anderson I know.

    K. OF S.   Thou art my subiect and doest [3] meane me good.   110

    S. CUT. AND.   But by your gratious[4] fauours grant me this :
To sweare vpon your sword [5] to do me right.

    K. OF ENG.   See, by my sword, and by a princes faith,
In euery lawfull sort I am thine owne!

    K. OF S.   And by my scepter and the Scottish crowne,   115
I am resolu'd to grant thee thy request!

    CUTB.   I see you trust me, princes, who repose
The waight of such a warre vpon my will.
Now marke my sute : a tender lyons whelpe,
This other day came stragling in the woods,   120
Attended by a young and tender hinde,
In courage hautie,[6] yet tyred like a lambe.
The prince of beasts had left this young in keepe,
To foster vp as louemate and compeere
Vnto the lyons mate, a [7] naibour friend.   125
This stately guide, seduced by the fox,
Sent forth an eger woolfe bred vp in France,
That gript the tender whelp, and wounded it.
By chance as I was hunting in the woods,

---

  [1] D. *suggests and reads* fiend; field *or* feud *is quite as probable; but the text is intelligible, and is retained by* G.
  [2] D. G. *transfer this line to the* KING OF SCOTS.
  [3] G. doost.   [5] D. sword[s].
  [4] G. gracious.   [7] D. *suggests* and.
  [6] D. *changes to* haught, *for metre ;* G. *keeps* hautie, *but prints* tyr'd.

I heard the moane the hinde made for the whelpe ;   130
I tooke them both, and brought them to my house ;
With charie care I haue recurde the one ;
And, since I know the lyons are at strife
About the losse and dammage of the young,
I bring her home ; make claime to her who list !   135

Hee discouereth her.

DORO.   I am the whelpe, bred by this lyon vp,
This royall English king, my happy sire ;
Poore Nano is the hinde that tended me.
My father, Scottish king, gaue me to thee,
A haplesse wife ; thou, quite misled by youth,   140
Haste sought sinister loues and forraine ioyes.
The fox Ateukin, cursed parasite,
Incenst your Grace to send the woolfe abroad,
The French-borne Iaques, for to end my daies.
Hee, traiterous man, pursued me in the woods,   145
And left mee wounded, where this noble knight
Both rescued me and mine, and sau'd my life.
Now keep thy promise ; Dorothea liues :
Giue Anderson his due and iust reward ;
And, since you kings your warres began by me,   150
Since I am safe, returne, — surcease your fight.
K. OF S.   Durst I presume to looke vpon those eies
Which I haue tired with a world of woes,
Or did I thinke submission were ynough,
Or sighes might make an entrance to my soule,   155
You heauens, you know how willing I wold weep !
You heauens can tell how glad I would submit !
You heauens can say how firmly I would sigh !
DO.   Shame me not, prince, companion in thy bed.
Youth hath misled ; tut, but a little fault !   160
Tis kingly to amend what is amisse.
Might I with twise as many paines as these
Vnite our hearts, then should my wedded lord
See how incessaunt labours I would take.

My gracious father, gouerne your affects,   165
Giue me that hand that oft hath blest this head,
And claspe thine armes, that haue embraced this,[1]
About the shoulders of my wedded spouse.
Ah, mightie prince, this king and I am one ;
Spoyle thou his subiects, thou despoylest me ;   170
Touch thou his brest, thou doest attaint this heart :
Oh, bee my father then in louing him !
    K. OF ENG.   Thou prouident kinde mother of increase,
Thou must preuaile, ah, Nature, thou must rule !
Holde, daughter, ioyne my hand and his in one,   175
I will embrace him for to fauour thee :
I call him friend, and take him for my sonne.
    DOR.   Ah, royall husband, see what God hath wrought :
Thy foe is now thy friend !   Good men-at-armes,
Do you the like ; these nations if they ioyne,   180
What monarch with his liegemen in this world
Dare but encounter you in open fielde ?
    K. OF S.   Al wisedom, ioynde with godly pietie !
Thou, English king, pardon my former youth ;
And pardon, courteous queen, my great misdeed :   185
And, for assurance of mine after-life,
I take religious vowes before my God
To honour thee for father,[2] her for wife.
    SIR CUTHB.[3]   But yet my boones, good princes, are not past :
First, English king, I humbly do request   190
That by your meanes our princesse may vnite
Her loue vnto mine alder-truest [4] loue,
Now you will loue, maintaine and helpe them both.
    K. OF ENG.   Good Anderson, I graunt thee thy request.
    SIR CUTHB.[3]   But you, my prince, must yeelde me mickle
        more :   195
You know your nobles are your chiefest staies,[5]
And long time haue been bannisht from your court ;

---

[1] D. G. *read* embrac'd this [neck].   [3] Cr. L. AND. ; *emend. by* D.
[2] Cr. fauour ; *emend. by* D.   [4] G. aldertruest.
[5] Cr. D. (1st ed.) states ; D. (2d ed.), G. staies, *without note.*

Embrace and reconcile them to your-selfe, —
They are your hands, whereby you ought to worke.
As for Ateukin and his lewde compeeres,   200
That sooth'd you in your sinnes and youthly pompe,
Exile, torment and punish such as they,
For greater vipers neuer may be found
Within a state then such aspiring heads,
That reck not how they clime, so that they clime.   205
    K. OF S.   Guid knight, I graunt thy sute: first, I submit
And humble[1] craue a pardon of your Grace;
Next, courteous queene, I pray thee by thy loues,
Forgiue mine errors past, and pardon mee;
My lords and princes, if I haue misdone, —   210
As I haue wrongd indeed both you and yours, —
Heereafter, trust me, you are deare to me;
As for Auteukin, who-so findes the man,
Let him haue martiall lawe and straight be hangd,
As all his vaine abetters[2] now are dead.[3]   215
And Anderson our treasurer shall pay
Three thousand markes for friendly recompence.
    NANO.[4]   But princes, whilst you friend it thus in one,
Me thinks of friendship Nano shall haue none.
    DORO.   What would my dwarfe that I will not bestow?   220
    NANO.   My boone, faire queene, is this: that you would
       go;
Altho my bodie is but small and neate,
My stomacke[5] after toyle requireth meate.
An easie sute, dread princes; will you wend?
    K. OF S.   Art thou a pigmey borne, my prettie frend?   225
    NANO.   Not so, great king, but Nature, when she framde
      me,
Was scant of earth, and Nano therefore namde me;
And, when she sawe my bodie was so small,
She gaue me wit to make it big withall.

---

[1] D. G. humble[y].
[2] Cr. arbetters; *corr. by* D.
[3] Cr. diuided; *corr. by* D.
[4] Cr. L. ANDR.; *emend. by* D.
[5] G. stomache,

K.   Till time when —
Dor.   Eate then.[1]   230
K.   My friend, it stands with wit
To take repast when stomacke [2] serueth it.
Dor.[8] Thy pollicie, my Nano, shall preuaile.
Come, royall father, enter we my tent.
And, souldiers, feast it, frolike it like friends ;   235
My princes, bid this kinde and courteous traine
Partake some fauours of our late accord.
Thus warres haue end, and, after dreadfull hate,
Men learne at last to know their good estate !

Exeunt.

FINIS.

[1] *In* Cr. *this line stands thus :* K. Till time when, Dor. Eate then.
D. *suggests that there is a gap in the text.*

[2] G. stomache.

[8] Lines 234, 236 *seem to indicate that this speech belongs to the* King of
Scots ; *and besides, as* Kittredge *points out, one of the kings should speak
the closing lines,* — " *It is not the fashion to see the lady the epilogue* " *or
even the last speaker, in a play.*

THE
LOVE OF KING

DAVID AND FAIR

BETHSABE

With the Tragedie of Abſalon.

As it hath ben diuers times plaied on the ſtage.

Written by George Peele.

Vignette.

LONDON,
Printed by Adam Iſlip.
1599.

Printed from a copy of the first edition, in the Boston Public Library. This edition, printed by Islip, is indicated in the footnotes by Isl.; all important variants of the editions of Hawkins (Haw.), Dyce (D.), and Bullen (B.) are also recorded. The titlepage is not a facsimile.

[Dramatis Personae.

DAVID, *King of Israel.*

ABSOLON
AMMON
ADONIA } *sons of David.*
CHILEAB
SALOMON

HANON, *King of Ammon.*

MACHAAS, *King of Gath.*

IOAB
ABISAY } *David's captains.*

AMASA, *Absolon's captain.*

VRIAS, *husband of Bethsabe.*

CUSAY
ITHAY } *friends of David.*

ACHITOPHEL, *Counsellor of Absolon.*

IONADAB, *friend of Ammon.*

NATHAN, *a prophet.*

SADOC, *High-priest.*

AHIMAAS, *his son.*

ABIATHAR, *a priest.*

IONATHAN, *his son.*

SEMEI, *enemy of David.*

IETHRAY, *servant of Ammon.*

BETHSABE, *wife of Vrias.*

THAMAR, *sister of Absolon.*

A widow of Thecoa.

A maid-servant of Bethsabe.

Messengers, Soldiers, Shepherds, Attendants, Concubines of David, Chorus, etc.

SCENE: *Israel; and Ammon.*]

THE LOUE OF DAUID AND FAIRE BER–SABE,[1] WITH THE TRAGEDIE OF ABSOLON.

Prologue.

Of Israels sweetest singer now I sing,
His holy style and happie victories,
Whose muse was dipt in that inspiring deaw
Arch-angels stilled from the breath of Ioue,
Decking her temples with the glorious flowers   5
Heauens raind on tops of Syon and Mount Synai.
Vpon the bosome of his yuorie lute
The cherubins and angels laid their brests ;
And, when his consecrated fingers strooke
The golden wiers of his rauishing harpe,   10
He gaue alarum to the host of heauen,
That, wing'd with lightning, brake the clouds, and cast
Their christall armor at his conquering feet.

[1] *In the page-headings the alternation of the spellings* Bethsabe *and* Bersabe *is regular: this line is at the top of sign.* B r°; *the heading of* B v° *and* B ii r° *has* Bethsabe, B ii v° *and* B iii r° *have* Bersabe; *in other words, the inside of each sheet has* Bethsabe, *and the outside* Bersabe; *this holds true throughout sheet* G; *on sheet* H, *however, the inside headings have* Bersabe, *and the outside* Bethsabe; *of sheet* I *there is only one leaf,* pp. I r° *and* I v°, *both headings having* Bersabe. *The explanation is, perhaps, that the page-headings were not put in until the pages were arranged for the forms, and the insertion of them was then entrusted to two different persons. In the hasty examination I was able to make, I could find no evidence of two printing establishments. In the text the spelling* Bersabe *appears only on* pp. 441 ff., 478. *In connection with the change at the beginning of sheet* H, *see below,* p. 476, n. 1.

Of this sweet poet, Ioues musition,
And of his[1] beauteous sonne I prease to sing.   15
Then helpe, deuine Adonay, to conduct
Vpon the wings of my well-tempered verse
The hearers minds aboue the towers of heauen,
And guide them so in this thrice-haughty flight
Their mounting feathers scorch not with the fire   20
That none can temper but thy holy hand.
To thee for succour flies my feeble muse,
And at thy feet her yron pen doth vse.

[DAVID AND BETHSABE.]

[Act I.   Scene I.][2]

[Jerusalem.]

He[3] drawes a curtaine and discouers BETHSABE, *with her* MAID, *bathing
ouer a spring; she sings, and* DAUID *sits aboue, vewing her.*

THE SONG:

Hot sunne, coole fire, temperd with sweet aire,
Black shade, fair nurse, shadow my white haire!
Shine sun, burne fire, breathe, aire, and ease mee!
Black shade, fair nurse, shroud me and please me!
Shadow, my sweet nurse, keep me from burning,   5
Make not my glad cause cause of my mourning!
  Let not my beauties fire
  Enflame vnstaied desire,
  Nor pierce any bright eye
  That wandreth lightly!   10

[1] Isl. *misprints* bis.

[2] *The* CHORUS *and the express statements of the author divide the play
into three acts (see* pp. 440, 475).

[3] *That is, the Prologue, who, of course, goes off the stage immediately.
In* Isl. *this begins* B v°, *but there is no heading except the regular page-
heading, and no indication of a division between the prologue and the
play.*

BETHSABE.   Come, gentle Zephire, trickt with those per-
    fumes
That erst in Eden sweetned Adams loue,
And stroke my bosome with thy [1] silken fan.
This shade, sun-proofe, is yet no proofe for thee :
Thy body, smoother then this wauelesse spring   15
And purer then the substance of the same,
Can creepe through that his launces cannot pierse.
Thou, and thy sister, soft and sacred Aire,
Goddesse of life and gouernesse of health,
Keepes euery fountaine fresh and arbor sweet.   20
No brasen gate her passage can repulse,
Nor bushly [2] thicket bar thy subtle breath.
Then decke thee with thy loose delightsome robes,
And on thy wings bring delicate perfumes,
To play the wantons with vs through the leaues !   25
    DA.   What tunes, what words, what looks, what wonders
      pierce
My soule, incensed with a suddain fire?
What tree, what shade, what spring, what paradise
Enioyes the beautie of so faire a dame?
Faire Eua, plac'd in perfect happinesse,   30
Lending her praise-notes to the liberall heauens,
Strooke with the accents of arch-angels tunes,
Wrought not more pleasure to her husbands thoughts
Then this faire womans words and notes to mine.
May that sweet plaine that beares her pleasant weight   35
Be still enameld with discoloured flowers ;
That precious fount beare sand of purest gold ;
And, for the peble, let the siluer streames
That pierce earths bowels to mainteine the sorce
Play vpon rubies, saphires, chrisolites ;   40
The brims let be imbrac'd with golden curles
Of mosse that sleepes with sound the waters make
For ioy to feed the fount with their recourse ;

---

[1] Isl. the ; *emend. by* D.
[2] Haw. *emends to* bushy ; D. B. *follow him,* D. *proposing also* busky.

Let all the grasse that beautifies her bower
Beare manna euery morne in-steed of dew,   45
Or let the dew be sweeter far then that
That hangs, like chaines of pearle, on Hermon hill,
Or balme which trickled from old Arons beard! —
Cusay !   Come vp, and serue thy lord the king.

Enter Cusay.

Cus.   What seruice doth my lord the king command?   50
  Dauid.   See, Cusay, see the flower of Israel,
The fairest daughter that obeies the king
In all the land the Lord subdued to me!
Fairer then Isacs louer at the well,
Brighter then inside-barke of new-hewen cædar,   55
Sweeter then flames of fine perfumed [1] myrrhe,
And comelier then the siluer clouds that dance
On zephires [2] wings before the King of Heauen !
  Cus.   Is it not Bethsabe, the Hethites wife,
Vrias, now at Rabath [3] siege with Ioab?   60
  Dau.   Goe know, and bring her quickly to the king;
Tell her her graces hath [4] found grace with him.
  Cusay.   I will, my lord.

Exit Cusay *to* Bethsabe.

Dauid.   Bright Bethsabe shall wash, in Dauids bower,
In water mix'd with purest almond-flower,   · 65
And bath her beautie in the milke of kids.
Bright Bethsabe giues earth [5] to my desires,
Verdure to earth, and to that verdure flowers,

---

¹ D. *points out that* England's Parnassus (1600) *has the attractive reading* fire-perfumed.

² D. *points out that in* England's Parnassus *the reading is* Zephyrus.

⁸ D. Rabbah, *stating correctly that in the early part of the play the name is spelled* Rabath; B. *follows* D., *but implies that* Rabath *is the only form found in* Isl.; *see below,* p. 441, n. 5.

⁴ Haw. B. have, *without note;* D. *follows* Haw., *but records* Isl.

⁵ *The reading has been doubted, and* birth (*by* Collier) *and* heart (*by* Sprenger) *have been proposed; but* earth *is right; see Notes,* vol. III, *or* Engl. Stud., XVIII, 297. [See Publisher's Note].

To flowers sweet odors, and to odors wings,
That carrie pleasures to the hearts of kings.   70

CUSAY to BETHSABE; she starting, as something afright.

CUSAY.   Faire Bethsabe, the king of Israell
From forth his princely tower hath seen thee bath,
And thy sweet graces haue found grace with him.
Come then, and kneele vnto him where he stands :
The king is gracious and hath liberall hands.   75
    BETH.   Ah! what is Bethsabe, to please the king?
Or what is Dauid that he should desire
For fickle beuties sake his seruants wife?
    CUSAY.   Dauid, thou knowest, faire dame, is wise and iust,
Elected to the heart of Israels God ;   80
Then doe not thou expostulate with him
For any action that contents his soule.
    BETHSABE.   [1] My lord the king, elect to Gods owne heart,
Should not his gracious ielousie incense
Whose thoughts are chast.   I hate incontinence.   85
    CUSAY.   Woman, thou wrongst the king *and* doubtst his
            honour
Whose truth mainteines the crowne of Israel,
Making him stay that bad me bring thee strait.
    BETHSABE.   The kings poore handmaid will obey my lord.
    CUSAY.   Then come, and doe thy dutie to his Grace,   90
And doe what seemeth fauour in his sight.

Exeunt, [and ascend to DAVID].

    DAUID.   Now comes my louer tripping like a roe,
And brings my longings tangled in her haire.
To ioy her loue Ile build a kingly bower
Seated in hearing of a hundred streames,   95

---

1 *The text of this passage has been misunderstood by some commenta-*
tors and emended by others. Keltie (Brit. Dram., p. 60) *thinks* his *and*
whose *refer to* URIAS; Sprenger (Engl. Stud., XVII, 319) *thinks* whose *re-*
fers to BETHSABE *herself, and suggests that a line has fallen out.* D. *and*
B., *to judge from their punctuation, saw clearly that* his *and* whose *refer*
to God; but B. *records a conjecture of* P. A. Daniel's *on* l. 85 : and hate
for I hate.

That, for their homage to her souereine ioies,[1]
Shall, as the serpents fold into their nests
In oblique turnings, wind their [2] nimble waues
About the circles of her curious walkes,
And with their murmure summon easefull sleepe   100
To lay his golden scepter on her browes. —
Open the dores and enterteine my loue ;
Open, I say ; and, as you open, sing :
Welcome, faire Bethsabe, King Dauids darling !

Enter CUSAY, *with* BETHSABE.

DAUID.   Welcome, faire Bethsabe, King Dauids darling !   105
Thy bones faire couering, erst discouered faire,
Afar [3] mine eyes with all thy beuties pierst.
As heauens bright eye burnes most when most he climes
The crooked Zodiake with his fierie sphere
And shineth furthest from this earthly globe,   110
So, since thy beautie scorcht my conquerd soule,
I cald thee neerer for my neerer cure.

BETHSA.   Too neere, my lord, was your vnarmed heart,
When furthest off my haplesse beautie pierc'd.
And would this drerie [4] day had turnd to night,   115
Or that some pitchie cloud had clok'd the sun,
Before their lights had caus'd my lord to see
His name disparag'd and my chastitie !

DAUID.   My loue, if want of loue haue left thy soule
A sharper sence of honor then thy king, —   120
For loue leads princes sometimes from their seats, —
As erst my heart was hurt, displeasing thee,
So come and tast thy ease with easing me !

BETH.   One medicine cannot heale our different harmes,

[1] D. *suggests, for* ioies, charms *or* eyes.   Sprenger *wishes to read* sovereign's joy (= BETHSABE).   *I agree with* B. *that no emendation is necessary ; see my note,* Engl. Stud., XVIII, 299.

[2] Isl. the ; *emend. by* Walker.

[3] Isl. And all ; B. *suggests* Enthrall'd ; D. *thinks a line has dropped out ; a friend of his suggested* Have all.

[4] B. *suggests* garish.

But rather make both ranckle at the bone.   125
Then let the king be cunning in his cure,
Least, flattering both, both perish in his hand.
   DAUID.   Leaue it to me, my deerest Bethsabe,
Whose skill is conuersant in deeper cures.
And, Cusay, hast thou to my seruant Ioab,   130
Commanding him to send Vrias home
With all the speed can possibly be vsed.
   CUSAY.   Cusay will flie about the kings desire.

                                                 Exeunt.

[Act I.   Scene II.]

[*Rabath.*]

Enter IOAB, ABISAY, VRIAS, *and others, with drum and ensigne.*

   IOAB.   Courage, ye mightie men of Israel,
And charge your fatall instruments of war
Vpon the bosomes [1] of prowd Ammons sonnes,
That haue disguised your kings embassadors,
Cut halfe their beards and halfe their garments off,   5
In spight of Israel and his daughters sonnes.
Ye fight the holy battels of Iehoua,
King Dauids God, and ours and Iacobs God,
That guides your weapons to their conquering strokes,
Orders your footsteps and directs your thoughts   10
To stratagems that harbor victorie.
He casts his sacred eiesight from on high
And sees your foes run seeking for their deaths, —
Laughing their labours and their hopes to scorne,
While [2] twixt your bodies and their blunted swords   15
He puts on armor of his honors proofe,
And makes their weapons wound the sencelesse winds.
   ABIS.   Before this citie Rabath we will lie,
And shoot forth shafts as thicke and dangerous
As was the haile that Moises mixt with fire   20

    1 Haw. bosom.   2 Isl. B. While; Haw. D. Whilst.

And threw with furie round about the fields,
Deuouring Pharoes friends and Egypts fruits.

   VRIAS.   First, mighty captaines, Ioab and Abisay,
Let vs assault and scale this kingly tower
Where all their conduits and their fountains are;   25
Then may we easily take the citie too.

   IOAB.   Well hath Vrias counseld our attempts;
And, as he spake vs, so assault the tower!
Let Hanon now, the king of Ammons sonnes,[1]
Repulse our conquering passage if he dare!   30

       HANON, *with* KING MACHAAS *and others, vpon the wals.*

   HANON.   What! would the shepheards dogs of Israel
Snatch from the mighty issue of King Ammon,
The valiant Amonites and haughty Syrians?
Tis not your late successiue victories
Can make vs yeeld or quaile our courages.   35
But, if ye dare assay to scale this tower,
Our angrie swords shall smite ye to the ground,
And venge our losses on your hatefull liues.

   IOAB.   Hanon, thy father Nahas gaue releefe
To holy Dauid in his haplesse exile,   40
Liued his fixed date, and died in peace;
But thou, in-steed of reaping his reward,
Hast trod it vnder foot and scornd our king.
Therefore thy daies shall end with violence,
And to our swords thy vitall bloud shall cleaue.   45

   MACH.   Hence, thou that bearst poor Israels shepherds
       hook,
The prowd lieutenant of that base-borne king;
And kep within the compasse of his fold!
For, if ye seeke to feed on Ammons fruits
And stray into the Syrians fruitfull medes,   50
The mastiues of our land shall werry [2] ye
And pull the weesels from your greedy throtes.

---

[1] Isl. sonne; *corr. by* D., *because* Ammons sonnes = the Ammonites.
[2] Haw. worry; D. B. *follow* Haw., *but record* Isl.

ABIS.　Who can indure these pagans blasphemies?
VRIAS.　My soule repines at this disparagement.
IOAB.　Assault, ye valiant men of Dauids host,　　55
And beat these railing dastards from their dores!

Assault; and they win the tower; and IOAB *speakes aboue.*

[IOAB.]　Thus haue we won the tower; which we will
　　keepe
Maugre the sonnes of Ammon and of Syria.

Enter CUSAY, *beneath.*

CUS.　Where is Lord Ioab, leader of the host?
IOAB.　Here is Lord Ioab, leader of the host.　　60
Cusay, come vp, for we haue won the hold.

He comes.

CUSAY.　In happie hower, then, is Cusay come.
IOAB.　What news, then, brings Lord Cusay from the
　　king?
CUSAY.　His Maiestie commands thee out of hand
To send him home Vrias from the wars　　65
For matter of some seruice he should [1] doe.
VRIAS.　Tis for no choler hath surpris'd the king,
I hope, Lord Cusay, gainst his seruants truth?
CUSAY.　No; rather to prefer Vrias truth.
IOAB.　Here, take him with thee, then, and goe in peace.　　70
And tell my lord the king that I haue fought
Against the citie Rabath with successe
And skaled where [2] the royall pallace is,
The conduit-heads and all their sweetest springs.
Then, let him come in person to these wals　　75
With all the souldiers he can bring besides,
And take the city as his owne exploit,
Least I surprise it, and the people giue
The glory of the conquest to my name.

---

[1] Haw. shall.
[2] B. *suggests* sealed, where; *but the text is correct.*

Cus.   We will, Lord Ioab ; and great Israels God   80
Blesse in thy hands the battels of our king !
   Ioab.   Farewel,[1] Vrias ; hast away the king.
   Vrias.   As sure as Ioab breaths a victor here,
Vrias will hast him and his owne returne.

                                   Exeunt [Cusay *and* Vrias].

   Abisa.   Let vs descend, and ope the pallace gate,   85
Taking our souldiors in to keepe the hold.
   Ioab.   Let vs, Abisay.   And, ye sonnes of Iuda,
Be valiant and mainteine your victory !   *Exeunt.*

[Act I.   Scene III.]

[Jerusalem : the house of Ammon.]

Ammon,[2] Ionadab, Iethray, *and* Ammons Page.[3]

Ionad.   What meanes my lord, the kings beloued son,
That weares vpon his right triumphant arme
The power of Israel for a royall fauor,
That holds vpon the tables of his hands
Banquets of honor and all thoughts content,   5
To suffer pale and grisely abstinence
To sit and feed vpon his fainting cheekes
And sucke away the bloud that cheeres his lookes?
   Ammo.   Ah ! Ionadab, it is my sisters lookes,
On whose sweet beutie I bestow my bloud,   10
That makes [4] me looke so amorously leane.
Her beautie, hauing seasd vpon my heart,
So merely [5] consecrate to her content,
Sets now such guard about his vitall bloud
And viewes the passage with such piercing eyes   15
That none can scape to cheare my pining cheekes,
But all is thought too little for her loue.

---

[1] Isl. Earewel.
[2] *So consistently in* Isl.; D. B. *emend to* Amnon.
[3] *I am inclined to suggest that* Iethray *and the* Page *go out after* l. 8.
[4] D. B. make, *without note.*   [5] Isl. merrily ; *corr. by* D.

IONADAB. Then from her heart thy lookes shall be re-
    leeued,
And thou shalt ioy her as thy soule desires.

  AMMON. How can it be, my sweet friend Ionadab,   20
Since Thamar is a virgine and my sister?

  IONADAB. Thus it shall be : lie downe vpon thy bed,
Faining thee feuer-sicke and ill at ease ;
And, when the king shall come to visit thee,
Desire thy sister Thamar may be sent   25
To dresse some deinties for thy maladie ;
Then, when thou hast her solely with thy-selfe,
Enforce some fauour to thy manly loue. —
See, where she comes ! intreat her in with thee.

Enter THAMAR.

  THAMAR. What aileth Ammon with such sickly lookes   30
To daunt the fauour of his louely face?

  AM. Sweet Thamar, sick, *and* wish some wholesome cates
Drest with the cunning of thy daintie hands.

  THAM. That hath the king commanded at my hands.
Then, come and rest thee, while I make thee readie   35
Some dainties easefull to thy crased soule.

  AM. I goe, sweet sister, eased with thy sight.

Exeunt ; restet [1] IONADAB.

  ION. Why should a prince whose power may command
Obey the rebell passions of his loue
When they contend but gainst his conscience   40
And may be gouernd or supprest by will?
Now, Ammon, lose those louing knots of bloud
That sokte [2] the courage from thy kingly heart,
And giue it passage to thy withered cheekes.
Now, Thamar, ripened [3] are the holy fruits   45
That grew on plants of thy virginitie,
And rotten is thy name in Israel.

---

[1] Isl. B. restet; Haw. D. restat.

[2] *So* Isl.; Haw. soak'd ; B. D. suck'd; lokte, *which comes very near*
sokte, *is attractive.*

[3] B. *substitutes* rifled ; *but* l. 47 *supports* ripened.

Poore Thamar! little did thy louely hands
Foretell an action of such violence
As to contend with Ammons lusty armes,   50
Sinnewd with vigor of his kindlesse loue!
Faire Thamar, now dishonour hunts thy foot
And followes thee through euery couert shade,
Discouering thy shame and nakednesse
Euen from the valeyes of Iehosophat   55
Vp to the loftie mounts of Libanon,
Where cædars, stird with angir of the winds,
Sounding in stormes the tale of thy disgrace,
Tremble with furie and with murmure shake
Earth[1] with their feet and with their heads the heauens,   60
Beating the clouds into their swiftest racke,
To beare this wonder round about the world.   *Exit.*

AMMON *thrusting out* THAMAR.

AM. Hence from my bed, whose sight offends my soule
As doth the parbreake of disgorged beares!

THAMA.   Vnkind, vnprincely and vnmanly Ammon,   65
To force and then refuse thy sisters loue,
Adding vnto the fright of thy offence
The banefull torment of my publisht shame!
O, doe not this dishonor to thy loue,
Nor clog thy soule with such increasing sinne!   70
This second euill far exceeds the first.

AM.   Iethray, come thrust this woman from my sight,
And bolt the dore vpon her if she striue![2]

IETHRAY.   Go, madame, goe! away! you must be gone,
My lord hath done with you; I pray, depart!   75

He shuts her out.[2]

---

[1] *Misprinted* Eearth *in* Isl.

[2] *After* ll. 73, 75, D. B. *insert* Exit, *noting the absence of these directions in* Isl. *I follow* Isl., *because it seems superfluous to mark an exit which consists in shutting a door, — an action distinctly indicated in* Isl. *Lines 63–75 are spoken at the stage-door;* Thamar *is thrust out upon the stage and the door closes. That* Ammon *disappears at* l. 73 *is by no means certain; his attitude during* ll. 74, 75 *forms part of a striking tableau.*

THAM.   Whether, alas! ah, whether shall I flie,
With folded armes and all-amased soule?
Cast, as was Eua from that glorious soile
Where al delights sat bating, wingd with thoughts,
Ready to nestle in her naked breasts,   80
To bare and barraine vales, with floods made wast,
To desart woods, and hils with lightning scorcht;
With death, with shame, with hell, with horror sit;[1]
There will I wander from my fathers face;
There Absolon,[2] my brother Absolon,   85
Sweet Absolon, shall heare his sister mourne ;
There will I lure [3] with my windie sighs
Night-rauens and owles to rend my bloudie side,
Which with a rusty weapon I will wound
And make [4] them passage to my panting heart.   90
Why talkst thou, wretch, and leau'st the deed vndone?

Enter ABSOLON. [THAMAR *continues her lament.*]

Rend haire and garments, as thy heart is rent
With inward furie of a thousand greefes,
And scatter them by these vnhallowed dores
To figure Ammons resting [5] crueltie   95
And tragicke spoile of Thamars chastitie!
   ABS.   What causeth Thamar to exclaime so much?
   THAM.   The cause that Thamar shameth to disclose.
   ABSA.   Say! I, thy brother, will reuenge that cause.
   THAM.   Ammon, our fathers son, hath forced me,   100
And thrust me from him as the scorne of Israel.
   ABS.   Hath Ammon forced thee?   By Dauids hand,
And by the couenant God hath made with him,
Ammon shall beare his violence to hell!
Traitor to heauen, traitor to Dauids throne,   105

---

[1] B. *suggests and reads* rife; *the text seems possible, but, if any emendation must be made, it might be well to read* Where death, *etc.*

[2] *This, of course, is the spelling of* Isl.; *see* p. 441, n. 5.

[3] Isl. liue; *emend. by* D.

[4] *Misprinted* makee *in* Isl.

[5] B. *suggests* wresting.

Traitor to Absolon and Israel!
This fact hath Iacobs ruler seene from heauen;
And through a cloud of smoake and tower of fire, —
As he rides vaunting him vpon the greenes, —
Shall teare his chariot-wheeles with violent winds, 110
And throw his body in the bloudy sea.
At him the thunder shall discharge his bolt,
And his faire spouse with bright and fierie wings
Sit euer burning on his hatefull bones.
My-selfe, as swift as thunder or his spouse, 115
Will hunt occasion with a secret hate
To worke false Ammon an vngracious end.
Goe in, my sister; rest thee in my house;
And God, in time, shall take this shame from thee.

THAM.   Nor God nor time will doe that good for me. 120

Exit THAMAR; *restat* ABSOLON.

Enter DAUID *with his train.*

DAUID.   My Absolon, what makst thou here alone,
And beares [1] such discontentment in thy browes?

ABS.   Great cause hath Absolon to be displeasd
And in his heart to shrowd the wounds of wrath.

DAUID.   Gainst whom should Absolon be thus displeased? 125

ABS.   Gainst wicked Ammon, thy vngracious sonne,
My brother and faire Thamars by the king,
My stepbrother by mother and by kind!
He hath dishonoured Dauids holinesse,
And fixt a blot of lightnesse on his throne, 130
Forcing my sister Thamar, when he faind
A sickenesse, sprung from root of heinous lust.

DAUID.   Hath Ammon brought this euill on my house,
And suffered sinne to smite his fathers bones?
Smite, Dauid, deadlier then the voice of heauen! 135
And let hates fire be kindled in thy heart,
Flame [2] in the arches of thy angrie browes,
Making thy forehead like a comet shine,

1 Haw. D. B. bear'st.   2 Isl. Haw. D. B. Frame.

To force false Ammon tremble at thy looks!
Sin, with his seuenfold crowne and purple robe,　　140
Begins his triumphs in my guiltie throne;
There sits he watching with his hundred eyes
Our idle minuts and our wanton thoughts;
And with his baits, made of our fraile desires,
Giues vs the hooke that hales our soules to hell.　　145
But with the spirit of my kingdomes God
Ile thrust the flattering tyran from his throne,
And scourge his bondslaues from my hallowed court
With rods of yron and thornes of sharpened steele.
Then, Absolon, reuenge not thou this sin;　　150
Leaue it to me, and I will chasten him.

　　ABS.　I am content.　Then graunt my lord the king
Himselfe with all his other lords would come
Vp to my sheepe-feast on the plaine of Hazor.

　　DA.　Nay, my faire sonne, my-selfe with all my lords　　155
Will bring thee too much charge; yet some shall goe.

　　ABS.　But let my lord the king himselfe take paines;
The time of yeare is pleasant for your Grace,
And gladsome summer in her shadie robes,
Crowned with roses and with painted[1] flowers,　　160
With all her nimphs shall enterteine my lord,
That from the thicket of my verdant groues
Will sprinckle hony-dewes about his brest
And cast sweet balme vpon his kingly head:
Then grant thy seruants boone and goe, my lord.　　165

　　DAU.　Let it content my sweet sonne Absolon
That I may stay; and take my other lords.

　　ABS.　But shall thy best-beloued Ammon goe?

　　DAU.　What needeth it that Ammon goe with thee?

　　ABS.　Yet doe thy sonne and seruant so much grace.　　170

　　DAU.　Ammon shall goe, and all my other lords,
Because I will giue grace to Absolon.

　　　　　　[1] Isl. planted; *emend. by* D.

Enter CUSAY *and* VRIAS, *with others.*[1]

CUSAY.   Pleaseth my lord the king, his seruant Ioab
Hath sent Vrias from the Syrian wars.

DAU.   Welcome, Vrias, from the Syrian wars ;   175
Welcome to Dauid as his dearest lord !

VRIAS.   Thankes be to Israels God and Dauids grace,
Vrias finds such greeting with the king.

DAU.   No other greeting shall Vrias find
As long as Dauid[2] swaies the elected seat   180
And consecrated throne of Israel.
Tell me, Vrias, of my seruant Ioab :
Fights he with truth the battels of our God
And for the honor of the Lords annointed?

VRIAS.   Thy seruant Ioab fights the chosen wars   185
With truth, with honour and with high successe,
And gainst the wicked king of Ammons sonnes
Hath, by the finger of our souereines God,
Besieg'd the citie Rabath, and atchieu'd
The court of waters, where the conduits run   190
And all the Ammonites delightsome springs.
Therefore he wisheth Dauids mightinesse
Should number out the host of Israel,
And come in person to the citie Rabath,
That so her conquest[3] may be made the kings,   195
And Ioab fight as his inferior.

DAVID.   This hath not God and Ioabs prowesse done
Without Vrias valour,[4] I am sure,
Who, since his true conuersion from a Hethite
To an adopted sonne of Israel,   200
Hath fought like one whose armes were lift by Heauen
And whose bright sword was edgd with Israels wrath.
Goe therefore home, Vrias ; take thy rest ;

---

[1] *This shows clearly how undefined were the scenes in plays of this date.
The location, which so recently was* AMMON'S *house, has now become the
royal palace; see* l. 237.   [4] Isl. valours; *corr. by* D.

[2] Isl. Dauids; *corr. silently by* Haw. D.; *recorded by* B.

[3] Haw. conquests, *perhaps misprint.*

Visit thy wife and houshold with the ioies
A victor and a fauorite of the kings   205
Should exercise with honor after armes.
    VRIAS.   Thy seruants bones are yet not halfe so crasde
Nor constitute on such a sickly mould
That for so little seruice he should faint
And seeke, as cowards, refuge of his home;   210
Nor are his thoughts so sensually stird
To stay the armes with which the Lord would smite
And fill their circle with his conquered foes
For wanton bosome of a flattering wife.
    DA.   Vrias hath a beauteous, sober wife,   215
Yet yong and framd of tempting flesh and bloud:
Then, when the king hath summond thee from armes,
If thou vnkindly shouldst refraine her bed,
Sinne might be laid vpon Vrias soule
If Bethsabe by frailtie hurt her fame.   220
Then goe, Vrias; solace in her loue:
Whom God hath knit to thee tremble to lose.
    VRIAS.   The king is much too tender of my ease.
The arke and Israel and Iuda dwell
In pallaces and rich pauillions,   225
But Ioab and his brother in the fields,
Suffering the wrath of winter and the sun:
And shall Vrias, of more shame than they,
Banquet, and loiter in the worke of Heauen?
As sure as thy soule doth liue, my lord,   230
Mine eares shall neuer leane to such delight
When holy labour cals me forth to fight.
    DAUID.   Then be it with Vrias manly heart
As best his fame may shine in Israel.
    VRIAS.   Thus shall Vrias heart be best content: 235
Till thou dismisse me backe to Ioabs bands,
This ground before the king my masters dores

He lies downe.

Shall be my couch, and this vnwearied arme
The proper pillow of a souldiours head;

For neuer will I lodge within my house   240
Till Ioab triumph in my secret vowes.[1]

DAUID.   Then fetch some flagons of our purest wine,
That we may welcome home our hardie friend
With full carouses to his fortunes past
And to the honours of his future armes.   245
Then will I send him backe to Rabath siege,
And follow with the strength of Israel.

Enter one with the flagons of wine.

Arise, Vrias ; come, and pledge the king.

He riseth.[2]

VRIAS.   If Dauid thinke me worthy such a grace,
I will be bold and pledge my lord the king.   250

DAU.   Absolon and Cusay both shall drinke
To good Vrias and his happinesse,

ABS.   We will, my lord, to please Vrias soule.

DAU.   I will begin, Vrias, to thy-selfe,
And all the treasure of the Ammonites,   255
Which here I promise to impart to thee,
And bind that promise with a full carous.

VRIAS.   What seemeth pleasant in my souereines eyes,
That shall Vrias doe till he be dead.

DAU.   Fill him the cup ; follow, ye lords that loue   260
Your souereines health, and doe as he hath done.

ABS.   Ill may he thriue, [n]or liue in Israel,
That loues not Dauid, or denies his charge !
Vrias, here is to Abisais health,
Lord Ioabs brother *and* thy louing friend ![3]   265

VRIAS.   I pledge Lord Absolon : and Abisais health !

He drinkes.

CUS.   Here now, Vrias : to the health of Ioab,
And to the pleasant iourny we shall haue

---

[1] B. *says:* " *The words*, my secret vows, *are to me unintelligible. Were it not that a rhyme seems to be required for* house, *I would read*, in thy sacred cause." *But the text is right.*

[2] *In* Isl. *this is at the end of* l. 248 ; Haw. D. *put it after* 249 ; B. *after* 250.   [3] Lines 264, 265 *as one in* Isl. ; *corr. by* Haw.

When we returne to mightie Rabath siege!

VRIAS.   Cusay, I pledge thee all with all my heart.   270
Giue me some drink, ye seruants of the king;
Giue me my drinke.   *He drinkes.*

DA.   Well done, my good Vrias! Drinke thy fill,
That in thy fulnesse Dauid may reioice!

VRIAS.   I will, my lord.   275

ABS.   Now, Lord Vrias, one carouse to me!

VRIAS.   No, sir, Ile drinke to the king;
Your father is a better man then you.

DAU.   Doe so, Vrias; I will pledge thee straight.

VRIAS.   I will indeed, my lord and souereine,   280
I will[1] once in my daies be so bold.

DAUID.   Fill him his glasse.

VRIAS.   Fill me my glasse.

He giues him the glasse.

DAU.   Quickly, I say.

VRIAS.   Quickly, I say.[2]

[*His glass is filled.*]

VRIAS.   Here, my lord:
By your fauour now I drinke to you.[3]   285

DAU.   I pledge thee, good Vrias, presently.

He drinkes.

ABS.   Here then, Vrias: once againe for me,
And to the health of Dauids children!

VRIAS.   Dauids children?

ABS.   I, Dauids children; wilt thou pledge me, man?   290

---

[1] Isl. I; Haw. D. B. I 'll.

[2] *In* Isl. *printed thus:*

Dau. Quickly, I fay. *Vrias.* Quickly, I fay.

As Isl. *does not use italics for names that are a part of the text, this is full confirmation of D.'s suggestion that* Urias *repeats David's words, if so excellent a suggestion needed such support. That* VRIAS *is also prefixed to the next speech* (ll. 284, 285, — *printed as one in* Isl.) *is perhaps due to its not being regarded as a continuation, but as a new speech; I have indicated the separation by a stage-direction.*

[3] Lines 284, 285 *as one in* Isl.

VRIAS.   Pledge me, man?

ABS.   Pledge me, I say, or else thou louest vs not.

VRIAS.   What doe you talke — doe you talke —
Ile no more ; Ile lie downe here.

DAUID.   Rather, Vrias, goe thou home and sleepe.   295

VRIAS.   O, ho, sir, would you make me break my sentence?

He lies downe.

Home, sir?   No, indeed, sir ; Ile sleepe vpon mine arme
Like a souldiour, sleepe like a man as long as I liue in Israel.[1]

DAUID. [*aside*]   If nought will serue to saue his wiues re-
        nowne,
Ile send him with a letter vnto Ioab   300
To put him in the forefront of the wars,
That so my purposes may take effect. —
Helpe him in, sirs.   *Exeunt* [2] DAUID *and* ABSOLON.

CUSAY.   Come, rise, Vrias ; get thee in and sleepe.

VRIAS.   I will not goe home, sir ; thats flat.   305

CUSAY.   Then come and rest thee vpon Dauids bed.

VRIAS.   On afore, my lords ; on afore!

Exeunt.

CHORUS.

O prowd reuolt of a presumptious man,
Laying his bridle in the necke of sin,
Ready to beare him past his graue to hell.
Like as the fatall rauen, that in his voice
Carries the dreadfull summons of our deaths,   5
Flies by the faire Arabian spiceries,
Her pleasant gardens and delightsome parkes,[3]
Seeming to curse them with his hoarse exclaimes,
And yet doth stoope with hungrie violence
Vpon a peece of hatefull carrion,   10
So wretched man, displeased with those delights
Would yeeld a quickning sauor to his soule,

---

[1] D. B. *print the whole of this speech as prose ; I follow* Isl.

[2] Isl. Haw. Exit ; D. B. Exeunt.

[3] D. *records that* England's Parnassus *has, in this passage,* delightfull
parts.

Pursues with eagre and vnstanched thirst
The greedie longings of his lothsome flesh.
If holy Dauid so shoke hands with sinne,   15
What shall our baser spirits glorie in?
This king, by giuing vnto lust her raigne,[1]
Pursues the sequell with a greater ill:
Vrias in the forefront of the wars
Is murthered by the hatefull heathens sword,   20
And Dauid ioies his too deere Bethsabe.
Suppose this past, and that the child is borne,
Whose death the prophet solemnly doth mourne.   [*Exit.*]

[Act II.   Scene I.][2]

[*The palace at Jerusalem.*]

Enter BETHSABE, *with her handmaid.*

BETH.   Mourne, Bethsabe! bewaile thy foolishnesse,
Thy sinne, thy shame, the sorrow of thy soule!
Sinne, shame and sorrow swarme about thy soule;
And in the gates and entrance of thy[3] heart
Sadnesse, with wreathed armes, hangs her complaint.   5
No comfort from the ten-string'd instrument,
The tinckling[4] cymball or the yuorie lute;
Nor doth the sound of Dauids kingly harpe
Make glad the broken heart of Bersabe.[5]

---

[1] Isl. This kingly giuing lust her raigne; *so* Haw.; D. *suggests* king by *for* kingly; B. *keeps* kingly, *inserting* ruler *after it;* P. A. Daniel *keeps* kingly, *inserting* unto *after* giuing.

[2] *See above,* p. 422, n. 2; B., *who does not divide the play into acts, calls this* Scene iv.   [3] Isl. D. B. my; Haw. thy, *without note.*

[4] Isl. twinckling; *corr. silently by* Haw.

[5] *This is the first appearance in the text of the spelling* Bersabe, *which is the usual form in this scene and the next (the only exceptions being in the stage-directions at the beginning and the end of this scene).   The name does not occur in either of its forms in the rest of this act.   In Act iii the usual form is* Bethsabe, *only one instance of* Bersabe *occurring*

Ierusalem is fild with thy complaint,   10
And in the streets of Syon sits thy greefe.
The babe is sicke, sicke to the death, I feare,
The fruit that sprung from thee to Dauid's house;
Nor may the pot of honny and of oyle
Glad Dauid or his handmaids countenance.   15
Vrias — woe is me to thinke hereon!
For who is it among the sonnes of men
That sayth not to my soule the king hath sind,
Dauid hath done amisse and Bersabe
Laid snares of death vnto Vrias life?   20
My sweet Vrias, falne into the pit
Art thou, and gone euen to the gates of hell
For Bersabe, that wouldst not shroud her shame!
O, what is it to serue the lust of kings!
How lyonlike they[1] rage when we resist!   25
But, Bersabe, in humblenesse attend
The grace that God will to his handmaid send.

           Exit BETH[SABE, *with* MAID].

[Act II.   Scene II.][2]

[*The palace.*]

DAUID *in his gowne, walking sadly ; to him* NATHAN.

DAUID.   The babe is sicke, and sad is Dauids heart
To see the guiltlesse beare the guilties paine.
Dauid, hang vp thy harpe, hang downe thy head

(iii. 2, 15). *If to these differences we add the noteworthy fact that in this second act several proper names regularly appear in forms different from those of Acts i and iii, it may seem not improbable that the* MS. *sent to the printer was prepared by two persons, one of whom copied Act ii : in Act i the city* Rabath *is defended by its king,* Hanon; *in Act ii the city* Rabba *is defended by its king,* Hannon; *the spelling of* Absolon *becomes* Absalon (*not regularly, but frequently*), *and* Abisai *varies similarly ; many other words also show variation in the two parts. It may be noted further that it is at the end of Act ii that the puzzling fragment of a scene appears ; see below, p. 476, n. 1, and also p. 452, n. 2.*

     [1] Isl. thy ; *corr. silently by* D.   [2] B. *calls this* Scene v.

And dash thy yuorie lute against the stones!
The dew that on the Hill of Hermon fals   5
Raines not on Syons tops and lofty towers :
The plaines of Gath and Askaron reioice,[1]
And Dauids thoughts are spent in pensiuenesse.
The babe is sicke, sweet babe that Bersabe
With womans paine brought forth to Israel.   10

Enter NATHAN.

But what saith Nathan to his lord the king?

NATHAN *to* DAUID.

NATHAN.   Thus Nathan saith vnto his lord the king :
There were two men, both dwellers in one towne ;
The one was mighty and exceeding rich
In oxen, sheepe and cattell of the field ;   15
The other poore, hauing nor oxe nor calfe
Nor other cattell saue one little lambe
Which he had bought and nourisht by the hand,
And it grew vp and fed with him and his,
And eat and dranke as he and his were wont,   20
And in his bosome slept and was to him[2]
As was his daughter or his deerest child.
There came a stranger to this wealthy man ;
And he refused and spar'd to take his owne,
Or of his store to dresse or make him meat,   25
But tooke the poor mans sheepe, the[3] poore mans store,
And drest it for this strangar in his house.
What, tell me, shall be done to him for this?
    DAU.   Now, as the Lord doth liue, this wicked man
Is iudgd, and shall become the child of death!   30
Foure-fold to the poore man shall he restore

---

1 *In* Isl. l. 8 *precedes* l. 7 ; *corr. by* D.

2 Isl. liue ; *corr. by* D.

3 *Instead of* the, Isl. *has* partly, *which is unintelligible.* Sprenger *proposes to make the line read :* But took the poor man's lamb, his only store ; *but this departs too far from the transmitted text, and in Elizabethan English* store *means* all one has, *as well as* abundance.

That without mercy tooke his lambe away!
    NATH.   Thou art the man, and thou hast iudgd thy-selfe!
Dauid, thus sayth the Lord thy God by me:
" I thee annointed king in Israel,   35
And sau'd thee from the tyranny of Saul;
Thy maisters house I gaue thee to possesse,
His wiues into thy bosome did I giue,
And Iuda and Ierusalem withall;
And might, thou knowest, if this had ben too small,   40
Haue giuen thee more:
Wherefore then hast thou gone so far astray,
And hast done euill and sinned in my sight?
Vrias thou hast killed with the sword, —
Yea, with the sword of the vncircumcised   45
Thou hast him slaine: wherefore from this day forth
The sword shall neuer goe from thee and thine.
For thou hast tane this Hethites wife to thee,
Wherefore,[1] behold, I wil," saith Iacobs God,
" In thine owne house stir euill vp to thee, —   50
Yea, I before thy face will take thy wiues
And giue them to thy neighbour to possesse:
This shall be done to Dauid in the day,
That Israel openly may see thy shame." [2]
    DAUID.   Nathan, I haue against the Lord, I haue   55
Sinned, O, sinned greeuously, and, loe!
From heauens throne doth Dauid throw himselfe
And grone and grouell to the gates of hell.

He fals downe.

    NATH.   Dauid, stand vp; thus saith the Lord by me:
" Dauid, the king, shall liue," for he hath seene   60
The true repentant sorrow of thy heart.
But, for thou hast in this misdeed of thine
Stird vp the enemies of Israel
To triumph, and blaspheme the God of Hosts,
And say he set a wicked man to reigne   65

---

[1] *Qy.* Therefore.   [2] B. *closes the quotation at* l. 52.

Ouer his loued people and his tribes,
The child shall surely die that erst was borne,
His mothers sin, his kingly fathers scorne.　　*Exit* NATHAN.

DA.　How iust is Iacobs God in all his workes!
But must it die that Dauid loueth so?　　70
O that the Mighty One of Israel
Nill change his dome, and sayes the babe must die!
Mourne, Israel, and weepe in Syon gates;
Wither, ye cædar-trees of Libanon;
Ye sprouting almons with your flowring tops,　　75
Droope, drowne and drench in Hebrons fearefull streames!
The babe must die that was to Dauid borne,
His mothers sin, his kingly fathers scorne.

DAUID *sits sadly.*

Enter CUSAY *to* DAUID *and his traine.*

SERUUS.　What tidings bringeth Cusay to the king?
CUSAY.　To thee, the seruant of King Dauids court,　　80
This bringeth Cusay: As the prophet spake,
The Lord hath surely stricken to the death
The child new-borne by that Vrias wife
That by the sonnes of Ammon erst was slaine.

SERUUS.　Cusay, be still; the king is vexed sore:　　85
How shal he speed that brings this[1] tidings first,
When, while the child was yet aliue, we spake,
And Dauids heart would not be comforted?

DA.　Yea, Dauids heart will not be comforted!
What murmure ye, the seruants of the king?　　90
What tidings telleth Cusay to the king?
Say, Cusay: liues the child, or is he dead?

CUSAY.　The child is dead that of Vrias wife
Dauid begat.[2]

DA.　　　　Vrias wife, saiest thou?
The child is dead! Then ceaseth Dauids shame.　　95
Fetch me to eat, and giue me wine to drinke,

---

[1] Haw. these, *without note.*
[2] *In* Isl. *this is part of the preceding line; corr. silently by* Haw.

Water to wash, and oyle to cleere my lookes;
Bring downe your shalmes, your cymbals and your pipes;
Let Dauids harpe and lute, his hand and voice,
Giue laud to him that loueth Israel, 100
And sing his praise that shendeth [1] Dauids fame,
That put away his sinne from out his sight,
And sent his shame into the streets of Gath.
Bring ye to me the mother of the babe,
That I may wipe the teares from off her face, 105
And giue her comfort with this hand of mine;
And decke faire Bersabe with ornaments,
That she may beare to me another sonne,
That may be loued of the Lord of Hosts.
For where he is, of force must Dauid go; 110
But neuer may he come where Dauid is.

They bring in water, wine and oyle; musike and a banquet.

[Enter BETHSABE.]

[DAUID.] Fair Bersabe, sit thou, and sigh no more.
And sing and play, you seruants of the king.
Now sleepeth Dauids sorrow with the dead,
And Bersabe liueth to Israel. 115

They vse all solemnities together, and sing, &c.

DAUID. Now armes and warlike engins for assault
Prepare at once, ye men of Israel,
Ye men of Iuda and Ierusalem,
That Rabba may be taken by the king,
Least it be called after Ioabs name 120
Nor Dauids glory shine in Syon streets.
To Rabba marcheth Dauid with his men
To chastise Ammon and the wicked ones.

Exeunt omnes.

[1] Sprenger, *not knowing* protect *as a meaning of* shend, *wishes to read* shield; *but see* Engl. Stud., XVIII, 300, *for several examples of this use.*

[Act II.   Scene III.] [1]

[A field : AMMON'S *sheep-feast.]*

Enter ABSOLON *with two or three.*

ABS.   Set vp your mules, and giue them well to eat,
And let vs meet our brothers at the feast.
Accursed is the maister of this feast,
Dishonour of the house of Israel,
His sisters slander and his mothers shame!   5
Shame be his share that could such ill contriue
To rauish Thamar, and, without a pause,
To driue her shamefully from out his house.
But may his wickednesse find iust reward !
Therefore doth Absolon conspire with you   10
That Ammon die, what time he sits to eat ;
For in the holy temple haue I sworne
Wreake of his villany in Thamars rape.
And here he comes.   Bespeake him gently, all,
Whose death is deepely graued in my heart.   15

Enter AMMON, *with* ADONIA *and* IONADAB, *to* ABSOLON *and his companie.*

AM.   Our shearers are not far from hence, I wot ;
And Ammon to you all, his brethren,
Giueth such welcome as our fathers erst
Were wont [2] in Iuda and Ierusalem, —
But specially, Lord Absolon, to thee,   20
The honour of thy house and progenie.   .
Sit downe and dine with me, King Dauids sonne,
Thou faire young man, whose haires shine in mine eye
Like golden wyers of Dauids yuorie lute.
ABS.   Ammon, where be thy shearers and thy men,   25
That we may powre in plenty of thy vines, [3]

---

[1] B. *calls this* Scene vi.   [2] *In* Isl. *the* t *looks like* r.
[3] Isl. vines ; Haw. D. B. wines ; *but* Kittredge *points out that* plenty of
thy vines (= the increase of thy vines, *i.e.* wine) *is better.*

And eat thy goats-milke and reioice with thee?

AM.   Here commeth Ammons shearers and his men.
Absolon, sit and reioice with me.[1]

Here enter a company of sheepeheards, and daunce and sing.

AM.   Drinke, Absolon, in praise of Israel !   30
Welcome to Ammons fields from Dauids court !

ABS.   Die with thy draught !   Perish and die accurst,
Dishonour to the honour of vs all !

[Stabs him.]

Die for the villany to Thamar done !
Vnworthy thou to be King Dauids sonne.   35

Exit ABSA.

IONAD.   O, what hath Absolon for Thamar done?
Murthred his brother, great King Dauids sonne!

ADON.   Run, Ionadab ; away and make it knowne
What cruelty this Absolon hath showne.
Ammon, thy brother Adonia shall   40
Bury thy body among the dead mens bones,
And we will make complaint to Israel
Of Ammons death and pride of Absolon.

Exeunt omnes.

[Act II.   Scene IV.][2]

[Before the city Rabba.]

Enter DAUID, *with* IOAB, ABYSHAI,[3] CUSAY, *with drum and ensigne,
against Rabba.*

[DAUID.]   This is the towne of the vncircumcised,
The citie of the kingdome, this is it, —
Rabba, where wicked Hannon sitteth king.
Dispoile this king, this Hannon, of his crowne ;
Vnpeople Rabba and the streets thereof ;   5

---

[1] *For metrical reasons* B. *inserts* Come *before* Absolon; D. *suggests* sit
down.

[2] *According to* B. *this is* Scene vii.

[3] Isl. B. Abyssus; Haw. D. Abisai.

For in their bloud and slaughter of the slaine
Lyeth the honor of King Dauids line.
Ioab, Abyshai, and the rest of you,
Fight ye this day for great Ierusalem.

[*Enter* HANNON *and others on the walls.*]¹

IOAB.   And see where Hannon showes him on the wals!   10
Why then do we forbeare to giue assault,
That Israel may, as it is promised,
Subdue the daughters of the Gentils tribes?
All this must be performd by Dauids hand.

DA.   Harke to me, Hannon, and remember well!   15
As sure as he doth liue that kept my host
What time our young men by the poole of Gibeon
Went forth against the strength of Isboseth,
And twelue to twelue did with their weapons play,
So sure art thou and thy men of war   20
To feele the sword of Israel this day;
Because thou hast defied Iacobs God,
And suffered Rabba with the Philistine
To raile vpon the tribe of Beniamin.

HANNON.   Hark, man! As sure as Saul, thy maister, fell   25
And gor'd his sides vpon the mountaine tops,
And Ionathan, Abinadab and Melchisua
Watred the dales and deepes of Askaron
With bloudy streames, that from Gilboa ran
In channels through the wildernesse of Ziph,   30
What time the sword of the vncircumcised
Was drunken with the bloud of Israel,
So sure shall Dauid perish with his men
Vnder the wals of Rabba, Hannons towne.

IOAB.   Hannon, the God of Israel hath said   35
Dauid, the king, shall weare that crowne of thine,
That weighs a talent of the finest gold,
And triumph in the spoile of Hannons towne,
When Israel shall hale thy people hence,

¹ *Supplied by* D.

And turne them to the tile-kill, man and child,   40
And put them vnder harrowes made of yron,
And hew their bones with axes, and their lims
With yron swords deuide and teare in twaine.
Hannon, this shall be done to thee and thine,
Because thou hast defied Israel. —   45
To armes! to armes! that Rabba feele reuenge,
And Hannons towne become King Dauids spoile.

> *Alarum, excursions, assault; exeunt omnes. Then the trumpets, and*
> DAUID *with* HANNONS *crowne.*

DAU.   Now clattering armes and wrathfull stormes of war
Haue thundred ouer Rabbaes raced towers
The wreakefull ire of great Iehouaes arme,   50
That for his people made the gates to rend,
And clothed the cherubins in fierie coats
To fight against the wicked Hannons towne.
Pay thankes, ye men of Iuda to the King,
The God of Syon and Ierusalem,   55
That hath exhalted Israel to this,
And crowned Dauid with this diademe.

IOAB.   Beauteous and bright is he among the tribes:
As when the sunne, attir'd in glist'ring robe,
Comes dauncing from his orientall gate,   60
And, bridegroom-like, hurles through the gloomy aire
His radiant beames, such doth King Dauid shew
Crownd with the honour of his enemies towne,
Shining in riches like the firmament,
The starrie vault that ouerhangs the earth: 65
So looketh Dauid, king of Israel.

ABYSHAI.   Ioab, why doth not Dauid mount his throne,
Whom Heauen hath beautified with Hannons crowne?
Sound, trumpets, shalmes and instruments of praise,
To Iacobs God for Dauids victory!   70

> *Enter* IONADAB.[1]

IONADAB.   Why doth the king of Israel reioice?

[1] P. A. Daniel *suggests that* IONADAB *does not enter until about* l. 82;
he assigns this speech to a messenger. His view seems probable.

Why sitteth Dauid crownd with Rabbaes·rule?
Behold, there hath great heauinesse befalne
In Ammons fields by Absolons misdeed;
And Ammons shearers and their feast of mirth　　75
Absolon hath ouerturned with his sword;
Nor liueth any of King Dauids sonnes
To bring this bitter tidings to the king!

DAUID.　Ay me! how soone are Dauids triumphs dasht!
How suddenly declineth Dauids pride!　　80
As doth the daylight settle in the west,
So dim is Dauids glory and his gite!
Die, Dauid, for to thee is left no seed
That may reuiue thy name in Israel!

IONA.　In Israel is left of Dauids seed.　　85

Enter ADONIA, with other sonnes.

Comfort your lord, you seruants of the king.
Behold, thy sonnes returne in mourning weeds,
And only Ammon Absalon hath slaine.

DA.　Welcome, my sonnes: deerer to me you are
Then is this golden crowne or Hannons spoile.　　90
O, tell me then, tell me, my sonnes, I say:
How cometh it to passe that Absolon
Hath slaine his brother Ammon with the sword?

ADO.　Thy sonnes, O king, went vp to Ammons fields
To feast with him and eat his bread and oyle;　　95
And Absalon vpon his mule doth come,
And to his men he sayth: "When Ammons heart
Is merry and secure, then strike him dead,
Because he forced Thamar shamefully,
And hated her and threw her forth his dores."　　100
And this did he and they with him conspire,
And kill thy sonne in wreake of Thamars wrong.

DAUID.　How long shall Iuda and Ierusalem
Complaine and water Syon with their teares?
How long shall Israel lament in vaine,　　105
And not a man among the mighty ones
Will hear the sorrowes of King Dauids heart?

Ammon, thy life was pleasing to thy lord
As to mine eares the musike of my lute
Or songs that Dauid tuneth to his harpe!   110
And Absalon hath tane from me away
The gladnesse of my sad distressed soule.   *Exeunt omnes.*[1]

Manet DAUID; *Enter* WIDDOW *of Thecoa.*[2]

WIDDOW.   God saue King Dauid, king of Israel,
And blesse the gates of Syon for his sake!
    DAU.   Woman, why mournest thou? Rise from the earth; 115
Tell me what sorrow hath befalne thy soule.
    WIDDOW.   Thy seruants soule, O king, is troubled sore,
And greeuous [3] is the anguish of her heart;
And from Thecoa doth thy handmaid come.
    DAUID.   Tell me, and say, thou woman of Thecoa,   120
What aileth thee, or what is come to passe.
    WIDDOW.   Thy seruant is a widow in Thecoa,
Two sonnes thy handmaid had; and they, my lord,
Fought in the field where no man went betwixt,

---

[1] *It can hardly be necessary to alter this in the interest of truth; see the next words.*

[2] P. A. Daniel *says:* " *One or more scenes are wanting here; the loss deprives the scene with the* Widow *of all motive.* David *has not banished* Absalon *nor taken any course to revenge the death of* Ammon. *The fragment* (p. 476) *may have formed part of one of those missing scenes." That* David, *at the end of this episode, is still before Rabba seems to make impossible the assumption of a mere loss of scenes. It may, however, not be amiss to bring into connection with this difficulty the peculiar forms of certain names in this act (see p.* 441, *n.* 5), *and the fact observed by every one and recorded by* B., *that the sheep-feast at which* Ammon *is killed is not held by* Absalon, *as originally planned, but by* Ammon. *A simple hypothesis accounting for all these peculiarities is a desideratum. But for the style, which seems distinctly* Peele's, *one might suggest that* Act ii *is an insertion by another hand. Of two remaining possibilities the latter seems the more probable:* Peele *himself rewrote* Act ii, *without sufficiently considering its relations to the rest of the play; another hand entirely remodeled what is now* Act ii, *but was originally* Acts ii, iii *and* iv *of a five-act play (note the comparative length of this act, the number of themes it contains, and the presence of the figure* 5 *before the* CHORUS, p. 475), *rewriting, however, only* Scene iii *and* ll. 74, 75, 94, 95, 96 *of* Scene iv.

[3] Isl. greenous.

And so the one did smite and slay the other.   125
And loe, behold, the kindred doth arise
And crie on him that smote his brother [1]
That he therefore may be the child of death,
" For we will follow and destroy the heire."
So will they quench that sparkle that is left,   130
And leaue nor name nor issue on the earth
To me or to thy handmaids husband dead.

    DAU.   Woman, returne ; go home vnto thy house :
I will take order that thy sonne be safe.
If any man say otherwise then well,   135
Bring him to me, and I shall chastise him ;
For, as the Lord doth liue, shall not a haire
Shed from thy sonne or fall vpon the earth !
Woman, to God alone belongs reuenge :
Shall then the kindred slay him for his sinne?   140

    WIDDOW.   Well hath King Dauid to his handmaid spoke !
But wherefore, then, hast thou determined
So hard a part against the righteous tribes
To follow and pursue the banished,
When-as to God alone belongs reuenge?   145
Assuredly thou saist against thy-selfe.
Therefore call home againe the banished ;
Call home the banished, that he may liue
And raise to thee some fruit in Israel.

    DAU.   Thou woman of Thecoa, answere me,   150
Answere me one thing I shall aske of thee :
Is not the hand of Ioab in this worke?
Tell me : is not his finger in this fact?

    WID.   It is, my lord ; his hand is in this worke :
Assure thee, Ioab, captaine of thy host,   155
Hath put these words into thy handmaids mouth ;
And thou art as an angel from on high
To vnderstand the meaning of my heart.
Lo, where he commeth to his lord the king !

---

[1] B. *suggests* And cry upon him that did smite his brother ; *equally good
is* And crie out vpon him that smote his brother.

Enter IOAB.

DAUID.   Say, Ioab, didst thou send this woman in   160
To put this parable for Absalon?

IOAB.   Ioab, my lord, did bid this woman speake;
And she hath said, and thou hast vnderstood.

DAUID.   I haue, and am content to do the thing.
Goe fetch my sonne, that he may liue with me.   165

IOAB *kneeles.*

IOAB.   Now God be blessed for King Dauids life!
Thy seruant Ioab hath found grace with thee
In that thou sparest Absolon thy child :
A beautifull and faire young man is he ;
In all his bodie is no blemish seene,   170
His haire is like the wyer of Dauids harpe
That twines about his bright and yuorie necke, —
In Israel is not such a goodly man ;
And here I bring him to entreat for grace.

Enter ABSOLON *with* IOAB.

DAUID.   Hast thou slaine Ammon[1] in the fields of Hazor — 175
Ah, Absalon, my sonne! ah, my sonne Absolon!
But wherefore doe I vexe thy spirit so?
Liue, and returne from Gesur to thy house,
Returne from Gesur to Ierusalem.
What boots it to be bitter to thy soule?   180
Ammon is dead, and Absolon suruiues.

ABS.   Father, I haue offended Israel,
I haue offended Dauid and his house ;
For Thamars wrong hath Absolon misdone.
But Dauids heart is free from sharpe reuenge,   185
And Ioab hath got grace for Absalon.

DAUID.   Depart with me, you men of Israel,
You that haue followed Rabba with the sword,
And ransacke Ammons richest treasuries.
Liue, Absalon, my sonne, liue once in peace ;   190
Peace with thee and with Ierusalem.   *Exeunt omnes.*

---

[1] B. *inserts* Ammon.

Manet ABSOLON.

ABS.   Dauid is gone, and Absolon remaines,
Flowring in pleasant spring-time of his youth.
Why liueth Absalon and is not honoured
Of tribes and elders and the mightiest ones,   195
That round about his temples he may weare
Garlands and wreaths set on with reuerence,
That euery one that hath a cause to plead
Might come to Absolon and call for right?
Then in the gates of Syon would I sit,   200
And publish lawes in great Ierusalem;
And not a man should liue in all the land
But Absolon would doe him reasons due.
Therefore I shall addresse me as I may
To loue the men and tribes of Israel.   205

Exit.

[Act II.   Scene V.] [1]

[The Mount of Olives.]

Enter DAUID, ITHAY, SADOC, AHIMAAS, IONATHAN, *with others ;* DAUID
barefoot, with some lose couering ouer his head, and all mourning.

DA.   Proud lust, the bloudiest traitor to our soules,
Whose greedie throte nor earth, aire, sea or heauen
Can glut or satisfie with any store,
Thou art the cause these torments sucke my bloud,
Piercing with venome of thy poysoned eies   5
The strength and marrow of my tainted bones!
To punish Pharoh and his cursed host,
The waters shrunk [2] at great Adonaies voice,
And sandy bottom of the sea appeard,
Offering his seruice at his seruants feet: 10
And, to inflict a plague on Dauids sinne,
He makes his bowels traitors to his breast,
Winding about his heart with mortall gripes.

[1] Scene viii *in* B.
[2] *So* Haw. D.; Isl. shrinke, *which* B. *retains.*

Ah, Absalon, the wrath of Heauen inflames
Thy scorched bosome with ambitious [1] heat,   15
And Sathan sets thee on a lustie [2] tower,
Shewing thy thoughts the pride of Israel,
Of choice to cast thee on her ruthlesse stones!
Weepe with me, then, ye sonnes of Israel,

He lies downe and all the rest after him.

Lie downe with Dauid, and with Dauid mourne   20
Before the Holy One that sees our hearts!
Season this heauie soile with showers of teares,
And fill the face of euery flower with dew!
Weepe, Israel! for Dauids soule dissolues,
Lading the fountaines of his drowned eyes,   25
And powres her substance on the sencelesse earth.

SADOC.   Weepe, Israel! O weepe for Dauids soule,
Strewing the ground with haire and garments torne
For tragicke witnesse of your heartie woes!

AHIMAAS.   O, would our eyes were conduits to our hearts,   30
And that our hearts were seas of liquid bloud,
To powre in streames vpon this holy mount
For witnesse we would die for Dauids woes!

IONA.   Then should this Mount of Oliues seeme a plaine
Drownd with a sea, that with our sighs should rore,   35
And, in the murmure of his mounting waues,
Report our bleeding sorrowes to the heauens
For witnesse we would die for Dauids woes!

ITH.   Earth cannot weepe ynough for Dauids woes.
Then weepe, you heauens, and, all you clouds, dissolue,   40
That pittious stars may see our miseries
And drop their golden teares vpon the ground
For witnesse how they weepe for Dauids woes!

SADOC.   Now let my soueraigne raise his prostrate bones,

---

[1] B. *suggests* ambition's; *but see next note.*
[2] B. *follows* D. *in emending to* lofty; *but in Elizabethan English* a
lustie tower *means* a tower of lust, *just as* ambitious heat *means* the heat of
ambition.

And mourne not as a faithlesse man would doe ;   45
But be assurd that Iacobs righteous God,
That promist neuer to forsake your throne,
Will still be iust and pure in his vowes.

    DA.   Sadoc, high-priest, preseruer of the arke,
Whose sacred vertue keepes the chosen crowne,   50
I know my God is spotlesse [1] in his vowes
And that these haires shall greet my graue in peace;
But that my sonne should wrong his tendred soule
And fight against his fathers happinesse,
Turnes all my hopes into despaire of him,   55
And that despaire feeds all my veines with greefe.

    ITHAY.   Thinke of it, Dauid, as a fatall plague
Which greefe preserueth but preuenteth not ;
And turne thy drooping eyes vpon the troupes
That, of affection to thy worthinesse,   60
Doe swarme about the person of the king.
Cherish their valours and their zealous loues
With pleasant lookes and sweet encouragements.

    DA.   Me thinkes the voice of Ithay fils mine eares!

    ITH.   Let not the voice of Ithay loth thine eares,   65
Whose heart would baulme thy bosome with his teares!

    DAUID.   But wherefore goest thou to the wars with vs?
Thou art a stranger here in Israel
And sonne to Achis, mightie king of Gath :
Therefore returne, and with thy father stay.   70
Thou camst but yesterday ; and should I now
Let thee partake these troubles here with vs?
Keepe both thy-selfe and all thy souldiors safe ;
Let me abide the hazards of these armes.
And God requite the friendship thou hast shewd!   75

    ITH.   As sure as Israels God giues Dauid life,
What place or perill shall containe the king,
The same will Ithay share in life and death!

    DA.   Then, gentle Ithay, be thou still with vs,
A ioy to Dauid, and a grace to Israel!   80

       [1] *Misprinted* spotlefle *in* Isl.

Goe, Sadoc, now and beare the arke of God
Into the great Ierusalem againe.
If I find fauour in his gratious eyes,
Then will he lay his hand vpon my heart
Yet once againe before I visit death,   85
Giuing it strength and vertue to mine eies,
To tast the comforts and behold the forme
Of his faire arke and holy tabernacle.
But, if he say : " My wonted loue is worne,
And I haue no delight in Dauid now,"   90
Here lie I armed with an humble heart
T' imbrace the paines that anger shall impose,
And kisse the sword my Lord shall kill me with.
Then, Sadoc, take Ahimaas, thy sonne,
With Ionathan, sonne to Abiathar,   95
And in these fields I will repose my-selfe
Till they returne from you some certaine newes.
   SADOC.   Thy seruants will with ioy obey the king,
And hope to cheere his heart with happy newes.

                     Exeunt [1] SADOC, AHIMAAS *and* IONATHAN.

   ITH.   Now that it be no greefe vnto the king,   100
Let me for good enforme his Maiestie
That with vnkinde and gracelesse Absalon
Achitophel, your auncient counsellor,
Directs the state of this rebellion.
   DAUID.   Then doth it aime with danger at my crowne.   105
O thou that holdst his raging bloody bound [2]
Within the circle of the siluer moon

---

  [1] Isl. Exit ; *emend. by* D.
  [2] B. *says: " Very corrupt.* — *Qy.* sea's ranging body bound ? *That*
raging *is a misprint for* ranging *I am convinced ; but the rest is dark."*
Psalm lxxxix *prevents me from sharing* B.*'s conviction in regard to* raging.
*The rest is dark enough ; for, in the first place, the passage is not so much
worse than many others in* Peele *as to guarantee that it did not come from*
Peele's *pen in its present form ; but, on the other hand,* bloody *may, as* B.
suggests, be a misprint for body, *or* bloody bound *may be a distortion of*
flood ybound (*past participles with* y- *are not unknown in Elizabethan
English*). *At any rate, his* (106) *is correlative with* that (108).

That girds earths centre with his watrie scarfe,
Limit the counsell of Achitophel,
No bounds extending to my soules distresse ;   110
But turne his wisdome into foolishnesse !

Enter Cusay *with his coat turnd and head couered.*

 Cusay. Happinesse and honour to my lord the king!
 Dauid. What happinesse or honor may betide
His state that toiles in my extremities?
 Cus. O, let my gracious soueraine cease these greefes,   115
Vnlesse he wish his seruant Cusayes death,
Whose life depends vpon my lords releefe.
Then let my presence with my sighs perfume
The pleasant closet of my soueraignes soule.
 Da. No, Cusay, no ; thy presence vnto me   120
Will be a burthen, since I tender thee
And cannot brooke[1] thy sighs for Dauids sake.
But, if thou turne to faire Ierusalem
And say to Absalon, as thou hast been
A trusty friend vnto his fathers seat,   125
So thou wilt be to him and call him king,
Achitophels counsell may be brought to naught.
Then, hauing Sadoc and Abiathar,
All three may learne the secrets of my sonne,
Sending the message by Ahimaas   130
And friendly Ionathan, who both are there.
 [Cusay.][2] Then rise, referring the successe to Heauen!
 Da. Cusay, I rise, though with vnweldie bones :
I carrie armes against my Absalon.

            Exeunt.

   [1] Isl. breake ; *corr. by* Haw.
   [2] *Not in* Isl. ; *supplied by* Haw., *without note.*

[Act II.   Scene VI.] [1]

[Jerusalem : the palace.]

ABSALON, AMASA, ACHITOPHEL, *with the* CONCUBINES OF DAUID, *and others, in great state ;* ABSALON *crowned.*

ABS.   Now you, that were my fathers concubines,
Liquor to his inchast and lustfull fire,
Haue seene his honour shaken in his house,
Which I possesse in sight of all the world.
I bring ye forth for foiles to my renowne   5
And to eclipse the glorie of your king,
Whose life is with his honour fast inclosd
Within the entrailes of a ieatie cloud
Whose dissolution shall powre downe in showers
The substance of his life and swelling pride.   10
Then shall the stars light earth with rich aspects
And heauen shall burne in loue with Absalon,
Whose beautie will suffice to chast[2] all mists
And cloth the suns spheare with a triple fire
Sooner then his cleare eyes should suffer staine   15
Or be offended with a lowring day.
    [I][3] CONCUB.   Thy fathers honour, graceless Absalon,
And ours, thus beaten with thy violent armes,
Will cry for vengeance to the host of heauen,
Whose power is euer armed against the proud,   20
And will dart plagues at thy aspiring head
For doing this disgrace to Dauids throne.
    II [CONCUB.][3] To Dauids throne, to Dauids holy throne,
Whose scepter angels guard with swords of fire
And sit as eagles on his conquering fist,   25
Ready to prey vpon his enemies!
Then thinke not thou, the captaine of his foes, —

---

[1] Scene ix *in* B.   [3] *Not in* Isl.
    [2] *So* Isl.; Haw. D. B. *print* chase ; *but confusion of the verbs* chase *and* chaste *is so easy and some of the meaning*s *of* chaste *are so appropriate that it seems possible that* Peele *wrote* chaste.

Wert thou much swifter than Azahell was,
That could out-pace the nimble-footed[1] roe, —
To scape the furie of their thumping beakes   30
Or dreadfull scope[2] of their commanding wings.
   ACHIT.[3]   Let not my lord the king of Israel
Be angrie with a sillie womans threats ;
But, with the pleasure he hath erst enioied,
Turne them into their cabinets againe   35
Till Dauids conquest be their ouerthrow.
   ABS.   Into your bowers, ye daughters of disdaine,
Gotten by furie of vnbridled lust,
And wash your couches with your mourning teares
For greefe that Dauids kingdome is decaied.   40
   1 [CONCUB.][4]   No, Absalon ; his kingdome is enchaind
Fast to the finger of great Iacobs God,
Which will not lose it for a rebels loue.   *Exeunt* [CONCUBINES].
   AMASA.   If I might giue aduise vnto the king,
These concubines should buy their taunts with bloud.   45
   ABS.   Amasa, no ; but let thy martiall sword
Empty the veines[5] of Dauids armed men,
And let these foolish women scape our hands,
To recompense the shame they haue sustaind.
First, Absolon was by the trumpets sound   50
Proclaimd through Hebron King of Israel ;
And now is set in faire Ierusalem
With complete state and glorie of a crowne.
Fiftie faire footmen by my chariot run,
And to the aire, whose rupture rings my fame,   55
Where-ere I ride, they offer reuerence.
Why should not Absolon, that in his face
Carries the finall purpose of his God, —

---

   1 *Misprinted* nimple-footed *in* Haw.
   2 Swoop, *the suggestion of* P. A. Daniel, *is attractive ;* Kittredge *suggests* stoop *as another possibility, but thinks, as I do, that* Peele *wrote* scope.
   3 *Misprinted* Achip. *in* Isl.   4 *Not in* Isl.
   5 Isl. paines ; *emend. by* Haw. ; D. B. *put* veines *in the text, but* D., *in his first edition, suggests* plaines.

That is, to work him grace in Israel,—
Endeuour to atchieue with all his strength   60
The state that most may satisfie his ioy,
Keeping his statutes and his couenants pure?
His thunder is entangled in my haire,
And with my beautie is his lightning quencht:
I am the man he made to glorie in,   65
When by the errours of my fathers sinne
He lost the path that led into[1] the land
Wherewith our chosen ancestors were blest.

Enter Cusay.

Cus.   Long may the beautious king of Israel liue,
To whom the people doe by thousands swarme!   70
    Abs.   What meaneth Cusay so to greet his foe?
Is this the loue thou shewst[2] to Dauids soule,
To whose assistance thou hast vowed thy life?
Why leauest thou him in this extremitie?
    Cus.   Because the Lord and Israel chuseth thee.   75
And, as before I serued thy fathers turne
With counsell acceptable in his sight,
So likewise will I now obey his sonne.
    Abs.   Then welcome, Cusay, to King Absalon!
And now, my lords and louing counsellors,   80
I think it time to exercise our armes
Against forsaken Dauid and his host.
Giue counsell first, my good Achitophel,
What times and orders we may best obserue
For prosperous manage of these high exploits.   85
    Achi.   Let me chuse out twelue thousand valiant men,
And, while the night hides with her sable mists
The close endeuors cunning souldiers vse,
I will assault thy discontented sire,
And, while with weaknesse of their wearie armes,   90
Surchargd with toile to shun thy suddaine power,
The people flie in huge disordred troupes

---

¹ Haw. led him into.   ² Isl. shewdst ; *corr. by* D.

To saue their liues, and leaue the king alone,
Then will I smite him with his latest wound
And bring the people to thy feet in peace.   95
  ABS.   Well hath Achitophel giuen his aduise.
Yet let vs hear what Cusay counsels vs,
Whose great experience is well worth the eare.
  CUS.   Though wise Achitophel be much more meet
To purchase hearing with my lord the king   100
For all his former counsels then my-selfe,
Yet, not offending Absolon or him,
This time it is not good nor worth pursuit ;
For, well thou knowest, thy fathers men are strong,
Chafing as shee-bears robbed of their whelpes ;   105
Besides, the king himselfe a valiant man,
Traind vp in feats and stratagems of warre,
And will not, for preuention of the worst,
Lodge with the common souldiers in the field,
But now, I know, his wonted policies   110
Haue taught him lurke within some secret caue
Guarded with all his stoutest souldiers,
Which, if the forefront of his battle faint,
Will yet giue out that Absalon doth flie,
And so thy souldiers be discouraged.   115
Dauid himselfe, withall, whose angry heart
Is as a lyons letted of his walke,
Will fight himselfe, and all his men to one,
Before a few shall vanquish him by feare.
My counsell therefore is, with trumpets sound   120
To gather men from Dan to Bersabe,
That they may march in number like sea-sands
That nestle close in one [1] anothers necke :
So shall we come vpon him in our strength,
Like to the dew that fals in showers from heauen,   125
And leaue him not a man to march withall.
Besides, if any citie succour him,
The numbers [2] of our men shall fetch vs ropes,

---

[1] *Not in* Isl.; *supplied by* Haw.   [2] *Misprinted* nnmbers *in* Isl.

And we will pull it downe the riuers streame,
That not a stone be left to keepe vs out.   130
    ABS.   What says my lord[s] to Cusaies counsell now?
    AMASA.   I fancie Cusaies counsell better farre
Then that is giuen vs from Achitophel;
And so, I think, doth euery souldier here.
    ALL.   Cusaies counsell is better then Achitophels.   135
    ABS.   Then march we after Cusaies counsell all.
Sound trumpets through the bounds of Israel,
And muster all the men will serue the king,
That Absalon may glut his longing soule
With sole fruition of his fathers crowne.   *Exeunt.* 140
    ACH. [*aside*]   Ill shall they fare that follow thy attempts,
That skornes the counsell of Achitophel.   [*Exit.*]

Restat CUSAY.

    CUSAY.   Thus hath the power of Iacobs iealous God
Fulfild his seruant Dauids drifts by me
And brought Achitophels aduise to scorne.   145

Enter SADOC, ABIATHAR, AHIMAAS *and* IONATHAN.

    SADOC.   God saue Lord Cusay, and direct his zeale
To purchase Dauids conquest gainst his sonne!
    ABIA.   What secrets hast thou gleande from Absalon?
    CUSAY.   These, sacred priests that beare the arke of God:
Achitophel aduisd him in the night   150
To let him chuse twelue thousand fighting-men,
And he would come on Dauid at vnwares,
While he was wearie with his violent toile;
But I aduisd to get a greater host,
And gather men from Dan to Bersabe,   155
To come vpon him strongly in the fields.
Then send Ahimaas and Ionathan
To signifie these secrets to the king,
And will him not to stay this night abroad
But get him ouer Iordane presently,   160
Least he and all his people kisse the sword.

SADOC.   Then goe, Ahimaas and Ionathan,
And straight conuey this message to the king.
    AHIM.   Father, we will, if Absalons cheefe spies
Preuent not this deuise and stay vs here.   165

Exeunt.

[Act II.   Scene VII.] [1]

[*The highway.*]

SEMEI *solus.*

SEMEI.   The man of Israel that hath rul'd as king,
Or, rather, as the tyrant of the land,
Bolstering his hatefull head vpon the throne
That God vnworthily hath blest him with,
Shall now, I hope, lay it as low as hell,   5
And be depos'd from his detested chaire.
O that my bosome could by nature beare
A sea of poyson to be powr'de vpon
His cursed head that sacred baulme hath grac'd
And consecrated king of Israel!   10
Or would my breath were made the smoke of hell,
Infected with the sighs of damned soules
Or with the reeking of that serpents gorge
That feeds on adders, toads and venomous roots,
That, as I opened my reuenging lips   15
To curse the sheepeheard for his tyrannie,
My words might cast rancke poyson to his pores
And make his swolne and ranckling sinewes cracke,
Like to the combat-blowes that breake the clouds
When Ioues stout champions [do] [2] fight with fire!   20
See where he commeth that my soule abhors!
I haue prepard my pocket full of stones
To cast at him, mingled with earth and dust,
Which, bursting with disdaine, I greet him with.

[1] Scene x *in* B.
[2] P. A. Daniel *inserts* in air.

DAUID, IOAB, ABYSHAI, ITHAY, *with others.*

SEMEI.[1]   Come forth, thou murtherer, and wicked man!   25
The Lord hath brought vpon thy cursed head
The guiltlesse bloud of Saule and all his sonnes,
Whose royall throne thy basenesse hath vsurpt ;
And, to reuenge it deepely on thy soule,
The Lord hath giuen the kingdome to thy son,   30
And he shall wreake the traitrous wrongs of Saule.
Euen as thy sinne hath still importund heauen,
So shall thy murthers and adulterie
Be punisht in the sight of Israel,
As thou deserust, with bloud, with death and hell.   35
Hence, murtherer, hence!

He throws at him.[2]

ABIS.   Why doth this dead dog curse my lord the king?
Let me alone to take away his head !
DA.   Why medleth thus the son of Zeruia
To interrupt the action of our God?   40
Semei vseth me with this reproch
Because the Lord hath sent him to reproue
The sinnes of Dauid printed in his browes
With bloud, that blusheth for his conscience guilt :
Who dares then aske him why he curseth me?   45
SEMEI.   If then thy conscience tell thee thou hast sind
And that thy life is odious to the world,
Command thy followers to shun thy face,
And by thy-selfe here make away thy soule,
That I may stand and glorie in thy shame.   50
DA.   I am not desperate, Semei, like thy-selfe,
But trust vnto the couenant of my God,
Founded on mercie, with repentance built,
And finisht with the glorie of my soule.
SEMEI.   A murtherer, and hope for mercie in thy end?   55

[1] *So* Isl.; *omitted by* Haw. D. B.
[2] Isl. Hence murtherer, hence, he threw at him (*in italics, as stage-direction*) ; *corr. silently by* Haw.

Hate and destruction sit vpon thy browes
To watch the issue of thy damned ghost,
Which, with thy latest gaspe, theile take and teare,
Hurling in euery paine of hell a peece.
Hence, murtherer! thou shame to Israel!   60
Foule letcher, drunkard, plague to heauen and earth!

He throwes at him.

IOAB.   What! is it pietie in Dauids thoughts
So to abhorre from lawes of pollicie
In this extremitie of his distresse
To giue his subiects cause of carelesnesse?   65
Send hence the dog with sorrow to his graue!
   DAUID.   Why should the sons of Zeruia seeke to checke [1]
His spirit which the Lord hath thus inspir'd?
Behold, my sonne, which issued from my flesh,
With equall furie seekes to take my life: 70
How much more, then, the sonne of Iemini, —
Cheefely since he doth nought but Gods command?
It may be he will looke on me this day
With gracious eyes, and for his cursing blesse
The heart of Dauid in his bitternesse.   75
   SEMEI.   What! doest thou fret my soule with sufferance?
O that the soules of Isboseth and Abner,
Which thou sentst swimming to their graues in bloud,
With wounds fresh-bleeding, gasping for reuenge,
Were here to execute my burning hate!   80
But I will hunt thy foot with curses still:
Hence, monster, murtherer, mirror of contempt!

He throwes dust againe.

Enter AHIMAAS [2] *and* IONATHAN.

AHIM.   Long life to Dauid! to his enemies, death!
   DA.   Welcome, Ahimaas and Ionathan!
What newes sends Cusay to thy lord the king?   85

----

1 D. *suggests the omission of* seeke to; *but* B. *is clearly right in main-taining that* Zeruia *is not a quadrisyllable.*
2 Isl. AHIMAAAS.

AHIM.　Cusay, [my lord,] would wish my lord the king [1]
To passe the riuer Iordane presently,
Least he and all his people perish here ;
For wise Achitophel hath counsel'd Absalon
To take aduantage of your wearie armes　　　　　　　90
And come this night vpon you in the fields.
But yet the Lord hath made his counsell skorne,
And Cusaies pollicie with praise preferd :
Which was, to number euery Israelite
And so assault you in their pride of strength.　　　　95
　　IONAT.　Abiathar besides intreats the king
To send his men of warre against his sonne
And hazard not his person in the field.
　　DAUID.　Thankes to Abiathar, and to you both,
And to my Cusay, whom the Lord requite !　　　　100
But tenne times treble thankes to his soft hand
Whose pleasant touch hath made my heart to dance
And play him praises in my zealous breast, —
That turnd the counsell of Achitophel
After the praiers of his seruants lips !　　　　　　105
Now will we passe the riuer all this night,
And in the morning sound the voice of warre,
The voice of bloudy and vnkindly warre.
　　IOAB.　Then tell vs how thou wilt diuide thy men,
And who shall haue the speciall charge herein.　　110
　　DAU.　Ioab, thy-selfe shall for thy charge conduct
The first third part of all my valiant men ;
The second shall Abisaies valour lead ;
The third faire Ithay, which I most should grace
For comfort he hath done to Dauids woes ;　　　　115
And I my-selfe will follow in the midst.
　　ITH.　That let not Dauid ; for, though we should flie,
Tenne thousand of vs were not halfe so much
Esteemd with Dauids enemies as himselfe :

---

[1] B. *inserts* sovereign *before* lord ; *my insertion seems more in* Peele's
*manner ; but it is by no means clear that in plays of this date metrically
incomplete lines are to be filled out.*

Thy people, louing thee, denie thee this.   120
    DA.   What seemes them best, then that will Dauid doe.
But now, my lords and captaines, heare his voice
That neuer yet pierst pittious heauen in vaine, —
Then let it not slip lightly through your eares :
For my sake, spare the young man Absalon !   125
Ioab, thy-selfe didst once vse friendly words
To reconcile my heart incenst to him :
If then thy loue be to thy kinsman sound
And thou wilt proue a perfit Israelite,
Friend him with deeds, and touch no haire of him,   130
Not that faire haire with which the wanton winds
Delight to play and loues [1] to make it curle,
Wherein the nightingales would build their nests
And make sweet bowers in euery golden tresse
To sing their louer euery night asleepe.   135
O, spoile not, Ioab, Ioues faire ornaments,
Which he hath sent to solace Dauids soule !
The best, ye see, my lords, are swift to sinne !
To sinne our feet are washt with milke of roes
And dried againe with coales of lightening !   140
O Lord, thou seest the proudest sinnes poor slaue,
And with his bridle pulst him to the graue ! — [2]
For my sake then, spare louely Absalon !
    ITH.   Wee will, my lord, for thy sake fauour him.
Exeunt.

[1] D. *changes to* love.

[2] B. *says : "This line is hardly intelligible. I should prefer to read,* That with his bridle pulls him, *etc. A similar emendation was proposed by* Collier." *But* 2 Kings, xix, 28, *seems to lend some support to the present form of the text. The difference between* Collier's *emendation and* B.'s *is that* Collier *has* who *where* B. *has* that.

[Act II.   Scene VIII.][1]

[*The house of* ACHITOPHEL.]

ACHITOPHEL *solus, with a halter.*

ACHI.   Now hath Achitophel orderd his house
And taken leaue of euery pleasure there.
Hereon depends[2] Achitophels delights
And in this circle must his life be closde.
The wise Achitophel, whose counsell prou'd   5
Euer as sound for fortunate successe
As if men askt the oracle of God,
Is now vsde like the foole of Israel.
Then set thy angrie soule vpon her wings,
And let her flie into the shade of death!   10
And for my death let heauen for-euer weepe,
Making huge flouds vpon the land I leaue
To rauish[3] them and all their fairest fruits!
Let all the sighs I breath'd for this disgrace
Hang on my[4] hedges like eternall mists   15
As mourning-garments[5] for their maisters death!
Ope, earth, and take thy miserable sonne
Into the bowels of thy cursed wombe!
Once in a surfet thou diddest spue him forth ;
Now for fell hunger sucke him in againe,   20
And be his bodie poyson to thy vaines ! —
And now, thou hellish instrument of Heauen,
Once execute th' arrest of Ioues iust doome
And stop his breast[6] that curseth Israel!

Exit.

[1] Scene xi *in* B.
[2] D. *changes to* depend.
[3] B. *prefers* ravage.
[4] B. *suggests* thy, "*the word being addressed to* the land 1 leaue." *But*
l. 16 *seems to put* my *beyond suspicion.*
[5] Isl. *misprints* monrning.
[6] D. breath ; *but* Kittredge *remarks that* breast *is possible.*

[Act II. Scene IX.] [1]

[The battle-field before the battle.]

ABSALON, AMASA, *with all his traine.*

ABS. Now for the crowne and throne of Israel
To be confirmd with vertue of my sword
And writ with Dauids bloud vpon the blade!
Now, Ioue, let forth the golden firmament,
And looke on him with all thy fierie eyes,   5
Which thou hast made to giue their glories light!
To shew thou louest the vertue of thy hand,
Let fall a wreath of starres vpon my head
Whose influence may gouern Israel
With state exceeding all her other kings! —   10
Fight, lords and captaines, that your soueraignes face
May shine in honour brighter then the sunne,
And with the vertues of my beautious raies
Make this faire land as fruitfull as the fields
That with sweet milke and hony ouerflow'd.   15
God in the whissing of a pleasant wind
Shall march vpon the tops of mulberie-trees
To coole all breasts that burne with any greefes.
As whylome, he was good to Moyses men,
By day the Lord shall sit within a cloud,   20
To guide your footsteps to the fields of ioy;
And in the night a piller, bright as fire,
Shall goe before you like a second sunne,
Wherein the essence of his godhead is;
That, day and night, you may be brought to peace,   25
And neuer swarue from that delightsome path
That leads your soules to perfect happinesse :
This shall he doe for ioy, when I am king.
Then fight, braue captaines, that these ioies may flie
Into your bosomes with sweet victorie.   30

Exeunt.

1 Scene xii *in* B.

[Act II.   Scene X.][1]

[A forest.]

The battell; and ABSALON *hangs by the haire.*

[ABS.]   What angrie angel, sitting in these shades,
Hath laid his cruell hands vpon my haire,
And holds my body thus twixt heauen and earth?
Hath Absalon no souldier neere his hand
That may vntwine me this vnpleasant curle,   5
Or wound this tree that rauisheth his lord?
O God, behold, the glorie of thy hand
And choisest fruit of natures workemanship
Hang, like a rotten branch, vpon this tree,
Fit for the axe and ready for the fire!   10
Since thou withholdst all ordinarie helpe
To lose my bodie from this bond of death,
O, let my beautie fill these senceless plants
With sence and power to lose me from this plague,
And worke some wonder to preuent his death   15
Whose life thou madst a speciall miracle.

[Enter] IOAB, *with another* SOULDIER.

SOULD.   My lord, I saw the young prince Absalon
Hang by the haire vpon a shadie oke,
And could by no meanes get himselfe vnlosde.

IOAB.   Why slewst thou not the wicked Absalon,   20
That rebell to his father and to Heauen,
That so I might haue giuen thee for thy paines
Tenne siluer shekles[2] and a golden wast?

SOULD.   Not for a thousand shekles[2] would I slay
The sonne of Dauid, whom his father chargd   25
Nor thou, Abisay nor the sonne of Gath
Should touch with stroke of deadly violence.
The charge was giuen in hearing of vs all;

1 Scene xiii *in* B.
2 Isl. sickles; *corr. silently by* Haw.

And, had I done it, then, I know, thy-selfe,
Before thou wouldst abide the kings rebuke,   30
Would haue accus'd me as a man of death.

    IOAB. I must not now stand trifling here with thee.

[IOAB goes to ABSALON ; exit SOLDIER.]

    ABS. Helpe, Ioab, helpe!   O helpe thy Absalon!
Let not thy angrie thoughts be laid in bloud,
In bloud of him that sometimes nourisht thee   35
And softned thy sweet heart with friendly loue.
O, giue me once againe my fathers sight,
My deerest father and my princely soueraigne,
That, shedding teares of bloud before his face,
The ground may witnesse and the heauens record   40
My last submission sound and full of ruth!

    IOAB. Rebell to nature, hate to heauen and earth,
Shall I giue helpe to him that thirsts the soule
Of his deere father and my soueraigne lord?
Now see, the Lord hath tangled in a tree   45
The health and glorie of thy stubborne heart,
And made thy pride curbd with a sencelesse plant!
Now, Absalon, how doth the Lord regard
The beautie wherevpon thy hope was built
And which thou thoughtst his grace did glorie in?   50
Findst thou not now with feare of instant death
That God affects not any painted shape
Or goodly personage, when the vertuous soule
Is stuft with naught but pride and stubbornesse?
But preach I to thee, while I should reuenge   55
Thy cursed sinne that staineth Israel
And makes her fields blush with her childrens bloud?
Take that as part of thy deserued plague,
Which worthily no torment can inflict!

[Stabs him.]

    ABS. O Ioab! Ioab! cruell, ruthlesse Ioab!   60
Herewith thou woundst thy kingly soueraignes heart,
Whose heauenly temper hates his childrens bloud,

And will be sicke, I know, for Absalon.
O my deere father, that thy melting eyes
Might pierce this thicket to behold thy sonne,   65
Thy deerest sonne gor'de with a mortall dart!
Yet, Ioab, pittie me! pittie my father, Ioab;
Pittie his soules distresse that mournes my life
And will be dead, I know, to hear my death!

   IOAB.   If he were so remorsefull of thy state,   70
Why sent he me against thee with the sword?
All Ioab meanes to pleasure thee withall
Is to despatch thee quickly of thy paine.
Hold, Absalon, Ioabs pittie is in this!
In this, prowd Absalon, is Ioabs loue!   75

He [*stabs him again and*] *goes out.*

   ABS.   Such loue, such pittie Israels God send thee,
And for his loue to Dauid pittie me!
Ah, my deere[1] father, see thy bowels bleed,
See death assault thy deerest Absalon!
See, pittie, pardon, pray for Absalon!   80

Enter fiue or sixe SOULDIORS.

[SOULD.]   See where the rebell in his glorie hangs!
Where is the vertue of thy beautie, Absalon?
Will any of vs here now feare thy lookes,
Or be in loue with that thy golden haire,
Wherein was wrapt rebellion gainst thy sire   85
And cords prepar'd to stop thy fathers breath?
Our captaine, Ioab, hath begun to vs:
And heres an end to thee and all thy sinnes!

[*Stabs him; he dies.*]

Come, let vs take the beauteous rebell downe,
And in some ditch amids this darkesome wood   90
Burie his bulke beneath a heape of stones
Whose stonie heart did hunt his fathers death.

   [1] Haw. fear.

[*They take him down.*]

Enter in triumph, with drum and ensigne IOAB, ABYSHAI, *and* SOULDIERS, *to* ABSALON.

IOAB.　Well, done, tall souldiers! Take the traitor downe,
And in this myerie ditch interre his bones,
Couering his hatefull breast with heapes of stones.　　　95
This shadie thicket of darke Ephraim [1]
Shall euer lower on his cursed graue;
Night-rauens and owles shall ring his fatall knell,
And sit exclaiming on his damned soule;
There shall they heape their preyes of carrion　　　100
Till all his graue be clad with stinking bones,
That it may loth the sense of euery man:
So shall his end breed horror to his name
And to his traitrous fact eternall shame.

Exeunt. [2]

CHORUS. [3]

O dreadfull president of his iust doome
Whose holy heart is neuer toucht with ruth
Of fickle beautie or of glorious shapes, [4]
But with the vertue of an vpright soule,
Humble and zealous in his inward thoughts　　　5
Though in his person loathsome and deform'd!
Now, since this storie lends vs other store
To make a third discourse of Dauids life,
Adding thereto his most renowmed death
And all their deaths that at his death he iudgd,　　　10
Here we end this; and what here wants to please,
We will supplie with treble willingnesse.

[*Exit.*]

[1] Isl. Ephrami; *corr. silently by* Haw.

[2] Isl. Exit; *corr. silently by* Haw.

[3] Isl. 5 Chorus, *which is especially puzzling in view of the other facts which indicate that we have only a part of this play; but* l. 8 *below has been altered, if what is now* Act iii *was once* Act v.

[4] D. *changes to* shape.

¹ ABSALON *with three or foure of his* SERUANTS *or* GENTLEMEN.

ABS. What boots it, Absalon, vnhappie Absalon, —
Sighing I say, what boots it, Absalon,
To haue disclos'd a farre more worthy wombe
Then

[Act III. Scene. I.] ²

[DAUID's camp.]

Trumpets sound. Enter IOAB, AHIMAAS, CUSAY, AMASA, *with all the*
rest.

IOAB. Souldiers of Israel and ye sonnes of Iuda
That haue contended in these irkesome broiles
And ript old Israels bowels with your swords,
The godlesse generall of your stubborne armes
Is brought by Israels helper to the graue, —   5
A graue of shame and skorne of all the tribes.
Now then, to saue your honours from the dust
And keepe your blouds in temper by your bones,
Let Ioabs ensigne shroud your manly heads ;
Direct your eies, your weapons and your hearts   10
To guard the life of Dauid from his foes.
Error hath maskt your much-too-froward ³ minds,
And you haue sind against the chosen state,
Against his life for whom your liues are blest,
And followed an vsurper to the field,   15

¹ *This fragment is printed in* Isl. *at the bottom of* G 4 v°. *The word*
Then *is the catch-word for the next page, and its presence indicates that*
more of the copy than has been preserved to us was in the printer's hands,
if not actually set up — how much more is of course unknown. But for
the fact that the sheet following this is properly marked H, *the presence of*
this catch-word, the heading of the CHORUS *just above, and the peculiarities*
of the page-heading (see p. 421, *n.* 1) *would tempt one to believe that some*
sheets were printed but not bound. It is a remarkable fact that leaf C 4
is not left unmarked, as is usual, but is marked I, *and, strangely enough,*
the first word on the leaf is Then; *but the confusion extends only to the*
marking, not to the text.   ² Scene xiv *in* B.   ³ Isl. *forward.*

In whose iust death your deaths are threatened;
But Ioab pitties your disordered soules,
And therefore offers pardon, peace and loue
To all that will be friendly reconcil'de
To Israels weale, to Dauid and to Heauen.   20
Amasa, thou art leader of the host
That vnder Absalon haue raisde their armes;
Then be a captaine wise and polliticke,
Carefull and louing for thy souldiers liues,
And lead them to this honourable league.   25
   AMASA.   I will;[1] at least Ile doe my best.
And for the gracious offer thou hast made
I giue thee thankes as much as for my head. —
Then, you deceiu'd poore soules of Israel,
Since now ye see the errors you incurd,   30
With thankes and due submission be appeasde,
And, as ye see your captaines president,
Here cast we then our swords at Ioabs feet,
Submitting with all zeale and reuerence
Our goods and bodies to his gracious hands.   35

[The rebels kneel.][2]

   IOAB.   Stand vp and take ye all your swords againe!
Dauid and Ioab shall be blest herein.

All stand vp.[3]

   AHIM.   Now let me go enforme my lord the king
How God hath freed him from his enemies.
   IOAB.   Another time, Ahimaas; not now.   40
But, Cusay, goe thy-selfe and tell the king
The happie message of our good successe.
   CUS.   I will, my lord; and thanke thee for thy grace.

Exit CUSAY.

---

[1] D. *suggests* Ioab, I will, *or* I will, my lord; B. *prints* I will; [I will;];
but see p. 468, n. 1.
   [2] *Supplied by* B.
   [3] *In* Isl. Haw. *this precedes* l. 36; D. B. *put it after* l. 36 (D., *without note.*)

AHIM.   What if thy seruant should goe to, my lord?

IOAB.   What newes hast thou to bring, since he is gone?   45

AHIM.   Yet doe Ahimaas so much content

That he may run about so sweet a charge!   *Exit.*[1]

IOAB.   Run, if thou wilt; and peace be with thy steps. —

Now follow, that you may salute the king

With humble hearts and reconciled soules.   50

AMA.   We follow, Ioab, to our gracious king;

And him our swords shall honour to our deaths.

Exeunt.

[Act III.   Scene II.][2]

[DAUID's *camp.*]

DAUID, BETHSABE, SALOMON, NATHAN, ADONIA, CHILEAB, *with their traine.*

BETH.   What meanes my lord, the lampe of Israel,

From whose bright eyes all eyes receiue their light,

To dim the glory of his sweet aspects[3]

And paint his countenance with his hearts distresse?

Why should his thoughts retaine a sad conceit,   5

When euery pleasure kneeles before his throne

And sues for sweet acceptance with his Grace?

Take but your lute, and make the mountaines dance,

Retriue the sunnes sphere and restraine the clouds,

Giue eares to trees, make sauage lyons tame,   10

Impose still silence to the loudest winds,

And fill the fairest day with foulest stormes:

Then why should passions of much meaner power

Beare head against the heart of Israel?

DA.   Faire Bersabe, thou mightst increase the strength   15

Of these thy arguments drawne from my skill

By vrging thy sweet sight to my conceits,

Whose vertue euer seru'd for sacred baulme

---

[1] *Of course this stage-direction comes in too early, as is usual in the old editions.*

[2] Scene xv *in* B.   [3] D. B. *change to* aspect.

To cheere my pinings past all earthly ioies;
But, Bethsabe, the Daughter of the Highest,   20
Whose beautie builds the towers of Israel,
Shee that in chaines of pearle and vnicorne
Leads at her traine the ancient golden-world, —
The world that Adam held in paradise,
Whose breath refineth all infectious aires   25
And makes the meddowes smile at her repaire, —
Shee, shee,[1] my dearest Bethsabe,
Faire Peace, the goddesse of our graces here,
Is fled the streets of faire Ierusalem,
The fields of Israel and the heart of Dauid,   30
Leading my comforts in her golden chaines
Linckt to the life and soule of Absalon.
   BETH.   Then is the pleasure of my soueraignes heart
So wrapt within the bosome of that sonne
That Salomon, whom Israels God affects   35
And gaue the name vnto him for his loue,
Should be no salue to comfort Dauids soule?
   DAU.   Salomon, my loue, is Dauids lord,[2]
Our God hath nam'd him lord of Israel:
In him — for that, and since he is thy sonne —   40
Must Dauid needs be pleased at the heart,
And he shall surely sit vpon my throne;
But Absalon, the beautie of my bones,
Faire Absalon, the counterfeit of loue,
Sweet Absalon, the image of content,   45
Must claime a portion in his fathers care
And be in life and death King Dauids sonne.
   NAT.   Yet, as my lord hath said, let Salomon reign,

---

[1] D. *suggests* She, she, alas!

[2] D. *thinks the text corrupt;* B. *proposes* Salomon, my love, is David's
lovéd son; Sprenger (*loc. cit.*) *proposes* Salomon, my love, he that is
David's lord. *Commenting on* Sprenger, *I proposed* (Engl. Stud., XVIII,
301) Nay, Salomon, &c., *but held and still hold that this is a nine-syllabled verse. To the subject, there treated in a brief note, I shall recur in* vol.
III *of this book, in the notes on this play.* [See Publisher's Note].

Whom God in naming hath annointed king.
Now is he apt to learne th' eternall lawes,   50
Whose knowledge being rooted in his youth
Will beautifie his age with glorious fruits ;
While Absalon, incenst with gracelesse pride,
Vsurps and staines the kingdome with his sinne.
Let Salomon be made thy staffe of age,   55
Faire Israels rest, and honour of thy race.
   DA.   Tell me, my Salomon : wilt thou imbrace
Thy fathers precepts graued in thy heart,
And satisfie my zeale to thy renowne
With practise of such sacred principles   60
As shall concerne the state of Israel?
   SAL.   My royall father, if the heauenly zeale
Which for my welfare feeds vpon your soule
Were not sustaind by vertue of mine own, —
If the sweet accents of your cheerefull voice   65
Should not each hower beat vpon mine eares
As sweetly as the breath of heauen to him
That gaspeth scorched with the summers sunne,
I should be guiltie of vnpardoned sinne,
Fearing the plague of Heauen and shame of earth ;   70
But, since I vow my-selfe to learne the skill
And holy secrets of his mightie hand
Whose cunning tunes the musicke of my soule,
It would content me, father, first to learne
How th' Eternall fram'd the firmament,   75
Which bodies lead[1] their influence by fire,
And which are fild with hoarie winters yse,[2]
What signe is raignie, and what starre is faire,
Why by the rules of true proportion
The yeare is still diuided into months,   80
The months to daies, the daies to certaine howers,
What fruitfull race shall fill the future world,
Or for what time shall this round building stand,

---

   [1] D.'s *emendation,* lend, *is adopted, though with some doubt, by* B.
   [2] *Misprinted* use *in* Haw.

What magistrates, what kings shall keepe in awe
Mens minds with bridles of th' eternall law.   85
   DA.   Wade not too farre, my boy, in waues too [1] deepe!
The feeble eyes of our aspiring thoughts
Behold things present and record things past;
But things to come exceed our humane reach,
And are not painted yet in angels eyes: 90
For those, submit thy sence, and say: " Thou Power
That now art framing of the future world,
Knowest all to come, not by the course of heauen,
By fraile coniectures of inferiour signes,
By monstrous flouds, by flights and flockes of birds,   95
By bowels of a sacrificed beast,
Or by the figures of some hidden art,
But by a true and naturall presage,
Laying the ground and perfect architect [2]
Of all our actions now before thine eyes   100
From Adam to the end of Adams seed.
O Heauen, protect my weakenesse with thy strength!
So looke on me that I may view thy face
And see these secrets written in thy browes!
O Sun, come dart thy raies vpon my moone,   105
That now mine eyes, eclipsed to the earth,
May brightly be refin'd and shine to heauen!
Transforme me from this flesh, that I may liue
Before my death, regenerate with thee!
O thou great God, rauish my earthly sprite,   110
That for the time a more then humane skill
May feed the organons of all my sence,
That, when I thinke, thy thoughts may be my guide,
And when I speake, I may be made by choice
The perfect eccho of thy heauenly voice!" —   115
Thus say, my sonne, and thou shalt learne them all.
   SALO.   A secret fury rauisheth my soule,

----

[1] D. *changes to* so.
[2] D. *suggests* archetype; B. archi'ture; Sprenger *changes* and *to* a; *I have shown in* Engl. Stud., XVIII, 302, *that* architect *is right.*

Lifting my mind aboue her humane bounds,
And, as the eagle, roused from her stand
With violent hunger, towring in the aire   120
Seaseth her feathered prey and thinkes to feed,
But, seeing then a cloud beneath her feet,
Lets fall the foule, and is emboldened
With eies intentiue to bedare the sun,
And stieth close vnto his stately sphere, —   125
So Salomon, mounted on the burning wings
Of zeale deuine, lets fall his mortall food
And cheeres his sences with celestiall aire,
Treads in the golden, starrie labyrinth
And holds his eyes fixt on Iehouaes browes.   130
Good father, teach me further what to doe.
   NATH.   See, Dauid, how his haughtie spirit mounts,
Euen now of heigth to wield a diademe :
Then make him promise, that he may succeed,
And rest old Israels bones from broiles of warre.   135
   DAUID.   Nathan, thou prophet sprung from Iesses root,
I promise thee and louely Bethsabe
My Salomon shall gouerne after me.
   BETH.   He that hath toucht thee with this righteous
        thought
Preserue the harbour of thy thoughts in peace !   140

Enter MESSENGER.

   MESS.   My lord, thy seruants of the watch haue seene
One running hitherward from forth the warres.
   DAUID.   If hee bee come alone, he bringeth newes.
   MESS.   Another hath thy seruant seene, my lord,
Whose running much resembles Sadocs sonne.   145
   DA.   He is a good man, and good tidings brings.

Enter AHIMAAS.

   AHIM.   Peace and content be with my lord the king,
Whom Israels God hath blest with victory !
   DA.   Tell me, Ahimaas : liues my Absalon?

AHIMAAS.　I saw a troupe of souldiours gathered,　　150
But know not what the tumult might import.

　DAU.　Stand by, vntill some other may informe
The heart of Dauid with a happie truth.

Enter CUSAY.

CUSAY.　Happinesse and honour liue with Dauids soule,
Whom God hath blest with conquest of his foes!　　155

　DAUID.　But, Cusay, liues the yong man Absalon?

　CUSAY.　The stubborne enemies to Dauids peace,
And all that cast their darts against his crowne,
Fare euer like the young man Absalon!
For, as he rid the woods of Ephraim, ——　　160
Which fought for thee as much as all thy men, ——
His haire was tangled in a shadie oake,
And, hanging there, by Ioab and his men
Sustaind the stroke of well-deserued death.

　DAUID.　Hath Absalon sustaind the stroke of death?　　165
Die, Dauid, for the death of Absalon,
And make these cursed newes the bloudy darts
That, through his bowels, rip thy wretched[1] breast!
Hence, Dauid, walke the solitarie woods,
And in some cædars shade the thunder slew　　170
And fire from heauen hath made his branches blacke
Sit mourning the decease of Absalon!
Against the body of that blasted plant
In thousand shiuers breake thy yuorie lute,
Hanging thy stringlesse harpe vpon his boughs;　　175
And through the hollow, saplesse, sounding truncke
Bellow the torments that perplexe thy soule!
There let the winds sit sighing till they burst!
Let tempest, mufled with a cloud of pitch,
Threaten the forrests with her hellish face,　　180
And, mounted fiercely on her yron wings,
Rend vp the wretched engine by the roots
That held my dearest Absalon to death!

[1] *Misprinted* wtetched *in* Isl.

Then let them tosse my broken lute to heauen,
Euen to his hands that beats me with the strings,   185
To shew how sadly his poore sheepeheard sings!

He goes to his pauillion and sits close a-while.

BETH.   Die, Bethsabe, to see thy Dauid mourne,
To heare his tunes of anguish and of hell!
O helpe! my Dauid, helpe thy Bethsabe,

She kneeles downe.

Whose heart is pierced with thy breathie [1] swords,   190
And bursts with burthen of tenne thousand greefes!
Now sits thy sorrowes sucking of my bloud :
O, that it might be poison to their powers,
And that their lips might draw my bosome drie,
So Dauids loue might ease him, though she die!   195
NAT.   These violent passions come not from aboue.
Dauid and Bethsabe offend the Highest
To mourne in this immeasurable sort.
DAU.   O Absalon, Absalon!   O my sonne, my sonne!
Would God that I had died for Absalon !   200
But he is dead! ah, dead! Absalon is dead,
And Dauid liues to die for Absalon !

He lookes forth, and at the end sits close againe.

Enter IOAB, ABISAY, ITHAY, *with their traine.*

IOAB.   Why lies the queene so prostrate on the ground?
Why is this companie so tragicke-hew'd?
Why is the king now absent from his men,   205
And marcheth not in triumph through the gates?

He vnfolds the pauillion.

Dauid, awake, if sleepe haue shut thine eies,
Sleepe of affection, that thou canst not see
The honour offerd to the victors head.
Ioab brings conquest pierced on his speare   210
And ioy from all the tribes of Israel.

───────────

[1] Mitford, *reviewing* D.'s *first edition, proposed* breathed words, *but* D. *properly refused to change the present reading.*

DAU.   Thou man of bloud! thou sepulchre of death,
Whose marble breast intombe[s] [1] my bowels quicke,
Did I not charge thee, nay intreat thy hand
Euen for my sake to spare my Absalon?   215
And hast thou now, in spite of Dauids health
And skorne to do my heart some happinesse,
Giuen him the sword, and spilt his purple soule?

IOAB.   What! irkes it Dauid that he victor breaths,
That Iuda and the fields of Israel   220
Should cleanse their faces from their childrens bloud?
What! art thou wearie of thy royall rule?
Is Israels throne a serpent in thine eyes,
And he that sets thee there so farre from thankes
That thou must curse his seruant for his sake?   225
Hast thou not said that as the morning light,
The cloudlesse morning, so should be thine house,
And not as flowers by the brightest raine,
Which growes vp quickly and as quickly fades?
Hast thou not said the wicked are as thornes,   230
That cannot be preserued [2] with the hand,
And that the man shall touch them must be armd
With coats of yron and garments made of steele
Or with the shaft of a defenced speare?
And art thou angrie he is now cut off   235
That led the guiltlesse swarming to their deaths,
And was more wicked then an host of men?
Aduance thee from thy melancholy denne,
And decke thy bodie with thy blisfull robes,
Or, by the Lord that swaies the heauen I sweare   240
Ile lead thine armies to another king
Shall cheere them for their princely chiualrie,
And not sit daunted, frowning, in the darke,
When his faire lookes, with oyle and wine refresht,
Should dart into their bosomes gladsome beames,   245
And fill their stomackes with triumphant feasts,
That when elsewhere sterne warre shall sound his trumpe

---

[1] *Corr. silently by* Haw.   [2] D. *suggests* repressed.

And call another battaile to the field,
Fame still may bring thy valiant souldiers home,
And for their seruice happily confesse   250
She wanted worthy trumpes to sound their prowesse.
Take thou this course, and liue; refuse, and die!

    ABISAY.   Come, brother; let him sit there till he sincke:
Some other shall aduance the name of Ioab.

Offers to goe out.

    BETH.   O, stay, my lords! stay; Dauid mournes no more, 255
But riseth to giue honour to your acts.

Stay. He riseth vp.

    DAUID.   Then happie art thou, Dauids fairest sonne,
That, freed from the yoke of earthly toiles
And sequestred from sence of humane sinnes,
Thy soule shall ioy the sacred cabinet   260
Of those deuine ideas that present
Thy changed spirit with a heauen of blisse.
Then thou art gone! ah, thou art gone, my sonne!
To heauen, I hope, my Absalon is gone.
Thy soule there plac'd in honour, of the saints   265
Or angels, clad with immortalitie,
Shall reape a seuenfold grace for all thy greefes.
Thy eyes, now no more eyes but shining stars,
Shall decke the flaming heauens with nouell lampes.
There shalt thou tast the drinke of seraphins   270
And cheere thy feelings with archangels food.
Thy day of rest, thy holy Sabboth day
Shall be eternall.   And, the curtaine drawne,
Thou shalt behold thy soueraigne face to face,
With wonder knit in triple vnitie,   275
Vnitie infinite and innumerable. —
Courage, braue captaines! Ioabs tale hath stird
And made the suit of Israel preferd.

    IOAB.   Brauely resolued, and spoken like a king!
Now may old Israel and his daughters sing!   280

Exeunt.

FINIS.

THE
SPANISH TRAGE-

die, Containing the lamentable

end of *Don Horatio*, and *Bel-imperia:*

with the pittifull death of

olde *Hieronimo.*

Newly corrected and amended of fuch groffe faults as

paffed in the firft imprefsion.

At London

Printed by *Edward Allde*, for

Edward White

487

Printed from the earliest extant edition, the titlepage of which is here reproduced, though not in facsimile. This edition is undated; it has been called the second edition, and so perhaps it is, but the titlepage proves only that it is not the first. In the footnotes it is indicated by A. Occasionally the readings of the editions of 1618, 1623, 1633 are given in the footnotes, the two first on the authority of Hawkins; but as these editions rarely, if ever, present a better text than A., their readings are in general omitted. There is no list of *Dramatis Personae* in A. or 1633.

[DRAMATIS PERSONAE.

GHOST OF ANDREA ⎫ *the Chorus.*
REVENGE ⎭

KING OF SPAIN.

VICEROY OF PORTUGAL.

DON CIPRIAN, *duke of Castile.*

HIERONIMO, *knight-marshall of Spain.*

BALTHAZAR, *the Viceroy's son.*

LORENZO, *Don Ciprian's son.*

HORATIO, *Hieronimo's son.*

ALEXANDRO ⎫ *lords of Portugal.*
VILLUPPO ⎭

PEDRINGANO, *servant of Bel-imperia.*

SERBERINE, *servant of Balthazar.*

Spanish General, Portuguese Embassador, Old Man, Painter Page, Hangman, Citizens, Soldiers, Attendants, &c.

BEL-IMPERIA, *Lorenzo's sister.*

ISABELLA, *Hieronimo's wife.*

SCENE: *Spain; and Portugal.*]

[THE SPANISH TRAGEDIE.]

Actvs Primvs.

Enter the GHOAST OF ANDREA, *and with him* REUENGE.

GHOAST.　When this eternall substance of my soule
Did liue imprisond in my wanton [1] flesh,
Ech in their function seruing others need,
I was a courtier in the Spanish court :
My name was Don Andrea ; my discent,　　　　　　　5
Though not ignoble, yet inferiour far
To gratious fortunes of my tender youth,
For there, in prime and pride of all my yeeres,
By duteous seruice and deseruing loue,
In secret I possest a worthy dame,　　　　　　　　10
Which hight sweet Bel-imperia by name.
But in the haruest of my sommer ioyes
Deaths winter nipt the blossomes of my blisse,
Forcing diuorce betwixt my loue and me ;
For in the late conflict with Portingale　　　　　　15
My valour drew me into dangers mouth
Till life to death made passage through my wounds.
When I was slaine, my soule descended straight
To passe the flowing streame of Acheron ;
But churlish Charon, only boatman there,　　　　　20
Said that, my rites of buriall not performde,
I might not sit amongst his passengers.
Ere Sol had slept three nights in Thetis lap,

[1] 1618, '23, '33, wonted.

489

And slakte his smoking charriot in her floud,
By Don [1] Horatio, our knight-marshals sonne,   25
My funerals and obsequies were done.
Then was the feriman of hell content
To passe me ouer to the slimie strond
That leades to fell Auernus ougly waues.
There, pleasing Cerberus with honied speech,   30
I past the perils of the formost porch.
Not farre from hence, amidst ten thousand soules,
Sate Minos, Eacus and Rhadamant;
To whome no sooner gan I make approch,
To craue a pasport for my wandring ghost,   35
But Minos in grauen leaues of lotterie
Drew forth the manner of my life and death.
"This knight," quoth he, "both liu'd and died in loue;
And for his loue tried fortune of the warres;
And by warres fortune lost both loue and life."   40
"Why then," said Eacus, "conuay him hence
To walke with louers in our fields of loue
And spend the course of euerlasting time
Vnder greene mirtle-trees and cipresse shades."
"No, no!" said Rhadamant, "it were not well   45
With louing soules to place a martialist.
He died in warre, and must to martiall fields,
Where wounded Hector liues in lasting paine,
And Achilles Mermedons do scoure the plaine."
Then Minos, mildest censor of the three,   50
Made this deuice, to end the difference:
"Send him," quoth he, "to our infernall king,
To dome him as best seemes his Maiestie."
To this effect my pasport straight was drawne.
In keeping on my way to Plutos court   55
Through dreadfull shades[2] of euer-glooming[3] night,
I saw more sights then thousand tongues can tell
Or pennes can write or mortall harts can think.

---

[1] A. 'Don.   [2] 1618, shapes.
[3] 1618, '23, '33, ever-blooming.

Three waies there were : that on the right hand side
Was ready way vnto the foresaid fields   60
Where louers liue and bloudie martialists,
But either sort contain within his bounds ;
The left hand path, declining fearfully,
Was ready downfall to the deepest hell,
Where bloudie Furies shakes their whips of steele,   65
And poore Ixion turnes an endles wheele,
Where vsurers are choakt with melting golde,
And wantons are imbraste with ougly snakes,
And murderers grone[1] with neuer-killing wounds,
And periurde wights scalded in boyling lead,   70
And all foule sinnes with torments ouerwhelmd ;
Twixt these two waies I trod the middle path,
Which brought me to the faire Elizian greene,
In midst whereof there standes a stately towre,
The walles of brasse, the gates of adamant.   75
Heere finding Pluto with his Proserpine,
I shewed my pasport, humbled on my knee.
Whereat faire Proserpine began to smile,
And[2] begd that onely she might giue my doome.
Pluto was pleasd, and sealde it with a kisse.   80
Forthwith, Reuenge, she rounded thee in th' eare,
And bad thee lead me through the gates of horn,[3]
Where dreames haue passage in the silent night.
No sooner had she spoke but we were heere,
I wot not how, in twinkling of an eye.   85
    REUENGE.   Then know, Andrea, that thou art ariu'd
Where thou shalt see the author of thy death,
Don Balthazar, the prince of Portingale,
Depriu'd of life by Bel-imperia :
Heere sit we downe to see the misterie,   90
And serue for Chorus in this tragedie.

[1] 1618, greeve, *according to* Haw.; *but he modernizes even his variant readings; the reading*, greene, *of* 1623, '33, *suggests that* 1618 *has* greeue.

[2] 1618, '23, '33, I.

[3] A. Hor; 1618, '23, '33, Horror; *corr. by* Haw.

[Act First.   Scene First.]

[The Spanish Court.]

Enter SPANISH KING, GENERALL, CASTILE, HIERONIMO.

KING.   Now say, l[ord] generall : how fares our campe?

GEN.   All wel, my soueraigne liege, except some few
That are deceast by fortune of the warre.

KING.   But what portends[1] thy cheerefull countenance
And posting to our presence thus in hast?   5
Speak, man : hath fortune giuen vs victorie?

GEN.   Victorie, my liege, and that with little losse.

KING.   Our Portingals will pay vs tribute then?

GEN.   Tribute, and wonted homage therewithall.

KING.   Then blest be Heauen, and Guider of the heauens,   10
From whose faire influence such iustice flowes!

CAST.   *O multum dilecte Deo, tibi militat aether,*
Et coniuratae[2] *curuato poplite*[3] *gentes*
Succumbunt : recti soror[4] *est victoria iuris!*

KING.   Thanks to my louing brother of Castile.   15
But, generall, vnfolde in breefe discourse
Your forme of battell and your warres successe,
That, adding all the pleasure of thy newes
Vnto the height of former happines,
With deeper wage and greater dignitie   20
We may reward thy blisfull chiualrie.

GEN.   Where Spaine and Portingale do ioyntly knit
Their frontiers, leaning on each others bound,
There met our armies in their proud aray :
Both furnisht well, both full of hope and feare,   25
Both menacing alike with daring showes,

---

[1] 1618, '23, '33, pretends, *which* Hazlitt, *in his edition of* Dodsley, *says
may be right, because* pretend *means* intend.

[2] A. coniurat œ.

[3] A. poplito.

[4] A. rectiforor ; Haw. *prints this Latin correctly, but gives no variants;
it is correctly printed in* 1633, *except* Succumbant *for* Succumbunt.

Both vaunting sundry colours of deuice,
Both cheerly sounding trumpets, drums and fifes,
Both raising dreadfull clamors to the skie,
That valleis, hils, and riuers made rebound　　　　　30
And heauen it-selfe was frighted with the sound.
Our battels both were pitcht in squadron forme,
Each corner strongly fenst with wings of shot ;
But, ere we ioynd and came to push of pike,
I brought a squadron of our readiest shot　　　　　35
From out our rearward to begin the fight;
They brought another wing to incounter vs ;
Meane-while our ordinance[1] plaid on either side,
And captaines stroue to haue their valours tride.
Don[2] Pedro, their chiefe horsemens corlonell,[3]　　40
Did with his cornet[4] brauely make attempt
To break the order of our battell rankes ;
But Don Rogero, worthy man of warre,
Marcht forth against him with our musketiers
And stopt the mallice of his fell approch.　　　　　45
While they maintaine hot skirmish too and fro,
Both battailes ioyne and fall to handie blowes,
Their violent shot resembling th' oceans rage
When, roaring lowd and with a swelling tide,
It beats vpon the rampiers of huge rocks,　　　　　50
And gapes to swallow neighbour-bounding lands.
Now, while Bellona rageth heere and there,
Thick stormes of bullets ran[5] like winters haile,
And shiuered launces darke[6] the troubled aire ;
Pede pes & cuspide cuspis,　　　　　　　　　　55
Arma[7] *sonant armis*[8] *vir petiturque viro ;*
On euery side drop[9] captaines to the ground,
And souldiers, some ill-maimde,[10] some slaine outright :

---

[1] 1633, ordnance, *to which* Haw. *corrects silently.*
[2] A. 'Don.　　　　　　　　　[6] 1618, '23, '33, dark'd.
[3] 1633, coronell; Haw. colonel, *without note.*
[4] 1618, '23, '33, coronet.　　[7] A. Anni.　　　　[8] A. annis.
[5] *Qy.* run.　　　　　　　　　[9] 1618, '23, '33, dropt.
[10] 1618, '23, '33, And souldiers ly maim'd.

Heere falles a body sundred from his head ;
There legs and armes lye bleeding on the grasse,   60
Mingled with weapons and vnboweld steeds,
That scattering ouer-spread the purple plaine.
In all this turmoyle, three long hovres and more
The victory to neither part inclinde,
Till Don Andrea with his braue launciers   65
In their maine battell made so great a breach
That, halfe dismaid, the multitude retirde.
But Balthazar, the Portingales young prince,
Brought rescue and encouragde them to stay.
Heere-hence the fight was eagerly renewd,   70
And in that conflict was Andrea slaine, —
Braue man-at-armes, but weake to Balthazar.
Yet, while the prince, insulting ouer him,
Breathd out proud vaunts, sounding to our reproch,
Friendship and hardie valour ioynd in one   75
Prickt forth Horatio, our knight-marshals sonne,
To challenge forth that prince in single fight.
Not long betweene these twaine the fight indurde,
But straight the prince was beaten from his horse
And forcst to yeeld him prisoner to his foe.   80
When he was taken, all the rest they fled,
And our carbines pursued them to the death,
Till, Phoebus waning [1] to the western deepe,
Our trumpeters were chargde to sound retreat.
    KING.   Thanks, good l[ord] generall, for these good newes!   85
And, for some argument of more to come,
Take this and weare it [2] for thy soueraignes sake.

Giue him his chaine.

But tell me now : hast thou confirmd a peace?
    GEN.   No peace, my liege, but peace conditionall,
That, if with homage tribute be well paid,   90
The fury of your forces wilbe staide.
And to this peace their viceroy hath subscribde,

---

[1] 1633, Haw. waving.   [2] 1633 *omits* it.

Giue the K[ING] *a paper.*

And made a solemne vow that during life
His tribute shalbe truely paid to Spaine.

 KING. These words, these deeds become thy person wel. 95
But now, knight-marshall, frolike with thy king,
For tis thy sonne that winnes this battels prize.

 HIERO. Long may he liue to serue my soueraigne liege!
And soone decay vnlesse he serue my liege!

A tucket[1] *a-farre off.*

 KING. Nor thou nor he shall dye without reward. 100
What meanes this warning of this trumpets sound?

 GEN. This tels me that your Graces men of warre,
Such as warres fortune hath reseru'd from death,
Come marching on towards your royall seate,
To show themselues before your Maiestie; 105
For so I gaue in[2] charge at my depart.
Whereby by demonstration shall appeare
That all, except three hundred or few more,
Are safe returnd and by their foes inricht.

The armie enters, BALTHAZAR *betweene* LORENZO *and* HORATIO, *captiue.*

 KING. A gladsome sight! I long to see them heere. 110

They enter and passe by.

Was that the warlike prince of Portingale
That by our nephew was in triumph led?

 GEN. It was, my liege, the prince of Portingale.

 KING. But what was he that on the other side
Held him by th' arme as partner of the prize? 115

 HIERO. That was my sonne, my gratious soueraigne;
Of whome though from his tender infancie
My louing thoughts did neuer hope but well,
He neuer pleasd his fathers eyes till now,
Nor fild my hart with ouercloying ioyes. 120

---

[1] 1618, '23, '33, trumpet.
[2] 1618, '23, '33, them: *a mere unauthorized modernization, like many of the variants of these editions.*

KING.　Goe, let them march once more about these walles,
That staying them we may conferre and talke
With our braue prisoner and his double guard.

[Exit a MESSENGER.]

Hieronimo, it greatly pleaseth vs
That in our victorie thou haue a share　　　　　　125
By vertue of thy worthy sonnes exploit.

Enter againe.

Bring hether the young prince of Portingale!
The rest martch on, but, ere they be dismist,
We will bestow on euery souldier
Two duckets, and on euery leader ten,　　　　　　130
That they may know our largesse welcomes them.[1]

Exeunt all [the army] but BAL[THAZAR], LOR[ENZO], HOR[ATIO].[2]

[KING.]　Welcome, Don Balthazar! welcome nephew!
And thou, Horatio, thou art welcome too !
Young prince, although thy fathers hard misdeedes
In keeping backe the tribute that he owes　　　　135
Deserue but euill measure at our hands,
Yet shalt thou know that Spaine is honorable.
　BALT.　The trespasse that my father made in peace
Is now controlde by fortune of the warres ;
And cards once dealt, it bootes not aske why so.　140
His men are slaine, — a weakening to his realme ;
His colours ceaz'd, — a blot vnto his name ;
His sonne distrest, — a corsiue to his hart :
These punishments may cleare his late offence.
　KING.　I, Balthazar, if he obserue this truce,　　145
Our peace will grow the stronger for these warres.
Meane-while liue thou, though not in libertie,
Yet free from bearing any seruile yoake ;
For in our hearing thy deserts were great,
And in our sight thy-selfe art gratious.　　　　　150
　BALT.　And I shall studie to deserue this grace.

---

[1] *In* A. 1633, Haw. *these three lines are so arranged as to end with*
duckets, know, them.　　　　　　[2] A. Flor.

KING.   But tell me, — for their holding makes me doubt:
To which of these twaine art thou prisoner?
LOR.   To me, my liege.
HOR.   To me, my soueraigne.
LOR.   This hand first tooke his courser by the raines.   155
HOR.   But first my launce did put him from his horse.
LOR.   I ceaz'd his weapon and enioyde it first.
HOR.   But first I forc'd him lay his weapons downe.
KING.   Let goe his arme, vpon our priviledge !

Let him goe.

Say, worthy prince : to whether didst thou yeeld?   160
BALT.   To him in curtesie ; to this perforce :
He spake me faire, this other gaue me strokes ;
He promisde life, this other threatned death ;
He wan my loue, this other conquerd me ;
And, truth to say, I yeeld my-selfe to both.   165
HIERO.   But that I know[1] your Grace for iust and wise,
And might seeme partiall in this difference,
Inforct by nature and by law of armes,
My tongue should plead for young Horatios right.
He hunted well that was a lyons death,   170
Not he that in a garment wore his skin ;
So hares may pull dead lyons by the beard.
KING.   Content thee, marshall ; thou shalt haue no wrong,
And for thy sake thy sonne shall want no right.
Will both abide the censure of my doome?   175
LOR.   I craue no better then your Grace awards.
HOR.   Nor I, although I sit beside my right.
KING.   Then by my iudgement thus your strife shall end :
You both deserue and both shall haue reward.
Nephew, thou tookst his weapons[2] and his horse :   180
His weapons and his horse are thy reward.
Horatio, thou didst force him first to yeeld :
His ransome therefore is thy valours fee ;
Appoint the sum as you shall both agree.

----

[1] A. knaw; 1633, know.   [2] *So* 1633; A. weapon.

But, nephew, thou shalt haue the prince in guard,   185
For thine estate best fitteth such a guest;
Horatios house were small for all his traine.
Yet, in regarde thy substance passeth his,
And that iust guerdon may befall desert,
To him we yeeld the armour of the prince.   190
How likes Don Balthazar of this deuice?
    BALT.   Right well, my liege, if this prouizo were:
That Don Horatio beare vs company,
Whome I admire and loue for chiualrie.
    KING.   Horatio, leaue him not that loues thee so.   195
Now let vs hence, to see our souldiers paide,
And feast our prisoner as our friendly guest.

                              Exeunt.

[Act First. Scene Second.]

[Portugal: the VICEROY'S *palace.]*

Enter VICEROY, ALEXANDRO, VILLUPPO.[1]

    VICE.   Is our embassadour dispatcht for Spaine?
    ALEX.   Two daies, my liege, are past since his depart.
    VICE.   And tribute paiment gone along with him?
    ALEX.   I, my good lord.
    VICE.   Then rest we heere a-while in our vnrest;   5
And feed our sorrowes with some inward sighes,
For deepest cares break neuer into teares.
But wherefore sit I in a regall throne?
This better fits a wretches endles moane.
Yet this is higher then my fortunes reach,   10
And therefore better then my state deserues.

               Falles to the ground.

I, I, this earth, image of mellancholly,
Seeks him whome fates adiudge [2] to miserie!

---

[1] 1633 *regularly spells this name with* i *instead of* u.
[2] A. aduidge.

Heere let me lye! Now am I[1] at the lowest!
Qvi iacet in terra non habet vnde cadat.   15
In me consumpsit vires fortuna nocendo,
Nil[2] superest vt iam possit obesse magis.
Yes, Fortune may bereaue me of my crowne, —
Heere, take it now; let Fortune doe her worst,
She will not rob me of this sable weed.   20
O, no, she enuies none but pleasant things.
Such is the folly of despightfull chance,
Fortune is blinde and sees not my deserts,
So is she deafe and heares not my laments;
And, could she heare, yet is she wilfull mad,   25
And therefore will not pittie my distresse.
Suppose that she could pittie me, what then?
What helpe can be expected at her hands
Whose foot is[3] standing on a rowling stone
And minde more mutable then fickle windes?   30
Why waile I, then, wheres hope of no redresse?
O, yes, complaining makes my greefe seeme lesse.
My late ambition hath distaind my faith,
My breach of faith occasioned bloudie warres,
Those bloudie warres haue spent my treasur[i]e,   35
And with my treasur[i]e my peoples blood,
And with their blood my ioy and best beloued, —
My best beloued, my sweet and onely sonne!
O, wherefore went I not to warre my-selfe?
The cause was mine; I might haue died for both.   40
My yeeres were mellow, his but young and greene:
My death were naturall, but his was forced.

   ALEX.   No doubt, my liege, but still the prince suruiues.
   VICE.   Suruiues! I, where?
   ALEX.   In Spaine, a prisoner by mischance of warre.   45
   VICE.   Then they haue slaine him for his fathers fault.
   ALEX.   That were a breach to common law of armes.
   VICE.   They recke no lawes that meditate reuenge.

---

[1] 1633, now I am, *which changes the construction, perhaps for the better.*
[2] 1633, Nihil.   [3] *Not in* A. 1633; *supplied silently by* Haw.

ALEX.   His ransomes worth will stay from foule reuenge.

VICE.   No ; if he liued, the newes would soone be heere.   50

ALEX.   Nay, euill newes flie faster still than good.

VICE.   Tell me no more of newes, for he is dead.

VILLUP.   My soueraign, pardon the author of ill newes,
And Ile bewray the fortune of thy sonne.

VICE.   Speake on ; Ile guerdon thee, what-ere it be.   55
Mine eare is ready to receiue ill newes,
My hart growne hard gainst mischiefes battery ;
Stand vp, I say, and tell thy tale at large.

VILLUP.   Then heare that truth which these mine eies
           haue seene :
When both the armies were in battell ioynd,   60
Don Balthazar amidst the thickest troupes,
To winne renowme,[1] did wondrous feats of armes ;
Amongst the rest I saw him hand-to-hand
In single fight with their lord generall,
Till Alexandro, that heere counterfeits   65
Vnder the colour of a duteous freend,
Discharged his pistoll at the princes back,
As though he would haue slaine their generall,
But therwithall Don Balthazar fell downe ;
And when he fell, then we began to flie ;   70
But, had he liued, the day had sure bene ours.

ALEX.   O wicked forgerie ! O traiterous miscreant !

VICE.   Hold thou thy peace ! But now, Villuppo, say :
Where then became the carkasse of my sonne?

VILLUP.   I saw them drag it to the Spanish tents.   75

VICE.   I, I, my nightly dreames haue tolde me this !
Thou false, vnkinde, vnthankfull, traiterous beast !
Wherein had Balthazar offended thee,
That thou shouldst thus betray him to our foes ?
Wast Spanish golde that bleared so thine eyes   80
That thou couldst see no part of our deserts?
Perchance, because thou art Terseraes lord,
Thou hadst some hope to weare this diademe [2]

---

[1] *Misprinted* remowne *in* A.   [2] *Misprinted* diadome *in* A.

If first my sonne and then my-selfe were slaine ;
But thy ambitious thought shall breake thy neck.   85
I, this was it that made thee spill his bloud !

Take [1] *the crowne and put* [1] *it on againe.*

But Ile now weare it till thy bloud be spilt.
   ALEX.   Vouchsafe, dread [2] soueraigne, to heare me speak!
   VICE.   Away with him! his sight is second hell!
Keepe him till we determine of his death.   90
If Balthazar be dead, he shall not liue.

[They take him out.]

Villuppo, follow vs for thy reward.   *Exit* VICE[ROY].
   VILLUP.   Thus haue I with an enuious forged tale
Deceiued the king, betraid mine enemy,
And hope for guerdon of my villany.   *Exit.*   95

[Act First.   Scene Third.]

[Spain: the palace.]

Enter HORATIO *and* BEL-IMPERIA.

   BEL.   Signior Horatio, this is the place and houre
Wherein I must intreat thee to relate
The circumstance of Don Andreas death,
Who liuing was my garlands sweetest flower,
And in his death hath buried my delights.   5
   HOR.   For loue of him and seruice to your-selfe,
I nill [3] refuse this heauy dolefull charge ;
Yet teares and sighes, I feare, will hinder me.
When both our armies were enioynd in fight,
Your worthie chiualier amidst the thikst,   10
For glorious cause still aiming at the fairest,
Was at the last by yong Don Balthazar
Encountred hand-to-hand.   Their fight was long,

---

[1] 1633, Haw. He takes . . . puts ; *so also the editors of* Dodsley, *but they*
(including Hazlitt) *seem usually to have neglected to collate plays printed*
by Hawkins.   [2] 1618, '23, '33, deare.   [3] 1618, '23, '33, Ile not.

Their harts were great, their clamours menacing,
Their strength alike, their strokes both dangerous;   15
But wrathfull Nemesis, that wicked power,
Enuying at Andreas praise and worth,
Cut short his life to end his praise and woorth.
She, she her-selfe, disguisde in armours maske,
As Pallas was before proud Pergamus,   20
Brought in a fresh supply of halberdiers,
Which pauncht his horse and dingd him to the ground.
Then yong Don Balthazar, with ruthles rage,
Taking aduantage of his foes distresse,
Did finish what his halberdiers begun;   25
And left not till Andreas life was done.
Then, though too late, incenst with iust remorce,
I with my band set foorth against the prince,
And brought him prisoner from his halba[r]diers.
    BEL.   Would thou hadst slaine him that so slew my loue!   30
But then was Don Andreas carkasse lost?
    HOR.   No; that was it for which I cheefely stroue,
Nor stept I back till I recouerd him.
I tooke him vp, and wound him in mine armes,
And, welding him vnto my priuate tent,   35
There laid him downe and dewd him with my teares,
And sighed and sorrowed as became a freend.
But neither freendly sorrow,[1] sighes nor teares
Could win pale Death from his vsurped right.
Yet this I did, and lesse I could not doe: 40
I saw him honoured with due funerall.
This scarfe I pluckt from off [2] his liueles arme,
And wear it in remembrance of my freend.
    BEL.   I know the scarfe: would he had kept it still!
For, had he liued, he would haue kept it still,   45
And worne it for his Bel-imperias sake;
For twas my fauour at his last depart.

────────

    [1] *Here, as often, the later editions change a singular noun to the plural
for the sake of uniformity.*
    [2] 1618, '23, '33, This scarfe pluckt off from.

But now weare thou it both for him and me;
For, after him, thou hast deserued it best.
But, for thy kindnes in his life and death,   50
Be sure, while Bel-imperias life endures,
She will be Don Horatios thankfull freend.
   HOR. And, madame, Don Horatio will not slacke
Humbly to serue faire Bel-imperia.
But now, if your good liking stand thereto,   55
Ile craue your pardon to goe seeke the prince;
For so the duke, your father, gaue me charge.   *Exit.*[1]
   BEL. I, goe, Horatio; leaue me heere alone,
For sollitude best fits my cheereles mood. —
Yet what auailes to waile Andreas death,   60
From whence Horatio proues my second loue?
Had he not loued Andrea as he did,
He could not sit in Bel-imperias thoughts.
But how can loue finde harbour in my brest,
Till I reuenge the death of my beloued?   65
Yes, second loue shall further my reuenge:
Ile loue Horatio, my Andreas freend,
The more to spight the prince that wrought his end;
And, where Don Balthazar, that slew my loue,
Himselfe now pleades for fauour at my hands,   70
He shall, in rigour of my iust disdaine,
Reape long repentance for his murderous deed, —
For what wast els but murderous cowardise,
So many to oppresse one valiant knight,
Without respect of honour in the fight?   75
And heere he comes that murdred my delight.

Enter LORENZO *and* BALTHAZAR.

   LOR. Sister, what meanes this melanchollie walke?
   BEL. That for a-while I wish no company.
   LOR. But heere the prince is come to visite you.
   BEL. That argues that he liues in libertie.   80

---

[1] *This* Exit, *like most stage-directions in the old editions, is two lines too high; Haw., as usual, transfers it.*

BAL. No, madame ; but in pleasing seruitude.
BEL. Your prison then, belike, is your conceit.
BAL. I, by conceit my freedome is enthralde.
BEL. Then with conceite enlarge your-selfe againe.
BAL. What if conceite haue laid my hart to gage?   85
BEL. Pay that you borrowed, and recouer it.
BAL. I die if it returne from whence it lyes.
BEL. A hartles man, and liue?[1] A miracle!
BAL. I, lady, loue can worke such miracles.
LOR. Tush, tush, my lord! let goe these ambages,   90
And in plaine tearmes acquaint her with your loue.
BEL. What bootes complaint, when thers no remedy?
BAL. Yes, to your gratious selfe must I complaine,
In whose faire answere lyes my remedy,
On whose perfection all my thoughts attend,   95
On whose aspect mine eyes finde beauties bowre,
In whose translucent brest my hart is lodgde.
BEL. Alas, my lord! these are but words of course,
And but deuise [2] to driue me from this place.

She, in going in, lets fall her gloue, which HORATIO, *comming out, takes*[3]
vp.

HOR. Madame, your gloue.   100
BEL. Thanks, good Horatio ; take it for thy paines.
BAL. Signior Horatio stoopt in happie time!
HOR. I reapt more grace then I deseru'd or hop'd.
LOR. My lord, be not dismaid for what is past ;
You know that women oft are humerous :   105
These clouds will ouerblow with little winde ;
Let me alone, Ile scatter them my-selfe.
Meane-while let vs deuise to spend the time
In some delightfull [4] sports and reuelling.
HOR. The king, my lords, is comming hither straight   110
To feast the Portingall embassadour ;

[1] 1618, '23, '33, liues, *which* Haz. *prefers and adopts. Here, and in
similar cases, I give the spelling of* 1633, *the only one of these three editions
that I have seen.*   [3] 1633 *has a superfluous* it.
[2] 1618, '23, '33, deuis'd.   [4] 1618, '23, '33, delightsome.

Things were in readines before I came.

BAL.   Then heere it fits vs to attend the king,
To welcome hither our embassadour,
And learne my father and my countries health.   115

Enter the banquet, TRUMPETS, *the* KING, *and* EMBASSADOUR.

KING.   See, lord embassador, how Spaine intreats
Their prisoner Balthazar, thy viceroyes sonne :
We pleasure more in kindenes then in warres.

EMBASS.   Sad is our king, and Portingale laments,
Supposing that Don Balthazar is slaine.   120

BAL. [*aside*]   So am I, slaine by beauties tirannie! —
You see, my lord, how Balthazar is slaine :
I frolike with the Duke of Castiles sonne,
Wrapt euery houre in pleasures of the court,[1]
And graste with fauours of his Maiestie.   125

KING.   Put off your greetings till our feast be done ;
Now come and sit with vs, and taste our cheere.

Sit to the banquet.

Sit downe, young prince, you are our second guest ;
Brother, sit downe ; and, nephew, take your place ;
Signior Horatio, waite thou vpon our cup,   130
For well thou hast deserued to be honored.
Now, lordings, fall too : Spaine is Portugall,[2]
And Portugall[2] is Spaine ; we both are freends ;
Tribute is paid, and we enioy our right.
But where is olde Hieronimo, our marshall?   135
He promised[3] vs, in honor of our guest,
To grace our banquet with some pompous iest.

Enter HIERONIMO *with a* DRUM, *three* KNIGHTS, *each his scutchin; then
he fetches three* KINGS; *they take their crownes and them captiue.*

Hieronimo, this maske contents mine eie,
Although I sound not well the misterie.

---

[1] *In* 1633 *this word has slipped up into the preceding line.*
[2] *So* A.; 1633, Haw. Portingale.
[3] *Misprinted* pcomised *in* A.

HIERO.   The first arm'd knight that hung his scutchin vp   140

He takes the scutchin and giues it to the KING.

Was English Robert, Earle of Glocester,
Who, when King Stephen bore sway in Albion,
Arriued with fiue and twenty thousand men
In Portingale, and, by successe of warre,
Enforced the king, then but a Sarasin,   145
To beare the yoake of the English monarchie.
    KING.   My lord of Portingale, by this you see
That which may comfort both your king and you,
And make your late discomfort seeme the lesse.
But say, Hieronimo : what was the next?   150
    HIERO.   The second knight that hung his scutchin vp

He doth as he did before.

Was Edmond, Earle of Kent in Albion.
When English Richard wore the diadem,
He came likewise and razed Lisbon walles,
And tooke the king of Portingale in fight, —   155
For which, and other such like seruice done,
He after was created Duke of Yorke.
    KING.   This is another speciall argument
That Portingale may daine to beare our yoake,
When it by little England hath beene yoakt.   160
But now, Hieronimo, what were the last?
    HIERO.   The third and last, not least in our account,

Dooing as before.

Was, as the rest, a valiant Englishman,
Braue Iohn of Gaunt, the Duke of Lancaster,
As by his scutchin plainely may appeare :   165
He with a puissant armie came to Spaine
And tooke our King of Castile prisoner.
    EMBASS.   This is an argument for our viceroy
That Spaine may not insult for her successe,
Since English warriours likewise conquered Spaine   170
And made them bow their knees to Albion.

KING.   Hieronimo, I drinke [1] to thee for this deuise,
Which hath pleasde both the embassador and me :
Pledge me, Hieronimo, if thou loue the king !

Takes the cup of HORATIO.

My lord, I feare we sit but ouer-long,   175
Vnlesse our dainties were more delicate, —
But welcome are you.to the best we haue.
Now let vs in, that you [2] may be dispatcht ;
I think our councell is already set.

Exeunt omnes.

[CHORUS.]

ANDREA.   Come we for this from depth of vnder ground, —
To see him feast that gaue me my deaths wound ?
These pleasant sights are sorrow to my soule :
Nothing but league and loue and banqueting !
REUENGE.   Be still, Andrea ; ere we goe from hence,   5
Ile turne their freendship into fell despight,
Their loue to mortall hate, their day to night,
Their hope into dispaire, their peace to warre,
Their ioyes to paine, their blisse to miserie.

Actus Secundus.   [Scene First.]

[*The* DUKE'S *castle.*]

Enter LORENZO *and* BALTHAZAR.

LORENZO.   My lord, though Bel-imperia seeme thus coy,
Let reason holde you in your wonted ioy :
In time the sauage bull sustaines the yoake,
In time all haggard hawkes will stoope to lure,
In time small wedges cleaue the hardest oake,   5
In time the flint [3] is pearst with softest shower ;
And she in time will fall from her disdaine,
And rue [4] the suffèrance of your freendly paine.

---

[1] *Misprinted* dtinke *in* A.   [3] 1618, '23, '33, In time the hardest flint.
[2] 1618, '23, '33, we.   [4] 1618, '23, '33, rule.

BAL.   No; she is wilder, and more hard withall,
Then beast or bird, or tree or stony wall !   10
But wherefore blot I Bel-imperias name?
It is my fault, not she that merits blame.
My feature is not to content her sight;
My wordes[1] are rude and worke her no delight;
The lines I send her are but harsh and ill,   15
Such as doe drop from Pan and Marsias[2] quill;
My presents are not of sufficient cost;
And, being worthles, all my labours lost.
Yet might she loue me for my valiancie.
I ; but thats slaundred by captiuitie.   20
Yet might she loue me to content her sire.
I ; but her reason masters his[3] desire.
Yet might she loue me as her brothers freend.
I ; but her hopes aime at some other end.
Yet might she loue me to vpreare her state.   25
I ; but perhaps she hopes[4] some nobler mate.
Yet might she loue me as her beauties[5] thrall.
I ; but I feare she cannot loue at all.
      LOR.   My lord, for my sake leaue these extasies,
And doubt not but weele finde some remedie.   30
Some cause there is that lets you not be loued :
First that must needs be knowne, and then remoued.
What if my sister loue some other knight?
      BALT.   My sommers day will turne to winters night.
      LOR.   I haue already found a stratageme   35
To sound the bottome of this doubtfull theame.
My lord, for once you shall be rulde by me;
Hinder me not what ere you heare or see :
By force or faire meanes will I cast about
To finde the truth of all this question out.   40
Ho, Pedringano !

---

[1] A. wodres.   [2] 1618, ’23, ’33, Marses.
[3] 1618, ’23, ’33, her; *possibly* fire *was read* fire (l. 21), *and* his *then became unintelligible; but* 1633 *has* Sire.   [4] 1623, ’33, loues.
[5] A. beauteous; *corr. silently by* Haw.; 1633, Beauties.

PED.   Signior.
LOR.   *Vien qui¹ presto !*

Enter PEDRINGANO.

PED.   Hath your lordship any seruice to command me?
LOR.   I, Pedringano, seruice of import.
And, not to spend the time in trifling words,
Thus stands the case : it is not long, thou knowst,   45
Since I did shield thee from my fathers wrath
For thy conueiance in Andreas loue,
For which thou wert adiudg'd to punishment;
I stood betwixt thee and thy punishment,
And since thou knowest how I haue fauoured thee.   50
Now to these fauours will I adde reward,²
Not with faire woords, but store of golden coyne
And lands and liuing ioynd with dignities,
If thou but satisfie my iust demaund ;
Tell truth and haue me for thy lasting freend.   55
    PED.   What-ere it be your lordship shall demaund,
My bounden duety bids me tell the truth,
If case it lye in me to tell the truth.
    LOR.   Then, Pedringano, this is my demaund :
Whome loues my sister Bel-imperia?   60
For she reposeth all her trust in thee.
Speak, man, and gaine both freendship and reward :
I meane, whome loues she in Andreas place?
    PED.   Alas, my lord, since Don Andreas death
I haue no credit with her as before,   65
And therefore know not if she loue or no.
    LOR.   Nay, if thou dally, then I am thy foe,
And feare shall force what frendship cannot winne.
Thy death shall bury what thy life conceales.
Thou dyest for more esteeming her then me!   70

[Draws his sword.]

PED.   Oh stay, my lord !

¹ A. 1633, Haw. que; *corr. silently in* Collier-Dodsley.
² A. addereward.

LOR.   Yet speak the truth, and I will guerdon thee
And shield thee from what-euer can ensue,
And will conceale what-ere proceeds from thee ;
But, if thou dally once againe, thou diest !   75
    PED.   If madame Bel-imperia be in loue —
    LOR.   What, villaine ! ifs and ands?
    PED.   O stay, my lord ! she loues Horatio.

                BALTHAZAR *starts back.*

    LOR.   What ! Don Horatio, our knight-marshals sonne?
    PED.   Euen him, my lord.   80
    LOR.   Now say but how knowest thou he is her loue,
And thou shalt finde me kinde and liberall.
Stand vp, I say, and feareles tell the truth.
    PED.   She sent him letters, — which my-selfe perusde, —
Full-fraught with lines and arguments of loue,   85
Preferring him before Prince Balthazar.
    LOR.   Sweare on this crosse that what thou saiest is true,
And that thou wilt conseale what thou hast tolde.
    PED.   I sweare to both, by him that made vs all.
    LOR.   In hope thine oath is true, heeres thy reward.   90
But, if I proue thee periurde and vniust,
This very sword whereon thou tookst thine oath
Shall be the worker of thy tragedie.
    PED.   What I haue saide is true, and shall, for me,
Be still conceald from Bel-imperia.   95
Besides, your Honors liberalitie
Deserues my duteous seruice euen till death.
    LOR.   Let this be all that thou shalt doe for me :
Be watchfull when and where these louers meete,
And giue me notice in some secret sort.   100
    PED.   I will, my lord.
    LOR.   Then shalt thou finde that I am liberall.
Thou knowst that I can more aduaunce thy state
Then she : be therefore wise and faile me not.
Goe and attend her as thy custome is,   105
Least absence make her think thou doost amisse.

                          Exit PEDRINGANO.

Why, so, *Tam armis quam ingenio* :
Where words preuaile not, violence preuailes.
But golde doth more than either of them both.
How likes Prince Balthazar this stratageme?   110
 BAL.   Both well and ill ; it makes me glad and sad :
Glad, that I know the hinderer of my loue ;
Sad, that I feare she hates me whome I loue ;
Glad, that I know on whom to be reueng'd ;
Sad, that sheele flie me if I take reuenge.   115
Yet must I take reuenge or dye my-selfe ;
For loue resisted growes impatient.
I think Horatio be my destinde plague :
First, in his hand he brandished a sword,
And with that sword he fiercely waged warre,   120
And in that warre he gaue me dangerous wounds,
And by those wounds he forced me to yeeld,
And by my yeelding I became his slaue ;
Now, in his mouth he carries pleasing words,
Which pleasing wordes doe harbour sweet conceits,   125
Which sweet conceits are lim'd with slie deceits,[1]
Which slie deceits smooth Bel-imperias eares,
And through her eares diue downe into her hart,
And in her hart set him, where I should stand.
Thus hath he tane my body by his force,   130
And now by sleight would captiuate my soule ;
But in his fall Ile tempt[2] the Destinies,
And either loose my life or winne my loue.
 LOR.   Lets goe, my lord ; your[3] staying staies reuenge.
Doe you but follow me, and gaine your loue ;   135
Her fauour must be wonne by his remooue.
          Exeunt.

---

[1] Haw.'s *statement that* 1618, '23, '33 *omit this line is inaccurate, at least in regard to* 1633, *which omits* are lim'd with slie deceits, Which slie deceits.   [2] A. temft.   [3] 1633, our.

[Act Second.   Scene Second.]

[The DUKE's *castle.]*

Enter HORATIO *and* BEL-IMPERIA.

HOR.   Now, madame, since by fauour of your loue
Our hidden smoke is turnd to open flame,
And that with lookes and words we feed our thought, —
Two chiefe contents where more cannot be had, —
Thus in the midst of loues faire blandeshments   5
Why shew you signe of inward languishments?

PEDRINGANO *sheweth all to the* PRINCE *and* LORENZO, *placing them in secret.*

BEL.   My hart, sweet freend, is like a ship at sea :
She wisheth port, where, riding all at ease,
She may[1] repaire what stormie times haue worne,
And, leaning on the shore, may sing with ioy   10
That pleasure followes paine, and blisse annoy.
Possession of thy loue is th' onely port
Wherein my hart, with feares and hopes long tost,
Each howre doth wish and long to make resort,
There to repaire the ioyes that it hath lost,   15
And, sitting safe, to sing in Cupids quire
That sweetest blisse is crowne of loues desire.

BALTHAZAR, *aboue.*[2]

BAL.   O sleepe, mine eyes ; see not my loue prophande !
Be deafe, my eares ; heare not my discontent !
Dye, hart ; another ioyes what thou deseruest !   20
LOR.   Watch still, mine eyes, to see this loue disioyned !
Heare still, mine eares, to heare them both lament !
Liue,[3] hart, to ioy at fond Horatios fall !
BEL.   Why stands Horatio speecheles all this while?

---

[1] A. mad; 1633, may ; *corr. silently by* Haw.
[2] Lorenzo, *of course, is with him, and their speeches are supposed not to be heard by* Horatio *and* Bel-imperia.
[3] 1618, '23, '33, Leave.

Hor.	The lesse I speak, the more I meditate.	25
Bel.	But whereon doost thou chiefely meditate?	
Hor.	On dangers past and pleasures to ensue.	
Bal.	On pleasures past and dangers to ensue!	
Bel.	What dangers and what plesures doost thou mean?	
Hor.	Dangers of warre and pleasures of our loue.	30
Lor.	Dangers of death, but pleasures none at all!	
Bel.	Let dangers goe ; thy warre shall be with me,	

But such a warring[1] as breakes no bond of peace.
Speak thou faire words, Ile crosse them with faire words ;
Send thou sweet looks, Ile meet them with sweet looks ;   35
Write louing lines, Ile answere louing lines ;
Giue me a kisse, Ile counterchecke thy kisse :
Be this our warring peace, or peacefull warre.

Hor.   But, gratious madame, then appoint the field
Where triall of this warre shall first be made.   40

Bal.   Ambitious villaine, how his boldenes growes !

Bel.   Then be thy fathers pleasant bower the field, —
Where first we vowd a mutuall amitie.
The court were dangerous ; that place is safe.
Our howre shalbe when Vesper ginnes to rise,   45
That summons home distresfull[2] trauellers.
There none shall heare vs but the harmeles birds :
Happelie the gentle nightingale
Shall carroll vs a-sleepe ere we be ware,
And, singing with the prickle at her breast,   50
Tell our delight and mirthfull[3] dalliance.
Till then, each houre will seeme a yeere and more.

Hor.   But, honie-sweet and honorable loue,
Returne we now into your fathers sight ;
Dangerous suspition waits on our delight.   55

Lor.   I, danger mixt[4] with iealous despite
Shall send thy soule into eternall night!

Exeunt.

---

[1] *Qy.* warre ; *but* 1633 *also has* warring.
[2] 1623, '33. distressed.   [3] 1623, '33, sportfull.
[4] *Qy.* mixëd ; *but* 1633 *has* mixt ; Kittredge *suggests* iealious, *which is better.*

[Act Second. Scene Third.]

[The Spanish court.]

Enter KING OF SPAINE, PORTINGALE EMBASSADOUR, DON CIPRIAN, *&c.*

KING.   Brother of Castile, to the princes loue
What saies your daughter Bel-imperia?
CIP.   Although she coy it, as becomes her kinde,
And yet dissemble that she loues the prince,
I doubt not, I, but she will stoope in time;   5
And, were she froward, — which she will not be, —
Yet heerein shall she follow my aduice,
Which is to loue him or forgoe my loue.
KING.   Then, lord embassadour of Portingale,
Aduise thy king to make this marriage vp   10
For strengthening of our late-confirmed league;
I know no better meanes to make vs freends.
Her dowry shall be large and liberall;
Besides that she is daughter and halfe heire
Vnto our brother heere, Don Ciprian,   15
And shall enioy the moitie of his land,
Ile grace her marriage with an vnckles gift,
And this it is: in case the match goe forward,
The tribute which you pay shalbe releast;
And, if by Balthazar she haue a sonne,   20
He shall enioy the kingdome after vs.
EMBAS.   Ile make the motion to my soueraigne liege,
And worke it if my counsaile may preuaile.
KING.   Doe so, my lord; and, if he giue consent,
I hope his presence heere will honour vs   25
In celebration of the nuptiall day, —
And let himselfe determine of the time.
EM.   Wilt please your Grace command me ought besid?
KING.   Commend me to the king; and so, farewell!
But wheres Prince Balthazar, to take his leaue?   30
EM.   That is perfourmd alreadie, my good lord.

KING. Amongst the rest of what you haue in charge,
The princes raunsome must not be forgot:
Thats none of mine, but his that tooke him prisoner, —
And well his forwardnes deserues reward: 35
It was Horatio, our knight-marshals sonne.
    EM. Betweene vs theres a price already pitcht,
And shall be sent with all conuenient[1] speed.
    KING. Then once againe farewell, my lord!
    EM. Farwell, my lord of Castile, and the rest!   *Exit.* 40
    KING. Now, brother, you must take some little paines
To winne faire Bel-imperia from her will:
Young virgins must be ruled by their freends.
The prince is amiable, and loues her well;
If she neglect him and forgoe his loue,   45
She both will wrong her owne estate and ours.
Therefore, whiles I doe entertaine the prince
With greatest pleasure that our court affoords,
Endeuour you to winne your daughters thought.[2]
If she giue back, all this will come to naught.   50
                                    Exeunt.

[Act Second. Scene Fourth.]

[HIERONIMO's *garden.*]

Enter HORATIO, BEL-IMPERIA, *and* PEDRINGANO.

HOR. Now that the night begins with sable wings
To ouer-cloud the brightnes of the sunne,
And that in darkenes pleasures may be done,
Come, Bel-imperia, let vs to the bower,
And there in safetie passe a pleasant hower.   5
    BEL. I follow thee, my loue, and will not backe,
Although my fainting hart controles my soule.
    HOR. Why, make you doubt of Pedringanos faith?
    BEL. No; he is as trustie as my second selfe.
Goe, Pedringano, watch without the gate,   10
And let vs know if any make approch.

---

[1] *Misprinted* conueinent *in* A.   [2] *So* 1633, Haw.; A. thoughts.

PED. [*aside*] In-steed of watching, Ile deserue more golde
By fetching Don Lorenzo to this match.   *Exit* PED[RINGANO].
   HOR. What meanes my loue?
   BEL.   I know not what, my-selfe;
And yet my hart foretels me some mischaunce.   15
   HOR. Sweet, say not so; faire Fortune is our freend,
And heauens haue shut vp day to pleasure vs.
The starres, thou seest, holde back their twinckling shine
And Luna hides her-selfe to pleasure vs.
   BEL. Thou hast preuailde! Ile conquer my misdoubt,   20
And in thy loue and councell drowne my feare.
I feare no more ; loue now is all my thoughts!
Why sit we not?[1] for pleasure asketh ease.
   HOR. The more thou sitst within these leauy bowers,
The more will Flora decke it with her flowers.   25
   BEL. I; but, if Flora spye Horatio heere,
Her iealous eye will think I sit too neere.
   HOR. Harke, madame, how the birds record by night
For ioy that Bel-imperia sits in sight!
   BEL. No; Cupid counterfeits the nightingale,   30
To frame sweet musick to Horatios tale.
   HOR. If Cupid sing, then Venus is not farre,—
I, thou art Venus, or some fairer starre!
   BEL. If I be Venus, thou must needs be Mars;
And where Mars raigneth, there must needs be warres.[2]   35
   HOR. Then thus begin our wars: put forth thy hand,
That it may combat with my ruder hand.
   BEL. Set forth thy foot to try the push of mine.
   HOR. But, first, my lookes shall combat against thine.
   BEL. Then ward thy-selfe! I dart this kisse at thee.   40
   HOR. Thus I retort[3] the dart thou threwst at me!
   BEL. Nay then, to gaine the glory of the field,
My twining armes shall yoake and make thee yeeld.
   HOR. Nay then, my armes are large and strong withall :[4]

---

[1] A. nat.   [4] A. with ; 1633, Haw. withall.
[2] A. 1633, warre ; *corr. silently by* Haw.
[3] 1618, '23, '33, returne.

Thus elmes by vines are compast till they fall.   45
    BEL.   O, let me goe, for in my troubled eyes
Now maist thou read that life in passion dies!
    HOR.   O, stay a-while, and I will dye with thee ;
So shalt thou yeeld, and yet haue conquerd me.
    BEL.   Whose there? Pedringano?   We are betraide!   50

    Enter LORENZO, BALTHAZAR, CERBERIN, PEDRINGANO, *disguised.*

    LOR.   My lord, away with her! take her aside! [1]
O sir, [2] forbeare, your valour is already tride.
Quickly dispatch, my maisters.

           Th[e]y hang him in the arbor.

    HOR.   What, will you murder me?
    LOR.   I ; thus! and thus! these are the fruits of loue !

           They stab him.

    BEL.   O, saue his life, and let me dye for him !   55
O, saue him, brother ! saue him, Balthazar !
I loued Horatio, but he loued not me.
    BAL.   But Balthazar loues Bel-imperia.
    LOR.   Although his life were still ambitious, proud,
Yet is he at the highest now he is dead.   60
    BEL.   Murder! murder! helpe! Hieronimo, helpe!
    LOR.   Come, stop her mouth! away with her!
                              Exeunt.
    Enter HIERONIMO *in his shirt, &c.*

    HIERO. What outcries pluck [3] me from my naked bed,
And chill my throbbing hart with trembling feare,
Which neuer danger yet could daunt before?   65
Who cals Hieronimo? speak; heare I am !
I did not slumber ; therefore twas no dreame.
No, no ; it was some woman cride for helpe,
And heere within this garden did she crie,
And in this garden must I rescue her.   70

---

   [1] 1618, '23, '33 *have* take her aside *as a stage-direction.*
   [2] O sir, *in this line, and* my maisters, *in the next, seem to be hyper-*
metrical.   [3] 1618, '23, '33, outcry calles.

But stay! what murdrous spectacle is this?
A man hangd vp, and all the murderers gone!
And in my bower, to lay the guilt on me!
This place was made for pleasure not for death.

He cuts him downe.

Those garments that he weares I oft haue seene, —   75
Alas! it is Horatio, my sweet sonne!
O, no ; but he that whilome was my sonne!
O, was it thou that call'dst me from my bed?
O, speak, if any sparke of life remaine!
I am thy father.   Who hath slaine my sonne?   80
What sauadge monster, not of humane kinde,
Hath heere beene glutted with thy harmeles blood,
And left thy bloudie corpes dishonoured heere,
For me amidst these[1] darke and deathfull shades
To drowne thee with an ocean of my teares?   85
O heauens, why made you night, to couer sinne?
By day this deed of darkenes had not beene.
O earth, why didst thou not in time deuoure
The vilde[2] prophaner of this sacred bower?
O poore Horatio, what hadst thou misdoone   90
To leese thy life ere life was new begun?
O wicked butcher, what-so-ere thou wert,
How could[3] thou strangle vertue and desert?
Ay me, most wretched! that haue lost my ioy
In leesing my Horatio, my sweet boy!   95

Enter ISABELL.

ISA.   My husbands absence makes my hart to throb.
Hieronimo!
HIERO.   Heere, Isabella.   Helpe me to lament ;
For sighes are stopt, and all my teares are spent.
ISA.   What world of griefe — my sonne Horatio!   100
O wheres the author of this endles woe?

[1] A. this; 1633, these.   [3] 1633, couldst.
[2] 1618, '23, '33 *modernize the spelling to* vile.

HIERO.   To know the author were some ease of greefe,
For in reuenge my hart would finde releefe.

ISA.   Then is he gone? and is my sonne gone too?
O, gush out, teares! fountaines and flouds of teares! 105
Blow, sighes, and raise an euerlasting storme;
For outrage fits our cursed wretchednes![1]

1 *Between this line and the next occurs the first of a number of inser-tions, supposed to have been written by* Ben Jonson, *and said to appear first in the edition of* 1602. *I print them from a copy of the edition of* 1633, *now in the Library of Harvard University:*

Aye me! Hieronimo, sweet husband, speake!
    HIER.   He supt with us to-night frolicke and merry,
And said he would goe visit Balthazar
At the dukes pallace, — there the prince doth lodge.
He had no custome to stay out so late. 5
He may be in his chamber, — some goe see!
Roderigo, ho![2]
        Enter PEDRO *and* IAQUES.

    ISA.   Aye me, he raues! Sweet Hieronimo!
    HIER.   True, all Spaine takes note of it;
Besides, he is so generally beloved; 10
His Majesty the other day did grace him
With waiting on his cup: these be favours
Which doe assure me that he cannot be [3] short-lived.
    ISA.   Sweet Hieronimo!
    HIER.   I wonder how this fellow got his clothes. 15
Sirha, sirha, Ile know the truth of all!
Iaques, run to the Duke of Castiles presently,
And bid my sonne Horatio to come home;
I and his mother haue had strange dreames to-night:
Doe you hear me, sir?
    IAQUES.   I, sir.
    HIER.   Well, sir, begon. 20
Pedro, come hither. Knowest thou who this is?
    PED.   Too well, sir.
    HIER.   Too well! who? who is it? Peace, Isabella!
Nay, blush not, man!
    PED.   It is my lord Horatio.

2 *In* 1633 *these words are in* l. 5.   *I shall not record changes in the line divi-sion hereafter in these insertions.*
    3 *Misprinted* he *in* 1633.

HIERO.   Sweet louely rose, ill pluckt before thy time!
Faire, worthy sonne, not conquerd, but betraid!
Ile kisse thee now, for words with teares are staide.[1]   110
    ISA.   And Ile close vp the glasses of his sight;
For once these eyes were onely my delight.
    HIERO.   Seest thou this handkercher besmerd with blood?
It shall not from me till I take reuenge;
Seest thou those [2] wounds that yet are bleeding fresh?   115

    HIER.   Ha, ha! Saint Iames, but this doth make me laugh,   25
That there are more deluded then my-selfe!
    PED.   Deluded?
    HIER.   I; I would haue sworne my-selfe
Within this houre that this had bin my sonne Horatio,
His garments are so like: ha! are they not great perswasions?
    ISA.   O, would to God it were not so!   30
    HIER.   Were not, Isabella? dost thou dreame it is?
Can thy soft bosome entertaine a thought
That such a blacke deed of mischiefe should be done
On one so pure and spotlesse as our sonne?
Away! I am ashamed!
    ISA.   Deare Hieronimo,   35
Cast a more serious eye upon thy griefe:
Weake apprehension giues but weake beliefe.
    HIER.   It was a man, sure, that was hang'd up here,—
A youth, as I remember: I cut him downe.
If it should prooue my sonne now after all?   40
Say you, say you? Light!
Lend me a taper, let me looke againe.
O God!
Confusion, mischiefe, torment, death and hell,
Drop all your stings at once in my cold bosome,
That now is stiffe with horrour! kill me quickly!   45
Be gracious to me, thou infectiue night,
And drop this deed of murder downe on me!
Gird in my wast of griefe with thy large darknes,
And let me not surviue to see the light
May put me in the mind I had a sonne.   50
    ISA.   O sweet Horatio! O my dearest sonne!
    HIER.   How strangely had I lost my way to griefe!

[Line 108 follows.]

---

[1] A. stainde; 1633, staid.   [2] *Misprinted* thofs *in* A.

Ile not intombe them till I haue reueng'd :
Then will I ioy amidst my discontent,
Till then, my sorrow neuer shalbe spent.

    ISA.   The heauens are iust, murder cannot be hid ;
Time is the author both of truth and right,   120
And time will bring this trecherie to light.

    HIERO.   Meane-while, good Isabella, cease thy plaints,
Or, at the least, dissemble them awhile ;
So shall we sooner finde the practise out,
And learne by whom all this was brought about.   125
Come, Isabell, now let vs take him vp

They take him vp.

And beare him in from out this cursed place.
Ile say his dirge, — singing fits not this case.
O aliquis mihi quas pulchrum ver [1] *educet herbas*

HIERO[NIMO] *sets his brest vnto his sword.*

Misceat, et nostro detur medicina dolori;   130
Aut siqui faciunt annorum obliuia [2] *succos*
Prebeat; ipse metam magnum quaecunque [3] *per orbem*
Gramina sol pulchras eiecit lucis in [4] *oras.*
Ipse bibam quicquid meditatur saga veneni, [5]
Quicquid et irarum ui caeca nenia [6] *nectit.*   135
Omnia perpetiar, lethum quoque, dum semel omnis
Noster in extincto moriatur pectore [7] *sensus.*
Ergo tuos occulos nunquam, mea vita, videbo, [8]
Et tua perpetuus sepeliuit lumina somnus ?
Emoriar tecum : sic, sic iuuat ire sub vmbras !   140
Attamen absistam properato cedere letho,
Ne mortem vindicta tuam tum [9] *nulla sequatur.*

Heere he throwes it from him and beares the body away.

[1] A. var; 1633, ver.   [7] A. pectora; 1633, pectore.
[2] A. 1633, annum oblimia; *corr. by* Haw.
[3] A. 1633, metum magnam quicunque; *corr. by* Haw.
[4] A. 1633, effecit in luminis; *corr. by* Haw.
[5] A. veneri; 1633, veneni. .   [8] A. vi debo.
[6] A. irraui euecæca menia; 1633, iravi evecæca menia; *corr. by* Haw.
[9] A. vindictatuam tam; *corr. by* Haw.

[CHORUS.]

ANDREA.   Broughtst thou me hether to increase my paine?
I lookt that Balthazar should haue been slaine ;
But tis my freend Horatio that is slaine,
And they abuse faire Bel-imperia,
On whom I doted more then all the world,   5
Because she lou'd me more then all the world.
    REUENGE.   Thou talkest of haruest, when the corne is
        greene :
The end is crowne[1] of euery worke well done ;
The sickle comes not till the corne be ripe.
Be still, and, ere I lead thee from this place,   10
Ile shew thee Balthazar in heauy case.

Actus Tertius.   [Scene First.]

[The Portuguese court.]

Enter VICEROY OF PORTINGALE, NOBLES, ALEXANDRO, VILLUPPO.

VICEROY.   Infortunate condition of kings,
Seated amidst so many helpeles doubts !
First, we are plast vpon extreamest height,
And oft supplanted with exceeding hate,[2]
But euer subiect to the wheele of chance ;   5
And at our highest neuer ioy we so
As we both doubt and dread our ouerthrow.
So striueth not the waues with sundry winds
As fortune toyleth in the affaires of kings,
That would be feard, yet feare to be beloued,   10
Sith feare or loue to kings is flatterie.
For instance, lordings, look vpon your king,
By hate depriued of his dearest sonne,
The onely hope of our successiue line.[3]
    NOB.   I had not thought that Alexandros hart   15

---

[1] 1618, '23, '33, growne.   [3] 1618, '23, '33, liues.
[2] A. heat: 1633, hate.

Had beene enuenomde with such extreame hate ;
But now I see that words haue seuerall workes,
And theres no credit in the countenance.

  VIL. No ; for, my lord, had [1] you behelde the traine
That fained loue had coloured in his lookes   20
When he in campe consorted Balthazar,
Farre more inconstant had you thought the sunne,
That howerly coasts the center of the earth,
Then Alexandros purpose to the prince.

  VICE. No more, Villuppo ! thou hast said enough, 25
And with thy words thou slaiest our wounded thoughts.
Nor shall I longer dally with the world,
Procrastinating Alexandros death.
Goe, some of you, and fetch the traitor forth,
That, as he is condemned, he may dye.   30

    Enter ALEXANDRO, *with a* NOBLE-MAN *and* HALBERTS.

  NOB. In such extreames will nought but patience serue.
  ALEX. But in extreames what patience shall I vse ?
Nor discontents it me to leaue the world,
With whome there nothing can preuaile but wrong.
  NOB. Yet hope the best.
  ALEX.   Tis heauen is my hope : 35
As for the earth, it is too much infect
To yeeld me hope of any of her mould.
  VICE. Why linger ye ? bring forth that daring feend,
And let him die for his accursed deed.
  ALEX. Not that I feare the extremitie of death — 40
For nobles cannot stoop to seruile feare —
Doo I, O king, thus discontented liue ;
But this, O this, torments my labouring soule,
That thus I die suspected of a sinne
Whereof, as Heauens haue knowne my secret thoughts, 45
So am I free from this suggestion !
  VICE. No more, I say ; to the tortures ! when ?
Binde him, and burne his body in those flames,

    They binde him to the stake.

  [1] A. bad ; *corr. silently by* Haw. *from* 1633.

That shall prefigure those vnquenched fiers
Of Phlegiton prepared for his soule.   50
    ALEX.   My guiltles death will be aueng'd on thee!
On thee, Villuppo, that hath malisde thus,
Or for thy meed hast falsely me accusde!
    VIL.   Nay, Alexandro, if thou menace me,
Ile lend a hand to send thee to the lake   55
Where those thy words shall perish with thy workes,
Iniurious traitour, monstrous homicide!

Enter EMBASSADOUR.

    [EM.] [1]   Stay! hold a-while! and heer, with pardon of
His Maiestie, lay hands vpon Villuppo!
    VICE.   Embassadour,[2] what newes hath vrg'd this sodain
        entrance?   60
    EM.   Know, soueraigne l[ord], that Balthazar doth liue.
    VICE.   What saiest thou? liueth Balthazar, our sonne?
    EM.   Your Highnes sonne, L[ord] Balthazar, doth liue,
And, well intreated in the court of Spaine,
Humbly commends him to your Maiestie.   65
These eies beheld; and these my followers,
With these, the letters of the kings commends,[3]

Giues him letters.

Are happie witnesses of his Highnes health.

The KING lookes on the letters, and proceeds.[4]

    VICE. [reads]   "Thy sonne doth liue; your tribute is receiu'd;
Thy peace is made, and we are satisfied.   70
The rest resolue vpon as things proposde
For both our honors and thy benefite."
    EM.   These are his Highnes farther articles.

He giues him more letters.

    VICE.   Accursed wretch to intimate these ills
Against the life and reputation   75

---

[1] *Supplied from* 1633.
[2] *Qy. extra metrum.*
[3] 1618, '23, '33, commend.
[4] *The blank-verse habit is strong.*

Of noble Alexandro! come, my lord, vnbinde him![1]
[*To* ALEXANDRO]   Let him vnbinde thee that is bound to death,
To make a quitall for thy discontent.

They vnbinde him.

ALEX.   Dread lord, in kindenes you could do no lesse,
Vpon report of such a damned fact;   80
But thus we see our innocence hath sau'd
The hopeles life which thou, Villuppo, sought
By thy suggestions to haue massacred.
VICE.   Say, false Villuppo, wherefore didst thou thus
Falsly betray Lord Alexandros life?   85
Him whom thou knowest that no vnkindenes els
But euen the slaughter of our deerest sonne
Could once haue moued vs to haue misconceaued.
ALEX.   Say, trecherous Villuppo; tell the king!
Or wherein hath Alexandro vsed thee ill?   90
VIL.   Rent with remembrance of so foule a deed,
My guiltie soule submits me to thy doome,
For, not for Alexandros iniuries,
But for reward and hope to be preferd,
Thus haue I shamelesly hazarded his life.   95
VICE.   Which, villaine, shalbe ransomed with thy deeth,
And not so meane a torment as we heere
Deuisde for him who thou saidst slew our sonne,
But with the bitterest torments and extreames
That may be yet inuented for thine end.   100

ALEX[ANDRO] *seemes to intreat.*

Intreat me not!   Goe, take the traitor hence !   *Exit* VIL[LUPPO].
And, Alexandro, let vs honor thee
With publique notice of thy loyaltie.
To end those things articulated heere
By our great l[ord], the mightie king of Spaine,   105
We with our councell will deliberate.
Come, Alexandro, keepe vs company.   *Exeunt.*

---

[1] *Qy. an Alexandrine ; or, as* Kittredge *suggests,* my lord *is hypermetrical.*

[Act Third.   Scene Second.]

Enter HIERONIMO.

HIERO.   Oh eies! no eies but fountains fraught with
    teares ;
Oh life! no life, but liuely fourme of death ;
Oh world ! no world, but masse of publique wrongs,
Confusde and filde with murder and misdeeds ;
Oh sacred heauens, if this vnhallowed deed,   5
If this inhumane and barberous attempt,
If this inçomparable [1] murder thus
Of mine, but now no more my sonne
Shall vnreueald and vnreuenged passe,
How should we tearme your dealings to be iust,   10
If you vniustly deale with those that in your iustice trust?
The night, sad secretary to my mones,
With direfull visions wake my vexed soule,
And with the wounds of my distresfull sonne
Solicite me for notice of his death ;   15
The ougly feends do sally forth of hell,
And frame my steps to vnfrequented paths,
And feare my hart with fierce inflamed thoughts ;
The cloudie day my discontents records,
Early begins to regester my dreames   20
And driue me forth to seeke the murtherer.
Eies, life, world, heauens, hel, night and day,
See, search, shew, send, some man, some meane, that may! [2]

A letter falleth.

Whats heere? a letter?   Tush, it is not so !
A letter written to Hieronimo.   *Red incke.* 25
[*Reads*] [3] " For want of incke receiue this bloudie writ.

---

[1] A. incompaeable.

[2] *As two lines in* A., *the first ending with* man.

[3] *Before this letter of* BEL-IMPERIA'S, A. *has* BEL., *as if she were present as a speaker.*

Me hath my haples brother hid from thee.
Reuenge thy-selfe on Balthazar and him,
For these were they that murdered [1] thy sonne.
Hieronimo, reuenge Horatios death,   30
And better fare [2] then Bel-imperia doth ! " —
[3] What meanes this vnexpected miracle?
My sonne slaine by Lorenzo and the prince?
What cause had they Horatio to maligne?
Or what might mooue thee, Bel-imperia,   35
To accuse thy brother, had he beene the meane?
Hieronimo, beware ! thou art betraide,
And to intrap thy life this traine is laide.
Aduise thee therefore, be not credulous :
This is deuised to endanger thee,   40
That thou, by this, Lorenzo shouldst accuse,
And he, for thy dishonour done, should draw
Thy life in question and thy name in hate.
Deare was the life of my beloued sonne,
And of his death behoues me be aueng'd :   45
Then hazard not thine owne, Hieronimo,
But liue t' effect thy resolution !
I therefore will by circumstances trie
What I can gather to confirme this writ,
And, harkning [4] neere the Duke of Castiles house,   50
Close if I can with Belimperia,
To listen more, but nothing to bewray.

Enter PEDRINGANO.

HIERO.   Now, Pedringano !
PED.   Now, Hieronimo !
HIERO.   Wheres thy lady?
PED.   I know not ; heers my lord.

Enter LORENZO.

LOR.   How now, whose this? Hieronimo?

---

[1] *So* 1633 ; A. murdred.   [3] *Before this line* A. *has* HIERO.
[2] *So* A. ; Haw. *prints* far, *which, though it is the reading of* 1633, *is clearly wrong.*   [4] 1618, '23, '33, hearken.

HIERO.   My lord.   55

PED.   He asketh for my lady Bel-imperia.

LOR.   What to doo, Hieronimo?   The duke, my father, hath,

Vpon some disgrace, a-while remoou'd her hence ;

But, if it be ought I may enforme her of,

Tell me, Hieronimo, and Ile let her know it.   60

HIERO.   Nay, nay, my lord, I thank you, it shall not need.

I had a sute vnto her, but too late ;

And her disgrace makes me vnfortunate.

LOR.   Why so, Hieronimo?   Vse me.[1]

HIERO.   Oh, no, my lord, I dare not. it must not be ;   65

I humbly thank your lordship.

LOR.   Why then, farewell!

HIERO.   My griefe no hart, my thoughts no tung can tell.

Exit.

LOR.   Come hither, Pedringano ; seest thou this?

PED.   My lord, I see it, and suspect it too.

LOR.   This is that damned villain Serberine,   70

That hath, I feare, reuealde Horatios death.

PED.   My lord, he could not ; twas so lately done,

And since he hath not left my company.

---

[1] *In* 1618, '23, '33 ll. 64–66 *are replaced by the following,* — *I print from* ed. 1633 :

LOR.   Why so, Hieronimo ?, Use me.

HIERO.   Who? You, my lord?

I reserue your favour for a greater honour ;

This is a very toy, my lord, a toy.

LOR.   All's one, Hieronimo ; acquaint me with it.

HIERO.   Y faith, my lord, tis an idle thing.   5

I must confesse I ha bin too slacke, too tardy,

Too remisse unto your Honour.

LOR.   How now, Hieronimo?

HIERO.   In troth, my lord, it is a thing of nothing :

The murder of a sonne or so, my lord, — [2]   10

A thing of nothing.

LOR.   Why then, farewell!

[2] *In* 1618, '23, '33 my lord *comes after* nothing, l. 11.

LOR.   Admit he haue not; his conditions such
As feare or flattering words may make him false.   75
I know his humour, and there-with repent
That ere I vsde him in this enterprise.
But, Pedringano, to preuent the worst,
And cause I know thee secret as my soule,
Heere, for thy further satisfaction, take thou this!   80

Giues him more golde.

And harken to me; thus it is deuisde:[1]
This night thou must — and prethee so resolue —
Meet Serberine at S. Luigis[2] Parke, —
Thou knowest tis heere hard by behinde the house;
There take thy stand, and see thou strike him sure,   85
For dye he must, if we do meane to liue.
  PED.   But how shall Serberine be there, my lord?
  LOR.   Let me alone, Ile send to him to meet
The prince and me where thou must doe this deed.
  PED.   It shalbe done, my l[ord]; it shall be done;   90
And Ile goe arme my-selfe to meet him there.
  LOR.   When things shall alter, as I hope they wil,
Then shalt thou mount for this, thou knowest my minde.[3]

Exit PED[RINGANO].

Che le Ieron![4]

Enter PAGE.

PAGE.   My lord.
  LOR.   Goe, sirra,
To Serberine, and bid him forthwith meet   95
The prince and me at S. Luigis[2] Parke,[5]
Behinde the house, this euening, boy.
  PAGE.   I goe, my lord.

---

[1] 1618, '23, '33, thus it is: disguis'd.
[2] A. Haw. Liugis; 1633, Luges.
[3] *One would expect a couplet here; but perhaps identical rhyme seemed undesirable.*
[4] A. Che le Ieron; Haw. Che le Jeron; 1633, Che le Ieron. *I suppose this to be a call to the* PAGE, *not, as* Hazlitt *thinks, a remark to* LORENZO.
[5] *Two lines in* edd., Goe ... forthwith, Meet ... Parke.

LOR.[1]   But, sirra, let the houre be eight a-clocke.
Bid him not faile.

    PAGE.   I flye, my lord.   *Exit·*

    LOR.   Now to confirme the complot thou hast cast   100
Of all these practises, Ile spread the watch,
Vpon precise commandement from the king
Strongly to guard the place where Pedringano
This night shall murder haples Serberine.
Thus must we worke that will auoide distrust,   105
Thus must we practise to preuent mishap,
And thus one ill another must expulse.
This slie enquiry of Hieronimo
For Bel-imperia, breeds suspition;[2]
And this[3] suspition boads a further ill.   110
As for my-selfe, I know my secret fault,
And so doe they, but I haue dealt for them.
They that for coine their soules endangered
To saue my life, for coyne shall venture theirs;
And better tis[4] that base companions dye   115
Then by their life to hazard our good haps.
Nor shall they liue for me to feare their faith;
Ile trust my-selfe, my-selfe shalbe my freend;
For dye they shall, —
Slaues are ordein[e]d to no other end.[2]   120

                                    Exit.

[Act Third.   Scene Third.]

[San Luigi's Park.]

Enter PEDRINGANO *with a pistoll.*

    PED.[1]   Now, Pedringano, bid thy pistoll holde;
And holde on, Fortune!   Once more fauour me!
Giue but successe to mine attempting spirit,

    [1] *So* 1633; *not in* A.
    [2] *These two lines as one in* A. 1633; *no note in* Haw. *as to* 1618, '23.
    [3] A. thus.
    [4] A. its.

And let me shift for taking of mine aime.
Heere is the golde !   This is the golde proposde!   5
It is no dreame that I aduenture for,
But Pedringano is possest thereof.
And he that would not straine his conscience
For him that thus his liberall purse hath stretcht,
Vnworthy such a fauour may he faile,   10
And, wishing, want when such as I preuaile !
As for the feare of apprehension,
I know, if need should be, my noble lord
Will stand betweene me and ensuing harmes.
Besides, this place is free from all suspect.   15
Heere therefore will I stay and take my stand.

Enter the WATCH.

I WATCH.[1]   I wonder much to what intent it is
That we are thus expresly chargde to watch.
II WATCH.   Tis by commandement in the kings own
          name.
III WATCH.   But we were neuer wont to watch and ward   20
So neere the duke his brothers [2] house before.
II WATCH.   Content your-selfe, stand close, theres some-
          what int.

Enter SERBERINE.

SER. [*aside*]   Heere, Serberine, attend and stay thy pace ;
For heere did Don Lorenzos page appoint
That thou by his command shouldst meet with him.   25
How fit a place, if one were so disposde,
Me thinks this corner is to close with one.
PED. [*aside*]   Heere comes the bird that I must ceaze vpon ;
Now, Pedringano, or neuer play the man !
SER. [*aside*]   I wonder that his lordship staies so long,   30
Or wherefore should he send for me so late.
PED.   For this, Serberine ; and thou shalt ha'te !

---

[1] *In* A. 1633 *the speeches of the* WATCHMEN *are merely marked* 1, 2, 3.
[2] 1618, '23, '33 *omit* brothers.

Shootes the dagge.

So ! there he lyes ; my promise is performde.

The WATCH.

I WATCH.   Harke, gentlemen, this is a pistol shot !
II WATCH.   And heeres one slaine ; stay the murderer !   35
PED.   Now, by the sorrowes of the soules in hell,

He striues with the WATCH.

Who first laies hand on me, Ile be his priest !
III WATCH.   Sirra, confesse, and therein play the priest.
Why hast thou thus vnkindely kild the man?
PED.   Why, because he walkt abroad so late.   40
III WATCH.   Come, sir, you had bene better kept your bed
Then haue committed this misdeed so late.
II WATCH.   Come to the marshals with the murderer !
I WATCH.   On to Hieronimos! helpe me heere
To bring the murdred body with vs too.   45
PED.   Hieronimo?   Carry me before whom you will ;
What ere he be, Ile answere him and you.
And doe your worst, for I defie you all!   *Exeunt.*

[Act Third.   Scene Fourth.]

[*The* DUKE'S *castle.*]

Enter LORENZO *and* BALTHAZAR.

BAL.   How now, my lord? what makes you rise so soone?
LOR.   Feare of preuenting our mishaps too late.
BAL.   What mischiefe is it that we not mistrust?
LOR.   Our greatest ils we least mistrust, my lord,
And in-expected [1] harmes do hurt vs most.   5
BAL.   Why, tell me, Don Lorenzo, — tell me, man,
If ought concernes our honour and your owne!
LOR.   Nor you nor me, my lord, but both in one ;
For I suspect — and the presumptions great —

[1] 1633, unexpected.

That by those base confederates in our fault   10
Touching the death of Don Horatio
We are betraide to olde Hieronimo.

    BAL.   Betraide, Lorenzo? tush! it cannot be.

    LOR.   A guiltie conscience vrged with the thought
Of former euils, easily cannot erre :   15
I am perswaded — and diswade me not —
That als reuealed to Hieronimo.
And therefore know that I haue cast it thus—

[Enter PAGE.]

But heeres the page.   How now? what newes with thee?

    PAGE.   My lord, Serberine is slaine.   20

    BAL.   Who? Serberine, my man?

    PAGE.   Your Highnes man, my lord.

    LOR.   Speak, page: who murdered him?

    PAGE.   He that is apprehended for the fact.

    LOR.   Who?

    PAGE.   Pedringano.   25

    BAL.   Is [1] Serberine slaine, that lou'd his lord so well?
Iniurious villaine! murderer of his freend!

    LOR.   Hath Pedringano murdered Serberine?
My lord, let me entreat you to take the paines
To exasperate and hasten his reuenge   30
With your complaints vnto my l[ord] the king.
This their dissention breeds a greater doubt.

    BAL.   Assure thee, Don Lorenzo, he shall dye,
Or els his Highnes hardly shall deny.
Meane-while, Ile haste the marshall sessions,   35
For die he shall for this his damned deed.

Exit BALT[HAZAR].

    LOR. [aside]   Why, so! this fits our former pollicie;
And thus experience bids the wise to deale.
I lay the plot, he prosecutes the point;
I set the trap, he breakes the worthles twigs,   40

[1] 1618, '23, '33, I.

And sees not that wherewith the bird was limde.
Thus hopefull men, that meane to holde their owne,
Must look, like fowlers, to their dearest freends.
He runnes to kill whome I haue holpe [1] to catch,
And no man knowes it was my reaching fatch.[2]   45
Tis hard to trust vnto a multitude, —
Or any one, in mine opinion,
When men themselues their secrets will reueale.

Enter a MESSENGER *with a letter.*

LOR.   Boy.
PAGE.   My lord.
LOR.   Whats he?
MES.   I haue a letter to your lordship.
LOR.   From whence?   50
MES.   From Pedringano that 's imprisoned.
LOR.   So he is in prison then?
MES.   I, my good lord.
LOR.   What would he with vs?

[Reads the letter.]
                              He writes vs heere
To stand good l[ord] and help him in distres.[3]
Tell him I haue his letters, know his minde ;   55
And what we may, let him assure him of.
Fellow, be gone ; my boy shall follow thee.

Exit MES[SENGER].

[Aside] This works like waxe ! Yet once more try thy wits. —
Boy, goe conuay this purse to Pedringano, —
Thou knowest the prison, — closely giue it him,   60
And be aduisde that none be there-about.
Bid him be merry still, but secret ;
And, though the marshall sessions be to-day,
Bid him not doubt of his deliuerie.
Tell him his pardon is already signde,   65

___

[1] 1623, '33, hope.   [2] Haw. fetch, *without note.*
[3] 1633 *prints* to stand . . . distres, &c., *in italics, as if a quotation,
the* &c. *indicating perhaps liberty of improvisation.*

And thereon bid him boldely be resolued;
For, were he ready to be turned off, —
As tis my will the vttermost be tride, —
Thou with his pardon shalt attend him still.
Shew him this boxe, tell him his pardons int;   70
But opent not, and if thou louest thy life,
But let him wisely keepe his hopes vnknowne.
He shall not want while Don Lorenzo liues.
Away! [1]

    PAGE.   I goe, my lord, I runne!

    LOR.   But, sirra, see that this be cleanely done.   75

                         Exit PAGE.

Now stands our fortune on a tickle point,
And now or neuer ends Lorenzos doubts.
One onely thing is vneffected yet,
And thats to see the executioner, —
But to what end?   I [2] list not trust the aire   80
With vtterance of our pretence therein,
For feare the priuie whispring of the winde
Conuay our words amongst vnfreendly eares,
That lye too open to aduantages.
Et quel che [3] *voglio io,* [4] *nessun lo* [5] *sa,*   85
Intendo io quel [che] *mi basterà.* [6]   *Exit.*

[Act Third. Scene Fifth.]

[*A street.*]

Enter BOY *with the boxe.*

My maister hath forbidden me to look in this box, and, by
my troth,[7] tis likely, if he had not warned me, I should not
haue had so much idle time; for wee mens-kinde [8] in our
minoritie are like women in their vncertaintie: that they are

---

[1] *In* edd. *this word is in* l. 73.
[2] 1618, '23, '33 *omit.*
[3] Edd. que.
[4] A. Ii; 1633, il; Haw. io.

[5] A. nessun le; 1633, nessum le.
[6] A. 1633, bassara; Haw. bastara.
[7] 1618, '23, '33, honesty.
[8] 1618, '23, '33, men-kind.

most forbidden, they wil soonest attempt; so I now.   By my   5
bare honesty,[1] heeres nothing but the bare emptie box!
Were it not sin against secrecie, I would say it were a peece
of gentlemanlike knauery.   I must goe to Pedringano and
tell him his pardon is in this boxe!   Nay, I would haue sworne
it, had I not seene the contrary.   I cannot choose but smile   10
to thinke how the villain wil flout the gallowes, scorne the
audience, and descant on the hangman, and al presuming of
his pardon from hence.   Wilt not be an odde iest, for me to
stand and grace euery iest he makes, pointing my finger at
this boxe, as who would [2] say : " Mock on, heers thy warrant ! "   15
Ist not a scuruie iest that a man should iest himselfe to death ?
Alas, poore Pedringano !   I am in a sorte sorie for thee, but, if
I should be hanged with thee, I cannot [3] weep.

Exit.

[Act Third.   Scene Sixth.]

[*The court of justice.*]

Enter HIERONIMO *and the* DEPUTIE.

HIERO.   Thus must we toyle in other mens extreames
That know not how to remedie our owne,
And doe them iustice, when vniustly we
For all our wrongs can compasse no redrese.
But shall I neuer liue to see the day   5
That I may come by iustice of the Heauens
To know the cause that may my cares allay?
This toyles my body, this consumeth age,
That onely I to all men iust must be,
And neither gods nor men be iust to me!   10
DEP.   Worthy Hieronimo, your office askes
A care to punish such as doe transgresse.
HIERO.   So ist my duety to regarde his death
Who when he liued deserued my dearest blood.

[1] 1618, '23, '33, credit.   [3] 1618, '23, '33, could **not**.
[2] 1618, '23, '33, should.

But come ; for that we came for, lets begin ;   15
For heere lyes that which bids me to be gone.

Enter OFFICERS, BOY, *&* PEDRINGANO *with a letter in his hand, bound.*

DEPU.   Bring forth the prisoner for the court is set.
PED.   Gramercy, boy! but it was time to come,
For I had written to my lord anew
A neerer matter that concerneth him,   20
For feare his lordship had forgotten me ;
But, sith he hath remembred me so well,
Come, come, come on ! when shall we to this geere?
HIERO.   Stand forth, thou monster, murderer of men,
And heere, for satisfaction of the world,   25
Confesse thy folly and repent thy fault,
For ther 's thy place of execution.
PED.   This is short worke!   Well, to your marshallship
First I confesse, nor feare I death therfore,
I am the man, — twas I slew Serberine.   30
But, sir, then you think this shalbe the place
Where we shall satisfie you for this geare?
DEPU.   I, Pedringano.
PED.   Now [1] I think not so.
HIERO.   Peace, impudent! for thou shalt finde it so ;
For blood with blood shall, while I sit as iudge,   35
Be satisfied, and the law dischargde.
And, though my-selfe cannot receiue the like,
Yet will I see that others haue their right.
Dispatch ! the faults [2] approued and confest,
And [3] by our law he is condemned to die.   40
HANG.   Come on, sir ! [4] are you ready?
PED.   To do what, my fine officious knaue?
HANG.   To goe to this geere.
PED.   O, sir, you are to forward ; thou wouldst faine fur-
nish me with a halter, to disfurnish me of my habit. [5]   45

---

[1] 1618, '23, '33, No.   [3] A. Hnd.
[2] 1633, fault.   [4] A. sit ; 1633, sir.
[5] *In the paragraphing of this prose I follow* A. 1633.

So I should goe out of this geere, my raiment, into that geere, the rope.

But, hangman, now I spy your knauery, Ile not change without boot ; thats flat.

HANG.   Come, sir.   50

PED.   So then I must vp?

HANG.   No remedie.

PED.   Yes, but there shalbe for my [1] comming downe.

HANG.   Indeed heers a remedie for that.

PED.   How? be turnd off?   55

HANG.   I, truely.   Come, are you ready?
I pray,[2] sir, dispatch, the day goes away.

PED.   What, doe you hang by the howre?   If you doo, I may chance to break your olde custome.

HANG.   Faith, you haue [3] reason, for I am like to break   60
your yong neck.

PED.   Dost thou mock me, hangman?   Pray God I be not preserued to break your knaues-pate for this !

HANG.   Alas, sir, you are a foot too low to reach it, and I hope you will neuer grow so high while I am in the office.   65

PED.   Sirra, dost see yonder boy with the box in his hand ?

HANG.   What, he that points to it with his finger?

PED.   I, that companion.

HANG.   I know him not; but what of him?   70

PED.   Doost thou think to liue till his olde doublet will make thee a new trusse? [4]

HANG.   I, and many a faire yeere after, to trusse vp many an honester man then either thou or he.

PED.   What hath he in his boxe, as thou thinkst?   75

HANG.   Faith, I cannot tell, nor I care not greatly.
Me thinks you should rather hearken to your soules health.

PED.   Why, sirra hangman, I take it that that is good for the body is likewise good for the soule : and it may be in that box is balme for both.   80

---

[1] 1618, '23, '33 *omit* my.   [3] 1618, '23, '33, haue no.
[2] 1633, Haw. I pray you.   [4] A. truffs.

HANG. Wel, thou art euen the meriest peece of mans flesh that ere gronde at my office-doore.

PED. Is your roaguery become an office, with a knaues name?

HANG. I, and that shall all they witnes that see you seale 85
it with a theeues name.

PED. I prethee, request this good company to pray with [1]
me.

HANG. I, mary, sir, this is a good motion! My maisters,
you see heers a good fellow.   90

PED. Nay, nay, now I remember me, let them alone till
some other time; for now I haue no great need.

HIERO. I haue not seen a wretch so impudent.
O monstrous times where murders set so light,
And where the soule that should be shrinde in heauen   95
Solelie delights in interdicted things,
Still wandring in the thornie passages
That intercepts it-selfe of hapines!
Murder? O bloudy monster! God forbid
A fault so foule should scape vnpunished!   100
Dispatch and see this execution done;
This makes me to remember thee, my sonne.

                              Exit HIERO[NIMO].

PED. Nay, soft! no hast!

DEPU. Why, wherefore stay you? haue you hope of life?

PED. Why, I!   105

HANG. As how?

PED. Why, rascall, by my pardon from the king.

HANG. Stand you on that? then you shall off with this.

             He turnes him off.

DEPU. So, executioner, conuey him hence;
But let his body be vnburied.   110
Let not the earth be choked or infect
With that which Heauens [2] contemnes and men neglect.

                                   Exeunt.

---

[1] 1618, '23, '33, for.   [2] Haw. heaven.

[Act Third.   Scene Seventh.]

[Hieronimo's house.]

Enter HIERONIMO.

HIER.[1]   Where shall I run to breath abroad my woes, —
My woes whose weight hath wearied the earth,
Or mine exclaimes that haue surcharged the aire
With ceasles plaints for my deceased sonne?
The blustring winds, conspiring with my words,   5
At my lament haue moued the leaueles trees,
Disroabde the medowes of their flowred greene,
Made mountains marsh with spring-tides [2] of my teares,
And broken through the brazen gates of hell;
Yet still tormented is my tortured soule   10
With broken sighes and restles passions,
That, winged, mount, and, houering in the aire,
Beat [3] at the windowes of the brightest heauens,
Solliciting for iustice and reuenge.
But they are plac't in those imperiall heights,   15
Where, countermurde with walles of diamond,
I finde the place impregnable, and they
Resist my woes and giue my words no way.

Enter HANGMAN *with a letter.*

HANG.   O Lord, sir ! God blesse you, sir ! the man, sir, —
Petergade, sir : he that was so full of merrie conceits —   20
   HIERO.   Wel, what of him?
   HANG.   O Lord, sir ! he went the wrong way; the fellow
had a faire commission to the contrary. Sir, heere is his
pasport, I pray you, sir; we haue done him wrong.
   HIERO.   I warrant thee; giue it me.   25
   HANG.   You will stand between the gallowes and me?
   HIERO.   I, I !

---

[1] *Not in* A.; *supplied from* 1633.
[2] 1618, '23, '33, spring-tide.
[3] 1618, '23, '33, But; *perhaps caught up from* l. 15.

HANG.   I thank your l[ord] worship.   *Exit* HANGMAN.
HIERO.   And yet, though somewhat neerer me concernes
I will, to ease the greefe that I sustaine,   30
Take truce with sorrow while I read on this.
[*Reads*] " My lord, I writ,[1] as mine extreames requirde,[2]
That you would labour my deliuerie :
If you neglect, my life is desperate,
And in my death I shall reueale the troth.   35
You know, my lord, I slew him for your sake,
And was confederate with the prince and you ;
Wonne by rewards and hopefull promises,
I holpe to murder Don Horatio too." —
Holpe he to murder mine Horatio ?   40
And actors in th' accursed tragedie
Wast thou, Lorenzo ? Balthazar and thou,
Of whom my sonne, my sonne deseru'd so well ?
What haue I heard ? what haue mine eies behelde ?
O sacred heauens, may it come to passe   45
That such a monstrous and detested deed,
So closely smootherd and so long conceald,
Shall thus by this be venged[3] or reueald ?
Now see I, what I durst not then suspect,
That Bel-imperias letter was not fainde,   50
Nor fained she, though falsly they haue wrongd
Both her, my-selfe, Horatio and themselues.
Now may I make compare twixt hers and this
Of euerie accident.   I neere could finde
Till now, and now I feelingly perceiue,   55
They did what Heauen vnpunisht would[4] not leaue.
O false Lorenzo ! are these thy flattering lookes ?
Is this the honour that thou didst my sonne ?
And, Balthazar, — bane to thy soule and me ! —
Was this the ransome he reseru'd thee for ?[5]   60

---

[1] All edd. write.   [2] *So* A. ; Haw. require.
[3] 1618, Shall thus be this revenged ; 1623, '33, Shall thus be thus
revenged.   [4] 1618, '23, '33, should.
[5] 1618, '23, '33, for thee.

Woe to the cause of these constrained warres!
Woe to thy basenes and captiuitie!
Woe to thy birth, thy body and thy soule,
Thy cursed father, and thy conquerd selfe!
And band with bitter execrations be   65
The day and place where he did pittie thee!
But wherefore waste I mine vnfruitfull words,
When naught but blood will satisfie my woes?
I will goe plaine me to my lord the king,
And cry aloud for iustice through the court,   70
Wearing the flints with these my withered feet,
And either purchase iustice by intreats
Or tire them all with my reuenging threats.

Exit.

[Act Third.   Scene Eighth.] [1]

[HIERONIMO'S *house.*]

Enter ISABELL *and her* MAID.

ISA.   So that you say this hearb will purge the eye, [2]
And this the head? ah! but none of them will purge the
       hart!
No, thers no medicine left for my disease,
Nor any phisick to recure the dead!

She runnes lunatick.

Horatio! O, wheres Horatio?   5
   MAIDE.   Good madam, affright not thus your-selfe
With outrage for your sonne Horatio:
He sleepes in quiet in the Elizian fields.
   ISA.   Why did I not giue you gownes and goodly things,
Bought you a wistle and a whipstalke too,   10
To be reuenged on their villanies?
   MAID.   Madame, these humors doe torment my soule.

---

[1] *Here* Haw. *begins Act iv. I have not followed him, because the*
CHORUS *does not appear here, and because it is not certain that* Kyd *felt
any obligation to make his play consist of five acts.*
   [2] 1618, '23, '33, **eyes.**

ISA.   My soule? poore soule, thou talkes of things
Thou knowest not what!   My soule hath siluer wings,
That mounts me vp vnto the highest heauens —   15
To heauen?   I, there sits my Horatio,
Backt with a troup of fiery cherubins
Dauncing about his newly healed wounds,
Singing sweet hymns and chaunting heauenly notes,
Rare harmony to greet his innocence,   20
That dyde,[1] I, dyde a mirrour in our daies!
But say, where shall I finde, the men, the murderers,
That slew Horatio? whether shall I runne
To finde them out, that murdered my sonne?

Exeunt.

[Act Third.   Scene Ninth.]

[The DUKE'S castle.]

BEL-IMPERIA at a window.

BEL.   What meanes this outrage that is offred me?
Why am I thus sequestred from the court?
No notice? shall I not know the cause
Of these[2] my secret and suspitious ils?
Accursed brother! vnkinde murderer!   5
Why bends thou thus thy minde to martir me?
Hieronimo, why writ[3] I of thy wrongs,
Or why art thou so slacke in thy reuenge?
Andrea! O Andrea, that thou sawest
Me for thy freend Horatio handled thus,   10
And him for me thus causeles murdered!
Wel, force perforce, I must constraine my-selfe
To patience, and apply me to the time,
Till Heauen, as I haue hoped, shall set me free.

Enter CHRISTOPHILL.[4]

CHRIS.   Come, Madame Bel-imperia, this may[5] not be !   15

Exeunt.

---

[1] 1618, '23, '33, liv'd.   [3] 1618, '23, '33, write.   [5] 1618, '23, '33, must.
[2] *So* 1633; A. this.   [4] 1633, Christophel.

[Act Third.   Scene Tenth.]

[A room in the DUKE'S *castle.]*

Enter LORENZO, BALTHAZAR *and the* PAGE.

LOR.   Boy, talke no further ; thus farre things goe well.
Thou art assurde that thou sawest him dead?
 PAGE.   Or els, my lord, I liue not.
 LOR.   Thats enough.
As for his resolution in his end,
Leaue that to him with whom he soiourns now.   5
Heere, take my ring, and giue it Christophill,
And bid him let my sister be enlarg'd,
And bring her hither straight.   *Exit* PAGE.
This that I did was for a policie,
To smooth and keepe the murder secret,   10
Which as a nine daies wonder being ore-blowne,
My gentle sister will I now enlarge.
 BAL.   And time, Lorenzo ; for my lord the duke,
You heard, enquired for her yester-night.
 LOR.   Why ! and, my lord, I hope you heard me say   15
Sufficient reason why she kept away ;
But thats all one.   My lord, you loue her?
 BAL.   I.
 LOR.   Then in your loue beware ; deale cunningly ;
Salue all suspitions ; onely sooth me vp,
And, if she hap to stand on tearmes with vs,   20
As for her sweet-hart, and concealement so,
Iest with her gently ; vnder fained iest
Are things concealde that els would breed vnrest.
But heere she comes.

Enter BEL-IMPERIA.

LOR.   Now, sister.
 BEL.   Sister? No![1]
Thou art no brother, but an enemy,   25

1 *In* edd. *these two words are in* l. 25.

Els wouldst thou not haue vsde thy sister so :
First, to affright me with thy weapons drawne,
And with extreames abuse my company ;
And then to hurry me like whirlewinds rage
Amidst a crew of thy confederates,   30
And clap[1] me vp where none might come at me,
Nor I at any to reueale my wrongs.
What madding fury did possesse thy wits?
Or wherein ist that I offended thee?
 Lor. Aduise you better, Bel-imperia ;   35
For I haue done you no disparagement, —
Vnlesse, by more discretion then deseru'd,
I sought to saue your honour and mine owne.
 Bel. Mine honour? Why, Lorenzo, wherein ist
That I neglect my reputation so   40
As you, or any, need to rescue it?
 Lor. His Highnes and my father were resolu'd
To come conferre with olde Hieronimo
Concerning certaine matters of estate
That by the viceroy was determined.   45
 Bel. And wherein was mine honour toucht in that?
 Bal. Haue patience, Bel-imperia ; heare the rest.
 Lor. Me, next in sight, as messenger they sent
To giue him notice that they were so nigh :
Now, when I came, consorted with the prince,   50
And vnexpected in an arbour there
Found Bel-imperia with Horatio —
 Bel. How than?
 Lor. Why then, remembring that olde disgrace
Which you for Don Andrea had indurde,   55
And now were likely longer to sustaine
By being found so meanely accompanied,
Thought rather, for I knew[2] no readier meane,
To thrust Horatio forth my fathers way.
 Bal. And carry you obscurely some-where els,   60
Least that his Highnes should haue found you there.

   [1] 1633, clapt.   [2] 1618, '23, '33, know.

Bel.   Euen so, my lord?   And you are witnesse
That this is true which he entreateth of?
You, gentle brother, forged this for my sake?
And you, my lord, were made his instrument?   65
A worke of worth! worthy the noting too!
But whats the cause that you concealde me since?
    Lor.   Your melancholly, sister, since the newes
Of your first fauourite Don Andreas death
My fathers olde wrath hath exasperate.   70
    Bal.   And better wast for you, being in disgrace,
To absent your-selfe and giue his fury place.
    Bel.   But why had I no notice of his ire?
    Lor.   That were to adde more fewell to your fire,
Who burnt like Aetne for Andreas losse.   75
    Bel.   Hath not my father then enquirde for me?
    Lor.   Sister, he hath ; and thus excusde I thee.

He whispereth in her eare.

But, Bel-imperia, see the gentle prince ;
Looke on thy loue ; beholde yong Balthazar,
Whose passions by thy presence are increast,   80
And in whose melanchollie thou maiest see
Thy hate, his [1] loue, thy flight, his following thee.
    Bel.   Brother, you are become an oratour —
I know not, I, by what experience —
Too pollitick for me, past all compare,   85
Since last I saw you.   But content your-selfe ;
The prince is meditating higher things.
    Bal.   Tis of thy beauty, then, that conquers kings,
Of those thy tresses, Ariadnes twines,[2]
Wherewith my libertie thou hast surprisde,   90
Of that thine iuorie front, my sorrowes map,
Wherein I see no hauen to rest my hope.
    Bel.   To loue and feare, and both at once, my lord,
In my conceipt, are things of more import
Then womens wits are to be busied with.   95

1 1618, is.   2 1618, '23, '33, twinnes.

BAL.   Tis I that loue.

BEL.   Whome?

BAL.   Bel-imperia.

BEL.   But I that feare.

BAL.   Whome?

BEL.   Bel-imperia.

LOR.   Feare your-selfe?

BEL.   I, brother.

LOR.   How?

BEL.   As those [1]

That, what [2] they loue, are loath and feare to loose.

BAL.   Then, faire, let Balthazar your keeper be.   100

BEL.   No, Balthazar doth feare as well as we;

Et [3] tremulo metui pauidum [4] iunxere [5] timorem,

Et [3] vanum stolidae proditionis opus.   *Exit.*

LOR.   Nay, and you argue things so cunningly,

Weele goe continue this discourse at court.   105

BAL.   Led by the loadstar of her heauenly lookes,

Wends poore oppressed Balthazar,

As ore the mountains walkes the wanderer

Incertain to effect his pilgrimage.   *Exeunt.*

[Act Third.   Scene Eleventh.]

[*A street.*]

Enter two PORTINGALES, *and* HIERONIMO *meets them.*

1 PORT.[6]   By your leaue, sir.[7]

---

[1] A. 1633, Haw. *have these two words in* l. 99.

[2] 1618, '23, '33, when.   [4] 1633, me tui pauidem.

[3] A. 1633 *have* Est *in the first line and* Et *in the second;* Haw. Et *in both, without note.*   [5] A. iunx ei e.

[6] *Here and below* A. *has only* 1, 2.

[7] *Between this line and the next* 1618, '23, '33 *have the following passage:*

HIER.   Tis neither as you thinke, nor as you thinke,

Nor as you thinke: you'r wide all:

These slippers are not mine, they were my sonne Horatios.

My sonne?   And what's a sonne?   A thing begot

HIERO.   Good leaue haue you; nay, I pray you goe,

Within a paire of minutes, there-about;   5
A lump bred up in darkenesse, and doth serue
To ballance those light creatures we call women,
And at the [1] nine moneths end creepes foorth to light.
What is there yet in a sonne to make a father
Dote, rave or runne mad?   Being borne, it pouts,   10
Cries, and breeds teeth.   What is there yet in a sonne?
He must be fed, be taught to goe and speake.
I, or yet?   Why might not a man love
A calfe as well, or melt in passion over
A frisking kid, as for a sonne?   Me thinkes   15
A young bacon or a fine smooth little [2] horse-colt
Should moove a man as much as doth a son;
For one of these in very little time
Will grow to some good use, whereas a sonne,
The more he growes in stature and in yeares,   20
The more unsquar'd, unleavelled [3] he appeares,
Reckons his parents among the ranke of fooles,
Strikes cares [4] upon their heads with his mad ryots,
Makes them looke old before they meet with age. —
This is a son!   And what a losse were this,   25
Considered truely!   Oh, but my Horatio
Grew out of reach of those insatiate humours:
He loved his loving parents, he was my comfort
And his mothers joy, the very arme that did
Hold up our house, our hopes were stored up in him.   30
None but a damned murderer could hate him!
He had not seene the backe
Of nineteene yeere, when his strong arme unhorst
The proud prince Balthazar; and his great minde,
Too full of honour tooke him unto [5] mercy,   35
That valiant but ignoble Portingale.
Well!   Heaven is Heaven still!   And there's [6] Nemesis, and Furies,
And things called whippes, and they sometimes doe meet
With murderers!   They doe not alwayes scape, —
That is [7] some comfort!   I, I, I; and then   40
Time steales on, and steales and steales, till violence
Leapes foorth like thunder wrapt in a ball of fire,
And so doth bring confusion to them all.

[Line 2 follows.]

[1] Haw. *omits* the.   [4] *So* 1623, '33; 1618, care.
[2] 1633, little smooth.   [5] 1633, us to.
[3] *So* 1623, '33; 1618, unbeveled.   [6] 1633, there is.   [7] 1633, that's.

For Ile leaue you,[1] if you can leaue me so.

   II Port.   Pray you, which is the next way to my l[ord]
       the dukes?

   Hiero.   The next way from me.

   I Port.   To his house, we meane.   5

   Hiero.   O hard by ; tis yon house that you see.

   II Port.   You could not tell vs if his sonne were there?

   Hiero.   Who? my lord Lorenzo?

   I Port.   I, sir.

He goeth in at one doore and comes out at another.

   Hiero.   Oh, forbeare,[2]

For other talke for vs far fitter were!

But, if you be importunate to know   10

The way to him and where to finde him out,

Then list to me, and Ile resolue your doubt :

There is a path vpon your left hand side

That leadeth from a guiltie conscience

Vnto a forrest of distrust and feare,—   15

A darkesome place and dangerous to passe, —

There shall you meet with melancholy thoughts,

Whose balefull[3] humours if you but vpholde,[4]

It will conduct you to dispaire and death :

Whose rockie cliffes when you haue once behelde,   20

Within a hugie dale of lasting night,

That, kindled[5] with the worlds iniquities,

Doth cast vp filthy and detested fumes,—

Not far from thence where murderers haue built

A habitation for their cursed soules,   25

There, in a brazen caldron fixt by Ioue

In his fell wrath vpon a sulpher flame,

---

   [1] 1618, '23, '33 *omit* you.

   [2] A. 1633, Haw. *have these two words in* l. 9. *I regard* who, l. 8, *as hypermetrical.*

   [3] 1618, '23, '33, palefull.

   [4] 1618, '23, '33, behold.

   [5] 1618, '23, '33, That's kindled ; A. That kinded.

Your-selues shall finde Lorenzo bathing him
In boyling lead and blood of innocents.

    I PORT.   Ha, ha, ha!   30

    HIERO.   Ha, ha, ha! why, ha, ha, ha! Farewell, good ha,
        ha, ha!   *Exit.*

    II PORT.   Doubtles this man is passing lunaticke,
Or imperfection of his age doth make him dote.
Come, lets away to seek my lord the duke.   [*Exeunt.*]

[Act Third.   Scene Twelfth.]

[*The Spanish court.*]

Enter HIERONIMO *with a ponyard in one hand, and a rope in the other.*

    HIERO.   Now, sir, perhaps I come and see the king,
The king sees me, and faine would heare my sute:
Why, is not this a strange and seld-seene thing
That standers by with toyes should strike me mute?
Go too, I see their shifts, and say no more;   5
Hieronimo, tis time for thee to trudge!
Downe by the dale that flowes with purple gore
Standeth a firie tower; there sits a iudge
Vpon a seat of steele and molten brasse,
And twixt his teeth he holdes a fire-brand,   10
That leades vnto the lake where hell doth stand.
Away, Hieronimo; to him be gone:
Heele doe thee iustice for Horatios death.
Turne down this path, thou shalt be with him straite;
Or this, and then thou needst not take thy breth.   15
This way, or that way? Soft and faire, not so!
For, if I hang or kill my-selfe, lets know
Who will reuenge Horatios murther then!
No, no; fie, no! pardon me, ile none of that:

He flings away the dagger & halter.

This way Ile take; and this way comes the king,   20

He takes them vp againe.

And heere Ile haue a fling at him, thats flat!
And, Balthazar, Ile be with thee to bring;
And thee, Lorenzo!   Heeres the king; nay, stay!
And heere, — I, heere, — there goes the hare[1] away!

Enter KING, EMBASSADOR, CASTILE, *and* LORENZO.

KING.   Now shew, embassadour, what our viceroy saith :   25
Hath hee receiu'd the articles we sent?
HIERO.   Iustice! O, iustice to Hieronimo!
LOR.   Back! seest thou not the king is busie?
HIERO.   O! is he so?
KING.   Who is he that interrupts our busines?   30
HIERO.   Not I! [*aside*] Hieronimo, beware! goe by, goe
    by!
EMBAS.   Renowned king, he hath receiued and read
Thy kingly proffers and thy promist league,
And, as a man extreamely ouer-ioyd
To heare his sonne so princely entertainde,   35
Whose death he had so solemnely bewailde,
This, for thy further satisfaction
And kingly loue, he kindely lets thee know :
First, for the marriage of his princely sonne
With Bel-imperia, thy beloued neece,   40
The newes are more delightfull to his soule
Then myrrh or incense to the offended Heauens.
In person, therefore, will he come himselfe
To see the marriage rites solemnized
And in the presence of the court of Spaine   45
To knit a sure inexecrable[2] band
Of kingly loue and euerlasting league
Betwixt the crownes of Spaine and Portingale.
There will he giue his crowne to Balthazar,
And make a queene of Bel-imperia.   50

---

[1] 1633, haire.
[2] 1618, '23, '33, inexplicable ; Haw. inextricable.

KING.   Brother, how like you this our vice-roies loue?

CAST.   No doubt, my lord, it is an argument
Of honorable care to keepe his freend
And wondrous zeale to Balthazar, his sonne.
Nor am I least indebted to his Grace,   55
That bends his liking to my daughter thus.

EM.   Now last, dread lord, heere hath his Highnes sent —
Although he send not that his sonne returne —
His ransome due to Don Horatio.

HIERO.   Horatio? who cals Horatio?   60

KING.   And well remembred, thank his Maiestie!
Heere, see it giuen to Horatio.

HIERO.   Iustice! O iustice! iustice, gentle king!

KING.   Who is that?   Hieronimo?

HIERO.   Iustice! O iustice! O my sonne! my sonne!   65
My sonne, whom naught can ransome or redeeme!

LOR.   Hieronimo, you are not well aduisde.

HIERO.   Away, Lorenzo! hinder me no more,
For thou hast made me bankrupt of my blisse!
Giue me my sonne!   You shall not ransome him!   70
Away! Ile rip the bowels of the earth,

He diggeth with his dagger.

And ferrie ouer to th' Elizian plaines
And bring my sonne to shew his deadly wounds.
Stand from about me!   Ile make a pickaxe of my poniard,
And heere surrender vp my marshalship;   75
For Ile goe marshall vp the [1] feends in hell,
To be auenged on you all for this.

KING.   What meanes this outrage?
Will none of you restraine his fury?[2]

HIERO.   Nay, soft and faire; you shall not need to striue! 80
Needs must he goe that the diuels driue.   *Exit.*

KING.   What accident hath hapt [3] Hieronimo?

---

[1] 1618, '23, '33, my.
[2] A. 1633, Haw. *have these two lines as one.*
[3] 1618, '23, '33, hapt to.

I haue not seene him to demeane him so.

    LOR.   My gratious lord, he is with extreame pride
Conceiued of yong Horatio, his sonne,   85
And couetous of hauing to himselfe
The ransome of the yong prince, Balthazar,
Distract, and in a manner lunatick.

    KING.   Beleeue me, nephew, we are sorie for 't ;[1]
This is the loue that fathers beare their sonnes.   90
But, gentle brother, goe giue to him this golde,
The princes raunsome ; let him haue his due ;
For what he hath, Horatio shall not want.
Happily Hieronimo hath need thereof.

    LOR.   But if he be thus helpelesly[2] distract,   95
Tis requisite his office be resignde
And giuen to one of more discretion.

    KING.   We shall encrease his melanchollie so.
Tis best that we see further in it first ;
Till when, our-selfe will exempt the place.   100
And, brother, now bring in the embassador,
That he may be a witnes of the match
Twixt Balthazar and Bel-imperia,
And that we may prefixe a certaine time
Wherein the marriage shalbe solemnized,   105
That we may haue thy lord the vice-roy heere.

    EM.   Therein your Highnes highly shall content
His Maiestie, that longs to heare from hence.

    KING.   On then, and heare you,[3] lord embassadour.
                                   Exeunt.

1 *So* 1633 ; A. fort.
2 1618, '23, '33, haplesly.
3 1618, '23, '33, your.

[Act Third. Scene Thirteenth.]

[HIERONIMO'S *house.*]

[1] *Enter* HIERONIMO *with a book in his hand.*

Vindicta mihi.

I, heauen will be reuenged of euery ill,
Nor will they suffer murder vnrepaide!

[1] *At the beginning of this scene* 1618, '23, '33 *insert the following passage:*

Enter IAQUES *and* PEDRO.

IAQ.   I wonder, Pedro, why our master thus
At mid-night sends us with our torches light,
When man and bird and beast are all at rest
Save those that watch for rape and bloody murther?
PED.   O Iaques, know thou that our masters mind   5
Is much distraught since his Horatio died;
And, now his aged yeares should sleepe in rest,
His heart in quiet, like a desperate man,
Growes lunatike and childish for his sonne.
Sometimes as he doth at his table sit,   10
He speakes as if Horatio stood by him;
Then, starting in a rage, falles on the earth,
Cries out "Horatio! Where is my Horatio?"
So that, with extreame griefe and cutting sorrow,
There is not left in him one inch of man. —   15
See, heere he comes!

Enter HIERONIMO.

HIER.   I pry through every crevice of each wall,
Looke at each tree, and search through every brake,
Beat on the bushes, stampe our grandame earth,
Dive in the water, and stare up to heaven;   20
Yet cannot I behold my sonne Horatio.
How now? who's there?   Sprights! sprights!
PED.   We are your servants that attend you, sir.
HIER.   What make you with your torches in the darke?
PED.   You bid us light them and attend you here.   25
HIER.   No, no; you are deceiv'd! not I; you are deceiv'd!
Was I so mad to bid you light your torches now?
Light me your torches at the mid of noone,
When-as the sun-god rides in all his glory, —
Light me your torches then.

Then stay, Hieronimo, attend their will ;
For mortall men may not appoint their time.

   Ped.   Then we burne day-light.   30
   Hier. Let it be burnt ! Night is a murderous slut
That would not have her treasons to be seene ;
And yonder pale-fac'd Heccat there, the moone,
Doth give consent to that is done in darkenesse ;
And all those starres that gaze upon her face   35
Are aglots on her sleeve, pinnes on her traine,
And those that should be powerful and divine
Doe sleepe in darkenesse, when they most should shine.
   Ped. Provoke them not, faire sir, with tempting words !
The Heavens are gracious, and your miseries   40
And sorrow makes you speake you know not what.
   Hier. Villaine, thou lyest ! and thou doest nought
But tell me I am mad. Thou lyest ! I am not mad.
I know thee to be Pedro, and hee Iaques, —
Ile prove it to thee ; and, were I mad, hovv could I ?   45
Where was she the same night when my Hor[atio]
Was murdred ? She should have shone : search thou the booke !
Had the moone shone in my boyes face, ther was a kind of grace
That I know, nay I do know, had the murderer [1] seene him,
His weapon would have falne and cut the earth,   50
Had he bin fram'd of nought but blood and death.
Alacke ! vvhen mischiefe doth it knowes not what,
What shall we say to mischiefe ?

Enter Isabella.

   Isa. Deare Hieronimo, come in a-doores !
O, seeke not meanes so to increase thy sorrow !   55
   Hier. Indeed, Isabella, wee doe nothing here ;
I doe not crie, — aske Pedro and Iaques, —
Not I, indeed ; wee are very merry, very merry.
   Isa. How ? be merry here ? be merry here ?
Is not this the place, and this the very tree,   60
Where my Horatio died ? where hee was murdered ?
   Hier. Was — do not say vvhat. Let her weep it out.
This was the tree ; I set it of a kirnell ;
And, when our hote Spaine could not let it grow,
But that the infant and the humane sappe   65
Began to wither, duely twice a morning
Would I be sprinkling it with fountaine water.

[1] 1633, murderers.

Per scelus semper tutum est sceleribus iter :
Strike, and strike home, where wrong is offred thee ;

At last it grew and grew, and bore and bore,
Till, at the length, it grew a gallowes and did beare our son, —
It bore thy fruit and mine!   O wicked, wicked plant !   70

> *One knocks within at the doore.*

See who knocks there.
    PED.   It is a painter, sir.
    HIER.   Bid him come in and paint some comfort ;
For surely ther 's none lives but painted comfort.
Let him come in. — One knowes not what may chance.
Gods will, that I should set this tree !   75
But even so masters ungrateful servants reare[1] from nought,
And then they hate them that did bring them up.

> *Enter the* PAINTER.

    PAINT.   God bless you, sir.
    HIER.   Wherefore ?   Why, thou scornefull villaine,
How, where or by what meanes should I be blest ?   80
    ISA.   What wouldst thou have, good fellow ?
    PAINT.   Iustice, madame.
    HIER.   O ambitious beggar,
Wouldst thou have that that lives not in the world ?
Why, all the undelved mines cannot buy
An ounce of justice, 't is a jewell so inestimable.   85
I tell thee God hath ingrossed all justice in his hands,
And there is none but what comes from him.
    PA.   O then I see that God must right me for my murdred sonne.
    HIER.   How ? was thy sonne murdred ?
    PAIN.   I, sir ; no man did hold a sonne so deáre.   90
    HIER.   What, not as thine ?   That 's a lye
As massie as the earth !   I had a sonne
Whose least unvaluèd haire did weigh
A thousand of thy sonnes, and he was murdered.
    PAIN.   Alas, sir, I had no more but hee.   95
    HIER.   Nor I, nor I !   But this same one of mine
Was worth a legion.   But all is one. —
Pedro ! Iaques !   Goe in a-doores, Isabella, goe,
And this good fellow here and I
Will range this hideous orchard up and downe,   100
Like to two lyons reaved of their young.
Goe in a-doores, I say.   *Exeunt.*

---

[1] 1633 reard, *which may be right if* masters *be vocative, and the construction be loose.*

For euils vnto ils conductors be,
And death's the worst of resolution.

The PAINTER *and he sits downe.*

Come, let's talke wisely now.
Was thy sonne murdered?
    PAIN.   I, sir.
    HIER.   So was mine.
How dost thou take it?   Art thou not sometime mad?   105
I[s] there no tricks that comes before thine eyes?
    PAIN.   O Lord, yes, sir!
    HIER.   Art a painter? canst paint me a teare or a wound,
A groane or a sigh?   Canst paint me such a tree as this?
    PAIN.   Sir, I am sure you have heard of my painting: 110
My name's Bazardo.
    HIER.   Bazardo?   Afore God, an excellent fellow.   Looke you, sir,
Doe you see?   Ide haue you paint me [in] my gallery
In your oyle-colours matted, and draw me fiue
Yeares younger then I am, — doe you see, sir? let fiue   115
Yeares goe, — let them goe! — like the marshall of Spaine,
My wife Issabella standing by me,
With a speaking looke to my sonne Horatio,
Which should intend to this, or some such like purpose:
"God bless thee, my sweet sonne," and my hand leaning upon   120
His head, thus, sir; doe you see?   May it be done? [1]
    PAIN.   Very well, sir.
    HIER.   Nay, I pray, marke me, sir:
Then, sir, would I have you paint me this tree,
This very tree.   Canst paint a dolefull cry?
    PAIN.   Seemingly, sir.
    HIER.   Nay, it should cry.   But all is one!   125
Well, sir, paint me a youth run thorow and thorow
With villaines swords, hanging upon this tree.
Canst thou draw a murderer?
    PAIN.   Ile warrant you, sir;
I haue the patterne of the most notorious villaines
That ever lived in all Spaine.   130
    HIER.   O, let them be worse, worse!   Stretch thine art.
And let their beards be of Iudas his owne colour,
And let their eye-brows jutty over: in any case obserue that!
Then, sir, after some violent noise,
Bring me forth in my shirt, and my gown under mine arme,   135

[1] *As this speech is a very rude sort of verse, if indeed it is not, like the other
conversations with the* PAINTER, *prose, I leave the lines as they stand in* 1633.
The line division is, in general, that of 1633.

For he that thinks with patience to contend　　　10
To quiet life, his life shall easily end.
Fata si miseros iuuant, habes salutem ;
Fata si[1] *vitam negant, habes sepulchrum:*
If destinie thy miseries doe ease,
Then hast thou health, and happie shalt thou be ;　　　15

With my torch in my hand, and my sword reared up, thus!
And with these words :
　　　　　　" What noise is this?　Who calls Hieronimo?"
May it be done?
　　　PAIN.　　　Yea, sir.
　　　HIER.　Well, sir; then bring me foorth, bring me through ally and ally,　140
still with a distracted countenance going along, and let my haire heave up
my night-cap, —
　　　Let the cloudes scowle, make the moone darke, the stars extinct, the
windes blowing, the belles tolling, the owles shriking, the toads crooking, the
minutes jerring, and the clocke striking twelue, —　　　145
　　　And then, at last, sir, starting, behold a man hanging and tottring and
tottring, as you know the winde will weave a man, and I, with a trice, to
cut him downe, —
　　　And, looking upon him by the advantage of my torch, find it to be my
sonne Horatio.　　　150
There you may [shew] a passion, there you may shew a passion!
Draw me like old Priam of Troy,
Crying " The house is a-fire! the house is a-fire!"
As the torch over thy head.　Make me curse,
Make me rave, make me crie, make me mad!　　　155
Make me well againe, make me curse hell,
Invocate; and in the end leave me
In a trance, and so foorth.
　　　PAIN.　And is this the end?
　　　HIER.　O, no! there is no end!　The end is death and madnes;　160
As I am never better then when I am mad ;
Then me thinkes I am a brave fellow,
Then I doe wonders, — but reason abuseth me ;
And there's the torment, there's the hell!
At the last, sir, bring me to one of the murderers :　　　165
Were he as strong as Hector, thus would I
Teare, and dragge him up and downe!

　　　He beats the PAINTER *in ; then comes out againe with a booke in his hand.*

　　　　　　[Line 1 *follows.]*

　　　　　　[1] 1633, Futasi.

If destinie denie thee life, Hieronimo,
Yet shalt thou be assured of a tombe ;
If neither, yet let this thy comfort be :
Heauen couereth him that hath no buriall.
And, to conclude, I will reuenge his death!　　　　20
But how?　Not as the vulgare wits of men,
With open, but ineuitable ils ;
As by a secret, yet a certain meane,
Which vnder kindeship wilbe cloked best.
Wise men will take their oportunitie,　　　　　25
Closely and safely fitting things to time ;
But in extreames aduantage hath no time :
And therefore all times fit not for reuenge.
Thus, therefore, will I rest me in unrest,
Dissembling quiet in vnquietnes,　　　　　30
Not seeming that I know their villanies,
That my simplicitie may make them think
That ignorantly I will let all slip ;
For ignorance, I wot, and well they know,
Remedium malorum iners [1] *est.*　　　　　35
Nor ought auailes it me to menace them,
Who, as a wintrie storme vpon a plaine,
Will beare me downe with their nobilitie.
No, no, Hieronimo, thou must enioyne
Thine eies to obseruation, and thy tung　　　　　40
To milder speeches then thy spirit affoords,
Thy hart to patience, and thy hands to rest,
Thy cappe to curtesie,[2] and thy knee to bow,
Till to reuenge thou know when, where and how.
How now? what noise, what coile is that you keepe?　　45

A noise within.

Enter a Seruant.

SER.　Heere are a sort of poore petitioners
That are importunate, and it shall please you, sir,

---

[1] *So* A.; 1633, Haw. mors; *but* Sarrazin, Anglia, XIII, 127, *points out
that* A. *is right.*　　　　　[2] A. cuttesie.

That you should plead their cases to the king.

    HIERO.   That I should plead their seuerall actions?
Why, let them enter, and let me see them.   50

Enter three CITTIZENS and an OLDE MAN.

    I CIT.[1]   So I tell you this : for learning and for law
There is [2] not any aduocate in Spaine
That can preuaile or will take halfe the paine
That he will in pursuite of equitie.

    HIERO.   Come neere, you men, that thus importune me !   55
[*Aside*] Now must I beare a face of grauitie,
For thus I vsde, before my marshalship,
To pleade in causes as corrigedor. —
Come on, sirs, whats the matter?

    II CIT.   Sir, an action.

    HIERO.   Of batterie?

    I CIT.   Mine of debt.

    HIERO.   Giue place.   60

    II CIT.   No, sir, mine is an action of the case.

    III. CIT.   Mine an *eiectione firmae* [3] by a [4] lease.

    HIERO.   Content you, sirs ; are you determined
That I should plead your seuerall actions?

    I CIT.   I, sir ; and heeres my declaration.   65

    II CIT.   And heere is my band.

    III CIT.   And heere is my lease.

They giue him papers.[5]

    HIERO.   But wherefore stands yon silly man so mute,
With mournfull eyes and hands to heauen vprearde?
Come hether, father ; let me know thy cause.

    SENEX.   O worthy sir, my cause but slightly knowne   70
May mooue the harts of warlike Myrmydons,
And melt the Corsicke rockes with ruthfull teares!

    HIERO.   Say, father ; tell me whats thy sute!

---

    [1] *Here and below* A. *has only* 1, 2, 3.

    [2] A. Theres ; *corr. silently by* Haw.

    [3] A. 1633, Haw. eiectione firma ; Sarrazin, Engl. Stud., XV, 258, ejectio
firma.   [4] 1633 *omits* a.   [5] A. paper ; *corr. silently by* Haw.

SENEX.   No, sir, could my woes
Giue way vnto my most distresfull words,   75
Then should I not in paper, as you see,
With incke bewray what blood began in me.
    HIERO.   Whats heere? " The Humble Supplication
Of Don Bazulto for his Murdered Sonne."
    SENEX.   I, sir.
    HIERO.   No, sir, it was my murdred sonne!   80
Oh, my sonne, my sonne! oh, my sonne Horatio!
But mine or thine, Bazulto, be content;
Heere, take my hand-kercher and wipe thine eies,
Whiles wretched I in thy mishaps may see
The liuely portraict of my dying selfe.   85

                He draweth out a bloudie napkin.

O, no ; not this! Horatio, this was thine!
And when I dyde it in thy deerest blood,
This was a token twixt thy soule and me
That of thy death reuenged I should be.
But heere: take this, and this! what? my purse?   90
I, this and that and all of them are thine;
For all as one are our extremeties.
    I CIT.   Oh, see the kindenes of Hieronimo!
    II CIT.   This gentlenes shewes him a gentleman.
    HIERO.   See, see, oh, see thy shame, Hieronimo!   95
See heere a louing father to his sonne :
Beholde the sorrowes and the sad laments
That he deliuereth[1] for his sonnes dicease.
If loues[2] effects so striues in lesser things,
If loue enforce such moodes in meaner wits,   100
If loue expresse[3] such power in poore estates,
Hieronimo, as when[4] a raging sea,
Tost with the winde and tide, ore-turneth[5] then
The vpper billowes, course of waues to keep,

---

[1] 1618, '23, '33, deliuered.
[2] 1618, loue.   [3] 1618, '23, '33, enforce.
[4] Edd. when as; *corr. by* Kittredge.
[5] A. ore turnest; 1633, oreturned; Haw. o'erturneth, *without note.*

Whilest lesser waters labour in the deepe,　　　　　　　105
Then shamest thou not, Hieronimo, to neglect
The sweet[1] reuenge of thy Horatio?
Though on this earth iustice will not be found,
Ile downe to hell and in this passion
Knock at the dismall gates of Plutos court,　　　　　　110
Getting by force, as once Alcides did,
A troupe of furies and tormenting hagges,
To torture Don Lorenzo and the rest.
Yet, least the triple-headed porter should
Denye my passage to the slimy strond,　　　　　　　115
The Thracian poet thou shalt counterfeite :
Come on, olde father, be my Orpheus ;
And, if thou canst no notes vpon the harpe,
Then sound the burden of thy sore harts greefe
Till we do gaine that Proserpine may graunt　　　　　120
Reuenge on them that murd[e]red my sonne.
Then will I rent and teare them thus and thus,
Shiuering their limmes in peeces with my teeth !

Teare the papers.

　I CIT.　　Oh, sir, my declaration !

Exit HIERONIMO *and they after.*

II CIT.　　　　　　　　　　　Saue my bond !

Enter HIERONIMO.

　II CIT.　　Saue my bond !
　III CIT.　　　　　　　　Alas my lease, it cost me　　　125
Ten pound,[2] and you, my lord, haue torne the same !
　HIERO.　　That can not be, I gaue it neuer a wound ;
Shew me one drop of bloud fall from the same !
How is it possible I should slay it then ?
Tush, no ! Run after, catch me if you can !　　　　　130

Exeunt all but the OLDE MAN.

　　　[1] 1618, swift.
　　　[2] A. 1633, Haw. *haue these two words in* l. 125.

BAZULTO *remaines till* HIERONIMO *enters againe, who, staring him in the face, speakes:*

HIERO.   And art thou come, Horatio, from the depth,
To aske for iustice in this vpper earth?
T[o] tell thy father thou art vnreuenged?
To wring more teares from Isabellas eies,
Whose lights are dimd with ouer-long laments?   135
Goe back, my sonne, complaine to Eacus;
For heeres no iustice.   Gentle boy, begone;
For iustice is exiled from the earth.
H[i]eronimo will beare thee company.
Thy mother cries on righteous Radamant   140
For iust reuenge against the murderers.
 SENEX.   Alas, my l[ord], whence springs this troubled
   speech?
 HIERO.   But let me looke on my Horatio:
Sweet boy, how art thou chang'd in deaths black shade!
Had Proserpine no pittie on thy youth,   145
But suffered thy fair crimson-colourd spring
With withered winter to be blasted thus?
Horatio, thou art older then thy father:
Ah, ruthlesse father, that fauour thus transformess.
 BA.   Ah, my good lord, I am not your yong sonne.   150
 HIE.   What! not my sonne? thou then a Furie art
Sent from the emptie kingdome of blacke night
To summon me to make appearance
Before grim Mynos and iust Radamant,
To plague Hieronimo, that is remisse   155
And seekes not vengeance for Horatioes death.
 BA.   I am a greeued man, and not a ghost,
That came for iustice for my murdered sonne.
 HIE.   I, now I know thee, now thou namest thy[1]
   sonne;
Thou art the liuely image of my griefe: 160
Within thy face my sorrowes I may see;

---

[1] *So* 1633, Haw.; A. my.

Thy eyes are gum'd[1] with teares, thy cheekes are wan,
Thy forehead troubled, and thy muttring lips
Murmure sad words abruptly broken off
By force of windie sighes thy spirit breathes ;   165
And all this sorrow riseth for thy sonne,
And selfe-same sorrow feele I for my sonne.
Come in, old man ; thou shalt to Izabell.
Leane on my arme ; I thee, thou me shalt stay ;
And thou and I and she will sing a song,   170
Three parts in one, but all of discords fram'd, —
Talke not of cords ! — but let vs now be gone, —
For with a cord Horatio was slaine.   *Exeunt.*

[Act Third.   Scene Fourteenth.]

[*The Spanish court.*]

Enter KING OF SPAINE, *the* DUKE, VICE-ROY, *and* LORENZO, BALTHAZAR, DON PEDRO, *and* BELIMPERIA.

KING.   Go, brother, it is the Duke of Castiles cause ;
Salute the vice-roy in our name.[2]
CASTILE.   I go.
VICE.   Go forth, Don Pedro, for thy nephews sake,
And greet the Duke of Castile.
PEDRO.   It shall be so.
KING.   And now to meet these Portaguise ;   5
For, as we now are, so sometimes were these,
Kings and commanders of the westerne Indies.
Welcome, braue vice-roy, to the court of Spaine!
And welcome, all his honorable traine !
Tis not vnknowne to vs for why you come,   10
Or haue so kingly crost the seas.
Suffiseth it, in this we note the troth
And more then common loue you lend to vs.
So is it that mine honorable neece,

----

¹ 1618, '23, '33, dim'd.   ² *One long line in* A.

For it beseemes vs now that it be knowne,   15
Already is betroth'd to Balthazar ;
And, by appointment and our condiscent,
To-morrow are they to be married.
To this intent we entertaine thy-selfe,
Thy followers, their pleasure, and our peace.   20
Speak, men of Portingale, shall it be so?
If I, say so ; if not, say flatly no.
    VICE.   Renowmed king, I come not, as thou thinkst,
With doubtfull followers, vnresolued men,
But such as haue vpon thine articles   25
Confirmed thy motion and contented me.
Know, soueraigne, I come to solemnize
The marriage of thy beloued neece,
Faire Bel-imperia, with my Balthazar, —
With thee, my sonne, whom sith I liue to see,   30
Heere, take my crowne, I giue it her and thee,
And let me liue a solitarie life,
In ceaselesse praiers,
To think how strangely heauen hath thee preserued.
    KING.   See, brother, see, how nature striues in him!   35
Come, worthy vice-roy, and accompany
Thy freend, [to strive] with thine extremities :
A place more priuate fits this princely mood.
    VICE.   Or heere or where your Highnes thinks it good.

                    Exeunt all but CAS[TILE] *and* LOR[ENZO].

    CAS.   Nay, stay, Lorenzo ; let me talke with you.   40
Seest thou this entertainement of these kings?
    LOR.   I doe, my lord, and ioy to see the same.
    CAS.   And knowest thou why [1] this meeting is?
    LOR.   For her, my lord, whom Balthazar doth loue,
And to confirme their promised marriage.   45
    CAS.   She is thy sister.
    LOR.   Who? Bel-imperia?
I, my gratious lord, and this is the day

              [1] *Qy.* for whom, *or* wherefore, *for metre.*

That I haue longd so happily to see.[1]
   CAS. Thou wouldst be loath that any fault of thine
Should intercept her in her happines?   50
    LOR. Heauens will not let Lorenzo erre so much.
   CAS. Why then, Lorenzo, listen to my words :
It is suspected, and reported too,
That thou, Lorenzo, wrongst Hieronimo,
And in his sutes towards his Maiestie   55
Still keepst him back and seeks [2] to crosse his sute.
    LOR. That I, my lord?
   CAS. I tell thee, sonne, my-selfe haue heard it said,
When to my sorrow I haue beene ashamed
To answere for thee, though thou art [3] my sonne.   60
Lorenzo, knowest thou not the common loue
And kindenes that Hieronimo hath wone
By his deserts within the court of Spaine?
Or seest thou not the k[ing] my brothers care
In his behalfe and to procure his health?   65
Lorenzo, shouldst thou thwart his passions,
And hee exclaime against thee to the king,
What honour wert in this assembly,
Or what a scandale wert among the kings,
To heare Hieronimo exclaime on thee !   70
Tell me, — and looke thou tell me truely too, —
Whence growes the ground of this report in court?
    LOR. My l[ord], it lyes not in Lorenzos power
To stop the vulgar liberall of their tongues :
A small aduantage makes a water-breach ;   75
And no man liues that long contenteth all.
   CAS. My-selfe haue seene thee busie to keep back
Him and his supplications from the king.
    LOR. Your-selfe, my l[ord], hath seene his passions,
That ill beseemde the presence of a king ;   80
And, for I pittied him in his distresse,

---

1 *This speech as two lines in* edd., *ending* lord, see.
2 Haw. seek'st, *without note.*
3 1618, '23, '33, wert.

I helde him thence with kinde and curteous words,
As free from malice to Hieronimo
As to my soule, my lord.

CAS.　Hieronimo, my sonne, mistakes thee then.　　85

LOR.　My gratious father, beleeue me, so he doth;
But whats a silly man, distract in minde
To think vpon the murder of his sonne?
Alas, how easie is it for him to erre!
But, for his satisfaction and the worlds,　　90
Twere good, my l[ord], that [1] Hieronimo and I
Were reconcilde, if he misconster me.

CAS.　Lorenzo, thou hast said; it shalbe so!
Goe, one of you, and call Hieronimo.

Enter BALTHAZAR *and* BEL-IMPERIA.[2]

BAL.　Come, Bel-imperia,[3] Balthazars content,　　95
My sorrowes ease, and soueraigne of my blisse, —
Sith heauen hath ordainde thee [4] to be mine,
Disperce those cloudes and melanchollie lookes,
And cleere [5] them vp with those thy sunne-bright eies,
Wherein my hope and heauens faire [6] beautie lies!　　100

BEL.　My lookes, my lord, are fitting for my loue,
Which, new begun, can shew no [7] brighter yet.

BAL.　New kindled flames should burne as morning sun.

BEL.　But not too fast, least heate and all be done.
I see my lord my father.

BAL.　　　　　　True,[8] my loue;　　105
I will goe salute him.[9]

CAS.　　　　　Welcome, Balthazar,
Welcome, braue prince, the pledge of Castiles peace! [10]
And welcome Bel-imperia! How now, girle?
Why commest thou sadly to salute vs thus?
Content thy-selfe, for I am satisfied.　　110

---

[1] 1623, '33 *omit* that.
[2] A. BŒL-IMPERIA.
[3] A. Bel-imperie.
[4] 1623, '33, thee ordained.
[5] 1618, '23, '33, cheare.

[6] *Misprinted* faite *in* A.
[7] A. *omits* no.
[8] A. Truce; *so* Haw., *without* **note.**
[9] *This speech as one line in* edd.
[10] *Two lines in* edd., *ending* prince, **peace.**

It is not now as when Andrea liu'd ;
We haue forgotten and forgiuen that,
And thou art graced with a happier loue.
But, Balthazar, heere comes Hieronimo ;
Ile haue a word with him.

Enter HIERONIMO *and a* SERUANT.

HIERO.   And wheres the duke?   115
SER. Yonder.
HIERO.   Euen so.[1]
[*Aside*] What new deuice haue they deuised, tro?
Pocas palabras! Milde as the lambe !
Ist[2] I will be reueng'd ?   No, I am not the man.
  CAS. Welcome, Hieronimo !   120
  LOR. Welcome, Hieronimo !
  BAL. Welcome, Hieronimo !
  HIERO. My lords, I thank you for Horatio.
  CAS. Hieronimo, the reason that I sent
To speak with you is this —
  HIERO.   What? so short?   125
Then Ile be gone ; I thank you fort !
  CAS. Nay, stay, Hieronimo ; goe call him, sonne.
  LOR.[3] Hieronimo, my father craues a word with you.
  HIERO. With me, sir? Why, my l[ord], I thought you
          had done.
  LOR. [*aside*] No ; would he had !
  CAS.   Hieronimo, I hear[4]   130
You finde your-selfe agreeued at my sonne,
Because you haue not accesse vnto the king,
And say tis he that intercepts your sutes.
  HIERO. Why, is not this a miserable thing, my lord?
  CAS. Hieronimo, I hope you haue no cause,   135
And would be loth that one of your deserts,
Should once haue reason to suspect my sonne,
Considering how I think of you my-selfe.

<hr>

1 *Part of* l. 117 *in* edd.   3 A. *omits* LOR.
2 1633, Hist.   4 *Part of* l. 131 *in* edd.

HIERO.   Your   sonne   Lorenzo?   whome,   my   noble
     lord?
The hope of Spaine? mine honourable freend?   140
Graunt me the combat of them, if they dare!

Drawes out his sword.

Ile meet him face-to-face to tell me so!
These be the scandalous reports of such
As loues [1] not me, and hate my lord too much.
Should I suspect Lorenzo would preuent   145
Or crosse my sute, that loued my sonne so well?
My lord, I am ashamed it should be said.
   LOR.   Hieronimo, I neuer gaue you cause.
   H[I]ERO.   My good lord, I know you did not.
   CAS.   There then pause,[2]
And, for the satisfaction of the world,   150
Hieronimo, frequent my homely house,
The Duke of Castile Ciprians ancient seat;
And when thou wilt, vse me, my sonne, and it.
But heere before Prince Balthazar and me
Embrace each other, and be perfect freends.   155
   HIERO.   I, marry, my lord, and shall!
Freends, quoth he? See, Ile be freends with you all!
Especially [3] with you, my louely lord;
For diuers causes it is fit for vs
That we be freends.   The world is suspitious,   160
And men may think what we imagine not.
   BAL.   Why this is freendly doone, Hieronimo.
   LOR.   And that I hope olde grudges are forgot.
   HIERO.   What els? it were a shame it should not
     be so!
   CAS.   Come on, Hieronimo, at my request;   165
Let vs entreat your company to-day!

Exeunt.

---

1 Haw. love, *without note.*
2 *Part of* l. 150 *in* edd.
3 A. 1633, Specially; *corr. silently by* Haw.

HIERO.   Yo[u]r lordships to commaund ! Pha ![1] keep your
               way ![2]
Chi mi fa più carezze che non suole
Tradito mi ha o tradir mi vuole.[3]

Exit.

[CHORUS.]

Enter GHOAST *and* REUENGE.

GHOST.   Awake Erictho ![4] Cerberus, awake !
[5] Sollicite Pluto, gentle Proserpine !
To combat, Achinon and Ericus [6] in hell !
For neere by Stix and Phlegeton :[7]

[1] 1633 *omits* Pha.

[2] *Two lines in* A. 1633 ; *perhaps because half is spoken before the others
go out and half after.*

[3] A. *has:*

> Mi. Chi mi fa?   Pui Correzza Che no fule
> Tradito viha otrade vule.

1633 *has:*

> Mi, chi mifa?   Pui Correzza Che non fult
> Tradito niha otrade vel.

The text follows Haw., *except that he retains* Mi *as the first word; it appears
in no version of the proverb that I have seen.*

[4] A. Erictha ; Hazlitt, Alecto.

[5] Hazlitt *prints:*

> Solicit Pluto, gentle Proserpine,
> To combat Acheron and Erebus in hell;
> Or near-by Styx and Phlegethon ;
> Nor ferried Charon to the fiery lakes
> Such fearful sights as poor Andrea sees.

This is certainly not right. Kittredge *suggests as barely possible:*

> Solicit Pluto, gentle Proserpine!
> To combat, Acheron and Erebus!
> For neere did Stix and Phlegeton in hell
> Nor Carons ferrie to the fierie lakes
> Such fearfull sights as poore Andrea see.

[6] *So* A.; 1633, Achmon and Erichus; Haw. Acheron and Erebus;
Ericus *suggests also* Orcus; *but the whole speech seems hopelessly corrupt.*

[7] *Qy.* For neere by Stix and Phlegeton there came.

Nor ferried Caron to the fierie lakes,   5
Such fearfull sights, as poore Andrea see?[1]
Reuenge awake!
    REUENGE.   Awake? for-why?[2]
    GHOST.   Awake, Reuenge! for thou art ill aduisde
To[3] sleepe away[4] what thou[5] art warnd to watch!
    REUENGE.   Content thy-selfe, and doe not trouble me.   10
    GHOST.   Awake, Reuenge, if loue, as loue hath had,
Haue yet the power or preuailance in hell!
Hieronimo with Lorenzo is ioynde in league,
And intercepts our passage to reuenge.
Awake, Reuenge, or we are woe-begone![6]   15
    REUENGE.   Thus worldlings ground what they haue
        dreamd vpon!
Content thy-selfe, Andrea; though I sleepe,
Yet is[7] my mood soliciting their soules.
Sufficeth thee that poore Hieronimo
Cannot forget his sonne Horatio.   20
Nor dies Reuenge although he sleepe a-while;
For in vnquiet, quietnes is faind,[8]
And slumbring is a common worldly wile.
Beholde, Andrea, for an instance how
Reuenge hath slept; and then imagine thou   25
What tis to be subiect to destinie.

Enter a Dumme-shew.

    GHOST.   Awake, Reuenge! reueale this misterie!
    REUENGE.   The two first [do] the nuptiall torches beare,[9]
As brightly burning as the mid-daies sunne;
But after them doth Himen hie as fast,   30
Clothed in sable and a saffron robe,

---

[1] *So* A.; 1633, sees. *In* ll. 4–6 *I retain the punctuation of* A.
[2] 1618, '23, '33 *omit this half-line, apparently by mistake.*
[3] A. Th.; 1633, Haw. To.
[4] 1633, Haw. awake.
[5] 1618, '23, '33, *omit* thou.
[6] A. degone.
[7] 1618, '23, '33, in.
[8] 1618, '23, '33, found.
[9] 1633, Haw. bore.

And blowes them out and quencheth them with blood,
As discontent that things continue so.
   Ghost.   Sufficeth me ; thy meanings vnderstood,
And thanks to thee and those infernall powers   35
That will not tollerate a louers woe.
Rest thee ; for I will sit to see the rest.
   Reuenge.   Then argue not ; for thou hast thy request.

Exeunt.

Actus Quartus. [Scene First.]

[*The* Duke's *castle.*]

Enter Bel-imperia *and* Hieronimo.

   Bel-imperia.   Is this the loue thou bearst Horatio?
Is this the kindnes that thou counterfeits,[1]
Are these the fruits of thine incessant teares?
Hieronimo, are these thy passions,
Thy protestations and thy deepe laments,   5
That thou wert wont to wearie men withall?
O vnkind father!   O deceitfull world !
With what excuses canst thou shew thy-selfe, —
With what dishonour, and the hate of men, —
From this dishonour and the hate of men,[2]   10
Thus to neglect the losse and life of him
Whom both my letters and thine owne beliefe
Assures thee to be causles slaughtered?
Hieronimo ! for shame, Hieronimo,
Be not a history to after times   15
Of such ingratitude vnto thy sonne!
Vnhappy mothers of such children then !
But monstrous fathers, to forget so soone
The death of those whom they with care and cost
Haue tendred so, thus careles should be lost![3]   20

---

[1] *So* A. 1633 ; Haw. counterfeit'st, *without note.*

[2] Hazlitt *says this line is a mistake, and should be omitted.*

[3] *Confusion of two constructions is probably responsible for the queer* syntax,

My-selfe, a stranger in respect of thee,
So loued his life as still I wish their deathes.
Nor shall his death be vnreuengd by me,
Although I beare it out for fashions sake ;
For heere I sweare in sight of heauen and earth,   25
Shouldst thou neglect the loue thou shouldst retaine
And giue it ouer and deuise no more,
My-selfe should send their hatefull soules to hel
That wrought his downfall with extreamest death !
 Hie. But may it be that Bel-imperia   30
Vowes such reuenge as she hath dain'd to say?
Why then, I see that heauen applies our drift,
And all the saints doe sit soliciting
For vengeance on those cursed murtherers.
Madame, tis true, and now I find it so.   35
I found a letter, written in your name,
And in that letter, how Horatio died.
Pardon, O pardon, Bel-imperia,
My feare and care in not beleeuing it!
Nor thinke I thoughtles thinke vpon a meane   40
To let his death be vnreueng'd at full.
And heere I vow, so you but giue consent
And will conceale my resolution,
I will ere long determine of their deathes
That causles thus haue murderd my sonne.   45
 Bel. Hieronimo, I will consent, conceale,
And ought that may effect for thine auaile,
Ioyne with thee to reuenge Horatioes death.
 Hier. On[1] then, [and] whatsoeuer I deuise,
Let me entreat you grace my practises,   50
For-why the plots already in mine head. —
Heere they are !

   Enter Balthazar *and* Lorenzo.

 Bal.   How now, Hieronimo?
What, courting Bel-imperia?[2]

   [1] 1618, '23, '33, O. [2] *One line in* edd.

Hiero.   I, my lord,
Such courting as, I promise you,[1]
She hath my hart, but you, my lord, haue hers.   55
    Lor.   But now, Hieronimo, or neuer we are to intreate
        your helpe.
    Hie.   My help? why, my good lords, assure your-selues
        of me ;
For you haue giuen me cause, — I, by my faith, haue you!
    Bal.   It pleasde you at the entertainment of the em-
        bassadour,
To grace the King so much as with a shew :   60
Now were your studie so well furnished
As, for the passing of the first nights sport,
To entertaine my father with the like,
Or any such like pleasing motion,
Assure yourselfe it would content them well.   65
    Hiero.   Is this all?
    Bal.   I, this is all.
    Hiero.   Why then ile fit you; say no more.
When I was yong I gaue my minde
And plide my-selfe to fruitles poetrie,   70
Which, though it profite the professor naught,
Yet is it passing pleasing to the world.
    Lor.   And how for that?
    Hiero.   Marrie, my good lord, thus. —
And yet, me thinks, you are too quick with vs ! —
When in Tolledo there I studied,   75
It was my chaunce to write a tragedie, —
See heere, my lords, —   *He shewes them a book.*
Which, long forgot, I found this other day.
Now would your lordships fauour me so much
As but to grace me with your acting it,   80
I meane each one of you to play a part.
Assure you it will proue most passing strange
And wondrous plausible to that assembly.
    Bal.   What, would you haue vs play a tragedie?

        [1] *One line in* edd.

HIERO.   Why, Nero thought it no disparagement,   85
And kings and emperours haue tane delight
To make experience of their wits in plaies!
    LOR.   Nay, be not angry, good Hieronimo;
The prince but asked a question.
    BAL.   In faith, Hieronimo, and you be in earnest,   90
Ile make one.
    LOR.   And I another.
    HIERO.   Now, my good lord, could you intreat,
Your sister, Bel-imperia, to make one, —
For whats a play without a woman in it?
    BEL.   Little intreaty shall serue me, Hieronimo,   95
For I must needs be imployed in your play.
    HIERO.   Why, this is well!   I tell you, lordings,
It was determined to haue beene acted,
By gentlemen and schollers too,
Such as could tell what to speak.   100
    BAL.   And now it shall be plaide by princes and courtiers,
Such as can tell how to speak,[1]
If, as it is our country manner,
You will but let vs know the argument.
    HIERO.   That shall I roundly.   The cronicles of Spaine   105
Recorde this written of a knight of Rodes:[2]
He was betrothed, and wedded at the length,
To one Perseda, an Italian dame,
Whose beauty rauished all that her behelde,
Especially the soule of Soliman,   110
Who at the marriage was [3] the cheefest guest.
By sundry meanes sought Soliman to winne
Persedas loue, and could not gaine the same.
Then gan he break his passions to a freend,
One of his bashawes whom he held full deere.   115
Her had this bashaw long solicited,
And saw she was not otherwise to be wonne
But by her husbands death, this knight of Rodes,

---

[1] Lines 101, 102 *as prose in* A.   *The metre is often imperfect in this scene.*
[2] 1618, of the Rhodes.   [3] *Misprinted* way *in* A.

Whome presently by trecherie he slew.
She, stirde with an exceeding hate therefore,   120
As cause of this, slew [Sultan] Soliman,
And, to escape the bashawes tirannie,
Did stab her-selfe.   And this [1] the tragedie.
    LOR.   O, excellent!
    BEL.   But say, Hieronimo:
What then became of him that was the bashaw? [2]   125
    HIERO.   Marrie thus: moued with remorse of his misdeeds,
Ran to a mountain top and hung [3] himselfe.
    BAL.   But which of vs is to performe that parte?
    HIERO.   O, that will I, my lords; make no doubt of it;
Ile play the murderer, I warrant you;   130
For I already haue conceited that.
    BAL.   And what shall I?
    HIERO.   Great Soliman, the Turkish emperour.
    LOR.   And I?
    HIERO.   Erastus, the knight of Rhodes.
    BEL.   And I?
    HIERO.   Perseda, chaste and resolute.   135
And heere, my lords, are seuerall abstracts drawne,
For eache of you to note your [seuerall] [4] partes,
And act it as occasion's offred you.
You must prouide [you with] [4] a Turkish cappe,
A black mustacio and a fauchion.   140

        Giues paper to BAL[THAZAR].

You with a crosse, like to a knight of Rhodes.

        Giues another to LOR[ENZO].

And, madame, you must [then] attire your-selfe

        He giueth BEL[-IMPERIA] *another.*

Like Phœbe, Flora, or the huntresse [Dian], [4]
Which [5] to your discretion shall seeme best.
And as for me, my lords, Ile looke to one,   145

    [1] 1618, '23, '33, this is.   [4] *Supplied by* Kittredge.
    [2] *This speech as two lines in* edd., *ending* him, bashaw.
    [3] 1618, '23, '33, hang'd.   [5] *Qy. insert* e'er *or read* unto *for* to.

And with the raunsome that the vice-roy sent
So furnish and performe this tragedie
As all the world shall say Hieronimo
Was liberall in gracing of it so.

   BAL.   Hieronimo, me thinks a comedie were better.   150
   HIERO.   A comedie? fie ! comedies are fit for common
        wits ;
But to present a kingly troupe withall,
Giue me a stately-written tragedie, —
Tragedia cothurnata,[1] fitting kings,
Containing matter, and not common things !   155
My lords, all this [our sport] must be perfourmed,
As fitting, for the first nights reuelling.
The Italian tragedians were so sharpe
Of wit [2] that in one houres meditation
They would performe any-thing in action.   160

   LOR.   And well it may, for I haue seene the like
In Paris, mongst the French tragedians.

   HIERO.   In Paris? mas, and well remembred ! —
Theres one thing more that rests for vs to doo.

   BAL.   Whats that, Hieronimo ?   165
Forget not any-thing.[3]

   HIERO.   Each one of vs
Must act his parte in vnknowne languages,[4]
That it may breede the more varietie :
As you, my lord, in Latin, I in Greeke,
You in Italian, and, for-because I know   170
That Bel-imperia hath practised the French,
In courtly French shall all her phraises be.

   BEL.   You meane to try my cunning then, Hieronimo !
   BAL.   But this will be a meere confusion,
And hardly shall we all be vnderstoode.   175

   HIERO.   It must be so ; for the conclusion

---

[1] A. cother nato ; *corr. silently by* Haw.
[2] *Part of* l. 157 *in* edd.
[3] *This speech as one line in* edd.
[4] *As two lines in* edd., *ending* part, languages.

Shall proue the inuention and all was good ;
And I my-selfe in an oration,
That I will haue there behinde a curtaine,
And with a strange and wondrous shew besides,   180
Assure your-selfe, shall make the matter knowne.
And all shalbe concluded in one scene,
For theres no pleasure tane in tediousnes.

    BAL. [*to* LOR.]   How like you this?

    LOR.   Why thus, my lord, we must resolue,   185
To soothe his humors vp.

    BAL.   On then, Hieronimo ; farewell till soone!

    HIERO.   Youle plie this geere?

    LOR.   I warrant you.   *Exeunt all but* HIERO.

    HIERO.   Why, so! now shall I see the fall of Babilon   190
Wrought by the heauens in this confusion.
And, if the world like not this tragedie,
Hard is the hap of olde Hieronimo.   *Exit.*

[Act Fourth.   Scene Second.]

[HIERONIMO'S *garden.*]

Enter ISABELLA *with a weapon.*

Tell me no more!   O monstrous homicides !
Since neither pietie nor pittie moues
The king to iustice or compassion,
I will reuenge my-selfe vpon this place,
Where thus they murdered my beloued sonne.   5

She cuts downe the arbour.

Downe with these branches and these loathsome bowes
Of this vnfortunate and fatall pine !
Downe with them, Isabella ; rent them vp,
And burne the roots from whence the rest is sprung!
I will not leaue a root, a stalke, a tree,   10
A bowe, a branch, a blossome, nor a leafe, —
No, not a hearb within this garden plot,

Accursed complot of my miserie !
Fruitlesse for-euer may this garden be,
Barren the earth, and blislesse whosoeuer   15
Immagines not to keep it vnmanurde !
An easterne winde comixt with noisome aires
Shall blast the plants and the yong saplings [here],
The earth with serpents shalbe pestered,
And passengers, for feare to be infect,   20
Shall stand aloofe, and, looking at it, tell
There murdred dide the sonne of Isabell.
I, heere he dide, and heere I him imbrace !
See where his ghoast solicites with his wounds
Reuenge on her that should reuenge his death !   25
Hieronimo, make haste to see thy sonne,
For Sorrow and Dispaire hath scited me
To heare Horatio plead with Radamant.
Make haste, Hieronimo, to holde excusde
Thy negligence in pursute of their deaths   30
Whose hatefull wrath bereu'd him of his breath.
Ah, nay ; thou dost delay their deaths,
Forgiues ¹ the murderers of thy noble sonne ;
And none but I bestirre me, — to no end !
And, as I cursse this tree from further fruit,   35
So shall my wombe be cursed for his sake ;
And with this weapon will I wound the brest, —
That haples brest that gaue Horatio suck!

She stabs her-selfe.

[Act Fourth.   Scene Third.]

[*The* DUKE'S *castle.*]

Enter HIERONIMO ; *he knocks vp the curtaine.*

Enter the DUKE OF CASTILE.

CAS.   How now, Hieronimo? wheres your fellows,
That you take all this paine?

---

¹ Haw. Forgiv'st, *without note.*

HIERO.　O sir, it is for the authors credit
To look that all things may goe well.
But, good my lord, let me intreat your Grace　　　5
To giue the king the coppie of the plaie:
This is the argument of what we shew.
　　CAS.　I will, Hieronimo.
　　HIERO.　One thing more, my good lord.[1]
　　CAS.　　　　　　　　　　　　Whats that?
　　HIERO.　Let me intreat your Grace　　　10
That, when the traine are past into the gallerie,
You would vouchsafe to throwe me downe the key.
　　CAS.　I will Hieronimo.　　　*Exit* CAS[TILE].
　　HIERO.　What, are you ready, Balthazar?
Bring a chaire and a cushion for the king.　　　15

　　　　　Enter BALTHAZAR *with a chaire.*

Well doon, Balthazar; hang vp the title:
Our scene is Rhodes.　What, is your beard on?
　　BAL.　Halfe on, the other is in my hand.
　　HIERO.　Dispatch, for shame! are you so long?

　　　　　　　　　　　　　Exit BALTHAZAR.
Bethink thy-selfe, Hieronimo,　　　20
Recall thy wits, recompt thy former wrongs
Thou hast receiued by murder of thy sonne,
And lastly, [but] not least, how Isabell,
Once his mother and thy [2] deerest wife,
All woe-begone for him, hath slaine her-selfe.　　　25
Behoues thee then, Hieronimo, to be
Reueng'd![3]　The plot is laide of dire reuenge:
On then,[4] Hieronimo; pursue reuenge,
For nothing wants but acting of reuenge!　　　*Exit* HIERONIMO.

　　　Enter SPANISH KING, VICE-ROY, *the* DUKE OF CASTILE, *and their traine,*
　　　[*to the gallery*].

　　KING.　Now, viceroy, shall we see the tragedie　　　30
Of Soliman, the Turkish emperour,

　　　[1] 1633, good my lord.　　　[3] *In* l. 26 *in* edd.
　　　[2] 1623, '33, nry.　　　[4] 1618, '23, '33, On them.

Performde of pleasure by your sonne the prince,
My nephew Don Lorenzo, and my neece.

VICE.   Who? Bel-imperia?

KING.   I; and Hieronimo our marshall,   35
At whose request they deine to doo 't themselues.
These be our pastimes in the court of Spaine.
Heere, brother, you shall be the booke-keeper :
This is the argument of that they shew.

He giueth him a booke.

Gentlemen, this play of HIERONIMO in sundrie languages
was thought good to be set downe in English more
largely, for the easier vnderstanding to euery
publique reader.

Enter BALTHAZAR, BEL-IMPERIA, *and* HIERONIMO.

BALTHAZAR.   Bashaw, that Rhodes is ours yeeld Heau-
        ens the honor   40
And holy Mahomet, our sacred prophet !
And be thou grac't with euery excelence
That Soliman can giue or thou desire !
But thy desert in conquering Rhodes is lesse
Then in reseruing this faire Christian [1] nimph,   45
Perseda, blisfull lamp of excellence,
Whose eies compell, like powerfull adamant,
The warlike heart of Soliman to wait.

KING.   See, vice-roy, that is Balthazar your sonne,
That represents the Emperour Solyman :   50
How well he acts his amorous passion !

VICE.   I ; Bel-imperia hath taught him that.

CASTILE.   That 's because his mind runnes all on Bel-
        imperia.

HIERO.   What-euer ioy earth yeelds betide your Maies-
        tie ! [2]
BALT.   Earth yeelds no ioy without Persedaes loue.   55
HIERO.   Let then Perseda on your Grace attend.
BALT.   She shall not wait on me, but I on her !
Drawne by the influence of her lights, I yeeld.

---

[1] 1633 *omits* Christian.   [2] *Misprinted* Meiestie *in* A.

But let my friend, the Rhodian knight, come foorth, —
Erasto, dearer then my life to me, —   60
That he may see Perseda, my beloued.

Enter ERASTO.

KING.   Heere comes Lorenzo : looke vpon the plot
And tell me, brother, what part plaies he.

    BEL.   Ah, my Erasto! Welcome to Perseda!
    LO.   Thrice happie is Erasto that thou liuest!   65
Rhodes losse is nothing to Erastoes ioy ;
Sith his Perseda liues, his life suruiues.
    BALT.   Ah, bashaw, heere is loue betweene Erasto
And faire Perseda, soueraigne of my soule !
    HIERO.   Remooue Erasto, mighty Solyman,   70
And then Perseda will be quickly wonne.
    BALT.   Erasto is my friend ; and, while he liues,
Perseda neuer will remooue her loue.
    HIERO.   Let not Erasto liue to greeue great Soliman !
    BALT.   Deare is Erasto in our princly eye.   75
    HIERO.   But, if he be your riuall, let him die !
    BALT.   Why, let him die ! so loue commaundeth me.
Yet greeue I that Erasto should so die.
    HIERO.   Erasto, Soliman saluteth thee,
And lets thee wit by me his Highnes will,   80
Which is, thou shouldst be thus imploid.   *Stab him.*
    BEL.   Ay, me, Erasto !   See, Solyman, Erastoes slaine !
    BALT.   Yet liueth Solyman to comfort thee.
Faire queene of beautie, let not fauour die,
But with a gratious eye beholde his griefe,   85
That with Persedaes beautie is encreast,
If by Perseda [1] griefe be not releast.
    BEL.   Tyrant, desist soliciting vaine sutes ;
Relentles are mine eares to thy laments
As thy butcher is pittilesse and base   90
Which seazd on my Erasto, harmelesse knight.
Yet by thy power thou thinkest to commaund,
And to thy power Perseda doth obey ;
But, were she able, thus she would reuenge

---

    [1] A. Persedaes ; 1633, Haw. Persedas.

Thy treacheries on thee, ignoble prince;   *Stab him.*   95
And on herselfe she would be thus reuengd.   *Stab herselfe.*

KING.   Well said, olde marshall! this was brauely done!
HIERO.   But Bel-imperia plaies Perseda well.
VICE.   Were this in earnest, Bel-imperia,
You would be better to my sonne then so.   100
    KING.   But now what followes for [1] Hieronimo?
    HIERO.   Marrie, this followes for Hieronimo!
Heere breake we off our sundrie languages,
And thus conclude I in our vulgare tung:
Happely you think — but bootles are your thoughts —   105
That this [2] is fabulously counterfeit,
And that we doo as all tragedians doo, —
To die to-day, for fashioning our scene,
The death of Aiax, or some Romaine peere,
And, in a minute starting vp againe,   110
Reuiue to please to-morrowes audience.
No, princes; know I am Hieronimo,
The hopeles father of a haples sonne,
Whose tung is tun'd to tell his latest tale,
Not to excuse grosse errors in the play.   115
I see your lookes vrge instance of these words:
Beholde the reason vrging me to this!

Shewes his dead sonne.

See heere my shew; look on this spectacle!
Heere lay my hope, and heere my hope hath end;
Heere lay my hart, and heere my hart was slaine;   120
Heere lay my treasure, heere my treasure lost;
Heere lay my blisse, and heere my blisse bereft.
But hope, hart, treasure, ioy and blisse, —
All fled, faild, died, yea, all decaide with this.
From forth these wounds came breath that gaue me life;   125
They murdred me that made these fatall markes.
The cause was loue whence grew this mortall hate:

---

[1] 1618, '23, '33 *omit* for.
[2] A. thus; 1633, this.

The hate, Lorenzo and yong Balthazar ;
The loue, my sonne to Bel-imperia.
But night, the couerer of accursed crimes,   130
With pitchie silence husht these traitors harmes,
And lent them leaue — for they had sorted leasure —
To take aduantage in my garden-plot
Vpon my sonne, my deere Horatio.
There mercilesse they butcherd vp my boy,   135
In black, darke night, to pale, dim, cruell death !
He shrikes ; I heard — and yet, me thinks, I heare –
His dismall out-cry eccho in the aire ;
With soonest speed I hasted to the noise,
Where, hanging on a tree, I found my sonne   140
Through-girt with wounds and slaughtred, as you see.
And greeued I, think you, at this spectacle?
Speak, Portaguise, whose losse resembles mine!
If thou canst weep vpon thy Balthazar,
Tis like I wailde for my Horatio.   145
And you, my l[ord], whose reconciled sonne
Marcht in a net and thought him selfe vnseene,
And rated me for brainsicke lunacie,
With [1] " God amend that mad Hieronimo! " —
How can you brook our plaies catastrophe?   150
And heere beholde this bloudie hand-kercher,
Which at Horatios death I weeping dipt
Within the riuer of his bleeding wounds !
It as propitious, see, I haue reserued,
And neuer hath it left my bloody [2] hart,   155
Soliciting remembrance of my vow
With these, O these accursed murderers !
Which now perform'd, my hart is satisfied.
And to this end the bashaw I became,
That might reuenge me on Lorenzos life,   160
Who therefore was appointed to the part
And was to represent the knight of Rhodes,

[1] 1618, '23, '33, which.
[2] 1618, '23, '33, bleeding.

That I might kill him more conueniently.
So, vice-roy, was this Balthazar thy sonne —
That Soliman which Bel-imperia   165
In person of Perseda murdered, —
So[le]lie appointed to that tragicke part,
That she might slay him that offended her.
Poore Bel-imperia mist her part in this:
For, though the story saith she should haue died,   170
Yet I, of kindenes and of care to her,
Did otherwise determine of her end.
But loue of him whom they did hate too much
Did vrge her resolution to be such.
And, princes, now beholde Hieronimo,   175
Author and actor in this tragedie,
Bearing his latest fortune in his fist;
And will as resolute conclude his parte
As any of the actors gone before.
And, gentles,[1] thus I end my play!   180
Vrge no more words, I haue no more to say.

He runs to hang himselfe.

KING.   O hearken, vice-roy; holde Hieronimo!
Brother, my nephew and thy sonne are [2] slaine!
VICE.   We are betraide! my Balthazar is slaine!
Breake ope the doores; runne saue Hieronimo!   185
Hieronimo, doe but enforme the king of these euents;
Vpon [3] mine honour, thou shalt haue no harme.
HIERO.   Vice-roy, I will not trust thee with my life,
Which I this day haue offered to my sonne:
Accursed wretch, why staiest thou him that was resolued to
   die?   190
KING.   Speak, traitor! damned, bloudy murderer, speak! —
For, now I haue thee, I will make thee speak!
Why hast thou done this vndeseruing deed?
VICE.   Why hast thou murdered my Balthazar?

---

[1] 1633, gentiles.   [3] *Misprinted* Ypon *in* A.
[2] *All* edd. *appear to have* are.

CAS.   Why hast thou butchered both my children thus? [1]   195
HIERO.   O good words!   As deare to me was my Horatio
As yours, or yours, my l[ord], to you.
My guiltles sonne was by Lorenzo slaine;
And by Lorenzo and that Balthazar
Am I at last reuenged thorowly, —   200
Vpon whose soules may Heauens be yet auenged
With greater far then these afflictions! [2]
CAS.   But who were thy confederates in this?

[1] *Between this line and the next* 1618, '23, '33 *insert the following*
passage:

HIER.   But are you sure that they are dead?
CAST.   I, slaine too sure!
HIER.   What! and yours too?
VICE.   I, all are dead; not one of them survive!
HIER.   Nay, then, I care not; come, and we shall be friends:
Let us lay our heads together!   5
See, heere's a goodly nooze will hold them all!
VICE.   O, damned devill, how secure he is!
HIER.   Secure?   Why dost thou wonder at it?
I tell thee, vice-roy, this day I have seene reveng'd,[3]
And in that sight am growne a prouder monarch   10
Then ever sate under the crowne of Spaine.
Had I as many lives as there be starres,
As many heavens to goe to as those lives,
Ide give them all, — I, and my soule to boot, —
But I would see thee ride in this red poole!   15
CAST.   Speake: who were thy confederates in this?
VICE.   That was thy daughter Belimperia;
For by her hand my Balthazar was slaine, —
I saw her stab him.

[2] *In* 1618, '23, '33 ll. 203–218 *are replaced by the following:*

Me thinkes, since I grew inward with Revenge,
I cannot looke with scorne enough on Death.
KING.   What! dost mock us, slave?   Bring tortures forth!
HIER.   Doe, doe, doe! and meane-time Ile torture you:
You had a sonne, as I take it; and your sonne   5
Should have bin married to your daughter, — ha! wast not so?
You had a sonne too; he was my lieges nephew;
He was proud and politike; had he lived,

[3] Dodsley, revenge.

Vice.   That was thy daughter Bel-imperia;
For by her hand my Balthazar was slaine,—   205
I saw her stab him.

    King.   Why speakest thou not?

    Hiero.   What lesser libertie can kings affoord
Then harmeles silence?   Then affoord it me!
Sufficeth I may not nor I will not tell thee.

    King.   Fetch forth the tortures!   Traitor as thou art,   210
Ile make thee tell! [1]

    Hiero.   Indeed? [2]
Thou maiest torment me as his wretched sonne
Hath done in murdring my Horatio;
But neuer shalt thou force me to reueale
The thing which I haue vowd inuiolate.   215
And therefore, in despight of all thy threats,
Pleasde with their deaths, and easde with their reuenge,
First take my tung, and afterwards my hart!

He bites out his tongue [3]

    King.   O monstrous resolution of a wretch!
See, Vice-roy, hee hath bitten foorth his tung   220

He might a come to weare the crowne of Spaine,—
I thinke twas so.   Twas I that killed him,—   10
Looke you, this same hand was it that stab'd
His heart,— doe you see this hand?—
For one Horatio, if you ever knew him,
A youth, one that they hanged up in his fathers garden,—
One that did force your valiant sonne to yeeld   15
While your valiant sonne did take him prisoner.

    Vice.   Be deafe, my senses, I can heare no more!

    King.   Fal, heaven, and cover us with thy sad ruines!

    Cast.   Rovvle all the world vvithin thy pitchie cloud!

    Hier.   Now doe I applaud vvhat I haue acted!   20
Nunc, mors,[4] *cedo manus!*
Now, to expresse the rupture of my part,
First take my tongue, and afterward my heart!

---

1 *This speech as two lines in* edd., *ending* tortures, tell.
2 *Part of* l. 212 *in* edd.   3 *So* 1633; *not in* A.

4 1618, mers cadae; 1623, '33, mens cadae; Haw. mors caede; Hazlitt, mors, [nunc] caede.

Rather then to reueale what we requirde.

CAS. Yet can he write.

KING. And if in this he satisfie vs not,
We will deuise the 'xtreamest kinde of death
That euer was inuented for a wretch. 225

Then he makes signes for a knife to mend his pen.

CAS. O, he would haue a knife to mend his pen.

VICE. Heere ; and aduise thee that thou write the troth, —
Looke to my brother ! saue Hieronimo !

He with a knife stabs the DUKE *and himselfe.*

KING. What age hath euer heard such monstrous deeds?
My brother and the whole succeeding hope 230
That Spaine expected after my discease!
Go beare his body hence, that we may mourne
The losse of our beloued brothers death,
That he may be entom'd, what-ere befall.
I am the next, the neerest, last of all. 235

VICE. And thou, Don Pedro, do the like for vs :
Take vp our haples sonne vntimely slaine ;
Set me with him, and he with wofull me,
Vpon the maine-mast of a ship vnmand,
And let the winde and tide hall[1] me along 240
To Sillas barking and vntamed gulfe[2]
Or to the lothsome poole of Acheron,
To weepe my want for my sweet Balthazar.
Spaine hath no refuge for a Portingale!

The trumpets sound a dead march, the KING OF SPAINE *mourning after his brothers body, and the* KING OF PORTINGALE *bearing the body of his sonne.*

[CHORUS.]

Enter GHOAST *and* REUENGE.

GHOAST. I ; now my hopes haue end in their effects,
When blood and sorrow finnish my desires :
Horatio murdered in his Fathers bower,

---

[1] 1633, hale. [2] *So* 1633 ; A. griefe ; Haw. gulph, *without note.*

Vilde Serberine by Pedringano slaine,
False Pedringano hang'd by quaint deuice,   5
Faire Isabella by her-selfe misdone,
Prince Balthazar by Bel-imperia stabd,
The Duke of Castile and his wicked sonne
Both done to death by olde Hieronimo,
My Bel-imperia falne as Dido fell,   10
And good Hieronimo slaine by himselfe!
I, these were spectacles to please my soule.
Now will I beg at louely Proserpine
That, by the vertue of her princely doome,
I may consort my freends in pleasing sort,   15
And on my foes work iust and sharpe reuenge.
Ile lead my freend Horatio through those feeldes
Where neuer-dying warres are still inurde ;
Ile lead faire Isabella to that traine
Where pittie weepes but neuer feeleth paine ;   20
Ile lead my Bel-imperia to those ioyes
That vestal virgins and faire queenes possess ;
Ile lead Hieronimo where Orpheus plaies,
Adding sweet pleasure to eternall daies.
But say, Reuenge, — for thou must helpe or none, —   25
Against the rest[1] how shall my hate be showne?
    REUENGE.   This hand shall hale them down to deepest
        hell,
Where none but furies, bugs and tortures dwell.
    GHOAST.   Then, sweet Reuenge, doo this at my request:
Let me be iudge and doome them to vnrest;   30
Let loose poore Titius from the vultures gripe,
And let Don Ciprian supply his roome ;
Place Don Lorenzo on Ixions wheele,
And let the louers endles paines surcease,
Iuno forget[2] olde wrath and graunt[2] him ease;   35
Hang Balthazar about Chimeras [3] neck,
And let him there bewaile his bloudy loue,

---

[1] A. therest.   [3] A. Chineras.
[2] All edd., forgets , . . graunts.

Repining at our ioyes that are aboue ;
Let Serberine goe roule the fatall stone
And take from Siciphus his endles mone ;   40
False Pedringano,[1] for his trecherie,
Let him be dragde through boyling Acheron,
And there liue dying still in endles flames,
Blaspheming gods and all their holy names.
   REUENGE.   Then haste we downe to meet thy freends and
     foes ;   45
To place thy freends in ease, the rest in woes.
For heere though death hath[2] end their miserie,
Ile there begin their endles tragedie.   *Exeunt.*

FINIS.

[1] *Misprinted* Pedringaco *in* A.
[2] 1623, '33, doth.

END OF VOL. II.

CATALOGUE OF DOVER BOOKS

Philosophy, Religion

GUIDE TO PHILOSOPHY, C. E. M. Joad. A modern classic which examines many crucial problems which man has pondered through the ages: Does free will exist? Is there plan in the universe? How do we know and validate our knowledge? Such opposed solutions as subjective idealism and realism, chance and teleology, vitalism and logical positivism, are evaluated and the contributions of the great philosophers from the Greeks to moderns like Russell, Whitehead, and others, are considered in the context of each problem. "The finest introduction," BOSTON TRANSCRIPT. Index. Classified bibliography. 592pp. 5⅜ x 8.
T297 Paperbound **$2.25**

HISTORY OF ANCIENT PHILOSOPHY, W. Windelband. One of the clearest, most accurate comprehensive surveys of Greek and Roman philosophy. Discusses ancient philosophy in general, intellectual life in Greece in the 7th and 6th centuries B.C., Thales, Anaximander, Anaximenes, Heraclitus, the Eleatics, Empedocles, Anaxagoras, Leucippus, the Pythagoreans, the Sophists, Socrates, Democritus (20 pages), Plato (50 pages), Aristotle (70 pages), the Peripatetics, Stoics, Epicureans, Sceptics, Neo-platonists, Christian Apologists, etc. 2nd German edition translated by H. E. Cushman. xv + 393pp. 5⅜ x 8.
T357 Paperbound **$1.85**

ILLUSTRATIONS OF THE HISTORY OF MEDIEVAL THOUGHT AND LEARNING, R. L. Poole. Basic analysis of the thought and lives of the leading philosophers and ecclesiastics from the 8th to the 14th century—Abailard, Ockham, Wycliffe, Marsiglio of Padua, and many other great thinkers who carried the torch of Western culture and learning through the "Dark Ages": political, religious, and metaphysical views. Long a standard work for scholars and one of the best introductions to medieval thought for beginners. Index. 10 Appendices. xiii + 327pp. 5⅜ x 8.
T674 Paperbound **$2.00**

PHILOSOPHY AND CIVILIZATION IN THE MIDDLE AGES, M. de Wulf. This semi-popular survey covers aspects of medieval intellectual life such as religion, philosophy, science, the arts, etc. It also covers feudalism vs. Catholicism, rise of the universities, mendicant orders, monastic centers, and similar topics. Unabridged. Bibliography. Index. viii + 320pp. 5⅜ x 8.
T284 Paperbound **$1.85**

AN INTRODUCTION TO SCHOLASTIC PHILOSOPHY, Prof. M. de Wulf. Formerly entitled SCHOLASTICISM OLD AND NEW, this volume examines the central scholastic tradition from St. Anselm, Albertus Magnus, Thomas Aquinas, up to Suarez in the 17th century. The relation of scholasticism to ancient and medieval philosophy and science in general is clear and easily followed. The second part of the book considers the modern revival of scholasticism, the Louvain position, relations with Kantianism and Positivism. Unabridged. xvi + 271pp. 5⅜ x 8.
T296 Clothbound **$3.50**
T283 Paperbound **$2.00**

A HISTORY OF MODERN PHILOSOPHY, H. Höffding. An exceptionally clear and detailed coverage of western philosophy from the Renaissance to the end of the 19th century. Major and minor men such as Pomponazzi, Bodin, Boehme, Telesius, Bruno, Copernicus, da Vinci, Kepler, Galileo, Bacon, Descartes, Hobbes, Spinoza, Leibniz, Wolff, Locke, Newton, Berkeley, Hume, Erasmus, Montesquieu, Voltaire, Diderot, Rousseau, Lessing, Kant, Herder, Fichte, Schelling, Hegel, Schopenhauer, Comte, Mill, Darwin, Spencer, Hartmann, Lange, and many others, are discussed in terms of theory of knowledge, logic, cosmology, and psychology. Index. 2 volumes, total of 1159pp. 5⅜ x 8.
T117 Vol. 1, Paperbound **$2.50**
T118 Vol. 2, Paperbound **$2.25**

ARISTOTLE, A. E. Taylor. A brilliant, searching non-technical account of Aristotle and his thought written by a foremost Platonist. It covers the life and works of Aristotle; classification of the sciences; logic; first philosophy; matter and form; causes; motion and eternity; God; physics; metaphysics; and similar topics. Bibliography. New Index compiled for this edition. 128pp. 5⅜ x 8.
T280 Paperbound **$1.00**

THE SYSTEM OF THOMAS AQUINAS, M. de Wulf. Leading Neo-Thomist, one of founders of University of Louvain, gives concise exposition to central doctrines of Aquinas, as a means toward determining his value to modern philosophy, religion. Formerly "Medieval Philosophy Illustrated from the System of Thomas Aquinas." Trans. by E. Messenger. Introduction. 151pp. 5⅜ x 8.
T568 Paperbound **$1.25**

LEIBNIZ, H. W. Carr. Most stimulating middle-level coverage of basic philosophical thought of Leibniz. Easily understood discussion, analysis of major works: "Theodicy," "Principles of Nature and Grace," "Monadology"; Leibniz's influence; intellectual growth; correspondence; disputes with Bayle, Malebranche, Newton; importance of his thought today, with reinterpretation in modern terminology. "Power and mastery," London Times. Bibliography. Index. 226pp. 5⅜ x 8.
T624 Paperbound **$1.35**

THE SENSE OF BEAUTY, G. Santayana. A revelation of the beauty of language as well as an important philosophic treatise, this work studies the "why, when, and how beauty appears, what conditions an object must fulfill to be beautiful, what elements of our nature make us sensible of beauty, and what the relation is between the constitution of the object and the excitement of our susceptibility." "It is doubtful if a better treatment of the subject has since been published," PEABODY JOURNAL. Index. ix + 275pp. 5⅜ x 8.
T238 Paperbound **$1.00**

PROBLEMS OF ETHICS, Moritz Schlick. The renowned leader of the "Vienna Circle" applies the logical positivist approach to a wide variety of ethical problems: the source and means of attaining knowledge, the formal and material characteristics of the good, moral norms and principles, absolute vs. relative values, free will and responsibility, comparative importance of pleasure and suffering as ethical values, etc. Disarmingly simple and straightforward despite complexity of subject. First English translation, authorized by author before his death, of a thirty-year old classic. Translated and with an introduction by David Rynin. Index. Foreword by Prof. George P. Adams. xxi + 209pp. 5⅜ x 8. T946 Paperbound **$1.60**

AN INTRODUCTION TO EXISTENTIALISM, Robert G. Olson. A new and indispensable guide to one of the major thought systems of our century, the movement that is central to the thinking of some of the most creative figures of the past hundred years. Stresses Heidegger and Sartre, with careful and objective examination of the existentialist position, values—freedom of choice, individual dignity, personal love, creative effort—and answers to the eternal questions of the human condition. Scholarly, unbiased, analytic, unlike most studies of this difficult subject, Prof. Olson's book is aimed at the student of philosophy as well as at the reader with no formal training who is looking for an absorbing, accessible, and thorough introduction to the basic texts. Index. xv + 221pp. 5⅜ x 8½. T55 Paperbound **$1.65**

SYMBOLIC LOGIC, C. I. Lewis and C. H. Langford. Since first publication in 1932, this has been among most frequently cited works on symbolic logic. Still one of the best introductions both for beginners and for mathematicians, philosophers. First part covers basic topics which easily lend themselves to beginning study. Second part is rigorous, thorough development of logistic method, examination of some of most difficult and abstract aspects of symbolic logic, including modal logic, logical paradoxes, many-valued logic, with Prof. Lewis' own contributions. 2nd revised (corrected) edition. 3 appendixes, one new to this edition. 524pp. 5⅜ x 8. S170 Paperbound **$2.00**

WHITEHEAD'S PHILOSOPHY OF CIVILIZATION, A. H. Johnson. A leading authority on Alfred North Whitehead synthesizes the great philosopher's thought on civilization, scattered throughout various writings, into unified whole. Analysis of Whitehead's general definition of civilization, his reflections on history and influences on its development, his religion, including his analysis of Christianity, concept of solitariness as first requirement of personal religion, and so on. Other chapters cover views on minority groups, society, civil liberties, education. Also critical comments on Whitehead's philosophy. Written with general reader in mind. A perceptive introduction to important area of the thought of a leading philosopher of our century. Revised index and bibliography. xii + 211pp. 5⅜ x 8½.
T996 Paperbound **$1.50**

WHITEHEAD'S THEORY OF REALITY, A. H. Johnson. Introductory outline of Whitehead's theory of actual entities, the heart of his philosophy of reality, followed by his views on nature of God, philosophy of mind, theory of value (truth, beauty, goodness and their opposites), analyses of other philosophers, attitude toward science. A perspicacious lucid introduction by author of dissertation on Whitehead, written under the subject's supervision at Harvard. Good basic view for beginning students of philosophy and for those who are simply interested in important contemporary ideas. Revised index and bibliography. xiii + 267pp. 5⅜ x 8½.
T989 Paperbound **$2.00**

MIND AND THE WORLD-ORDER, C. I. Lewis. Building upon the work of Peirce, James, and Dewey, Professor Lewis outlines a theory of knowledge in terms of "conceptual pragmatism." Dividing truth into abstract mathematical certainty and empirical truth, the author demonstrates that the traditional understanding of the a priori must be abandoned. Detailed analyses of philosophy, metaphysics, method, the "given" in experience, knowledge of objects, nature of the a priori, experience and order, and many others. Appendices. xiv + 446pp. 5⅜ x 8. T359 Paperbound **$2.25**

SCEPTICISM AND ANIMAL FAITH, G. Santayana. To eliminate difficulties in the traditional theory of knowledge, Santayana distinguishes between the independent existence of objects and the essence our mind attributes to them. Scepticism is thereby established as a form of belief, and animal faith is shown to be a necessary condition of knowledge. Belief, classical idealism, intuition, memory, symbols, literary psychology, and much more, discussed with unusual clarity and depth. Index. xii + 314pp. 5⅜ x 8. T235 Clothbound **$3.50**
T236 Paperbound **$1.75**

LANGUAGE AND MYTH, E. Cassirer. Analyzing the non-rational thought processes which go to make up culture, Cassirer demonstrates that beneath both language and myth there lies a dominant unconscious "grammar" of experience whose categories and canons are not those of logical thought. His analyses of seemingly diverse phenomena such as Indian metaphysics, the Melanesian "mana," the Naturphilosophie of Schelling, modern poetry, etc., are profound without being pedantic. Introduction and translation by Susanne Langer. Index. x + 103pp. 5⅜ x 8. T51 Paperbound **$1.25**

CATALOGUE OF DOVER BOOKS

AN ESSAY CONCERNING HUMAN UNDERSTANDING, John Locke. Edited by A. C. Fraser. Unabridged reprinting of definitive edition; only complete edition of "Essay" in print. Marginal analyses of almost every paragraph; hundreds of footnotes; authoritative 140-page biographical, critical, historical prolegomena. Indexes. 1170pp. 5⅜ x 8.
T530 Vol. 1 (Books 1, 2) Paperbound **$2.50**
T531 Vol. 2 (Books 3, 4) Paperbound **$2.50**
2 volume set **$5.00**

THE PHILOSOPHY OF HISTORY, G. W. F. Hegel. One of the great classics of western thought which reveals Hegel's basic principle: that history is not chance but a rational process, the realization of the Spirit of Freedom. Ranges from the oriental cultures of subjective thought to the classical subjective cultures, to the modern absolute synthesis where spiritual and secular may be reconciled. Translation and introduction by J. Sibree. Introduction by C. Hegel. Special introduction for this edition by Prof. Carl Friedrich. xxxix + 447pp. 5⅜ x 8.
T112 Paperbound **$2.25**

THE PHILOSOPHY OF HEGEL, W. T. Stace. The first detailed analysis of Hegel's thought in English, this is especially valuable since so many of Hegel's works are out of print. Dr. Stace examines Hegel's debt to Greek idealists and the 18th century and then proceeds to a careful description and analysis of Hegel's first principles, categories, reason, dialectic method, his logic, philosophy of nature and spirit, etc. Index. Special 14 x 20 chart of Hegelian system. x + 526pp. 5⅜ x 8.
T254 Paperbound **$2.75**

THE WILL TO BELIEVE and HUMAN IMMORTALITY, W. James. Two complete books bound as one. THE WILL TO BELIEVE discusses the interrelations of belief, will, and intellect in man; chance vs. determinism, free will vs. determinism, free will vs. fate, pluralism vs. monism; the philosophies of Hegel and Spencer, and more. HUMAN IMMORTALITY examines the question of survival after death and develops an unusual and powerful argument for immortality. Two prefaces. Index. Total of 429pp. 5⅜ x 8.
T291 Paperbound **$2.00**

THE WORLD AND THE INDIVIDUAL, Josiah Royce. Only major effort by an American philosopher to interpret nature of things in systematic, comprehensive manner. Royce's formulation of an absolute voluntarism remains one of the original and profound solutions to the problems involved. Part One, Four Historical Conceptions of Being, inquires into first principles, true meaning and place of individuality. Part Two, Nature, Man, and the Moral Order, is application of first principles to problems concerning religion, evil, moral order. Introduction by J. E. Smith, Yale Univ. Index. 1070pp. 5⅜ x 8.
T561 Vol. 1 Paperbound **$2.75**
T562 Vol. 2 Paperbound **$2.75**
Two volume set **$5.50**

THE PHILOSOPHICAL WRITINGS OF PEIRCE, edited by J. Buchler. This book (formerly THE PHILOSOPHY OF PEIRCE) is a carefully integrated exposition of Peirce's complete system composed of selections from his own work. Symbolic logic, scientific method, theory of signs, pragmatism, epistemology, chance, cosmology, ethics, and many other topics are treated by one of the greatest philosophers of modern times. This is the only inexpensive compilation of his key ideas. xvi + 386pp. 5⅜ x 8.
T217 Paperbound **$2.00**

EXPERIENCE AND NATURE, John Dewey. An enlarged, revised edition of the Paul Carus lectures which Dewey delivered in 1925. It covers Dewey's basic formulation of the problem of knowledge, with a full discussion of other systems, and a detailing of his own concepts of the relationship of external world, mind, and knowledge. Starts with a thorough examination of the philosophical method; examines the interrelationship of experience and nature; analyzes experience on basis of empirical naturalism, the formulation of law, role of language and social factors in knowledge; etc. Dewey's treatment of central problems in philosophy is profound but extremely easy to follow. ix + 448pp. 5⅜ x 8.
T471 Paperbound **$2.00**

THE PHILOSOPHICAL WORKS OF DESCARTES. The definitive English edition of all the major philosophical works and letters of René Descartes. All of his revolutionary insights, from his famous "Cogito ergo sum" to his detailed account of contemporary science and his astonishingly fruitful concept that all phenomena of the universe (except mind) could be reduced to clear laws by the use of mathematics. An excellent source for the thought of men like Hobbes, Arnauld, Gassendi, etc., who were Descartes's contemporaries. Translated by E. S. Haldane and G. Ross. Introductory notes. Index. Total of 842pp. 5⅜ x 8.
T71 Vol. 1, Paperbound **$2.00**
T72 Vol. 2, Paperbound **$2.00**

THE CHIEF WORKS OF SPINOZA. An unabridged reprint of the famous Bohn edition containing all of Spinoza's most important works: Vol. I: The Theologico-Political Treatise and the Political Treatise. Vol. II: On The Improvement Of Understanding, The Ethics, Selected Letters. Profound and enduring ideas on God, the universe, pantheism, society, religion, the state, democracy, the mind, emotions, freedom and the nature of man, which influenced Goethe, Hegel, Schelling, Coleridge, Whitehead, and many others. Introduction. 826pp. 5⅜ x 8.
T249 Vol. I, Paperbound **$1.75**
T250 Vol. II, Paperbound **$1.50**

History, Political Science

THE POLITICAL THOUGHT OF PLATO AND ARISTOTLE, E. Barker. One of the clearest and most accurate expositions of the corpus of Greek political thought. This standard source contains exhaustive analyses of the "Republic" and other Platonic dialogues and Aristotle's "Politics" and "Ethics," and discusses the origin of these ideas in Greece, contributions of other Greek theorists, and modifications of Greek ideas by thinkers from Aquinas to Hegel. "Must" reading for anyone interested in the history of Western thought. Index. Chronological Table of Events, 2 Appendixes. xxiv + 560pp. 5⅜ x 8. T521 Paperbound **$2.50**

THE IDEA OF PROGRESS, J. B. Bury. Practically unknown before the Reformation, the idea of progress has since become one of the central concepts of western civilization. Prof. Bury analyzes its evolution in the thought of Greece, Rome, the Middle Ages, the Renaissance, to its flowering in all branches of science, religion, philosophy, industry, art, and literature, during and following the 16th century. Introduction by Charles Beard. Index. xl + 357pp. 5⅜ x 8. T40 Paperbound **$1.95**

THE ANCIENT GREEK HISTORIANS, J. B. Bury. This well known, easily read work covers the entire field of classical historians from the early writers to Herodotus, Thucydides, Xenophon, through Poseidonius and such Romans as Tacitus, Cato, Caesar, Livy. Scores of writers are studied biographically, in style, sources, accuracy, structure, historical concepts, and influences. Recent discoveries such as the Oxyrhinchus papyri are referred to, as well as such great scholars as Nissen, Gomperz, Cornford, etc. "Totally unblemished by pedantry." Outlook. "The best account in English," Dutcher, A Guide to Historical Lit. Bibliography, Index. x + 281pp. 5⅜ x 8. T397 Paperbound **$1.65**

HISTORY OF THE LATER ROMAN EMPIRE, J. B. Bury. This standard work by the leading Byzantine scholar of our time discusses the later Roman and early Byzantine empires from 395 A.D. through the death of Justinian in 565, in their political, social, cultural, theological, and military aspects. Contemporary documents are quoted in full, making this the most complete reconstruction of the period and a fit successor to Gibbon's "Decline and Fall." "Most unlikely that it will ever be superseded," Glanville Downey, Dumbarton Oaks Research Lib. Geneological tables. 5 maps. Bibliography. Index. 2 volumes total of 965pp. 5⅜ x 8. T398, 399 Two volume set, Paperbound **$4.50**

A HISTORY OF ANCIENT GEOGRAPHY, E. H. Bunbury. Standard study, in English, of ancient geography; never equalled for scope, detail. First full account of history of geography from Greeks' first world picture based on mariners, through Ptolemy. Discusses every important map, discovery, figure, travel expedition, war, conjecture, narrative, bearing on subject. Chapters on Homeric geography, Herodotus, Alexander expedition, Strabo, Pliny, Ptolemy, would stand alone as exhaustive monographs. Includes minor geographers, men not usually regarded in this context: Hecataeus, Pytheas, Hipparchus, Artemidorus, Marinus of Tyre, etc. Uses information gleaned from military campaigns such as Punic Wars, Hannibal's passage of Alps, campaigns of Lucullus, Pompey, Caesar's wars, the Trojan War. New introduction by W. H. Stahl, Brooklyn College. Bibliography. Index. 20 maps. 1426pp. 5⅜ x 8. T570-1, clothbound, 2-volume set **$12.50**

POLITICAL PARTIES, Robert Michels. Classic of social science, reference point for all later work, deals with nature of leadership in social organization on government and trade union levels. Probing tendency of oligarchy to replace democracy, it studies need for leadership, desire for organization, psychological motivations, vested interests, hero worship, reaction of leaders to power, press relations, many other aspects. Trans. by E. & C. Paul. Introduction. 447pp. 5⅜ x 8. T569 Paperbound **$2.00**

A HISTORY OF HISTORICAL WRITING, Harry Elmer Barnes. Virtually the only adequate survey of the whole course of historical writing in a single volume. Surveys developments from the beginnings of historiographies in the ancient Near East and the Classical World, up through the Cold War. Covers major historians in detail, shows interrelationship with cultural background, makes clear individual contributions, evaluates and estimates importance; also enormously rich upon minor authors and thinkers who are usually passed over. Packed with scholarship and learning, clear, easily written. Indispensable to every student of history. Revised and enlarged up to 1961. Index and bibliography. xv + 442pp. 5⅜ x 8½. T104 Paperbound **$2.25**

Prices subject to change without notice.

Dover publishes books on art, music, philosophy, literature, languages, history, social sciences, psychology, handcrafts, orientalia, puzzles and entertainments, chess, pets and gardens, books explaining science, intermediate and higher mathematics, mathematical physics, engineering, biological sciences, earth sciences, classics of science, etc. Write to:

Dept. catrr.
Dover Publications, Inc.
180 Varick Street, N.Y. 14, N.Y.